The Invention of the Newspaper

The Invention of the Newspaper

English Newsbooks 1641–1649

JOAD RAYMOND

CLARENDON PRESS · OXFORD

OXFORD
UNIVERSITY PRESS
Great Clarendon Street, Oxford OX2 6DP

Oxford University Press is a department of the University of Oxford
It furthers the University's objective of excellence in research, scholarship,
and education by publishing worldwide in

Oxford New York
Athens Auckland Bangkok Bogotá Buenos Aires Calcutta
Cape Town Chennai Dar es Salaam Delhi Florence Hong Kong Istanbul
Karachi Kuala Lumpur Madrid Melbourne Mexico City Mumbai
Nairobi Paris São Paulo Singapore Taipei Tokyo Toronto Warsaw
with associated companies in Berlin Ibadan

Oxford is a registered trade mark of Oxford University Press
in the UK and in certain other countries

Published in the United States
by Oxford University Press Inc., New York

Reprinted 1999

ISBN 0-19-813002-3

Printed in Great Britain
on acid-free paper by
Biddles Short Run Books
King's Lynn

Mercury (*Mercurius*) the son of *Jupiter* and *Maia*; he was the messenger of the gods, the god of Eloquence, Merchandize, Chivalry, and Thievery; also author of the Harp, and guider of the way, he was said to have wings on his arms and feet. It is commonly used for a swift messenger, or for a book of news, because such books are (as it were) the messengers of the news.

(Thomas Blount, *Glossographia*, 1656)

eloquence ought to be banish'd out of *civil societies* as a thing fatal to Peace and good Manners.

(Thomas Sprat, *History of the Royal Society*, 1667)

I am to yield thus much, that the Crisis *of eloquence is not a little altered; In* Senates *and* Harangues *to the people length was necessary, for the same men acted both parts, (and that in a single Citie) & that which was necessary to gain the people, degenerated in time to be in fashion in counsel, so that this was play'd for a* prize, *and was held so far unnecessary, that as if the best Masters had not been enough, it was the care of parents themselves to instruct their children, who seeing it the readiest way of advancement, were not like to be wanting in emulation and indeavour, whereas now the* Scene *is changed, and (in Civil matters) we are to speak to the* few *and not the* many: *For as the corruption of time hath diseas'd most Governments into* Monarchies, *so the least of these few populacies now in being, is too great to be included in the same walls, or brought to the hearing of one voice (long studied Orations being become uselesse) and therefore as men now endeavour to summe up their Notions, and draw them into a sharp angle, expecting reason should overcome, so in the management and conueiance of that reason, there must be needfull so many artifices, charms, masteries, and such subtle conducts, that without them a man cannot so well obtain his end, and a man of skill that brings not so much force of reason may easily avoid them.*

(John Hall, preface to *Peri hypsous Or Dionysius Longinus of the Height of Eloquence*, 1652)

THIS BOOK IS DEDICATED TO THE PILLARS OF THESE PAST FIVE YEARS

DAVID AND LAUREN

Preface

THIS book has been the product of much labour. There were numerous premature completions, and I look now upon its fruition less as upon the arrival of a newborn child than as the departure of a recalcitrant teenager who has overstayed its welcome.

One of the joys of its long stay is the number of debts I have incurred. I have roosted for many hours in the Bodleian and never been unwelcome. Bodley has found the misplaced, felicitously named volume Hope 8° 636, which I mentioned in the preface to *Making the News*. While I was working on several volumes of John Rushworth's newsbooks which formed part of the Fairfax deposit at Bodley they were withdrawn and put up to auction (adding insult to injury I was quoted in the auction catalogue); Bodley assuaged the wound by purchasing them. I render my appreciation to all the staff, at both the thin and thick ends of the wedge.

I also thank the British Library; the Public Record Office; the library of Worcester College, Oxford; the library of Magdalen College, Oxford; Durham University Library; the Library Company of Philadelphia; the library of the University of Pennsylvania; the McGill Library of Haverford College, Philadelphia; the Hayden Library at Arizona State University, Tempe, Ariz.; the Folger Shakespeare Library, Washington; the Library of Congress, Washington; the New York Public Library; the libraries of the University of Virginia. I was assisted in travelling to these by grants from Magdalen College and the English Faculty of the University of Oxford. The British Academy funded my doctoral research.

I am indebted to the President and Fellows of Magdalen College for a Fellowship by Examination, which gave me time to repent and revise my D.Phil. thesis. The talking culture of an Oxford college is an excellent environment for a broader education, as well as for learning how to make small talk. Of the tutors in English, John Fuller and Bernard O'Donoghue, I am particularly mindful. As I prepare to travel into the frozen north I reflect with valedictory pleasure on my two years here; most tenderly on those friends I shall not meet again.

Others have given their time to discussing an odd subject, I hope I did not too much resemble the Ancient Mariner: Susan Wiseman, David Underdown, Michael Harris, Christine Ferdinand, Terry Eagleton, Line Cottegnies. Carolyn Nelson contributed some very helpful correspondence, and I remain grateful to her and Matthew Seccombe for their superb STC. Don McKenzie read an early draft of Chapter 2 and offered valuable and insightful criticisms. The argument that most forms of censorship are broadly economic rather than narrowly political has helped me to understand the twentieth century as much as the seventeenth. Peter Burke examined me for the Magdalen Fellowship, and for his enthusiasm and support of interdisciplinary work I am beholden.

I thank Kevin Sharpe and Margaux Stocker for a characteristically generous viva, which influenced the shape the work adopted after its minimalist construction as a thesis. Kevin has been a tireless reader of this book, and without his very positive interventions it might never have appeared to the wider world.

Nigel Smith has been a constant companion in Oxford, intellectually generous and always encouraging; I owe much to his energetic espousing of seventeenth-century trashy writing, with which I have been infected.

Anyone who knows David Norbrook, my thesis supervisor, will realize how influential five years of his care and attention can be. He is a true and spontaneous critic. He has served as a model when I have been tempted by more raucous careers. Much of this book is his. What remains of bloody-minded impatience is definitely mine.

My long-suffering partner, Lauren Kassell, suffered to read many recensions of the typescript, while Marchamont endeavoured to turn them into papier mâché. To Lauren's intellectual and emotional support I owe a great deal. Marchamont has continuously reminded me of the brute realities of everyday life.

J.R.

Magdalen College
October 1995

Contents

Format of References

References to newsbooks are given in the following format: *Title* issue no., end date, page no., N&S no./LT shelfmark.

Shelfmarks for the Thomason collection in the British Library appear thus: E . . . /669 f.

In order to facilitate the consultation of the newsbooks cited I have given both the Nelson and Seccombe number and, where possible, the Thomason Tracts shelfmark. This does not indicate that I am quoting the Thomason copy. References to pamphlets are given in the format: *Title* (place and year; STC or Wing no./Thomason shelfmark [where relevant]), page no.

In references place of publication is London unless otherwise specified. These details make for inelegant notes, but assist in the location of the material. Dates remain in the old style, though the year is taken to begin on 1 January.

Abbreviations

AO	Anthony Wood. *Athenæ Oxonienses.* 3rd edn. Ed. Philip Bliss, 4 vols. London, 1813–20.
Astrology	Bernard Capp. *Astrology and the Popular Press: English Almanacs 1500–1800.* London, 1979.
Beginnings	Joseph Frank. *The Beginnings of the English Newspaper, 1620–1660.* Cambridge, Mass., 1961.
Berkenhead	P. W. Thomas. *Sir John Berkenhead 1617–1679: A Royalist Career in Politics and Polemics.* Oxford, 1969.
Birch	T. Birch, ed. *The Court and Times of Charles I.* 2 vols. London, 1848.
BL	British Library, London.
Bod.	Bodleian Library, Oxford.
British Monarchies	Conrad Russell. *The Fall of the British Monarchies 1637–1642.* Oxford, 1991.
CJ	*Commons Journals.*
Clyde	William M. Clyde. *The Struggle for the Freedom of the Press from Caxton to Cromwell.* London, 1934.
Constitutional Documents	S. R. Gardiner. *Constitutional Documents of the Puritan Revolution 1625–1660.* Oxford, 1906.
Cotton	A. N. B. Cotton. 'London Newsbooks in the Civil War: Their Political Attitudes and Sources of Information'. D.Phil. thesis. Oxford, 1971.
CPW	John Milton. *Complete Prose Works of John Milton.* 8 vols. General editor Don M. Wolfe. New Haven, 1953–82.
CSPD	*Calendar of State Papers Domestic.*
CSP Ven.	*Calendar of State Papers Venetian.*
Dahl	Folke Dahl, *A Bibliography of English Corantos and Periodical Newsbooks 1620–1642.* London, 1952.
Folger	Folger Shakespeare Library, Washington.
Gardiner[1]	S. R. Gardiner. *History of England from the Accession of James I to the Outbreak of the Civil War 1603–1642.* 10 vols. London, 1883–4.
Gardiner[2]	S. R. Gardiner. *History of the Great Civil War.* 4 vols. London, 1986–7.
Gardiner[3]	S. R. Gardiner. *History of the Commonwealth and Protectorate.* 4 vols. Adlestrop, 1988–9.
GCRO	Glamorgan County Record Office.
HC[1]	John Rushworth. *Historical Collections.* First Part. London, 1659; R2316.

HC[2]	John Rushworth. *Historical Collections.* Second Part. 2 vols. London, 1680; R2318.
HC[3]	John Rushworth. *Historical Collections.* Third Part. 2 vols. London, 1691; R2319.
HC[4]	John Rushworth. *Historical Collections.* Fourth Part. 2 vols. London, 1701.
History	J. B. Williams. *A History of English Journalism to the Foundation of the Gazette.* London, 1908.
HJ	*Historical Journal.*
HMC	*Historical Manuscripts Commission.*
HMSO	Her/His Majesty's Stationery Office.
KWI	*Kingdomes Weekly Intelligencer.*
L&R	Nigel Smith. *Literature and Revolution in England, 1640–1660.* New Haven, 1994.
LJ	*Lords Journals.*
LT	Thomason Tracts, British Library.
Madan	Falconer Madan. *Oxford Books: A Bibliography.* 3 vols. Oxford, 1895–1931.
MTN	Joad Raymond, ed. *Making the News: An Anthology of the Newsbooks of Revolutionary England.* Moreton-in-Marsh, 1993.
N&S	Carolyn Nelson and Matthew Seccombe. *British Newspapers and Periodicals: A Short Title Catalogue.* New York, 1987.
NYPL	New York Public Library.
OR	P. W. Thomas, ed. *English Revolution*[3], *Newsbooks*[1]*: Oxford Royalist.* 4 vols. London, 1971.
P&P	*Past and Present.*
Personal Rule	Kevin Sharpe. *The Personal Rule of Charles I.* New Haven, 1992.
PRO	Public Record Office, London.
PWA	*Perfect Weekly Account.*
Secret Rites	Lois Potter. *Secret Rites and Secret Writing: Royalist Literature, 1641–1660.* Cambridge, 1989.
Siebert	F. S. Siebert. *Freedom of the Press in England 1476–1776: The Rise and Decline of Government Controls.* Urbana, Ill., 1952.
STC	A. W. Pollard and G. R. Redgrave. *A Short-Title Catalogue of Books Printed in England, Scotland and Ireland: And of English Books Printed Abroad 1475–1640.* Rev. edn. 3 vols. London, 1976–91.
Wing	Donald Wing. *Short-Title Catalogue of Books Printed in England, Scotland, Ireland, Wales, and British America and of English Books Printed in Other Countries 1641–1700.* Rev. edn. 3 vols. New York, 1972–94.

Introduction: What News?

'WHAT news?' was probably one of the most frequently asked questions of early-modern Britain. It was the kind of question which only rarely left traces, being requested of passing travellers, neighbours, fellow drinkers, cousins, and correspondents. The sparse evidential residue suggests that it was a common currency of social exchange. In Norfolk in 1629 John Rous stopped his neighbour Mr Tayler to ask him 'what newes?' Tayler responded with something he had heard from a Mr Barret, who had shown him a printed sermon.[1] In 1642 Thomas Elliot, fleeing from London to the king at Oxford carrying the Great Seal, encountered John Rushworth. Trying to act inconspicuously, Elliot demanded, 'what News?'[2] John Smyth recorded that whenever any 'clothiers, horse carriers and wain men' arrived at Berkeley Hundred in Gloucestershire they were greeted with the question 'What news at London?', and their answers soon disseminated among locals.[3] A man from Cheshire arriving in London in 1659 was asked in turn 'what News there was in his Country'.[4] In 1657 when Oliver Cromwell encountered the state newswriter Marchamont Nedham he asked him, with a certain weight of irony, 'what news?'[5]

The profusion of this question was sufficiently evident for it to become the subject of satire. 'What news?' appeared as a refrain in satirical news pamphlets in 1641 and 1642.[6] This was not new. 'It is an itch in our natures to delight in newnes and varietie,' wrote Sir Richard Hawkins in 1622.[7] In his 1626 play *The Staple of Newes*, Ben Jonson represented news as the footing for social intercourse amongst simple rural folk and sophisticated town socialites. When Cymbal, the entrepreneur who runs the news office, asks a customer: 'What newes would she heare? | Or of what kind, Sir?', the answer is: 'Any, any kind. | So it

[1] *Diary of John Rous*, ed. Mary Anne Everett Green, Camden Society, 66 (1856), 44.

[2] *HC*[3], i. 718.

[3] Michael Frearson, 'The Distribution and Readership of London Corantos in the 1620s', in Robin Myers and Michael Harris, eds., *Serials and their Readers, 1620–1914* (Winchester, 1993), 17.

[4] *Politicus* 582, 11 Aug. 1659, 643–4, 361.582/E766(30).

[5] *CSPD 1656–1657*, 318; *The Writings and Speeches of Oliver Cromwell*, ed. Wilbur Cortez Abbott, 4 vols. (Cambridge, Mass., 1937–47), iv. 432.

[6] *Mercuries Message, or the Coppy of a Letter* (1641; M1748); *A new Play Called Canterbury His Change of Diot* (1641; N702/E177(8)); *The Last News in London* (1642; L498).

[7] Richard Hawkins, *Observations of Sir R. Hawkins in his Voiage* (1622; *STC* 12962), sig. X4. See also Susan Brigden, *London and the Reformation* (Oxford, 1989), 365.

be *newes*, the newest that thou hast.'[8] Jonson implicated himself, recognizing that the dramatist and poet, as well as the journalist, was involved in the business of selling news.[9] The greed of the vulgar for anything that might pass as news was a frequent refrain in seventeenth-century satire.[10] News was supposed to be consumed not only because it enabled social exchange, or facilitated rational behaviour, but as an end in itself. Though some social critics condemned the appetite as undiscerning, correspondence and conversation suggest that many people wished to be informed.

The desire for news, with its concomitant dangers, has probably been an aspect of most societies through history. News is a constituent of communication, and communication binds together societies and cultures.[11] It is a basic fact of sensuous human activity. But the ways of expressing and satisfying the desire for news are as diverse as those societies themselves. The role news plays in history is at once general and specific, open to abstract analysis and detailed micronarrative.

This study is concerned with the newsbooks printed in Britain in the 1640s, a closely circumscribed project, but large enough. It addresses newsbooks as a literary and material form, as books which were produced, circulated, and received in a society. Newsbooks are not simply historical documents the value of which is proportional to the degree of truth they contain; rather they are literary texts, which can provide historical information. Read against the grain of their authors' intentions they reveal much about the culture of print in the 1640s. But not only verbal information should be considered: if we are to understand writing as a historical phenomenon we must recognize that the meaning of a text is the transitory product of a particular relationship between a reader or group of readers within specific circumstances, who encounter not texts but books. In this creative encounter the material construction of a book, its typography, binding, the feel of the paper; the situation in which it is read, whether silent or out loud, in a library,

[8] Ben Jonson, *The Staple of Newes*, in *The Workes of Benjamin Jonson*, vol. ii (1631; *STC* 14753.5), 36; cf. *The Noble Soldier*, quoted Gerald Eades Bentley, *The Jacobean and Caroline Stage*, 7 vols. (Oxford, 1941–68), iii. 260; also iv. 631; vi. 25.

[9] D. F. McKenzie, '"*The Staple of News*" and the Late Plays', in W. Blissett, J. Patrick, and R. W. Van Fossen, eds., *A Celebration of Ben Jonson* (Toronto, 1973), 83–128; Mark Z. Muggli, 'Ben Jonson and the Business of News', *Studies in English Literature*, 32 (1992), 323–40.

[10] Richard Braithwait, *Whimzies: or, a New Cast of Characters* (1631; *STC* 3591), 15–24; 'A Character of a London Scriuenor', BL: Add. MS 25303, ff. 183ᵛ–184; *MTN*, 11–14; see also Thomas Nashe, *Pierce Penilesse*, where the devil is described as 'a greedy pursuer of newes'; (1592; 1924), 11–12.

[11] Claude Lévi-Strauss, *Structural Anthropology*, trans. Claire Jackson and Brooke Grundfest Schoepf (Harmondsworth, 1977), 296–315.

a crowd, or secluded room; in youth or in age; patiently or urgently; in a cloistered or revolutionary world; all these play upon the meanings which a reader and a text can produce between them.[12] The methodological difficulties generated by the return to concrete acts of reading are compensated for by recourse to unusual forms of evidence and inventive strategies.[13] The new bibliography has offered a useful corrective to reception theories which freeze the act of reading into a phenomenological ideal.

While literary critics and bibliographers have come to recognize that texts have a historicity and a fluidity, historians have acknowledged that historical writing has a textuality which implicates it in the same rhetorical dynamics as literary texts.[14] This is not to concede the historicity of texts and the textuality of history as parallel or equivalent epistemological phenomena.[15] Nor is it to concede that narrativity should replace a notion of historical reality as the guiding principle of historical research and writing. Rather it is to allow that the historian, literary or otherwise, must face the problem of communication him- and herself, and be bedevilled by the seductiveness of narrative, the artificiality of rhetoric, and the contingency of the unknown reader.[16] In short, the historian must find a way of creating understanding, despite the freedom of the publisher and reader to poach upon and transmit the text as they will. The shortcomings of history as a narrative of events derive not from its artificiality, but from the limited kinds of meanings which can

[12] D. F. McKenzie, *Bibliography and the Sociology of Texts*, The Panizzi Lectures, 1985 (1986); id., 'Speech—Manuscript—Print', *Library Chronicle*, 20 (1990), 87–109; Roger Chartier, *The Cultural Uses of Print in Early Modern France*, trans. Lydia G. Cochrane (Princeton, 1987); id., *Cultural History: Between Practices and Representations*, trans. Lydia G. Cochrane (Cambridge, 1988); id., ed., *The Culture of Print: Power and the Uses of Print in Early Modern Europe*, trans. Lydia G. Cochrane (Cambridge, 1989); id., *The Cultural Origins of the French Revolution*, trans. Lydia G. Cochrane (Durham, NC, 1991); id., *The Order of Books: Readers, Authors, and Libraries in Europe between the Fourteenth and Eighteenth Centuries*, trans. Lydia G. Cochrane (Cambridge, 1994); Robert Darnton, 'History of Reading', in Peter Burke, ed., *New Perspectives on Historical Writing* (Cambridge, 1991), 140–67; Harold Love, *Scribal Publication in Seventeenth-Century England* (Oxford, 1993); Arthur F. Marotti, *Manuscript, Print, and the English Renaissance Lyric* (Ithaca, NY, 1995).

[13] See Michel de Certeau, *The Practice of Everyday Life*, trans. Steven Rendall (Berkeley, 1988), 165–76.

[14] Paul Veyne, *Writing History: Essay on Epistemology*, trans. Mina Moore-Rinvolucri (Middletown, Conn., 1984); Hayden White, *Metahistory: The Historical Imagination in Nineteenth-Century Europe* (Baltimore, 1973); Michel de Certeau, *The Writing of History*, trans. Tom Conley (New York, 1988); Simon Schama, *Dead Certainties (Unwarranted Speculations)* (1991).

[15] See the essays in H. Aram Veeser, ed., *The New Historicism* (London, 1989).

[16] See Peter Burke, 'Overture: The New History, its Past and Future' and 'History of Events and the Revival of Narrative', in id., ed., *New Perspectives on Historical Writing*, 1–23, 233–48.

be embraced by traditional narrative modes.[17] This seems to me to reinforce rather than deny the relationship between history and reality.

The problems remain the same for modern historians as for ancient: how to conduct an inquiry and then how to communicate the fullness of the resulting material. One complexity of the history of news in the seventeenth century is the competing advantages of short- and long-term perspectives. Traditionally historians of the news have taken a telescopic view of the development of news media in the early-modern period, and identified a long-term development and increase in communication.[18] The story has all the properties of the classic Whig model of history: it tells of the move from an oral culture through a manuscript culture to a culture of print; of an expansion of political franchise being reflected in increasingly wide access to news; of the breakdown of censorship and the evolution of political liberty: in short of the move-

[17] Stuart Clark, 'The *Annales* Historians', in Quentin Skinner, ed., *The Return of Grand Theory in the Human Sciences* (1985; Cambridge, 1990), 179–96; Burke, 'History of Events'; Giovanni Levi, 'On Microhistory', in Burke, ed., *New Perspectives on Historical Writing*, 93–113; Fernand Braudel, 'History and the Social Sciences', in *On History*, trans. Sarah Matthews (Chicago, 1980), 25–54; Paul Ricoeur, *Time and Narrative*, 3 vols., trans. Kathleen McLaughlin and David Pellauer (Chicago, 1984–8).

[18] Alexander Andrews, *The History of British Journalism, from the Foundation of the Newspaper Press in England, to the Repeal of the Stamp Act in 1855* (1859; Grosse Point, Mich., 1968); James Grant, *The Newspaper Press: Its Origin—Progress—and Present Position*, 2 vols. (1871); H. R. Fox Bourne, *English Newspapers: Chapters in the History of Journalism* (1887); *History*; J. B. Williams, 'Beginnings of English Journalism', in A. W. Ward and A. R. Waller, eds., *The Cambridge History of English Literature*, vol. vii: *Cavalier and Puritan* (Cambridge, 1911), 389–415; J. G. Muddiman, *The King's Journalist 1659–1689: Studies in the Reign of Charles II* (1923); Mrs Herbert Richardson, *The Old English Newspaper* (1929); Stanley Morison, *The English Newspaper* (Cambridge, 1932); id., *Origins of the Newspaper* (1954); William M. Clyde, *The Struggle for the Freedom of the Press from Caxton to Cromwell* (1934); F. S. Siebert, *Freedom of the Press in England 1476–1776: The Rise and Decline of Government Controls* (Urbana, Ill., 1952); Harold Herd, *The March of Journalism: The Story of the British Press from 1622 to the Present Day* (1952); *Beginnings*; Michael McKeon, *The Origins of the English Novel 1600–1740* (1988), 47; for popular studies see Jane Soames, *The English Press: Newspapers and News*, preface by Hilaire Belloc (1936; 1938); Francis Williams, *Dangerous Estate: The Anatomy of Newspapers*, foreword by Michael Foot (1957; Cambridge, 1984); Jim Allee Hart, *Views on the News: The Developing Editorial Syndrome, 1500–1800*, foreword by Howard Rusk Long (Carbondale, Ill., 1970); Keith Williams, *The English Newspaper: An Illustrated History to 1900* (1977); Geoffrey A. Cranfield, *The Press & Society: From Caxton to Northcliffe* (1978); Anthony Smith, 'The Long Road to Objectivity and Back Again: The Kinds of Truth we Get in Journalism', in George Boyce, James Curran, and Pauline Wingate, eds., *Newspaper History: From the Seventeenth Century to the Present Day* (1978), 153–71; id., *The Newspaper: An International History* (1979); Dan Schiller, *Objectivity and the News: The Public and the Rise of Commercial Journalism* (Philadelphia, 1981); Mitchell Stephens, *A History of News: From the Drum to the Satellite* (New York, 1988); Ray Boston, *The Essential History of Fleet Street: Its History and Influence* (1990).

ment from an ancient regime to a democratic one.[19] The allure of this seamless narrative has elided some of the complexities of history.

There are elements of truth in the story. In the fourteenth century, before the introduction of printing into the British Isles, news was communicated by word of mouth, sometimes assisted by manuscript. It could travel with a surprising speed and degree of accuracy, but this accelerated in the sixteenth century with the introduction of occasional printed pamphlets.[20] These influenced the reception of news only among the social élite, however, as printed texts were a luxury product. Simultaneously, central governments were increasingly intervening in provincial affairs, which facilitated not only a sense of the local community but of the relation of locality to nationhood.[21]

News was seasonal: more plentiful during the summer when travel was easier, and sparse during the winter. It also depended on court sessions, permeating during regional assizes and when local gentry travelled to London to settle legal matters in a notoriously litigious age. This periodicity was significantly levelled by the development of the professional newswriter in Elizabethan London. Students at the Inns of Court were paid retainers to write formal letters of news to provincial gentry. The centre for news was St Paul's, surrounded by booksellers and the focus for leisurely walkers and professional scriveners, actively or passively giving and receiving the latest news.[22] In the words of John Earle, 'It is the eares Brothell and satisfies their lust, and ytch. The Visitants are all men without exceptions, but the principall Inhabitants and possessors, are stale Knights, and Captaines out of seruice, men of long Rapiers, and Breeches, which after all turne Merchants here and traffick for Newes.'[23] In 1630 a coranto publisher complained that

[19] e.g. Perez Zagorin, *The Court and the Country: The Beginning of the English Revolution* (1969), 106–8, 198–206.

[20] Matthias A. Shaaber, *Some Forerunners of the Newspaper in England 1476–1622* (Philadelphia, 1929); C. A. J. Armstrong, 'Some Examples of the Distribution and Speed of News in England at the Time of the Wars of the Roses', in R. W. Hunt, W. A. Pantin, and R. W. Southern, eds., *Studies in Medieval History: Presented Frederick Maurice Powicke* (Oxford, 1948), 429–54; F. J. Levy, 'How Information Spread among the Gentry, 1550–1640', *Journal of British Studies*, 21 (1982), 11–34; D. C. Collins, ed., *Battle of Nieuport*, Shakespeare Association Facsimiles, 9 (1935), pp. v–xxx.

[21] Victor Morgan, 'Country, Court and Cambridge University, 1558–1640: A Study in the Evolution of a Political Culture' Ph.D. thesis, 5 vols. (Norwich, 1983), i. 46–99; Clive Holmes, 'The County Community in Stuart Historiography', *Journal of British Studies*, 19 (1980), 54–73.

[22] For newsletters frequently referring to St Paul's, see Birch; for booksellers see Dagmar Freist, 'The World is Ruled and Governed by Opinion: The Formation of Opinions and the Communication Network in London 1637 to c.1645', Ph.D. thesis (Cambridge, 1992), 84–110.

[23] John Earle, *Micro-Cosmographie. Or, A Peece of the World Discovered; In Essayes and Characters* (1628; *STC* 7439), sigs. I11–K.

'the greatest talkers of Newes (as the *Pauls* walkers) are the poorest buyers'.[24]

During the last quarter of the sixteenth century, London publishers produced in increasing numbers occasional news pamphlets. These were for the large part sensationalistic or moralistic, concerned with trials and executions, witchcraft, and other anomalous phenomena.[25] Though there were also almanacs, ballads, some fiction, underground literature, and political controversy, the mainstay of British publishing remained theological works.[26] This 'popular' literature continued to flourish through the early seventeenth century.[27] On the Continent, meanwhile, the business of periodical publishing had begun. The preferred year of inception is 1594, when *Mercurius Gallobelgicus* was published in Cologne. The first issue of this Latin serial contained European, mainly military news of the previous six years.[28] Thereafter, under several editors, it appeared semi-annually until 1635. Unlike the later newsbook or newspaper, *Gallobelgicus* was a substantial volume: it was, however, both a serial and a periodical, superseding a number of irregular news publications which had appeared across Europe, in Paris, Poland, Venice, Vienna, Cologne, and Hungary. *Gallobelgicus* circulated widely in Britain amongst the educated, and several volumes were translated.[29] Today it is probably best known from John Donne's epigram:

> Like *Esops* fellow-slaves, O *Mercury*,
> Which could do all things, thy faith is; and I

[24] Quoted Dahl, 168.

[25] Sandra Clark, *The Elizabethan Pamphleteers: Popular Moralistic Pamphlets, 1580–1640* (1983); J. A. Sharpe, '"Last Dying Speeches": Religion, Ideology and Public Executions in Seventeenth-Century England', *P&P* 107 (1985), 144–67.

[26] In general: H. S. Bennett, *English Books and Readers*, 3 vols. (1965–70; Cambridge, 1989). More particularly: Gamini Salgado, ed., *Cony-Catchers and Bawdy Baskets: An Anthology of Elizabethan Low Life* (Harmondsworth, 1972); *The Elizabethan Underworld* (1977); *Astrology*; Neil Rhodes, *Elizabethan Grotesque* (1980); Charles Nicholl, *A Cup of News: The Life of Thomas Nashe* (1984); David Margolies, *Novel and Society in Elizabethan England* (1985); Paul Salzman, *English Prose Fiction 1558–1700: A Critical History* (Oxford, 1985); Tessa Watt, *Cheap Print and Popular Piety, 1550–1640* (Cambridge, 1991).

[27] Victor E. Neuburg, *Popular Literature: A History and Guide: From the Beginning of Printing to the Year 1897* (1977); Margaret Spufford, *Small Books and Pleasant Histories: Popular Fiction and its Readership in Seventeenth-Century England* (1981); John Carey, 'Sixteenth- and Seventeenth-Century Prose', in Christopher Ricks, ed., *English Poetry and Prose, 1550–1674* (1970; 1986), 329–411; Roger Pooley, *English Prose of the Seventeenth Century, 1590–1700* (1992); Bernard Capp, *The World of John Taylor the Water-Poet, 1578–1653* (Oxford, 1994).

[28] *Mercurius Gallobelgicus: siue, rerum in gallia & Belgio potissimum: Hispania quoque, Italia, Anglia, Germania, Polonia, vicinisque locis ab anno 1588 vsque ad Martium . . . 1594 gestarum, Nuncius* (Cologne, 1594). Later issues were printed in Frankfurt.

[29] Shaaber, *Some Forerunners of the Newspaper*, 310–11.

Like *Esops* selfe, which nothing; I confesse
I should have had more faith, if thou hadst lesse;
Thy credit lost thy credit: 'Tis sinne to doe,
In this case, as thou wouldst be done unto,
To beleeve all: Change thy name: thou art like
Mercury in stealing, but lyest like a *Greeke*.[30]

The earliest printed news periodical established a reputation for unreliability, a presage of things to come.

Continental Europe followed the precedent before Britain; Holland and Germany were soon producing monthly, or irregular, news periodicals. The Antwerp printer Abraham Verhoeven began producing his *Nieuwe Tydinghe* around 1605, initially at uneven intervals, then with increasing frequency; from 1610 a French edition appeared. It was at this time illegal to publish British news in Britain, a policy unevenly enforced by the Stationers' Company under the Star Chamber decree of 1586.[31] In 1620, however, a Dutch printer named Petrus Keerius published in Amsterdam a small, untitled folio broadsheet in English, containing news of continental Europe. Keerius' was the first of the early news serials known as corantos. It is not clear precisely when they appeared, though it was probably early in 1620. If the earliest surviving issue, dated 2 December, was the first, then it begins with what is probably the most profound anticlimax in the history of literature: 'The new tydings out of Italie are not yet com.'[32]

By the following year a number of competitors had appeared in the Low Countries. In January 1621, James VI and I, sensitive to the circulation of news, persuaded the States General to place a ban upon the export of corantos to Britain.[33] Nevertheless, between February and September of the same year the first London-printed news periodical, translated into English from the Dutch, was published by Thomas Archer. No copy survives, and its existence is inferred from contemporary correspondence.[34] In August 1621, John Chamberlain expressed contempt for the reliability of these domestic corantos, just as Donne had done for *Gallobelgicus*:

[30] John Donne, *The Satires, Epigrams and Verse Letters*, ed. W. Milgate (Oxford, 1967), 53.

[31] Cyprian Blagden, *The Stationers' Company: A History 1403–1959* (Stanford, Calif., 1960), 19–77.

[32] Dahl, 31; W. P. Van Stockum, Jr. ed., *The First Newspapers of England Printed in Holland 1620–1621* (The Hague, 1914).

[33] *Tercentenary Handlist of English & Welsh Newspapers, Magazines & Reviews* (1920), 9.

[34] For bibliographical information on corantos see Dahl, *passim*; id., 'Amsterdam: Cradle of English Newspapers', *Library*[5], 4 (1949), 166–78; Matthias Shaaber, 'The History of the First English Newspaper', *Studies in Philology*, 29 (1932), 551–87; Laurence Hanson, 'English Newsbooks, 1620–1642', *Library*[4], 18 (1938), 355–84.

there is come out a new proclamation against lavish and licentious talking in matters of state, either at home or abrode, which the common people know not how to understand, nor how far matter of state may stretch or extend; for they continue to take no notice of yt, but print every weeke (at least) corantos with all manner of newes, and as strange stuffe as any we have from Amsterdam.[35]

In September Archer was imprisoned for publishing the corantos, and was replaced by 'N.B.', either Nathaniel Butter or Nicholas Bourne, who obtained an official licence.[36] Until 1624, when a shift in foreign policy may have made foreign news less lucrative, Butter and Bourne collaborated with Thomas Archer, William Sheffard, and Bartholomew Downes in a publishing syndicate. Thereafter Butter and Bourne collaborated alone, while Archer produced a competing series between 1624 and 1628.[37]

The periodicity of these early corantos was irregular; they appeared at roughly weekly intervals, whenever there was enough news to fill them. They contained foreign news, translated from foreign gazettes and corantos and from original letters. Initially they followed the format of Continental folio sheets, but soon adopted the conventions of the domestic book trade, becoming quartos, usually three sheets (twenty-four pages) long, with full title-pages. Publishers evidently found these easier to produce; and it is possible that readers found them more familiar. New practices were gradually developed which adjusted to the specific requirements of transmitting news in a printed periodical. From 1622 corantos were numbered, and the editor, possibly Thomas Gainsford, began to 'digest' discrete items into a continuous, smooth narrative.[38] Corantos were a very successful enterprise, and quickly proliferated in numbers, presumably with concomitant profits. They swiftly and accurately communicated news to the provinces, via trade routes, carriers, and the post.[39]

[35] Chamberlain writing to Sir Dudley Carleton, the English Ambassador at The Hague. Cf.: 'The uncertaintie likewise and varietie of reports is such that we know not what to beleve of that is done here under our nose, and what is geven out to day for certain is to morrow contradicted: for since two yeares that the forge or mint was set up at Amsterdam we have never left off coyning, so apish are we in imitation of what is worst.' This reference to corantos in Feb. 1622 suggests that they first appeared early in 1620. Quoted Dahl, 49.

[36] BL: Harl. MS 389, f. 122.

[37] D. F. McKenzie, 'The London Book Trade in the Later Seventeenth Century', unpublished Sandars Lectures, 1976; Dahl, 266–78.

[38] See Butter and Bourne's first numbered series; Dahl, 86–113; Frearson, 'London Corantos in the 1620s', 5.

[39] Judith Simmons, 'Publications of 1623', *Library*[5], 21 (1966), 207–22; Frearson, 'London Corantos in the 1620s', 6–15; Richard Cust, 'News and Politics in Early Seventeenth-Century England', *P&P* 112 (1986), 60–90; Tom Cogswell, 'The Politics of Propaganda: Charles I and the People in the 1620s', *Journal of British Studies*, 29 (1990), 187–215; Howard Robinson, *The British Post Office: A History* (Princeton, 1948).

Despite the success of corantos, they did not simply evolve into the domestic newsbook. There were few direct continuities. The digestive editing of 1622 corantos was rediscovered or reinvented by the newsbook in 1642–3. The first newsbooks of 1641 were not numbered: this was introduced in January 1642.[40] Yet the London *Bills of Mortality* were consistently numbered through this period. Newsbooks publishers invented consecutive pagination and signatures, which had never been employed in corantos. Newsbooks introduced regularity in length, exact periodicity, and the brief, unchanging title. Corantos tended to vary in all these characteristics of the periodical. Like corantos and pamphlets, however, the first newsbooks did have title-pages. Newsbooks also followed, though not at first, the use of section headings to indicate the date and place of origin of letters.

Newsbooks partly inherited a readership from corantos. Some readers did move from corantos to newsbooks. Yet the newsbook, as I argue in Chapter 2, initially addressed a specific audience, without which it would not have appeared; and to a large extent a new readership was generated in 1642. It is not in these formal continuities that the relationship between newsbooks and corantos subsists. There was in fact a much closer relationship between newsbooks and non-periodical pamphlets. Except for a very brief period of collaboration between Butter and John Thomas, and one or two interventions by Bourne, the publishers of corantos did not move on to produce newsbooks and therefore transmit their experience directly.[41] The most important continuities lie not in the objects or texts themselves, but in the means employed to distribute them rapidly and widely across the country. In 1641 it was already a convention to accompany a personal letter with a printed text; carriers had become used to moving books along trade routes, and publishers had become accustomed to sending them.[42] Provincial booksellers had already established relations with publishers in the metropolis. The provision of an infrastructure for distribution was probably the most useful precedent which corantos provided for newsbooks.

Though the coranto was a commercial and informational success, the government did not endeavour to take advantage of the form for propa-

[40] The publisher Humphrey Blunden started the fashion with *A True Diurnall of the Last Weeks Passages in Parliament*, 17 Jan. 1642, 623.01A (see also 623.01B). He was followed by at least three others the next week: see N&S 104.2, 69.2, 99.02.

[41] Butter collaborated for three weeks with Thomas on the continuation of *Heads of Severall Proceedings* (181.104B–06); he also produced the single issue newsbook *The Passages in Parliament*, 10 Jan. 1642, 494.1; and he continued to produce his foreign-news coranto, *Continuation of the Forraine Occurrents*, N&S 64.348–432, Dahl, 367–83; and the unnumbered series described by Dahl, 384–9. Bourne was involved with *Generall Newes* (N&S 167); *Nouvelles ordinaires* (N&S 454), and *Mercure anglois* (N&S 258).

[42] See Ch. 5, below.

ganda purposes. The newsletter-writer John Pory was among a group who petitioned as early as 1621 for a 'Gazette or weekly occurants'.[43] Domestic news remained proscribed. The news of the Protestant cause in the Thirty Years War could reflect on British affairs, and comment unfavourably on the king's policy of non-intervention. Corantos were implicitly anti-Catholic, and their hero was Gustavus Adolphus, who to some seemed the antitype of Charles I. Charles remained cautious, nervous even, about the 'promiscuous' circulation of printed news, and no one suggested that it was an untypical eccentricity when in October 1632 the Privy Council issued a decree prohibiting the printing of pamphlets of overseas news.[44] News was not meant for the common people: the king wrote that the foreign news presented in the corantos was 'unfit for popular view and discourse'.[45]

In continental Europe such restrictions did not operate: there the elasticity of news was primarily restricted by geography and economics.[46] In France the conceptual challenge presented by the power of print was grasped by Cardinal Richelieu, a case providing an enlightening contrast with Britain. The prehistory of news periodicals in France, like Britain, consisted of political and historical *occasionnels* and of Dutch imports. An official periodical, *Le Mercure français*, was founded in 1613; this was a large volume, published irregularly, the first volume containing retrospective news back to 1605. A more heterogeneous, that is, more newspaper-like periodical, *Nouvelles ordinaires*, appeared in January 1631, published by three members of the Parisian Corporation of Printers and Booksellers, Jean Martin, Louis Vendosme, and François Pommerai. In May the same year, following the division of the French royal family and the ensuing propaganda wars, Richelieu commissioned Théophraste Renaudot to edit a weekly *Gazette*. This soon became France's dominant news publication, and was reprinted in the provinces.[47]

[43] *CSPD 1619–1623*, 330; Andrew Mousley, 'Self, State, and Seventeenth-Century News', *Seventeenth Century*, 6 (1991), 159; William S. Powell, *John Pory 1572–1636: The Life and Letters of a Man of Many Parts* (Chapel Hill, NC, 1977).

[44] *CSPD 1631–1633*, 426.

[45] *Personal Rule*, 646.

[46] Fernand Braudel, *The Mediterranean and the Mediterranean World in the Age of Philip II*, trans. Siân Reynolds, 2 vols. (1949, 1966; New York, 1972), i. 355–71.

[47] Howard M. Solomon, *Public Welfare, Science, and Propaganda in Seventeenth Century France* (Princeton, 1972), 100–22; Solomon's work is very useful, but many of his dates are inaccurate. Also Folke Dahl, with Fanny Petibon and Marguerite Boulet, *Les Débuts de la presse française: Nouveaux Aperçus*, Acta Bibliothecae Gotoburgensis, 4 (Göteborg, 1951); Philip A. Knachel, *England and the Fronde: The Impact of the English Civil War and Revolution on France* (Ithaca, NY, 1967); Roger Chartier, 'Pamphlets et gazettes', in Henri-Jean Martin and Chartier, eds., *Histoire de l'édition français*, vol. i: *Le Livre conquérant* (Paris, 1982), 405–25; Gilles Feyel, *La 'Gazette' en province à travers ses réimpressions, 1631–1752*

Renaudot was both a true logomach and an idealist. Richelieu saw the press as a political instrument, and in November secured a monopoly for his creature. Martin, Vendosme, and Pommerai were ordered to stop publishing, and Renaudot purloined the title *Nouvelles ordinaires*. The *Gazette* became a tool of modern statecraft, engineering support for the regime of Louis XIII. The periodical was not respectable as an instrument of government, but contemporaries descried its effectiveness. One wrote of Richelieu: 'He has recognised his shortcoming and endeavoring to escape from it, has erected a school or, perhaps better, an aviary of Psaphon, the academy which meets at the house of the Gazeteer, the father of lies.'[48] Renaudot suggested that the periodical press could be used to control rumour and restrict false news, to drive a wedge between news and gossip: 'History is the account of things that have happened, the *Gazette* that only of their advance reports. The former is obliged always to tell the truth, the latter only to ward off falsehood.'[49] He undertook to spread news not only of political, military, and economic affairs, but also of cultural events, science, and medicine. As a Huguenot converted to Catholicism he was cautious about reporting matters of state, but managed nevertheless to combine his role as Richelieu's propagandist with projections for a scientific and philosophical academy open to the public. This became a threat to the Académie Française. Renaudot also founded a *Bureau d'Adresse*, an office which advertised goods and services and functioned as a trading post. The idea had initially been propounded by Montaigne.[50] Though his own profit and self-interest were involved, Renaudot was a philanthropist, devising projects for the good of mankind, including the poor. Although his *Gazette* was a propaganda machine, this did not exhaust its potential; he believed that news countered 'rumours' and therefore increased truth.[51] Samuel Hartlib was impressed by Renaudot's efforts, corresponded with him, and tried to establish comparable institutions in England.[52]

(Amsterdam, 1982); Anne-Marie Chouillet and Madeleine Fabre, 'Diffusion et réception des nouvelles et ouvrages britanniques par la presse spécialisée de langue française', in Hans Bots, ed., *La Diffusion et la lecture des journaux de langue française sous l'ancien régime* (Amsterdam, 1988), 177–201; Henri-Jean Martin, *Le Livre français sous l'ancien régime* (Paris, 1987), 135; Jeffrey K. Sawyer, *Printed Poison: Pamphlet Propaganda, Faction Politics, and the Public Sphere in Early Seventeenth-Century France* (Berkeley, 1990).

[48] Mathieu de Morgues, quoted Solomon, *Public Welfare, Science, and Propaganda*, 95.

[49] Quoted Erica Harth, *Ideology and Culture in Seventeenth-Century France* (Ithaca, NY, 1983), 165, also 173.

[50] Michel de Montaigne, 'Something Lacking in our Civil Administrations', *The Complete Essays*, trans. M. A. Screech (1991), 251–2.

[51] Solomon, *Public Welfare, Science, and Propaganda*, 62–5.

[52] Samuel Hartlib, *A further Discoverie of the Office of Pvblick Addresse for Accommodations* (1648; H987); G. H. Turnbull, *Hartlib, Dury and Comenius: Gleanings from Hartlib's Papers*

France therefore set a clear example of what could be done in Britain. Several projectors petitioned Charles I for a licence to follow Renaudot's precedent.[53] In 1634 George More and Walter Waldner appealed for a licence to publish an official newsbook, presenting the king with an opportunity to use propaganda to support controversial policies.[54] During the personal rule of 1632 to 1640 an interested public were starved of news.[55] When the dearth was remedied, it was all too easy for parliament to deploy news in its own interest, to encourage the reading public to sympathize with its reformism.

After the Star Chamber decree of 1632 the corantos stopped. Butter and Bourne continued to produce an irregular serial publication of recent history, variably entitled *The Swedish Intelligencer*, *The German History*, and *Diatelesma*.[56] The reading public returned to imports from Holland and France and to ballads and other occasional publications. Interest in news may have slightly abated with the death of Gustavus Adolphus in November 1632, with the non-sitting of parliament, and through accustomization to its absence.[57] In 1637 Star Chamber introduced new licensing legislation which enabled closer control of the press. The result was a more focused mechanism, devolving responsibility according to type of book. It was on paper a more effective system, and the penalties were more severe. It was also in 1637 that the threat to civil order began to loom over the horizon, when the Book of Common Prayer was imposed upon Scotland, precipitating a chain of events leading to war and ultimately the calling of a parliament in 1640.[58] In 1638 the Scots rebelled, and, perhaps surprisingly, Butter and Bourne were granted a Royal Patent:

(1947); H. R. Trevor-Roper, 'Three Foreigners: The Philosophers of the Puritan Revolution', *Religion, the Reformation and Social Change and Other Essays* (1967), 237–93; Charles Webster, ed., *Samuel Hartlib and the Advancement of Learning* (Cambridge, 1970); id., 'Macaria: Samuel Hartlib and the Great Reformation', *Acta Comenia*, 26 (Prague, 1970), 147–64; id., *The Great Instauration: Science, Medicine and Reform 1626–1660* (1975); id., 'Benjamin Worsley: Engineering for Universal Reform from the Invisible College to the Navigation Act', in Mark Greengrass, Michael Leslie, and Timothy Raylor, eds., *Samuel Hartlib and Universal Reformation: Studies in Intellectual Communication* (Cambridge, 1994), 213–46; Caroline Hibbard, *Charles I and the Popish Plot* (Chapel Hill, NC, 1983); Stephen Clucas, 'Samuel Hartlib's Ephemerides, 1635–59, and the Pursuit of Scientific and Philosophical Manuscripts: The Religious Ethos of an Intelligencer', *Seventeenth Century*, 6 (1991), 33–55.

[53] See *History*, 158–61; *CSPD 1637–1638*, 19–21.

[54] *CSPD 1634–1635*, 418; *Personal Rule*, 647.

[55] Cust, 'News and Politics', *passim*.

[56] Dahl, 221–2. The two kinds of publications, coranto and history, were obviously closely related.

[57] *Personal Rule*, 644–730.

[58] *British Monarchies, passim.*

> for the imprinting & publishing of all matter of History or Newes of any forraine place or Kingdome since the first beginning of the late German warres to this present. And also for the translating setting forth imprinting & publishing in the English tongue all Newes, Novells, Gazetts Currantos or Occurrences that concerne forraine p[ar]t[e]s &c, for the term of XXI^{ty} yeares.[59]

The resulting series of corantos was a diminished sequel: each issue consisting of four, albeit larger, pages. The title and periodicity remained irregular. Bourne withdrew in late 1639, suggesting that interest in domestic news had undermined the foreign-news market.

Butter continued to produce corantos until September 1641. He tried to revive a serial in 1642, which appears from the few extant copies to have been unsuccessful.[60] By then the market for news publications had changed dramatically. In November 1640 the Long Parliament met, and soon a commercially produced weekly manuscript of parliamentary proceedings was available in London. During the summer of 1641 many London presses allocated their resources to produce large numbers of small topical pamphlets, notably satires and news pamphlets about the Earl of Strafford and William Laud, Archbishop of Canterbury. In November 1641 the first newsbook appeared: a weekly periodical, initially published on Mondays, eight pages long, and containing domestic news. The bookseller George Thomason began to amass an enormous collection of cheap print that had previously been considered disposable ephemera. As a consequence the survival rate of news publications from the 1640s is considerably higher than that for corantos and ballads.[61] There rapidly developed a culture of the pamphlet, of which the newsbook was a central, driving feature.[62]

Editors of newsbooks rapidly engineered a repertoire for representing and organizing news events. The newsbook soon transformed from a plain and non-controversial narration of parliamentary proceedings into a bitter and aggressive instrument of literary and political faction. That is the story told below. Parliament regained control of the press in September 1649, and soon made efforts to intervene where Charles had

[59] Quoted Dahl, 223.

[60] Dahl, 262–5.

[61] G. K. Fortescue, ed., *Catalogue to the Thomason Tracts*, 2 vols. (1908); Lois Spencer, 'The Professional and Literary Connections of George Thomason', *Library*^{5}, 13 (1958), 102–18; ead., 'The Politics of George Thomason', *Library*^{5}, 14 (1959), 11–27; Stephen J. Greenberg, 'Dating Civil War Pamphlets, 1641–1644', *Albion*, 20 (1988), 387–401; Michael Mendle, 'The Thomason Collection: A Reply to Stephen J. Greenberg', and Greenberg, 'The Thomason Collection: Rebuttal to Michael Mendle', both in *Albion*, 22 (1980), 85–98.

[62] For example; *Secret Rites*; James Holstun, ed., *Pamphlet Wars: Prose in the English Revolution* (1992); Thomas Corns, *Uncloistered Virtue: English Political Literature, 1640–1660* (Oxford, 1992); *L&R*; Sharon Achinstein, *Milton and the Revolutionary Reader* (Princeton, 1994).

feared to tread, by allowing a limited number of licensed newsbooks.[63] This was taken a step further in June 1650 when *Mercurius Politicus* was founded. For ten years this was Britain's dominant publication; it moved away from the controversial writing of the 1640s, and instead supplied high-quality news, both domestic and foreign.[64] This was none the less propaganda, and its editor, Marchamont Nedham, occasionally incorporated editorials of republican political theory. *Politicus* had a monopoly between October 1655 and April 1659, when political disorder resulted in another pamphlet war and further mud-slinging.[65] The fortunes of this very remarkable journal were closely linked with those of the republic, and when Charles II returned to England and the throne in 1660, it was closed. The restored king nevertheless acknowledged the role of the modern newspaper, subjected the press to tight controls, and commissioned writers to supply his subjects; initially Henry Muddiman, then Roger L'Estrange.[66]

After the Restoration newsbooks were fewer and more conservative, and editorial material tamer, until the licensing act lapsed in 1679, and concerns over the Popish Plot led to a polemical mêlée resembling the days of the civil war.[67] In November 1665 Joseph Williamson, the under-secretary of Lord Arlington, one of the secretaries of state, took advantage of the court's retreat to Oxford from plague-ridden London and established the biweekly *Oxford Gazette.* Differing from the format of previous newsbooks, this was a newspaper, a half-sheet of paper printed in two columns on each side. In January 1666 the court returned to London and the next month the *Oxford Gazette* became the *London*

[63] For the 1640s newsbook in addition to the above see: Henry Plomer, 'Secret Printing during the Civil War', *Library*², 5 (1904), 373–403; id., 'An Analysis of the Civil War Newspaper "Mercurius Civicus"', *Library*², 6 (1905), 184–207; G. E. Manwaring, 'Journalism in the Days of the Commonwealth', *Edinburgh Review,* 244 (1926), 105–20; *Beginnings*; Joseph Frank, *Cromwell's Press Agent: A Critical Biography of Marchamont Nedham, 1620–1678* (Lanham, Md., 1980); *Berkenhead*; Cotton; id., 'John Dillingham, Journalist of the Middle Group', *English Historical Review,* 93 (1978), 817–34; David Stormer, 'The Faithful Scout, 1652–3: A Re-evaluation of a So-called Radical London Weekly', MA thesis (Victoria University of Wellington, 1987; I am grateful to Professor Colin Davies for this reference); Carolyn Nelson and Matthew Seccombe, *Periodical Publications 1641–1700: A Survey with Illustrations,* Occasional Papers of the Bibliographical Society, 2 (Oxford, 1986); *N&S.*

[64] I am currently at work on a study of Milton, Nedham, and *Politicus.*

[65] *MTN,* ch. 8.

[66] Muddiman, *The King's Journalist*; Peter Fraser, *The Intelligence of the Secretaries of State and their Monopoly of Licensed News, 1660–1688* (Cambridge, 1956); Ronald Hutton, *The Restoration: A Political and Religious History of England and Wales 1659–1667* (Oxford, 1985), 156–7; James Sutherland, *The Restoration Newspaper and its Development* (Cambridge, 1986).

[67] Jonathan Scott, *Algernon Sidney and the Restoration Crisis, 1677–1683* (Cambridge, 1991).

Gazette, which survived for over three hundred years.[68] Through the second half of the seventeenth century the newspaper continued to play a part in everyday life, editors using the form to embrace heterogeneous material. This was not a total innovation; many of the newsbooks of the 1640s and 1650s had been collocations of different kinds of reports and religious and cultural comment. But the later period can be seen to lead directly to the journalism of the eighteenth century, when the newspaper became an established factor in British politics; when the daily newspaper appeared, beginning with the *Daily Courant* in 1703; when leisurely journals, such as *The Tatler*, *The Female Tatler*, Swift and Sheridan's *The Intelligencer*, and *The Spectator*, began to fashion a literary discourse discrete from politics; and when the provincial newspaper developed.[69] The desire for news, and suspicions of it, continued: as Addison wrote in *The Spectator* in 1712, 'There is no Humour in my Countrymen, which I am more enclined to wonder at, than their general Thirst after News.'[70]

The decision to place the newsbook within broad historiographical parameters is limiting. Newsbooks could be seen alternatively in the more constrained contexts elaborated by civil war historiography. Recent studies of the civil war have replaced long-term causes with detailed political narrative.[71] The implications for our view of the broader history of early-modern Britain are profound.[72] Yet no historian has systematically outlined the relation between the appearance of the newsbook and the origins or outbreak of the war.

The newsbook has direct bearings on the issues of provincialism and neutralism. Information crossed the boundaries of the local communi-

[68] P. M. Handover, *A History of the London Gazette, 1665–1965* (HMSO, 1965).

[69] Michael Harris and Alan Lee, eds., *The Press in English Society from the Seventeenth to Nineteenth Centuries* (Cranbury, NJ, 1986); Christine Gerrard, *The Patriot Opposition to Walpole: Politics, Poetry, and National Myth, 1725–1742* (Oxford, 1994); for general accounts of the non-London press, see J. M. Sutherland, 'The Circulation of Newspapers and Literary Periodicals, 1700–30', *Library*[4], 15 (1934–5), 110–24; Geoffrey A. Cranfield, *The Development of the Provincial Newspaper, 1700–1760* (Oxford, 1962); R. M. Wiles, *Freshest Advices: Early Provincial Newspapers in England* (Columbus, Oh., 1965); Robert Munter, *The History of the Irish Newspaper, 1685–1760* (Cambridge, 1967); R. B. Walker, 'The Newspaper Press in the Reign of William III', *HJ* 17 (1974), 691–709; Christine Ferdinand, *Networking the News* (Oxford, forthcoming); for a sceptical account of the influence of the political press see Jeremy Black, *The English Press in the Eighteenth Century* (1987).

[70] *The Spectator*, ed. Donald F. Bond, vol. iv (Oxford, 1965), 90.

[71] Anthony Fletcher, *The Outbreak of the English Civil War* (1981; 1985); Conrad Russell, *The Causes of the English Civil War* (Oxford, 1990); *British Monarchies*; also Ann Hughes, *The Causes of the English Civil War* (Basingstoke, 1991); Richard Cust and Ann Hughes, eds., *Conflict in Early Stuart England: Studies in Religion and Politics 1603–1642* (1989).

[72] J. C. D. Clark, *Revolution and Rebellion: State and Society in England in the Seventeenth and Eighteenth Centuries* (Cambridge, 1986).

ties, and turned the provinces into parts of the nations. In 1640 the provincial gentry did not well understand the king's policies.[73] In 1649 the basis for grasping the political and religious motivations for the trial and execution of the king was firmly established. Provincialism is one of the keystones of Stuart revisionism, which should oblige us to consider the role of cheap print in integrating the national culture. The appearance of the newsbook in November 1641 made more information available, and for comparatively low prices. This was no revolution in print, and the short-term effects were modest. But not negligible: parliamentary debates and resolutions, the basis for modern arguments about the role of politics in the causes of the war, became more widely available. This underlines the asymmetry between effects and causes: as we see it today the newspaper is a large effect; in 1642 it seemed less so, though it received widespread comment as a new and remarkable thing. Yet the social implications were implicit in the first, unheralded appearance, with causes inauspicious and unintended. Those who work on the history of the newspaper and trace it back to the 1640s will distort matters.

If we wish to, then, we can see the development of the newspaper as a linear progress in the infrastructures of communication, from the limits of gossip to the facility of print. This stream is troubled, however, by shorter-term perspectives. Newspapers themselves are committed to the quotidian current of events, and they need to be understood in the context of how and what they represented on a daily premiss, and how this was read, as much as their role in transhistorical shifts. This is not merely to draw a distinction between structure and function, or between paradigmatic and syntagmatic interpretations; it is to suggest that a highly focused perspective on the development of the newsbook and newspaper will reveal very different information from a sweeping one. A series of close studies disturbs the narrative of emergent news, as newsbooks and newspapers were themselves subject to the vicissitudes of everyday history.

In this study I argue that the newsbooks of the 1640s were complex in function. They were part of the political culture of the civil war, and reflected at once a political and commercial interest. It seems a natural correlative of the focus on the material book enjoined by the new bibliography to consider the book as a commodity in society. Historians of the newsbook have, however, tended to recognize the role of political interest and profit to the exclusion of other simultaneous effects.[74] A

[73] J. S. Morrill, *The Revolt of the Provinces: Conservatives and Radicals in the English Civil Wars, 1630–1650* (1976; 1980), 21–6; id., *The Nature of the English Revolution* (1993), 179–241; Cust, 'News and Politics'.

[74] Herd, *March of Journalism*, 26.

closer perspective unfolds some of the involutions. Newsbooks were of course a commodity: if we understand a commodity as a status of an object, it is clear that commodities are not exclusive to industrialized societies.[75] The exaggerated contrast between industrialized and non-industrialized societies has led to an overstated difference between the commodity and what might be described as the 'gift'. Conceptions of news cannot be reduced to the objects of its transmission: they are found at the intersection between objects and practices. Messages are received as well as sent, and readers can be active and creative.[76] Not all exchanges within a society are constituted by the same intensity of cultural information; as Georg Simmel suggested, buyer and seller can fail to communicate in their contact.[77] Newsbooks, like all commodities, move in and out of commodity status.[78] This explains why the desire and supply of news was only partly shaped by economic factors: psychological, political, literary, and social needs were more than a supplement to these.[79] After all, the demand for news could be met by other, free modes of communication, hence the role of printed news was always eccentric.

This has several implications. First, historians should pay much less attention to what contemporaries said about newsbooks in the 1640s, and consider instead what they did with them. Secondly, the fact that newsbooks were a commodity did not prevent them from fulfilling ideals, such as Hartlib expressed, of improved communication.[80] The objects and their use also carried ideas. Thirdly, and consequently, it is not sufficient to consider a single function of the newsbook, such as its profit-making dimension or its communicative role; it is necessary to approach it from a series of parallel perspectives, as an object, as a text

[75] Arjun Appadurai, 'Introduction: Commodities and the Politics of Value', in id., ed., *The Social Life of Things: Commodities in Cultural Perspective* (Cambridge, 1986), 6–16; Joan Thirsk, *Economic Policy and Projects: The Development of a Consumer Society in Early Modern England* (Oxford, 1978).

[76] Carlo Ginzburg, *The Cheese and the Worms: The Cosmos of a Sixteenth-Century Miller*, trans. John and Anne Tedeschi (New York, 1982).

[77] Marcel Mauss, *The Gift: The Form and Reason for Exchange in Archaic Societies*, trans. W. D. Halls, foreword by Mary Douglas (1990); Simmel quoted by Appadurai, 'Introduction', 14; see also Pierre Bourdieu, *Outline of a Theory of Practice*, trans. Richard Nice (New York, 1977); id., *Distinction: A Social Criticism of the Judgement of Taste*, trans. Richard Nice (Cambridge, Mass., 1984).

[78] Igor Kopytoff, 'The Cultural Biography of Things: Commoditization as Process', in Appadurai, ed., *The Social Life of Things*, 64–91.

[79] Appadurai writes: 'we can state as a general rule that those commodities whose consumption is most intricately tied up with critical social messages are likely to be *least* responsive to crude shifts in supply or price, but most responsive to political manipulation at the societal level.' 'Introduction', 33.

[80] Cf. Steven Shapin, *A Social History of Truth: Civility and Science in Seventeenth-Century England* (Chicago, 1994).

amongst others, as a product, as a consumable. Newsbooks were predicated not only on a means of distribution but on the desire of individual readers; hence they played their part in the division between intimate and public aspects of life.[81] Such an approach will demonstrate that political instrumentalism can further disinterested ends; and this reminds us that seventeenth-century Britain was a society where economics did not necessarily compete with religion and ideals, and where ideas had force.

Newsbooks were, and newspapers continue to be, a central constituent of culture, the network of meanings which operate within a society and regulate communication within it, 'a signifying system through which necessarily (though among other means) a social order is communicated, reproduced, experienced and explored'.[82] Although newsbooks spoke of history operating at its fastest speed, *l'histoire événementielle*, they were also engaged with the slowly modulating real circumstances of communication within their society. If we wish to understand the latter we must, however, patiently reconstruct the former in detail. In doing so we inevitably, though not deliberately, comment on the dynamics of the present.

Thus I have two stories to tell. In the first chapter I present a general narrative of the development of the newspaper in the 1640s, balancing necessary detail with the need to make progress. This narrative will be to some extent familiar from the work of previous historians of the newsbook, notably J. G. Muddiman, sometimes writing under the pseudonym of J. B. Williams (when referring to him I accept his chosen guise), who in the early years of this century contributed two informed and deeply tendentious studies; Joseph Frank, whose *Beginnings of the English Newspaper* has been the standard work on the subject since 1961; and Anthony Cotton, whose untimely death prevented the development and publication of his 1971 doctoral thesis.[83] Stories are not everything; this chapter provides an immediate context for the rest of the book. There are also narrative elements to the ensuing chapters, which focus on particular aspects of the newsbook: its prehistory and invention; the nature of journalistic rhetoric and its evolution through the 1640s; the relationship between newsbooks and other forms of

[81] For a convenient account of some of the aspects and consequences of this development, mainly focused on France, see Roger Chartier, ed., *Passions of the Renaissance*, vol. iii of Philippe Ariès and George Duby, general eds., *A History of Private Life* (Cambridge, Mass., 1989); Norbert Elias, *The History of Manners*, trans. Edmund Jephcott (New York, 1978).

[82] Raymond Williams, *Culture* (Glasgow, 1981), 13; in addition to the works by Chartier, Lévi-Strauss, and Bourdieu cited above, see Clifford Geertz, *The Interpretation of Cultures* (New York, 1973).

[83] *History*; Muddiman, *The King's Journalist*; *Beginnings*; Cotton.

cheap print; the distribution and readership of newsbooks; the transmission of newsbooks into subsequent seventeenth-century histories of the civil war. These elaborations offer a more complete picture, though my emphases may initially appear perverse. Our second tour may take a long time, but an unfamiliar territory will accordingly be mapped, and a destination will be sighted, if not reached. I hope I follow the poetry of what happens.

1

A Narrative History of the English Newsbook, 1641–1649

THE first story this book tells is of the rapid proliferation of newsbooks after their initial appearance in November 1641. Within a few weeks there were many newsbooks produced by different publishers, competing with and counterfeiting each other, struggling to find a foothold in a potentially lucrative market. Writers began to express their opinions, and thereby to differentiate themselves from their competitors. Political antagonism played an increasingly significant role. At the same time novice readers rapidly acclimatized themselves to the new form, and became sensitive to rhetorical and political arguments. Newsbooks became very influential. Writers alluded to them, attacked them, and thereby acknowledged their literary potency.[1] To some readers newsbooks were worth collecting, to others they were ephemera, and they may even have reached the scatological end about which contemporaries joked.[2] Across the country, throughout social hierarchies, in many different ways, newsbooks left traces of their impact.

1641 and 1642

The first newsbook appeared on 29 November 1641, a few weeks after the reconvening of the Long Parliament after its autumn recess. *Heads of Severall Proceedings* was a sober publication, dedicated exclusively to reporting news of both Houses. The Long Parliament was at a turning point in its history: debates over the Irish Rebellion and over the publication of the Grand Remonstrance had brought political tensions to the surface. The uneasy rhetoric of compromise and consensus, which had characterized both parliamentary debate and political writing, was falling away to reveal conflict and faction.[3]

[1] See Joad Raymond, 'The Daily Muse; or, Seventeenth-Century Poets Read the News', *Seventeenth Century*, 11 (1995), 1–30.

[2] *Mercurius Mastix* 1, 27 Aug. 1652, 3, 339.1/E674(18); *Britanicus* 113, 12 Jan. 1646, 994, 286.113/E315(11).

[3] Elizabeth Skerpan, *The Rhetoric of Politics in the English Revolution 1642–1660* (Columbia, Mo., 1992), 60–80; Kevin Sharpe, *Politics and Ideas in Early Stuart England: Essay and Studies* (1989), 65–8.

Though the first newsbooks showed no signs of this shift, they represented the discussion of fraught, controversial subjects and were intimately bound into developing political conflict. This relationship, and the language used to describe politics, was fundamental to the origins and nature of the newsbook. The very existence of the newsbook was itself significant.[4]

John Thomas, the publisher of *Heads of Severall Proceedings*, stimulated rivals immediately. The next week Richard Herne produced two competitors: *A Continvation of the Most Remarkable Passages* (26 November to 3 December) and *Divrnall Occvrrances, Truly Relating the Most Remarkable Passages* (25 November to 5 December).[5] The second issue of Thomas's serial appeared with a slightly emended title, but it was in most respects like its predecessor: an eight-page small-quarto pamphlet with a full title-page (with a blank verso) and six pages of text, divided into chronological sections headed by day and date. News of proceedings in the Lords and Commons were interspersed. The next week (6–13 December) a newsbook entitled *The Diurnall, Or, The Heads of All the Proceedings in Parliament* was published by John Wright and Thomas Bates. Thomas's serial has either been lost or did not appear. These imitations of Thomas's publication, however, show that the formal elements which were combined to construct a newsbook were recognizable to other publishers. This was in part because the first newsbooks were printed from a manuscript serial.[6] The next week (13–20 December) three newsbooks, exhibiting little variety, appeared: Thomas collaborated with Bates to publish *Diurnall Occurrences, Or, The Heads of Severall Proceedings*; John Wright published *The Diurnall, Or, The Heads of All the Proceedings*; and Bates (again) co-operated with Francis Coules to publish *The Diurnall Occurrances: Or, The Heads of Proceedings.* The next week there were three newsbooks, the publisher John Hammond joining in, the next week at least four, the next week at least six, the next week seven or eight.[7]

Newsbooks, like pamphlets, were produced collaboratively, by an editor and a printer and a publisher, who was usually a bookseller. Each

[4] These literary and political implications of the newsbook are traditionally avoided by historians of 17th-cent. journalism. Clyde; Siebert; *History*; Muddiman, *The King's Journalist*; *Beginnings*; Cotton. Thomas's *Berkenhead* does deal with them within circumscribed limits.

[5] 64A.1 and 106A.1.

[6] See Ch. 2, below.

[7] 106.1; 109.3; 181.104A and B. For the week ending 3 Jan.: 97.1, 106.2A/B, 107.2, 181.105; for the week ending 10 Jan.: 97.2, 99.01, 98.2, 106.3, 181.106, 494.1; for the week ending 17 Jan.: 97.3, 101.1, 102.1, 104.1, 106.4, 181.107, 623.01A/B, and possibly 105.1. There is a possibility of missing issues, particularly as Thomason seems not to have realized just how many newsbooks there were concealed under such similar titles. John Rushworth, however, did.

had something to contribute to the form, style, and commercial success of a newsbook. In this triadic relationship the publisher usually took the dominant role, except in cases where the editor had a distinctive style or a considerable reputation. Most editors were anonymous, however: they were editors rather than authors. Titles of individual newsbooks, by which readers distinguished between them, could therefore be associated with either publishers or editors. As these men and women established their credentials they frequently faced competitors who stole their titles and imitated their typography in order to profit from their markets.

The rapid turnover in titles and the intervention of more publishers suggest a commercial roller-coaster. William Cooke, Nathaniel Butter, Humphrey Blunden, Robert Bryson, Humphrey Tucker, Thomas Banks, Francis Leach, and George Thompson all published newsbooks in January. Numbers fluctuated week by week, publishers and titles came and went. Only close reading reveals significant differences between these serials. They were fairly homogeneous, cheaply produced pamphlets of parliamentary news, though there were differences in the quality of news-gathering. The editors who were inadvertently inventing a new profession did not yet intervene to produce a journalistic style. The term 'journalism' is thus somewhat anachronistic, though it does suggest the amorphous variety of practices used by the newsbook editors of the time. Manuscripts of parliamentary news had circulated for some time, and this material was sent to the printers largely unaltered, perhaps simply cut to size. The first real effort to produce a distinctive periodical was made by Humphrey Blunden (or his editor) who for the week 10–17 January produced *A Trve Diurnall of the Last Weeks Passages in Parliament*. The title distinguished it from the various *Diurnall Occurrences* on the market.[8] This was the first newsbook to have consecutive pagination, signatures, and issue numbers.[9] Consecutive signatures, used for larger books, assisted binders in placing material in the correct order: this implied that newsbooks would be collected and bound as a set. Some readers took the hint.

Previous newsbooks had only implicitly been serials. The concept of seriality was familiar to readers of corantos, but newsbooks did not continue this practice immediately because they descended from an unnumbered manuscript serial.[10] Numbering was a typographical innovation which solidified the concept of the periodical. Perhaps Blunden

[8] 623.01A/B. The 'B' edition has the imprint 'Printed for C. B. W.'

[9] Frank, *Beginnings*, 279, is wrong.

[10] One MS 'Diurnall Occurrences' separate does appear to be numbered: 'Diurnall Proceedings in Parliam[t] the xxvi[th] pte'; BL: Sloane MS 3065, f. 7. From this numbering, issue 1 would have appeared in early Dec. 1640, which is not implausible. The title-page may, however, be later.

envisaged that it would encourage his readers to identify and purchase the next issue. Two other publishers saw the commercial advantage and a week later took the opportunity to add 'Numb. 2.' to the upper right-hand corner of the title-pages of their newsbooks. The practice of consecutive numbering has remained with the serial. For his second issue, entitled *A Continuation of the True Diurnall*, Blunden added the logical corollary, consecutive pagination. This did not catch on at first, perhaps because it was an awkward and irksome practice for printers and publishers. By the end of the year, however, it was the norm.

Late January and February also saw the abandoning of full title-pages. Title-pages were inherited from pamphlets, which served as the model for the first newsbooks probably because they were familiar to both printers and readers. To maximize the efficient use of space newsbook publishers first introduced news onto the verso of the title-page, which was not a standard printing practice, and then reduced the title to cover about a half of the front page. This considerably increased the amount of text, though it did not make for prestigious presentation.

This early period, then, was characterized by two contradictory tendencies: the instability and flux caused by shifting partnerships of publishers, editors, and printers and by the lack of traditional practices for producing newsbooks; and the uneven, sometimes rapid, improvisation and systematization of new practices which introduced regularity.[11] Editorial techniques remained amongst the least developed aspects. Editors did not yet contribute their own material and they remained anonymous. The first who rose to prominence and developed a distinctively professional, though impersonal, style was Samuel Pecke, who has been credited with responsibility for the first newsbook and the manuscripts of parliamentary news which circulated in 1628, 1640, and 1641. There is no real proof for this attribution, which is motivated largely by the desire to allocate authorial names to anonymous texts, though attribution enhances our understanding of neither.[12]

[11] On printing, haphazardness, and systematization see Elizabeth L. Eisenstein, *The Printing Press as an Agent of Change: Communications and Cultural Transformations in Early-Modern Europe*, 2 vols. (Cambridge, 1979); D. F. McKenzie, 'Printers of the Mind: Some Notes on Bibliographical Theories and Printing-House Practices', *Studies in Bibliography*, 22 (1969), 1–75; Chartier, *Order of Books*; Anthony T. Grafton, 'The Importance of Being Printed', *Journal of Interdisciplinary History*, 11 (1980), 265–86.

[12] The attribution derives from a pamphlet entitled *A Fresh Whip for all scandalous Lyers* (9 Sept. 1647; F2199/E406(10)), 2. The relevant passage is as follows: 'He was once a Stationer, till he crept into the little hole at Westminster-Hall, where indeed he began his trade of inditing or framing; and so rose at last to the stile of *Diurnall-Writer*. I must confesse at his first beginning to write, he was very industrious, and would labour for the best intelligence, as his large volumnes doe testifie, but when he found the sweetnesse of it, and how easily he could come by his Intelligence, he fell to his sports and pastimes, for you should hardly ever finde him at home all the weeke, till Saturday-morning, and then you shoud be sure to find him abed, panting and puffing as if he had over-rid himselfe,

Pecke enters into our knowledge in January 1642 with *A Perfect Diurnall of the Passages in Parliament*, published by William Cooke.[13] In this time of unstable commercial relationships he moved between publishers and was interrupted in his work, but he continued to edit *A Perfect Diurnall* in some form until September 1655, when the Protector and his council suppressed all unofficial newsbooks, leaving only *Mercurius Politicus, Publick Intelligencer*, and *Nouvelles ordinaires*.[14] Pecke was a scrivener, and is an interesting model for the early journalist not least because he was relatively uneducated. There are few classical references in his work, unlike that, for instance, of the polemicists Marchamont Nedham and Sir John Berkenhead. Pecke was also professionally dedicated, rather than being a pamphleteer who broadened his interests.[15] Like many of the anonymous and uninspired journalists of 1642, he was an artisan as much as a writer and aspired to neither literary fame nor political influence. He was simply doing his job.

Parliament did not always see it that way. The Commons had noted the increase in printing on several occasions. Then, in response to proto-royalism, and sheer insolence, in a single newsbook, they intervened on 28 March with relative effectiveness.[16] One newsbook appeared the next week followed by over six weeks of silence.[17] In the mean time the Commons pursued and punished seditious printers, and the scriveners enjoyed prosperous times.[18]

At the end of May the newsbooks returned, relatively unchanged, though renumbered as a new series. Thomas did experiment with an unusual title, *Five Matters of Note*, but it only appeared as a single issue.[19]

with riding too and agen from the Army, when God wot hee hath not been out of the Lynes of Communication.' Williams claims that this is a literal reference to Pecke (*History*, 37–8; 'Beginnings of English Journalism', 347). It may be that Williams had some evidence which he failed to present, but it is equally likely that this is a piece of undocumented academic fiction. Wallace Notestein and Frances Helen Relf (eds., *Commons Debates for 1629* (Minneapolis, 1921), pp. l–lii) are ambivalent about the case; W. H. Coates (ed., *The Journal of Sir Simonds D'Ewes* (New Haven, 1942), pp. xx–xxii, 403–4) sensibly passes over it. But a study of the evidence, including *A Presse full of Pamphlets* (1642; P3293), Samuel Sheppard, *The Weepers* (1652; S3171), and manuscripts circulating in 1641, does not, sadly, support the attribution.

[13] *Perfect Diurnall*, 31 Jan. 1642, 507.01/E201(12).

[14] N&S 507, 503, 504, 513, and 509; with a gap between 15 Aug. and 5 Sept. Interrupted for nos. 10 to 12 between serials 509 and 513; it is possible that these have not survived, or that Pecke was collaborating with another publisher for a short period, or even that he was idle. *CSPD 1655*, 318–19.

[15] Cotton, 104–5.

[16] See Ch. 3, below.

[17] Until *Some Speciall Passages* on 17 May, N&S 606.1; then *Many Remarkable Passages* on 20 May; to be included in Wing supplement.

[18] *HMC: Report on the Manuscripts of Lord Montagu of Beaulieu* (HMSO, 1900), 148.

[19] *Five Matters*, 23 May 1642, 153.1/E148(27).

Through the remainder of 1642 there were two main developments. Many newsbooks developed relatively explicit political allegiances. Newsbooks were centred around parliament, and they did not criticize what it was doing, but they did express hope for what it might do in the future, particularly in response to the rebellion in Ireland. Gradually political differences between newsbooks became apparent, and while these were not expressed in bitter or factional language, the basis of faction was already present. The change was less dramatic than that in the relationship between king and parliament. In January the king attempted to arrest the Five Members and then left London; in April Sir John Hotham refused the king entry to Hull, where the magazine collected for the Bishops' Wars was kept; armies were formed through the summer, resulting in conflicts at Manchester and Hull; the king raised his standard on 22 August and this official declaration was soon followed by earnest bloodshed.[20] This was a secure political basis for overt propaganda, but the newsbooks resisted such interventionism, retaining pretensions to the language of objectivity, interrupted mostly by expressions of apprehension and desire for peace.

The other development of 1642 was the accumulation and dissemination of divergent sources. Parliament ceased to be the sole focal point, particularly when there was military conflict in the provinces. Editors found rural correspondents who supplied regional information. Provincial postmasters probably played a large part in this. Many letters were sent to private correspondents in London, merchants for instance, who forwarded them to editors or publishers. The documents which in the spring and summer played an important part in the deteriorating relations between king and parliament also featured prominently. These were frequently juxtaposed as if engaged in dialogue, thereby underscoring the context of exchange and political disagreement.[21] This variety of sources increased the scope for editorial intervention by selection and presentation, resulting in covert ideological weighting. Complaints about newsbooks show that some readers felt them to be more factional than their superficial moderation initially suggests.[22]

Political interest was most marked in anti-royalist stories, accounts of cavaliers swearing oaths, raping, and pillaging, and anti-Catholic stories, frequently about Ireland, the potential influx of Irish troops into the king's army, and the danger of risings in the provinces. *Quotidian Occur-*

[20] For newsbook accounts of these events, see *MTN*, ch. 1.

[21] A practice followed by some historians: *HC*[1], preface, sigs. b[v]–b2; *HC*[3], i, 'To The Reader' (not written by Rushworth); Bulstrode Whitelocke, *Memorials of the English Affairs* (1682; W1986), 58; Thomas May, *The History of the Parliament of England Which began November the third, M.DC.XL.* (1647; M1410), ii. 45, 96. See Ch. 6, below.

[22] BL: Harl. MS 163, f. 52[v], a speech by Sir Simonds D'Ewes, quoted Zagorin, *Court and the Country*, 206; *A Presse full of Pamphlets.*

rences, later *England's Memorable Accidents*, which ran for nineteen issues between September 1642 and January 1643, was devoted more than most to this kind of partisanship. But because these weeklies were London-based, there was little room for strongly antithetical politics, though a close comparison with pamphlets published in the provinces would have indicated differences in representation. Despite the many counterfeit newsbooks which appeared in 1642, which poached on the markets of established publishers, there was as yet no underground press, nor a significant provincial press, and hence there was no opposition press.

1643

Mercurius Aulicus appeared in Oxford on 8 January 1643,[23] essentially as a counterblast to London newsbooks and parliamentary propaganda. It was intended to demoralize parliament's army and fracture the parliamentary coalition by identifying internal divisions, for instance, accusing parliament of pecuniary embezzlement, specifying large and unsubstantiated sums.[24] Its prose was distinguished by an elevated style, and pointed, calculated, and snobbish satirical criticism of its enemies. It was neatly presented, with running heads, even type, and fewer typographical errors. The Latinate title, which gestured back to *Mercurius Gallobelgicus* and to the 'Mercurius Britannicus' imprint of Butter and Bourne, was also an innovation. Its size fluctuated between one, one and a half, and two sheets; this swelling and deflating was mocked in the parliamentarian newsbook *Mercurius Britanicus*.[25] Size was equated with prestige.

The first issues were edited by the Laudian divine Peter Heylin, gradually succeeded by Sir John Berkenhead, who wrote in a more barbed and aggressive style.[26] Though the prose changed considerably with this transition, both editors presented material in an even style with substantial editorial comment. This was not yet the case with the London newsbooks. *Britanicus* suggested that *Aulicus* was a collaborative enterprise, in which Secretary Edward Nicholas, Sir Philip Warwick, Sir John Colepeper, and others were periodically involved.[27] This may merely have been a way of deriding their individual wit. Whatever the truth behind this, *Aulicus* was authorized by the king and represented a

[23] Frank gives the date 1 Jan., attributing *Aulicus* precedence over *KWI*, *Beginnings*, 33.

[24] *Aulicus* 26, 21 July 1643, 341; *OR* i. 365.

[25] *Britanicus* 23, 19 Feb. 1644, 177, 286.023B; *Britanicus* 25, 6 Mar. 1644, 191, 286.025/E35(28).

[26] *Berkenhead*, 30–5, 88–9.

[27] *Britanicus* 68, 3 Feb. 1645, 533, 286.068/E27(8).

sustained propaganda exercise the likes of which Charles had hitherto resisted, the only comparable effort being the posthumous *Eikon Basilike.*[28]

With its literary pretensions *Aulicus* equated stylistic difference with social difference. It associated false news with stereotypical puritan hypocrisy and lack of humour. It was nominally published on Sundays, according to *Britanicus* in order to mock observers of the Sabbath: 'a dutifull subject, he obeys the *Book of Recreation for the Sabbath* punctually; but you see, they make no conscience to lie upon Sundayes: Is *Aulicus* such a religious work that it must be begun upon the *Sabbath day*? I think he intends it for a *Court Catechisme*; Surely this is the second part of Doctor *Heylins Sunday no Sabbath.*'[29] Later *Britanicus* suggested that the Oxford court would soon replace a Sunday religious service with a masque by Jonson and Davenant, which perhaps conceded the royalist point.[30]

Aulicus was a success: it was widely distributed, sometimes admired, and in part imitated. The London press became more polished. A few days before *Aulicus*, on 3 January 1643, the *Kingdomes Weekly Intelligencer* first appeared.[31] This disappeared for September and October, but then emerged, to continue to October 1649. It was distinguished by a brief phrase summarizing a news item, placed just above the title: this antecedent of the headline was echoed by other newsbooks later in the year. The other London contemporaneous non-ephemeral serials were: *A Continvation of Certain Speciall and Remarkable Passages*, which appeared between October 1642 and June 1643; *Some Speciall and Considerable Passages* (later *Special Passages*), which appeared between August 1642 and June 1643, and *Certaine Informations* (January 1643 to February 1644).[32] In May *Mercurius Civicus* appeared, with London-based sources, content, and readership. Its title specified opposition to *Aulicus*, the well-digested news of which it imitated.[33] From its third issue *Civicus* was

[28] *Aulicus* was soon followed by another Oxford newsbook, the repetitious *Mercurius Rusticus, or the Covntries Complaint*, beginning 20 May 1643, 384.01/E103(3); *OR* iv. 117–32. This was dedicated to describing at length and usually tardily the destruction caused by the parliamentary army.

[29] *Britanicus* 11, 9 Nov. 1643, 81, 286.011/E75(14).

[30] *Britanicus* 12, 16 Nov. 1643, 89, 286.012/E75(38).

[31] Who edited *KWI* is uncertain: Richard Collings, editor of *Civicus*, is traditionally associated with it: *History*, 43; *Beginnings*, 36, 37, 40, 308 n. 13; *KWI* 229, 12 Oct. 1647, 214.229/E410(17), claims to be 'Collected by R. C.'. Cotton suggested that Captain Thomas Audley was responsible, as he was sent to prison, accompanied by the publisher Robert White, when it was censured. Cotton, 61–2, 68; id, 'John Dillingham', 829; *LJ* vi. 595, 597. The preponderance of military news might also favour Audley. It is plausible that responsibility changed at some point.

[32] N&S 54, 605, and 36.

[33] *Civicus* 1, 11 May 1643, sig. A2, 298.001/E101(15).

singularly distinguished by one or two woodcut portraits on the title-page. Prior to 1640 engraved illustrations were generally restricted to more expensive publications, though many ballads incorporated cheaper woodcuts.[34] In the 1640s such woodcuts were more common in occasional pamphlets and satires. Other 1640s newsbooks which presented woodcuts on their title-pages were *A Perfect Diurnall* (the only one before *Civicus*), *The London Post*, *The Scotish Dove*, and *The Faithfull Scout*. *Civicus* also had a rhymed outline of contents in the top left-hand corner of its title-page.[35]

Except for faint traces of increasing professionalism the London newsbooks continued in the uneven and disjointed fashion of 1642. Their anti-royalism became increasingly focused and in April they began to respond directly to *Aulicus*, *Kingdomes Weekly Intelligencer* being among the most eager. This was an important move, as it recognized the outbreak of a war on paper. Whereas disagreement had long been apparent, direct criticism, increasingly bitter recrimination, and *ad hominem* attacks soon became an important and resource-consuming aspect of journalism.

In April the Stationers' Company, internally divided since 1640, submitted to parliament a remonstrance, *To the High Court of Parliament: the Humble Remonstrance of the Company of Stationers*.[36] This requested powers to curtail the wayward press. Though generally diffident in actions, parliament could be sympathetic to the problem when it wanted to be, and on numerous occasions in 1641 and 1642 it had expressed concern over the flourishing of scandalous printed books. On 22 March 1641 the Commons received a petition concerned with printing patents; on 5 June it ordered the Stationers' Company to hinder the licence of printing; on 29 January 1642 it ordered that nothing be printed without the name and consent of the author; in March 1641 the Lords appointed a committee to examine unlicensed publications; on 26 August 1642 both Houses issued a joint declaration intended to suppress seditious and scandalous pamphlets.[37] There are many more examples of actions against individual writers, printers, and publishers.[38] Coles, Leach, and Pecke spent January to April 1643 in the Fleet prison for publishing 'false and scandalous Pamphlets and under

[34] Watt, *Cheap Print and Popular Piety*, *passim*.

[35] Frank's typographical argument for attributing *Civicus* to Richard Collings is nonsensical; *Beginnings*, 41.

[36] Siebert, 165–7; Cyprian Blagden, *The Stationers' Company*, 130–4; [Henry Parker?], *To the High Court of Parliament* (1643; P425).

[37] *CSPD 1640–1641*, 508-9; *CJ* ii. 168; *CJ* ii. 402; Willson H. Coates, Anne Steele Young, and Vernon F. Snow, eds., *The Private Journals of the Long Parliament*, i: *3 January to 5 March 1642* (New Haven, 1982), 165–6; *LJ* iv. 180, 182; *LJ* iv. 398.

[38] Siebert, 180–6, 205–7.

the Title and Name and Order of the Parliament'.[39] This was an unusually harsh sentence.[40] On 14 June 1643 parliament responded to the Stationers' remonstrance with an Ordinance for the Regulation of Printing, which established controls over the press administered jointly by parliament and the Stationers' Company, to replace the crown controls dismantled in 1641.[41] All works were to be licensed before publication, and powers were granted to punish offenders, including that of seizing a press which printed an unlicensed work. Henry Walley was the first licenser to be responsible specifically for newsbooks; he was replaced in April 1644 by John Rushworth.

Newsbook publishers responded by registering their titles. *Kingdomes Weekly Intelligencer*, *Civicus*, and *A Continvation of Certain Speciall and Remarkable Passages* continued without interruption. On 3 July Pecke and Coles made a public reappearance with a new series of *A Perfect Diurnall*, which then continued more or less uninterrupted until October 1649. The licensing act apparently precipitated the appearance of one new newsbook, from the staple of Robert White (like *Kingdomes Weekly Intelligencer* and *Certaine Informations*). This was John Dillingham's *The Parliament Scout*, which announced itself:

> Having perused an Ordinance of Parliament, I perceive a generall prohibiting of Printing any thing but what is Licensed, which had it been agreed unto sooner, would have prevented many inconveniences that have befalne the Parliament by divers things mistaken that have been made publique, and by some things published by disaffected persons to the Parliament, as it were in favour to their proceedings, yet of purpose to being scandall upon them.[42]

Parliament Scout was attacked for being the first newsbook licensed following the act. It was a distinctive newsbook, marked with the personality of its editor.

Like John Stow, Dillingham was by original profession a tailor, and was therefore, like many MPs and army officers in the 1640s, vulnerable to satire directed at his low social status.[43] Dillingham believed what

[39] *LJ* v. 533, 547; vi. 16.

[40] Frank suggests that the offence involved promoting an apprentices' petition; *Beginnings*, 36. John Bond was another newsbook editor who was imprisoned in 1642 as 'A Contriver of false and scandalous libels'; *LJ* iv. 681. He 'averred' *True Diurnal Occvrances*, N&S 621. His main offence was publishing *A Copie of the Queens Letter from the Hague* (1642; H1456). This occurred immediately before the Mar. 1642 intervention, and, though an anti-royalist publication, it may have contributed to the Commons' general irritation and ultimately to the bad reputation of newsbooks. Bond's punishment is reported in *Perfect Diurnall* 12, 4 Apr. 1642, 3, 507.12/E202(1).

[41] The Commons agreed on 10 June, the Lords on 14 June: *CJ* ii. 123, 129; *LJ* vi. 95–7.

[42] *Parliament Scout* 1, 27 June 1643, 1, 485.01/E56(7).

[43] All authors were prone to such satire. Stow was a significant autodidact, though it did not protect him from criticism by those who relied upon others to supply their

most commentators on newsbooks have ignored or denied, that the spread of information had its role in a good political cause. His opening editorial continued to outline his purpose:

considering withall the condition the Kingdome now stands in, when the *Times* is the only study, and that then I finde a necessity, that a right Intelligence be kept and imparted throughout the Kingdome, of the proceedings of the Parliament, and their Armies, to the end the well-affected party, who are willing to sacrifice life and fortune for their Religion and Liberty, and the good of the King and Kingdome, may from time to time be informed, and receive encouragement.[44]

Dillingham saw nothing wrong with the times being the only study: if people wanted news, then it was to the good of the kingdom that right intelligence be distributed to bolster the cause and consciences of those who fought for religion and liberty. The ideal was partisan, in so far as the news informed the well affected, but in that sense God was partisan too. Later, in the first issue of his newsbook *The Moderate Intelligencer*, Dillingham offered to 'represent an extract weekly of such things as come to knowledge, and are fit for publike view . . . which shall ever be according to intelligence, and without invectives'.[45] These statements need not be interpreted as the calculated self-legitimization of avaricious motives. Dillingham certainly had political interests, though as they developed he repudiated earlier allegiances. His patronage connections in the early 1640s, with Edward Lord Montagu, the Earl of Manchester,[46] Oliver St John, and the 'Middle Group', also involved political sympathies. Initially Dillingham's political ideals made him a well-informed and effective correspondent, but they subsequently led him into unpopularity, marginalization, and eventual unemployment.[47] He maintained an ideal of the importance of news, qualified with reservations which echoed criticisms made of newsbooks. The protestations in favour of an educative role of newsbooks, over and above instrumental or financial interests, were consistent through

education. Sir Henry Savile mocked 'the Dregs of the Common People' who had compiled the 1687 edition of Holinshed's *Chronicles*, and Edmund Bolton quoted him with approval; Annabel Patterson, *Reading between the Lines* (1993), 121–2.

[44] *Parliament Scout* 1, 1. For his newsletters, see *HMC: Montagu, passim.*

[45] *Moderate Intelligencer* 1, [6 Mar. 1645], 1, 419.001/E271(15).

[46] *Aulicus* accused Dillingham of having been the Earl's 'pensioner'; *Aulicus* 23, 8 June 1644, 1009, 275.223A&B/E52(7); *OR* iii. 101.

[47] These associations preceded the meeting of the Long Parliament: his newsletters to Montagu began while he was in Paris, probably being discreet after being found sheltering a Scottish knight in August 1638. Cotton, 'John Dillingham', 818–19. These political associations parallel those of another writer of newsletters who held strong ideals about the value of information and communication: Samuel Hartlib. In 1639 Hartlib had also been in trouble in relation to his role in distributing news: Hibbard, *Charles I and the Popish Plot*, 119; *CSPD 1639*, 104; *CSP Ven. 1636–9*, 538.

Dillingham's career.[48] After all, there was probably money to be made in tailoring, with less trouble and danger of imprisonment, particularly for someone with connections in the army.[49]

Another personality appeared on the scene in August 1643, one who was to have the greatest impact on seventeenth-century journalism. This was Marchamont Nedham, who began his writing career as co-editor of *Mercurius Britanicus: Communicating the Affaires of Great Britaine: for the Better Information of the People* (published by Robert White). *Britanicus* looks like parliament's answer to *Aulicus*, and in effect it was, though it is not clear whether it began with official sanction. Certainly it managed to avoid being licensed through the usual means, instead receiving the patronage of the Earl of Essex, Lord General of the army.[50] It was nominally edited by Captain Thomas Audley, who supervised its production and gathered the information, to whom Nedham was an assistant.[51] After issue 51 Audley withdrew: the change in *Britanicus*' railing style at that point of transition was not particularly marked, so it seems likely that Nedham was responsible for the writing all along. According to *Mercurius Academicus* Nedham received an official salary of £3 per week.[52] Nedham's editorial in issue 52, after a brief absence, certainly suggests continuity:

Now if I should lay a side my pen, and they hear of it, they would dare to be *Voting* there again, if so be his Majestie make a shift to quarter there this *Winter*, according to *Aulicus* his expectation: Therefore I give fair warning, I will deal with as little mercy as I have done formerly: my pen, ink, and paper, are still the same; I onely loyter'd a while to take *Physick*; but I'le promise you, I *purg'd* away nothing but *Phlegme*, and such drowsie humours; I have as much *Choler* and *Gall* left as ever, which must serve to quicken and keep me warm this winter; and you shall finde that I am able to *spin* more whip-cord for *Aulicus* and his friends.[53]

[48] He favoured vocational systems of education: *Moderate Intelligencer* 49, 12 Feb. 1646, 287, 419.049/E322(19). A 1652 revival, possibly by Dillingham, continued this tradition; *Moderate Intelligencer* 166, 8 Dec. 1652, 417.166/E683(19).

[49] In fact he continued, in a small way, as a tailor, and was required to inspect the uniforms of the army, a subject upon which he was prone to comment in his opinionated editorials. *CSPD 1648–1649*, 309. If the John Dillingham who in 1672 donated money to the City of Leicester for the foundation of a young men's school of riding, fencing, vaulting, and other exercises was the erstwhile newsbook writer, then perhaps the trade of tailoring later proved a lucrative one. Cotton, 'John Dillingham', 833–4; Manwaring, 'Journalism in the Days of the Commonwealth', 105–20.

[50] Cotton, 30–1, 74–5; Frank refers to 'the men who hired' Nedham, without stating who they were; *Beginnings*, 48.

[51] A newsbook entitled *The Spie* suggested that it was produced by a committee of four or five; *Spie* 4, 20 Feb. 1644, 32. This is plausible: Nedham and Audley may very well have liaised with MPs and army officers in order to gather news, and to present the correct political arguments. Nedham would still have written it. Moreover Nedham had his own points to make, as his subsequent troubles indicate.

[52] *Academicus* 6, [19 Jan. 1646], 56, 260.06/E316(25); *OR* iv. 390.

[53] *Britanicus* 52, 7 Oct. 1644, 407–8, 286.052/E13(10).

Britanicus projected a barbed and witty style, frequently described as 'railing'. This style was something new in journalism, raising the mixture of bitterness and bile to a new height and making the controversy funny: there had always been an edge of stiltedness to *Aulicus*. *Britanicus* abandoned the modest restraint of *Aulicus*, and while it was distinctly boastful it made no attempt to imitate the self-righteous uprightness of its rival. Its criticisms and satires were sufficiently successful to provoke sustained responses from Oxford, which the other London newsbooks were only occasionally seen to merit.

The title *Britanicus* addressed the country, differentiating itself from the implicitly corrupt, courtly *Aulicus*. This effect may have been weakened by the printer's omission of an 'n' from the title.[54] This caused some amusement, and it provided grounds for comments on a lack of erudition.[55] Nevertheless the misspelling was recognized in the community of readers and writers, and the majority of contemporary allusions misspelt the name correctly. In 1643 newsbooks became increasingly individualized: mercury became a character.[56]

The identity of individual newsbooks was enhanced by the different days on which they appeared. The first newsbooks were published on Mondays, and covered a week of parliamentary news which was written up through the week and on the weekend; the same had been the case with manuscript serials. They were then printed over the weekend and on Monday morning, which conveniently allowed them to be purchased, read, and then sent to the provinces by the Tuesday post. *Kingdomes Weekly Intelligencer*, on the other hand, appeared on Tuesdays; *A Continvation of Certain Speciall and Remarkable Passages* on Wednesdays; *Mercurius Civicus* on Thursdays; *Parliament Scout* initially on Thursdays and later on Fridays; *Britanicus* and *Aulicus* both appeared on Mondays, though the latter claimed to run from Sunday to Sunday. From September 1643 *The True Informer* appeared on Saturdays. By 1652 this weekly

[54] Or was it a mistake? An identical orthographical unorthodoxy had been committed by the printers of Butter and Bourne's third, fourth, and fifth series of corantos, 1625–7. See Dahl, 133–53. In the imprint of these corantos, 'for Mercurius Britannicus', the printer had misspelt the troublesome word both 'Brittanicus' and 'Britanicus'. Yet there seems to be no reason, other than ignorance, why this should have been imitated. Contemporary comments suggest that it cannot simply be put down to non-standardized spelling. Nor did Nedham ever justify it, though he did suggest that he stuck to it as a matter of political principle: see *Britanicus* 73, 10 Mar. 1645, 587, 286.073/E271(21).

[55] e.g. *Queres to be Considered* (24 June 1647; Q175/669f.11(33)). In fact Nedham's Latin was at least serviceable.

[56] *MTN* 20–2. See Ch. 3, below, on play-pamphlets. There were other forms of personification not involving mercuries: *Parliament Scout* repeatedly referred to 'our Scout', meaning not a person but the anthropomorphized newsbook itself. For example: 'Our Scouts work is to give you a Narration of the affairs of the Armies, and Actions of war'; *Parliament Scout* 13, 22 Sept. 1643, 97, 485.13/E67(34).

spread caused an irritated Samuel Sheppard to comment on the way mercuries 'come over one anothers backs, as if they were playing at Leap-frog'.[57] This division of labour had two commercial points: first it broadened the market by slightly varying the product, and secondly it differentiated within the market by enabling midweek publications to present news which would otherwise not appear for a few days. In other words, it enabled the early-modern equivalent of the 'exclusive'. There was an increase in news material at this time, as new sources were developed, attention to detail increased, and editorial comment extended. Though there was considerable repetition from day to day, for those who could afford it perhaps one eight-page newsbook per week was not really enough.

After the transient and disorderly commercial relations of early 1642, the production of newsbooks had settled into stable patterns. There were fly-by-nights, ephemeral series which lasted for one or a few issues, but the centre of the metaphorical marketplace was from 1643 onwards occupied by a cluster of long-term titles. Some editors who would make their mark on the form over a period of years had established themselves (Nedham, Dillingham, Pecke, Daniel Border). Certain London publishers dominated the market, having established advantageous economies of scale and operational infrastructures. These publishers (Robert White, Francis Coles, Francis Leach, both printer and publisher, Thomas Bates, Bernard Alsop, the John Wrights) were typically publishers of cheap print, for whom newsbooks were a further specialization. Most London newsbooks which survived for long series arose out of partnerships between one or two or three publishers and their editors. Distinctions between serials produced by the same group, therefore, may have been the consequence of a deliberate publishing strategy, as well as of the limited availability of printers.

On 6 September 1643 another Wednesday newsbook appeared: *The Weekly Account* (which continued, changing its title to *The Perfect Weekly Account* in May 1647, until January 1648).[58] It was edited by Daniel Border, previously a scrivener and subsequently, like Nedham, a physician. His sympathies lay with parliament, and he used mainly parliamentary sources, commenting that it was impossible anyone 'should meet with such variety of intelligence as not to fall upon the rehearsal of some occurrences which have beene heretofore imparted'.[59] He also attacked *Aulicus*, and found his attentions returned. Early issues of *Weekly Account*

[57] *Mastix*, 2.

[58] Probably not related to two single-issue serials: *A Weekly Accompt*, 3 Aug. 1643, 673.1/E63(14), though also published by Bernard Alsop; and *A Weekly Accompt*, 10 July 1643, 676.1/E249(25). Frank is contradictory: *Beginnings* 53, 311 n. 66.

[59] *Weekly Account* 5, 4 Oct. 1643, 1, 671.105/E250(17).

were typographically distinct in having a full title-page with a numbered list of contents, plus each page was surmounted by a headline. Border also distinguished himself by periodically moving to Tuesdays in order to avoid Wednesday Thanksgivings.[60]

Several other non-ephemeral newsbooks appeared in late 1643. Also on Wednesdays in July and August was *Wednesday's Mercury* (also entitled *The Speciall Passages Continued*), lasting four issues. *Remarkable Passages* appeared through November and December; *The Kingdomes Weekly Post* (distinguished by a woodcut of a postman blowing a bugle) lasted a month longer.[61] Both of these serials were irregular in their periodicity. *The True Informer* appeared on Saturdays between September 1643 and February 1645.[62] Unlike the mercuries, and like *Perfect Diurnall* and *Weekly Account*, it had few literary aspirations. These newsbooks did not have factional interests: they were not intended to deceive but to inform, at a reasonable profit.

The Scotish Dove was edited by George Smith and published by Laurence Chapman on Fridays between October 1643 and December 1646. It appears to have been a continuation of *The Scotch Mercury*, which appeared on 5 October 1643, fifteen days before the first *Scotish Dove*, published by Chapman and Laurence Blaicklocke.[63] *The Scotish Dove* expressed an initial intention to focus on Scottish and northern affairs, but this objective soon paled and was only sporadically fulfilled. Nevertheless it was with Scotland that Smith's sympathies generally resided, and he adopted an increasingly Presbyterian stance through the three years of his editorship. His editorials frequently inclined to expressions of sometimes cloying piety. Religious interventions had been subdued in newsbooks until this point, and in most newsbooks continued to be marginal. Anti-Catholicism was of course a popular theme, and appeals to providence found their way into military accounts. But, quite unlike many other forms of pamphlets, secular concerns overwhelmingly predominated. Newsbooks were concerned with political affairs, and managed to sustain a remarkably political language. Theological concerns were important, but this was not the language which the newsbooks generally spoke.

The Scotish Dove was striking in its appearance: its title-page carried a large woodcut of a dove carrying an olive branch, incorporating the motto 'holy inocency is blessed'. Just below this was the sententia 'Be

[60] *Weekly Account* 9, [5 Mar. 1645], sig. Iiii, 671.209/E271(14).

[61] N&S 669, 582. *Kingdomes Weekly Post* was resurrected between Oct. and Dec. 1645 and Dec. 1647 and Mar. 1648: N&S 217, 216, and 215 respectively.

[62] Not to be confused with James Howell's historiographical treatise of the same name, published in Oxford the same year: though this suggests the close proximity between the languages of newsbooks and of history.

[63] *Scots Dove* N&S 594, first issue 20 Oct. 1643, E71(24); *Scotch Mercury* 591.1/E69(23).

Wise as Serpents, Innocent as Doves.' This emblematic image distinguished the *Dove* from other newsbooks, and made the typography immediately attractive. In the days when printed images were few and expensive, the impact of these cheap woodcuts on a weekly basis should not be scorned. *Mercurius Civicus* was often identified by allusion to its portraits, and until the same representation was repeatedly used for different persons there is no reason to assume that many readers did not find the illustration informative. The same is true of the magnificent impression of the House of Commons which appeared on Pecke, Coles, and Blaicklocke's *Perfect Diurnall*, mocked by the royalist penman John Cleveland in *The Character of a London Diurnall* (1645).[64] It gave the newsbook an identity which the publishers were reluctant to abandon, even when the quality of the block deteriorated through sustained use. *Perfect Diurnall* remained attentive to parliamentary news, and the picture of parliament conjured a sense of place unknown to most readers. It also emphasized debate, and authority: the Speaker's chair and the royal coat of arms surmounting it were the focus of the image, above the title, at the apex of the lines formed by the sitting members. This was an early fragment of parliamentary iconography, an attempt to represent the authority of parliament in an image in which monarchy was implicit, but from which the king was absent.

These strands do not represent the whole story of 1643. In September appeared a single issue of *An Antidote Against the Malignant Influence of Mercurius (Surnamed) Aulicus*; its devotion to countering another newsbook was imitated in November by *Britanicvs Vapvlans: Or, the Whipping of Poore British Mercury* (the second and final issue was entitled *Mercurivs Vrbanvs Communicating the Several Lies, Mistakes and Absurdities of Brittannicus and Others, to the Abused People*). The same month five issues of *The Compleate Intelligencer and Resolver* introduced a question-and-answer section after presenting the news. This was later adopted by other newsbooks, including *The Parliament Scout* and *Britanicus*. Also in November, a single issue of *Informator Rusticus* addressed rural readers.[65] In February *A Perfect Tiurnall: Or Welch Post* pandered to English xenophobia by satirizing the Welsh accent. In October that year a nine-issue serial (lasting until January 1644) entitled *The Welch Mercury* (changing to *Mercurius Cambro-Britannus*) purveyed more news while employing a similar satirical format.[66] In August a single-issue newsbook entitled *The Northerne Nuntio* may have been uniquely printed in York. In June there

[64] Serial 513; Cleveland, *Character of a London Diurnall* (Oxford, 1644[5]; C4659), 2; *MTN* 474.

[65] N&S 15.1; 29.1–2; 52.1–5; 198.1. On *Britanicvs Vapvlans*, see Ernest Sirluck, 'Shakespeare and Jonson among the Pamphleteers of the First Civil War', *Modern Philology*, 53 (1955–6), 88–99.

[66] N&S 532.1; 708.1–9.

appeared a single issue of *The Parliaments Scouts Discovery*; in October *New Christian Vses*, the contents of which were less distinctive than its title; in January, *The Daily Intelligencer of Court, City, and Countrey*; on 9 June, *A Coranto from Beyond Sea*, which contained a dedication, possibly unique in a newsbook, to the Earl of Warwick.[67] These scattered single issues were relatively few and uncomplicated in comparison to those of early 1642 and 1647–8, when the press raged more fiercely.

1644

By the end of 1644 newsbooks were a familiar part of pamphlet culture. In a postscript to an attack on puritan pamphleteers, projected in the ghostly voice of Thomas Nashe, John Taylor wrote:

> *so have I also written Answers to the nimble, villanous, quicke, pretty, little witted* Mercurius Britanicus, *the* Scotish Dove, *(Pigeon or Widgeon) the* Scout, *and all the rabble of lying, railing Rascals and Rebells, all these things are laid (like rods in pisse) till I can get them printed: and could I but have meanes, and the Presse leasure, I doe undertake with my poore Goose quill, to stop the mouthes or cut the throates of all the seditious Pulpiteers, and roguish Pamphleteers in* England *or else I would lose my labour.*[68]

He was spitting in the wind.

At the beginning of 1644 one of a dozen familiar titles could be purchased on six days of the week: *True Informer, Kingdomes Weekly Intelligencer, Mercurius Civicus, Scotish Dove, Perfect Diurnall, Mercurius Aulicus, Parliament Scout, Certaine Informations, Continuation, Weekly Account. Weekly Account* commented, 'There were never more books abroad then now, and never lesse newes.'[69] *Kingdomes Weekly Post* disappeared in January. The same month *Mercurius Britanicus* was absent, but it soon returned to engage with *Aulicus* which itself began to fail through the year, fluctuating in size and sporadically vanishing. In January *The Spie, Communicating Intelligence from Oxford* appeared, lasting six months. Edited by Durant Hotham, it attacked *Aulicus* for adhering to a bad cause, and *Britanicus* for incompetence.[70] *The Spie* claimed that it travelled to Oxford to gather intelligence; *Britanicus* accused it of travelling with Oxford. Nedham warned: 'it is a more dangerous designe to our State and affaires, to print malignity from our owne

[67] N&S 453.1; 488.1; 439.1; 86.1; 77.1. For the missing *Northerne Nuntio* see N&S 453.1.

[68] John Taylor, *Crop-Eare Curried, or, Tom Nash His Ghost* (1644[5]; T446), 40.

[69] *Weekly Account* 35, 29 Feb. 1644, sig. A4^v, 671.135/E34(22).

[70] For the attribution to Hotham see LT copy of *Spie* 5, 27 Feb. 1644, 609.05/E34(15).

Presses, then from enemies', accusing *The Spie* of 'a wry, a crooked, and a King *Richards* wit'.[71] Whatever the value of its news, its jocular bar-room style followed in the wake of the innovations of *Aulicus* and *Britanicus*.

The social logic of the newsbook was carrying it further and further away from *Heads of Severall Proceedings*. In January two other newsbooks appeared: on Fridays *Occurrences of Certain Speciall and Remarkable Passages in Parliament* (later *Perfect Occurrences*); and on Tuesdays *Mercvrivs &c.* (later *Mercurius Veridicus*) for nine issues. *Perfect Occurrences* was written by Henry Walker,[72] an ironmonger turned Independent minister, famous for throwing a pamphlet entitled *To Your Tents, O Israel!* into the king's carriage in 1642,[73] and for a polemical engagement with John Taylor. Walker grew more professionally competent through the year. His was an earnest publication, unlike *Mercvrivs &c.*, which, while it did present news, also indulged in artful rhetorical flourishes. Equally serious and even more uncontroversial was a Thursday newsbook which appeared in May and ran until March 1646: *An Exact Diurnall*, which, after the first issue, changed title to *A Diary, Or an Exact Iovrnall*.[74]

In February the first of six issues of *The Military Scribe* appeared, with an emphasis on military news, both domestic and overseas. The foreign news-market had been vacated with the demise of Butter's final series of corantos in September 1641, though there were a few occasional and unsuccessful publications in 1642.[75] Gradually newsbooks were beginning to allocate space to the Continent. In June 1644 Bourne launched *Le Mercure anglois*, a French-language periodical of English news addressed to overseas readers, which may have been edited by John Cotgrave. Its publication was announced by a handbill, which represents an ingenious innovation on Bourne's part; newsbooks were not usually advertised. This handbill suggested that, like much foreign news, it was addressed to merchants. *Mercure anglois* disap-

[71] *Britanicus* 23, 19 Feb. 1644, 176, 286.023A/E33(21).

[72] Possibly with John Saltmarsh. Cotton, 220–1; LT copy of *Perfect Occurrences* 15, 5 Apr. 1644, 465.1015/E40(26). There are numerous contemporary references to Walker's editorship. For Saltmarsh see N&S 465.

[73] Ernest Sirluck, '*To Your Tents, O Israel*: A Lost Pamphlet', *Huntington Library Quarterly*, 19 (1955–6), 301–5.

[74] The first issue appeared on Wed., the second changed to Thurs. Frank attributes this to Rushworth on evidence which does not survive scrutiny. See *Beginnings*, 82, 321 n. 53.

[75] Serial 64; for the 1642 publications, see Dahl, 384–9. Internal evidence suggests that a number have not survived. In Jan. 1643 Butter was imprisoned in the Fleet under the charge of being an 'Intelligencer and Spy'; see *CJ* ii. 943; iii. 307; and Leona Rostenberg, 'Nathaniel Butter and Nicholas Bourne, First "Masters of the Staple"', *Library*[5], 12 (1957), 33.

peared, certainly not because of any lull in news, in December 1648.[76]

On 2 July 1644 *The Court Mercurie* began its four-month run. Like *The Spie*, this was a London publication focused on Oxford news. On this same day the Battle of Marston Moor instigated the first stage in the destruction of royalist military morale. As *Aulicus* was soon to discover, Oxford was no longer an ideal focus for a newsbook, and *Court Mercurie* increasingly returned to the usual sources. In April John Rushworth had replaced Walley as licenser to newsbooks. With the formation of the New Model Army Rushworth would become secretary to Sir Thomas Fairfax, thus assisting the development of close relations between London newsbooks and the army. At the end of 1643 *Britanicus* had defended Nathaniel Fiennes, who had been condemned to death then pardoned for surrendering Bristol to Prince Rupert. Fiennes was son to Lord Saye and Sele, the Independent leader of the 'commonwealth party' in the Lords. Nedham was attacked in February by William Prynne in *A Checke to Brittanicus, For His Palpable Flattery and Prevarication, in justifying condemned Nat: Fiennes.*, which accused Nedham of accepting bribes to defend Fiennes. Prynne contributed much to the myth that Nedham performed services for money. Nedham responded at the end of the month with *A check to the checker*. In these exchanges Nedham's more ideologically radical future was foreshadowed.[77]

In August *The London Post* appeared, a Tuesday newsbook published by Gilbert Bishop, lasting ten months.[78] It was divided into two sections: an editorial entitled 'Preface', the rest 'Intelligence'. *London Post* had distinctly literary aspirations, though it kept them separate from the presentation of news. The only other lasting serial of the later half of 1644 was *Perfect Passages of Each Dayes Proceedings in Parliament*, which ran from October 1644 to March 1646. Marked by Independent inclinations, it followed *Weekly Account* in appearing on Wednesday, except on the monthly day of Thanksgiving, when it was brought forward to

[76] N&S 258. *History*, 49–50, 228; *Beginnings*, 70–1, 78–9, 318; Cotton, 98. If it was Cotgrave, then Dillingham may have been involved: see 147 and n. 70, below. *Court Mercurie* has also been attributed to Cotgrave.

[77] *A Checke to Brittanicus* (1644; P3926). Frank accepts the bribe accusation: *Cromwell's Press Agent*, 19–20. He also credits Prynne's suggestion that during the silence of *Britanicus* in Jan., Nedham had been working as Fiennes's press agent; *Beginnings*, 60, 314 n. 68. This is an interesting suggestion but there appears to be no corroborating evidence. Nedham's motivation during these months is consistent with his politics, so we need not accept the view that he was motivated by avarice and prudence.

[78] Attributed by Frank, unreliably, to Rushworth and Mabbott; *Beginnings*, 82–3, 321 nn. 53 and 56, 96, 324 n. 134. Frank is following *History*, 59. Loose attributions rapidly accumulate other loose attributions; see P. N. Furbank and W. R. Owens, *The Canonization of Daniel Defoe* (New Haven, 1988), 14–15, 47, and *passim*. Cotton, 121, suggests that the editor was Daniel Border.

Tuesday. Its praise of the army was another warning of the possibility of fractures within the anti-royalist ranks being publicized and perhaps aggravated by newsbooks. This reached a climax in 1645.

There were remarkably few ephemeral serials in 1644. They included: *A Particular Relation/Continuation of True Intelligence* (May to August 1644); *Anti-Aulicus* (two issues in February); *Mercurius Aulico-Mastix* (12 April 1644); *Mercurius Anglicus* (two issues in February); *Britaines Remembrancer* (two issues in March and April); *A True and Perfect Journall of the Warres in England* (two issues in April); *Chiefe Heads of Each Dayes Proceedings* (one issue, 15 May); *The Flying Post Conveying Weekly Packets to All Forraigne Nations* (one issue, 10 May 1644, decorated with a woodcut of a postman).[79] Longer-lived newsbooks dominated the market, and economics impeded any challengers who might have wanted to stay the distance.

1645

The newsbooks of 1645 began by reporting without remorse on the execution of William Laud, former Archbishop of Canterbury, and Sir John Hotham, who in 1643 had attempted to surrender Hull, the city he famously defended in 1642, into royalist hands.[80]

Early 1645 witnessed no upheaval in newsbook production. A dozen established periodicals continued. *The True Informer* ceased to appear in February, *The Weekely Post-Master* (formerly *London Post*) in May.[81] *Parliament Scout* disappeared at the end of January; Dillingham and his publisher, Robert White, were taken into custody for offending the Lords with 'great defamation of the Honour of the Lord General'.[82] In fact this appears to have been a misreading, perhaps a deliberate one, as the offending newsbook did not mention Essex, and the passage sometimes identified actually refers to the Prince of Orange.[83] Dillingham, however, had been voicing opposition to peace talks, and it seems likely that his militaristic line had provoked the hostility of the Earl of Manchester and his colleagues, who caused the charges to be brought.[84] *Britanicus* expostulated at the action: White was its printer.[85] Dillingham was soon released and in March began to edit *The Moderate Intelligencer*, which appeared on Thursdays until October 1649. In February 1646 it in-

[79] N&S 492, 14, 272, 265, 28, 618, 41, 155.
[80] *MTN* 299–307.
[81] N&S 629, 233
[82] *LJ* vii. 164–5.
[83] *Parliament Scout* 84, 23–30 Jan. 1645, 675, 485.84/E26(12).
[84] Cotton, 90; id., 'John Dillingham', 824–5; Clyde, 86–7.
[85] *Britanicus* 68, 3 Feb. 1645, 539, 286.068/E27(8).

creased in size by four pages, admitting foreign news. While *Moderate Intelligencer* was a staunchly pro-army newsbook, at the same time it expressed Dillingham's religious moderation and desire for peace.

At the beginning of the year the publisher Richard Harper established the first monthly serial: it lasted three issues.[86] In February *Mercvrivs Hibernicvs, Or, The Irish Mercurie* became the only single-issue serial in the first half of the year. *The Exchange Intelligencer*, presenting foreign news particularly for merchants and travellers, appeared in May through July. *Mercurius Veridicus: Or, True Informations, of Speciall and Remarkable Passages* appeared on Saturdays between April 1645 and March 1646. This was more or less a continuation of the *Mercvrivs &c./Mercurius Veridicus* which had ceased in April 1644; both were printed and published by Bernard Alsop. The name was also used in 1648, 1660, and 1681.[87] In April *A Perfect Declaration of the Proceedings in Parliament* appeared, the second issue of which changed its name to *The True Informer*. Like *Veridicus*, the publishers, Thomas Bates and John Wright, had resurrected a recently deceased title.[88] In both cases the identity of the editor is uncertain, which signifies that continuity was as likely to inhere in publishers as in editors. This matter was to stimulate controversy in 1648 when Dillingham and White struggled for proprietary control over the title *Moderate Intelligencer*. In February 1646, a month before it disappeared, *The True Informer* argued that the day of St Valentine, 'Patron of copulation', should be abolished, suggesting its editor's sincere anti-ecclesiastical opinions. Elsewhere it adopted a Presbyterian standpoint, attacking, for instance, the Leveller John Lilburne and those who would create 'Anarchy' while pursuing a 'phantasticall Utopia'. It also presented some lengthy foreign news reports.[89]

The Parliaments Post: Faithfully Communicating to the Kingdome the Proceedings of the Armies, printed and published by George Bishop, appeared in May and disappeared in October. It was concerned mostly with the newly formed New Model Army, supporting its progress and defending the integrity of its soldiers from the impugnments of royalist propaganda.[90] It also carried anti-feminist accounts of witchcraft, and cavalier

[86] N&S 205.1–3; respectively titled: *Ianuaries Accovnt*; *The Monthly Account of February*; *The General Account*.

[87] *Mercvrivs Hibernicvs, Or, The Irish mercurie* (1645). Not in Wing or N&S, LT, E269(16), dated 'Feb: 14. 1644'. The others: N&S 145, 394; the later *Veridicus* were N&S 391, 392, 393.

[88] N&S 498, 629.

[89] *True Informer* 42, 14 Feb. 1646, 329, 498.42/E322(25); *MTN* 387. For Lilburne; *True Informer* 27, 25 Oct. 1645, 211, 498.27/E307(6). For foreign news see *MTN* 261–3, a story with anti-Independent implications.

[90] *Parliaments Post* 9, 8 July 1645, 2, 487.09/E292(14).

atrocities.[91] The presentation was self-righteous and impassioned, its style artful, as this account of the siege of Basing House suggests:

> they are all Papists in that Garrison, and if there were ever Purgatory on earth the Papists doe finde it and feele it there, for besides the thicke and perpetuall darknesse which the wet and smoaking straw doth make the burning of Brimstone and Arsenicke, and other dismall ingredients doth infinitely annoy the besieged, which makes them to gnash their teeth for indignation, in the meane time the Canons do perpetually thunder one against another, On every side desolation dwels about them, and to subdue the place there are those things are put in Execution which the nature of man doth tremble at.[92]

The anti-royalism of *Parliaments Post* verged on anti-monarchism. This was a general drift of newsbooks: as they became more polemically fierce, more radical ideological implications entered their prose. Editors no longer sought to suppress these implications.

In July the newsbook form was directly exploited by the army, when two serials were apparently produced under the agency of its officers: *Mr. Peters Report* was the first issue of a serial documenting the progress of the army, partly written by the Independent chaplain Hugh Peters. This appeared at uneven intervals, with various titles, until around November. The second, produced by another chaplain, Edward Bowles, was *The Proceedings of the Army Under the Command of Sir Thomas Fairfax*, which appeared, also irregularly, until mid-August. A related publication appeared on 30 October, entitled *A Packet of Letters from Sir Thomas Fairfax his Quarter*.[93]

With the rise of the New Model Army newsbooks were increasingly associated with sectarianism, due in part to the influence of Thomas Edwards's *Gangræna*, which blamed them for protecting and promoting heresy. Edwards described *The Moderate Intelligencer* as 'the great Historian and Chronicler of the sectaries'.[94] Seventeenth-century periodicals depended on heroes, generally military leaders, to encourage a continuing market week after week. In January 1645 Cleveland described William ('the Conqueror') Waller as 'the *Diurnalls delight*'.[95] In early 1645 the army formed a collective hero for some reporters, and the newsbook became loosely bound to its fortunes. Some newsbooks encouraged this perception, while others were conspicuously Presbyterian: those who attacked newsbooks in general for Independency were mistaken. In June 1645 the New Model Army vanquished the king's forces at Naseby, establishing new heights of military confidence in the

[91] *MTN* 153–4, 112–14.
[92] *Parliaments Post* 20, 30 Sept. 1645, 4, 487.20/E303(23).
[93] N&S 411, 565, 479.1; see Ch. 4, below.
[94] *Gangræna* (1646; E228), 11.
[95] *Character of a London Diurnall*, 4.

parliamentary newsbooks at the same time as it made the army, and its albeit loose connection with religious toleration, a potential threat.

In November the Presbyterian *Mercurius Civicus* temporarily dropped its illustrations, on the grounds that it was 'not conceived now so fit to represent the effigies of pictures of our worthy Commanders in the frontispeece of this Intelligence as formerly', adding that it hoped the reader would not 'refuse to buy the Booke for the omission of a shaddow, when the same information for substance is committed to your view'.[96] It is possible that the editor was sensitive to increasing political polarization and did not wish to appear a partisan of the army. This may have adversely affected the sales of the publication, however, as the woodblocks reappeared nine issues later.

In August *Britanicus* found itself under attack by three issues of an Oxford serial entitled *Mercurius Anti-Britanicus*. This witty and snobbish attack was intended to bolster the waning fortunes of *Mercurius Aulicus*. *Aulicus* had appeared only twice in May, once in June, once in July, and once in August; its history would conclude (excepting revivals of the title in 1648, 1649, 1654, and 1660) with a single, final issue in September. Its imminent demise was apparent in this irregularity, though the publishers had endeavoured to conceal the fact by not numbering the nineteen issues which appeared in 1645 (and, with greater sophistication, by paginating as if intermediate issues had appeared). Throughout most of its lifespan the Oxford edition had been reprinted at London, probably because this was less dangerous than transporting large numbers of copies down the closely watched routes from Oxford.[97] Milton famously commented on the apparent ease with which this was done: 'Do we not see, not once or oftner, but weekly that continu'd Court-libell against the Parlament and City, Printed, as the wet sheets can witnes, and dispers't among us, for all that licencing can doe?'[98] While Milton's point held true, his example did not, as a few days after the publication of his words, the last London reprint appeared. There were none in 1645.

When *Aulicus* ceased to appear Nedham lost his direction and floundered while looking for a new way of writing. Some have suggested that Nedham had little to say when not controverting *Aulicus*: yet his imprisonment in August 1645 demonstrates that this was not the case.[99] Nedham's offence was to publish a 'Hue and Cry' after the king, accus-

[96] *Civicus* 131, 27 Nov. 1645, 1145, 298.131/E310(8). The woodblocks were first absent from issue 130.

[97] There was also a problem in supplying paper to Oxford: *Civicus* 6, 16 June 1643, 41, 298.006/E106(13).

[98] *CPW* ii. 528; dated 23 Nov.

[99] Cotton, 100–1; *Beginnings*, 100.

ing him of '*a guilty Conscience, bloody hands, a Heart full of broken Vowes and protestations*', and mocking the king's speech defect.[100] The Lords had their attention drawn to this *ad hominem* attack, and decided that the passage was 'scandalous to the kings person'. White, the printer, was sent for; he blamed Audley, the licenser; and Audley named Nedham as the author.[101] Audley spent about nine days in prison and was forbidden to license thereafter, which injunction he soon ignored; White was imprisoned for an unknown but probably short period; and Nedham after a short incarceration was released, having written, apparently under orders, a public apology, published as *Mercurius Britanicus, His Apologie to All Well-Affected People.*[102] *Mercurius Anti-Britanicus* mocked the single-week hiatus in *Britanicus,* though it continued to remonstrate with the comments Nedham had been making for the previous few weeks on the king's letters which had been seized at the Battle of Naseby.[103] Walker expressed his political sympathies by publishing a defence of Nedham in *Perfect Occurrences,* which suggested that the offending issue of *Britanicus* was a counterfeit.[104]

This was not Nedham's sole offence. On 10 March the Lords resolved to investigate *Britanicus* for 'unfitting expressions about the King'. One passage was found to be 'very derogatory and scandalous' and Audley was brought in as its 'supposed Author'. He presumably disabused them upon that occasion.[105] Moreover on 23 October the Lords heard from one Walter Gouge who had an affadavit to arrest Nedham as author of *Britanicus.* He went to 'James Ketterell's house near Temple Bar' where Nedham had been seen. Ketterell forcibly removed Gouge using 'reviling' language, not caring for the Lords' order.[106] Nedham had been of Cromwell's party since around the spring, though as his defection in 1647 would show, he was apprehensive about those who followed behind Cromwell. In early 1644 he had argued for mixed monarchy.[107] By

[100] *Britanicus* 92, 4 Aug. 1645, 825–6, 286.092/E294(29); *MTN* 348–9.

[101] *LJ* vii. 523, 525, 528. See also William M. Clyde, 'Parliament and the Press', *Library*[4], 13 (1932–3), 416–19.

[102] 1645; M1756. 'Published according to Order' by 'R. W.', presumably Robert White. Nedham's defence was predictably disingenuous. In a volume of *Britanicus* owned by William Penn, possibly given him by the famous book collector James Logan, to whose library it was returned in 1803, a copy of this appears in place of issue 84. In response to this appeared *Aulicus His Hue and Cry Sent forth After Britanicus, Who is Generally Reported to be a Lost Man* (1645; C3808). Wing attributes this to Francis Cheynell, though it may have been written by Berkenhead himself. It was, remarkably, licensed. Recriminations were evidently open to all. For a brief account of these events see *Beginnings,* 98–100; and Frank, *Cromwell's Press Agent,* 26–7.

[103] *Anti-Britanicus* [3], [22 Aug. 1645], 21–32, 267.3/E297(17); *OR* iv. 323–34.

[104] *Occurrences* 32, 8 Aug. 1645, 465.3032/E262(40).

[105] *LJ* vii. 267, 272

[106] *LJ* vii. 657.

[107] *Britanicus* 25, 6 Mar. 1644, [198], 286.025/E35(28).

1645 his writings were developing anti-monarchical tendencies and his attacks on the king were as harsh as any at this time. These beliefs appear to have been his own, and he would soon find the voice that was temporarily eluding him.

After the demise of *Aulicus* another Oxford newsbook ventured to carry the standard: this was *Mercurius Academicus,* which appeared in fourteen issues on Mondays between December 1645 and March 1646.[108] It varied between one and two sheets, and *Britanicus* commented on its ebbing and flowing.[109] Edited probably by Richard Little, another clergyman, and Thomas Swadlin, it followed *Aulicus* in undermining enemy morale: reporting for instance that the New Model Army was plagued by famine.[110] *Academicus* mocked *Britanicus* for wasting his paper in animadverting with it, ironically using a comparable amount of space.[111] It focused on criticizing London newsbooks, playing with their names, and identifying contradictions between them. According to *Britanicus* it was 'A *fondling Intelligencer,* made up of the *broken ends* of our *London* Pamphlets', and he suggested that when the malignant humour was purged, as it inevitably would be, *Academicus* could serve its turn in the privy.[112]

Four other serials appeared late in 1645. For three issues on Tuesdays in December there was *The Kingdomes Scout. Perfectly Communicating the Proceedings in Parliament.*[113] Also with an interest in the army was *The Kingdomes Weekly Post; Faithfully Communicating the Affaires of the Armies,* which appeared on Tuesdays for ten issues between October and December.[114] The same week this serial departed, *The Citties Weekly Post Faithfully Communicating the Affaires of the Armies* arrived, surviving until March 1646.[115] Finally, in September Samuel Pecke and Francis Leach revived *A Continuation of Certaine Speciall an* [*sic*] *Remarkable Passages,* which had disappeared in May 1644, apart from a possible revival in July

[108] N&S 260; Madan, 2065.

[109] *Britanicus* 118, 16 Feb. 1646, 1033, 286.118/E322(28).

[110] *Academicus* 4, [5 Jan. 1646], 36–7, 260.04/314(17); *OR* iv. 370–1. Nedham responded farcically by suggesting that the king's army were suffering from gout; *Britanicus* 112, 5 Jan. 1646, 990, 286.112/E314(19).

[111] *Academicus* 5, [12 Jan. 1646], 41, 260.05/E315(10); *OR* iv. 375.

[112] *Britanicus* 113, 12 Jan. 1646, 993–4, 286.113/E315(11).

[113] Frank relates this to *Mr Peters Report* (retitled *Heads of Some Notes of the Citie Scout;* then *The City-Scout*). Both were published by Robert Austin and Jane Coe. N&S 213, 411 respectively. *Beginnings,* 114.

[114] *Beginnings,* 152; Cotton describes it as a continuation of *London Post* and *Parliaments Post,* the latter two at least being written by the same author, possibly Border; Cotton, 121; N&S 216 note its attribution to John Harris.

[115] Frank describes this as a change in title, but they did overlap for a week, and the first issue of the supposed successor was published on a Mon., though the successive ten were published on Tues. N&S 45; *Beginnings,* 114.

and August 1644.[116] Professional and uninspired, this now lasted until March 1646.

The only newsbook to appear in 1645 which lasted longer than a year was *The Moderate Intelligencer.* Yet it was still a plentiful year, in which between eleven and sixteen newsbooks were available every week. This perhaps suggests the maximum numbers that the market could support. Several new newsbooks disappeared quickly: some publishers tried to revive old titles, and returned them to storage after a few weeks or months. Presumably profit lay at the centre of this. There is nothing to say, however, that existing newsbooks were not produced in greater numbers. What is certain is that by 1645 the newsbook was well established as a literary and journalistic form: and like any other literary form it could be manipulated. By 1645 the success of the newsbook had broadened its application. Whereas newsbook controversy previously had subsisted in the opposition between king and parliament, it was now prepared to embrace other conflicts, such as that between parliament and army. This may reflect the influence of the Self-Denying Ordinance of 3 April 1645, which sought to disqualify MPs from holding office in the army.

1646

The turbulent military and political events of 1646 advised caution. Nedham chose not to heed this advice, and he was not the only editor to change career during the year. The war ended, the king's disingenuousness in negotiating for peace did not. The abolition of episcopacy and the debate over what kind of Presbyterian Church should be established invited theological discussion: the negotiations of the Scottish commissioners in London required some commentary on church government and war guilt. Though the war was over it would be long before the consequences were settled, and editors strove to steer between unseen perils. Everyone, except Nedham, fostered caution.

Several unsuccessful serials containing foreign news arrived and departed: *The Phœnix of Europe, Or the Forraigne Intelligencer* for one issue on 16 January; *General Newes, from All Parts of Christendome* for four issues in May; and *The Military Actions of Europe* for two issues in October and November. *The Moderate Intelligencer,* on the other hand, introduced an extra four pages in February, and increased its attention to foreign news, until this frequently occupied more than half of the twelve pages.

In February and March four issues of *The Moderate Messenger* appeared

116 In chronological sequence: N&S 59, 60, 61.

from the stable of Robert Austin and Jane Coe. It was focused on military affairs, though it did contain some foreign news, and one issue defended William Lilly and astrology against the criticisms of *Academicus.*[117] The editorials were as pious and unwieldy as George Smith's: '*Samsons* Militia lay in his haire, ours in the Parliament, everie thing flourishes in its proper Orb; the fabricke will tumble downe if the Foundation be undermined, be not too confident of the enemies smiles, the smoothest words in such a case, is most suspicious, but to intelligence.'[118] The opening comment of the final issue, however, might have been a warning text for newsbooks for the rest of the year: 'As sacred things prohibit polluted fingers, so matters of State are verie unseasonable in Priests hands.'[119]

Nine other newsbooks consigned themselves to silence that same March. *Academicus* gave up the ghost, perhaps out of sympathy with the king's army, perhaps because the siege of Oxford had effectively restricted supplies. *An Exact and True Collection* appeared for the second and last time on 2 March. The first issue had been fourteen pages in length, covering six weeks, the second eight pages covering two weeks. Like *Moderate Messenger* it died of causes unknown. The same is true of *The Westerne Informer* which appeared for a single issue around 7 March.[120] The afflictions were probably economic. Six more established London newsbooks were victim to a parliamentary purge. *Civicus* had rejoiced at the prospect of this:

We heard also of something concerning the weekly Pamphlets, which are now to be regulated, or (if you please) in better sence, to be contracted into a shorter number. It is a good worke, and it will coole the heate of the blood, and Ring-worme of any who shal for private gaine have a desperate itch to infect and abuse the Kingdome.

There is no man more willing to stoope unto authority then my self.[121]

Civicus indeed did not suffer. *Mercurius Veridicus, The True Informer, A Diary, Perfect Passages, Citties Weekly Post,* and *A Continuation of Certaine Speciall and Remarkable Passages,* however, did. *The Scotish Dove* summarized the resulting situation:

First, I shall acquaint you that upon the suppressing of many weekly sheets, that formerly went abroad; there are now only 8. allowed, *viz.* the *Diurnall, Britanicus,* the Kingdoms *Intelligence,* the *Account,* the *Moderate-Intelligencer, Civicus,* the *Occuerences,* and the *Dove:* And each of these have the day appointed for comming forth: it falling to the *Doves* lot to bee of Saterday, which must

[117] *Moderate Messenger* 3, 17 Feb. 1646, 18–19, 424.3/E322(29).
[118] *Moderate Messenger* 2, 10 Feb. 1646, 9–10, 424.2/E322(7).
[119] *Moderate Messenger* 4, 3 Mar. 1646, 25, 424.4/E325(21).
[120] N&S 142 and 709.
[121] *Civicus* 145, 4 Mar. 1646, 2062, 298.145/E325(22).

accordingly be observed: therefore I shall as long as she flies send her out every Saterday.[122]

The apparent cause of the purge was the concern of the Scottish commissioners over the unfavourable publicity given to their negotiations with parliament for a peace settlement.[123] Yet *The Moderate Intelligencer*, which the commissioner Robert Baillie, and Thomas Edwards, in his *Gangræna*, had singled out for criticism, was not affected.[124] Parliament's response to the complaints was therefore lukewarm. Half-hearted attempts to control the press had been made at frequent intervals in the early 1640s, showing both that there was a will to restrict newsbooks, but also that it was difficult, onerous, and frequently undesirable to halt them. The result looks like complacency. The March 1646 intervention was an attempt to curtail a perceived excess, an excess frequently equated with the dispersal of untruths.[125] Yet the selection of victims had no overall political theme. *Perfect Passages* had been increasingly open in its Independency; *True Informer*, on the other hand, had been increasingly pro-Presbyterian, sympathizing with the Scots and earnestly attacking Lilburne. Its suppression was hardly a favour to the commissioners. The ordinance, though it may have been precipitated by the Scots, was haphazardly directed at limiting the licence of discourse and at suppressing open controversy. If there was any overall result, it was an increasingly Presbyterian face to the newsbook, though there were conspicuous exceptions, notably *Britanicus* and *The Moderate Intelligencer*. William Clyde describes the period of 1645 through 1646 as one of 'Presbyterian tyranny over the press'.[126] The continuing newsbooks endeavoured to be circumspect, though they could not ignore the fact that parliament and the army were determining a future for the king and that a propaganda war between Presbyterian and Independent was breaking out.[127]

Circumspection was not at this point one of Nedham's most exercised talents. His consistent anti-Presbyterianism and intense Scotophobia must have irritated the peace negotiators. Whether this was the entire story behind his suppression is uncertain. Nedham's journalism was remarkable. He had made his own Independent politics more explicit, and warned the Independents against courting royalist support.[128] He

[122] *Scotish Dove* 127, 28 Mar. 1646, 606, 594.127/E330(3).

[123] On the intervention of the commissioners in licensing see Clyde, 95–100; *Beginnings*, 111.

[124] See Ch. 5, below.

[125] e.g. *KWI* 172, 3 Nov. 1646, 281, 214.172/E360(3).

[126] Clyde, 95–100.

[127] Cotton, 165–8.

[128] *Britanicus* 120, 2 Mar. 1646, 286.120/325(18): after which there was an unexplained interval of two weeks before the appearance of the next issue.

had called for revenge, and barely fallen short of describing Charles as a 'man of blood'.[129] In the final issue of *Britanicus* he accused the king of attempting to rob the commons of England of their liberties and invoked the neo-republican theory of George Buchanan, associated closely with resistance theory in the 1640s, to deduce that he was therefore a tyrant. The last straw was the king's apparent reconciliation with the Scots, which signified either a secret design to overthrow parliament by force or his intention to set Scots and English upon each other, and pick up the pieces himself.[130]

The insight was probably true, but Nedham and Audley were brought before the Lords. The offending issue had not been licensed, so Audley was released, while Nedham confessed to authorship of *Britanicus* since issue 52. After nearly two weeks in prison Nedham was released on bail of £200 with a promise not to write again without the Lords' permission.[131] He turned to practising physic and parliament did not regret its decision for sixteen months.

Other newsbooks avoided this fate by being non-committal. *Moderate Intelligencer* was cautious, conservative, and increasingly devoted to foreign news. When it did speak out on religious affairs it was in favour of an Erastian settlement rather than a Presbyterian one. *Perfect Occurrences* was dense and erudite, and though written by a fervent Independent made gestures, through qualification and counter-example, towards a balanced analysis. *Perfect Diurnall* continued to highlight parliamentary consensus. This did not always appear as a neutral position: for its account of the king's flight to the Scots it was accused of Independent tendencies.[132] Such an accusation would have been increasingly accurate through 1646, as Pecke voiced criticism of Presbyterian activity and showed a sensitivity to the Leveller cause.

Whereas *Scotish Dove* turned to innocuous editorials, *Kingdomes Weekly Intelligencer* sought security by avoiding editorial comment, but fell foul of the authorities none the less. On 20 October *Kingdomes Weekly Intelligencer* concluded with a report that Prince Rupert had been made governor of Dunkirk, adding, 'He hath deceived the Presage of Mr. *Lilly*', and that 10,000 men stood ready to invade England.[133] On 26

[129] *Britanicus* 92, 4 Aug. 1645, 286.092/E294(29); *MTN*, 348–9. Patricia Crawford, '"Charles Stuart, That Man of Blood"', *Journal of British Studies*, 16 (1977), 41–61; Christopher Hill, *The English Bible and the Seventeenth-Century Revolution* (1993), 324–31.

[130] *Britanicus* 130, 18 May 1646, 286.130/E337(24); *MTN* 349–50.

[131] *LJ* viii. 321, 325, 341, 355, 373; Clyde, 'Parliament and the Press' (1932–3), 419. Standing surety were John Partridge and William Lipthorpe. At the same time Lilburne was committed to Newgate for *The Freeman's Freedom Vindicated*, and for contempt shown to the House.

[132] *Perfect Diurnall* 150, 15 June 1646, 1200, 504.150/E511(11); *Beginnings*, 118.

[133] *KWI* 170, 20 Oct. 1646, 272, 214.170/E358(8).

October *Perfect Diurnall* suggested that 'the trade of writing *Aulicus* at Court failing', Berkenhead had become 'journey man to the Kingdomes Intelligencer'.[134] Pecke's metaphor suggested that *Kingdomes Weekly Intelligencer* had employed the spirit of Berkenhead, by writing royalist propaganda.[135]

On 27 October *Kingdomes Weekly Intelligencer* defended itself:

> Reader, The Late *Oxford* Mercurialist, being sweld with invie at the truth of Mr. *Lillies* predictions, and striving to disgorge; had last weeke (by a *Bachanalian* stratagem) bespattered the taile of this Pamphlet with some of his owne language, according to the old stile, *viz.* That Prince *Rupert* was made Governour of *Dunkerke,* and so had prevented the presage of Mr. *Lillie.* Thus you see Aulicus cannot decline his lying; let us therefore decline this Adjective Birkenhead, Brekenhead, Brokenhead.[136]

The allusion to Berkenhead responded to Pecke's accusation: the defence was squeezed into the last paragraph on the final page, so the editor had had time to read *Perfect Diurnall.* This was an inadequate, albeit amusing excuse, and the authorities did not repent of their umbrage. On 29 October *Mercurius Civicus* defended *Kingdomes Weekly Intelligencer*:

> He hath advised me to declare, that he utterly disclaimes the last passage in the book which this last week came forth. He much admired to finde the next morning, hee knows not what stuffe thrust in, when he had laboured for, and over-night sent in, such Intelligence, as he beleeved would satisfie the expectation of the people. He doth not know of any infallibility in Mr. *Lilly,* nor because he is pleased to make himself the Intelligencer of the Starres, will he therefore conclude that he is of the privy Counsell of GOD; He much lamenteth the vanity of some men, who, instead of loving their friends, do almost adore them. He knows very well in what reputation the Professors of that Art have lived, both before and after the Incarnation of our Saviour; And besides this, he hath read the Bible. He doth not know of any Stratagem of the late *Oxford Mercurialist,* and I dare undertake for him, he had something else to doe than in the close of all, to make a vile declension on the name of Mr. *Birkenhead.*[137]

Kingdomes Weekly Intelligencer had clearly been attacked on a number of grounds, including supporting astrology, which *Civicus* repudiated.

134 *Perfect Diurnall* 169, 26 Oct. 1646, 1356, 504.169/E513(20).

135 Frank interprets this literally as an accusation: Cotton accepts it as true. *Beginnings,* 122; Cotton, 171–2, citing *KWI* 170, the offending passage. Cotton also writes that *Civicus* picked up Berkenhead. This is improbable, and the evidence is ambiguous.

136 *KWI* 171, 27 Oct. 1646, 280, 214.171/E358(21). *Pragmaticus* 18, 25 1 Aug. 1648, 369.218/E456(7), also claimed that the copy of its previous issue had been tampered with by the man who carried it to press. This is a much more plausible scenario, as *Pragmaticus* was an underground publication.

137 *Civicus* 179, 29 Oct. 1646, 2427–8, 298.179/E359(9).

Nothing corroborates the suggestion that the offending report had been inserted without the editor's knowledge.

In the first week in November, *Kingdomes Weekly Intelligencer* stuck very closely to a detailed account of the negotiation with the Scots, with a prefatory comment on the elusiveness of truth in this age. The editor refused to speak of Scotland:

but from other places I have almost daily seene Letters, which doe rather expresse the humour, or the passion of the Writers, then any wayes serve to advance the publick, and these I conceive in discretion ought not to be so hastilly committed to the Presse, because they tend to nothing, but to increase the differences which are too many, and are too great already.[138]

This was too true in divisive times. Merely presenting the news could itself be perilous, as he found out again that week, when his detailed and responsible reporting incurred further recriminations. The next week *Kingdomes Weekly Intelligencer* opened: 'It is true, in naturall Philosophy, that the Stars in their Orbes are moved by their Intelligences.' This prefaced an apology 'for having too liberally presented some part of the Scottish Papers unto the world'. Towards the end of the same issue it interjected, without apparent motivation, a melancholy reflection: 'Though Warres cannot be licensed, nor Swords run into even numbers as doe Letters, yet this war will be recorded into Letters, and receive a lasting Monument, to preserve the Innocence of his Excellencies Sword from the Inhumane apetite of blood and desolation and shall sanctifie his atchievements.'[139] It concluded by quoting the 'noble Sidney' on the 'wast of Fire in the midst of Water', a disappointingly literal reference to a burning ship. The editor was unhappy with both the times and his own, precarious position.

Despite its pessimism, *Kingdomes Weekly Intelligencer* survived the year, and two more: its defender did not. The charitable behaviour of *Civicus* was out of character, and it had attacked a number of other London newsbooks and editors through the year.[140] In these times of anti-factional sentiment, this may have made its existence tenuous. The full causes of its demise, however, remain unknown. Joseph Frank suggests 'induced suicide'; Anthony Cotton proposes that *Civicus* refused to bow its head and reign in its independence 'with the rest of the Fleet Street mob'.[141] *Civicus* may have disappeared for a congeries of reasons, including economic ones, like many other newsbooks. In early November, it presented a diligent summary of the negotiations, concluding:

[138] *KWI* 172, 3 Nov. 1646, 281, 214.172/E360(3).

[139] *KWI* 173, 10 Nov. 1646, 289, 296, 214.173/E361(8).

[140] *Civicus* 160, 25 June 1646, 2284, 2290, 298.160/E341(18); *Civicus* 163, 23 July 1646, 2320, 298.163/E345(17); *Civicus* 170, 2369.

[141] *Beginnings*, 125; Cotton, 178.

> I have now given you the heads of the Papers lately delivered by the Commissioners of the Kingdome of Scotland: what is omitted (for, all the paper is full of brain) is conceived to be too strong in sinnues for public apprehension, and Independent digestion. I have travailed with my pen to satisfie the Kingdome, and let no man throw more durt upon me, which will be inhumanely done, for I have found the way (by so many years travailes) to be deep and troublesome enough, neither, doe I hope, will my old Host be angry (although I hear he intends to stop my passage) if hereafter I shall lodge at the Heart, or at the signe of the Kings-Head; But signes are Signes, and Hearts are Hearts.[142]

The publisher Thomas Bates was located at the Maiden-head (*sic*): so the 'Kings-Head' and the 'Heart' (punning on 'hart') might just refer to royalist iconography: though earlier in the year *Civicus* had adopted an extremely hostile attitude to the king.[143] These oblique comments perhaps simply referred to the editor's self-loyalty. The next issue plagiarized from *Kingdomes Weekly Intelligencer*, repeating the 'wast of Fire in the midst of Water'; and the next was followed by two weeks of silence.[144] *Civicus* returned in its final issue, more dull and bland than usual, commented on this absence, and then permanently ceased.

Also in November, *The Scotish Dove* folded. There were no signs of foul play, but Smith predictably complained about the sinfulness of the world, and the lonely plight of the good man amidst such flourishing opposition.

Five new titles appeared in late 1646, indicating that no parliamentary ordinance would have effect without continuous intervention. Two appeared only as single issues: *Perfect Passages of State* on 4 August; and *Mercurius Candidus* on 20 November, which anounced in its only issue that a new mercury entitled 'Candidus' was intended to appear on Wednesday, 'but was hindred by the Press' and would now appear on Friday. *Candidus* re-processed news from *Civicus* and elsewhere, and was distinguished primarily by a platitudinous editorial on the inevitability and occasional necessity of war. It also contained a critical reference to Shakespeare.[145] For six issues in October and November *Papers from the Scots Quarters* represented at length the burden of the Scottish troops on the suffering English. The newcomer with the most extended future was *Diutinus Britanicus*: which title was changed to *Mercurius Diutinus (not Britanicus)* in the third issue, presumably intended ironically. Perhaps edited by Thomas Audley, this appeared in eleven issues between November and February 1647: lively and acerbic at first, it was soon

142 *Civicus* 180, 5 Nov. 1646, 298.180/E360(11).

143 e.g. *Civicus* 147, 18 Mar. 1646, 2071, 298.147/E328(13).

144 *Civicus* 181, 12 Nov. 1646, 2446, 298.181/E362(3).

145 *Candidus* 1, 20 Nov. 1646, 1–2, 8, 292.1/E362(21). The allusion to Shakespeare has led to the inference that it was written by John Harris; *History*, 232; J. Frank, 'An Early Newspaper Allusion to Shakespeare', *Shakespeare Quarterly*, 7 (1956), 456.

tamed.[146] Finally, *The London Post* appeared in December, lasting for seven issues until February 1647. It appeared to be a continuation of the earlier *Citties Weekly Post*, which had disappeared in March. The first issue expressed the nature of the succession: 'His language is still the same, neither in the change of time can he change his Temper. After almost a years absence he comes on his old Errand, which is to bring you weekly Intelligence.'[147] Like Pecke, the editor warned against partisanship, and chose caution.

1647

In 1646 the press moved towards discretion and silence; in 1647 it reacted by swinging towards the opposite extreme of bitter and vitriolic mercurialness. The first eight months were sedate, but from September the marketplace was frenzied. At the new year titles were few: *Perfect Diurnall, Kingdomes Weekly Intelligencer, Moderate Intelligencer, Weekly Account, Perfect Occurrences.*[148] *Mercurius Diutinus* and *London Post* continued, though the last two were to disappear in February. These were augmented in January by another issue of *Mercurius Candidus*, probably by a different author. In January and February two undated issues of *Englands Remembrancer of Lon[d]ons Integritie* purveyed pro-Presbyterian and anti-sectarian sentiments. The author, apparantly influenced by Edwards's *Gangræna*, attacked newsbooks, specifically *Perfect Diurnall* and *Kingdomes Weekly Intelligencer*, for promoting and transmitting 'newfangled' heresies.[149]

Papers of the Resolution/Surrendring/Kings Majesties appeared in five issues between January and March, each with a different title. Much in the vein of *Papers from the Scots Quarters*, it was composed of various documents central to the news, as had been common in 1642. *Civicus* had once sensibly commented: 'The most unquestionable way to make

[146] For authorship, see the comment that he had often remarked 'both in *Britanicus* and in my *Diutinus*'; *Diutinus* 9, 27 Jan. 1647, 111.09/E373(11). As Nedham is unlikely to have been involved in journalism at this time, the comment implies Audley: so Frank (*Beginnings*, 130–1) and Williams (*History*, 69–70) judge. The statement may be unreliable, however.

[147] *London Post* 1, 31 Dec. 1646, 1, 232.1/E369(7); see also *London Post* 2, 21 Jan. 1647, 232.2/E371(17).

[148] In Jan. Walker adopted the anagrammatic pseudonym 'Luke Harruney', under which name he pretended the journal was under a different editorship: no one was fooled.

[149] See e.g. *Englands Remembrancer* 2, '11 Feb.' 1647, 17–18, 126.2/E375(9). These targets are odd to say the least: *Perfect Diurnall* was still a judicious publication, though now supporting toleration; *KWI* underwent a period of soft-royalism in the summer, and expressed sympathy to the king on the Isle of Wight.

good intelligence, is to deliver it in the same Letters from which it was received.'[150] In this way, reporting in newsbooks relied on a notion of documentation which was becoming increasingly important to historiography.[151]

For three issues in June, a *Mercurius Britanicus Representing the Affaires of Great Britajne* appeared, which did not attempt to recover the famous style and personality of Nedham's original. Of greater longevity was Pecke's revival of *A Continuation of Certain Speciall and Remarkable Passages*, which ran for thirteen issues on Fridays between June and September. It focused on publishing existing documents. Pecke soon had competition himself on Mondays from a newsbook that might just have been edited by Walker, *A Perfect Summary of Chiefe Passages in Parliament*, which appeared between July and August. June also saw a single-issue newsbook entitled *The Armies Post*, and two issues of *A Diarie, Or an Exact Iournall, of the Proceedings of the Treaty*.[152] Between August and September seven issues of the curiously titled *The Moderne Intelligencer* appeared on Thursdays. This allocated about half its space to foreign news, and expected wide distribution, commenting that its news 'will be worthy your observation, both in *England, Scotland*, and *Ireland*'.[153] If an audience was specified for foreign news it was usually one of merchants, and therefore predominantly London based.[154]

What happened to the newsbook between September 1647 and the spring of 1648 apparently ensued from changes in press controls, though the precise connections are unclear. In 1647 and 1648 an outburst of royalist mercuries followed the devolution of licensing to the army. Importantly, these royalist newsbooks were no longer published in Oxford, but under the army's very feet in London. Yet the bulk of the initial newcomers were not royalist, and the real force of the royalist ephemerals was confined to the spring of 1648. Perhaps this was because provincial insurrections prevented the army from exerting any effective controls: but in fact the army seems to have been as complacent as parliament, relying on economic censorship, and was only truly concerned to stop the royalist periodicals which appeared to be permanent, and had established their polemical credentials. A royalist re-

150 *Civicus* 146, 10 Mar. 1646, 2067, 298.146/E327(16).

151 See Ch. 6, below.

152 N&S 289, 62, 528, 20, 94.

153 *Moderne Intelligencer* 1, 19 Aug. 1647, 431.1/E402(24).

154 Unfortunately Robert Brenner does not tackle the issue of information distribution, or the use of propaganda in pursuit of the merchants' political objectives; *Merchants and Revolution: Commercial Change, Political Conflict, and London's Overseas Traders, 1550–1653* (Cambridge, 1993). Cf. Warren McDougall, 'Scottish Books for America in the Mid 18th Century', in Robin Myers and Michael Harris, eds., *Spreading the Word: The Distribution Networks of Print 1550–1850* (Winchester, 1990), 21–46.

cently returned to England described the situation in October 1647 thus: 'the safety & freedome wch we finde here is beyond expectation till a fewe dayes agoe all libells against ye times walked freely up and downe ye streets, & since ye restraint, the inquiry seemes nothing strict.'[155]

On 3 February the Commons appointed a committee to suppress the licence of the press, particularly pamphlets and ballads, which were scandalous to and critical of parliament. On 10 March, incensed by their ineffectiveness, they revoked the appointment as licensers of Rushworth and his assistants, including Gilbert Mabbott.[156] In July the army entered London, placing the House, and particularly the Presbyterian party, under threat of a purge or reform. On 4 September the first issue of *Mercurius Melancholicus*, the first of the royalist trinity of 1647–9, appeared. Its opening words asked: 'And must invention labour into infinites? what, no respite from the tired Presses?', and parliament must have sympathized.[157] Both royalist and Presbyterian publications attacked the negotiations between the parliamentary leaders and officers in the army and the king.[158] On 20 September, concerned with the proliferation of royalist pamphlets, Sir Thomas Fairfax wrote to the Earl of Manchester, Speaker of the House of Lords (not for the first time that year), suggesting that some reform of the press was necessary:

> I have sent inclosed some Printed Pamphlets, that are not only very scandalous and abusive to this Army in particular, but indeed to the whole Kingdom in general. My Desire is, That these and all of the like Nature may be suppresed for the future; and yet, That the Kingdom's Expectation may be satisfied in relation to Intelligence, till a firm Peace be settled . . . That (if the House shall see it fit) some Two or Three Sheets may be permitted to come out Weekly, which may be licensed, and have some Stamp of Authority with them; and in respect the former Licencer Mr. *Mabbott* hath approved himself faithful in that Service of Licence, and likewise in the Service of the House and of this Army, I humbly desire that he may be restored and continued in the said Place of Licencer.[159]

The Commons had been discussing reform for some time, and on the same day they drew up an ordinance, which the Lords eventually confirmed, after some reminding, on 30 September, and Mabbott was appointed licenser to the weekly newsbooks. The punishments estab-

[155] Durham University Library: MS Cosin Letter Book 1A, 46.

[156] *CJ* v. 72–3 109.

[157] *Melancholicus* 1, [4 Sept. 1647], 1, 344.01/E405(24).

[158] Gardiner², iii. 353–74.

[159] *LJ* ix. 441; see also 312. Clyde, 120, suggests that the resurgence of royalist newsbooks led to the army intervention. This is unlikely, as only *Melancholicus* had appeared at the time of this letter.

lished by the ordinance included a fine of 40*s*. or forty days' imprisonment for authors/editors; 20*s*. or twenty days for printers; and 10*s*. or ten days for stationers and booksellers; street vendors were to be whipped.[160]

Around 9 September an anonymous writer lacerated *Perfect Diurnall* and *Perfect Occurrences* with *A Fresh Whip for all scandalous Lyers*, suggesting that there had been a general decline in responsibility in presenting news, and that the excess of printing had inflicted great damage upon the kingdom.[161] The author was premature: the worst was yet to come.

Nedham chose 21 September to return to his preferred trade, and having been officially forgiven by the king he appeared in a royalist guise as *Mercurius Pragmaticus*. Nedham followed John Hackluyt, editor of *Melancholicus*, in using poetry as an important element of his newsbook. *Melancholicus* had a full title-page, with a central poem, and incorporated poetry in the text. This poetry was frequently in Latin. Nedham introduced a ballad-like four-quatrain poem just below the half-title on the front page, which soon became the model for the newsbook poem. After the Restoration he published these as a sequence, *A Short History of the English Rebellion*.[162] They were simple, witty, and Nedham had a good sense of metre. The sentiments were not subtle:

> For *Liberty*, and *Priviledge*,
> *Religion*, and the *King*.
> We fought: but *ô* the *golden Wedge*!
> That is the only thing.
>
> There lies the *Creame* of all the CAUSE
> *Religion* is but a *Whigg*;
> Pure '*Priviledge* eates up the *Lawes*.
> And cryes for *Kings* a *Figg*,
>
> The *Houses* may a CHRISTMAS keep,
> The Countrimen a LENT;
> The *Citizens* (like silly *Sheep*)
> Must FAST, and be content.
>
> Then where is *Liberty* (I pray.)
> With *Justice, Truth*, and *Right?*
> Sure. They and *Conscience* fled away
> With *CHARLES* to th'Isle of *Wight*.
> ———Nemo me impune lacessit.[163]

[160] *CJ* v. 292, 305, 309, 318–19; *LJ* ix. 440–1, 451–2, 456–8. *An Ordinance of the Lords and Commons . . . against unlicensed or scandalous pamphlets* (28 Sept. 1647; E1802).

[161] See n. 12, above.

[162] *A Short History of the English Rebellion* (1661; N404).

[163] *Pragmaticus* 11, 30 Nov. 1647, sig. L, 369.11A/E417(20).

Nedham continually mocked the government agents who chased after and could not find him: he was an underground force, the scourge of the army grandees. The complaints acknowledged his importance, as he repeatedly informed his readers. The response was swift: the Stationers' Company were ordered to discover the author and printer of *Pragmaticus* on 7 October. Such recognition was not given to *Mercurius Clericus, Mercurius Diabolicus*, or *Mercurius Vapulans*, other royalist newsbooks of 1647.[164] On 16 October Richard Lowndes was committed to Newgate for publishing and vending *Pragmaticus*.[165] These efforts indicate the noxiousness of *Pragmaticus*, its style an extension of *Britanicus*: witty, urbane, and sexually slanderous, but also proficient at changing to sudden seriousness, in order to make earnest political points.[166]

The same distinction was accorded to *Melancholicus*; on 19 October its printer was fined 20*s*. and had his press broken.[167] Yet *Mercurius Anti-Pragmaticus* observed in mid-October that this 'new broome' had not swept the exchange clean.[168] In early November *Mercurius Populi* paradoxically complained that only he had been suppressed.[169] *Mercurius Vapulans* celebrated the ordinance with expressions of high expectations, which were no doubt disappointed.[170] Nedham mocked the action: 'Fie upon't what a *Litter* of *Pamphlets* have beene swept away by one single *Ordinance* against *Printing*!'[171] The irony lay in the fact that he was not one of them. Though it was relatively easy to identify the printers of scandalous material, as each London printer had a distinguishable letterpress type, the royalist mercuries had an underground existence, employing secret presses. When one editor or publisher was thrown in prison, another would take his place. The resources invested in stopping the royalist newsbooks were inadequate, as Gilbert Mabbott evidently thought when he submitted, in August 1648, proposals to the Commons for the suppressing of the offending publications, 'Provided he may be enabled with power to do the same'.[172] The powers and provisions were granted to Francis Bethan and a considerable number of deputies, who did a better, though imperfect job, unable to stop the three most vocal malignants.

[164] *LJ* ix. 172. N&S 302.1/E408.21; (1647; M1764); 390.1/E417(6); 390.2 not in LT.

[165] *CJ* v. 335.

[166] See e.g. the editorial to *Pragmaticus* 36, 37, 12 Dec. 1648, 369.236/E476(2).

[167] *CSPD 1645–1647*, 602.

[168] *Anti-Pragmaticus* 1, 19 Oct. 1647, 1–2, 270.01/E411(10).

[169] Presumably he refers to another newsbook, though the author's identity is unknown; *Populi* 1, 11 Nov. 1647, 6, 364.1/E413(14).

[170] *Vapulans* 2, no date, 11, 390.2.

[171] *Pragmaticus* 3, 6 Oct. 1647, sig. C, 369.103/E410(4).

[172] *Perfect Diurnall* 266, 4 Sept. 1648, 2140, 504.266/E526(2); *CJ* v. 695; *History*, 99–100; Clyde, 158–9.

On 5 November the unholy trinity was completed by the appearance of *Mercurius Elencticus*, edited by George Wharton, sometimes replaced by Samuel Sheppard. This endeavoured to fit the same mould as *Pragmaticus* and *Melancholicus*, but was too pedantic and dull, despite Wharton's use of it to vilipend the parliamentarian astrologer William Lilly. Poetry was integral to its censorious style, as a cruel elegy on the assassinated Leveller Colonel Thomas Rainsborough shows:

> Thus he, whose *Reaching thoughts*, nor *Sea* nor *Land*
> Could ever *terminate*, the dexterous hand
> Of some *bless'd* body in an instant *bounded*,
> And through his *sydes* both *Cause* and *Senate* wounded:
> Hee the Grand *Pilate* to the *Iuncto blocks*,
> Is now *cast ore-board*, they upon the *Rocks*.
> The *Saints* are well nigh *shipwrackt*, and the *State*
> Is at her prayers to *divert* the *fate*.
> Her *Anchor's* split, and on the *Ocean* tost,
> Her *Main-mast* broke, and all the tackling lost.
> The vessell *leekes*, the *Members* pump by *turns*,
> Whilst all on *shelves* and *sands* to *ruine* runs.
> Say *Reader*! was not this a strange *event*,
> Should cause the *Members* say they would *repent*?
> Was't not a *cruell storme*, a *Dismall* day,
> Which (in good *earnest*) made those *Heathens* Pray?
> O yes! the losse of *Rainsborough* is more,
> Than all the *rabble* that *expir'd* before.
> For they rebelled only on the *shoare*,
> He both at *sea*, and *land* could serve the *Whore*.
> But now the *traytor* has his just *reward*.
> *'Treasons not alwaies shelterd by a Guard*.
> For though they *stripp's* of all things but our *life*,
> Hard is his *fortune* never finds a *knife*.[173]

The satirical journalism of all three royalist newsbooks reflected a world of dishonesty, hypocrisy, greed, violence, incontinence, and rapacity. Even when numerous malignant serials were being spawned, the primacy and longevity of these three royalist newsbooks was recognized, not least by counterfeits. The short-lived *Mercurio Volpone*, for instance, advertised itself in October 1648 as 'a reserve to the grand *Mercury* of the Times', meaning *Pragmaticus*.[174] On 27 November 1647 parliament appointed a committee 'to inquire after the Licensers, Authors, Printers, and Publishers of the Pamphlets, intituted, "*Mercurius Elenchichus*," "*Mercurius Pragmaticus*," or any other Pamphlet of the like scandalous or

[173] *Elencticus* 52, 22 Nov. 1648, 504, 312.52/E473(9); see also the mock elegy for the Long Parliament, *MTN* 114–15; for Lilly see *MTN* 139–40.

[174] *Volpone* 2, 12 Oct. 1648, 259.2/E467(22).

seditious Nature; and all unlicensed Pamphlets'.[175] The committee had powers to seize and burn all pamphlets and to break the presses and type. On 19 February 1648 the Committee of Both Houses issued a search warrant authorizing the bearer to search any premises 'where they shall hear that Pragmaticus, Melancholicus, Elencticus, or any other unlicensed pamphlets are to be printed or sold and seize on them', and apprehend any involved.[176] But *Elencticus* survived to witness the beginning of the king's trial, and the others even longer.

The old hand now an understudy, Berkenhead resurfaced with *Mercurius Bellicus. Or, an Alarum to All Rebels,* which appeared between November 1647 and July 1648. This never reached great notoriety, though it was witty enough.[177] Like other royalists it indulged in bad poetry, political satire, and false optimism: though in May it reported news that the king was dead.[178]

These mercuries soon precipitated their antinomies. The single issue of *Mercurius Anti-Melanchollicus. Or, Newes from Westminster, and All Other Parts* was, oddly, more or less royalist. It advocated humour, as the envoi suggests:

To the Book.
Flie merry Booke about this sable Towne,
Untill dull Melancholy be put downe:
Laugh at all Vice, and let thy quainter Rimes
Turne Dr. *Merry-man* to *Cure* the Times.
Apply all speedy Remedies untill
The wound be whole, from whence proceeds our ill.[179]

It also employed a nonsensical imprint, a common device in anti-mercuries and play-pamphlets: 'Printed where I was, and where I will be.' This absurdist comedy was not apolitical. It implied that the world was mad, and that in order to make sense in a mad world madness had to be spoken. The madness was associated with the symbolic inversion of the world, and hence with disruption to the social and monarchical order. In other words, although it was an ambivalent stance which blamed all who participated in the disruption to linguistic sanity represented by cheap print, it was much more likely to be an implicitly royalist position. This was also the case with the two issues of *Mercurius*

[175] *CJ* v. 371.
[176] *CSPD 1648–1649,* 19.
[177] e.g. *MTN* 115–16. *Berkenhead,* 151–60, suggests that the first two issues were by another author, though the internal evidence is thin. Berkenhead's role in other mercuries at this time is thoroughly uncertain. The title had been used for one issue of a serial in May 1643, 640.4/E100(7).
[178] *Bellicus* 16, 16 May 1648, 8, 279.16/E443(2).
[179] *Anti-Melanchollicus* 1, 24 Sept. 1647, 268.1/E408(9).

Medicus: Or, a Soveraigne Salve for These Sick Times which appeared in October.[180] The medical metaphor was a central aspect of the satirico-political language of the newsbooks of the late 1640s: there was a sickness in the state, and many offered reparatives.

Beginning in October, *Mercurius Anti-Pragmaticus* appeared for nine issues. This inversion of *Pragmaticus*, modelled upon it and intended to refute it, also purveyed news. It was a witty publication, and supplied Anthony Wood with some endearing abuse of Nedham, which he plagiarized for *Athenæ Oxonienses*.[181] Half a dozen other ephemeral newsbooks participated in the frenzied spirit of the times. September saw two newsbooks entitled *Mercurius Clericus*, both royalist, but probably by different authors. Two issues of *Mercurius Morbicus*, possibly by Henry Walker, appeared in September, provoking a response entitled *A Recommendation to Mercurius Morbicus Together with a Fair Character Upon His Worth*, possibly by John Taylor.[182] The first issue of *Morbicus* was numbered '1, 2, 3', because it was predominantly an attack on the first three issues of *Melancholicus*.[183] In November *Mercurius Populi. Or Newes Declaring Plain Truth to the People* aspired to egalitarianism, while lamenting the irrational appetite for newsbooks; it promised to introduce news into the next issue, which never appeared.[184] The undated and royalist *Mercurius Vapulans* appeared for two issues in November and probably December; in the same months two issues of *Mercurius Rusticus* attacked the army.[185] Though these publications were numerous enough, the real torrent of royalist ephemerals commenced in 1648.

1648

The year 1648 saw the recrudescence of royalist newsbooks. The spring brought a chaos of printed texts, both evocative and tedious. There were around sixty-seven distinct serials in the year. *Perfect Diurnall*, *Kingdomes Weekly Intelligencer*, *Moderate Intelligencer*, *Perfect Occurrences*, *Mercurius Elencticus*, and *Mercurius Pragmaticus* survived the year. *Perfect Weekly Account* terminated in January, to be replaced in March by another serial with the same name.[186] *Kingdomes Weekly Post* ceased in

[180] Possibly by Henry Walker, N&S 340.

[181] *AO* iii. 1180–90.

[182] For Walker, see *Beginnings*, 142; *A Recommendation to Mercurius Morbicus* (6 Oct. 1647; T502); see also Cotton, 214–19, 239.

[183] *Morbicus* 1, 2, 3, 350.1/E407(30); dated 20 Sept. in LT.

[184] *Mercurius Populi* [or *Populus*] 1, [11 Nov. 1647], 364.1/E413(14).

[185] N&S 390.1–2. The title echoed *Britanicvs Vapvlans. Beginnings*, 283.

[186] This led to some confusion, as the printer of the revived serial (probably Bernard Alsop, who acknowledged himself in imprints in 1649) put the date 1647 on the front

March; *Mercurius Anti-Pragmaticus* in February; *Bellicus* in July; *Melancholicus* in November, though it did reappear in December. In July the Leveller *The Moderate* appeared, and ran until September 1649. *A Declaration* appeared in December and saw the year out. In addition to this another fifty or so newsbooks made brief manifestations, about forty-five of them lasting five issues or less.[187] The longer-lived serials were *Heads of Chiefe Passages/Kingdoms Weekly Account, Mercurius Aulicus, Mercurius Britanicus Alive Again, Mercurius Psitacus, Packets of Letters.* The shorter-lived were: *Linx Brittanicus, Mercurius Dogmaticus, Perfect Summarie, Mercurius Insanus Insanissimus, Mercurius Anti-Mercurius, Mercurius Critticus,*[188] *Ieremiah Revived, A Jovrnal of Parliament, Mercurius Academicus, Mercurius Veridicus, Mercurius Militaris, Mercurius Urbanus, Mercurius Poeticus, Mercurius Publicus, Mercurius Gallicus, Mercurius Honeštus, Parliament-Kite, Mercurius Censorius, Mercurius Domesticus, Westminster Projects, New News, The Parliaments Vulture, The Parliaments Scrich-Owle, Perfect Diary of Passages, A Wonder a Mercury Without a Lye In's Mouth, Mercurius Scoticus, Royall Divrnall, Mercurius Anglicus, Mercurius Aquaticus, The Colchester Spie, Hermes Stratjcus, Mercurius Fidelicus, The Parliament-Porter, Mercurius Catholicus, The Treaty Traverst: Or, Newes from Newport, Mercurio Volpone, The True Informer, Mercurius Pacificus, Mercurius Militans, Martin Nonsence, A Declaration, Collected out of the Journals, Mercurius Impartialis.* Some titles were used for more than one serial. Most were royalist. Many paid little attention to the news, but indulged in sexual and political satire, and criticized other newsbooks for scurrility and inaccuracy. The English commissioners in Scotland none the less complained in March about the 'diurnals printing all their doings'. In response parliament ordered 'That no Person do presume to print or publish any of the Proceedings, or other Matters, agitated in Both or Either of the Houses of Parliament, but by the special Order and Direction of Both or Either of the said Houses: And that no Person do presume to license any such Things.'[189]

In April 1648, for the first time in over a year, *Weekly Account* was entered in the Stationers' Register; a formality which *The Moderate Intelligencer* alone had observed since the preceding September. The reluctance to follow this weekly procedure stemmed from the cost: a fee

page. This led Williams (*History*, 52) to assume this was a competitor to the 1647 serial, which caused the addition of 'perfect' to the name. Frank repeated the error; *Beginnings*, 128, 150. Cotton, ch. 6, corrected it.

[187] *Beginnings*, appendix D, identifies 35. In addition to those see N&S 206, 201, 219, 269, 274, 345, 442, 499, 529, 531.

[188] Two or three issues in Apr. and May, N&S 303; attributed to John Crouch, whom the Commons ordered the Committee of Printing to investigate on 18 Nov. 1648; *CJ* vi. 80.

[189] *CJ* v. 493; *LJ* x. 111.

of 6*d*. was charged for each entry, and each issue of a serial was considered a separate publication, requiring a separate payment.[190] The return of *Weekly Account* to the Register probably indicates that the editor was nervous that parliament or the army would one day make the significant intervention they threatened. This was delayed until September 1649. Meanwhile ordinances against unlicensed printing, stage-plays, and interludes were passed; and George Thomason, the seller and collector of books, sold for £500 a collection of books in 'Eastern languages' to the library of Cambridge University, thus funding his further purchase of all the newsbooks he could find.[191] In November Thomason, with a number of 'mercury women', was summoned to Derby House to answer charges that he had dispersed unlicensed books.[192]

The recrudescence of royalist mercuries predominantly coincided with the royalist uprisings in the provinces which have become known as the second civil war. This broke out in April, and was concluded when the Scottish forces were defeated at Preston in August. There followed a period of treating with Charles, discontinued when the army purged parliament and set up a court to try the king.[193] The appearance of the royalist newsbooks proceded these events, suggesting that they reflected the same general dissatisfaction which led to support of the royalist forces.

Early February brought a revival of *Mercurius Aulicus*, not by Berkenhead but probably by Samuel Sheppard. This lasted until mid-May, though it was revived for four issues in August. Its satire included sexual slander, notably of Hugh Peters and the republican Henry Marten, both of whom received egregious and unfavourable notice in newsbooks. Like *Pragmaticus*, this *Aulicus* used a catch-phrase, positioned just below the opening poem. Nedham's was 'Nemo me impune lacessit', an exit line from Webster's *The White Devil*;[194] Sheppard's was 'Quis me impune lacessit'. The same phrase appeared on *The Parliament-Kite* (between May and August), perhaps indicating the same author. *Mercurius Publicus* (three issues in May) repeated, 'Si Natura

[190] Clyde, 144.

[191] *LJ* x. 40–2; *Ordinance . . . for the Utter Suppression and Abolishing of All Stage Plays and Interludes . . . 11 Feb. 1647* (1648; E2070); *LJ* x. 130, 157, 158, 160, 162, 342; *CJ* v. 512, 518.

[192] *CSPD 1648–1649*, 327–8, 331.

[193] Robert Ashton, *Counter Revolution: The Second Civil War and its Origins, 1646–1648* (New Haven, 1994); David Underdown, *Pride's Purge: Politics in the Puritan Revolution* (1971; 1985).

[194] Lois Potter, 'The Plays and the Playwrights, 1642–1660', in Philip Edwards, Gerald Eades Bentley, Kathleen McLuskie, and Lois Potter, eds., *The Revels History of Drama in English*, vol. iv: *1613–1660* (1981), 285.

negat, facit indignatio versum'; and *Domesticus* (one issue in June), 'Sequitur post gaudia luctus'; *The Parliaments Scrich-Owle* (three issues in June and July), 'Quis vetat hoc verum'. Such phrases had become, along with satirical locatives and the intermingling of verse with prose, stock elements of the royalist mercury. Some, including *The Parliaments Scrich-Owle, The Parliament-Kite, Mercurius Melancholicus, Westminster Projects,* and *Mercurius Psitacus,* had full title-pages, the former two with poems on the versos. *Mercurius Honestus* (two issues in May) had the appearance of a royalist mercury, a full title-page with poetry, and, unusually, was written in dialogue form. It attacked *Elencticus* and *Pragmaticus,* suggesting that anti-royalism was not the same as supporting parliament: instead this newsbook participated in the language of chaos, inversion, and madness which was associated with the attack on journalism and on the political differences which led to the war.

On 16 May John Hall responded to the revived *Aulicus* by writing *Mercurius Britanicus Alive Again,* which appeared for sixteen issues between May and August.[195] Hall had recently moved to London from Cambridge, and was celebrated as the prodigious author of a volume of poems, a collection of essays, a satire upon Presbyterianism, an edition of Robert Hegge, and a translation of Johann Christian Andreæ.[196] His biographer, John Davies of Kidwelly, wrote that in 1648 Hall:

> contributed somthing to the revivall of BRITANNICUS, which must needs be taken very hainously by the party against whom it was directed . . . it came abroad in a conjuncture of time when the affections of the City were extreamly retrograde, absolutely alienated from an adored Parliament to a persecuted King, whose cause was devolved from Arms to Pens. The wits of the ruin'd party had their secret *Clubs,* these hatched *Mercuries, Satyres,* and *Pasquinado's,* that travelled up and down the streets with so much impunity, that the poor weekly *Hackneyes,* durst hardly communicate the ordinary Intelligence. This was the true state of affairs when Mr. *Hall* made that appearance for the State, not disconsonant to his former principles, even in the University, which were sufficiently anti-monarchicall, and subservient to the interest of a Commonwealth.[197]

This is a sensitive analysis. Hall endeavoured to repossess the literary journalism which the royalists had pretended to be their own, using

[195] To Hall has also been doubtfully attributed a single issue of *Mercurius Britannicus* (7 Apr. 1648; 284.1/E435(3)), which began with a poem: '*Come old* Britanicus *here sings, | Who long ha's slept, but now | Again is wakened, and he brings | Intelligence to you.*' Despite the poem, this was not a polemical newsbook.

[196] See Joad Raymond, 'John Hall's "Method of History": A Book Lost and Found', *ELR,* forthcoming.

[197] The biography is printed in preface to Hall's posthumously published translation, *Hierocles upon the golden verses of Pythagoras; Teaching a vertuous and worthy life* (1657; H1938), sig. b3^{v}. See also *AO* ii. 457–60.

poetry and witty satire, written in a jovial, comradely style. Though he used classical allusions the prose was less erudite, strained, and convoluted than his normal style. Hall quickly engaged with *Pragmaticus, Melancholicus, Elencticus,* and *Bellicus,* beginning by accusing them of pandering to vulgar appetite.[198] He also defended William Lilly, traducing Lilly's royalist opposite Wharton, editor of *Elencticus.* At the end of May *Elencticus* responded: 'Come away *Lilly,* and bring that *Apostate Hyreling* with thee, *Iack Hall,* the *Rymeing,* Whistle-cap of *Grayes-Inne.*' He accused Hall of ripping the '*Bowells*' of his '*mother*', Cambridge University, echoing Cleveland's *Character of a London Diurnall,* and asked: 'Am I ignorant that *William Lilly* put this *meritorious* work upon thee & promised *Bolstrode Whitlock's* assistance to procure thee a weekly *stipend* from the *Rebells,* to gratifie thy paines?'[199] Wharton later wrote that he had not seen the third issue of *Britanicus* 'for there was but 200. in all printed for his owne use, which he run a *begging* with amongst the *Members*', as Lilly's stipend was insufficient.[200] Wharton knew a fair amount about Hall, including his association with the royalists Lovelace, Shirley, and Stanley, but the suggestion of Lilly's patronage is unconfirmed. Lilly did not mention Hall in his albeit patchy autobiography, written late in life, though he did complain about being abused by 'many lewd *Mercurys*' in 1646.[201] Davies recorded that Hall became acquainted with Lilly after writing *Britanicus.*[202]

Hall may have written the three issues of *Mercurius Censorius,* which appeared in June. This defended Lilly, reproached the usual enemies, and commented on Hall himself:

Elencticus thinks he hath done sufficiently, for now he supposes he hath eternally engratiated himself to those of the Party, in fathering *Britanicus* on *Jack Hall* of *Greisinne,* and makes it the businesse of his sheet (as a matter that much concerneth the affairs of the Royallists his Masters) to rail at and traduce a person of such eminent parts and excellencies, that to have a serious thought of *Elencticus,* were the most inexcusable fault he ever committed: But he scornes thee, and the rest of the litter of flattering *spaniels,* who are fed with the *excesse*

[198] *Britanicus Alive Again* 1, 16 May 1648, 2, 282.01/E442(19).

[199] *Elencticus* 27, 31 May 1648, 205–6, 312.27/E445(23); see also *Elencticus* 28, 7 June 1648, 213–14, 312.28/E446(16); *Elencticus* 29, 14 June 1648, 222, 312.29/E447(11); *Elencticus* 30, 21 June 1648, 233, 312.30/E449(7); *Elencticus* 34, 19 July 1648, 261–4, 312.34/E453.23. The story is tacitly supported by Williams, 'Beginnings of English Journalism', 405; *History,* 103; *Beginnings,* 334 n. 38; Cotton, 185. See also Hyder E. Rollins, *Cavalier and Puritan: Ballads and Broadsides Illustrating the Period of the Great Rebellion, 1640–1660* (New York, 1923), 44, where it is suggested that Hall was paid the extraordinary fee of £5 per week for his services.

[200] *Elencticus* 29, 14 June 1648, 222, 312.29/E447(11).

[201] *Mr. William Lilly's History of His Life and Times, From the Year 1602, to 1681* (1715), 58.

[202] Davies in Hall, *Hierocles,* sigs. b3^{v}–b4.

of that money which a sort of *needy* Gentlemen, your Patrons, should have spent upon their *Whores*: And such is the violence of this weekly drudge (whom the *silly madcaps* of *Greisinne* admire, and are astonished at, and whose *learned writings* they prefer before *Ployden* or *Littleton*) that he blushes not to raise horrid falshoods of his carriage in the *Vniversity*, when 'tis well known 'twas such, that it had indeared the greatest men in the *Vniversity* to his acquaintance; and his worthy contributions to the Common-wealth of learning while he was there, have not undeservedly conciliated a precious memory of him among all good men.[203]

This concedes Hall to be author of *Britanicus* if not *Censorius*, and suggests an attempt to establish his literary credentials as an equal opponent to any royalist journalist.

The same issue of *Censorius* mentioned that *Elencticus* cost 2*d*. This is plausible, though it is certainly meant to be juxtaposed against the penny charged for *Britanicus*. Allusions to the prices of newsbooks are usually found only in derogatory comments, yet it is safe to assume that most single-sheet newsbooks cost a penny, those in two sheets twice as much. The royalist mercuries of 1648 are supposed to have cost 2*d*. because of the dangers involved in selling them, and because they were in greater demand; there is evidence for the former point, little for the latter.[204] In 1649 *Mercurius Pragmaticus (For King Charles II)* advertised itself as costing 2*d*.[205] Less reliable is the description of *Aulicus* in *The spie* as a 'peniworth of *slander*'.[206] The term 'pennyworth' was a common slur.[207] When *Britanicus* suggested in 1645 that the difficulties in obtaining *Aulicus* caused it to sell for 6*d*. a copy, it was probably a pure fabrication.[208] On the other hand, *The True Character of Mercurius Aulicus* suggested in 1645 that *Aulicus* retailed for as much as 18*d*.[209] These figures should be compared with the shilling a building or agricultural labourer could earn in a day; perhaps 16*d*. for a skilled builder.[210] A strikingly wide audience could afford to purchase the cheapest publica-

[203] *Mercurius Censorius* 2, 8 June 1648, 13–4, 296.2/E446(20).

[204] Clyde, 129; *History*, 93, 169; Plomer, '"Mercurius Civicus"', 187; *Beginnings*, 23, 39, 75, 136, 194, 206, 314 n. 54; Cotton, 9, 245; *Secret Rites*, 36; PRO: SP 16/493/62; *CSPD 1641–1643*, 428.

[205] *Pragmaticus (For King Charles II)* 18, 21 Aug. 1649, 370.18/E571(8).

[206] *Spie* 2, 30 Jan.–5 Feb. 1644, 609.02/E31(12). *Aulicus* was one and a half sheets at the time.

[207] *The Actors Remonstrance* (24 Jan. 1642; A454/E86(8)), 7; *Britanicus* 47, 19 Aug. 1644, 367–8, 286.047/E6(26); Bod.: MS Tanner 60, f. 354; John Cleveland, *A Character of a Diurnal-Maker* (1654; C4657), 5; *Pragmaticus* 21, 8 Feb. 1648, sig. X^{v}, 369.121/E426(6). *Severall Proceedings* 85, 15 May 1651, 1295, 599.085/E785(24), refers to a single-sheet pamphlet costing a penny, without insult.

[208] *Britanicus* 95, 1 Sept. 1645, 852, 286.095/E298(24).

[209] *The True Character of Mercurius Aulicus* (1645; T2601).

[210] Figures for 1640: E. H. Phelps Brown and Sheila V. Hopkins, 'Seven Centuries of Building Wages', in Eleanor M. Carus-Wilson, ed., *Essays in Economic History*, ii (Economic

tions, though it might involve making sacrifices, as the notebooks of the puritan wood-turner Nehemiah Wallington show.[211] Of course interested parties did not have to buy a copy to read it: newsbooks certainly had a high circulation as a result of being passed from hand to hand, and also read aloud to the illiterate. Furthermore, second-hand copies of newsbooks may have been available a week or two belatedly at a reduced cost: there was a significant trade in used books in the seventeenth century.[212]

In June a conflict between John Dillingham and his printer Robert White resulted in a 'counterfeit' or alternative *Moderate Intelligencer*, and eventually in the founding in June of a salient newsbook. In May, sympathy for the maltreatment of John Lilburne led Dillingham to make a contentious comment: 'Upon the whole, fully agreed by both judges, Lieut. Col. Lilburne was sent back to the Tower, they declaring it was against law for them either to baile him, or set him at libertie. If the case be thus then: Dieu nous donne les Parlyaments briefe, Rois de vie longue.'[213] Mabbott subsequently refused to license Dillingham. Someone, perhaps Mabbott, then proceeded to produce a newsbook of the same name with the collaboration of the original publisher Robert White. Dillingham petitioned the Lords who upheld his complaint, ordering Mabbott to license Dillingham's book in future, and no other by that name.[214] White then went on to publish instead *The Moderate*, perhaps still working with Mabbott; and Dillingham continued his newsbook with the publisher Robert Leybourne.

Historians disagree over the authorship of *The Moderate*. Mabbott is accepted by J. B. Williams and Frank, rejected by Cotton, and doubted by Carolyn Nelson and Matthew Seccombe and Jurgen Diethe.[215] There are no overwhelming reasons why Mabbott could not have had some role in the publication, which was the product of collaboration. The style of the political editorials has played a key element in attribution,

History Society, 1962), 177; Joan Thirsk, ed. *The Agrarian History of England and Wales*, vol. iv: *1560–1640* (Cambridge, 1967), 864.

[211] Paul Seaver, *Wallington's World: A Puritan Artisan in Seventeenth-Century London* (1985), 156; Ch. 5, below.

[212] Watt, *Cheap Print and Popular Piety*, 260–4; Keith Wrightson, *English Society 1580–1680* (1982), 32–4.

[213] *Moderate Intelligencer* 164, 11 May 1648, 1314, 419.164/E441(30). Dillingham's sympathy for the king can be gauged from a newsletter to Lord Montagu dated 21 Sept. 1648, expressing hopes for a personal treaty; *HMC: Montagu*, 163–4. The same letter reveals that he was still working as a tailor.

[214] *LJ* x. 345; *Beginnings*, 152–60; Cotton, 120, 239–41; id., 'John Dillingham', 829–30; Siebert, 215–16.

[215] *History*, 104; *Beginnings*, 153–60; Cotton, 258–66, 280; N&S 413; Jurgen Diethe, '*The Moderate*: Politics and Allegiances of a Revolutionary Newspaper', *History of Political Thought*, 4 (1983), 247–9, 251, 267.

and the editorials were most unlikely to have been written by him. But the writer of the editorials was not necessarily responsible for gathering the news and co-ordinating the production, a role Mabbott might have undertaken. *The Moderate* denied any acquaintance with Mabbott: 'I professe I know him not, nor to my knowledge ever saw him.'[216] On 23 September the Lords moved to make enquiries after the authorship of *The Moderate*, 'wherein the King and Parliament is much dishonoured', and to do this they requested the assistance of Dillingham.[217] This makes their suspicions clear. There is, however, no record of any resulting report. It is just conceivable that Mabbott was protected by the support of Fairfax, who had been responsible for his appointment.

Another inconclusive hint lies in Henry Walker's petition to the Lords on 30 June 1648, complaining about Mabbott's activity as a licenser.[218] Walker seems to have been concerned over his possession of the title *Perfect Occurrences*, perhaps in response to Mabbott's officiousness, though his complaint may have been an opportune attempt to shrug the licenser off, following Dillingham's successful move. He argued that:

> Mabbot, besides his licensing, which is alone worth nearly 100.*l.* per annum, collects the intelligence of Monday's Journal and other sheets of news, which is worth much more; and being both writer and licenser he has liberty to make use of what he pleases to advance his own writing, and to leave out to disparage others; for these reasons, when he licensed under his master John Rushworth, the House of Commons put him out.[219]

Walker's complaint was successful, and he was granted the right to publish his newsbook by special licence, without Mabbott's interference. 'Monday's journal' refers to Pecke's *Perfect Diurnall*, so perhaps Mabbott had a hand in supplying news to Pecke, who later supported him against his former ally Theodore Jennings in a struggle for the position of official licenser.

Mabbott is not otherwise known as a Leveller, but the garnering of news could be distinct from editing and writing, and need not indicate political allegiance. It is perhaps worth noting that *The Moderate* is attributed to Mabbott in Crouch's *Man in the Moon*.[220] This is not a reliable source; but all of the other attributions made by Crouch in the same issue are correct, or at least uncontested. Crouch was well in-

[216] *Moderate* 12, 3 Oct. 1648, 96, 413.2012/E465(25).
[217] *LJ* x. 508.
[218] *LJ* ix. 441; x. 354, 494.
[219] *HMC: Seventh Report* (HMSO, 1879), appendix, 45; dated 16 Aug. 1648; cf. *LJ* x. 442.
[220] *Man in the Moon* 26, 24 Oct. 1649, 218, 248.26/E575(32); also *Elencticus* 44, 27 Sept. 1648, 351, 312.44/E464(46).

formed, though possibly relying on popular rumour. Though a name is convenient, it does not much matter who the author was; as is the case with the many ephemeral royalist mercuries of 1648, authorship should not determine the way we read anonymous, and possibly collaborative, texts.

The Moderate began like its precursor, *The Moderate Intelligencer*, twelve pages long with much foreign news. After three issues it was reduced to eight pages, moved from Thursday to Tuesday, and began a new series, numbering from one. The sixth issue of this series introduced a regular editorial, with which *The Moderate* became a mouthpiece of, and forum for, Leveller arguments, advocating a broad franchise and religious toleration.[221] These clear and trenchant statements of radical political theory frightened the Earl of Leicester, father to the republican Algernon Sidney, into exclaiming that *The Moderate* 'endeavours to invite the people to overthrow all propriety, as the original cause of sin; and by that to destroy all government, magistracy, honesty, civility, and humanity'.[222] They were the natural ancestor of Nedham's republican editorials in *Mercurius Politicus*, and make *The Moderate* one of the half-dozen or so newsbooks which reward detailed study.[223]

The royalists pursued their war with the licensers. From July to November, *Pragmaticus* proudly appeared in a sheet and a half. Nedham was certainly successful at avoiding those whom he claimed were pursuing him, but his exaggerated optimism developed hollow resonances in the second half of the year, and moments of darkness were allowed to interrupt. His news, however, was excellent, suggesting that he may have had a sympathetic contact inside the Commons.[224] *Melancholicus* and its counterfeits, by Crouch and possibly Sheppard, continued to purvey invective, sometimes one editor expending it on the other who usurped his place in the market.[225] *Elencticus* broadcast his sense of outrage, much of it in verse. In August the rhetoric of encouragement and confidence in the royalist press was replaced with anger and pessimism. The same month Francis Bethan and twenty-one deputies were ap-

[221] J. Frank, *The Levellers* (Cambridge, Mass., 1955), 169–70; and *Beginnings*, 154–60, 178–82; Roger Howell, Jr., and David E. Brewster, 'Reconsidering the Levellers: The Evidence of *The Moderate*', *P&P* 46 (1970), 68–86; H. N. Brailsford, *The Levellers and the English Revolution*, ed. Christopher Hill (1961; Nottingham, 1983), 401–16; Diethe, '*The Moderate*', 247–94. As Howell and Brewster and Diethe argue, the Levellers were not a unified party with fixed and universal policies.

[222] *Sydney Papers*, ed. R. W. Blencowe (1825), 79.

[223] *MTN* 210–13, 399.

[224] Cotton, 311, proposed Speaker William Lenthal as a candidate. They had connections through their home town of Burford in Oxfordshire.

[225] See e.g. the two *Melancholicus* 31, 24 July 1648, 344.48A, 344.48B/E453(43); for authorship of the counterfeits, see *Melancholicus* 51, 14 Aug. 1648, sig. Ggv, 344.51B/E458(10).

pointed to chase down scurrilous pamphlets. *Pragmaticus* particularly took to ridiculing the efforts of these 'beagles'.[226]

The beagles were soon to chase after a Leveller newsbook which appeared five times in October and November: *Mercurius Militaris*, edited by John Harris, a former actor.[227] The title had been used once by a royalist newsbook in April, and would be used again twice in 1649, by both a Leveller, possibly Harris, and an anti-Leveller journalist. In *Militaris* Harris attacked *Elencticus* as a means of deceiving the people, and was in turn attacked by *Melancholicus.* He attacked *Pragmaticus* for a report of the king touching to cure the King's Evil.[228] His account of the last stand of the murdered Rainsborough was magnificent:

> while he strugled, they ran him through the Body, and yet he commanded the Sentinel to stick to him, and he said he had no match, then again they run him through the belly, and he with both his hands pulling the sword out of his body, had well nigh forced it from the villain, but 12. or 20. of them falling in, they run him through again, and mangled his flesh.[229]

Harris claimed both to undeceive the people by uncovering guile, and to speak on their behalf, discovering the treason and conspiracies of both the army grandees and the king. *Militaris* was also attacked on 12 December, the week after it disappeared, by *Mercurius Impartialis,* which represents the developing tendencies of royalist journalism. *Impartialis* impugned Harris for daring 'to Blaspheme that Sacred Person, who is the very expresse Signe and Type of God'.[230] After Pride's Purge on 6 December the iconography of Charles as a martyr, which had been accreting at least since 1646, had rapidly crystallized.[231] *Impartialis* also attacked *The Moderate,* attributing it to Mabbott, as 'a most immoderate Piece', a pun many historians have repeated. Though promising a second issue, it was ephemeral: many mercuries of 1648 were conceived as transitory. Though some may have been forcibly stopped, editors internalized the principle of the ephemeral publication, and the brief run followed by poignant silence became part of the character of the royalist mercury. There was not much news or exposition in *Impartialis,* just a peroration in poetry and prose; that was the point of the mercury. It warned that society would soon turn into community, and that the

[226] *Pragmaticus* 34, 21 Nov. 1648, 369.234/E473(7); *Pragmaticus* 43, 27 Feb. 1649, 369.243.

[227] *Militaris* 5, 21 Nov. 1648, 33, 346.5/E473(8).

[228] *MTN* 178–9; see also 116–17.

[229] *Militaris* 4, 8 Nov. 1648, 30, 346.4/E470(14); see also the hostile account of his funeral, including a mock elegy, in *Elencticus* 52, 22 Nov. 1648, 312.52/E473(9).

[230] *Impartialis* 1, 12 Dec., 3, 333.1/E476(3); see also *The Royall Diurnall (For King Charls the II.)* 1, 25 Feb. 1650, sig. A^v, 587.1/E594(6).

[231] For the newsbook coverage see Ch. 5, below.

army were resolved to 'have a speedy period put to this Parliament, and then up goeth the Tower of *Babell*, every man then shall be a King'.[232]

In reciprocation, journalism as reporting never disappeared. Those newsbooks which had been around for months or years continued to retail detailed news. They could be inaccurate, but this should not occlude the total effect of their service. One newsbook which appeared between March and November, entitled *Packets of letters from . . . to members of the House of Commons*, reveals the opposite tendency to royalist journalism. It was not space-efficient: it employed a full title-page and the text was in large, uneven type. It had no editorial content, and consisted entirely of letters, mostly from Scotland and the north, and a few other documents. Though it presented useful information on royalist disturbances, it was not rhetorically or formally vigorous; but it persisted for some thirty-seven issues, discontinuing when northern news ceased to be urgent. It was rapidly succeeded by another sober newsbook, also printed by Robert Ibbitson, *A Declaration, Collected Out of the Journalls of Both Houses of Parliament.* Both were probably edited by Henry Walker, who knew how to efface himself as an editor.[233]

When the army took parliament in hand in December, the newsbooks were generally quiet. The year 1648 was a prolific one, but its conclusion produced only a handful of newsbooks, most of them, excepting the arch-royalists, subdued in tone. Despite the claims which newsbooks made for their own influence, it seemed that for the time being they were powerless.

1649

'The Triall of the King is the great Hinge on which for this weeke the Doore of this Intelligence must move,' reported *Kingdomes Weekly Intelligencer* in January 1649, incontrovertibly.[234] An official account of the trial and execution of the king was prepared by authority, perhaps written by Gilbert Mabbott, and published in three parts as *A Perfect Narrative/A Continvation of the Narrative* in January. Most newsbooks presented derivative texts little altered.[235] The royalist newsbooks wrote elegiacally, but *Elencticus* and *Melancholicus* disappeared in January. An *Elencticus*, apparently written by Samuel Sheppard,[236] appeared sporadi-

[232] *Impartialis* 1, 4, 7.

[233] N&S 480, 90 respectively. The latter appeared in six issues in Dec. and Jan., changing its title in the fourth issue to *Heads of a Diarie.*

[234] *KWI* 295, 23 Jan. 1649, 1225, 214.295/E539(6).

[235] *Perfect Narrative*, 518.1–3; for the accounts see *MTN*, ch. 5.

[236] *CSPD 1649–1650*, 529, 534; a warrant to seize Sheppard as author and William Wright as printer on 11 May; another, without names, on 29 May.

cally in February and was revived between May and November; two issues of *Melancholicus, For King Charles the Second* appeared in May and June. Nedham resigned *Pragmaticus* in January, though someone else stepped in until May. Nedham returned in April with *Mercurius Pragmaticus (For King Charles II)*, which lasted until June or July 1649, when he was captured and imprisoned.[237]

None of the newsbooks which started the year saw its end: *Perfect Diurnall, Kingdomes Weekly Intelligencer, The Moderate, Moderate Intelligencer, Perfect Occurrences*, and *Perfect Weekly Account* were terminated in September and October by the efficacious parliamentary Act for which carpers against print had waited. Nevertheless there were around thirty newcomers through the year. One with greater longevity, appearing between February and October, was *The Kingdomes Faithfull and Impartiall Scout* (initially *Kingdomes Faithfull Scout*), published by Robert Wood and probably edited by Daniel Border. The *Scout* interspersed news with pious editorial asides, '(*There is now some hopes of amendment, and that the Disease being at its full height, a soveraign Balsome will be applyed to the almost dying and bleeding hearts of the poor Inhabitants of this Nation*)',[238] and from April onwards with Lilly's astrological reports. Border imitated the transliterative Hebrew word-games with which Henry Walker began *Perfect Occurrences*, later changing to Greek.[239] When the *Scout*, following *Perfect Diurnall*, represented at length the reasons for Gilbert Mabbott's resignation as censor in June,[240] Walker, who had in January petitioned to be his own licenser,[241] chose to take revenge, using the new licensers Henry Walley and Theodore Jennings as his authorities. After some counter-accusations *Perfect Occurrences* carried a statement from Jennings:

> I desire all people to take notice that I denie to give any authority to a Pamphlet called *The Kingdomes Weekly Scout*, because the Common-wealth hath been so abused by it, by *Rob. Wood* of *Grubstreet*, who contrives false inventions at an Alehouse to adde to it what he fancies as news, after *M. Border* the author hath write it, and the Licenser perused it.[242]

The statement added that Border refused to write it henceforth; though in fact Border acknowledged later issues. Jennings also licensed it. Only

[237] *AO* iii. 1181; *CSPD 1649–1650*, 507, 537; Frank, *Cromwell's Press Agent*, 64.

[238] *Kingdomes Faithfull and Impartiall Scout* 21, 22 June 1649, 162, 210.21/E530(46).

[239] On these see Nigel Smith, 'The Uses of Hebrew in the English Revolution', in Peter Burke and Roy Porter, eds., *Language, Self and Society* (Oxford, 1991), 50–71.

[240] *Perfect Diurnall* 304, 28 May 1649, 2500, 504.304/E530(21); *Kingdomes Faithfull and Impartiall Scout* 18, 1 June 1649, 143, 210.18/E530(26).

[241] The Lords granted him the right on 16 Jan., but suspended it until further consideration: *LJ* x. 645.

[242] *Perfect Occurrences* 129, 22 June 1649, 1128, 465.5129/E530(44); for the preceding controversy see *Perfect Occurrences* 127, 8 June 1649, 1094, 465.5127/E530(32); *Kingdomes Faithfull and Impartiall Scout* 20, 15 June 1649, 143–4 210.20/E530(40).

specific offences resulted in the termination of a newsbook, and the *Scout* had merely irritated.

Four other licensed serials lasted for six months or so. They were *A Perfect Summary*, with modulating title, appearing between January and October; *The Impartiall Intelligencer*, between March and September; *England's Moderate Messenger* and *A Modest Narrative of Intelligence*, both of which appeared between April and September. All four journals had some innocuous editorial content.[243] All relied on sanctioned sources, and were written in what would today be described as 'officialese'. From henceforth this manner of cautiousness, quite different from the individual but no less cautious style of *The Scotish Dove*, became common in those newsbooks which intended to subsist from week to week without offending the licenser.

Other newsbooks were less supine. *Kingdomes Weekly Intelligencer* contained accounts of the court in exile and of the Levellers which hinted at suppressed sympathy. Dillingham's *Moderate Intelligencer*, though apparently a closet royalist through much of 1648, adopted an intensely pro-Cromwell line.[244] More strikingly, *The Moderate* continued to be licensed, and, though its political stance wavered, it remained in support of the Levellers and continued to voice criticism of the government. When on 7 May Sir Henry Mildmay suggested to the Commons that Mabbott, too loose with his licence, be displaced, he recommended care to suppress 'dangerous' books and pamphlets, 'especially that known as "The Moderate"'.[245] The Council of State agreed and set in motion the preparations which would result in the licensing Act of September 1649;[246] but *The Moderate* remained. A few days later, however, Mabbott resigned for several purported reasons: because his name and reputation were being defamed by being attached to 'thousands' of malignant publications; because licensing was a popish means to enslave free people by keeping them in ignorance; because licensing was a monopoly; and because any punishment should be incurred after a book was published, rather than pre-emptively.[247] Mabbott's statement harked back to *Areopagitica*, and its republican overtones were all the more remarkable because it was written when the press was more malignant than in 1644.

In April John Crouch made his portentous début as editor of *The Man*

243 *A Modest Narrative* was probably the least circumspect: see the relatively sympathetic treatment of Lilburne in *Modest Narrative* 21, 25 Aug. 1649, 162–3, 433.21/E571(23). It was also attacked for supporting the Independent party by Clement Walker, *The History of Independency* (1648; W329), 198.

244 See Cotton, 'John Dillingham', 832.

245 *CSPD 1649–1650*, 127.

246 *CJ* vi. 249.

247 *Perfect Diurnall* 304, 28 May 1649, 2500, 504.304/E530(21); quoted *Beginnings*, 180–1.

in the Moon.[248] This caused army and parliament much consternation, and yet it persisted until June 1650, a month longer than *Pragmaticus (For King Charles II).* These two were distinguished by being the only newsbooks to survive the September 1649 Act against unlicensed and scandalous books and pamphlets. *The Man in the Moon* first appeared on 16 April, and on 26 April a warrant was issued for the arrest of the author and publisher.[249] Crouch vowed to interrupt the silence which followed the execution of the king: 'The *Lyons* in the *Tower,* (since the King was murdered) have mourned extreamly, Roar'd out his *obsequies,* and are now (all but the Princes) dead: shall man, endued with *reason,* be more unnaturall then bruit beasts? must the best of Kings, goe to his silent *grave* with nothing but KING CHARLES, 1648?'[250] Crouch contributed political and sexual satire, rather than news. David Underdown characterizes the serial as a voice of popular conservatism, though its genuine popularity has yet to be established.[251]

Before September ephemeral newsbooks flourished; not as plentifully as in 1648, but with more diverse political orientations. In January *The Armies Modest Intelligencer,* later *Armies Weekly Intelligencer,* advocated radical reform. It soon became subdued, and fell silent after five issues. At the beginning of August a single issue of *The Armies Painfull-Messenger. Affording True Notice of All Affairs* came and went unremarked. A related publication, with a different publisher, appeared for two issues at the end of the same month as *Great Britaines Paine-Full Messenger, Affording True Notice of All Affaires.* Several of the provincial contributors to this commented on the lack of news in their parts. Despite a single, pious editorial, it was an undistinguished publication.[252] The same was true of *Mercurius Pacificus* (one issue in May), *Mercurius Republicus* (one issue in May), *A Moderate Intelligence* (two issues in May), *The Moderate Mercury* (two issues in June), and Henry Walker's *Tuesdaies Journall of Perfect Passages in Parliament* (five issues in July and August). Slightly more quarrelsome were two serials, each lasting three issues, entitled *Mercurius Militaris,* one in favour of, one opposed to the Levellers, which appeared in April and May and in May and June, respectively.[253] More

[248] Though *Mercurius Critticus* 303.1–3 (Apr. and May 1648) and a single issue of *Mercvrjvs Melancholicvs* 345.1/E455(1) in July 1648 have also been speculatively attributed to Crouch.

[249] *CSPD 1649–1650,* 530; including *Pragmaticus.*

[250] *Man in the Moon* [1], 16 Apr. 1649, [8], 248.01/E550(26).

[251] '*The Man in the Moon*: Levelling, Gender and Popular Politics 1640–1660', Ford Lecture, delivered in Oxford, Hilary Term, 1992; I am grateful to Professor Underdown for supplying me with a transcript of this unpublished lecture.

[252] *Great Britains Paine-Full Messenger* 2, 24 Aug. 1649, 9, 12, 173.2A/E571(21); *Great Britains Paine-Full Messenger* 3, 30 Aug. 1649, 20–21, 173.2B/E572(9).

[253] N&S 348, 349; the latter entitled *Militaris* for one issue, changing to *The Metropolitan Nuncio.*

tenacious was the *Mercurius Brittanicus* which appeared for seven issues in May and June.[254] Though it abandoned the traditional spelling, it retained the tradition of anti-royalist philippic, in this instance attacking *Pragmaticus.*

Two serials in 1649 were more concerned with politics than news: the one issue of *First Decade of Vseful Observations Raised Out of Modern Experience,* and the two parts of *A Book without a Title,* both in June.[255] With these publications the concept of the serial was being broadened beyond the parameters of the newsbook.[256] The most important early example of this process appeared in April 1654: John Streater's *Observations Historical, Political, and Philosophical, Upon Aristotles First Book of Political Government: Together, with a Narrative of State Affairs in England, Scotland and Ireland.*[257]

The royalist ephemerals were most plentiful in the summer. Newsbooks with the familiar titles *Elencticus, Melancholicus,* and *Pragmaticus* appeared sporadically, written probably by a variety of editors, and bearing ambiguous relationships to the more stable versions.[258] Warrants were sent out for the arrest of editors, and *Pragmaticus* had the honour of being referred to the examination of Mr John Milton.[259] This was the precursor to a long friendship between the journalist and the pamphleteer. A *Mercurius Aulicus. (For King Charls II.)* appeared for three issues in August and September; *Mercurius Carolinus* for one issue on 26 July; *Mercurius Philo-Monarchicus* for two issues in April and May; *Mercurius Hybernicus* for one issue on 6 September;[260] *The Royall Divrnall,* possibly by Samuel Sheppard, for five issues in July and August;[261] and *The Divine Penitential Meditations . . . of his Late Sacred Majestie,* by 'E[dward]. R[eynolds].', for one issue on 18 June.

It may have been affairs in Ireland which precipitated the parliamentary Act, brewing for some months. It was passed, for a period of two

[254] N&S 285; written by Mabbott, according to *Pragmaticus, (For King Charles II.)* 4, 15 May 1649, sig. D2, 370.04A/E555(13); this *Pragmaticus* attacks Nedham as a turncoat.

[255] *First Decade,* 152.1/E562(5); *Book without a Title,* 26.1/E559(12); 26.2.

[256] Cf. also *The Moderate Intelligencer,* which between Feb. and Apr. 1649 contained a serial history of the Thirty Years War.

[257] See a forthcoming work by David Norbrook; and Nigel Smith, 'Popular Republicanism in the 1650s: John Streater's "Heroick Mechanicks"', in David Armitage, Armand Himy, and Quentin Skinner, eds., *Milton and Republicanism* (Cambridge, 1995).

[258] See N&S for details on these: 311, 313, 314, 315, 316, 317, 343, 371.

[259] *CSPD 1649–1650,* 204, dated 23 June; also 534, 537, naming Nedham; and 541, identifying Francis Heldersham and Martha Harrison as the printers and publishers of *Pragmaticus.*

[260] *Hybernicus* 1, 6 Sept. 1649, 329.1/E572(25).

[261] N&S 588.1–2; there was a *Royall Diurnall (For King Charls the II.)* between Feb. and Apr. 1650; 587.1–7B.

years, on 20 September.[262] All newsbooks were, in effect, immediately outlawed, and over the next two months they were expunged. Publishers, printers, booksellers, and binders were bound with recognizances and sureties in most cases of £300 each, a severe and effective threat.[263] Authorization was given to the Master and Wardens of the Stationers' Company to search shops for seditious and unlicensed pamphlets, to investigate premises and break open doors, locks, and chests, and to search and seize the packs of carriers.[264] *The Man in the Moon*, on 24 October, celebrated the purge: '*Ha, ha, ha*; What is become of our *Weekly Legends of Lies*? all quash'd on the sudden; lost in a mist.' According to Crouch, the newsbooks were to be pursued, and imprisoned 'till His Majesty Regains His Right', when they were to be whipped, except Walker, who was to be hanged. Crouch abused editors and publishers by name, concluding:

> *Those that contend to write against their King,*
> *Should in their* Lines *learn first the* Art *to* swing.[265]

The exact causes of the September Act are hazy, perhaps inexact. The Levellers had been dispersed, and Cromwell had just taken Drogheda, though initial reports had probably not been confirmed by 20 September. Earlier in the year *Kingdomes Weekly Intelligencer* had commented on the great interest in Irish news.[266] There were rumours in London that Cromwell had been defeated at Drogheda: but newsbooks were more likely to quash the rumours than encourage them. The royalist publications spread spurious stories, of course, but these were less susceptible to parliament's intervention.[267] Williams identifies concern over the reporting of the bloodshed at Drogheda as the main factor, identifying a critical strain in Pecke's *Perfect Diurnall* of 8 October.[268] This newsbook could, of course, only affect the enforcing of the Act, not its devising. Williams, reacting against S. R. Gardiner's heroic portrait of Cromwell, overestimates the sympathy which the contemporary reader felt for the Irish.[269] They were more likely to have applauded Cromwell's conquest

262 *CJ* vi. 298; *An Act against unlicensed and scandalous books* (1649; formerly E971, though not separately published according to Wing 1994); Cotton, 318–22.

263 *CSPD 1649–1650*, 522–4; a list of recognizances.

264 *CSPD 1649–1650*, 385–6, 545, 553.

265 *Man in the Moon* 26, 217–18; also *Man in the Moon* 25, 17 Oct. 1649, 209, 248.25/575.14.

266 *KWI* 317, 26 June 1469, 1401, 214.317/E561(18).

267 Cotton, 'John Dillingham', 832–3. Soon after the Act the Council of State issued a warrant for the arrest of the authors and printers of *Elencticus, Man in the Moon*, and *Pragmaticus* under the old system; *CSPD 1649–1650*, 550.

268 *History*, 123–4.

269 [J. G. Muddiman], 'S. R. Gardiner's Historical Method', *Notes and Queries*[13], 1 (1923), 23–5, 45–8, 69–70, 86–8, 107–8, 127–9, 149–50, 169–71, 185–8; see also J. S.

than questioned his methods: stories of the 1641 massacre still reverberated in their minds.[270]

Gardiner suggests that the Act was a response to the 'virulence' of Lilburne's pamphlets and of the royalist press. He writes: 'The Act was directed not against opinion, but against false news and misrepresentation of the proceedings and intention of the Government.'[271] Yet this hardly explains the timing of the Act, which had been in preparation since May, and which was enforced with greater consistency and effectiveness than any hitherto, including that of March 1642. No doubt all of these irritations were necessary causes, along with the accumulated frustration of numerous feckless interventions on previous occasions. The causes probably have less to do with nervousness and anger than with the positive desire by members of the Council of State to use the press as a means of intelligent propaganda, to reconcile an uncertain people to a dramatic change in government.[272] In other words, to use letters to make them fit citizens of a commonwealth. This could not be done until it could be made certain that people would read the official, sanctioned newsbooks; and the easiest way to do this was to eradicate competition. In other words, it was the first step on the path which led to *Mercurius Politicus.*

When the Act had taken effect, and the bookshelf was swept clean, two authorized newsbooks were introduced. The first appeared on 2 October, entitled *A Briefe Relation of Some Affaires and Transactions, Civill and Military, Both Forraigne and Domestique.* It was edited by Gualter (or Walter) Frost, who on 21 September had been empowered to produce an official 'weekly intelligence'.[273] Published on Tuesdays, it lasted for just over a year. The second, with less foreign news and a focus on parliamentary affairs, was *Severall Proceedings in Parliament,* edited at first by Henry Scobell, clerk to the parliament, and subsequently by Henry Walker.[274] This first appeared on Tuesday 9 October; though spotting the presumably accidental coincidence, by the fourth issue it was moved to Friday, then, early in 1650, to Thursdays. These two official newsbooks were the prototypes for *Mercurius Politicus* and *The Publick*

A. Adamson, 'Eminent Victorians: S. R. Gardiner and the Liberal as Hero', *HJ* 33 (1990), 641–57.

[270] See e.g. Sir John Temple, *The Irish Rebellion* (1646; T627).

[271] Gardiner[3], i. 173; Frank essentially follows Gardiner; *Beginnings*, 197–8.

[272] For the political context see Blair Worden, *The Rump Parliament 1648–1653* (Cambridge, 1974), chs. 10 and 11.

[273] *CSPD 1649–1650*, 316.

[274] The Earl of Leicester recorded that 'Generall proceedings', as he called it, was both 'by Scobell' and 'licensed by Scobell'. It is not clear whether this indicates a change or whether, significantly, he simply did not distinguish between the two roles. *Sydney Papers*, ed. Blencowe, 128.

Intelligencer under the Commonwealth and Protectorate. Commentators have condemned them both as dull,[275] but they served their purpose: to quell rumour with information. Their literary qualities may have been restricted, but they were informative and reliable; aspects which Frank and Cotton tend to overlook, but which were important to contemporaries. Gardiner comments: 'Both papers were eminently respectable, and are among our most valuable sources of information.'[276]

In December Samuel Pecke returned to edit *A Perfect Diurnall of Some Passages and Proceedings of, and in Relation to the Armies*, which continued to appear on Mondays until September 1655.[277] In 1650 this doubled in size from eight pages to two sheets, finding more room for foreign news. It respected the wishes of its licensers, and presented large quantities of official news. Two other newsbooks appeared after the act. The first, published by Francis Leach, also partly responsible for *Perfect Diurnall*, was *A Perfect and More Particular Relation of the Proceedings of the Army in Ireland*. This licensed publication appeared only twice.[278] It was probably produced to disseminate official information, and dropped when its purpose disappeared. A similar purpose was subsequently fulfilled by *The Irish Monthly Mercury*, which appeared in December 1649 and February 1650. This claimed to have been reprinted from an original printed at Cork: if true, this refers to a lost Irish newsbook which considerably precedes the earliest known periodical printed in Ireland, in 1660.[279]

1649: end of the line?

It becomes every day more and more necessary, to put the public news-papers under some better regulation . . . I would not have the liberty of writeing turned into Licentiousness . . . Neither am I averse to hearing of news, which is so naturall to all men, and so necessary in a free government: but I wou'd not

[275] *Beginnings*, 200–2; Cotton, 322–3.

[276] Gardiner[3], i. 174.

[277] N&S 503. Frank writes that Pecke was only the sub-editor and that it was mainly edited by Rushworth, presenting only circumstantial evidence: Rushworth licensed it, and Frank has a habit of confusing this with editing. There is no real evidence that Rushworth edited any newsbook, though he was involved in gathering and distributing news and certainly associated with editors closely in his role as licenser. As Frank himself admits, this *Perfect Diurnall* has all the marks of Pecke's editorship; *Beginnings*, 202–3. He is following Williams, who also has an unwieldy axe to grind; *History*, 126.

[278] *Perfect and More Particular Relation* 2, licensed 17 Nov., 497.2. The first issue has not been found, though N&S suggest that it may be Wing L56B.

[279] *Irish Monthly Mercury*, 2041–2/E592(5)/E594(5); the 1660 Irish newsbook is *An Account of the Chief Occurrences of Ireland*, published in Dublin by William Bladen, N&S 5.1–5; Munter, *History of the Irish Newspaper*, 6–7.

have seditious insinuations spread under this pretext, nor private persons, much less public ministers, abus'd with impunity.[280]

These words were not written in the 1640s, though the problem they encapsulate was defined then: they are from a 'Proposal for better regulating of News-papers' written, probably between 1714 and 1722, by John Toland, sometime editor of Milton and James Harrington. They show the enduring nature of preoccupations with licence, liberty, the freedom to hear news, and the propensity to distort news. The same concerns crossed the Atlantic, and are still with us today.[281] Within certain parameters the issues remained unchanging, despite the significant transformations in newsbooks during and after the 1640s.

I have chosen 1649 as a point of division carefully. Historians of the newsbook have been disappointed by the 1650s. They see it as a barren and dull period, devoid of the scurrilous *argumentum ad hominem* which fascinates them, and pay it cursory attention. Frank and Williams give the second decade a fraction of the space they give the first. Frank concluded that in the 1650s 'the early newspaper never regained that smell of health it had briefly acquired in the later 1640's'.[282] The Interregnum appears only as a prelude to the Restoration in Harold Herd's account.[283] Cotton, like Frank, sees only dullness in what is left after the purge of September 1649.[284] This is blinkered.

The 1649 act was a Rubicon for two reasons. Previous historians have overestimated the significance of censorship in the history of the newsbook. The Act proved that it was possible to control newsbooks, and like the effective suppression of newsbooks in April 1642 it influenced their development. These incidents also show that most of the time there was insufficient consensus and care prevalent to suppress sedition, slander, and libel. There were actions against individuals, and several publishers, printers, and editors spent time in prison. The periodic nature of the newsbook made it a particular focus for attempts to control the press: in the 1640s newspapers were central to conceptions of press control. Yet attempts to license newsbooks were profoundly limited in their impact. On 29 January 1642 the Commons legislated that every publication should bear the name of its author. This had no apparent effect on newsbooks. In June 1643 parliament passed its Ordinance for the Regulation of Printing which empowered the Stationers' Company to ensure that all newsbooks were licensed. This did

[280] BL: MS Add. 4295, f. 49.

[281] Jeffery A. Smith, *Printers and Press Freedom: The Ideology of Early American Journalism* (New York, 1988); *MTN* 23–5.

[282] *Beginnings*, 198.

[283] Herd, *March of Journalism*, 22–6.

[284] Cotton, 322.

cause the disappearance of some serials: but after a week or two business returned to normal. The 1646 ordinance had considerable short-term consequences, but it did not change the nature of the newsbook or the way in which it was produced. The ordinance of September 1647 occasioned consternation for *Pragmaticus* and *Elencticus*, but they continued to be available. The army's control was as lax as parliament's, and newsbooks proliferated. In the summer of 1648 Gilbert Mabbott requested an increase in resources which was not met, and in May 1649 he resigned, objecting to censorship in principle. This tendency to appoint officers who had a limited interest in controlling publications was continued in January 1651 when Milton, author of *Areopagitica*, was appointed a licenser of newsbooks, thus creating the deceptive spectre of the half-blind censor. Charles II made no such mistake with Roger L'Estrange.[285]

Secondly, the Act was a positive move. It precipitated a shift in style, a return to predominantly cautious journalism, resulting in reliable reporting with a minimum of scurrility. Probably for the first time a British government took stock of the empowering, authorizing potential of a controlled press. On 13 June 1650 *Mercurius Politicus* appeared. The disregard of the 1650s by historians of the newsbook is above all a failure to recognize the significance of Nedham's *magnum opus*. Royalist propaganda endeavoured to maintain wit in writing as a royalist preserve.[286] Dullness accordingly has a political content. In January 1650 a royalist newswriter remarked that newsbooks had 'grown so dull of late, and so timorously . . . intermeddle with the public concernments of the infant Commonwealth, that they hardly deserve the expense of so much time as to read them'.[287] The comment says more about aesthetics and economics than intellectual stimulation.

[285] In addition to sources cited above, see Leona Rostenberg, *Literary, Political, Scientific, Religious and Legal Publishing, Printing and Bookselling in England, 1551–1700: Twelve Studies*, 2 vols. (New York, 1965); D. F. McKenzie, 'The Economies of Print, 1550–1750: Scales of Production and Conditions of Constraint', in *Productione e commercio della carta e del libro secc. XIII–XVIII* (Prato, 1992), 414–25; Sheila Lambert, 'The Printers and the Government, 1604–1657', in Robin Myers and Michael Harris, eds., *Aspects of Printing from 1600* (Oxford, 1987), 1–29; C. H. Firth and R. S. Rait, *Acts and Ordinances of the Interregnum, 1642–1660*, 3 vols. (HMSO, 1911); Lyman Ray Patterson, *Copyright in Historical Perspective* (Nashville, 1968); John Feather, *A History of British Publishing* (1988), 43–9; Michael Mendle, 'De Facto Freedom, De Facto Authority: Press and Parliament, 1640–1643', *HJ* 38 (1995), 307–32.

[286] Steven N. Zwicker, *Lines of Authority: Politics and English Literary Culture, 1649–1689* (Ithaca, NY, 1993), 9–36; Blair Worden, '"Wit in a Roundhead": The Dilemma of Marchamont Nedham', in Susan D. Amussen and Mark A. Kishlansky, eds., *Political Culture and Cultural Politics in Early-Modern England: Essays Presented to David Underdown* (Manchester, 1995), 301–37.

[287] BL: Loan MS 331, f. 23^{v}: quoted Worden, *Rump Parliament*, 403.

Politicus was an extraordinary, multi-generic text, with a wide and diverse audience, a more complex beast than any previous newsbook.[288] Instead of complimenting it with a cursory visit like those paid by other historians, I intend to address it in a future volume. Deferring that tale, let us return once more to 1641 and scrutinize the incipience of the newsbook in detail.

[288] Worden acknowledges some of its complexities in 'Marchamont Nedham and the Beginnings of English Republicanism, 1649–1656', in David Wootton, ed., *Republicanism, Liberty, and Commercial Society, 1649–1776* (Stanford, Calif., 1994), 45–81.

2

The Outbreak of the English Newsbook

On 29 November 1641 a publisher and bookseller named John Thomas released a small pamphlet entitled *Heads of Severall Proceedings in this Present Parliament from the 22 of November, to the 29. 1641.*[1] The next week he produced another, and faced two competitors. With some fluctuation the quantity of weekly newsbooks continued to escalate. A considerable number of publishers of cheap print entered the skirmish, all capable of recognizing the formal qualities of the newsbook and of reproducing its typography and typical contents. *Heads of Severall Proceedings* was the first printed periodical to contain domestic news, and with some justification therefore can be described as the first newsbook, the immediate predecessor of the newspaper.[2] The newspaper press has not stopped since: Thomas's intervention set in motion an avalanche, which, with no more than a few weeks of interruption, rolls right up to this morning.

Modern historians of the newspaper have stupefyingly little to say about the events of 29 November 1641. Hence the origins of the English newsbook have been widely misunderstood.[3] In this chapter I will provide a worm's-eye view of what constitutes the first newsbook and how and why it appeared on 29 November, and of why it looked the way it did.

The prevalent account, which attributes the appearance of the newsbook to a breakdown in censorship, needs some revising. The newsbook did not lie as a dormant seed under deliberate suppression until a political thawing allowed it to sprout and blossom. The

[1] 181.101/E201(1).

[2] Not a newspaper because it was a quarto pamphlet; cf. *MTN* 2.

[3] I refer to it as the 'English' newsbook because it was in the English language, produced in London mostly by English men and women. News of Ireland was crucial to its existence, news from Scotland and Wales was prominent at several points during the decade. But the attitude of most journalists to the Irish, Welsh, and Scots was bigoted, and though newsbooks found their way to these other kingdoms and the dominion of Wales it would be an overstatement to say that these nations were addressed other than with lack of interest or contempt. Given these characteristic prejudices, and the lack of native-language publications and a developed printing trade, an 'archipelagic' history of the newsbook in the 1640s would actually be a study of the impact of the English newsbook on these places. The role of 17th-cent. newsbooks in Scotland, Ireland, and Wales deserves separate study, and I will not do it injustice here.

newsbook was, in effect, invented in 1641, though under conditions established earlier. The coranto, usually seen as the immediate, and sometimes sole, parent of the newsbook, bearing for the silent years of the personal rule all the genetic genres and elements which would enter the 1640s newsbook, was in fact only distantly related. The continuity between corantos and newsbooks has been overstated by historians looking for a good story. The newsbook was the product of a particular political moment; not a release of old pressures, but a response to something new. The appearance of the newsbook was the result of the actions of a few individuals as well as the consequence of long-term developments in print and political consciousness: great effects need not have great causes.

Previous explanations

The orthodox account of the origins of the newsbook begins with J. B. Williams (a pseudonym of J. G. Muddiman), the first historian of the newsbook this century, followed by William Clyde, and Frederick Siebert, who in the 1930s and 1950s presented overviews of censorship.[4] It was most clearly articulated by Siebert, who argued that there were three distinct causes specific to newsbooks. The first involved a historically contextualized demand:

> As the breach between the king and Parliament widened, the desire of the subjects to participate in governmental problems naturally increased. The public demand for information and discussion of the vital issues led inevitably to the publication of domestic news, just as a few years before the prevailing interest in the religious wars on the continent had produced the corantos of foreign news.

Political events caused an increase in the demand for news. Secondly, newsbooks were an ideal medium for parliamentarian propaganda, and MPs recognized them as such. This assertion is not supported with any evidence of parliamentary involvement in newsbooks. The final cause is the 'breakdown of the royal regulations for the control of printing'.[5] This third factor is most commonly repeated in histories of the mid-seventeenth century.

These three principles outline a convenient model, to which most analyses of, and allusions to, the newsbook correspond. Perez Zagorin writes:

[4] Siebert, *passim*; Clyde, *passim*; Don McKenzie and Sheila Lambert have, as I note below, substantially challenged Siebert's narrative: but we remain in need of a full study.

[5] Siebert, 202–3.

The appearance of the newspaper in 1641 was an indication of how far political life had broken through its former limits. Opposition to the regime had engendered a broad public which wished both to participate and to be informed. To mobilize popular support and stiffen conviction, the press was indispensable. The systematized provision of news, the presence of the journalist and publicist, were the necessary adjuncts of an energized politics.[6]

Zagorin follows Siebert in interpreting the appearance of the newsbook (critics show a reluctance to employ exact terminology[7]) as evidence of the consolidation and reifying of political differences. They are right to emphasize the role of the press in lubricating the mechanisms of oppositional politics: but this, of course, does not imply causation. For Zagorin, as for Siebert, the coming of the newsbook reveals a readership sympathetic to parliament, which in turn required effective means of propaganda to pursue an 'energized' prospectus. Just as the foreign-affairs 'newspaper or coranto' of 1620 was intertwined with a newly awakened political consciousness, so the 1641 newsbook represented the interests of popular politics against authoritarianism.[8] Historians have avoided confronting the moment at which the newsbook was invented by chronological vagueness or the invocation of an evolutionary process; and by suggesting that newsbooks were the produce of changes in a public sphere, itself rather difficult to locate.[9]

Williams was less unambiguously erroneous than those following him. Like Siebert he emphasized the role of public demand:

The nation wished to know what was being said and done in Parliament—the Cavalier no less than the Roundhead. The demand was for news, nothing but news, and as a result the whole literature of the next year [after November 1640] is confined to printed pamphlets of 'speeches' in Parliament or 'relations' of this or that incident connected with them.[10]

From such pamphlets 'step by step was evolved the "newsbook"'.[11]

[6] Zagorin, *Court and the Country*, 206.

[7] The reluctance is symptomatic of an insensitivity to form; cf. James Woolley's editorial comments in Jonathan Swift and Thomas Sheridan, *The Intelligencer* (Oxford, 1992), 6 n. 22.

[8] Zagorin, *Court and the Country*, 106–7.

[9] Derek Hirst, *Authority and Conflict: England, 1603–1658* (Cambridge, Mass., 1986), 194; Ivan Roots, 'English Politics 1625–1700', in T. G. S. Cain and Ken Robinson, eds., *Into Another Mould: Change and Continuity in English Culture 1625–1700* (1992), 20; Susan Wiseman, ' "Adam, the Father of All Flesh," Porno-Political Rhetoric and Political Theory in and after the English Civil War', in Holstun, ed., *Pamphlet Wars*, 134; and many others.

[10] *History*, 30. Williams is exaggerating, but excusably.

[11] *History*, 29. Cf. C. V. Wedgwood: 'Manuscript summaries of debates had been compiled in earlier Parliaments by practised scriveners for those who paid for them. But, when the abolition of the Star Chamber court relieved printers of the fear of prosecution for rash political statements, several of them gratified the news hunger of the public and the vanity of members of Parliament by issuing, in authentic or pirated forms, any

Williams gestures towards a gradual evolution, admitting the chronological rupture between the appearance of pamphlets and the appearance of newsbooks, and leaves it at that: implying, perhaps, that such things happen. Yet in passing he characterizes the newsbook as the evolution of the scrivener's newsletter. This is essentially accurate, but with the exceptions of W. H. Coates, Carolyn Nelson, and Matthew Seccombe, the suggestion has been overlooked.[12] Williams provided no evidence and it is accordingly difficult to judge exactly what he meant by his assertion. It is true, as I shall argue, that the immediate predecessor of the newsbook was not the printed coranto but a manuscript. But Williams also accepts wholesale the argument presented in two vitriolic pamphlets which attribute Thomas's *Heads of Several Proceedings* to an opportunistic scrivener dissatisfied with the profits available from small script-runs.[13] Thus when Williams writes that one of the scriveners 'instead of having his letter of news copied . . . obtained permission to have it printed', he is either speculating or reading literally a semi-metaphorical tirade. It is a quaint moment of naïvety from a writer who is generally sceptical of the evidence provided by the likes of Henry Walker and Marchamont Nedham.[14] Nevertheless the conclusion was correct.

The modern historian of the newsbook, Joseph Frank, who elsewhere relies very heavily on Williams, ignores this passage. Frank feels no obligation to provide analysis. He writes:

> Between July 1641, when the Star Chamber and the Court of High Commission were abolished, and March 1642, when Parliament itself got a temporary grip on the reins of censorship, there was a period during which the press, though still harassed, was comparatively free. Newsstands did not immediately appear on the streets of London, but in November 1641 the first newspaper dealing with events in England could be bought in the vicinity of Parliament.[15]

Here censorship is represented as the overwhelming determinant factor. Yet this passage foregrounds its own contradiction, drawing attention to the simple problem of chronology. The gap between the events usually associated with the 'breakdown in censorship', and the appear-

speeches they could lay their hands on. From this it was an easy step to issuing weekly bulletins of happenings at Westminster.' There was no such 'easy step'. Wedgwood is also wrong to claim that parliament denounced this as a breach of privilege; *The King's War, 1641–1647* (1958; 1983), 37–8.

[12] Coates, ed., *Journal of Sir Simonds D'Ewes*, pp. xx–xxii; Nelson and Seccombe, *Periodical Publications*, 20.

[13] See Ch. 1 n. 12, above.

[14] *History*, 33–4. Later, 145–6, Williams accepts Crouch's newsbooks as evidence of the great number of brothels on the outskirts of Commonwealth London. His scepticism is partial, consonant with his ultra-royalist agenda.

[15] *Beginnings*, 21.

ance of *Heads of Severall Proceedings* is manifest.[16] Anthony Cotton, whose unpublished thesis partly superseded Frank's book, did not challenge Frank on this point, and this bland and unhistorical account has been perpetuated into the arguments of all those who have relied on secondary material to comment on the appearance of the newsbook.[17]

Let me summarize my criticisms. There are three issues: demand, deliberate supply, and censorship. Though superficially simple, demand is a complex issue. The focus on popular appetite echoes the repetitive criticisms of newsbooks by contemporary readers.[18] Any desire to 'participate' must also have been satisfied, in some fashion, by non-periodical news pamphlets, to which the arguments of Siebert and Zagorin could also apply.[19] An explanation of the appearance of the newsbook must address the fundamental and distinguishing characteristic of periodicity.[20] Some distinction should be made between the form, origins, and impact of newsbooks and of other pamphlets and manuscripts, not least because the increase in the production of pamphlets pre-dated the appearance of the first periodical newsbook. The same is possibly true of the increase in preaching, another means of news distribution.[21]

The orthodoxy, moreover, has nothing to offer on the creation of demand. The vagueness in chronology obscures the means by which the desire for news was manufactured; implying that such a response to political events is in some way natural, or innately public. Anthony Fletcher has shown that a popular sphere of political discourse was being created in the early 1640s, and should by no means be accepted as a transhistorical given.[22] The historical transition by which proceedings of parliament became public property, and a suitable object for discussion by private people, has yet to be adequately mapped.[23] The existing accounts of the appearance of the newsbook assume that the

[16] See e.g. *British Monarchies*, 279, 341.

[17] It is very easy to miss the significance of what Williams argues, not least because of his paradoxical emphasis on the evolution of print: many refer to him as an authority without even mentioning the scriveners' manuscripts.

[18] Cf. *MTN* 12–14.

[19] Note the number of pamphlets in Fletcher, *Outbreak of the English Civil War*, 125–57.

[20] A serious flaw, for example, in Mendle's otherwise helpful 'De Facto Freedom'.

[21] On preaching as a means of distributing news in 1641 see e.g. Seaver, *Wallington's World*, 37–9; H. R. Trevor-Roper, 'The Fast Sermons of the Long Parliament', *Religion, the Reformation and Social Change*, 294–344.

[22] Fletcher, *Outbreak of the English Civil War*, chs. 4 and 6.

[23] Jürgen Habermas, while recognizing the complex interaction of news with the public and the private, erroneously attributes the creation of the public sphere to the end of the 17th and 18th cents.; *The Structural Transformation of the Public Sphere: An*

creation of demand for and of a format for transmitting news was simple and inevitable.

Next is the question of a deliberate supply. Siebert, Zagorin, and Hirst intimate suspicions that parliament was somehow involved in the publication of newsbooks, offering two reasons: newsbooks initially worked in the interest of parliament and were later to bear the authority of the imprint of the clerk to the Commons. They present no evidence that parliament was directly involved during November 1641.

Finally there is the question of censorship. Michael Wilding writes, quoting William Haller: 'The breakdown in censorship after 1640 was a liberation: "Nothing gave more resounding emphasis to the overthrow of Laud's power in the state than the collapse of his power over the press".'[24] Wilding and Haller rightly acknowledge the backlash against Laud. Between 1633 and 1640 Laud, as Archbishop of Canterbury, in principle supervised 'censorship', meaning pre-publication licensing, the attempted control over what could be said in print.[25] But the loosening of press controls did not simply follow as an immediate consequence: Laud was imprisoned in December 1640, and the reaction took some months. The courts through which censorship operated were abolished in July 1641, but the licensers of the press under Laud continued to approve books in 1642, and there is even one licence for 1643.[26] Clearly other factors were involved. The history of licensing and censorship was not a tidy one, and the actual series of events which

Inquiry into a Category of Bourgeois Society, trans. Thomas Burger (Cambridge, Mass., 1989). For a similar timetable see Terry Eagleton, *The Function of Criticism: From the Spectator to Post-structuralism* (1984), 9–27. See also the criticisms of Habermas in David Zaret, 'Religion, Science, and Printing in the Public Spheres of Seventeenth-Century England', in Craig Calhoun, ed., *Habermas and the Public Sphere* (Cambridge, Mass., 1992), 212–35; and 'Critical Theory and the Sociology of Culture', *Current Perspectives in Social Theory*, 11 (1992), 1–28. I am most grateful to David Zaret for sending me proofs of these articles. See also David Norbrook, '*Areopagitica*, Censorship, and the Early Modern Public Sphere', in Richard Burt, ed., *The Administration of Aesthetics: Censorship, Political Criticism, and the Public Sphere*, Cultural Politics, 7 (Minneapolis, 1994), 3–33; id., *The Penguin Book of Renaissance Verse, 1509–1659* (1992), 23–4; Achinstein, *Milton and the Revolutionary Reader*.

[24] Michael Wilding, *Dragons Teeth: Literature in the English Revolution* (Oxford, 1987), 90; quoting William Haller, *Liberty and Reformation in the Puritan Revolution* (New York, 1955), 33.

[25] 'Attempted' because it was frequently ineffective; Dennis B. Woodfield, *Surreptitious Printing in England, 1550–1640* (New York, 1973). It was possible, moreover, to negotiate restrictions linguistically; Annabel Patterson, *Censorship and Interpretation* (Madison, 1984).

[26] Sheila Lambert, 'The Beginning of Printing for the House of Commons, 1640–42', *Library*[6], 3 (1981), 47; McKenzie, 'Economies of Print', 389–425; id., Lyell Lectures (1988). I am grateful to Professor McKenzie for sending me this material.

constituted it are still uncharted. Imprecise chronology has foregrounded long-term causes and continuities.[27] As soon as we are more specific about dates the explanations invoking censorship as the dominant factor fall apart. Nature abhors a vacuum.

Let me summarize. Archbishop Laud, who nominally supervised the Caroline press, was impeached and imprisoned in December 1640. Acts abolishing the Courts of Star Chamber and High Commission, two of the institutions though which licensing operated, were passed on 5 July 1641, taking effect from 1 August; this was a retrospective action, formally removing non-functioning institutions.[28] In the same month the Commons showed much concern over the manuscript dissemination of speeches and proceedings.[29] The State Papers, Stationers' Company registers, and parliamentary journals show a persisting concern over licensing through 1641. By the summer of 1641 the press had already begun to produce in large numbers the torrent of small-quarto political and satirical pamphlets with which we associate the collapse of censorship. This was evident to contemporaries: George Thomason and John Rushworth were already collecting their textual testimonies to posterity. The so-called 'breakdown in censorship' and the so-called 'explosion of print' were old, dog-eared news by 29 November. Causes do not take vacations and there were no marketing managers to delay publication until a more convenient season.

The invention of the newsbook has been distorted by historians who kept an eye on what happened next. Newsbooks and the political and publishing contexts in which they found themselves shifted rapidly after 1641. These were unstable times, and it is a historiographical misfortune that the newsbooks published between November 1641 and March 1642 should have been characterized without distinction from those published later in 1642, and those in turn interpreted in anticipation of the newsbook wars of 1643, when the mercurial paper bullets fired between king and parliament offered no quarter.[30] Other historians have written the story backwards. I will temporarily avert my eyes from these developments and reconsider the long-term context for the first newsbooks.

[27] e.g. McKeon, *Origins of the English Novel*, 39–50. Williams observes that 'in its origin the printed "paper" of news was but auxiliary to the newsletters'; *History*, 192. This evades the question of readership, and the impact of newsbooks.

[28] *Constitutional Documents*, 178–89; Mendle, 'De Facto Freedom', 313.

[29] *CJ* ii. 208–9, 220; on 13 and 22 July.

[30] Kevin Sharpe and Steven N. Zwicker write that 'the newspaper as a polemical and literary medium was essentially a product of the civil wars'. 'Politics of Discourse: Introduction', in eid., eds., *Politics of Discourse: The Literature and History of Seventeenth-Century England* (Berkeley, 1987), 14. This is exactly right: the newsbook itself was not a product of the civil war.

Prehistory of the newsbook: newsletters and corantos

The political moment which created the newsbook was shaped by the personal rule of Charles I. This prehistory determined that when the newsbook appeared it would be perceived as subversive to the monarch. The extraordinary success of *Eikon Basilike* shows that propaganda could work very much in Charles's interest.[31] The success of *Mercurius Aulicus* reveals that news-propaganda as a form was not intrinsically opposed to the king's cause. Under the shrewd hand of Sir John Berkenhead, *Aulicus* became, if we are to believe many partisan contemporary sources, a powerful, persuasive force on the king's side: undefeated in the field, unlike the royalist army.[32] In fact *Aulicus* was the first officially patronized and sanctioned journal of either side, and was the product of direct participation by the king and his ministers more than any London newsbook was that of parliament. P. W. Thomas, Berkenhead's biographer, characterizes it as an organ of Laudian propaganda after the fact.[33] Yet Charles through the 1630s neglected many positive opportunities to use propaganda. By this means news acquired a political complexion.[34]

How can something as diaphanous and undefined as 'news' be described as 'political'? Anything new to the hearer counted as news, as seventeenth-century satirists, including Jonson, were quick to point out. In his 1620 masque *Newes From the New World Discover'd in the Moone* Jonson presented two stereotypes of the 'Factor' or scrivener and the 'Printer' of news. The first argues that on printing news ceases to be news; the latter that it is only turned into news by being printed.[35] For these interested parties, news is whatever makes a profit. A practical definition is that news is anything which can be said in answer to that oft-repeated early-modern question 'what news?' When John Rous met a Mr Tayler and asked him 'what newes?', Tayler responded that a Mr Barret had shown him a sermon by Dr Lushington lately preached before the king. Rous recorded in his diary: 'I asked what was remarkeable; he said, first the beginning. "What newes? Every man askes what newes? Every man's religion is knowne by his newes; the

[31] Cf. Corns, *Uncloistered Virtue*, 80–91.

[32] On *Aulicus* see *Berkenhead*, chs. 2–4. On the sentiment see Corns, *Uncloistered Virtue*, 128.

[33] *Berkenhead*, 76–9.

[34] Michael Wilding also allies the potential power of the press with 'Puritans', *Dragons Teeth*, 89–90; on 1632 see ibid. 28–9. When suppressing corantos Charles also made the decision to embark on a programme of enforcing religious uniformity. For this context, see *British Monarchies*, 37.

[35] *Ben Jonson*, ed. C. H. Herford and Percy and Evelyn Simpson, 11 vols. (Oxford, 1925–52), vii. 514–15.

Puritan talkes of Bethlehem Gabor, &c.".'[36] Jonson made this same point in *The Staple of Newes*, suggesting that the supplier altered his material according to the religious tendencies of his audience.[37] Rous's report is particularly revealing because the sermon had actually been preached five years earlier at Oxford, not before the king.[38] In Mondeford, where Rous met Tayler, this was none the less news. It is in the structure of the question 'what news?' that anything responding to it becomes, in exchange, news.

News is defined by its transmission, by the act of communication in a given context. It is never unmediated, but always passed on via a particular medium with its own ideological weighting, in a context which must be reconstructed. Richard Cust has argued that 'news contributed to a process of political polarization in the early seventeenth century'.[39] The circulation of manuscript separates concerning parliament, Cust argues, enhanced the reputation and status of parliament.[40] While making its members more accountable to their constituencies, it also served a propaganda function. Information did not lead to demystification, with its deleterious consequences.[41] In the late 1620s news reports ignored 'evidence of everyday agreement and co-operation', which set them at variance with the predominant parliamentary rhetoric of unity and consent.[42] In this respect news reports clearly differed from individually printed speeches.

Most of Cust's evidence, as his focus on parliament implies, is drawn from the 1620s. Observing this anomaly, Kevin Sharpe suggests that while the newsletters of the 1620s may have reflected considerable political division, the newsletters of the 1630s suggest a less discordant

[36] *Diary of John Rous*, 44.

[37] *Ben Jonson*, vi. 293–4. Readers often purchased newsbooks with views opposed to their own. Ian Atherton, moreover, has argued that Pory's newsletters did not really suit their news to their recipient: 'Viscount Scudamore and the Collection of Newsletters in the Seventeenth Century', an unpublished paper delivered at the History of the News seminar, Magdalen College, Oxford, 25 Nov. 1993.

[38] Levy, 'How Information Spread among the Gentry', 24.

[39] Cust, 'News and Politics', 87. Atherton has contested Cust's conclusions; see n. 37, above.

[40] Cust, 'News and Politics', 71–2. Cust's account focuses on newsletters rather than corantos, which might be associated with a more explicitly ideological position because of their suppression in 1632.

[41] In the French Revolution, 'common usage desacralized the attributes and symbols of royalty, depriving it of all transcendent significance'; Chartier, *Cultural Origins of the French Revolution*, 85. This is not a direct consequence of increased information exchange. There is an element of historical contingency in these relations. See also Jeremy D. Popkin, *Revolutionary News: The Press in France, 1789–1799* (Durham, NC, 1990).

[42] Cust, 'News and Politics', 73. To an even greater extent subsequent historians focused on atypical events, emphasizing conflict.

political nation.[43] This is a consequence of the combined effect of a cancelled, or at least indefinitely postponed, political and financial crisis, and the absence of parliaments. Parliaments generated news, and facilitated its transmission by bringing the provincial gentry to the metropolis.

The professional newsletter writers of the 1630s polished their wares with a minimal gloss.[44] This was also the case with the first newsbooks. The style did not attest to a buried stratum of conflict. But whereas the content of the early newsbooks was exclusively restricted to parliamentary proceedings, newsletters, at least during the interim of parliaments, comprehended a variety of material. In the vein of Jonson's Staple there was gossip and courtly news; news about trials, much foreign news, providential stories and strange deaths, accounts of mortality from the plague, news of Gustavus Adolphus and the much-touted death of the Emperor Tilly, news of bee stings.[45] Many stories were openly copied from other letters, creating a wide network of multiple transmissions, which may easily have slipped from repetition to a game of Chinese whispers. The Reverend Joseph Mead passed on to Sir Martin Stuteville what he admitted to be 'stale news' from a letter written by Mr Dinely to Sir Henry Wotton.[46] Earlier he had sent to Stuteville the 'original letter' he had received from John Pory, to which he added 'some principal and remarkable pieces' of 'my own', which he had also received in another letter.[47] A letter from Sir George Gresley to Sir Thomas Puckering referred to 'Mr. Pory's intelligence', from which it might plausibly be inferred that Pory's newsletter was enclosed, or that the writer knew that Puckering subscribed to the same.[48] The same correspondent wrote to Puckering: 'The news of this place and time I presume you have from better pens. Yet, I had rather be a little troublesome than condemned of neglect.'[49] This might simply be dismissed as a formulaic self-deprecation common to newswriters; but Puckering's correspondence included letters from Mr Beaulieu and Gresley reporting the death of the King of Sweden, the former several times.[50] Pory probably communicated the same story. At the Exchange in London, punters placed bets on whether the news was true. What finer example of the uncertainty of even the best informed could be expected? If the news was certain, then the newsletter writers could have expected a more substantial profit from the odds than from mere scribing of news. Manuscript news, however

[43] *Personal Rule*, 684. Cf. Brenner on the relative co-operation in the 1630s; *Merchants and Revolution*, 290–2 and ch. 6 *passim*.

[44] *Personal Rule*, 685.

[45] For the last see Birch, ii. 123. The ghost of Tilly was ubiquitous: ibid. ii. 150. See also Jonson's *Staple of Newes* in *Ben Jonson*, vi. 329.

[46] Birch, ii. 26–7.

[47] Birch, i. 436, and *passim*.

[48] Birch, ii. 181.

[49] Birch, ii. 35.

[50] Birch, ii. 200–3.

exclusive, was no more based on absolute certainty than printed reports.

Before the suppression of corantos in 1632, newsletter writers would pass on foreign news from printed sources.[51] As would later become common with newsbooks, they might enclose a coranto. Mead wrote to Stuteville from Cambridge in the summer of 1625: 'I send you a corranto brought me besides expectation and almost against my will; but it was well aired and smoked before I received it, as all our letters used to be; nor was the plague then at St. Paul's Churchyard, whence it came.'[52] Gresley wrote to someone, probably Puckering, in February 1632: 'Here is no foreign news at this instant, but what this enclosed aviso advertiseth.'[53] Newswriters recognized the adequate coverage offered by Butter and Bourne's corantos: a month previously Sir Gilbert Gerard apologized to Thomas Barrington for having no news 'but what you may find in the Swedish intelligencer or the last new currant'.[54] In February 1626 Mead wrote to Stuteville: 'For news, I can hear no more foreign than the last Corante afforded you.'[55] News was easily transferred from one form of communication to another.[56] This commonality explains the casual treatment of affairs of state in amateur letters sent to friends and relations.[57] The same news was transmitted in different styles and in different forms, and with different implications.

Despite the overlap in content, newsletters do not appear to have been threatened by the existence of corantos. The newsletter trade was partly insulated from corantos, as more could be said in a newsletter.[58] Newsletters frequently enclosed corantos, implying a functional differentiation. John Dillingham's cheerful response to the suppression of newsbooks in March 1642 suggests that the overlap had more serious implications in the case of the newsbook.[59] An exception occurred in February 1633, five months after Star Chamber's decree against the publication of corantos, which had a domino effect. Gresley wrote to Puckering: 'I hoped to have sent you, this week, a very true relation which is lately come over of the King of Sweden's death and battle. But Butter having got it to his hands, and thinking to have printed it, it is

[51] Frearson, 'London Corantos in the 1620s', 17–19.

[52] Birch, i. 44.

[53] Birch, ii. 95. The 'aviso' was probably either *The Continuation of our forraine avisoes* or *The Continuation of our forraine newes*, published on 24 and 30 Jan. respectively, *STC* 18507.238, 239. On the enclosing of newsbooks in letters, see Ch. 5, below.

[54] Qu. *Personal Rule*, 646. See also the other references in Sharpe's valuable analysis.

[55] Birch, i. 82.

[56] Manwaring observes that newsletters were 'similar to the printed "corantos" of the day'; 'Journalism in the Days of the Commonwealth', 106.

[57] Morrill, *Revolt of the Provinces*, 22.

[58] Love, *Scribal Publication*, 10.

[59] *HMC: Montagu*, 148.

there stopped both from publishing it in print or copying.'[60] It is ambiguous whether copyists were restricted because of Butter's possession of the text, or because an embargo was likewise placed upon them by implication. Nevertheless Gresley's remark suggests that there were moments when private correspondents were obliged to look sideways to the censor.

We do not have enough information about the distribution and economics of corantos and newsletters to assess whether printed texts potentially threatened the scribal market.[61] Yet it is important that there were substantial differences in prices. Manuscripts required more costly ink and paper,[62] and authors charged considerable fees. John Pory received £20 a year from Viscount Scudamore for his weekly newsletter.[63] Edward Rossingham[64] was rumoured to earn a similar sum in 1640.[65] On the eve of the Restoration the embittered Earl of Newcastle estimated that Rossingham's pre-war income was £500 per annum.[66] Few writers of printed texts could expect to earn such a sum from their profession.[67] Prior to the book-price inflation of the late 1630s, printed texts were considerably cheaper.[68] A bill of disbursements from 1641 or 1642 gives the price of 'two printed declaracons' as *2d.*, and a 'diurnall of parliament Occurrences', evidently a manuscript, as 1*s.* 6*d.* The purchaser also gave 6*d.* to the post boy.[69] The real economic overlap between printed books of domestic news and periodical manuscript newsletters is suggested by the fact that after the Restoration newsletter writers, including Henry Muddiman, Giles Hancock, and Will Urwin, charged much less for their services.[70] This may have been the effect of inroads made into the newsletter market by the cheaper newsbook.

[60] Birch, ii. 225–6.

[61] Frearson quotes Pory as evidence to the contrary; 'London Corantos in the 1620s', 17–18.

[62] Love, *Scribal Publication*, 104–5.

[63] Powell, *John Pory*, 55.

[64] Rossingham succeeded Pory as a newsletter writer to Sir Thomas Puckering. For a selection of his newsletters see Birch, ii, *passim.* His style was highly professional; extended, detailed, and systematic. He also had extensive sources of information.

[65] *Proceedings of the Short Parliament of 1640*, ed. Esther S. Cope and Willson H. Coates, Camden Society[4], 19 (1977), 35.

[66] Thomas P. Slaughter, ed., *Ideology and Politics on the Eve of Restoration: Newcastle's Advice to Charles II* (Philadelphia, 1984), 56. The figure is presumably a substantial overestimate.

[67] Love, *Scribal Publication*, 58.

[68] Francis R. Johnson, 'Notes on English Retail Book-Prices, 1550–1640', *Library*[5], 5 (1950), 83–112.

[69] PRO: SP 16/493/62. In *CSPD 1641–1643*, 428, the date is given as probably 1642; as manuscript diurnals survive exclusively for 1641, it seems that the undated item, bound in with later material, is from the earlier year.

[70] Love, *Scribal Publication*, 11.

The greater liberty available in private newsletters has perhaps been overestimated, as has the monolithic aspect of Caroline censorship. Recently, in reaction, it has been questioned whether political, as opposed to economic, censorship was a significant phenomenon in the early seventeenth century. Certainly the Caroline government did not attempt to silence all criticism; and complaints were made only against inept interventions by licensers, not against the basic premiss of the right to intervene.[71] When John Selden spoke on censorship in the 1629 parliament, in response to a booksellers' and printers' petition against Laud's autocratic restraint on the publishing of books against Arminianism and popery, he criticized the absence of a law 'to prevent the printing of any Books in *England*, onely a Decree in the *Star-Chamber*'. The Star Chamber decree was an 'invasion upon the Liberty of the Subject', and he proposed that a more just censorship law might be formulated.[72]

The suppression of corantos in 1632 has been given a prominent place in histories of the 1640s newsbook. The anxieties which Jonson expressed in the 1620s over the power of the journalist to supplant the poet as the counsellor to princes[73] were not fully realized by the corantos of the 1620s or 1630s: but they were by the 1640s newsbook. While corantos played little part in the invention of the newsbook in 1641, the decree which more or less removed them from the bookshelves between 1632 and 1638 set the long-term context into which the newsbook was received.

The Star Chamber decree had discomforting implications. On 25 October 1632, John Pory wrote from London to Lord Brooke at Warwick Castle: 'Yesterday was sennight, my lord keeper, my lord privy seal, my Lord of Arundel, my Lord of Kelly, my Lord Wimbledon, my Lord of London, my Lord Cottington, and Secretary Windebanke, signed an order at the council-board in these words . . .'[74] Pory went on to quote from the decree of 17 October, which follows in full:

[71] Blagden, *The Stationers' Company*; McKenzie, unpublished Lyell Lectures (1988) and 'Economies of Print'; Patterson, *Censorship and Interpretation*; A. B. Worden, 'Literature and Political Censorship in Early Modern England', in A. C. Duke and C. A. Tamse, eds., *Too Mighty to be Free: Censorship and the Press in Britain and the Netherlands* (Zutphen, 1987), 45–62; Lambert, 'The Printers and the Government, 1604–1657', 1–29; eid., 'Richard Montagu, Arminianism and Censorship', *P&P* 124 (1989), 36–68; eid., 'State Control of the Press in Theory and Practice: The Role of the Stationers' Company before 1640', in Robin Myers and Michael Harris, eds., *Censorship and the Control of Print: In England and France, 1600–1910* (Winchester, 1992), 1–32.

[72] *HC*[1] 655. Gardiner[1], vii. 51.

[73] Jonson, *The Staple of News*, in *Ben Jonson*, vi. McKenzie, 'The London Book Trade'; id., ' "The Staple of News" and the Late Plays'.

[74] For Pory's letter see Birch, ii. 185–6.

Upon Considerac[i]on had at the Board of the greate abuse in the printing & publishing of the ordenary Gazetts and Pamphletts of newes from forraigne p[ar]t[e]s, And upon significa[ti]on of his ma[jes]t[ie]s expresse pleasure and Com[m]aund for the p[re]sent suppressing of the same, It was thought fitt and hereby ordered that all printing and publishing of the same be accordingly suppress and inhibited. And that as well Nathaniell Butter & Nicholas Bourne Booke Sellers, under whose names the said Gazetts have beene usually published, as all other Stationers, Printers and Booke Sellers, p[re]sume not from henceforth to print publish or sell any of the said Pamphletts, &c, as they will answer the Contrary at theire p[e]rills. And Mr Secr[etary]e Windebanke is lykewise prayed to send for the said Butter and Bourne, and to lay a strict Com[m]aund upon them on that behalfe.[75]

Pory provided a context for this action:

They say the occasion of this order was the importunity of the Spanish and archduchess's agents, who were vexed at the soul to see so many losses and crosses, so many dishonours and disasters, betide the House of Austria, as well in the Upper as in the Lower Germany; but this smothering of the Currantos is but a palliation, not a cure, of their wounds. They will burst out again one of these days.

Arundel, Cottington, and Windebank, later a Catholic convert, were prominent members of the Spanish faction.

Excessive schematization of factional politics in the 1630s is a perilous exercise.[76] But contemporary perceptions, however simplistic, should be acknowledged; and the 1632 move was perceived as a continuation of the pro-Spanish, Arminian policy which in 1626 both prohibited responses to Richard Montagu and proscribed Calvinist teaching at Cambridge. Pory's gesture towards the involvement of a Spanish interest in the suppression of corantos is transparent. He found it 'ominous' that a minister at St Mary's in Oxford had recently prayed that 'it would please God to inspire the Courantiers with the spirit of truth, that we might know when to pray and where to praise'.[77] Now the source of information had dried, and this was an injury to the Protestant cause. The same cause was championed by the coranto-hero Gustavus Adolphus, who would not live long. In the winter of 1631–2 Charles had decided not to call a parliament in order to support Gustavus Adolphus in a campaign against the Habsburgs, to restore the Palatinate to its Protestant prince.[78] The corantos, though unreliable, disseminated news of Protestant triumphs which embarrassed the Spanish faction and

[75] Dahl, 'Amsterdam: Cradle of English Newspapers', 173–4.
[76] *Personal Rule*, 173–4.
[77] Birch, ii. 185–6.
[78] L. J. Reeve, *Charles I and the Road to Personal Rule* (Cambridge, 1989), 275–91.

some prominent Catholics. Their suppression was ill news, suggesting the presence of popery in domestic politics.

Pory wrote to Sir Thomas Lucy on 1 November:

> Since my last, Nathaniel Butter told me that a gentleman of his acquaintance having dined this day sennight in company of Mr. Taylor, the archduchess's agent, and asked him the reason of calling in the Currantos, he answered the news was so ill, as the Lords would not have it known. And besides, he told me that he would (if he dare be so good as his word) complain to their lordships how much Taylor had abused them in this answer. Besides he is getting to be translated divers Antwerp Currantos, to show their lordships how they lie upon us and their friends, and we in the mean time must be muzzled and our mouths stopped. But yesternight I met him at Whitehall, after he had been in Mr. Secretary Coke's chamber; and he told me he hoped ere long his Currantos would be revived.[79]

The agent 'abused' the Lords because he implied that they had placed Spanish interests above those of their own country. Coke favoured amicability with the Dutch and a hostile foreign policy towards Spain. Pory, apparently sympathetic to the latter, felt that he too had been 'muzzled', along with Butter and perhaps the nation in general.[80]

Neither Butter nor Pory felt that this suppression would be final. Butter appealed, but the Privy Council remained firm, later in the decade instituting licensing controls on almanacs, another form of news transmission.[81] Just as no one realized that 1629 instigated an eleven-year interval of parliaments, the purveyors of news did not realize that they would have to wait six years for Butter's next series of corantos.[82]

Charles I and public opinion

The silencing of the corantos contributed to the development of an opposition to the government: post-revisionist historians have appealed to contemporary perceptions in defence of the historiographical tradition of an emergent court-versus-country opposition.[83] Growing popular disaffection is suggested by the case of John Rous, the Suffolk clergyman sympathetic to Charles, who was forced into an oppositional position, after trying in vain to defend the king and his foreign policy to

[79] Birch, ii. 188.

[80] But cf. *Personal Rule*, 682.

[81] *Personal Rule*, 647 and refs.

[82] For the ninth and tenth series of corantos, and the irregular serial publication which Butter did publish in this period, see Dahl, 221–3; also Morison, *Origins of the Newspaper*, 33; and id., *The English Newspaper*, 7–14.

[83] Zagorin, *Court and the Country*, 74–118; Cust and Hughes, eds., *Conflict in Early Stuart England*, *passim*. On the conversion of erstwhile supporters see *British Monarchies*, 53.

his parishioners. Rous had no explanations from central government, no assistance to help him make sense of a series of apparently contradictory policies. The attempt to persuade his conversants of the coherence of Charles's outlook eventually forced him into rethinking his position and ultimately into agreeing with them.[84]

Robert Woodford, a Northampton puritan, also formed his political views through limited official government sources in conjunction with more plentiful gossip and newsletters, some of which may have been sent by Dillingham. This juxtaposition stressed conflict, and Woodford perceived the politics of the 1630s as a conspiracy against the commonwealth by popery and Arminianism, assisted by the bishops and particularly Laud. In 1640 he was a signatory to a petition of county grievances.[85] In this case perceived conflict became the basis for later social division and actual conflict.[86] Charles favoured the prohibition of corantos because he felt them to be against his interests: a deliberate use of them as state propaganda might have had very different effects.

It may have been a 'failure to stem the tide of puritan polemic and a growing awareness that he was in danger of losing the argument' that led to the king granting a patent to Butter and Bourne on 20 December 1638.[87] Responding to their petition he allowed them the sole right 'for the imprinting & publishing of all matter of History or News of any forraine place or Kingdome since the first beginning of the late German warres to this present'.[88] The publishers immediately released a coranto which proclaimed it had 'long been silenced' and was now 'permitted by Authority to speake again'.[89] A cessation in censorship was undeniably a cause of this periodical. The publishers were granted the sole right to print a weekly gazette, subject to the scrutinization of a secretary of state. What Charles did not do even at this point, which is quite remarkable, was to grant a patent for a newsbook written in his interests. The question of Charles's failure positively to use the press is more germane than the issue of censorship.

[84] Cogswell, 'The Politics of Propaganda', 187–215; *Diary of John Rous*, ed. Green, *passim*.

[85] John Fielding, 'Opposition to the Personal Rule of Charles I: The Diary of Robert Woodford, 1637–1641', *HJ* 31 (1988), 769–88.

[86] Cf. Richard Cust and Ann Hughes, 'Introduction: After Revisionism', in eid., eds., *Conflict in Early Stuart England*, 13–15.

[87] *Personal Rule*, 653. Cf. Hibbard's comments on the changing atmosphere in and shifting perceptions of the court in the summer and autumn of 1638; *Charles I and the Popish Plot*, 88. Elsewhere Sharpe has argued that Charles was inconsistent in his public orientation; 'The King's Writ: Royal Authors and Royal Authority in Early Modern England', in Sharpe and Peter Lake, eds., *Culture and Politics in Early Stuart England* (1994), 131–8.

[88] *CSPD 1638–1639*, 182; Dahl, 223–4.

[89] *An abstract of some speciall forreigne occurrences* 1, 20 Dec. 1638, [3], *STC* 18507.277.

Some writers closely associated with the king's cause admitted that news publications and the expansion of the sphere of political debate represented a threat. The continuity in this resistance to news media is revealed in a treatise of advice to the prospective king, written just before the Restoration by William Cavendish, first Earl of Newcastle. Cavendish recommended that the prince adopt a more severe position than his father: 'there is an other Error that doth over heate your people Extreamly And doth your Majestie much hurte, which is that Every man now Is becomed a state man, & itt is merly with the weekly Corants, Both att home & a broad, therefore they should bee forbid Eyther Domesticke or forayne news.'[90] Newcastle's use of the somewhat outdated term 'Corants' may have been an affected archaism, a refusal to come to terms with a modern industry. In distinguishing between foreign and domestic news, he implied that the permission given to the 1620s and 1630s corantos of Nathaniel Butter and their syndicate was the straw on the overburdened camel of state. He continued: 'as also such fellowes As Captaine Rosingame, that made £500 a yeare with writting Newes to severall persons, this did as much hurte as the other if not more, for in a letter hee might bee bolder Then they Durst bee in printe this too, not only to bee For-biden absolutly butt to bee punisht, severly if they offend in this, kinde.' However subversive the content of manuscripts, it was only the sheer numbers which were available from the printed press which facilitated the creation of a forum for public opinion. It was not safe to be explicit even in personal correspondence during the civil war, when the searching of mail was a fact of life.[91] While the printed word should not be privileged, neither should the written and the printed be taken as equivalent phenomena, with similar effects, though both contributed to the outbreak of the war.[92] Newcastle continued: 'this will so Coole the nation & quiett state speritts, as your Majestie & your subiects will finde greate Ease in itt,—so all our discourse will bee of Hunting & Hawkeing, Boling, Cocking, & such things, & bee

[90] Slaughter, ed., *Ideology and Politics*, 56.

[91] *Secret Rites* discusses coded exchanges and the opening of mail. *History*, 11–29, overstates the distinction between uncensored manuscripts and censored print; *Personal Rule*, 682–3. GCRO: D/DF F/241, a letter from Evan Seys to his father-in-law Robert Bridges dated 2 Feb. 1641[2], in which a politically sensitive paragraph concerning Warwickshire and Gloucestershire petitions against episcopacy is obliterated.

[92] Cf. Cogswell, 'The Politics of Propaganda', 198; Eisenstein, *The Printing Press as an Agent of Change*, Walter J. Ong, *Orality & Literacy: The Technologizing of the Word* (1982); Jack Goody, *The Domestication of the Savage Mind* (Cambridge, 1977); id., *The Logic of Writing and the Organization of Society* (Cambridge, 1986). John Taylor, *A Swarme of Sectaries and Schismatiqves: Wherein is discovered the strange preaching (or prating) of such as are by their Trades Coblers, Tinkers, Pedlers, Weavers, Sowgelders, and Chymney-Sweepers* (1641; T514), 2; 'I write of some, that with tongue, pen, and print | Have writ and rail'd, as if the devill were in't.'

Ever ready To serve your Majestie—.' Public discourse should have been devoted to holiday pastimes, if the king was successfully to subject his people. After the Earl's notorious military humiliation at Marston Moor, sporting activities may have been a preferable pastime.[93] Newcastle's advice invites interpretation as an interlinear commentary on the 1630s and early 1640s, and suggests just how the rejection of news publications ensured that their eventual appearance was in the interest of parliament.[94]

A glance across the Channel would have shown how successfully Richelieu had influenced popular opinion with the *Gazette* and *Mercure*, produced by Théophraste Renaudot, his long-standing communications genius, as one dimension of Richelieu's ambitious public-relations policy.[95] Renaudot claimed that Louis XIII not only read his *Gazettes*, but regularly sent him 'mémoires' to use in them.[96] *Mercure français* circulated widely in England in translation, presumably due to lack of domestically produced material, so the administration cannot have been unaware of it.[97] Prynne used it in his notorious *Newes from Ipswich* (1636), and later in *Popish Royall Favourite* (1643);[98] Rushworth cited it in his *Historical Collections*.[99] Yet the king neglected the opportunity to persuade and coerce his subjects. Hence Andrew Mousley is wrong to argue that there is 'a natural progression from Pory's empiricist stance and appeals to his version of events as the reliable and correct version, to the production of official, institutionalized news'.[100] This is to overlook both the institutional and international contexts. A 'natural progression' would have been understandable, but did not happen; official news eventually sprang from semi-unofficial news, and both were most unlike Pory's newsletters. At least since 1631, when Renaudot produced the *Gazette* and *Nouvelles ordinaires*, there was a glaringly obvious model for the British government: but the British chose not to invent their

[93] Gardiner², i. 374–82.

[94] Sir Philip Warwick complained that the propaganda campaign of Viscount Falkland, Colepeper, and Hyde was excessively witty and elegant. Ultimately it would make the readers more uncomfortable and suspicious than compliant. *Memoires of the reigne of King Charles I. With a Continuation to the Happy Restauration of King Charles II* (1701), 9, 195–9. He followed Hobbes in this; *Behemoth, or the Long Parliament*, ed. Ferdinand Tönnies (Chicago, 1990), 125.

[95] See Introduction, n. 47, above.

[96] Solomon, *Public Welfare, Science, and Propaganda*, 186.

[97] See Hibbard, *Charles I and the Popish Plot*, 24 and n.

[98] Prynne, *Newes from Ipswich* ('Ipswich' [Edinburgh], 1636; *STC* 20469), reprinted 1641, P4021A; Prynne, *The Popish Royall Favourite* (1643; P4039). If Wallington did not read *Mercure de France* then he knew about it from *Newes from Ipswich*; his deposition in Star Chamber revealed he owned a copy; Seaver, *Wallington's World*, 159–60.

[99] *HC*² i. 28.

[100] Mousley, 'Self, State, and Seventeenth-Century News', 159.

newspapers on the rational lines of the French, and instead allowed them to enter the world semi-illicitly.

Charles conspicuously rejected propaganda. Renaudot is relevant not as an illuminating parallel, but because we need to understand why Charles chose not to follow his example. Here silence speaks loudly enough. Some observations on Charles's policy early in his reign provide a useful context. The anti-controversy tendencies of government policy were received with greater indignation by Calvinists than by Catholics or Arminians. In 1626 Charles expressed a concern over seditious publications and attempted to suppress critics of Richard Montagu's *A Gagg for the New Gospell? No: A New Gagg for an Old Goose* (1624) and *Apello Caesarem* (1625). In the same year he suppressed Calvinist teaching at Cambridge University, within a fortnight of the election of Buckingham as Chancellor.[101] In January 1629 he issued a proclamation calling in Montagu's book, condemning 'reading, preaching, or making Bookes, either *pro* or *contra*, concerning these differences'.[102] Montagu had politicized religious controversy, and it is possible that Charles's 'tolerant' attitude was neither particularly temperate nor well counselled. For some, an imposed silence stimulated anxiety.[103]

There were other attempts to restrict public discussion. In November 1628, the month that Prynne was brought to court for his unlicensed anti-Arminian publishing, Charles prefaced a new edition of the Thirty-Nine Articles with a declaration forbidding disputation of their meaning.[104] In a sense Charles was only following his father, who had issued proclamations 'against the disorderly Printing, uttering, and dispersing of Bookes, Pamphlets, &c.' and 'against Seditious, Popish, and Puritanicall Bookes and Pamphlets' in 1623 and 1624. Perhaps more significantly in December 1620 and July 1621 James issued two proclamations 'against excesse of Lavish and Licentious Speech of matters of State', attempting to stem 'a greater opennesse, and libertie of discourse' than had existed in earlier times.[105] Charles's policy was, however, both more extensive and combined with more controversial religious tendencies. Whether these attempts to intervene in popular

[101] *STC* 18038 and 18030 respectively; Nicholas Tyacke, *Anti-Calvinists: The Rise of English Arminianism, c.1590–1640* (1987; Oxford, 1990), 48–9, and foreword to 1990 edn., pp. xii–xiii; Lambert, 'Richard Montagu, Arminianism and Censorship'.

[102] James F. Larkin, ed., *Stuart Royal Proclamations*, vol. ii: *Royal Proclamations of King Charles I, 1625–1646* (Oxford, 1983), 218–20.

[103] *Personal Rule*, 275–84, 292–301, qu. 297. Montagu's own correspondence perhaps suggests a greater political sensitivity; Durham University Library: Mickleton & Spearman MS 26, pp. 47 and following.

[104] Reeve, *Road to Personal Rule*, 63.

[105] James F. Larkin and Paul L. Hughes, eds., *Stuart Royal Proclamations*, vol. i: *Royal Proclamations of King James I, 1603–1625* (Oxford, 1973), 583–5, 599–600, 495–6, 519–21, qu. 495.

political debate were successful does not matter: Charles's actions reflect his suspicion of debate, and that is how the case was perceived by contemporaries. A liberty of discourse seemed to be incompatible with the personal rule. Yet Charles was not always opposed to encouraging public opinion as an alternative to preventing it. He published sermons preached at court in order to defend the largely indefensible forced loan.[106] In 1628, moreover, he used the press to deflect the impact of the Petition of Right. The series of events around this and the 1628 remonstrance, I suspect, hold the key to Charles's suspicion of his people's allegiance and his distaste for self-justification.

The king's passing of the Petition of Right in June 1628 was celebrated by the parliament, and they deviated from precedent by seeking to have it printed before they were prorogued, as if it were not a petition but an Act. On 26 June, at the close of the session, the king's speech expressed new reservations: 'Since that I see that even the House of Commons begins already to make false constructions of what I granted in your petition lest it be worse interpreted in the country I will now make a declaration concerning the true intent hereof.' As was reported to the House when it reconvened, the king subsequently had the issue of 1,500 copies seized at press and 'made waste paper'. The petition was then printed with other material, including the king's speech and the royal answer of 7 June. So the king undermined the intended impact of the printed petition and effectively turned it to the royal interest.[107] Many MPs were appropriately angered, and the incident destroyed any prospects of a lasting settlement between king and parliament.[108]

In the context of this intervention it is significant that Charles did not respond to the remonstrance. This was debated in the Commons in June 1628, the same month as the Petition of Right. In spite of Charles's efforts, Buckingham was named as the root of the kingdom's evils. Touching on sensitive nerves, the remonstrance grew to be more important than the petition. Laud drafted an answer upon the king's orders, but Charles declined to publish it.[109] Laud expressed bewilderment over this change of mind.[110]

The motivation was no doubt complex, but the contrast suggests a critical moment in the development of Charles's suspicion of his subjects' allegiance.[111] The second session of the 1628 parliament met in

[106] Richard Cust, *The Forced Loan and English Politics, 1626–1628* (Oxford, 1987), *passim*; Reeve, *Road to Personal Rule*, 14.

[107] Elizabeth Read Foster, 'Printing the Petition of Right', *Huntington Library Quarterly*, 38 (1974), 81–3; qu. 82, 83; Reeve, *Road to Personal Rule*, 20–1, 91–2.

[108] Cust, *Forced Loan*, 332.

[109] Reeve, *Road to Personal Rule*, 24–30.

[110] *Personal Rule*, 40–2, esp. 42 n. 248.

[111] Reeve and Cust both identify Charles's psychological vulnerableness about this. See also Sharpe on his uneven and ambivalent attitude to Sir Robert Cotton and the

the same factious mood which produced the remonstrance, and was dissolved in March 1629. The same month the king issued *A Proclamation for suppressing of false Rumours touching Parliament*, stating that he would be more inclined to their sitting 'when such as have bred this interruption shall have received their condigne punishment'.[112] Sir John Eliot was imprisoned in the Tower after the dissolution and acquired the status of a parliamentary martyr. Fear of Eliot's popular influence persuaded Charles not to free him, and subsequently not to call a parliament in the winter of 1631–2.[113] Charles felt that his honour might be impugned; and his counsel no doubt encouraged him. Eliot was further promoted in his hagiological status when he died in prison in November 1632: the same month as Frederick of Bohemia and Gustavus Adolphus, heroes of the Protestant cause.[114] The corantos had recently been suppressed. The Grand Remonstrance of 1641, a critical document in the history of the newsbook, was the sequel to the 1628 remonstrance, and the bitter and logical culmination of the opposition policies of the 1630s.[115] It cited the dissolution of parliament, the (mis-)printing of the Petition of Right, and the imprisonment and death of Eliot amongst its grievances.[116]

These interconnections suggest that his experience of the 1628 parliament, and his public exchanges with it, made Charles cynical about the use of propaganda. This critical period formed his attitudes to public opinion. In this context the suppression of corantos had political tremors; it explains why Charles resisted suggestions for an official news publication; and it provided the consumers of 1641 news with a framework in which news publications were perceived as a polarizing, seditious, and predominantly parliamentarian force.[117]

'Diurnall Occurrences' and Diurnall Occurrences

A number of writers have suggested that manuscripts are important antecedents of the newsbook, though none has explicated the circum-

Cottonian library; *Sir Robert Cotton 1586–1631: History and Politics in Early Modern England* (Oxford, 1979), 80–2, 140–6.

[112] Larkin, ed., *Stuart Royal Proclamations*, ii. 226–8; qu. on 228; *By the King. A Proclamation* . . . (1639; *STC* 8921).

[113] Reeve, *Road to Personal Rule*, 280–1.

[114] Reeve, *Road to Personal Rule*, 289–90.

[115] Cust, *Forced Loan*, 334; Fletcher, *Outbreak of the English Civil War*, 81–90.

[116] *Constitutional Documents*, 202–32.

[117] Hence the need for G. E. Aylmer's cautioning: 'It should not be assumed that all [newsbooks] were ultra-radical.' *Rebellion or Revolution? England 1640–1660* (Oxford, 1986), 65.

stances.[118] No one has explained why it was printed, nor explored earlier appearances of these manuscripts in print, nor enquired what the first newsbook really was. The forms of parliamentary manuscripts have been neglected. It was from one particular genre of manuscript, distinguishable from others contemporaneously proliferating and diversifying, that the first newsbooks were made.

Manuscript accounts of proceedings in parliament multiplied in the late 1620s.[119] This continued with the parliaments of 1640. At the same time the official journals, taken by the clerk of the Commons, were increasingly restricted to cover only the essential, skeletal actions of the House: motions, orders, and resolutions. The rigid and narrowing definition of the role of the journals excluded personal details, debates, and speeches.[120] They represented empirical details, not the process or the engagement of ideas and principles. Perhaps for this reason the members kept their own records, which spilled out to the public.

At the same time parliament was concerned with secrecy. The Short Parliament ruled against any member taking notes in the House.[121] Upon its dissolution the clerk, Henry Elsynge, surrendered a number of books and papers pertaining to the proceedings of the parliament, including the journal and a bundle of notes made by his assistant, John Rushworth.[122] Rushworth's able shorthand made him a liability to the secrecy of parliament, and the newly sitting Long Parliament ordered an investigation of him. On 1 December 1640, his notes were referred to a committee, and Elsynge and Rushworth were ordered to 'suffer no Copies to go forth of any Argument or Speech whatsoever: They are likewise to examine, what Copies have heretofore been delivered out, and to whom.'[123] Nevertheless individual members surreptitiously released copies of their speeches to printers, and sometimes printers would lay their hands on unofficial, often inaccurate copies.[124] These printed speeches were the primary source of printed parliamentary news for the reading public.[125]

But there were manuscript sources for readers who could afford

[118] Williams, 'Beginnings of English Journalism', 343–65, and *History*, 30–4; Notestein and Relf, eds., *Commons Debates for 1629*, pp. xlii–lv; Nelson and Seccombe, *Periodical Publications*, 20, following Coates, ed., *Journal of Sir Simonds D'Ewes*, pp. xx–xxii.

[119] See the introduction to Notestein and Relf, eds., *Commons Debates for 1629*.

[120] *Journal of Sir Simonds D'Ewes*, ed. Coates, pp. xix–xx; David Underdown, 'Popular Politics in Seventeenth-Century England', Ford Lectures, delivered in Oxford, 1992.

[121] *CJ* ii. 12.

[122] PRO: SP 16/452/30.

[123] *CJ* ii. 42.

[124] A. D. T. Cromartie, 'The Printing of Parliamentary Speeches November 1640–July 1642', *HJ* 33 (1990), 23–44.

[125] *Catalogue to the Thomason Tracts*, ed. Fortescue; Wing.

them.[126] These items came in many forms. There were speeches, sometimes mixed with accounts of proceedings; information such as might be found in a professional newsletter, though increasingly of a highly impersonal kind; accounts of Strafford's trial; almanacs with political commentary; occasional poems; manuscript dialogues on news events; accounts of proceedings in the Commons or both Houses, of uneven periodicity; weekly accounts of proceedings starting on Wednesday;[127] and, most significantly, weekly accounts running from Monday to Monday, without speeches.[128] Many forms which were to become familiar in print in the later 1640s appeared in manuscript in 1640 and 1641.

Certain items possessed the generic title 'Diurnall Occurrences or the Heads of Proceedings in Parliament'. Sometimes the subtitle stood on its own.[129] Occasionally other variants are found, such as 'Diurnal Occurrences in Parliament', and 'Diurnall Occurrences or The proceedings in Parliament'.[130] This slight deviation from a largely consistent title suggests that the title was recognized, and thus identified the form. Readers knew what 'Diurnall Occurrences' were.

These periodical manuscripts probably first appeared at the beginning of the Long Parliament in November 1640. Copies of similar texts dating back to that first week survive in subsequently transcribed volumes, but not as separate items.[131] The earliest separate I have found which conforms to the rules of the genre, other than in duration, covers the period Thursday 25 February to Saturday 6 March. This is a copy of a distinct text, in an entry book in a uniform hand.[132] An item from three weeks later appears to be a commercially produced separate. That is, it represents the source of copies in entry books.[133] This manuscript consists of two small-folio sheets headed 'diurnall Occurrences or the heads of proceedings in Parliament from the 15th of March to the 22th

[126] See Love, *Scribal Publication*, 19–22; though Love is primarily concerned with earlier material.

[127] BL: Sloane MS 3317, ff. 21–22^{v} (red foliation); BL: Sloane MS 1467, ff. 25–8, 37–40^{v}, 70–3, 76–79^{v}, 80–2, 85–8. These are also distinguished from 'Diurnall Occurrences' manuscripts by having no heading.

[128] For almanacs, poems, and Strafford see BL: Lansdowne MS 20, ff. 90–99^{v}, 108–108^{v}; cf. Marotti, *Manuscript, Print, and the English Renaissance Lyric*, 75–126. For everything else see BL: Sloane MS 1467, which nicely illustrates the formal diversity of the material circulating in 1640–1; BL: Sloane MS 3065.

[129] BL: Stowe MS 361, ff. 94–95^{v} and ff. 96–97^{v}.

[130] BL: Add. MS 33468, ff. 35–40^{v}; Bod.: Tanner MS 66, ff. 61–62^{v}; PRO: SP 16/484/26; PRO: SP 16/485/66; BL: Add. MS 34485, ff. 78–88^{v}.

[131] BL: Add. MS 6521.

[132] BL: Lansdowne MS 1232, pp. 290–6. The following item, 296–301, covers the week Mon. 22–9 Mar., suggesting that the preceding item is actually a distortion of the Mon. to Mon. genre. Internal evidence suggests that the copyist was confused over dates.

[133] Bod.: MS Tanner 65, ff. 285–288^{v}.

of March 1640'. Uniquely, it summarizes the contents just below the title: 'The greatest part of this weeke was spent in meetings, & consultacons about the Earle of Straffords Triall.' This brief summary of the import of the week's news anticipated later summaries of contents on the title-pages of printed newsbooks. In these later instances it has generally been assumed that the summary was an advertising function: this may also be true of the scribal text. There were formal, commercial, and functional overlaps between scribal products and printed books,[134] and manuscripts of 'Diurnall Occurrences' might have been sold next to printed products on booksellers' stalls. Muddiman, feeling no compunction to cite evidence, suggests that prior to 1641 the scrivener Samuel Pecke sold manuscript copies of parliamentary speeches at a stall in Westminster Hall, in the face of all supposed restrictions.[135] It is an absurdity worth contemplating.

Manuscripts of the same script-run as this one for 15–22 March were copied into a number of large, fair volumes of parliamentary proceedings.[136] Like all later issues of this scribal serial, and like most copies made from them, the days of the week were indented into the margin. When copies were made the text varied: it could vary substantially, with some items missing, and other passages nearly identical. The aetiology is complex, but certain important features can be generalized. We cannot tell what was happening with 'Diurnall Occurrences' in its first few weeks. For later weeks for which multiple copies survive there is a clearer picture. Two or more copies survive in the same hand; the quality of scripts suggests that professionals may have been involved in their multiplication; a number of textual errors appear. These three attributes are associated with entrepreneurial publication.[137] At the same time there are collections of extended series of 'Diurnall Occurrences' copied in a fair hand into uniform volumes, in which weeks overlap on the same page.[138] These were probably commissioned by individual customers from professional scribes. This is a sub-category of

[134] See Love, *Scribal Publication*; McKenzie 'Speech—Manuscript—Print'.

[135] Muddiman, *The King's Journalist*, 10. I suspect his source may have been an issue of *Kingdomes Weekly Post* 5, 6 Dec. 1643, 39, 217.5/E77(32): 'This day came out a Pamphlet called *A perfect Diurnall*, written by one *Pecke* an Anabaptist that sometime kept a Scriveners stall at Westminster, that hath layne this half yeare and above in the Fleet, for writing of Lyes, where he complyed so far with the Cavaliers there, that they made him often so drunke that he hath beene faine to bee led to his chamber: he lay so long there, that his wife was faine to pawne her gownes, and begge pardon in her petticoat and wastcoat for him; and now his place of greatest residency is at a Stationers in the Old Baily.'

[136] BL: Add. MS 36828, f. 55; BL: Add. MS 6521, p. 137 (f. 64).

[137] Love, *Scribal Publication*, 77.

[138] BL: Add. MS 6521; BL: Add. MS 36828; BL: Add. MS 36829; BL: Harleian MS 4262; PRO: 30/53/12; Durham University Library: Mickleton & Spearman MS 30.

user-publication.[139] Another form of user-publication was the frequent transcription into private copy books.[140]

'Diurnall Occurrences' covered a week beginning on Mondays. They were presumably published on the following Monday or soon after. They were periodical news publications, but they could also serve as reference works. It was because of these manuscripts and not because of the Tuesday post that the first newsbooks appeared on Mondays. Their periodicity was determined by their subject. The week was a convenient time in politics, particularly as the Houses sat only infrequently on Sundays, leaving that day free for the labour-intensive act of copying. Journalism and respect for the Sabbath have long been antipathetic. Some narratives of proceedings would originally have circulated among members of the parliament, particularly of the Lower House which was represented in more detail, and among their friends in the city and provinces.[141] The content would predominantly have been relevant to someone already in possession of considerable information. Some manuscripts were too inaccurate to have been useful to MPs.

'Diurnall Occurrences' did not contain speeches, and this self-denial is a key to understanding their audience. Either they were intended as personal substitutes for the official journals of the Commons, or they were produced by scriveners for the broader public, who had to buy speeches separately. These speeches were available in cheaper, printed forms. When copied into books the occurrences are most commonly found with speeches. By late 1641 these periodical manuscripts were in fairly wide circulation, costing about 1 *s.* 6*d.*, depending on length. They were mentioned in a Commons order on 21 August; and on 18 November, less than a fortnight before *Heads of Severall Proceedings* appeared, it was ordered:

> That the Committee for Printing, where Sir *Edward Deering* has the Chair, do meet Tomorrow at Seven of Clock, in the inner Star-chamber; and do take some speedy Course for the Preventing the great Abuses that happen by the licentious Printing of Pamphlets; and especially, that they take care to suppress the Printing, or Venting in Manuscript, the diurnal Occurrences of Parliament.[142]

The fact that the committee met in Star Chamber is not the only irony here: Dering was himself a repeated offender against the ordinances restricting the printing of parliamentary materials. We must not take too seriously the strictures of MPs against publication and printing:

[139] Love, *Scribal Publication*, 47, 79–83.

[140] BL: Lansdowne MS 1232, 290–301, 324–9; PRO: SP 16/450/94, 11.

[141] Three are to be found among William Lenthal's papers; Bod.: MS Tanner 66, ff. 61–62^{v}, 113–122^{v}; MS Tanner 65, ff. 285–288^{v}.

[142] *CJ* ii. 319.

objections were only raised when convenient. On 2 February 1642 a resolution to send Dering to the Tower for his *Collection of Speeches* was passed by eighty-five votes to sixty-one.[143] In this debate Bulstrode Whitelocke intervened with a round condemnation: 'no member of this house ought to publish any speech or passages in this house though it be very frequent, and this book is against the honor and privileges of the house.'[144] The same month *The Speech of Bulstrode Whitelocke Esquire* appeared.[145] John Pym authorized the publication of his speeches, favouring, at least in the autumn of 1641, the same John Thomas who would later publish the first newsbook. George, Lord Digby, Denzil Holles, Sir Simonds D'Ewes, Benjamin Rudyerd, and Edmund Waller, to name a few, also authorized publication of their speeches.[146] After his expulsion from the House, Dering made notes of an angry conversation, recording himself as saying: 'You have burnt my booke, and thereby raysed the price, and raised the desires of such as would have [it]. Alas, the burning of my booke cannot confute me, nor silence me in the way I go.'[147] Dering appears to have revelled in the publicity, for on 3 February Richard Fitche wrote to Sir John Penington: 'the most ridiculous thing that ever Sir Edward committed was his manner of going to the Tower this day, who, when he might have gone in his coach, went up and down the streets and the Exchange in London, with hundreds of boys and girls at his heels, to see him, crying out, "Which is Sir Edward Deering?"'[148] Individual members expressed reservations over and outright condemnation of public dissemination of parliamentary information while also courting publicity. Such qualifications should modify any reading of the order of 18 November 1641, which reveals an awareness of the circulation of manuscript 'Diurnall Occurrences', and a concern over their printing.

[143] *A Collection of speeches made by Sir Edward Dering in matter of religion* (1642; D1103,4); *CJ* ii. 411; see also 419, 426. On 20 Jan. 1642, moreover, a printed speech with Dering's name on it was referred to the Committee for Printing, which was revived especially for the occasion, though it was not clear whether he was responsible for this; *CJ* ii. 267, 387.

[144] *Private Journals of the Long Parliament*, i: *3 January to 5 March 1642*, ed. Coates *et al.*, 262. Dering's speeches savoured of party royalism.

[145] *The Speech of Bulstrode Whitelocke Esquire, To The Right Honourable the Lords, At a Conference of both Houses on Thursday the seventeenth of February last* (1642; W1992). As Whitelocke did not mention this in his *Remains* or diary it is possible that it was fabricated or published without his permission. Cromartie classifies it as a probable fabrication; 'Printing of Parliamentary Speeches', 42–3.

[146] Cf. Lambert, 'Beginning of Printing', 44, 57. On 6 Jan. 1642 D'Ewes said that it was 'the highest treacherie and breach of priviledge for any member of that howse to witnes or reveale what was done or spoken in that howse', and then had his speech printed as a separate; *Journal of Sir Simonds D'Ewes*, ed. Coates, p. xxi.

[147] Lambert B. Larking, ed., *Proceedings Principally in the County of Kent in connection with the Parliaments Called in 1640*, Camden Society, 80 (1862), 75.

[148] *CSPD 1641–1643*, 273; PRO: SP 16/489/3.

Sheila Lambert, in an important article on parliamentary printing, has used the wording of this order to suggest that the first newsbooks appeared before 29 November 1641, probably in September.[149] Lambert is right to gesture towards the chronological incoherence of previous explanations of the newsbook, but her conclusions are wrong. First, there were very strong reasons why periodical newsbooks appeared when they did, though these have not been recognized heretofore. Secondly, the survival rate for serials after 1641 is higher than Lambert acknowledges.[150] Lambert suggests that the apparent 'disappearance' of newsbooks in March 1642 is also an illusion caused by uneven survival:[151] yet, as I show below, contemporaries remarked upon this disappearance. Thirdly, the November order alludes not to weekly newsbooks, but to a large volume entitled *The Diurnall Occurrences, or Dayly Proceedings of both Houses, in this Great and Happy Parliament* published by William Cooke in early November 1641.[152] Finally, the similarity between this volume and newsbooks, which Lambert acutely identifies, does not mean that the large volume was printed from now lost newsbooks. Instead both Cooke's *Diurnall Occurrences* and John Thomas's *Heads of Severall Proceedings* were sourced from manuscript 'Diurnall Occurrences'.

In another respect Lambert is right. The manuscripts which became *Diurnall Occurrences* and *Heads of Severall Proceedings* did appear in print before November 1641; not in September, as she suggests, but in August. I examine these publications below. These are almost but not quite newsbooks: they are not periodicals.

Diurnall Occurrences was the sequel to Cooke's *Speeches and Passages Of this Great and Happy Parliament From the third of November, 1640, to this Instant June, 1641*, which reprinted numerous printed separates.[153] It appeared in late June or early July, and perhaps caused Cooke to be called before the Commons on 21 August. On that day parliament first expressed concern over the circulation of 'Diurnall Occurrences' manuscripts:

[149] Lambert, 'Beginning of Printing', 52.

[150] N&S; not available to Lambert. There are remarkably few issues missing from known serials, which demonstrates a much higher survival rate than the 0.013% for corantos, given by Dahl, 22. The survival is possibly owing to the incipience of the collecting impulse among readers of printed texts, an impulse no doubt benefiting from the fashion for serial publications.

[151] Lambert, 'Beginning of Printing', 56.

[152] Wing E1526.

[153] At least one speech was released simultaneously as a pamphlet, with the same pagination (351–8). *Sir Thomas Rowe His Speech At the Councell-Table touching Brasse-Money . . . Iuly, 1640* [i.e. 1641]. This employed two formes from *Speeches and Passages* with an added title leaf. Wing lists it as part of *Speeches and Passages*, E2309. Separates of course had to be newsworthy.

Ordered, That *T. Harper* in *Little Britain, Edw. Griffin* in the *Old Bailey, Paine* and *Symonds* in *Red-cross-street, Wm. Cooke* and *Lawrance Chapman*, be sent for, to give their Attendance upon the Committee for the Bill of Printing: And That Committee has likewise Power, not only to consider of what Passages of this House has been printed, or by whom, but also to inquire after those that have published the Occurrences of Parliament in Writing.[154]

In his diary D'Ewes recorded that the committee, of which he was a member, would sit 'to advize of some meanes to restraine this licentious printing'.[155] But equally important is the allusion to scribally produced Occurrences: those '*in Writing*'.

Diurnall Occurrences brought the speeches up to date, and presented parliamentary proceedings, often referring the reader to *Speeches and Passages.* The speeches and proceedings were not integrated. The texts of proceedings derived from 'Diurnall Occurrences', though the printed version is frequently compacted and does not always correspond exactly to extant texts.[156] Copies of 'Diurnall Occurrences' vary among themselves, generally differing more at the end of the week than at the beginning.

There are other sources for *Diurnall Occurrences,* some of them printed, but not for these passages of proceedings. They were set to type for the first time with a certain amount of daring. This information was not yet in the public domain, though by the summer of 1641 the manuscripts were probably intended as much for a politically conscious public interested in parliamentary proceedings as for the politicians themselves.[157]

Two members of this participating public were William Montagu and Edward Lord Montagu: the former wrote to the latter on 9 December: 'There is a Journal of this Parliament come forth from the beginning. I have not time now to send it, but if you please to have it next week I shall send it.'[158] This refers to *Diurnall Occurrences,* but this matter-of-factness should not conceal the risk which the publisher Cooke was conceivably taking. Parliament had several times expressed hostility to the printing of its 'Occurrences', yet Cooke had had, and continued to have, an interest in parliamentary material and some loose connections with individual members. Printing 'Diurnall Occurrences' might have provoked severe censure. Yet, despite the wording of the 18 November order, Cooke was not summoned to parliament.

[154] *CJ* ii. 267. All of the named printers except Harper subsequently produced newsbooks. The latest item in *Diurnall Occurrences* is dated 22 June.

[155] *Journal of Sir Simonds D'Ewes*, ed. Coates, 164.

[156] Cf. e.g. PRO: SP 16/483/29, f. 1; with *Diurnall Occurrences,* 334–5.

[157] Notestein and Relf (eds.), *Commons Debates for 1629*, p. xlv.

[158] *HMC: Report on the Manuscripts of the Duke of Buccleuch and Queensberry* (1899), i. 289.

Cooke's *Diurnall Occurrences* was not a newsbook. Though it contained material identical in nature to that in *Heads of Severall Proceedings*, and though parts of it were very recent, it fell short on several accounts. It may have appealed to a similar audience to a newsbook, but it did so in a different way. It was expensive. It was not a serial publication. Above all, it was not particularly a news item. It was a reference work, a volume of history, like the slimmer volume which Cooke published the same month, *The Diurnall Occurrences of every dayes proceeding in Parliament since the beginning thereof, being Tuesday the twentieth of Ianuary, which ended the tenth of March. Anno Dom. 1628.*[159]

Heads of Severall Proceedings*: the first newsbook?*

The first newsbook was not altogether unprecedented. One of the complexities of the babble of print in late 1641 is the degree to which texts overlapped in form and function. 'Diurnall Occurrences' manuscripts benefited from inexpensive multiplication by the printing press before *Heads of Severall Proceedings*.

Instrvctions Given Vnto the Commissioners of the Lords and Commons appointed to be imployed in the Parliament of Scotland, August. 18. 1641. Together With the proceedings in Parliament on Thursday, August 19. with order for the disbanding of the Armies in the Northerne Parts appeared without any indication of the identity of the publisher or printer.[160] Uneconomical in its use of paper, the last of the four pages of text contained, as advertised in the title, an account of the proceedings in parliament on 19 August. It was presumably published soon after that date. This last page appears to have been taken from a 'Diurnall Occurrences' manuscript.[161]

This fragment was followed by another in a similar publication, *The Heads Of severall Petitions delivered by many of the Troopers against the Lord General And some other Officers of the Army. With the Answer which Mr. Pym Made to the severall Heads or Petitions, before the Committee on Tuesday, October 5. 1641.* This was published by John Thomas.[162] The similarities suggest that Thomas may also have been responsible for August's *Instrvctions Given Vnto the Commissioners*; conspicuously Thomas is credited with no other publications in August. He was averse neither to anonymity nor to spurious imprints. *The Heads Of severall Petitions* reports on a petition delivered to the standing committee appointed to

[159] Nov. 1641; E1525.
[160] 1641; I252/E169(10).
[161] Though it does not correspond with PRO: SP 16/483/54.
[162] 1641; H1289/E172(14).

deal with business during the recess of 11 September to 20 October. The appearance of the petition and Pym's response in print suggests that one of the members of the standing committee chose to release it to Thomas. Pym, named in very large type on the title-page, is the most obvious candidate.

The young John Thomas was probably no politician, but he certainly had sources, including Pym, for parliamentarian propaganda. His publications in 1641, when he began his career, included: *The Wren's Nest defil'd; or, Bishop Wren anatomiz'd, his life and actions dissected and laid open* (July); *A learned and witty Conference betwixt a Protestant and a Papist* (September); *The Discovery of a Conspiracy at Edenburg in Scotland. Related in a letter, from the Committees for Scotland* (October, with a woodcut portrait of Pym); *A Coppie of the Bill against the XIII Bishops, presented to the Lords, by the Commons* (October, with a portrait of Laud); *The last Newes from Ireland, being a relation of the proceedings of the rebellious Papists there* (October); *Sir Iohn Holland his Speech in Parliament, declaring the grievances of this Kingdome* (November); *Irelands Complaint against Sir George Ratcliffe, delivered in Parliament by Captaine Audley Mervin. Wherein is declared the grievances occasioned by him and the late Earl of Strafford* (November); *A late and true Relation from Ireland of the warlike and bloody proceedings of the rebellious Papists in that Kingdome, from Novemb. 1. to this present* (9 November); *Most fearefull Newes from the Bishoppricke of Durham, being a relation of one Margaret Hooper of Edenbyres, who was possessed and tormented with a devil* (November); *More Newes from Ireland, or the bloody practices of the Papists* (November); *The Petition of Parliament presented to the King with the Remonstrance. Concerning the present state of this kingdome* (December).[163] Up to this last item, all Thomas's publications suggest consistent political inclinations, as the titles indicate. He might be described as an unofficial printer to parliament. This does not mean he was committed on grounds of personal belief: in December he managed to get a foot in the king's camp while maintaining a relationship with Pym.[164] Notably he was responsible in 1642 for one of the editions of *The Copie of a Letter Written unto Sir Edward Deering, lately put out of the House, and committed*

[163] W3681/E165(14); L799/E172(8); D1637/E173(13); C6206/E173(21); L492/E175(2); H2430/E198(6); M1882/E176(8); L541/E176(16); M2889/E180(11); M2712/E177(16); E2180/E181(10); see also L3085, N1236, N682, H1288A, E1286, L2324, R1425, C6868, D1642, W3377, E3933, C1706, C2064, D1636.

[164] Including *The Kings Maiesties most gratious Speech to both Houses of Parliament. Whereunto is added the King and Queenes Royall loves returned to the worthy members of the City of London* (2 Dec. 1641; C2522/E199(28)); and *His Majestie's speciall Command to the Lord Major of London for the sending of precepts into the city to suppresse the tumultuous assemblies. With a relation of the uproars made by the Brownists and Separatists within the City of London and Westminster* (9 Dec. 1641; C2772/E179(19)). Hunscott, who seems never to have printed a newsbook, succeeded Thomas as the Commons' favoured printer.

unto the Tower, February 2. 1641.[165] Like many publishers, he put out what he could lay his hands on. The distinct political bias evident in his publications stemmed from his personal connections and sources, which in November 1641 lay with Pym and the reforming party in the Commons.

By far the most significant proto-newsbook publication was also published by Thomas. It appeared in late October 1641 and was entitled *The Coppy of a Letter Sent by the Lords and Commons in Parliament to the Committees, now attending his Royall Majestie in Scotland. October 23. 1641. With certaine Instructions to the Committees there, to acquaint his Majestie with the Affayres of both Kingdomes at this present. Whereunto is annexed the Heads of severall proceedings in Parliament now Assembled, from October 20. to the 26.*[166] Even the title of the 'first newsbook' is embedded in this apparently innocuous pamphlet. The letter is just over a page in length, the instructions cover slightly more than two, and about a page and a half are occupied by the annexed 'heads of severall proceedings' (the versos of the title-page and the last leaf are blank). This covers the week 19–25 October, and is a severely abridged text of a 'Diurnall Occurrences'. *The Coppy of a Letter* cannot, however, be described as the first newsbook, not because of the brevity of the proceedings, but because it is not a serial. This reminds us of what lies at the heart of the newsbook: periodicity. In other respects *The Coppy of a Letter* is the progenitor of *Heads of Severall Proceedings.* The demarcations in print culture are rarely sharp or convenient.

About four weeks later, towards the end of November 1641, John Thomas decided to publish in print the manuscript of 'Diurnall Occurrences' for the preceding week. He entitled it *The Heads of Severall Proceedings in this Present Parliament from the 22 of November, to the 29. 1641. Wherein is contained the substance of severall Letters sent from Ireland, shewing what distresse and misery they are in With diverse other passages of moment touching the Affaires of these Kingdomes.*[167] For this there exists a corresponding manuscript, entitled 'Diurnall Occurences or The heads of proceedings in Parlam^t^ from the 22th of novemb<u>er</u> to the 29th 1641'.[168] Most of the text is identical, varying only in spelling and, particularly,

[165] (1642; P4257A). Another edition has the imprint 'For Iohn Tompson', P4257. There is little evidence of a John Thompson active in this period, though one did publish a single issue of *The Daily Intelligencer* in Feb. 1643; 86.1/E86(37). Plomer records a bookseller of this name reported for not paying his poll tax in 1641; Henry R. Plomer, *A Dictionary of the Booksellers and Printers who Were at Work in England, Scotland and Ireland from 1641 to 1667* (Oxford, 1968), 178; *CSPD 1641–1643*, 73. It is plausible that both editions were published by Thomas.

[166] E1286/E173(19).

[167] 181.101/E201(1).

[168] BL: Add. MS 33468, ff. 71–81v; see appendix, below.

the deployment of paragraphs. Under the Tuesday heading the printed text mentions some Irishmen not in the manuscript, though they appear again on Wednesday in both versions. The manuscript mentions Sir John Little, the bill against recusants, and the bill for subsidies where *Heads of Severall Proceedings* does not. The most significant difference is the more extended version of the king's reception in London in the printed text. The manuscript mentions this only briefly, and in a subordinate position. The manuscript, moreover, in explaining why the king did not attend upon parliament gives reasons in greater detail, mentioning that the queen had refused to stay at Whitehall, 'vpon some discontentm^{t} conceiued to be taken ag^{t} the Cittie at her Mothers departure'.[169] These variations result in difference of political weighting. The manuscript expresses less sympathy with the king, ignoring the ceremonial detailed in the newsbook, and speculating about the king's marriage. This last may have stood beyond the legitimate jurisdiction of print, but the differences are as likely to stem from different texts in 'Diurnall Occurrences' manuscripts, as from the different roles of manuscript and print.[170] *Heads of Several Proceedings* was therefore set not from the 'Diurnall Occurrences' in Add. MS 33468, but from its sibling, another manuscript stemming from a shared parent.

We have therefore arrived at a new premiss for the newsbook. I have explored in brief the development of a formally distinctive manuscript through 1641. 'Diurnall Occurrences' is a fascinating series, not to be confused with newsletters, or understood as a continuation of the non-periodical 'True Relation' manuscripts of 1629.[171] Evidence of the audience is largely internal, but some of these readers were increasingly sensitive to the possibility of printing it, realized in Thomas's separate news publications, Cooke's *Diurnall Occurrences*, and then in *Heads of Severall Proceedings*. This prehistory of the newsbook establishes the lineage. What we have left to explain is why this particular issue found its way to Thomas's press on the weekend of 27–9 November 1641, and why he produced a sequel the next week.

The 'public sphere', public good, and the Irish Rebellion

Some clues to the reasons for printing *Heads of Severall Proceedings* can be deduced from internal evidence. The format was directly derived from 'Diurnall Occurrences', some copies of which even had title-pages.[172]

[169] BL: Add. MS 33468, f. 79^{v}. [170] See Ch. 1 n. 11, above.

[171] An error made by Notestein and Relf (eds.), *Commons Debates for 1629*, pp. xlii–lv.

[172] BL: Sloane MS 3065, f. 7; Add. MS 33468, f. 41; PRO: SP 16/484/26; SP 16/485/66. The last is apparently in a different hand.

Thomas dropped the title 'Diurnall Occurrences' and used the extended subtitle, possibly because it was more in keeping with his earlier publications, possibly because it was more descriptive. It began, like all the manuscripts, with the word 'Monday'. The news of that week indicated the concerns which led to its printing.

On Monday, letters from Ireland expressed fears that the rebels were going to swamp the English. The news of the Irish Rebellion had broken on 1 November, twelve days after parliament reconvened from its autumnal recess, and the stories of a massacre motivated many members to reconsider their position in relation to the proposed remonstrance declaring the grievances of the kingdom.[173] The remonstrance, in some form or other, had been the subject of protracted debate through the summer, and Pym and his friends had finally conceived hopes of pushing it through parliament in November. The Irish news had a twofold effect. First, the debate on the remonstrance was postponed. Secondly, many members who previously had taken a neutral position felt that it was necessary to act very quickly in response to the Irish situation. They were nervous that a Scottish army, or an army commanded by Charles to crush the Irish, might afterwards be turned to suppress the differences in England and Wales. The earlier unity fostered by opposition to Strafford was revitalized. The situation was aggravated by the news of the 'Incident', a plot against Hamilton and Argyle in Edinburgh, which Pym brought before the recess committee on 19 October. This news was publicized by John Thomas, in a pamphlet which included a portrait of Pym.[174] This was followed by news of the Second Army Plot in the summer of that year, which Pym presented to the House of Commons on 30 October.[175] Two serious attempts to influence parliament by force were followed by the pressing problem of Ireland. Moderate members of both houses were encouraged to draw parallels.[176] All this gave Pym political leverage.

After the issue of the troops for Ireland was tentatively resolved, the lower house turned to the Grand Remonstrance. The religious differences thrown into relief by the rebellion were translated into positions taken on the remonstrance. Clarendon noted that the remonstrance was passionately urged by its party 'making doubtful glances and reflec-

[173] See Fletcher, *Outbreak of the English Civil War*, 125–57 and *passim*. Gardiner[1], x. 64, 74–9.

[174] *The Discovery of a Conspiracy at Edenburg in Scotland*, D1637; also *The Earl of Craford his Speech before the Parliament in Scotland*, printed for John Thomas (1641; L2324/E199(19)).

[175] Fletcher, *Outbreak of the English Civil War*, 130–9; *British Monarchies*, 150–4.

[176] *A Parallel Between the Late Troubles in Scotland, and the Present Trovbles in England* (1642; P336/A) did just that.

tions upon the rebellion in Ireland'.[177] Consequently Pym and his friends won the day, and the bitter recriminations against the king in this history of his malpractices were given the authority of a small Commons majority. This was on 22 November 1641. The debate was so acrimonious that Sir Philip Warwick later wrote: 'I thought, wee had all sat in the valley of the shadow of death; for wee, like Joab's and Abner's young men, had catcht at each others locks, and sheathed our swords in each other's bowels.'[178] According to Warwick, who may have been guilty of some retrospective exaggeration, Hampden skilfully diverted disaster. It was without doubt a histrionic moment. It was also the first day to be represented in a newsbook. John Thomas showed some confidence in putting his initials on the title-page.

The conflict was more subdued in the newsbook than in Warwick's memory:

> After this, in the house of Commons they read the declaration of the State of the Kingdom; and how farre the grievances had beene reduced by this Parliament. there was a great debate about divers clauses in it, and it was first put to the question that those clauses wherein the Bishops are tearmed malignant persons to the well-farre, and peace of this Kingdome in the particulars named should be altered, and the house being divided it was carried by the Majors part that it should so stand.
>
> Afterwards the house was twice divided upon the question for the passing of the said Remonstrance without any alteration, and for the publishing thereof, and the greater part carried it, in both there being great oppositions, and debate about it.[179]

Joab and Abner would have been inappropriate references in a kingdom avoiding armed confrontation.[180] The newsbook, being a more public document, had a different set of restrictions from the diary.[181] For the rest of the year newsbooks were characterized by the same

[177] Edward Hyde, Earl of Clarendon, *History of the Rebellion and Civil Wars in England*, ed. W. Dunn Macray, 6 vols. (Oxford, 1888), i. 417–18.

[178] Warwick, *Memoires*, 202; Thomas Carlyle, ed., *The Letters and Speeches Oliver Cromwell with Elucidations*, ed. S. C. Lomas, 3 vols. (1845; New York, 1904), i. 107–8. The moderate Thomas Fuller later preached on Joab and Abner, from 2 Sam. 2; *A Fast Sermon Preached On Innocents day* (1642; F2423).

[179] *Heads of Severall Proceedings*, 29 Nov. 1641, [3–4], 181.101/E201(1).

[180] Russell argues in *British Monarchies* and *Causes* that the prospect of war was essentially secured by the summer of 1641 and actively deferred for a year. This is consonant with the rapid developments in the pamphlet press through the summer.

[181] The Commons resolved on 29 Nov. that the remonstrance could be published but not printed: this enabled manuscripts to be circulated. On 15 Dec. they permitted its printing. Gardiner[1], x. 100; Fletcher, *Outbreak of the English Civil War*, 169; *British Monarchies*, 429, 439. These decisions concerning publication emphasize the distinction between the private and public versions of texts. Newsbooks managed to blur this distinction by representing the remonstrance in some detail.

restraint. *Heads of Severall Proceedings* on 6 December represented the news from Ireland and of the remonstrance in much the same fashion, though it also covered the protests of the citizens of London. *The Diurnall*, which appeared on 13 December, covered the usual news of debates over the Irish affairs, petitions, and bills against protections and for the defence of parliament.[182] The next week saw three similar newsbooks, reporting news from Scotland, the committee on Ireland, a bill against the bishops, and one concerning tonnage and poundage.[183]

Heads of Severall Proceedings provided its own immediate political context, and in the convergent effects of these two very public events, the Grand Remonstrance and the Irish Rebellion, subsist the factors which made the newsbook a socially inflected, politically utile, and economically feasible proposition.

In Gardiner's monumental narrative, October and November are the crucial months during which two parties emerged out of the chaos of the political nation.[184] The autumn recess was a pivotal moment for the Long Parliament, as almost all of its legislation until that point was accepted at the Restoration, and everything subsequent was rejected. This change suggests the fracture of unity and the beginning of majority politics. It was at this time that the stereotypes of Cavalier and Roundhead also appeared, as Clarendon noted.[185] Thomas May, the republican historian of parliament, placed the critical polarization of 'ordinary discourse', by which he meant popular political debate, at this point.[186] Conrad Russell argues that this period saw the rapid formulation of parties and the development of 'rival demonologies', the intolerant modes of representation which brought on the war.[187] Newsbooks were one of the cultural means by which these new oppositions were engineered. They did not need to underscore conflict as their very presence admitted and amplified it.

Newsbooks can usefully be contrasted with speeches. Ian Cromartie, in a study of the decision to print parliamentary speeches, has argued that the prevalence of speeches was not a good measure of public interest, and that peaks in their production indicate periods of political

[182] *Heads of Severall Proceedings*, 6 Dec. 1641, 181.102/E202(2); *The Diurnall*, 13 Dec., 109.1.

[183] *The Diurnall*, 109.2; *The Divrnall Occurrances*, 103.1; *Divrnall Occvrrences, or, the Heads of Severall Proceedings*, 181.103/E201(3). All 20 Dec. 1641. *The Diurnall* differed slightly in format by printing the supposed Irish Covenant as a separate document on the last page.

[184] Gardiner[1], x. 34, 43–79.

[185] Clarendon, *History*, i. 457.

[186] Thomas May, *The History of the Parliament of England: Which began November the third, M.DC.XL.* (1647; M1410), 18.

[187] *British Monarchies*, 400–53.

consensus, or at least 'contributed to an imagined consensus.'[188] By restricting analysis to speeches Cromartie ignores a critical innovation during this period. Published parliamentary speeches declined in number around the debate on the Grand Remonstrance, when 'political division militated against publication'.[189] Yet the figures for newsbooks dovetail with those for speeches. Newsbooks, which importantly did not contain speeches, functioned as a partial substitute for them, and when conflict discouraged the latter, it encouraged the former. Speeches represented oratory: newsbooks represented debate. Whereas printed pamphlets of speeches contributed to an imagined consensus, and were used in support of unanimity, newsbooks enervated political consensus, and focused on conflict.

Hence *Heads of Severall Proceedings* evoked conflict in its restrained prose by reporting the 'great oppositions and debate', a phrase which appears twice, over the remonstrance:

> Then *Master Peard* moved to have the remonstrance printed.
> *Master Palmer*, presently standing up, offered eight times to make a certificate in the behalfe of himselfe, and the rest of that part; against the vote of the house, as was conceived for the publishing of the same, Presently thereupon the house rose having sate in debate about it, till three of the clocke in the morning, the trayned Band attending the House all that time.

The very public dissemination of the debate surrounding the Irish Rebellion and the Grand Remonstrance in November 1641 encouraged the London apprentices who demonstrated against bishops the next month.[190] Public accusations that the king was stalling on Ireland created a situation in which a group of women could petition the parliament over the social effects of the consequent decay in trade. The petition was positively reported in a newsbook.[191] These protesters were an immediate audience for the newsbook. As news publications incorporated a greater number of people into the arena of political debate this debate was increasingly polarized. The production of news, like the remonstrance, generated conflicting opinions and permitted those divergent opinions already existing to become public.[192]

The Irish Rebellion was central to this development. Like informa-

[188] Cromartie, 'Printing of Parliamentary Speeches', 39–40.

[189] Cromartie, 'Printing of Parliamentary Speeches', 33, 37 and tables 1 and 2.

[190] Gardiner[1], x. 117; and *Heads of Severall Proceedings*, 6 Dec., 181.102. Also in Dec. 1642, when the citizens petitioned for peace; Gardiner[2], i. 74–5.

[191] Reported in *Diurnall Occurrences, Or, The Heads of the Proceedings* 5, 7 Feb. 1641[2], 181.205. Also Gardiner[1], x. 162–3. This does not fit the case presented by Anne Marie McEntee, '"The [Un]Civill-Sisterhood of Oranges and Lemons": Female Petitioners and Demonstrators, 1642–53', in Holstun, ed., *Pamphlet Wars*, 92–111.

[192] Fletcher, *Outbreak of the English Civil War*, 145. Cf. Brenner, *Merchants and Revolution*, 353–9.

tion from Scotland in 1639–40, news from Ireland was rare and it was in demand. Historians have not sufficiently emphasized the role played by news and rumour in the response of Britain to the uprising.[193] Unconfirmed reports, wild stories, and rumours were generated, fervid imaginations conjectured what they would. The impact on printing was enormous.[194] Both parliamentary debate and popular opinion responded to scarcity. Simultaneous shortage and excess is a recurrent trope in the history of newspapers.

There was much scrutiny of news. On 16 December Sidney Bere wrote to Sir John Penington, mentioning the order for printing the remonstrance, and enclosing the 'proceedings of the Parliament', probably meaning a newsbook. Penington was sent the same news by Captain Robert Slingsby on the same day.[195] Thomas Smith felt that the news in December was dividing king and parliament. He wrote to Penington on 17 December:

> For news, all I can say is here enclosed in two things, about which here is much discourse in Court, Parliament, and City, nay, and country too, and much discontent in all of them; factions increasing as men's humours vary, most men governing themselves rather by passion than judgement, and few regarding either religion or honesty in their censures of affairs of state, yet some such there be, and they much scandalized.[196]

Evan Seys, later Attorney-General under Cromwell, wrote from London to his father-in-law Robert Bridges at Woodchester through early 1642, passing on all the news he could gather, but rarely found any that was not in print. On 2 May he wrote:

> Since my letter on fryday laste to you, there is some very good newes brought out of Irelande as newe in printe you may read: there is since that time a message from the Kinge sent to the parlemt, w[ch] (when warranted by printe) I will alsoe sende you by the first: (it is concernenge the businesse & Magazin att Hull:) besides the printed pages I nowe sende I haue att this time noe more of newes to certify you.[197]

News was scarce, which made it a valuable commodity. Scarcity also

[193] Russell does gesture towards the problem of delayed communication in relation to negotiations with Scotland, *British Monarchies*, 27–146. The plot in Ireland was uncovered 22 Oct.: it broke in England on 1 Nov.; Gardiner[1], x. 41–4.

[194] See K. J. Lindley, 'The Impact of the 1641 Rebellion upon England and Wales 1641–5', *Irish Historical Studies*, 18 (1972), 143–76. Cromartie, and Lambert, 'Beginning of Printing', neglect the importance of this factor.

[195] *CSPD 1641–1643*, 201; PRO: SP 16/486/61; PRO: SP 16/486/63.

[196] *CSPD 1641–1643*, 206; PRO: SP 16/486/69.

[197] GCRO: D/DF F/244. Note 'warranted' by print. For this correspondence see D/DF F/241–5; On Seys see Geraint H. Jenkins, *The Foundations of Modern Wales* (Oxford, 1987), 33.

charmed news, giving it social and political moment, despite its mechanical reproduction. Brilliana, Lady Harley strained to know more, but was restricted as much by the paucity available to her husband as by the surprisingly efficient means of transmission.[198] News quickly found its way into print, as all those who enclosed pamphlets with correspondence testified, and MPs were little better informed than any literate Londoner.

A shortage of news meant an excess of rumour. Readers became reflexive about the nature of news. Thomas Wiseman wrote to Penington on 11 November, sending him printed news, and qualified it with the observation that 'oftimes we have much more printed than is true, especially when anything concerns the Papists, whom, though they are bad enough, our Preciser sort strive to make yet worse; and between them in no discoveries can we meet with truth'.[199] Wiseman, Sir Edward Nicholas, and Henry Cogan all reported, in letters dated 18 November, the supposed plots devised against parliament, behind the news of which no substance was discovered. Nicholas wrote that they were but the 'fictions of brain-sick Brownists'.[200] The very immaterial nature of information became fundamental to debate between politicians, capable of swinging the pendulum of advantage between Pym and his circle and those closer to the king. Fletcher writes, 'Pym and those close to him did not fabricate the plots they laid before the Commons, as Thomas Wiseman scoffed at them for doing. They were merely frightened men who gathered and circulated some of the combustible material of a bewildered nation.'[201] Concurrently anxieties were growing in London over responses to the rebellion: Fletcher writes of a 'general mood' generated in response to the news, of 'common gossip', amongst a group of 'informed Londoners'.[202] Opinion plays a comparable role in the accounts of Valerie Pearl and Robert Brenner.[203] Contemporary correspondence suggests that 'news', both name and thing, became more prominent and weighted.

The news led to the expectation of unity and to a desire for action. On 3 November Sir Henry Vane wrote to Nicholas expressing a hope that the news from Ireland would 'unite mens minds'. Three days later he was anxious to hear something concerning 'what good resolution'

[198] Jacqueline Eales, *Puritans and Roundheads: The Harleys of Brampton Bryan and the Outbreak of the English Civil War* (Cambridge, 1990), 121, 129–41, 152–3, and ch. 6.

[199] *CSPD 1641–1643*, 163; PRO: SP 16/485/72.

[200] PRO: SP 16/486/90, 92, 93 respectively. Cogan was Sir Henry Vane's clerk.

[201] Fletcher, *Outbreak of the English Civil War*, 139.

[202] Fletcher, *Outbreak of the English Civil War*, 137, 170.

[203] Brenner, *Merchants and Revolution*, 312, 333–4, 353–70; Valerie Pearl, *London and the Outbreak of the Puritan Revolution: City Government and National Politics, 1625–1643* (Oxford, 1961), *passim*.

parliament had taken touching Ireland.[204] The news demanded political action and foregrounded political inactivity. On 4 November Nicholas wrote to Penington juxtaposing news of the rebellion in Ireland 'made by the Papists' with an enclosed 'little pamphlet' containing an extract of a letter from the king 'declaring his constancy in the Protestant religion'.[205] Vane and Nicholas implied that the rebellion was a consequence of Catholics being flattered and tolerated for too long.[206] Petitions flooded in from the counties, showing that not only Londoners were informed and anxious. Just as parliament petitioned Charles with the remonstrances of 1628 and 1641, now the people resorted to demanding what John Milton called 'thir due'. They wanted action. Petitions were not a ritual process, but an overtly political one. In April 1642 Milton praised the Long Parliament:

> Insomuch that the meanest artizans and labourers, at other times also women, and often the younger sort of servants assembling with their complaints, and that sometimes in a lesse humble guise then for petitioners, have gone with confidence, that neither their meannesse would be rejected, nor their simplicity contemn'd, nor yet their urgency distasted . . . nor did they depart unsatisfi'd.[207]

Neither the sincerity nor the symbolic importance of these petitions should be underestimated.[208]

The news of the rebellion did at first achieve an ephemeral parliamentary harmony, all to Pym's advantage. With king and parliament divided space was created for a political faction to achieve ascendancy by responding in the most practical means. Fears and jealousies generated pressure for an appropriate response to the rebellion. Far from uniting the people, as Vane had hoped, the news from Ireland ultimately divided men's minds. According to Thomas Smith, writing to Penington on 29 December, the news had severed the king from his people:

> Though the storms are ceased at sea, they are not so on shore, for here with us such jealousies and discontents are daily raised by the Malignant party between the King and people, that we talk now of nothing but drawing of swords, and a

[204] PRO: SP 16/485/52; PRO: SP 16/485/64.

[205] PRO: SP 16/485/56.

[206] Vane to Nicholas, 9 Nov., PRO: SP 16/485/67; SP 16/485/56.

[207] *CPW* iii. 461; i. 926.

[208] Fletcher, *Outbreak of the English Civil War*, 191–227. Hughes, *Causes of the English Civil War*, 173; Pearl, *London and the Outbreak of the Puritan Revolution*, 210–28; Robert Ashton, *The English Civil War: Conservatism and Revolution 1603–1649* (1978; 1989), 142–3. Ashton wilfully accuses Pym of organizing the petitioning. The publication of petitions also helped to define a public political sphere in the sense that it encouraged other counties to present their own petitions. See also Patterson, *Reading between the Lines*, 57–79; Skerpan, *Rhetoric of Politics*, 73–6.

war between the Protestants and Papists, which God forbid; for though we may know the beginning no man can [foretell] the end and consequences of an intestine war.[209]

The rebellion and the remonstrance had stimulated great interest in news and in the political process, and then polarized popular political opinion. According to Smith, the division was not between king and parliament but between king and people. This was precisely the interpretation encouraged by the remonstrance and accompanying petition.

The news, as the petitioning shows, foregrounded the responsibility of parliament. Certain members encouraged this and used it to effect. The news from Ireland determined the allegiances of the City militants, and made the control of the London streets an important political objective.[210] On the first news of the rebellion Lord Mayor Gurney requested that the aldermen pursue contributions requested by both houses; to which request the City consented, providing that certain actions be taken against Catholic lords and bishops.[211] Trade in London had been disrupted since the spring of 1639 and the approach of war with Scotland.[212] At the end of 1641 indecision over Ireland had severely curtailed profits from foreign trade, the future of which was suspended in uncertainty.[213] The publication of the Grand Remonstrance was partly motivated by the desire to secure the citizens' continuing financial support. Money was necessary to raise troops, and propaganda was necessary to raise money. The remonstrance promised political solutions in return for immediate assistance. The king felt it succeeded: when he left London, after a belated effort to regain some control over the press, he believed that the city was his enemy.[214]

This public exposure worked to demystify government, empowering humble petitioners to express their own opinions.[215] This none the less heightened the prestige of parliament. This was an opportunity which Pym seized, for instance in his demands for a militia to protect the Houses.[216] A popular sphere of political debate, as it is familiar to us from the 1640s, was more than anything formed by the sudden impact

[209] *CSPD 1641–1643*, 215; PRO: SP 16/486/102.

[210] Brenner, *Merchants and Revolution*, 353–62.

[211] Reginald R. Sharpe, *London and the Kingdom*, 3 vols. (1894), ii. 146–7.

[212] Gardiner[1], ix, *passim*. C. V. Wedgwood, *The King's Peace 1637–1641* (1955), 265.

[213] John Taylor argued that the outbreak in preaching caused by the division between king and parliament aggravated the decay in trade by taking humble people away from their callings; *New Preachers, New* (Dec. 1641; T486), sigs. A3–A3[v].

[214] Fletcher, *Outbreak of the English Civil War*, 189; *British Monarchies*, 457; Mendle, 'De Facto Freedom', 328.

[215] See the accounts of the French revolutionary press cited in Introduction, n. 12, above; Vincent Price, *Public Opinion*, Communication Concepts, 4 (Newbury Park, Calif., 1992), 80–1.

[216] Gardiner[1], x. 80–106; Fletcher, *Outbreak of the English Civil War*, 158–90.

of the Irish Rebellion. This, and the way some members of parliament deliberately mediated concern over it, guaranteed a sustained market for news reports. A periodical update on the news from Ireland became both necessary and profitable, and pamphlets of news from Ireland were produced with frequency. A similar, though less significant, set of conditions developed with Scottish news earlier that year, and between 1638 and 1640, when the Scots printed and circulated a large body of propaganda in England.[217]

In this way news, means of its dissemination, and its role in political processes became more prominent. Demand for it became more urgent. Political configurations were redefined through November and December 1641, and the newsbook was endowed with special significance in these relations. The ritualized county petitions, published after their presentation, were also implicated. News of petitions from one county, disseminated in print, encouraged others to follow their example. Newsbooks and petitions helped to define a public sphere, one which many thought they could influence.[218]

A further foundation for periodicity was the newly promised permanence of parliament. The Triennial Act, 'for the preventing of inconveniences happening by the long intermission of Parliaments', in February 1641, and the 'Act to prevent inconveniences which may happen by the untimely adjourning, proroguing, or dissolving this present Parliament' in May 1641, were distant factors which assisted the appearance of the newsbook.[219] With this stability, a serial documenting the progress of the Long Parliament became more commercially viable. It is no coincidence that the parliament made Fast Sermons a regular, monthly event in December 1641.[220] With the Irish Rebellion we find a context in which periodicity was both valuable and necessary; we have an audience; we have the material waiting for us; we have a publisher. All that is left to be explained is the precipitating factor.

[217] Much 1641 material is in LT; for 1638–40, see *British Monarchies*, 68–9; *Personal Rule*, 813–17, 884, 902–9; Brenner, *Merchants and Revolution*, 333–4. On Scottish propaganda and interest in Scottish news in London see Freist, 'The World is Ruled and Governed by Opinion', 23, 209–28.

[218] Seaver, *Wallington's World*, 150–1. Wallington copied the messages of many petitions out of newsbooks into his notebooks. See Nehemiah Wallington, *Historical Notices of Events Occurring Chiefly in the Reign of Charles I*, 2 vols. ed. R. Webb (1869), ii. 1–21; BL: Add. MS 21935. Gardiner suggests that the London newsbooks directly reflected public opinion among London citizens: after describing the Battle of Nantwich, he writes, 'The London newspapers did but echo the sentiments of their readers.' Gardiner², i. 296.

[219] *Constitutional Documents*, 144–5, 158–9.

[220] Trevor-Roper, 'Fast Sermons', in *Religion, the Reformation and Social Change*, 306–8.

Newsbooks and the Grand Remonstrance

The Grand Remonstrance was central to the 'great debate and oppositions' which were offered to the public by *Heads of Severall Proceedings.* The debate crystallized the opposition between the king and parliament, and it required all the political resources of Pym to convince the Commons of its necessity.[221] A recriminatory history of the king's misdeeds throughout his reign, Thomas Carlyle correctly observed that however 'torpid' the 206 articles of the Grand Remonstrance seem to later readers, 'every line' of it 'once thrilled electrically into all men's hearts'.[222] Thomas May, writing around 1647, referred his readers to the remonstrance as a full account of the grievances of the people in the eight or nine years after the dissolution of the third Caroline parliament, thereby attributing to it the status of a true and non-instrumental narrative.[223] Yet instrumental it certainly was. Russell is right that the remonstrance 'is a manifesto of politics and religion rather than a landmark in the history of ideas', but, as Brenner has noted, 'in this case the medium was the message'.[224] It was preceded by a petition addressed to the people, and was intended to achieve an effect. Its historical significance lies in its breaking the bubble of parliamentary debate and addressing the public.

With hindsight Clarendon chose rather to criticize its divisive nature than the truth of its contents:

It contained a very bitter representation of all the illegal things which had been done from the first hour of the King's coming to the crown to that minute, with all those sharp reflections which could be made upon the King himself, the Queen, and Council; and published all the unreasonable jealousies of the present government, of the introducing Popery, and all other particulars which might disturb the minds of the people, which were enough discomposed.[225]

His analysis paralleled that of James Howell, who drew attention to the way the remonstrance surprised the king on his return from Scotland:

though he was brought in with a *Hosanna* at one end of the Town, he found a *Crucifige* at the other: For at *Westminster* ther was a Remonstrance fram'd, a work of many weeks, and voted in the dead of night, when most of the moderat and

[221] Fletcher, *Outbreak of the English Civil War,* 145–51; Gardiner[1], ix, *passim;* x. 64, 74–9. Gardiner emphasizes the long-term process of transformation of the proposed remonstrance through 1641. On the nature of the debates of 8–22 Nov., see *British Monarchies,* 425–7.

[222] Carlyle, ed., *Cromwell's Letters and Speeches,* i. 120.

[223] May, *History,* 16.

[224] Russell, *Causes,* 113; Brenner, *Merchants and Revolution,* 357.

[225] Clarendon, *History,* i. 417.

well-thoughted Members were retired to their rest, wherein with as much aggravation and artifice as could be, the least moat in Government was exposed to publick view, from the first day of His Majesties Inauguration to that very hour: Which Remonstrance as it did no good to the Publick but fill peoples heads with doubts, their hearts with gall, and retard the procedure of all businesse besides, so you may well think it could expect but cold entertainment with His Majesty.[226]

The remonstrance indicated an innovation in strategy, as Howell suggested, not only in the terms in which it outlined the king's policies, but in that it addressed not the object of its reproach, but the people.[227] The king's proposals were not intended for mass distribution: the remonstrance exposed him 'to publick view'.

This gives us pause to consider briefly the common principles behind *Heads of Severall Proceedings* and the Grand Remonstrance. The latter reflected back upon parliament's virtues as much as the king's failings. Both newsbook and remonstrance addressed an extra-parliamentary readership and exposed the role and workings of parliament to the public view. They encouraged the public to consider and understand. They happened the same week. A public sphere of political opinion was not created on 22 November, but the debate that day, and on 15 December, involved a symbolic leap in attitudes towards the polity. Without this expansion of the intellectual franchise to include a wider body of people, and hence of opinions, the newsbook would have made less sense. The development of a radical and political literature through the 1640s was only possible on this foundation.[228]

Printing was a subject of parliamentary contention, and this concern reflected notions of publicity. On 17 November John Thomas and Bernard Alsop were called on to defend themselves against a charge of printing scandalous pamphlets. On 18 November the committee for the printing of books met to advise on 'some meanes to restraine this licentious printing'.[229] The next day printing was discussed by the Lords.[230] On 24 November Pym complained of a 'false pamphlet', and separately Ralph Goodwin and Robert Reynolds complained about two printed books.[231] The Houses assumed they had power to influence

[226] *The Tru Informer*, written in 1642/3, first published in 1643; reprinted in *Divers Historical Discourses* (1661; H3068), 38; see 292–3, below.

[227] *Constitutional Documents*, 202–32. Fletcher, *Outbreak of the English Civil War*, 150. See also Christopher Hill, 'Political Discourse in Early Seventeenth-Century England', in Colin Jones, Malyn Newitt, and Stephen Roberts, eds., *Politics and People in Revolutionary England: Essays in Honour of Ivan Roots* (Oxford, 1986), 57–8.

[228] Corns, *Uncloistered Virtue*, 146.

[229] *LJ* iv. 443; *Journal of Sir Simonds D'Ewes*, ed. Coates, 164; *CJ* ii. 319.

[230] *LJ* iv. 447.

[231] *Journal of Sir Simonds D'Ewes*, ed. Coates, 191–2; *CJ* ii. 224.

printed debate even if manuscript publication was more difficult to control. That printing was considered to be more public than writing is indicated by the fact that on 22 November permission was extended to publish the remonstrance but not to print it. The decision to address the public, and in a potentially disreputable medium, indicates a deliberate strategy devised by the leaders in the Commons engaged in a self-marketing exercise. This strategy was fully realized on 15 December when William Purefoy ('None was more zealous in that dreadful catastrophe of the king's murder than Colonel Purefoy') successfully proposed that the remonstrance be printed.[232] George Peard, an expeditious parliamentarian during the war, followed him by proposing that the petition should also be printed. This encapsulated in miniature the changed focus of the radical leadership within the house, emphasizing the importance of broad support from the citizens of London, if not from the provinces.[233] The king's party persevered in their tradition of resisting appeals to public opinion and did not take a comparable propaganda initiative. Edward Hyde's official response to the remonstrance was written, according to its author, 'only to give vent to his own indignation, and without the least purpose of communicating it, or that any use should be made of it'. It was not published until January, impractically late in propaganda terms.[234] The horse had bolted.

The debate over Purefoy's proposal resulted in Pym's most important victory that month, with a majority of 52; the same motion had been defeated by 23 votes on 22 November. D'Ewes commented that 'if God had not prevented it there was a very great danger that mischiefe might have been done'.[235] In the earlier debate Sir John Colepeper said, 'All Remonstrances should bee addressed to the king, and not to the people, because hee only can redresse our grievances.'[236] The next month Purefoy suggested that the airing of the criticisms of the king would facilitate the raising of money for the Irish conflict. He made no efforts to conceal his meaning. Parliament was momentarily taking over the

[232] Purefoy was a republican, relatively inactive during the Protectorate but a supporter of the Long Parliament after Cromwell's death; and he was a puritan who, when governor of Warwick, was said 'to have signalized a furious fanatical zeal against the harmless cross in that town'. Mark Noble, *The Lives of the English Regicides*, 2 vols. (1798), ii. 134–7.

[233] See also Brenner, *Merchants and Revolution*, ch. 7.

[234] Clarendon, *History*, i. 492–6; *The Life of Edward Earl of Clarendon*, 2 vols. (Oxford, 1857), i. 79–81. An anonymous newsletter sent to Montagu, 29 Dec., comments on the king's written response; *HMC: Montagu*, 136–7.

[235] Fletcher, *Outbreak of the English Civil War*, 169; *British Monarchies*, 427–9; *Journal of Sir Simonds D'Ewes*, ed. Coates, 186.

[236] Sir Ralph Verney, *Notes of Proceedings in the Long Parliament Temp. Charles I*, ed. John Bruce, Camden Society, 31 (1845), 122.

traditional place of the monarch in exchanging political concessions for supply.

Acording to D'Ewes, Purefoy 'saied that hee conceived ther was [no] readier meanes to bring in monie then to cause our declaration to be printed that soe wee might satisfie the whole kingdome'. Parliament would expose its honesty and good intentions to the political nation. D'Ewes added, significantly, 'It seemes that many members weere privie to his intended motion.'[237] His intimation of a conspiracy is persuasive. The two debates over the printing of the remonstrance suggest that the appearance of the newsbook was deliberately timed. A group in parliament may have been directly responsible for the newsbook.

In both debates the appeal to the people in the prefatory petition annexed to the remonstrance caused the fiercest disputation. Remember Colepeper's words: 'All Remonstrances should be addressed to the king.' Rudyerd agreed with the history offered in the remonstrance, but feared that the 'prophetical part' would arouse unrealistic expectations in the people, which could not then be satisfied or controlled. Dering said: 'I did not dream that we should remonstrate downward, tell tales to the people, and talk of the King as a third person.' Colepeper agreed with him, complaining, 'This is a Remonstrance to the people.' Dering then had his speech printed.[238]

The importance of publicity was clearly articulated by the supporters of the remonstrance. Whereas Dering stated that 'Noe man can expresse the sense of the common people', Pym countered deftly, by denying that they were acting as a popular mouthpiece. Instead they were being publicly displayed in order that their audience might judge their virtue:

> The honour of the king lies in the saifety of the people, and wee must tell the truth . . .
>
> Remonstrances are not directed either to the king or the people, but shew the acts of this house.
>
> This declaration will binde the peoples hearts to us, when they see how we have been used.[239]

These three statements define his attitude to parliamentary publicity. Sir John Hampden stood firmly behind Pym: 'Noe counter remonstrance can come against us, being 'tis wholy true.' Holles honestly spoke in praise of publication: 'The kingdom consists of three sorts of men, the bad, the good, and the indifferent, and these wee hope to

[237] *Journal of Sir Simonds D'Ewes*, ed. Coates 294.

[238] Fletcher, *Outbreak of the English Civil War*, 151; *Journal of Sir Simonds D'Ewes*, ed. Coates, 184 n. 14; *British Monarchies*, 427–8.

[239] Verney, *Proceedings*, 122–3.

satisfie. They can turne the scales.' He added, 'All the necessary truth must be told.'[240] These were heady words.

An identifiable minority, Pym, Holles, Hampden, and Glyn, who referred back to the remonstrances of 1626 and 1628, all voiced pertinent beliefs, presenting a manifesto for the Grand Remonstrance. These were no doubt D'Ewes's 'privie members'. They wished to exculpate the honesty of some parliament men; they believed that the presentation of recent parliamentary proceedings would endear both the institution and certain individuals to the people; they suggested that the support of the people would vindicate the proceedings of the House. The publication of parliamentary proceedings would provide a context for reading the remonstrance and facilitate these three objectives. The remonstrance was like a speech, to be understood in the context of a debate. The debate on the remonstrance constitutes a manifesto for the newsbook: all the necessary truth must be told, the kingdom must be satisfied.

John Thomas had connections with parliament, and particularly Pym. He was a likely outlet for a semi-licit propaganda exercise.[241] He had repeatedly offended against printing ordinances, illicitly publishing speeches, sometimes omitting his name, sometimes borrowing someone else's.[242] Yet in this instance there were no sanctions against his action. In spite of numerous minatory gestures parliament was deafeningly silent: in effect, the debate about the propriety of Thomas's action had already been held. So on 29 November he released *Heads of Severall Proceedings* and put his initials on the title-page. The next week he did the same, and the history of the newspaper began to steamroller away. The scriveners must have been displeased, but parliament did not whisper a complaint.

Conclusions

The long-standing parallel between news and historical publications was extended in November 1641.[243] History had always teemed with meaning. After the Irish Rebellion it was necessary to have a weekly update. If such a history as the Grand Remonstrance contained was to be made public, and to be addressed to 'the people' as competent judges of

[240] Verney, *Proceedings*, 124–5; see also Patricia Crawford, *Denzil Holles, 1598–1680: A Study of his Political Career* (1979), 59–61.

[241] Cf. Lambert, 'Beginning of Printing', 53.

[242] *CJ* ii. 546, 801; Cromartie, 'Printing of Parliamentary Speeches', 38. Thomas was criticized by D'Ewes, *Two Speeches Spoken* (1642; D1256), title-page, for printing an earlier, inaccurate version of one of the speeches.

[243] *Personal Rule*, 646; Dahl, 223.

political matters, then the political moment was primed for an inexpensive weekly news publication. The history offered by the remonstrance, like that in Cooke's large volume of *Diurnall Occurrences*, brought the story forward to the point at which the newsbook appeared.

Heads of Several Proceedings is not, on the surface of it, a radical or a partisan document. Yet set in context of parliamentary encouragement of popular support and of Charles's neglect to court his subjects, this is how it appeared.[244] Hence it would be appropriate if the first newsbook appeared at the semi-official direction of a group within the Commons. In 1641 parliamentary opinion and public opinion cannot be entirely separated.[245] Newsbooks were not caused by the civil war, nor did they cause it, but they do have their own complex role in the circumstances out of which war arose.

James Howell thought that not only the Grand Remonstrance but attitudes to news in general contributed to the outbreak of war. He did not simply repeat the formulaic complaint about vulgar thirst for news. Instead he claimed that those men who were predisposed to oppose the Church and monarchy, essentially stereotypical puritans, were 'great listners after any Court-news'.[246] They deliberately sought to expose the weaknesses of the government. Simultaneously, 'Their greatest masterpiece of policy is to forge counterfeit news, and to divulge and disperse it as far as they can to amuse the world, for the advancement of their designs, and strengthing their party.' Likewise the Scots had 'punctual intelligence of every thing that passed at Court, as farre as what was debated in the Cabinet Councel, and spoken in the bedchamber'.[247] This way the rebels had the advantage of machiavellian policy over the king, who remained honestly ignorant of media manipulation. The Grand Remonstrance was a continuation of this aggressive policy. And the newsbook was the corollary of the remonstrance.

[244] Wallington and George Thomason are obvious examples: Seaver, *Wallington's World*, 34, 48, 153, 156; Spencer, 'Professional and Literary Connections of George Thomason', and ead., 'Politics of George Thomason'.

[245] Fletcher, *Outbreak of the English Civil War*, 191–227; Derek Hirst, 'The Defection of Sir Edward Dering, 1640–1641', *HJ* 15 (1972), 193–208.

[246] Ironically Howell was suspected of being the author of *Mercurius Melancholicus*; *Secret Rites*, 134–5.

[247] Howell, *Divers Historical Discourses*, 12, 13, 23.

3

Newsbooks, Style, and Political Rhetoric

> Since it is the opinion of some friends, that (as things now stand) it is better to invite those of a contrary opinion to the Parliament, by gentle expressions to see their errors, then to give them still tart language (which upon some natures (who are resolved in their Malignancy) do rather hurt then good) I shall for the future observe the first, and decline the latter, and give you simply a narration of affaires.[1]

NEWS events are not born but made.[2] As studies of modern newspapers have shown, a number of criteria determine the newsworthiness of any given event; from its unambiguity through its unexpectedness to its conformity to the reader's world-view.[3] All the news that's fit to print is too uncircumscribed; so editors print what fits. Once an event has been selected, it is transformed by diverse rhetorical practices into the kind of item found in newspapers, into a 'public idiom'.[4]

In news reporting, then and now, a plain narration utterly purged of opinion, a language without traces of tartness, is an ideal rather than a practical reality. In the mid-seventeenth century, before the institutionalization of newspapers, and before the development of journalistic and editorial techniques by centuries of approved practice, the process of constructing events as news was more diverse and haphazard. Printed news was probably then much closer to its oral counterpart than it is today, when newspapers inherit a longer tradition of rhetorical manufactures which give reporting an artificial flavour of orality.[5] This ensured rhetorical and linguistic heterogeneity.

Critics have long underscored the propaganda function of

[1] *KWI* 69, 27 Aug. 1644, 555, 214.069/E7(14).

[2] Roger Fowler, *Language in the News: Discourse and Ideology in the Press* (1991); Gaye Tuchman, *Making News: A Study in the Construction of Reality* (New York, 1978).

[3] Johann Galtung and Mari Ruge, 'Structuring and Selecting News', in Stanley Cohen and Jock Young, eds., *The Manufacture of News: Social Problems, Deviance, and the Mass Media* (1973), 62–72.

[4] Stuart Hall *et al.*, *Policing the Crisis: Mugging, the State, and Law and Order* (1978), 61.

[5] Fowler, *Language in the News*, ch. 4.

newsbooks, and associated it with lying and deception. Echoing the criticisms of contemporaries who had their own interests, newsbooks have been accused of facile ideological false-representation. 'For what is your weekly imployment but to smother the cleare truth of all proceedings at Court, and set a varnish upon all the Machiavellian cheats, unchristian practices, and horrible out-rages committed by the Plunderers and their complices in the Citie . . . ?' So asked Daniel Featley, in his *Sacra Nemesis, The Levites Scourge, or, Mercurius {Britan. Civicvs} Disciplined* (1644), and then it seemed a fair rhetorical question.[6] The accusation that newsbooks were machiavellian stuck, and this has prevented recognition of their complexity. They were not simply the instruments of faction, nor were they based upon an antiquated, unsceptical epistemology.[7]

There is no early manifesto for newsbooks, but their composition and intent were a complex mixture of idealism and instrumentalism. The first newsbooks presented news in an understated, non-interventionist manner, and their politics was predominantly shaped by the selection and juxtaposition of material and by the ways in which their readers received them. With the radicalization of civil war politics, newsbooks themselves were radicalized, and their objectives and rhetoric shifted.[8] The pretence to objectivity was fractured, and newsbook editors increasingly emphasized the premisses they did not share. Newsbook-editing became newsbook-writing. We should therefore ask not what percentage of the facts in newsbooks were true, but how did newsbooks imagine and accumulate a repository of rhetorical strategies for presenting information?

In 1641 the use of the vernacular in popular writing was a relatively recent practice. The creation of a domestic periodical news press was an important stage in the shift towards a vernacular printed culture which would still take decades to complete. Hence the rhetoric of newsbooks was improvised. The linguistic and generic ingredients of the early newsbooks were drawn from three main sources: oral transmission of news, the manuscript newsletter trade, and the indigenous tradition of pamphleteering, which had first risen to prominence in the 1580s.

The input from learned culture was minimal. This was for two rea-

[6] Daniel Featley, *Sacra Nemesis* (Oxford, 1644; F594), 2–3.

[7] Herd, *March of Journalism*, 26. 'News reporting', McKeon writes, 'retains its ties to non-typographical modes and to the relatively nonhistoricist epistemologies with which they are associated'; he associates 'uncriticial subjectivism' with an 'old' scribal culture; *Origins of the English Novel*, 48–50. Contrast *Secret Rites*; Love, *Scribal Publication*; *L&R*; Watt, *Cheap Print and Popular Piety*.

[8] David Wootton, 'From Rebellion to Revolution: The Crisis of the Winter of 1642/3 and the Origins of Civil War Radicalism', *English Historical Review*, 105 (1990), 654–69.

sons. First, many editors were not learned men. Secondly, a large constituency of their readers was not well educated. For newsbooks as well as pamphlets an accessible language had to be generated for the purposes of effective communication. This language did derive from longer-term developments in the history of rhetoric and political thought, but only through the popular repercussions of widely disseminated shifts.

The language of newsbooks was not plucked from the air. Aristotle's virtues of style, clarity, brevity, and appropriateness were all more or less manifested by newsbooks. Editors borrowed from a tradition of anti-Ciceronian or 'attic' prose, a vernacular plain style which they transformed into journalism.[9] This plain style was in part a consequence of the pamphleteer's need to exile ambiguity. During the civil war this increased, along with the need for clarity and proselytizing persuasiveness.[10] The tradition of vernacular political writing which fed into journalism also registered the influence of Tacitist European thought. While this strain was important to newsbooks as a genre, it was seldom important to individual editors, not all of whom had read Tacitus let alone Lipsius, who established Tacitus as a central figure in the new humanism of the late sixteenth century.[11] Newsbooks appeared towards the end of the Tacitist revival, when its intellectual tremors had, more or less, been popularized. There was also an important indigenous tradition: the continuities between the Lollards, the Levellers, and William Blake have been traced largely in terms of ideas, but there may have been an equal linguistic inheritance.[12] The plain speaking of this radical tradition influenced vernacular journalism in style, though not necessarily in radical thought.

Elizabeth Skerpan has outlined the use of simplified forms of neo-Ramist rhetoric in political pamphlets before and during the civil wars. She shows how pamphleteers deployed epideictic, deliberative, and forensic rhetoric, and how the use and success of these genres was influenced by political context. Her study suggests how complex rhetorical theories could inform and be subsumed under notions of style.[13] Many readers did not understand the rules and implications of formal

[9] Morris W. Croll, '"Attic Prose" in the Seventeenth Century', in *Style, Rhetoric, and Rhythm: Essays by Morris W. Croll*, ed. J. Max Patrick, Robert O. Evans, John M. Wallace, and R. J. Schoek (Princeton, 1966), 51–101.

[10] Hugh Macdonald, 'Another Aspect of Seventeenth-Century Prose', *Review of English Studies*, 19 (1943), 40–1.

[11] Richard Tuck, *Philosophy and Government 1572–1651* (Cambridge, 1993).

[12] Christopher Hill, 'From Lollards to Levellers', in *Religion and Politics in 17th Century England* (Brighton, 1986), 89–116; E. P. Thompson, *Witness against the Beast: William Blake and the Moral Law* (Cambridge, 1993).

[13] Skerpan, *Rhetoric of Politics*; review by Tom Corns, *RES*[2] 44 (1995), 94–5.

rhetoric.[14] Illocutionary force could also be applied through the use of literary genre, to which a wider group of readers were sensitive, particularly in the 1640s, when the flux and reformation of literary genres were open to manipulation by writers of pamphlets. Genres developed precise political significations.[15] Literature was polemicized in the 1640s, and all forms of writing expressed political allegiances through the deployment of generic patterns.[16]

These rhetorical, stylistic, and generic contexts are requisite to understanding the newsbook. Yet the mechanics of representation must also be analysed on a micro-scale, through the particulars of individual usage. An exhaustive description of the changing rhetoric of newsbooks would be illimitable, stretching from the abstract heights of eloquence to the exiguous dribbles of accidental slips, caused by the circumstances of early-modern printing houses. To give a universal account would be to shipwreck on Brobdingnag. This chapter, then, gives a general account of the varieties of rhetorical strategies deployed in newsbooks and how they developed and expanded through the decade.

The plain style of the factious newsbook

Though they were increasingly the voice of faction, the dominant styles of 1642 newsbooks combined familiar elements: plain narrations of fact, and, increasingly, the reproduction of documents; occasional commendations of the monumental efforts made for the good of the kingdom by the dedicated and godly members of parliament; sometimes they twitched at the threat of sanctions or recriminations. Early newsbooks were written in a number of stylistic strains uneasily deriving from diverse sources. The following example, dated 23 July, is from John Thomas's *A Perfect Diurnall, Or the proceedings in Parliament*:

> This day, the Earle of *HOLLOND* brought a Message from his Majesty, in Answer to the late Petition of both Houses; consisting of fower points, *Viz.*
>
> I.
>
> *That the Towne of* Hull *should be surrendred vnto Him.*
>
> II.
>
> *That the sole claime and interest in the* Militia, *by the* Parliament; *should be vtterly disclaimed.*

[14] Contrary to Clark, *Elizabethan Pamphleteers*, 225.

[15] *Secret Rites*; *L&R*; Achinstein, *Milton and the Revolutionary Reader*, David Quint, *Epic and Empire: Politics and Generic Form from Virgil to Milton* (Princeton, 1993).

[16] Zwicker, *Lines of Authority*, 9–36.

III.

That all the Shipps now at Sea, should be Delivered up, into His Maiesties Hands.

IIII.

That the Parliament *should be adiourned to some other place, where His Maiesty should thinke fit.*

And after mature deliberation hereof, both Houses Voted.

I.

That it was not for the Kingdomes safety, to deliver up the Towne of *Hull*, until such time as his Majesties Forces were disbanded.

II.

That for the *Militia*, they held it most fitting (according to his Majesties former desires) to settle it by Bill.

III.

For the Shipping, they thought it could not be put into more surer hands then now it is both for the defence of his Majesty and Kingdome.

IIII.

Fourthly that the Parliament was in the most Eminent place of the Kingdome, and where his Maiestie might abide in most peace and safetie, and there upon both Houses ordered that the Earle of *Essex* should forth with raise forces for the defence of his Maiestie and Kingdome.[17]

The editorial material was non-inflammatory, particularly in comparison with the content. The typography gestured towards the format of the original documents. This authenticated the report, implicitly referencing the editor's sources. *A Perfect Relation, or Svmmarie of all the Declarations, Messages, And Answers, Passages and Proceedings between the Kings Majesty, and both Houses of Parliament*, a short-lived serial by Francis Coles, claimed this authenticity in its title.[18] From the very earliest newsbooks, this typographical strategy, along with a parallel emphasis on eye-witnessing, was used to legitimize the contents. As *Civicus* professed: 'The most unquestionable way to make good intelligence, is to deliver it in the same Letters from which it was received.'[19]

The point-for-point response not only looked good on the page: it evoked a dialogue. The authentic voices of the king and parliament found a public stage in the newsbook. The dialogue was manipulated by the editor, as if in invisible parentheses, but none the less purported to allow the conversants to speak for themselves. The reproduction of

17 *Perfect Diurnall*, 25 July 1642, 7–8, 517.2/E202(24).

18 Beginning 29 Sept. 1642, 527.1–2/E240(15, 39).

19 *Civicus* 146, 10 Mar. 1646, 2067, 298.146/E327(16).

speeches and petitions invited readers to follow and interpret events as they unfolded.[20] The juxtaposition of texts performed a correlation function, bringing together contrasting ideas and views and co-ordinating public reactions. In this way the mass media is a principal means by which the public communicates and spectators interact.[21] The presentation of original documents created an interpretative space, permitting the reader freedom to respond. Readers were meant to make up their own minds: and the evidence suggests that they did.

The language of newsbooks could be thoroughly passive, such as when representing proceedings in parliament, the staple diet of any 1642 newsbook:

Wednesday.

It was ordered by the Commons, that the moneyes raised in the severall Countreys, for Coat, and Conduct-money, should be forthwith disposed of by the Deputy Lieutenants for the County.

Then the Committee appointed to make the Propositions to the City of *London* for the raising of Horse, made report to the House, that they the Citizens did very chearefully accept of the same; there being already great store of Plate and Moneyes brought into *Guild-hall* for that purpose.

Then there was a Petition presented to the House by the Committee to be sent to His Majestie, with some inlargements upon the *Yorke-shire* Petition, and to desire His Majestie to accept of the same, which was ordered to bee forthwith sent to *Yorke.* And a vote then passed by both Houses, That the Committee at *Yorke* should be sent for backe to the Parliament. Whereupon there was a Committee of both Houses appointed to frame a Letter to that purpose.

Then a new Booke of Rates was brought into the Commons, and once read.

There were then Instructions drawne up to bee sent to the Deputie Lieutenants of the severall Countyes, to tender the Propositions for the raising of Horse for the service of the King and Parliament, to the Countreyes.[22]

This typical example illustrates the 'style' in which parliamentary orders were represented, in tone not unlike the printed journals of the Commons. This is not the explosive, scurrilous writing likely to start or perpetuate a war: it was factual, mundane, and betrayed no signs of restlessness. Nothing suggests a writer restricting himself from speaking out. Yet a 1642 reader would have been confronting an unfamiliar genre and typographical format, and the unadorned news, in a contemporary context, would have been exciting and politically charged in itself. What is now buried under three and a half centuries might once have been electrifying.

Not all newsbooks were so purely literal. The following dates from 13 July 1642, when commissioners from the Lords were in the north negotiating with the king:

[20] Cf. Skerpan, *Rhetoric of Politics*, 79. [21] Price, *Public Opinion*, 81.

[22] *Perfect Diurnall* 1, 20 June 1642, 3–4, 509.1/E202(8).

As the King was Bowling, there was scatter'd a paper with Verses, very scandalous against Mr. Pym, and shewed the King, who having read them, tore them in pieces, and with a sad looke said, *such libellous Rascals hath broke the peace of the Kingdom, and if Iustice did but lay hold of them, peoples minds would be quickly calm'd*, he that showed them very likely looked for better thankes.

The Lords here sit as close, as the Houses of Parliament doe at *London*, let every good heart pray their consultations may meet in the Glory of God and this Kingdome.[23]

The king's speech was demarked, implying exact quotation, by the use of italic, and the newsbook writer incorporated an aside into the same sentence. The writer at once sought to position his own opinion, deferential to the parliament, while presenting the incident in a dramatic framework. The king's sporting activity is interrupted, and the original libel destroyed, leaving the reader with only the king's interpretation; then the scene is juxtaposed with the pious and industrious Houses. This emphasizes the distance between the two in geographical, political, and perhaps sentimental terms. Men are depicted to signify ideas. The device is fairly novelistic.

It was normative to be partisan when reporting on Ireland. The original reports were themselves likely to be naïvely brutal: 'wee killed the Lord *Dunboynes* brother, Colonell *Berne*, and Colonell *Butler*, and brought their heads along, this being done, every one of us fell on our knees, and gave God thankes for a safe deliverance, and so wee marched.'[24] Pecke's *Continvation Of certain Speciall and Remarkable Passages* concluded a report of a military victory at Galloway thus:

A chiefe thing remarkeable in this victory was, when our forces sett upon the Rebells they were in their quarters making merry, and had a great feast provided in Tryumph that they had brought *Galloway* to so low a condition, that they were not able to keep it from them two dayes later, in which time they presumed they would be all starved, but it fell out with these Rebels as it once did with the Isralites, when they Rebelled against God for [w]hen the meat was in their mouthes, the wrath of God fell amongest them.[25]

Providentialism was a useful means to expediency for a cautious newsbook writer in 1642. Before the war it was in such asides that the author or editor's political position was most clearly audible.

The subtleties of this self-control are illustrated by comparison with a passage from *Mercurius Aulicus* in February 1643, describing the reception of news at the court in Oxford:

[23] *Diurnall out of the North*, 18 July 1642, 7, 110.1/E107(11).

[24] *Occvrrences from Ireland* 3, 22 Apr., published 3 May 1642, sig. A3v, 464.3.

[25] *Continvation* 10, 29 Sept. 1642, 7, 638.10/E240(16).

This day was plentifull in newes, and from severall parts. From *London* it was signified by Letters of the fourth of February, that the severe proceedings of the two Houses of Parliament, in the manner formerly expressed, had very much alienated the affections of their owne party, who began to be somewhat sensible of the oppression and calamities which they had drawne upon themselves: and that it was conceived if that course went on, (so generall an aversenesse was growne among them) there would be fewer prisoners there then Freemen. And it was very confidently reported by some, who came from thence since the returne of the Committee, that some had caused the Propositions, with His Majesties Answer, to be printed by a different Copie from that which was sent hither, and returned to them: the Propositions being made more moderate than those sent hither by the Houses, and the King's Answer more unpleasing then He gave them here. A very pestilent devise whosoever it was, to abuse the subject.[26]

This passage can probably be ascribed to Peter Heylin's 'mannered' and 'copious style' and 'leisurely narration' rather than John Berkenhead's 'racy phrasing and spicy humour'.[27] While there is a careful polemical structure and a clear propagandistic intent behind this paragraph, it has none of the purely aggressive, polemical content that would later be found in Berkenhead's *Mercurius Bellicus* (1648), which would admit of no comparison with a plain-style 1642 newsbook. The source of the news was, once again, a letter. Here, however, the editor moved away from the parameters of strict reporting and blended the information with other material, confident in tone. This imposition of the writer's own emotion was rare in 1642 newsbooks. Furthermore, the syntactical structure implied a more considered response to the information. The reported speech of early London newsbooks, like the repetitive lists of parliamentary orders, made way for awkwardness. Formally clumsy prose suggested that the news was raw and un-intermediated. The facts were spare, curt, and devoid of active preparation. Heylin by contrast introduced long, periodic sentences; which, if not always elegant, showed an awareness of the role of linguistic registers in maintaining social and moral differentiation.[28] The digested prose implied a reader already committed to a view of the truth, and was a challenge to the plain style of the London newsbooks. The language communicated a level of information beyond and above the facts.

Selection and juxtaposition formed the basis of political balance in the 1642 newsbooks, as illustrated in the following two examples, dated 6 September. The first is from *True and Remarkable Passages from Several places in this Kingdome*:

Tuesday came letters from *Nottingham*, intimating that his Maiesty hath confined the Earle of Lecester, and refuseth to let him goe for Ireland; by which

[26] *Aulicus* 6, [11 Feb. 1643], 74, 275.106A&B/E246(26); *OR* i. 96.
[27] *Berkenhead*, 33. [28] e.g. *MTN* 92–5.

means the rebels are like to be much incouraged, and the Protestants disheartned, who daily expect his comming with assistance. Vpon debate thereof it was ordered, a Message should be forthwith sent to his Maiesty, to desire him not to make any longer stay of the Lord Deputy; and if he shall, the danger is so great that may fall by the same, that such course must be taken by both houses of Parliament, that shal prevent future danger threatned, and secure that bleeding Kingdome with speedy reliefe, desiring a speedy answer from his Maiesty to the same.[29]

The interpretation of this episode depends on the reader's inference of the motivation of the king and Leicester. In this instance, the latter was represented as passive. It also depends on whether the reader infers that the second half of this extract should have been in quotation marks. If not, then the passage clearly established the writer's allegiance to the parliament: he adopts an antagonistic attitude to the king, for instance in the term 'bleeding'. This personal perspective was not yet the role of a newsbook editor, hence parliament's words were being spoken as the writer's own.[30] Quite a different effect was produced by the corresponding report in Coles and Leach's *Continvation Of certain Speciall and Remarkable passages*:

The Houses also received advertisement by Letters from *Nottingham*, that the Earle of *Leicester*, upon pretence of going to His Majesty to take his leave, hath assisted His Majesty with moneys and other provisions, for the maintaining of the Warre against the Parliament, and done other ill offices betwixt His Majesty and the Parliament, whereupon the Commons at a conference, declared to the Lords that in respect of His carriage in that perticular and his neglect of setting forward for *Ireland*, having so long had his dispatches, and an Order of Parliament, for His departure by such a time; That they conceive him altogether unfit of such a trust, and desires the Lords to take the same into consideration, that there may bee an other appointed in his place.[31]

The use of alternative sources possibly furnished this newsbook with a substantially different interpretation. In this reading, Leicester himself is blamed for the bleeding kingdom of Ireland, and it is towards him that the hostility of the newsbook writer and parliament is directed. These examples, through their contrast, show the limits of criticism and linguistic hostility which the 1642 newsbook-editor respected.

The style of the early newsbooks can be characterized as the absence of 'style'. The horizons of the newsbook were outwardly, not inwardly,

[29] *True and Remarkable Passages* (10 Sept. 1642; T2577/E116(28)), sig. A3. Thomason added '& abroad' to the title.

[30] For an overview based on secondary material, see Hart, *Views on the News*.

[31] *Continvation Of certain Speciall and Remarkable passages* 6, 9 Sept. 1642, 2, 638.06/E116(26); probably written by Pecke. Leicester later retaliated by attacking *The Moderate*; *Sydney Papers*, ed. Blencowe, 79.

defined: they were anthologies of other modes of speech and writing, loosely bound in a small quarto. It was the formal, typographical elements, the title and the daily heads, which defined it as a newsbook, while the text was essentially heterogeneous, given thrust and coherence only by inclusion and juxtaposition. The early newsbook was all surface and no depth.

Contemporaries saw these texts as intrinsically divisive, and their authors as a generation of vipers, spreading plague and consternation. This was something of a rhetorical overstatement, conforming to the rules of a vituperative genre, but it does suggest something about the reception of this plain, undecorative style. There was a sharp division between the apparent intentionality of newsbooks and their social significance. Speech acts are always open to interpretation and misappropriation.

The fall of the newsbook

Hostile accounts suggested that newsbooks exacerbated the deterioration of political exchange through 1642. The practical relationship between rhetoric and reality was a complex one, but these critiques are a necessary though limited source. *A Presse full of Pamphlets*, published in April 1642, suggested that newsbooks were initially honest publications which turned to fabrication for the sake of profit. A similar point was iterated five years later in *A Fresh Whip For all scandalous Lyers.*[32] These interesting commentaries should not be read literally, but they do reflect a genuine shift in the character of newsbooks during the first year of their existence. The fantastic attacks of the later 1640s are difficult to reconcile with the bland, zero-degree texts of 1641, which accommodated differences of argument in a non-controversial diction and syntax:

> The Citizens and Prentices gathering againe about the Houses, occasioned the House of Commons to enter againe into consideration thereof, and upon scanning of their desires, there was a Conference with the Lords upon it, they moving the Lords that there might be a speedy calling of the Bishops that were delinquents to their answers, which might give some satisfaction to the Citizens in present, while some time might be spared for the further consultation of their Petition, which the Lords desired time to consider of.
>
> The House of Commons then entred upon the dispatch of reliefe for *Ireland*, and agreed upon convenient moneys to be raised, for the more speedy hasting thereof.

[32] Ch. 1 n. 12, above. There was greater continuity in the anti-newsbook literature than in the newsbooks themselves.

This Evening the Prentices broke into the *Abbey*, forcing open one of the doores, but finding some resistance by the Archbishop of *Yorkes* servants (still resident at the Deane of *Westminsters* house) they were for that time repulsed, not without some hurt, Sir *Richard Wiseman* and others being hurt by the flinging of stones and otherwise.

Whereupon it was ordered, that a competent part of the Trayned Band should guard the Cathedrall (words being given out of a pulling it downe) till time might redresse those disorders, which watched in the body of the Church all that night, having divers of the Officers of the Church, who stood in the Battlements thereof, all that night for assistance.

Wednesday the Citizens and Prentices gathered againe together about the Houses of Parliament, many of them being armed with Halberds and other offensive weapons very early in the morning before the Houses met, and upon their going to the Houses, they clamoured (as the two dayes before) against the Bishops and the Popish Lords for their removall.[33]

Editors and publishers made a serious attempt to purvey news. They steered a course far from pamphlet satires and evangelical sermons decrying malignancy. They were, none the less, circumstantially allied to the parliament. They employed consensual rhetoric, yet followed the lead of parliament; and when parliamentary disunity was exposed, they discovered literary means of partisanship.

The proliferation of pamphlets and newsbooks was repeatedly drawn to the attention of the Commons, but the resulting ordinances were ineffectual.[34] Until March newsbooks reported printing restrictions with remarkable unreflexiveness. On 28 March the Commons intervened directly and harshly:

Resolved, upon the Question, That the *Diurnal* from the Fourteenth of *March* last to the One-and-twentieth, printed by *Robert Wood*, is false and scandalous to the King's Majesty, and the Parliament; and contains in it divers seditious Passages, and of dangerous Consequence.

Resolved, That *Robert Wood* shall be forthwith sent for, as a Delinquent, by the Serjeant at Arms attending on this House, for printing the said Diurnal.

Resolved, upon the Question, That what Person soever shall print . . . sell any Act or Passages of this House under the Name of a *Diurnal*, or otherwise, without the particular Licence of this House, shall be reported a high Contemner and Breaker of the Privilege of Parliament, and so punished accordingly.[35]

[33] *Divrnal Occurrences: Or, The Heads of severall proceedings*, 3 Jan. 1642, sigs. A2ᵛ–A3, 181.105/E201(5).

[34] Siebert, 180–3; Ch. 1 n. 285, above.

[35] Ellipsis in original; *CJ* ii. 500–1. Four other printers of pamphlets were also sent for as delinquents on the same day: John Franc, John Wright, Gregory Dexter, and William Humphreyvile.

Sir Simonds D'Ewes, conscious of a decline in the quality of newsbooks, observed that in the early days, 'ther came out but one each weeke, & then ther was some moderate truth in them. But now ther are sometimes printed twelve or fourteene in a week, & they commonlie labour in that worke all the Lords day, to gett them readie by monday morning.'[36] His sentiment was echoed throughout the decade. Like *A Fresh Whip For all scandalous Lyers*, D'Ewes associated the breaking of the Sabbath with the decline into poor quality and falsehood.[37]

But the Commons were reacting to a specific offence. There were seven newsbooks for the week 14–21 March;[38] only one was named in the Commons' resolution, the *Continuation* printed by Robert Wood.[39] Wood's *Continuation* showed some sign of incipient royalism. This was probably accidental, as Wood put his name on the title-page at a time when this was uncommon. The news for Monday 14 March included the following items:

In the Lords House was read a Message from his Majesty, resident at *Huntington*, importing his Majesties intention to go to *Yorke*, and containing his Majesties Answer to the Declaration of both Houses of Parliament, sent by them, and presented to his Majesty the week before: Wherin his Majesty declared, that he desired the Parliament to expedite withall speed their intended Aid and Assistance for *Ireland*; that his Majesty was informed, nothing Enacted or Ordered by the Parliament, without his Assent therto, was binding to the Subject, or ought by them to be Obeyed; That the *Militia* of the Kingdome ought not to be Ordered without his consent; and that his Message of the 20. of *Ianuarie* is a sufficient Answer to their Declaration; as is by his Majesty conceived, which is in this Declaration again reiterated: which being read, was by the Lords sent down to the House of Commons. . . .

This day also was read in the House of Commons a Letter from *Ireland* to his Majesty: wherein is contained that the Rebels intentions in wageing of war, was not as the Scots, for lucre of gain, to raise there own fortunes by the ruine of others, but for Conscience sake, in duty to God and his Majesty, the preservation of his honour and Prerogatives, and rightfull government over them, and that they had none other intentions, should in time be made manifest to the whole world.

This day also there came Letters from *Spain, France*, and *Italy*, to his Majesty: profering in the same Aid and Assistance to his Majesty for the defence of his

[36] BL: Harl. MS 163, f. 52ᵛ, qu. Zagorin, *Court and the Country*, 206.

[37] *A Fresh Whip*, 3. Unlike the majority of critics, D'Ewes believed that piety could be maintained through an increase in preaching; Fletcher, *Outbreak of the English Civil War*, 105.

[38] *Continuation*, 67.10, 68.10A, 68.10B, 623.10; *A Perfect Diurnall*, 507.10A&B; *True Diurnall*, 625.2, 626.10.

[39] *Continuation* 10, 21 Mar. 1642, 68.10A; Bod.: Hope adds. 1136(29). Frank, always limited by his sources, glosses briefly over the incident because the offending item is not in LT: *Beginnings*, 22.

Regall Power, and prerogatives if intrenched upon, and individed to be abridged by his Parliament . . .

The publicity given to the king's 'Answer', the respect paid to the Irish rebels, and the demoralizing threat of foreign troops was likely to antagonize some active members of parliament. The text expressed distinct partisanship through its presentation of news. The other newsbooks for this week were quite different, either ignoring this news or passing briefly over it. *A Continuation* did not detail the Commons' unanimous response to the king's 'Answer', because 'the particular Votes' were already 'published in Print'.[40]

The most galling item, sufficient to galvanize the Commons, was dated Saturday 19 March:

In the House of Commons they received a Message from the Lords, wherein the Lords desired that house to take into their considerations the great abuses of printing scandalous and libellous Pamphlets: in defamation and abuse of the persons and honours of divers of the Lords: And the mixing the Lords with the Commons in the *Occurrences:* upon which it was Ordered by the house of Commons, that warrants should issue out for divers Printers to bring them before the house to answer the same.

In his copy John Rushworth marked this item, noting in shorthand 'observe'.[41] It is possible that this journalist had his story confused. A different *Continuation of the true Diurnall* reported:

The Lords then received a Complaint which was made to the House concerning the printing of some passages betwixt his Majesty and the late Committee, imployed with the Declaration, over and above his Message sent in answer to it, which upon debate they found not fitting, and therefore ordered the Printer should bee brought to the House as a delinquent. . . .

Order issued out this day from the Lords House for the bringing in of a Printer before them, for printing a private Conference betwixt his Majesty and the Lords, sent to him with the Houses last Declaration.[42]

William Gaye and Robert Fowler were sent for by the Commons.[43] The very different details suggest either that Wood's author was writing utter

[40] *Continuation* 10, 63–4, 65.

[41] *Continuation* 10, 69. Neither Lords nor Commons journals record this incident: though printers were sent for on Thurs. and Fri. Rushworth's copy formerly Bod.: Fairfax newsbooks 1; now Arch. H e.108, f. 128.

[42] *Continuation* 10, 21 Mar. 1642, 77–9, 68.10B, Bod.: Wood 373(41). Cf. *LJ* iv. 652–3. On 18 Mar. the Lords also ordered the judges to prepare a draft for a bill regulating printing.

[43] 18 Mar.; *CJ* ii. 485. The contentious book was *Some Passages that happened the 9th. of March between the Kings Majestie, and the committee* (1642; S4552/669f.3(54)). Gaye claimed that he received the copy from Edward Littleton's clerk; *LJ* iv. 653. Fowler published another edition dated 1641; Wing S4551, not in LT. Given Gaye's source, his was the first edition. Fowler was probably already a marked man for having published another edition of Robert Barker's *His Majesties Message to Parliament upon his Removall to the Citie of York* (15 Mar.; C2467/669f.3(57)). Fowler's reprint is Wing C2471, not in LT.

fiction or that he provided a unique source for a complaint about newsbooks nine days before the resolution which led to their suppression.

The complaint was about the mixing of the proceedings in the Upper and Lower Houses. In other words, as far as Lords were concerned, newsbooks were developing too active an editorial technique. They wanted to reverse the long-standing custom of including proceedings of both Houses in 'Occurrences', which stemmed right back to the manuscripts of early 1641. When a publisher had the nerve to report the Lords' dissatisfaction in a quasi-royalist publication which blatantly combined the proceedings of both Houses within adjacent paragraphs the Commons objected.

Many printers and publishers were charged, and it may be erroneous to distinguish between newsbooks and other cheap print which caused offence. On the other hand it took not six pro-parliament *Diurnalls*, but one unflattering newsbook, to provoke censure and effective prohibition. The specific offence was matched by a wider perception of decay. All newsbooks were blackened by the punishment, whereas occasional pamphlets suffered no such fate.

The next week, the first week in April, *A Perfect Diurnall* appeared alone, and then there were no newsbooks until May.[44] Rushworth commented on the gap, 'From Aprill 2 unto June 6th', in his collection of newsbooks.[45] Dillingham wrote to Lord Montagu, 'The printers being frighted, the diurnals cease, which, though to me trouble yet joy for I endure not news common.'[46] As with the Commons' decision to restrict printing of the remonstrance, the scriveners were gratified.

Six months after the newsbook had been invented the myth of the golden age, of the pre-lapsarian newsbook, was already in place. Newsbooks rose suddenly, and within half a year they fell. The honest scribes had bitten the apple, 'drownd their wits' in ale, and been succeeded by a certain 'stampe of English-men, who think a thing to be never well enough do[ne] till it be overdone, and prove uselesse or hurtfull'.[47] The first victim was truth, the second was the king.

Overt political allegiance in newsbooks developed through 1642.

[44] See the chronological list in N&S, p. 622. I am rejecting Lambert's proposition that the newsbooks for April have simply been lost. 'Beginning of Printing', 56. Take Dillingham's comment which follows, for example. Dillingham was in a position to know, and it was to his pecuniary advantage to know. It is improbable that all newsbooks for Apr. would disappear, leaving a massive dent in average survival figures. Moreover the recommencement of issue numbers in May 1642 is evidence for discontinuity.

[45] Bod.: Arch. H e.108, f. 143^{v}.

[46] Written between 12 and 16 Apr. 1642, *HMC: Montagu*, 148.

[47] *A Presse full of Pamphlets*, sigs. A3–A3^{v}.

Though March was a significant turning point in attitudes, the more substantial changes were gradual. Frank attributes to the second half of the year 'the growth of partisanship, the move away from cautious neutrality'.[48] The tidy typography of the 1641 and early 1642 issues, with neat, regular headings and uniform type size, was another casualty of the period (though it was to reappear in some newsbooks in 1643). The situation worsened after the intervention of parliament. Despite the impressive turnover in titles within this tough but reputedly lucrative market, none held that competition improved the service. Even after a brief six months of existence newsbooks reflected if not a fading glory, at least a diminished respectability. But as this respectability dwindled, the attributions of extraordinary power over the vulgar grew until Marchamont Nedham could vie with the Devil with a pen as big as a weaver's beam.[49]

Editorial techniques: Weekly Intelligence

Weekly Intelligence from Severall parts of this Kingdome was a short-lived serial appearing just twice in October 1642, distinguished by short, lucid reports and very clear typography.[50] The news items were broken up into fragments, each with its own heading indicating date and place of origin. White space divided the page. This was typical of 1642 newsbooks. Later in the decade editors frequently used linking phrases within and between reports: in 1645 *Mercurius Veridicus* promised 'his weekly Mercury shall not be disjoynted'.[51] The careful use of space in *Weekly Intelligence* made the text easier to comprehend for the less proficient reader.

One of the more lucid correspondents to *Weekly Intelligence* was an anonymous officer in the Earl of Essex's army, who wrote from near Worcester.[52] One report provides a useful insight into the nature of the style of this and similar newsbooks, as it can be shown to derive from a letter sent from Nehemiah Wharton, also an officer in the Earl of Essex's army, to George Willingham, a London merchant.[53] Wharton

[48] *Beginnings*, 26; cf. Hart, *Views on the News*, 26–7.

[49] The phrase is from [?Roger L'Estrange], *A Rope For Pol. Or, A Hue and Cry after Marchemont Nedham. The late Scurrulous News-writer* (1660; L1299A), p. [iv]. Wood quoted this passage, without acknowledgement, in his biography of Nedham; *AO* iii. 1181–2. Wood's copy is Bod.: Wood 622(24).

[50] 11 and 18 Oct. 1642, respectively; 686.1–2/E121(34), E123(6).

[51] *Veridicus* 32, 6 Dec. 1645, 244, 394.132/E311(14).

[52] He refers to 'one of our Souldiers', suggesting his rank; *Weekly Intelligence*, 18 Oct. 1642, 12, 686.2/E123(6).

[53] The letters are printed in *Archæologia*, 35 (1853), 310–34.

was a godly man who looked with equanimity upon the destruction of false idols. His view of the people of Hereford: 'The inhabitants are totally ignorant in the waies of God, and much addicted to drunkkenness and other vices, but principally unto swearinge, so that the children that have scarce learned to speak doe universally sweare stoutlye. Many here speake Welsh.'[54] These two linguistic profanities were evidently more or less morally equivalent to Wharton.

Weekly Intelligence reported thus:

> *Worcester Octob. the* 9
>
> You have heard of the taking in the City of *Heriford*, Sep. the 30. through the petitio̲n̲ of divers of the Knights and Gentlemen, of that County petitioners to his Excellency, who sent about 900 Foote, three Troopes of Horse, and two peeces of Ordinance, with which we marched (a forlorne hope) towards *Heriford*; we had some opposition by the Citizens for a time, being for the most part malignants; but one of the Aldermen perswading the wise Maior that my Lord Generall was at hand with all his Forces, Whereupon he opened the Gates, and let us in, we found the dores shut against us, & could scarce get a little quarter; and wet and weary, we were faine to guard the City that night: on Sunday about the time of Morning Prayer, we went to the Minster, where we heard the Organs play, and the Queristers sing so sweetely that some of our Souldiers could not forbeare dancing in the holy Quire; the Anthome being ended they fell to praying devoutly for the King and Bishops, and one of our Souldiers said with a loud voyce, what never a fit for the Parliament, which offended them greatly.[55]

This resembles Wharton's account, dated 7 October from Worcester:

> Fryday, Sept. 30, was my last to you. This day a company of knights, gentlemen, and yeomen of the county of Hereford, came to his Excelency, petitioners for strength to be sent spedily to Hereford, and forthwith we were commaunded to draw out fifteen out of every company in our regiments, in all about nine hundred, with three troopes of horse and two peeces of ordinance, with which we marched (a forlorne hope) towards Hereford. . . . In this poore condition comminge to Hereford, the gates were shut against us, and for two houres we stood in dirt and water up to the midde legge, for the city were all malignants, save three, which were Roundheads, and the Marquesse of Harford had sent them word the day before that they should in no wise let us in, or if they did we would plunder their houses, murder their children, burne their Bibles, and utterly ruinate all, and promised he would relieve them himself with all speede; for which cause the citizens were resolved to oppose us unto the death, and having in the city three peeces of ordinance, charged them with neyles, stones, &c., and placed them against us, and wee against them, resolvinge either to enter the city or dye before it. But the Roundheads in the city, one of them an alderman, surnamed Lane, persuaded the silly maior (for so hee is indeed) that

[54] *Archæologia*, 35 (1853), 332; cf. *CSPD 1641–1643*, 399.

[55] *Weekly Intelligence*, 18 Oct. 1642, 11–12.

> his Excellency and all his forces weere at hand, wherupon he opened unto us, and we entered the city at Bysters Gate, but found the dores shut, many of the people with their children fled, and had enuffe to do to get a little quarter. . . . This night, though weet and weary, wee were faine to guard the city. . . . Sabbath day, about the time of morninge prayer, we went to the Minster, when the pipes played and the puppets sange so sweetely, that some of our soildiers could not forbeare dauncinge in the holie quire; whereat the Baallists were sore displeased. The anthem ended, they fell to prayer, and prayed devoutly for the Kinge, the bisshops, &c.; and one of our soildiers, with a loud voice, saide, 'What! neiver a bit for the Parliament?' which offended them much more.[56]

This extract represents less than a third of the letter, from which the report in *Weekly Intelligence*, which self-evidently corresponds to it, was whittled down. Though the dates on the letters differ, both refer to a previous letter of the same date. They describe the same sequence of events. The number of troops, the forlorn hope, the malignancy of the city, the shutting of the gates and the role of the alderman in opening them, the 'wet and weary' guarding of the city, and the incident in the Minster all correspond, with considerable linguistic exactness. There are also substantial differences, and it is not absolutely certain that this letter was the copy which arrived in the newsbook editor's hands. None of the other letters from Wharton as closely match *Weekly Intelligence*. It is possible that another officer transcribed passages from Wharton's letter and sent them on to London. This would none the less represent an editing process, a selection of material suitable for the newsbook. Either way, and it is more probable that an editor rewrote Wharton's account, it is possible to use these two texts to trace through the process of editorial preparation of material for inclusion in a newsbook.

The alterations are significant. The 'silly maior (for so hee is indeed)' becomes the 'wise major' of *Weekly Intelligence*. This is a discretionary emendation. The mayor is only wise because he follows the advice of the alderman: to describe him as 'silly' in print may have been impolitic. The critical comments on the Marquis are also omitted in the newsbook. Whereas in modern journalism issues are frequently reduced to or equated with individuals, in this newsbook this identification is avoided. The references to 'Roundheads', not meant to be pejorative, are removed, presumably because they emphasize faction too strongly. Unlike modern journalism, *Weekly Intelligence* resisted using convenient stereotypes. Wharton, in contrast, could rely on his intended reader to interpret his meaning and sentiments exactly. The term 'Baallists', meaning a worshipper of false idols, is dropped, presumably because it is too hostile. The editor is carefully distinguishing

[56] *Archæologia*, 35 (1853), 331–2; cf. *CSPD 1641–1643*, 298–9.

between criticism and abusive language. There is also a certain standardization in diction: the metonym 'pipes' and the colloquialism 'puppets' are translated into 'Organs' and 'Queristers'.

Detail and conflict are curtailed. Wharton's graphic accounts of the misery of the soldiers are impressive. The editorial processing of *Weekly Intelligence* removed the two hours knee-deep in water. This was certainly economical. It is possible that it would have lowered morale and impaired the function of the newsbook as propaganda. The editing process involved massive compression, generally incompatible with vivid detail. The phrase 'wet and weary' suffices to note the miserable conditions. The reasons of the inhabitants of Hereford for their resistance are elided and simplified to unmotivated malignancy: this may also have had a propagandistic basis. The edited text falls into three parts: it begins with the facts of the capture of Hereford; it continues with a personal account of the brief siege; and it concludes with an anecdotal report capturing very economically the spirit of the town and perhaps justifying the army's actions. This definite structure is surely not fortuitous. It is a well-constructed and efficient narrative.

Weekly Intelligence is a good example of what could anachronistically be described as the more professional style of non-literary journalism. Clarity and compression are the two dominant objectives, with the minor aims of verity (emphasizing the eye-witness basis of the report), vividness, and godliness. It is systematic and does not ramble. While it may not have a startling aesthetic appeal as prose, it does have compositional, and functional, cohesion.

The writing is neither formal nor colloquial. The subjective position of the writer is not effaced, though the opinions expressed by Wharton are modified to seem more moderate. Wharton's detailed account, his descriptions of the architecture, landscape, the populace, his lists of names, and his pieties, would make for interesting, extended travel-writing. As it stood, however, his letter was not sufficiently brief or pithy for *Weekly Intelligence*. Nevertheless, it was edited down, and the resultant report preserves some of the excellencies of Wharton's prose; with an alternative structure retaining a variety of information and detail but also generating the immediate impact of skilled journalism.

Foreign news

The publication of domestic news was an event of some political significance, but foreign news also played a part in the constitution of newsbooks. If news from Ireland and Scotland is considered more or less domestic, the first newsbooks did not contain foreign news.[57] This underscores their difference from corantos. Foreign and domestic news were not the same thing, and though public appetites for both could be made to look similar, the former was to some extent a specialization in the 1640s.

The continuities and discontinuities were identified in an important statement in the first issue of *The Exchange Intelligencer* in the middle of the decade:

Wee had (some yeares agone) no *Diurnals* of our owne affaires in *England*. We did live then in so blessed a Time, that wee were onely curious, and desirous to heare forraigne Newes, and to know the state of other Kingdomes and Nations. And now by a strange alteration and vicissitude of Times, wee talke of nothing else, but of what is done in *England*: and perhaps once in a fortnight, wee hearken after Newes out of *Scotland*. It is true our owne Domestique affaires are of a greater concernment, then forraigne businesses; but yet, we may looke farther than home; partly to comfort us, when we heare that although our neighbours are not imbroyled with Civill warres as we are: yet they are so wel imployed and so farre ingaged by their Interests and pretences one against another, that they cannot very well frame any grand designe against us. Moreover, according as our severall inclinations and interests move us to rejoyce for the good successe, or to sorrow for the disasters that happen to our friends we desire to have some intelligence, by which we may heare either of their welfare, or ill fortunes. Besides, it is requisite for Marchants, and for those that travell beyond Sea, or upon the Sea, to know (as neere as intelligence can be given) what forces are upon the Seas, and where the Armies quarter, that they may prevent many dangers, shun the meeting of foes, and seeke to joyne with their friends. These reasons have moved me to undertake this Weekly labour for the delight and profit of whom it may concerne; but I would wish you use the wise Travellers method; *First to travell at home, and then abroad*. You shall know our owne affaires first, and in the next have Informations almost from all parts of the world. The best of the *French* and *Dutch* Coranto's shall be imparted to you, besides many other things out of Marchants and Gentlemens letters. The worke I hope will be acceptable, and I dare say profitable, if not to all, at least to a great many.[58]

It is worth considering seriously the suggestion that in the 1620s and 1630s readers had desired foreign news over and above domestic. The editorial makes no comment on the role of censorship, and though this is no doubt partly motivated by a desire not to appear disloyal, it none the less provides a corrective to the view that all readers wanted domes-

[57] Irish news was both foreign and domestic. It was as an outside force that Irish affairs first influenced the newsbook, and contributed to its appearance; yet Irish news was so closely integrated with domestic that it would be unhelpful to differentiate between them here.

[58] *Exchange Intelligencer* 1, 15 May 1645, 1–2, 145.1/E284(12). The implication that Irish news did not figure largely in newsbooks is very wrong.

tic news, but, due to the intervention of the king, were forced to satisfy themselves with foreign news as a substitute. Just as the progress of the civil war would later highlight questions of providence, the fate of international Protestantism in the Thirty Years War could be of immediate soteriological concern to readers. When corantos were revived in 1638, so far from rekindling interest thwarted by six years of relative silence, they were economically unsuccessful. Conflict was brewing closer to home.[59]

The Exchange Intelligencer made the important point that economic factors determined the appeal of certain kinds of news. Foreign news was important to trade, though it is difficult to assess the real appeal of newsbooks to merchants.[60] Newsbooks occasionally contained lists of cargoes held by ships docked in London harbour. This evidently held a general interest, but it would have been professionally relevant to merchants, and thieves. Later periodicals devoted to cargoes and prices may indicate that traders found the information useful.[61]

Fragments of foreign news crept into newsbooks through 1642–3. Few publications were systematic in their inclusion of it. Thomas Underhill identified a gap in the market, as in October 1642 he released *Special and Late Passages From the Most Eminent Places in Christendome.* This was a neat and systematic newsbook, divided into short, headed paragraphs. It presented a list of the cargo of eight ships recently arrived from Brazil; including gold, wood, ivory, copper, tobacco, and sugar.[62] *Aulicus* and *Britanicus* had little cause to include foreign news, and the same is true of most highly polemical newsbooks. *Mercurius Civicus* occasionally incorporated it in small quantities, without clear typographical demarcation.[63] *Perfect Diurnall* contained foreign news in variable quantities, sometimes with long reports; *Kingdomes Weekly Intelligencer, The Kingdomes Faithfull and Impartiall Scout, Certain Informations,* and others irregularly contained varying quantities.[64] Some newsbooks regularly presented small quantities of foreign news: for example *The Impartiall Intelligencer, Containing, A Perfect Account of the*

[59] 'Relative' because *The Swedish Intelligencer* had been published during these years: a poor substitute; Dahl, 221–2; *STC* 23521–23525.9. Rostenberg, 'Nathaniel Butter and Nicholas Bourne', 32.

[60] Cf. the 1644 handbill for the London-published, French-language newsbook *Le Mercure anglois*: 'These are to signifie, that all merchants and others that are desirous weekely to impart beyond seas the certain condition of affairs here and of the proceedings of the war, they shall have it weekely published in print, and in the French tongue.' Qu. *History*, 50.

[61] e.g. *Publick Adviser*, between May and Sept. 1657; N&S 573.

[62] *Special and Late Passages* (Oct. 1642; S4836/E240(24)), 2.

[63] e.g. *Civicus* 40, 29 Feb. 1644, 419, 298.040/E34(20), introduced a paragraph with the phrase 'From beyond Sea it is advertised'; *Civicus* 105, 29 May 1645, 939–40, 298.105/E286(8).

[64] *MTN*, ch. 6.

Weekly Passages in Parliament, which, like a number of others, mentioned the inclusion of foreign news towards the end of its long title.[65] Others tended to shun foreign news.[66] These publications had no systematic means of gathering foreign news or of translating it out of foreign corantos: hence they probably printed material only when it presented itself. Some items were taken directly from other newsbooks. Three newsbooks specializing in foreign news appeared in 1646, probably prompted by the winding-down of the war.[67] *The Phœnix of Europe*, like *Exchange Intelligencer*, specified merchants as part of its potential audience.[68] Judging by their transience, they did not find their market.

The 1640s newsbook which most effectively carried foreign news was *The Moderate Intelligencer*. The extra four pages (beginning in issue 51) enabled reasonably detailed inclusion of both foreign and domestic news. By sustaining this coverage over years, Dillingham was able to establish continuing relations with foreign correspondents. He had practical experience from writing newsletters in the late 1630s, and had spent time in Paris.[69] According to *The Man in the Moon* Dillingham was assisted in reading and translation by John Cotgrave.[70] Readers interested in foreign news would have bought *The Moderate Intelligencer*; those who were not would have chosen another serial. In this respect it was a specialist publication: from issue 60 onwards, it drew attention to the provenance of the foreign items with clear headings. The factors constraining the inclusion of foreign news can be illustrated by looking at the split between Dillingham and Mabbott and White, and the appearance of an alternative edition of *The Moderate Intelligencer* which subsequently became *The Moderate*. When White first split from Dillingham to produce *The Moderate* it had twelve pages and included foreign news. Three issues later *The Moderate* started a new series and was reduced to a single sheet, containing little foreign news. The constraint on space increased with its sixth issue, when lengthy political editorials were introduced. In the nineteenth issue, however, the extra half-sheet was restored and foreign news returned in plenty, possibly facilitated by the publisher's continuing connections with overseas sources.[71]

This shows that space was a primary concern in the inclusion of

[65] Feb. to June 1649; N&S 194.

[66] e.g. *Armies Modest Intelligencer*, Jan. and Feb. 1649; N&S 18.

[67] N&S 540, 167, 401. Some domestic news was included. Also *Weekly News* for three issues in May 1644; N&S 696.1–3.

[68] *Phoenix* 1, 16 Jan. 1646, 2, 540.1/E316(11).

[69] Cotton, 'John Dillingham', 818–19.

[70] *Man in the Moon* 26, 24 Oct. 1649, 218, 248.26/E575(32). See Ch. 1 n. 76, above.

[71] *Moderate* 171, 29 June 1648, 413.1171/E450(8); *Moderate* 1, 18 July 1648, 413.2001/E453(8); *Moderate* 6, 22 Aug. 1648, 413.2006/E460(18); *Moderate* 19, 21 Nov. 1648, 413.2019/E473(1).

foreign news. Only those newsbooks which were durable and economically successful could sustain it. Certain editors included items in order to fill up space and distract attention from controversial issues, but this was not advisable in the long term.[72] Foreign news could also be a means to comment upon domestic affairs,[73] particularly when the court was in exile:

We received this day some Intelligence from France, which is that the Prince of *Wales* (although he hath lately given a visite to the young King of *France*, and Queene Mother Regent now at *Paris*) is in some distresse for want of moneys. The company of English players that he had are for want of pay dissolved. The *French* desiring to see an English play acted but once; And the English Audience being there so poore and few, that they were not able to maintaine the charges of the Stage.[74]

While corantos could not report on British figures in the country, they did comment on their actions while on the Continent.[75] This, for instance in the case of the Spanish Match and the Isle de Rhé expedition, did enable the London press to comment, though indirectly, on British politics.[76] Even the absence of British connections was a criticism of non-participation in the Thirty Years War.[77] Yet in the summer of 1648 the greatest quantity of foreign news was presented by *The Moderate Intelligencer*, which was increasingly adopting a neutral position,[78] and by *The Moderate*, which was earnestly Leveller. While individual deployments of foreign news items could be political, there was no general correspondence to a particular political orientation.

Spilt ink

Decorative writing, like undecorative writing, has many forms. The most important form of non-literal style for the newsbook in the 1640s was as

[72] e.g. *MTN* 143–8.

[73] Notably in the 1620s, but also during Cromwell's Western Design; David Armitage, 'The Cromwellian Protectorate and the Languages of Empire', *HJ* 35 (1992), 531–55; id., 'John Milton: Poet against Empire', in id. *et al.*, eds., *Milton and Republicanism*, 206–25.

[74] *Civicus* 181, 12 Nov. 1646, 2450, 298.181/E362(3).

[75] For example, see *The Continvation of our forreine Newes* 39, 19 Sept. 1631 (Dahl, 238; *STC* 18507.223), which has an item on James, Duke of Hamilton, a report purporting to be from London, and an account of British adventures in Greenland.

[76] Though the corantos were circumspect. See also Alastair Bellany, '"Raylinge Rymes and Vaunting Verse": Libellous Politics in Early Stuart England, 1603–1628', in Sharpe and Lake, eds., *Culture and Politics*, 284–310.

[77] Cotton, 3; *Personal Rule*, 646–7.

[78] Though Dillingham's circumspection may indicate that he had swung away from his Cromwellian inclinations towards a pragmatic soft-royalism. Cf. *Beginnings*, 168–70.

likely to be perceived as 'unliterary' as the most mundane, journalistic prose. This was the fierce polemic. In 1643 the linguistic restraint of the 1642 *Diurnalls* was torn down, and writers turned to the aggressive controversialism of the *Mercury*. Commentators have distinguished between mercuries and diurnals as if they were self-evidently distinct forms.[79] This is misleading, as no such concrete division existed. The newsbook was a single form, and 'mercuries' and 'diurnals' were stylistic tendencies, always in mixed proportions, within that unity.[80] The relationship developed over time: *Diurnall Occurrences* became *Britanicus* vs. *Aulicus*.

A comparatively large amount of attention has been devoted to *Mercurius Aulicus*, which appeared in Oxford on 8 January 1643. In the nineteenth century it was regarded as unreliable, though ably written.[81] Twentieth-century accounts of the newsbook, however, have been Aulicocentric, praising Berkenhead's skill and paradoxically overlooking the rhetorical presentation in order to accept *Aulicus*' information as reliable.[82]

Aulicus has been ascribed improbably high print-runs; because it was printed in two subsidized editions and because historians like to think it was popular.[83] Some have even given *Aulicus* primacy as the first regular periodical. This probably stems from a desire to make *Aulicus* independent from London-based propaganda. Williams writes that it 'at once struck a higher literary note'.[84] Even Cotton makes the fallacious claim that: 'It was not intended to be a means of counter-propaganda, but simply a weekly dose of "faire play above board".'[85] Cotton is quoting Charles I, who was being economical with the truth. The second sentence of the first issue of *Aulicus* describes itself as a form of counter-propaganda. Though Heylin's first few issues may not have been as barbed and spiked as Berkenhead's, it was propaganda none the less.

Aulicus was not the first regular newsbook. Samuel Pecke had been editing *A Perfect Diurnall* in some form since January 1642, and would

[79] Morison, *The English Newspaper*, 15–29; Hart, *View on the News*, 24–35.

[80] *MTN* 19.

[81] Lord Nugent, *Some Memorials of John Hampden, his Party, and his Times*, 2nd edn., 2 vols. (1832), ii. 359, 361; Gardiner², i, pp. vi–vii.

[82] Frederick John Varley, *Mercurius Aulicus* (Oxford, 1948); Williams, 'Beginnings of English Journalism', 348; *History*, 41; Wedgwood, *King's War*, 163–6; *Berkenhead*, 43–7, 66–72, and *passim*. The same sometimes happens with *Mercurius Rusticus* (July 1646; R2448/E1099); *OR* iv. 117–302. Reprinted 1648 and 1685. Historians frequently cite the collected volume, obscuring its less prestigious origins.

[83] *Beginnings*, 7; *Berkenhead*, 49–52; Joyce Lee Malcolm, *Caesar's Due: Loyalty and King Charles 1642–1646* (1983), 126; and others. Cotton, 38, rightly queries this. Double editions do not necessarily mean significantly greater circulation. Nelson and Seccombe, *Periodical Publications*, 44–52.

[84] *History*, 41. [85] Cotton, 36.

continue to do so until September 1655, ten years after the demise of *Aulicus*.[86] Moreover, *The Kingdomes Weekly Intelligencer*, which claimed in March 1642 that it was established specifically to repudiate *Aulicus*, first appeared on 3 January, five days before its avowed rival.[87] It therefore gave strange authority to the myth of *Aulicus*' precedence.

What was important about *Aulicus* was its language, which departed from the clumsy reportage of London newsbooks. It played a provocative role in changing the presentation of news.[88] Through the year *Aulicus* heated up the 'cool element of prose',[89] writing emotively about the sufferings of the wronged monarch. The London newsbooks soon took the defensive. *Aulicus* even went so far as to correct the errors of its competitors.

Heylin, in his opening editorial, linked the exploitation of the reading public by the London diurnals with the perpetration of the war itself: 'there's a weekly cheat put out to nourish the abuse amongst the people, and make them pay for their seducement.'[90] When Berkenhead took over, the stakes were raised, and even Heylin's spurious politeness was dispensed with.[91] As a consequence of the increasingly aggressive royalist offence, London newsbooks turned to satire, sarcasm, scatology, and brought in animadversion to accompany them. Through 1643 London and Oxford made corresponding attempts to control local postal services.[92]

On Tuesday 29 August 1643 parliament's official defender appeared, playing David to *Aulicus*' Goliath, entitled *Mercurius Britanicus: Communicating the Affaires of Great Britaine*. The first fifty-one issues of this were produced by Captain Thomas Audley and the 23-year-old Marchamont Nedham; from issue 52 Nedham took sole responsibility. Nedham was a superbly gifted polemicist, whose language and ideas became the focus of irritable attacks. Modern critics have sympathized with the royalist perspective on Nedham's 'rough billingsgate'.[93]

The conflict between London and Oxford became more and more personal. It assumed the unprestigious[94] form of prose controversy, as much as reportage. Newsbooks became more book than news. *Britanicus* attacked a London edition of *Aulicus* thus:

This *new Aulicus* by vertue of his Commission, *railes* most abominably, prophanes most prodigiously, lies most incredibly, and though I am loathe to

86 Ch. 1 n. 14 above.
87 *KWI* 12, 21 Mar., 214.012/E93(19). Cf. Cotton, 46.
88 *Berkenhead*, 35–41, 88–90, and *passim*.
89 According to Milton; *CPW* i. 808.
90 *Aulicus* 1, [7 Jan. 1643], 1, 275.001B; *OR* i. 17; *MTN* 92.
91 *Berkenhead*, 89 and *passim*.
92 J. M. W. Stone, *The Inland Posts, 1392–1672* (1987), 94–9.
93 Hart, *Views on the News*, 32.
94 *CPW* i. 821–2.

write upon such foule *paper* as this late *Diurnall*, yet I will spit the wast of my inke in his face, and leave him with this *Caracter*.

He is one so full of *lying* and *railing*, that I think he is assisted by all the Pimps, Players, Poets and Oyster women in the Towne, and he *talks* so against the Scripture, and of the divell, that I thinke it is one of his spirits which hath assumed the body of a dead Cavalier, and walkes now in *London*, and *writes Aulicuses*.[95]

Aulicus was equally satirical, and frequently pornographic, anticipating the obscene writing of John Crouch in *The Man in the Moon*.[96]

Wee told you not long since of a *London* Committee of Ladyes and other publick Gentlewomen for the service of the pretended *Houses*, who have now proceeded so farre, that if any of their sex refuse to contribute, they have legislative power to compell their obedience; in pursuance whereof, Sir *Arthur Haslerig* (his Mothers own sonne) finding a handsome Merchants Wife at *Bristol* (I spare her name for her Husbands sake) did not onely passe his vote at *Bristol*, that shee was a handsome Gentlewoman, but tooke her away with him in a ship when he fled thence a little before the taking of the Towne, and are now to the joy of the *honourable Committee* safely arrived at *London*. But where Sir *Arthur* and his fellow traveller have beene all this while, was not yet certified, onely this we heare for certaine, that before Sir *Arthur* took this voyage with his friend, Colonell *Nathaniel Fines* was Governour of *Bristol*.[97]

By 1643 the common language of public political debate had begun to disintegrate.[98] By 1648 newsbooks freely explored the literary potentials of hostility, abjuring gestures of reconciliation: but even in the newsbook war of 1643 the executioner's axe seemed already sharp.[99]

The conflict was rhetorical: it is in the arena of political propaganda that the ideological strain of early-modern thought is most prominent. Heylin and Nedham went to the same school in Burford; it belonged to Nedham's stepfather.[100] Heylin later sheltered Nedham, in his passing royalist guise, when he was on the run.[101] The 'war without an enemy', as William Waller described it,[102] was in some ways impersonal. In the spring of 1648 aggression was conventional. Once this was the case,

[95] *Britanicus* 8, 17 Oct. 1643, 57, 286.008/E71(10). This reads like an invitation to Cleveland to write his *Character of a London Diurnall* (Oxford, 1645; C4659).

[96] *MTN* 98–9.

[97] *Aulicus* 38, [17–23 Sept. 1643], 519, 275.138A&B/E69(18); *OR* ii. 55.

[98] Skerpan, *Rhetoric of Politics*, 80. Cf. Sharpe, *Politics and Ideas*, 65–8; on the language of consensus in the 1630s, id., *Criticism and Compliment: The Politics of Literature in the England of Charles I* (Cambridge, 1987); for an account of criticism and dissonance in the 1630s see David Norbrook's forthcoming study.

[99] Cf. Wootton, 'Rebellion to Revolution', 668–9.

[100] Frank, *Cromwell's Press Agent*, 4.

[101] I believe that Nedham was at heart a republican and circumstantially a royalist; for a precedent for this view, see G. P. Gooch, *English Democratic Ideas in the Seventeenth Century*, 2nd edn. with additions by H. J. Laski (1898; Cambridge, 1927), 159–60.

[102] Quoted Gardiner², i. 168.

linguistic pugnacity was part of the formula of decorum for newsbooks, their war-paint. The extravagant figure of the mercury was a persona, freely available to all writers, which could be adopted in order to write with ink brewed with vitriol and poison.[103] The real significance of *Aulicus* lay not in its popularity or improved standards of accuracy, but in its incipient violence. In 1645, the anonymous author of a pamphlet-poem entitled *The Great Assises Holden in Parnassus* drew up essentially accurate charges against *Aulicus*, also suggesting that *Aulicus* had lost the war with *Britanicus*:

> Hee was accus'd, that he with slanders false,
> With forged fictions, calumnies and tales,
> Had sought the *Spartane Ephori* to shame,
> And added fewell to the direfull flame
> Of civill discord, and domesticke blowes,
> By the incentives of malicious prose.
> For whereas, hee should have compos'd his inke
> Of liquours, that make flames expire, and shrinke
> Into their cinders, it was there objected,
> That hee had his of burning oile confected,
> Of Naphtha, Gunpowder, Pitch, and Saltpeter,
> Which those combustions raised, and made greater.
> Hee was accus'd to have unjustly stung
> The sage *Amphictyons* with his venom'd tongue;
> And that he like the fierce Albanian curre,
> Did stubbornly choose rather to demurre,
> And bee dismembred by anothers wit,
> Then loose his teeth from those, whom first hee bit.[104]

The punishments meted out to the newsbooks at the conclusion of this poem averruncate their eloquence and dismantle the available print technology in order to make them harmless.

Britanicus *his railing*

Prior to the institutionalization and industrialization of journalistic discourse, styles were more individual, and could be associated with an author or a mercury figure. *Perfect Diurnall* and *Perfect Occurrences* are to some extent stylistically similar, and might be taken to represent a lowest common denominator of unadulterated reportage. Yet one contemporary wrote that the editor of the latter was more careful in 'com-

[103] *MTN* 19–21.

[104] *The Great Assises Holden in Parnassus* (1645; W3160); ed. Hugh Macdonald (Oxford, 1948), 12: references to this edition.

pacting his relations together', indicating a stylistic divergence.[105] *Mercurius Insanus, Insanissimus* referred to 'Walkerisme, Harrunayanisme' as if it were something distinctive.[106] As nuanced as any newsbook was *Britanicus*, whose jocular aggression served as a role-model for later royalist mercuries.

Britanicus was witty, that was its point. Attacks on *Britanicus* usually said either that it was offensive to nature, pathologically regicidal, or that it was not funny. The workings of *Britanicus* are a key to the workings of newsbooks in general, which is a testimony to Nedham's considerable influence.

Mercurius Anti-Britanicus repeatedly described *Britanicus* as 'Rayling', uttering abusive language with overtones of both jesting and boasting.[107] This is a useful and accurate characterization. According to *Anti-Britanicus*, Nedham made 'weekly sport' for 'the Rout and Scumme of people' by 'rayling at all that's Noble'. This was not gentlemanly. With Audley, his partner in malice, Nedham had 'abused' many 'great Names'.[108] Railing became the common characterization of his style. *Mercurius Britanicus His Welcome to Hell* adjudicated amongst parliamentary newsbooks:

> Amongst all these (deare Son *Britanicus*)
> Th' hast shew'd thy selfe the best *Mercurius*.
> Thou hast out-slander'd slander, and prevail'd,
> And every railing rogue thou hast out-rail'd.[109]

Anthony Wood generously agreed that *Britanicus* 'might very well have challenged the precedency of Satan, to have thrust him out of his chair, the seat of the scornful, wherein he sate several years, and out-railed all the Shimeis and Rabsekehs, and out-lyed all the Simmiasses and Pseudolusses that ever sate in that chair'.[110] *Mercurius Academicus* accused *Britanicus* of 'Rayling', suggesting that Audley was *Britanicus* and Nedham *Mercurius*.[111] *Academicus* also claimed that *Britanicus* was the 'provoker', his Oxford enemies the 'provok'd', but that it was better to avoid railing in response to *Britanicus* because the crime would in the end be the same.[112] The style was associated with *Britanicus* sufficiently

[105] *A Fresh Whip*, 5; disagreeing with Frank, who thought this 'crowding' a failing; *Beginnings*, 109.

[106] *Mercurius Insanus, Insanissimus* [4], [24 Apr. 1648], '9' i.e. 26, 335.4/E436(24); possibly a reference to Walker's Hebrew transliterations.

[107] *OED* 'Rail', v^4: 1*a*, 2*a*, 2*b*.

[108] *Anti-Britanicus* 3, [22 Aug. 1645], 25, 27, 267.3/E297(17); *OR* iv. 327, 329.

[109] [?Sir Francis Wortley], *Mercurius Britanicus His Welcome to Hell* (1647; W3641).

[110] *AO* iii. 1181.

[111] *Academicus* 5, 41–2; *OR* iv. 375–6; cf. *Academicus* 3, [29 Dec. 1645], 30–1, 260.03/E313(26); *OR* iv. 364–5. Cf. *Anti-Britanicus* 3, 25. See 31, above.

[112] *Academicus* 7, [26 Jan. 1646], 64, 260.07/E318(4); *OR* iv. 398.

closely for John Hall to imitate it in his *Mercurius Britanicus Alive Again,* and *Elencticus* responded: 'Alas poore Thread-bare *Britanicus*! What would become of thee, if thou had'st not the *Scots,* and *Elencticus* to *rayle* at?'[113] The criticisms remained the same.

Nedham knew he was witty, and attacked others for not being so. This had a dilated meaning: not to be witty was to fall into derangement. After the triumph at Naseby, *Britanicus* proclaimed: 'Sure, *Aulicus* is out of his *wits.*'[114] Defeat meant a loss of confidence and of humour, which meant madness. Polemical newsbooks had to be confident to the extent of overoptimistic, hubristic absurdity.

Railing implied an affable familiarity with the reader. Frequent repetitions, colloquialisms, and an occasional emphasis on the spoken word projected the image of an oral use of language. *Britanicus* ventured to be conversational, presenting dialogues of question and answer, implying a community of shared words, ideas, and values. This was achieved by rhetorical questioning; 'Dost thou thinke seriously': by inclusive pronouns; 'He tells us . . .', 'Is it true that we heare . . . ?': by common sense and an implied community; 'There is but *one LORD, one Faith,* good reason then but *one Confession,* that we all speak the same thing as touching the *Principles* of *Religion.* Though we may divide the *Circumference,* let us unite in the *Center.*'[115] The readers of *Britanicus* always knew what was right: 'he [*Academicus*] Communicates his own feeble *Phantsies* upon our Weekly *News books.*'[116] *Britanicus* summarized the contents of its enemy's publication in some detail: 'he sayes . . . he says . . . he sayes.' *Britanicus* did not fear what *Aulicus* had to say and repeated it without concern that readers might be seduced. This literally diminished the value of *Aulicus,* which was available more cheaply in this epitome.[117] Sure of his readers' allegiances, Nedham's railing could alienate a community who were not present in order more tightly to bind together his community of assenting readers. Nevertheless many royalists found it funny as well as offensive.[118]

This projected community of readers were bound together by three aspects of editorial style: first, the satirical wit directed at enemies;

[113] *Elencticus* 34, 12–19 July 1648, 261, 312.34/E453(23).

[114] *Britanicus* 87, 23 June 1645, 785, 286.087/E288(49); cf. *Britanicus* 81, 5 May 1645, 737, 286.081/E281(14).

[115] *Britanicus* 81, 737; *Britanicus* 6, 3 Oct. 1643, 44, 286.006/E69(19); *Britanicus* 17, 21 Dec. 1643, 131, 286.017/E79(2); *Britanicus* 79, 21 Apr. 1645, 726, 286.079/E278(21).

[116] *Britanicus* 115, 26 Jan. 1646, 1009, 286.115/E318(8).

[117] *Britanicus* 47, 19 Aug. 1644, 370–4, 286.047/E6(26); quotes at length a declaration and speech by the king; cf. Taylor, *Mercvrivs Aqvaticvs; Or, the Water-Poets Answer to All that hath or shall be Writ by Mercurius Britanicus* (Oxford, 1643; T481).

[118] *AO* iii. 1181–3; and the pamphlet attacks of 1660, some by Roger L'Estrange.

secondly, the implied agreement on the near side of the fictional barricades; thirdly, the linguistic markers of conversation. In attacking this 'railing' style, *Anti-Britanicus* perceptively identified some of its key terms:

As for his writings . . . we cannot say, that this Fellow writes, but vomits. His compositions have not that thing which we call Salt, but a kind of boysterous Gall, which makes them venemous, not sharpe. . . . There is as much difference, between his Invectives, and a true Satyre, as between the prick of a Needle, and the biting of Mad-Dogge, the one is all poynt, the other all Rage.[119]

Gentle irony was not always Nedham's priority; rather sometimes a boisterous impudence:

indeed the grand *Mercury Faulkland* is slaine, yet we hear her Majesty intends to summon all Poets and Schollers of any competency of wit, from the age of sixteen to sixty, to be aiding and assisting to the next *Diurnall*, for Master *Aulicus* is put upon such a *vast duty* every weeke, *viz.* the telling of at least an hundred lies, together with fine conceits, that he is not able to undergoe it, unlesse a *Sub-Committee* for lying and jesting be added to him. . . .

He tells us of the battell neare *Newberry*, and the thanks given for the preservation of his Majesties person, we must note, they had nothing else to give thanks for.[120]

In the end *Britanicus* won the war: vomiting could make more effective satire than the pricking of a needle.

Style and orality

Elements of this railing style were borrowed by other newsbooks. Nedham of course took his truculent skill with him to *Pragmaticus*. *Mercurius Anti-Mercvrivs* wrote of *Pragmaticus* (though, plausibly at this late date, attributing it to Cleveland) that he 'hath more wit then honesty', and that 'He spews poison in every ones face he meets', and that *Elencticus* likewise 'railes at the Almanack-makers in folio'.[121] *Elencticus* tried to rail, but was too awkward and verbose, turning the

[119] *Anti-Britannicus* 2, [11 Aug. 1645], 11, 267.2/E296(9); *OR* iv. 313; *MTN* 337–8. This claimed Nedham's writing was recognizable by its 'impudence'.

[120] *Britanicus* 6, 3 Oct. 1643, 41, 44. *Britanicus* repeatedly emphasized that his Oxford enemies employed a team of writers against him; *Britanicus* 23, 19 Feb. 1643, 177, 286.023B; *Britanicus* 25, 6 Mar. 1644, 194, 286.025/E35(28). When he observed that *Aulicus* had appeared in two sheets, he was sometimes emphasizing the disproportion of his position: he was a lone writer appearing in a single sheet, and none the less their equal.

[121] *Mercurius Anti-Mercvrivs* (Apr. 1648; M1752), sigs. A2–A2^v. It also accurately predicted that *Pragmaticus* was soon to die (of a consumption).

fireworks of the style into damp squibs: 'He explicates a jeer so largely, with so many circumlocutions, letting on't out by little and little, that he makes it, from the sounding fart of a jest, become the stinking fizle of a ridiculous sentence.' *Perfect Diurnall* was 'an old standing Pool', full of lies, but not witty, and 'seldome railes but at Presbytery'. *The Moderate Intelligencer*, on the other hand, consisted of lies plain and simple, 'the epitome of nothing'.[122] *Anti-Mercvrivs* characterized nicely the stylistic variations between these newsbooks.

Many newsbooks made gestures to oral speech, conveying a sense of immediacy. Mock-Welsh newsbooks reproduced accents.[123] The representation of laughter also used non-linguistic markers to suggest the spoken word. Printed laughter acquired a textual dimension through its inappropriateness to its context, but it none the less retained an association with pronounced speech. After an opening poem, *Mercurius Carolinus* began: 'Ha, ha, ha . . .'[124] The first and only issue of *Mercvrivs Anti-Melanchollicus* asked: 'Why how now Country-men? What i'th'sudds? All a-mort; Cheere up your drooping hearts, too much sorrow will kill a Cat; cast away care, laugh and be merry . . . Ha, ha, ha I laugh to thinke . . .'[125] Wit and laughter tended to go together: the laughter perhaps corresponds to the orthographical representation of vomiting in play-pamphlets. Laughter usually appeared near the beginning of newsbooks, where the editorial voice was most inflected, in order to set the tone.

Exclamations frequently conveyed a spoken quality: 'Alas poore STATE! How 'tis *cripled* in the *Hams*'; 'Good *Lord*! what shall I doe?'; even tongue-tied *Melancholicus* expostulated, 'O Ye imperious Tyrants!'; 'Courage *Royalists*, lift up your voices and *laugh* . . .'; 'O Heavens!'; 'Tush, Malignants!'; 'Why so—'; 'SEE what it is to have a *New-Model*!'[126]

[122] *Anti-Mercvrivs*, sig. A3^{v}.

[123] *The Welch Mercury*, N&S 708.1–9; *A Perfect Tiurnall: or VVelch Post*, N&S 532.1. This derived from a pamphlet tradition: *The Welshmens Prave Resolution* (7 June 1642; W1334); *The Welch-Mans Warning-Piece* (1642; W1339); *The Welch-mans publike Recantation* (Dec. 1642; W1338); *The Welch Plunderer* (1 Mar. 1643; W1344); *The Welchmens Lamentation and Complaint* (10 May 1643; W1326); *The Welsh Physitian* (11 Feb. 1647[8]; W1343); see also F. P. Wilson, 'Some English Mock-Prognostications', *Library*^{4}, 19 (1938–9), 39.

[124] *Carolinus* 1, 26 July 1649, sig. A, 294.1/E566(6).

[125] *Anti-Melancholicus* 1, 24 Sept. 1647, 1, 268.1/E408(9); 'Printed where I was, and where I will be.'

[126] *Pragmaticus* 14, 27 4 July 1648, sig. O, 369.214/E450(27); could this possibly be an obscure reference to Hamlet? *Elencticus* 29, 14 June 1648, 221, 312.29/E447(11); *Melancholicus* 51, 14 Aug. 1648, 143, 344.51B/E458(10), perhaps meant to evoke classical rhetoric and Latinity rather than speech; *Pragmaticus* 48, 3 Apr. 1649, sig. Mmm, 369.248/E549(13); *Pragmaticus* 45, 13 Mar. 1649, sig. Iii, 369.246D/E546(18); *Britanicus* 52, 7 Oct. 1644, 407, 286.052/E13(10); *Mercurius Vapulans* 2, [Dec.?] 1647, 11, 390.2; *Britanicus* 91, 28 July 1645, 823, 286.091/E294(5).

Other forms of speech implied a projected voice, either because of their colloquialism, their theatricality, or because they addressed the reader: 'You have heard of Mr *Peters* the mad *Preacher*. . .'; 'HELP help a little, pray lend me your hands (dear freinds) . . .'; 'Come, come, 'tis good children, do not cry, though I whipt you last week, I will now give you an apple . . .'; 'What have we here?'; 'Avaunt *Jack Pudding*, thy sport is dull . . .'; 'Heavens bless my eye-sight, what strange Beast is this?'; 'So, hoe, Whither so fast?'[127] *Britanicus* wrote of *Aulicus*: 'Henceforth then (perhaps) he will be able to *speake* plaine to his *Parliament*, and not brand them any more with that *S'tammering, crooked, Wry-mouth'd slaunder* of *Rebels*.'[128] This rather brilliant imputation gestured over the shoulder of *Aulicus* to the famous speech impediment of its paymaster. *The Moderate* was formal in tone; nevertheless when necessary it addressed readers directly: 'Reader, In obedience to the Order of the House of Lords . . .'; 'Reader, I am desired to change my day . . .'.[129] These paragraphs were italicized to identify them as slightly different kinds of speech acts.

The Man in the Moon manipulated the illusion of a projected voice, laughing, crying treason, calling for his boots, and shouting 'Ha-loo *Towzer*' to his dog.[130] The voice was a performance, indicating the public nature of the newsbook. It also had a repetitive, ritualistic tenor, reminding its readers that *The Man in the Moon* was an enduring witness to the wrongdoings of the regicides.

Many newsbooks did not share this oral quality: *Moderate Intelligencer*, *Kingdomes Weekly Intelligencer*, *Perfect Diurnall*, *Perfect Occurrences*, *Civicus*, etc. Their editorial voices were formal, reserved, or elevated in style, perhaps intended as a marker of social prestige. This distinction can be illuminated by the opening sentence of *Mercurius Rusticus*: 'It is the great Wisedome and Iustice of God to punish men in those very things which in a kind of secret Idolatry they set up in their hearts in a Competition with their maker.'[131] While this may owe a debt to Ciceronian oratory, its formal, deliberative periodicity carries it far from ordinary speech or conversationalism. *Rusticus* was conscious of social

[127] *Academicus* 12, [2 Mar. 1646], 109, 260.12/E325(16); *OR* iv. 443; *Mercurius Populi* 1, 11 Nov. 1647, 1, 364.1/E413(14); *Britanicus Alive Again* 2, 25 May 1648, 9, 282.02/E444(7); *Anti-Britanicus* 2, 9; *OR* iv. 311; *Anti-Pragmaticus* 6, 25 Nov. 1647, 1, 270.06/E416(38); *Mercurius Aulicus Againe* 5, 2 Mar. 1648, sig. E^v, 273.05/E430(7); *Mercurius Militaris* 1, 28 Apr. 1648, sig. A, 347.1 (not by John Harris).

[128] *Britanicus* 87, 785.

[129] *Moderate* 171, 29 June 1648, 1409, 413.1171/E450(8); *Moderate* 1, 18 July 1648, 1, 413.2001/E453(8).

[130] *Man in the Moon* 4, 7 May 1649, 25, 248.04/E554(4); *Man in the Moon* 6, 21 May 1649, 51, 248.06/E555(33); *Man in the Moon* 16, 8 Aug. 1649, 135, 248.16/E568(13); *Man in the Moon* 33, 13 Dec. 1649, 259, 248.33.

[131] *Rusticus* 1, 20 May 1643, 'To the Reader', sig. A2, 384.01/E103(3).

registers.[132] But a formal style also characterized the political-theoretical editorials of the Leveller newsbook *The Moderate*: 'The Oracle of *Apollo* at *Delphos*, being demanded why *Jupiter* should be the chief of Gods, sith *Mars* was the best souldier. Answered, *Mars* is valiant, but *Jupiter* wise; to get by Conquest is much, but to Conquer the Conqueror by policy is more.'[133] This organized, decorative, premeditated writing is associated more with royalism than with radicalism. Between 1643 and 1646 *Britanicus* spoke railingly, while *Rusticus* and *Aulicus* adopted self-consciously well-spoken though abusive voices. Formality could indicate a resistance to journalism and to Mercurialness, to the political style of cheap print.

Yet orality should not simply be equated with a general, and prodigious, journalistic populism. The model of speech was central to early-modern journalism, and in some cases may have represented a genuine proximity between speech and writing. But colloquialism also had important rhetorical effects. For *Britanicus*, an oral-animated style embraced his readers for propagandistic purposes. It boasted his confident personality, marked in the grain of his eloquence: mercuries were essentially ventriloquists, projecting a fictitious voice. They addressed readers personally, implicating them in ideological conflict. The public idiom of seventeenth-century newspapers articulated a new mode of writing and perhaps the sense of a public forum for the exchange of politics and news.

Information and the 'Intelligencer'

After Mercury had permeated the ink of newsbook writers, it was necessary for them to rationalize the problem of Intelligence. During the first civil war they therefore confronted the dichotomy between facts and interpretation, seeking to reconcile their claim to represent pure truth with the tendency to deploy that truth in order to achieve a desired effect. One approach to this dilemma involved the configuration of the terms 'news', 'information', and 'intelligencer'.

Despite the contemporary collective term 'newsbooks', individual serials rarely used the term 'news' in their titles. Foreign affairs were

[132] Cf. the opening to issue 18, 16 Dec. 1643, 136, 384.18/E78(21): 'The Author of the French History relating that horrid *Rebellion* of the *Holy League* in *France*, the *Prototype* of the present *Rebellion* in *England*, gives this definition or Character of one of those *Zealots*...' Only a limited readership could have identified this reference to Enrico Caterino Davila, *Historia delle guerre civili di Francia* (Venice, 1630).

[133] *Moderate* 6, 22 Aug. 1648, 41, 413.2006/E460(18).

more frequently described as news.[134] Some earlier publications calling themselves 'news' were sensationalist writings, wonder-pamphlets, *Strange News but True*, containing no real news.[135] By 1641 'news' could be pejorative. After the satires of the public desire for news by Jonson, Richard Braithwaite, and others, publishers were tentative about associating their serious newsbooks with whimsical appetites.

Some 'mercuries' and satirical newsbooks, notably in 1648, often ephemeral, were prepared to use the term, providing exceptions which reinforce the point: *Mercurius Clericus, or, Newes from Syon* (1647); *Mercurius Honestus. Or, Newes from Westminster* (1648); *New News, Strange News, True News* (1648); *The Parliaments Vulture. Newes from all parts of the Kingdome* (1648).[136] Editors and publishers of less vituperative newsbooks were consistent in preferring terms such as 'occurrences', 'transactions', 'proceedings', 'passages', 'affairs', 'relations', and particularly 'intelligence' and 'informations' to the less sophisticated 'news', elevating themselves above public cravings.

Francis Bacon alluded to the knowledge obtained from experiment as 'intelligencers of nature'; John Winthrop, Jr. described Hartlib as 'the Great Intelligencer of Europe'.[137] Newsbooks were also Intelligencers; the term was used in too many titles to enumerate. But the Intelligencer was not someone who plainly passed on information. To inform meant to convey knowledge or news of a particular fact or event. To inform could also mean to mould a mind or character. Intelligence was a more complex term: it could mean knowledge of events, or understanding; but it also had more dynamic meanings, such as the apprehension or interchange of knowledge, or a relation of understanding between parties; and significantly the obtaining or communicating of information by spies or other agents.[138] These distinctions facilitate understanding of the role of the 'Intelligencer'.

The first *Kingdomes Weekly Post*, which appeared 9 November 1643, advertised: 'this honest Post ventures in his travelling weeds to present his newes to the City, as well as to the rest of the Kingdome, without any gilded glosings, invented fixions, or flattering Commentaries, and in plain truth communicates to the kingdome such newes as is intrusted

[134] N&S 145, 696, 167. See also *The Newes, or the Full Particulars of the Last Fight*, 12 Aug. 1653, 449.1/E710(16), barely a newsbook.

[135] Shaaber, *Some Forerunners of the Newspaper*, 215–16; Jerome Friedman, *Miracles and the Pulp Press during the English Revolution: The Battle of the Frogs and Fairford's Flies* (1993).

[136] N&S 301 (see also 302), 331, 442, 490; see also 307, 389, 708.

[137] Francis Bacon, *The Advancement of Learning and New Atlantis*, ed. Arthur Johnston (Oxford, 1974), 63–4; Webster, ed., *Samuel Hartlib and the Advancement of Learning*, 3.

[138] *OED*, though sparse on 1640s examples.

with his packet.'[139] Plain truth without rhetoric was a formula to which other newsbooks claimed they adhered. In January 1645 *Civicus* wrote that it was his 'intention rather to search out the naked Truth (as neer as is possible) then to study Rhetoricall flourishes'.[140] *The Welch Mercury* claimed to be 'carryed on te wings of wit and truth' and promised to 'freely discover our new Inteligencers, free from passions or affections'.[141] *Pragmaticus* asked, 'What need we *belye* an *enemy*, when ther is *Truth* enough to undoe him?'[142] Some newsbooks, including *Britanicus*, recognized that language was complicit with issues, but most assumed the existence of the unmediated fact, a body to be dressed in functional clothing.

Informator Rusticus claimed to offer 'rusticall intelligence, plainly dressed', and claimed that 'Plaine Truth is the best Newes, and will doe most good in the publishing thereof'. Yet it also suggested that 'wit' was integral to conveying intelligence: 'I have adventured according to my rusticall wit, and my certaine information, to relate what I know, or have credibly heard thereof.'[143] Wit was the partner of information. These are exact terms. Wit is the editor's linguistic skill at evaluating and shaping the news; information is the presented, informed material. Wit soon became politicized, the opposite of fool, corresponding with Tory and Whig.[144]

The Moderate Intelligencer distinguished between 'Intelligence' and 'News', though implying that both were prone to manipulation or economizing: 'Intelligence or Newes, whosoever looks upon it, must be considered in this manner: no man, be he what he will, but will be apt to speake the most and best of what he likes, and conceal the worst, and so of the contrary.'[145] *The Compleat Intelligencer* also discriminated between them: 'Because there are so many Pamphlets that the Reader cannot well get through the crowde of them to the newes, nor come handsomely at the Intelligence for the multitude of those that relate it.'[146] Under the guise of saying that the reader had a difficult choice to make in selecting from a wide variety of newsbooks, the editor suggested that he alone was sufficiently competent, or witty, for the discerning reader. Intelligence was more mediated than mere news, and conformed to an accepted process of shaping.

139 *Kingdomes Weekly Post* 1, [9 Nov. 1643], 1–2, 217.1/E75(17).

140 *Civicus* 85, 9 Jan. 1645, 775, 298.085/E24(9).

141 *Welch Mercury* 3, 11 Nov. 1643, 2, 708.3/E75(27).

142 *Pragmaticus* 12, 20 June 1648, sig. M, 369.212/E448(7).

143 *Informator Rusticus* 1, 3 Nov. 1643, 8, 1, 198.1/E74(15).

144 John Dryden, *Absalom and Achitophel* (1681; D2122 etc.), 'To the Reader'; Zwicker, *Lines of Authority*, 9–36.

145 *Moderate Intelligencer* 101, 11 Feb. 1647, 912, 419.101/E375(10).

146 *Compleat Intelligencer* 2, 7 Nov. 1643, 17, 52.2/E75(6).

Several newsbooks had discrete sections of Intelligence. The twelfth issue of *Britanicus* introduced a division headed 'Intelligence' distinct from editorial material.[147] In *Pragmaticus* the 'Intelligence' followed Nedham's opening polemic.[148] He attacked the 'weekly *Romances*' in the London newsbooks, which contained only the 'Intelligence' that the Junto in the Commons decided was 'canonical'.[149] In *Mercurius Pragmaticus (For King Charles II)*, he claimed that: '*Prag.* is neither *scandalous* nor *seditious*, but the very truth of *Intelligence*.'[150] Nedham's Intelligence was as polemical as his editorials: this was less true of *The London Post*, the opening section of which was headed 'Preface', the rest 'Intelligence'.[151] A 1647 *Mercurius Britanicus* also had a 'Preface' followed by 'intelligence'.[152]

Intelligence was a mark of an editor's expertise, a point of competition. It was not freely available: an Intelligencer was also a spy. Cleveland began *The Character of a Moderate Intelligencer*: 'An Intelligencer is a State-spie.' A newsbook entitled *The Spie, Communicating Intelligence from Oxford* appeared in February 1644.[153] In 1653 Nedham was not only the preferred 'Intelligencer' of John Thurloe, head of the Cromwellian secret service, he worked for him as an undercover agent.[154] *Civicus* reported on the apprehension of 'a woman who is expected to be a spie or a she-Intelligencer for Oxford', and speculated on how many other 'Female-Intelligencers' there might be.[155] *Mercurius Aulicus Communicating the intelligence, and affaires of the Court*, used the word 'intelligence' to denote secret affairs, particularly military information, which might itself be gathered by a 'Scout', another term which recurred in newsbook titles.

Newsbooks attacked other newsbooks for presenting manipulative untruths as Intelligence. *Britanicus* accused *Aulicus* of cozening the kingdom with '*lies* and *slanders*, instead of *Intelligence*'.[156] *Aulicus* was 'patcht up with such pittifull *Rags* of *Intelligence*, that he shames all his friends'.[157] When his enemy disappeared Nedham lamented: 'Not an *Aulicus*, nor a *Declaration*, nor a *Proclamation*, nor a *tel-tale Epistle*, not so

147 *Britanicus* 12, 16 Nov. 1643, 286.012/E75(38).

148 See e.g. *Pragmaticus* 11, 13 June 1648, 369.211/E447(5).

149 *Pragmaticus* 12, sig. M^v.

150 *Pragmaticus (For King Charles II)* 3, 8 May 1649, 370.03/E554(12).

151 *London Post* 23, 11 Feb. 1645, 1, 233.123/E269(8).

152 *Britanicus* 2, 1 July 1647, 289.2/E396(2).

153 John Cleveland, *The Character of a Moderate Intelligencer* (1647; C4668), 1; *The Spie*, N&S 609.01–22.

154 [?Roger L'Estrange], *A True Catalogue* (1659; T2593/E999(12)), 14, 53; *CSPD 1653–1654*, 304–7, 393; and, though wrong, Frank, *Cromwell's Press Agent*, 107–10.

155 *Civicus* 110, 3 July 1645, 298.110/E292(1).

156 *Britanicus* 73, 10 Mar. 1645, 587, 286.073/E271(21).

157 *Britanicus* 98, 22 Sept. 1645, 873, 286.098/E302(15).

much as a *Royall ragge* of *Intelligence.*'[158] In 1652 Samuel Sheppard published an anti-newsbook entitled *Mercurius Mastix: Faithfully Lashing All Scouts, Mercuries, Posts, Spyes, and others; who cheat the Common-wealth under the name of Intelligence.*[159] In 1645 the first and only issue of the hubristically titled *The Best and Most Perfect Intelligencer* began by addressing 'my deare Brethren of the Waste-Paper Fraternitie'.[160] William Prynne, in *A Checke to Brittanicus, For His Palpable Flattery and Prevarication, in justifying condemned Nat: Fiennes,* complained that the defence of Fiennes by 'Brittannicus' was 'no wayes pertinent to his weekly Intelligence'.[161] Intelligence is not only what newsbooks aspired to: it is what they deviated from. When they did so they were rags, or waste paper.

The 'Intelligencer' actively gathered and communicated news. A distinction was maintained between Information and Intelligence. Juxtaposed against 'news', 'Information' and 'Intelligence' might look synonymous: played off against each other, the relationship of Information to Intelligence was an extension of that between Information/Intelligence and news. Information referred to editorial matter, informing the judgement of the readers: Intelligence was a relationship, a footing of intercourse established with the reader in which the editor was responsible for gathering and passing on news as well as interpreting it. This distinction was clearest in George Smith's *Scotish Dove*: the purpose of which was 'to inform the judgements of the ignorant'. The ignorant were not simply ignorant of the news or Intelligence, they were ignorant in their judgement. Truth was clear enough for Smith: *Aulicus* was 'the opposit of truth', for he 'engrosseth all untruth; and as maliciously suppresseth truth'. The news was not a sufficient path to truth, the reader had to be guided through it: 'if men were as diligent to search out truth, as they are desirous to here Newes, our Dove may give light enough.'[162] Intelligence led to Information which in turn led to understanding and action. Question-and-answer sections in newsbooks implied this. Smith's 'Intelligence' was often as little newsworthy as his 'Information', but the gesture was significant.[163] Perhaps defending himself against criticisms on this point, he developed an explicit formulation of the relationship between Information and Intelligence, which illustrates the widely held distinction:

It may be some will tell me, (as they have) that I digresse from the way of intelligence, &c. to them I answer; That I digresse not from the way of informa-

[158] *Britanicus* 100, 6 Oct. 1645, 889, 286.100/E304(2).
[159] *Mastix* 1, 27 Aug. 1652, 339.1/E674(18).
[160] *Best and Most Perfect Intelligencer* 1, 8 Aug. 1650, 1, 23.1/E609(6).
[161] [William Prynne], *A Checke to Brittanicus* (1644; P3926), 4.
[162] *Scotish Dove* 4, 10 Nov. 1643, 25, 29–30, 26, 594.004/E75(21).
[163] *Scotish Dove* 130, 22 Apr. 1646, 629, 594.130/E334(1).

tion, which I have ever propounded to my selfe to mix with my intelligence; information to cleare the judgement, is better then intelligence to please the fancie; and by such information the evill causes may be removed, from whence flow evill effects and sad intelligences; But till mens judgements are right they will erre in action: and erroneous actions bring forth severall disasters. But if we, everie one of us, would forsake our own ends, and seeke (in our places) to further Gods Worke, to set up truth in our hearts, and seeke to be at peace one with another, as we have Covenanted before God; all our intelligence will be joyous, and God will make us a happie and blessed people.[164]

Intelligence for Intelligence's sake may be entertaining: better Information may lead to clearer judgement, and end the war. These linguistic categories constitute a meaningful, coherent, and precise distinction in popular, post-Ramist rhetoric.[165] Their meaning reified between the years 1643 and 1645, as a result of editors' conscientious attempts to rationalize their role in the presentation of news.

Editorial intervention did not run counter to objective reporting, as is sometimes suggested today. The framing of Intelligence was a legitimate practice for an editor; it led to greater, rather than less, truth. It was less an act of distortion than of bringing out the hidden thread of divinity in the news. Editors were not, like Hartlib, 'disinterested promoters of knowledge', but then disinterested is perhaps too strong a term for Hartlib himself, who worked for the good of international Protestantism.[166] The Intelligencer parallels, perhaps, the poet who uses newsbooks to write poetry, using the historiographical licence of fictional speeches, and the poet's right to informed partiality, and thereby approaching more closely the truth; as perhaps Cowley felt he did.[167] The Intelligencer was a facilitator, a reader immersed in books yet a public-spirited agent of the action of another.[168] Actors in politics provide, in Gabriel Harvey's words, 'Particular matters of counsell, and pollicye, besides daylye freshe newes, and A thousande both ordinary, and extraordinary occurrents, and accidents in ye world', but they in turn need professionals to assess them.[169] The same is true of newsbook-readers and their Intelligencers. Political agents need their counsellors, political spectators need their commentators. The journalist mediated between political actors and their public.

[164] *Scotish Dove* 92, 25 July 1645, 723, 594.092/E293(29).

[165] For a background see Skerpan, *Rhetoric of Politics*, 1–31.

[166] Clucas, 'Samuel Hartlib's Ephemerides', 33.

[167] Abraham Cowley, *The Civil War*, ed. Allan Pritchard (Toronto, 1973), 19–35; Gerald M. MacLean, *Time's Witness: Historical Representation in English Poetry, 1603–1660* (Madison, 1990), 177–267.

[168] Lisa Jardine and Anthony Grafton, '"Studied for Action": How Gabriel Harvey Read his Livy', *P&P* 129 (1990), 48; Sawyer, *Printed Poison*, 17–21.

[169] Jardine and Grafton, 'How Gabriel Harvey Read his Livy', 52.

Poetry and the newsbook rebellion of 1648

> Since many Diurnals (for which we are griev'd)
> Are come from both Houses, and are not believ'd,
> The better to help them for running and flying,
> We have put them in Verse to authorize their lying:
> For it has beene debated and found to be true,
> That lying's a Parliament priviledge too.
> And that they may the sooner our conquests rehearse,
> We are minded to put them in galloping verse.
> But so many maim'd souldiers from Reading their came,
> That in spite of the Surgeons make our verses run lame.
> We have ever us'd factions; and now it is knowne,
> Our poverty has made us poeticall growne.[170]

The opening lines of *A new Diurnall of Passages more exactly drawne up then heretofore* (1643) borrow an equation between verse and fictitiousness at least as old as Plato, the formula Sir Philip Sidney cunningly overturned in his *Defence of Poetry*. The author of *A new Diurnall* played gamesomely with the inappropriateness of writing parliamentary news in verse, gesturing towards the exaggeration and romanticizing of the news-ballad:

> Thus far we have gone in rhyme to disclose
> What never was utter'd by any in prose . . .[171]

In Sir William Davenant's *Preface to Gondibert*, and in Hobbes's response, poetry and history were clearly distinguished in the kinds of truth each represented. Perhaps because recent history had been unkind, they preferred the historical fictions available to the poet.[172]

Where poetry did intermingle with a news-discourse prior to 1647, the clash of genres was usually deployed to satiric effect. In *A Description Of the Passage of Thomas late Earle of Strafford, over the River of Styx*, a 1641 play-pamphlet which Anthony Wood dismissed as 'Nothing but fooleries & rascallitiy', Strafford breaks down into verse when narrating the news from the world of the living to Noy.[173] The chaotic nature of worldly affairs dictates that the most appropriate genre in which to

[170] [?Alexander Brome], *A new Diurnall* (Oxford, 1643; N631), sig. A; reprinted in *The Rump* (1660; B4850B); and *Rump Songs* (1662; B4851).

[171] *A new Diurnall*, 8. On ballads prior to 1640 see Watt, *Cheap Print and Popular Piety*, 11–127; for a general account, though not particularly useful for the 1640s, see Natascha Würzbach, *The Rise of the English Street Ballad, 1550–1650*, trans. Gayna Walls (Cambridge, 1990).

[172] C. R. Orchard, 'Literary Theory in the English Civil War 1642–1660', Oxford M.Phil. thesis (1989), 39; Zwicker, *Lines of Authority*, 17–26; C. V. Wedgwood, *Poetry and Politics under the Stuarts* (Cambridge, 1960), 71–103.

[173] *A Description Of the Passage* (May 1641; D1166/E156(21)), sig. A3; Bod.: Wood 366(11).

represent the news is a low-verse satire. The truth is so inverted it paradoxically needs a debased, deceiving form to convey it.

Assisted by the publishing efforts of Humphrey Moseley, poetry remained in name an élite, royalist form, but the trials of the civil war demanded that it signify defeat and ignominy as much as heroism and education.[174] The cavaliers were determined to preserve their aesthetic rights, but in the process the heroic verse became the drinking song. Poetry in cheap publications was prone to absorb a vituperative, plain style. By 1647 the political implications of genre had shifted such that newsbooks began to use poetry for a serious-satirical purpose, and by mid-1648 this had become a broad convention.

Poetry had been used in newsbooks before 1647. Elegies were respectable in the context of a news publication: *Britanicus* had printed an elegy for Pym; *Scotish Dove* occasionally included poems.[175] In 1646 *Kingdomes Weekly Intelligencer* printed a verse satire on the cowardice of Prince Rupert's cavaliers; *Mercurius Cambro-Britannus* printed a verse prophecy in 1643.[176] Many newsbooks quoted and translated fragments of Greek or Latin verse, but these generally were more a proof of erudition than a manner of verbal assault.

Royalists took the initiative. The first newsbook systematically to incorporate poetry as integral to its identity was *Mercurius Melancholicus* by John Hackluyt. *Melancholicus* first appeared in September 1647 with a full title-page, complete with Latin and English poems. This established it as a 'literary' newsbook. *Elencticus* and *Pragmaticus*, though without title-pages, soon followed with four-quatrain, ballad-like poems preceding the editorial of each issue. In 1648 Nedham suggested that poetry could be singularly effective as communication: 'Not that I am a whit opinionated of this way of *Riming* constantly, but only to tickle and charme the more *vulgar phant'sies*, who little regard *Truths* in a grave and serious *garb*, have I hitherto been thus light and *Phantastick*, both in *Verse* and *Prose*.'[177] One 'counterfeit' *Melancholicus* claimed 'I sing to cure the times', giving an instrumental power to poetry.[178] These newsbooks commonly proclaimed the aesthetic superiority of royalist writers and readers.[179] *Elencticus* satirized the conventions of parliamentary speeches in a poem entitled 'The Thanks of the Hovse':

[174] *Secret Rites*, 1–37, 113–55; *L&R* 250–94.

[175] *MTN* 105–6; *Scotish Dove* 110, 27 Nov. 1645, 872, 594.110/E310(9); *Scotish Dove* 127, 28 Mar. 1646, [610], 594.127/E330(3).

[176] *KWI* 140, 20 Mar. 1646, 214.140/E327(18); *Cambro Brittanus* 4, 20 Nov. 1643, 708.4/E76(14).

[177] *Pragmaticus* 1, 4 Apr. 1648, 369.201/E434(17).

[178] *Melancholicus* 52, 21 Aug. 1648, 344.52A; attr. to Parker in *History*, 82.

[179] Accepted in subsequent criticism: Clyde, 129; *History*, *passim*; Wedgwood, *Poetry and Politics*, 106; Cranfield, *Press & Society*, 13; and others.

> O *Serjeant Wild*, we give the hearty *praise*
> For *justifying* all our *Lawlesse* wayes! . . .
> Thy *Ruffe we'le* count th'*Epitome* of *Law*,
> Thy *Poding-stick*, the *Scepter* that shall awe
> *Malignants*, that dare lift their *Clutched-fists*
> 'Gainst us so stately *Monarchomachists.*[180]

Two issues later *Elencticus* attacked those writers, journalists, and poets who endeavoured to dignify the parliamentarian cause:

> Who ist would take a *Pride* to represent
> *Luke Harruney* in's *Hæbrew complement?*
> Or *Dillingham*, or *Peck*, that *Idolize*
> The *Rebell-Iuncto*, and divulge their *Lyes*?
> Who ist desireth to attaine the *Glory*,
> Of *Tom May's* place; The *Rebells Secretary*?
> Who would their *Hystory* like him compile,
> Or be a *sprigge* in such *Hoofe-beate a style*?
> Who would be *Withers*, when his *captanic-ship*,
> Honest *John Taylor* shall both *strip* and *whip*?[181]

A few lines later *Elencticus* exclaimed: 'But I have no more roome to *ryme* in.' Though the author, Wharton, took the enemy to task for their creative deficiencies, he had few delusions about the quality of his verse. It is appropriately bad, and to the point. An *Elencticus* in September 1649 incorporated a poem about Cromwell's arrival in Dublin, asking: '*What though* George Wither's *croaking* Notes, | *Their* Actions *Magnifie*?' It notes that Wither had been 'Composing a *Hymne* of *Praises* for their great deliverance and Victory against *Ormond* . . . in hopes to get his Arreares', and expresses a preference for Wither's 'Royalist' verse, reproducing the galloping scansion of the republican material:

> I'm sure hee has shew'd himselfe a compleat Hypocrite, a dissembling Knave; as any man that Reads his *Campo-Musæ* and compares it with this *Oblation* may easily perceive, his verses prance it in this manner.
>
> *Withers a Dull and Drunken Sot,*
> *A Rustique-Rymer o're a Pot,*
> *Whose Barren* Genius *has the Rot;*
> *Hath writ a Thank-Oblation.*
> *And though his* Campo-Musæ *sings*

[180] *Elencticus* 25, 17 May 1648, sigs. Bb3–Bb3ᵛ, 312.25/E443(7).

[181] *Elencticus* 27, 31 May 1648, sig. Dd4ᵛ, 312.27/E445(23). The writers mentioned are Henry Walker (Luke Harruney was his anagrammatic pseudonym), John Dillingham, and Samuel Pecke, journalists; Thomas May, historian of the Long Parliament; Joshua Sprigge, historian of the New Model Army; George Wither, the parliamentarian soldier, poet, and pamphleteer; and John Taylor, the royalist poet and pamphleteer. There is also a pun on the name of Colonel Thomas Pride.

His Love and Loyaltie to Kings;
Yet now he calleth those vaine things.
To this brave Reformation.
Now honest Taylor *I commit*
This Brazen undigested bit
Unto thy, more deserving wit;
T' Examine *and* Retort:
And shew us how the Doting-Foole
Hath dabled in a dirty Poole,
To give the Common-wealth *a Stoole,*
And we will thank thee for't.[182]

This invocation recalled a passage from John Taylor's *Rebells Anathematized, and Anatomized* (1645):

Wither that dainty Darling of the Dolts,
The *Scout*, the *Scotish Dove*, and the Diurnall,
These (like to *Gothams* Archers) shoot their bolts,
And madly strive the Truth to overturne all . . .
The Scribe that writes the Weekes Intelligence
Th'Occurrents, and the flying lying Poste . . .
That poyson-framing Hound *Britannicus*,
That weekly snarling Whelpe of *Cerberus*,
That Microcosme of *Morbus Gallicus*,
That *Lernean* venom'd Snake of *Erebus*.[183]

Wither was a whipping-boy for anti-parliamentarian writing which linked bad poetry with newsbooks.

Newsbook poetry was not an exclusive ally to royalists. *Mercurius Anti-Pragmaticus* used poetry in 1647. Although the brief 1647 revival of *Britanicus* did not use verse, John Hall's 1648 *Mercurius Britanicus Alive Again* beat the royalists over the head with their own genres. Hall's *Britanicus* resembled a royalist publication, and after four quatrains cajoling those who would return to the 'bonds' of 'tyranny', he began in irony:

Thus do we according to the solemnity of a Pamphlet begin with verses; for if we should not retain the accustomed ceremonies of abusing the people, we should render them uselesse, and loose our labour. For I pray you, was there ever an Almanack that wanted an Anatomie, and could passe with the Country-men? or how many Ballads would sell without a formall wood cut? These general complyances must needs be observed, or else the people out of the rate of their madnesse will not be brought to parley.[184]

[182] *Elencticus* 19, 3 Sept. 1649, 145, 152, 316.19/E572(15).

[183] John Taylor, *Rebells Anathematized, And Anatomized* (Oxford, 25 May 1645; T501), 3, 5.

[184] *Britanicus Alive Again* 1, 16 May 1648, 1–2, 282.01/E442(19).

Mercurius Censorius (June 1648), after the now mandatory poem, began: 'Tis to be lamented that the *Royallists* continue yet so low and *miserable*, who have so long had such rare *comforters* as *Pragmaticus, Elencticus, Melancholicus, Publicus*, and a number more of them, who (if their words had had *force*) would have kept up a sick and *sinking* party.'[185] Poetry was associated with royalists not because they 'had a more flexible notion of poetic decorum',[186] but because they were first in on the act, and claimed territorial rights. Historians have tended to privilege the royalist aesthetic, perceiving the parliamentarian and republican as somewhat stiff and sombre, if not downright ugly.[187] Nedham, Hall, and Wither are neglected, distorted, or silenced in the process.

Poetry was important, not as a showcase for literary skills, but as a sign of disregard for the pretence of reporting and of readers' supposed appetite for news. Wharton's verse in *Elencticus* was in Latin, and thus exclusive, which dulled its vituperative edge. None the less it precipitated another shift in the dominant languages of the newsbooks; the Intelligencer was increasingly displaced by the forceful controversialist. The balance shifted away from news to editorial, news items were presented in a more aggressive tone, and more space was devoted to attacks on other newsbooks. Forceful metaphors usurped the remaining pretence to passing on intelligence, and the emergence of poetry was inseparable from this development. Poetry was freely mixed with prose, miscegenating political satire. In recognition of this, *Mercurius Poeticus* appeared on 13 May 1648, not entirely devoid of news, but swimming in contumely, and all in verse.

Persuasion, illumination, and prediction: Pride's Purge in newsbooks

In late 1648 the detailed reporting of news was concomitant with strong interpretation and passionate persuasion. Writers of newsbooks claimed that they were powerful. Their confidence was tested by the events of 6 December, when army officers excluded from parliament those members who were sympathetic to treating with the king, thereby opening the way for the trial that led to the regicide. The interventionist, instrumental role of newsbooks can be illuminated by a close scrutiny of the reporting of these events and the variety of rhetorical strategies available to their writers.

[185] *Censorius* 1, 1 June 1648, 1, 296.1/E445(31).

[186] Roger Pooley, 'The Poet's Cromwell', *Critical Survey*, 5 (1993), 226.

[187] David Norbrook, 'Lucan, Thomas May, and the Creation of a Republican Literary Culture', in Sharpe and Lake, eds., *Culture and Politics*, 45–66.

Nedham was immodest about his ability to affect the course of events at Westminster:

> *Last week* I was routed by the *Mirmydons*, but now you shall see me rout them, if they doe not rout themselves with these *wild courses*, and save me a labour: And therefore (to set them out in their proper Colours) I must needs re-collect part of the last weeks proceedings in the Houses and Army, that passed on *Friday*, *Saturday*, and *Monday*, December 1. 2. 4. which being matters of an eminent nature, the carriage of them must by no meanes be buried in *Oblivion*.[188]

He claimed his potency received official recognition:

> A little before the *House rose*, there was a heavy *Complaint* made by the godly Crew of Independents against *Mercurius Pragmaticus*, for revealing the Knavery of that *Faction*, in all their *Debates*, *Councells*, and *Proceedings*, whereby they are made odious in the eyes of the world; and therefore they pressed he might be severely dealt with, above all other *Malignant* and scandalous Authors, boasting, that now they had him in their *Clutches*.[189]

His Intelligence, 'the very *Cream* of all *Intelligence*',[190] revealed the true proceedings in parliament, exposed the knavery and double-dealings of Cromwell, the grandees, and the 'Faction', the 'Middle Group' in parliament,[191] and thereby enabled his readers to enlighten themselves.

The Leveller *Mercurius Militaris* had comparable conflicts with parliament:

> Last week even twenty Beagles from the State
> Pursued this Mercury with mortal hate.
> Where's that Rogue (said they) who dares speak Reason?
> When Cries for Justice are voted Treason?[192]

Elencticus argued, in turn, that the '*pretences* and *Reasons*' of the Levellers 'work wonderfully upon the fancy of the silly people, who cannot distinguish *Truth* from *Falsehood*, and have seduced very many from their *Obedience* and *Loyalty* to his Majesty'.[193] He admitted that '*Truth* sometimes must Lurke *in Angulis*, and watch opportunities'.[194]

The potency which newsbooks averred was not achieved simply through 'speaking', but through illumination, a metaphor closely fitting the Intelligencer's role. It relied on the participation of their readers' own vision. Accordingly *Elencticus* credited its readers with

188 *Pragmaticus* 36.37, 12 Dec. 1648, sigs. Ccc^{v}–Ccc2, 369.236/E476(2).

189 *Pragmaticus* 34, 21 Nov. 1648, sig. [Bb4], 369.234/E473(7).

190 *Pragmaticus* 34, sig. Bb; cf. *Pragmaticus* 32 & 33, 14 Nov. 1648, sig. Zz^{v}, 369.232/E470(33).

191 Underdown, *Pride's Purge*, 103.

192 *Militaris* 5, 21 Nov. 1648, 33, 346.5/E473(8).

193 *Elencticus* 49, 31 Oct. 1648, 399, 312.49/E469(15).

194 *Elencticus* 55, 12 Dec. 1648, 525, 312.55/E476(4).

superior eyesight; and *The Moderate* purported to address 'the opinion of wise men'.[195] Good news illuminated the understanding of readers, bad news clouded it. Light and darkness fought in politics, in language, and between rival newsbooks. Nedham's purpose in *Pragmaticus* was to vindicate 'the *best of Princes*':

This cannot be better done, than by representing the truth and sincerity of his Proceedings and endeavours for Peace by this *Treaty*, which must needs gain him so high an opinion in the hearts of his People, as will soone confute those nasty *Pamphleteers* now set on worke by the *new* STATES, to barke against the *Sun*, and blaspheme the royall Majesty of *England*.[196]

Accurate representation discovers reality. Language, the dress of thought, assumes the perfect transparency of the emperor's new clothes. This 'plain-style' philosophy of language which accepts the potential duplicity of words is simultaneously cross-threaded with the belief that words are inherently vital. Language is a glass, darkened or otherwise, upon reality and yet actively stimulates the reader.[197]

These terms were a common currency. *Militaris* used the metaphor of illumination to describe his revelation of the political machinations of the king and the deceptive propaganda of the royalist *Elencticus*:

But saith Elencticus, *Militaris* is a Traytor; and why I pray? because his poor Majesty cannot find a Cabs noddle dark enough to hammer a Chain in for the people, from the sight of *Militaris*; He cannot consult with any Grandees to deceive and enslave the people, but *Militaris* will tell them; He cannot counterfeit a sick fit in his conscience to gull the people with shews of piety, but *Militaris* will discover it, O horrid Treason.[198]

Militaris would break through the shadows in language sufficiently transparent to 'discover' to the people the truth behind the surface of shows, counterfeits, and feigned piety, he would become the eyes of his readers.

A letter from Scotland in *The Moderate* (linked with *Militaris* as 'those bawling Curres of the Levelling faction'[199]) used the millenarian language of illumination to describe political transformation:

When once the light breaks forth in this Kingdom, (and I think the sun is neer rising) it will warm and heal apace, but the clouds must be broken first, the foundation of this old fabrick must be shaken; and when the poore, blinde, dead people shall see the light, and feel the warmth of the sun (sweet liberty) to redeem them out of their present slavery, then the struglings of Scotland will

195 *Moderate* 16, 31 Oct. 1648, sig. Q4^v, 413.2016/E469(16).
196 *Pragmaticus* 32 & 33, sigs. Zz–Zz^v.
197 McKenzie, *Bibliography and the Sociology of Texts*, 24.
198 *Militaris* 5, 34.
199 *Melancholicus* 58–62, 21 Nov. 1648, 1, 344.59B/E472(26).

be as great as those of England, which hath overcome a few of those, but not yet gotten to the top of its glory.[200]

An editorial in the same issue argued that the people of England were still under the Norman Yoke, and that 'all the Laws of this Land, and most part of the earth, are Tyrannical and Arbitrary, being made and maintained by the sword'.[201] Any beneficial legislation must be forced from the rulers: *The Moderate* positioned itself as a theoretical spearhead to action.

Intelligence led to understanding and understanding to revelation and revelation led to action; that is the affirmation by writers of newsbooks of their own role. They also endeavoured to sway their readers' minds through prediction. A week before Pride's Purge the last, belated, and possibly counterfeit issue of *Mercurius Melancholicus* prophesied:

And verily it shall goe hard, but those Military Ghospell-men, will all be Iudges in Israel, since Duke *Oliver* is comming in Person (some say 'is already at *Westminster*) brim-full of malice against his Majesty, resolving to impeach all Treaters, as Traytors, and to make short work with all Peace-makers, as well in the Houses, and at *Westminster*, as in the Common Councell, and the City.

O brave Oliver,
O rare Oliver,
O fine Brewer.[202]

The considerable knowledge and high political expertise newsbook writers professed enabled them to judge the course of future events. *Anti-Pragmaticus* argued that the prophetic role of *Pragmaticus* was fundamental to the royalist cause.[203] These powers were mocked as early as 1643 in a satirical publication entitled: *Mercurius Propheticus, Or, A Collection of Some Old Predictions, O! May They Only Prove But Empty Fictions*.[204] This was not a metaphysical ability in the tradition of the prophetic pamphlets of Lilly and Wharton. The theoretical basis of their influence was articulated conveniently by Hobbes:

For the foresight of things to come, which is Providence, belongs onely to him by whose will they are to come. From him onely, and supernaturally, proceeds Prophecy. The best Prophet naturally is the best guesser; and the best guesser, he that is most versed and studied in the matters he guesses at: for he hath most *Signes* to guesse by.[205]

[200] *Moderate* 17, 7 Nov. 1648, sig. R2, 413.2017/E470(12).
[201] See Christopher Hill, *Puritanism and Revolution* (1958; 1968), 58–125.
[202] *Melancholicus*, 58–62, 1–2.
[203] *Anti-Pragmaticus* 3, 4 Nov. 1647, 2, 270.03/E412(27).
[204] 1643; M1769.
[205] Thomas Hobbes, *Leviathan*, ed. Richard Tuck (Cambridge, 1991), 22; see also 193–6, below.

Yet editors also mystified their role by claiming that they shaped events, through intervention as well as representation. Newsbooks rapidly manufactured an interpretation of Pride's Purge for posterity.

The eleven newsbooks published in the week 7–13 December show that the distinction between a 'pamphleteer' and a 'news retailer' is not an operable one. The binary opposition between truth and falsehood is not sufficient to describe accurately all the kinds of statements in newsbooks.[206] News and opinion were woven so closely that one could not be obtained without the other.

A Declaration Collected out of The Journalls of Both Houses of Parliament, an unassuming newsbook which first appeared in December 1648, was almost alone in reporting on the sermons preached on Sunday 10 December. The editor quoted the texts for two (Rev. 9: 2, 3; Eccles. 10: 18, 19) and prefaced the third, 'It was more seasonable councell that was given by another, for the remnant of Members that are not debarred the House.' The text was Amos 5: 15; 'Hate the evill, and love the good, and establish judgement in the gate, it may be that the Lord God of Hoasts will be gracious unto the remnant [of Joseph].'[207] This is a statement of opinion, made through a minor news item. The editor also expressed his own opinion, this time refracted through the precarious medium of another language, when he reported for 7 December: 'The Lords sate very little, and adjourned until Tuesday, *Sic transit gloria mundis.*'[208]

A similarly indirect comment was made in *The Perfect Weekly Account.* Under the heading '*Tuesday, Decemb.* 12', it begins 'I had almost forgotten . . .', and proceeds to relate a sermon preached the previous Sunday: 'Mr. *P.* in another discourse saith, that in the whole Book of God he findes not any text *of priviledge of Parliament,* which indeed came in with the conquest, and is now in the hands of the Conquerors.'[209] The confused and informal opening prefaced and concealed an editorial interjection. The editor also foregrounded his own beliefs by including an opinionated letter from Dover, expressing wonder that so much of the army remained unpaid and stating the expectation that they would soon 'hear of some eminent action performed by the Army at their approach so near the Parliament'. When the newsbook was published, the news of this 'eminent action', Pride's Purge, was already a week old.

[206] J. H. Hexter, *The Reign of King Pym* (Cambridge, Mass., 1941), 213; Brian Manning, *1649: The Crisis of the English Revolution* (1992), 27, 223 n. 52, 202, 265–6 n. 83.

[207] *A Declaration* 2, 13 Dec. 1648, 13, 90.2/E476(17), the last two words elided.

[208] *Declaration* 2, 11. This comment suggests that the author was not Henry Walker, as attributed in N&S. It also printed at length a speech by the king.

[209] *PWA* [39], 13 Dec. 1648, 312, 533.39/E476(15).

The complex texture of information and persuasion is evident in accounts of the morning of 6 December. Pecke's *Perfect Diurnall* is a useful benchmark because historians have credited it with greater objectivity than most newsbooks:

This day Col. *Riches* Regiment of horse and Col. *Prides* of Foot were a guard to the Parliament, and the City trained bands discharged.

Severall Members going to the House were seized upon and kept in custody by speciall Order from the Generall and Councell of the Army, which the house of Commons then sitting being informed of, it was ordered that the Serjeant at Arms attending the house of Commons should be required forthwith to go to the said Members so seized, and under a guard in the Queenes Court and Court of Wards, and acquaint them that it is the pleasure of the house that they forthwith attend the service of the house. The Serjeant returning brought answer that the Captaine of the guard had order to secure them, which order he was to obey before any other command, and therefore could not in prosecution thereof dismisse them til he had other orders to the contrary.[210]

Rushworth thought this sufficient to incorporate it verbatim in his *Historical Collections.*[211] The narrative is clear, though conspicuously the list of the 'seized' members follows two pages later. The report stages the conflict between two authorities as a drama, unfolding in the actions of the Sergeant at Arms who becomes the central character in that conflict. The Commons knew that the embassy of the sergeant would not accomplish the liberation of the captives. Ludlow presumed that they did it 'rather upon the account of decency, than from any desire they had that their message should be obeyed'.[212] The dramatization of the protest is enhanced by the use of direct speech: 'it *is* the pleasure . . .'. The remainder of the sentence is a quote. The reader witnesses, by proxy, the outcome as it unfolds.[213] The text is allowed, within certain confines, to speak for itself. This technique underlies the frequent reproduction of documents in newsbooks, and is fundamental to the way the newsbook works. It is not simply a case of editorial laziness. The presentation of the exchange in the *Diurnall* upholds the process of law, though the members remain imprisoned.

Drama was also the pith of *Kingdomes Weekly Intelligencer*:

early in the morning some Companyes of the Army appeared at Westminster under the Command of Collonel Pride and Collonel Rich, who dismissed the

[210] *Perfect Diurnall* 280, 11 Dec. 1648, 2252, 504.280/E526(40).

[211] *HC*[4] ii. 1353.

[212] See Gardiner[2] iv. 270–1; *The Memoirs of Edmund Ludlow*, ed. C. H. Firth, 2 vols. (Oxford, 1894), i. 211.

[213] See the analysis of 'witnessing' as a means of validating experiments in Steven Shapin and Simon Schaffer, *Leviathan and the Air-Pump: Hobbes, Boyle, and the Experimental Life* (Princeton, 1985); also Richard W. F. Kroll, *The Material Word: Literate Culture in the Restoration and Early Eighteenth Century* (Baltimore, 1991), ch. 5.

city Trayned Bands. Collonel Pride being on the toppe of the Staires as you goe unto the House of Commons, and having a List of those Members whom he was to apprehend, as they were entring the House, did give them, by course a courteous salutation, and with his hat in his hand he told them he had received orders to seize upon their persons, which having accordingly performed, he delivered them to some Officers that stood ready to receive them, who did secure them in the Queens Court, where they continued all day, and in the evening were conveyed into a House darke and low enough, a place of great Receipt, and knowne by the name of Hell.[214]

The image of imperious Pride doffing his hat is ironic; the failure to bare the head was a gesture used to characterize the godly. Pride's 'courteous salutation' to the members was surely meant to be comic.[215] The dramatic encounter between Pride and the members is presented with different emphases from Pecke's account. The strong incidental detail is unusual, as is the gesture towards the reader in second person. The author facilitates the visualization of the incident; he flatteringly implies that the reader will know the staircase, and emphasizes his own authority by indicating that he himself does. The picture of Pride at the top of the staircase is perhaps intended to evoke a familiar adage.

In a palpably symbolic episode, *Kingdomes Weekly Intelligencer* described the seizing of the treasuries on 8 December: 'The Souldiers also at the same time did come into Guild-Hall, the two Giants Corineus and Gogmagog, neither making resistance nor complaint. The Souldiers looked on them, and remembring what Giant-words were spoken before their comming to the City, they compared the vain confidence and Rhodomontadoes of the living to the statues of the Dead.'[216] Through the confusion, a message emerges. The statues in Guildhall were proverbial for lack of conscience.[217] The two icons lead into an open-ended meditation on the present. The 'vain confidence and Rhodomontadoes'[218] of the dead overshadow, in the soldiers' eyes and memories, 'the living', namely those who had spoken out before the advance on London, both MPs and officers. All is vanity, the editor urges, leaving the soldiers dwarfed by the towering, Ozymandias-like villains of the past. The statues were themselves destroyed by fire in 1666.

[214] *KWI* 289, 12 Dec. 1648, 1178–9, 214.289/E476(9).

[215] Contrary to Underdown, *Pride's Purge*, 136, 144, 146–7.

[216] *KWI* 289, 1183.

[217] *A Dialogue between the Two Giants in Guildhall* (1661; D1335).

[218] The same week Secretary Nicholas' correspondent John Lawrans (see n. 225 below) passed on a newsletter, apparently written by Nedham, which referred to the probability of an agreement between his Majesty and the Parliament, 'notwithst. ye Rodomont: of ye army'. Bod.: MS Clarendon 34, f. 7^v^.

This is a very creative piece of reporting. The statues are misnamed[219] because the incident alludes to a passage in Foxe's *Actes and Monuments* describing the celebration of the marriage of Queen Mary to Philip of Spain in 1554: 'and at London-bridge, as he entered at the draw-bridge, was a vain great spectacle set up, two images representing two giants, the one names Chorinæus, and the other, Gogmagog, holding between them certain Latin verses, which for the vain ostentation of flattery I overpasse.'[220] This was excerpted into the 1587 edition of Holinshed's chronicles.[221] The anecdote as told by Foxe and Holinshed is a reminder of royal transience; its deployment in the newsbook is meant to reflect back on the impermanence of the army's power. This is a covert royalist gesture, for those who recognize the echo.

The Moderate justified the purge as a logical clause in a long, historical sentence. A syntactical disturbance in the period introduces an ambiguity:

The Basis of a new warre thus laid, and a two yeares adiournment intended the next day to be concluded, the Army thus wounded for securing his Maiesty, and their Remonstrance waved, by their first Vote the King cleared, and this impudent Message from the City, grounded upon the whole, puts the Army upon much necessity, and no lesse Iustice to secure some of his Maiesties principall friends, and (Kingdomes enemies) in Parliament, against some of whom they had already preferred a Charge, and against the rest, another intended the next day. This put in execution, and about 40. Members apprehended the next day, *viz.* . . .[222]

Instead of the visual drama in the *Diurnall* and *Intelligencer*, there is a conceptual one. Necessity and justice cause the action, though the disruptive crux 'grounded upon the whole' suggests that the necessity is only apparent set in its undiminished context. With the assistance of the now-secluded members, parliament 'had then been able to have voted the Army Traytors the next day in plaine English', and 'consequently laid foundation for a new warre', which is plausible. The journalist states that infamous consequences would follow the Commons' acceptance of the king's concessions:

the grand Delinquent of the Kingdom excused from Iustice, contrary to the desire and Petition of all the well affected in the Kingdome, (which is the

[219] The statues were actually Gog and Magog, the last surviving giants of the race which had settled in Albion. They were slain by Brutus and his followers, one of which was Corineus, who had previously slain Goëmagot. Gog and Magog were said to have been brought to London and chained to Brutus' palace, on which site Guildhall was supposedly built.

[220] *The Acts and Monuments of John Foxe*, 4th edn., ed. Revd Josiah Pratt, introd. Revd John Stoughton, 8 vols. (1877), vi. 557.

[221] Raphael Holinshed, *The Third Volume of Chronicles* (1587; *STC* 13569), 1120.

[222] *Moderate* 22, 12 Dec. 1648, [197–8], 413.2022/E476(5).

Kingdome) The Arbytrary power of the House of Lords maintained (as a third Party in making a Law) and the King made equall in power with the whole Kingdome, by writing *Le Roy, Le veult,* which his Predecessors formerly got, and he now forfeited by Conquest.

The politically intense editorial preceding this report advocated an alternative: 'We finde in History, That the next in succession to the Crown, by Propinquity of blood, have oftentimes been put back by the Common wealth, and others farther off admitted in their places, even in those Kingdoms where succession prevaileth.'[223] A series of examples from biblical and British history ensue, reaching Richard II. *The Moderate* was not a simple and unified piece of polemic but the product of a collaborative enterprise, particularly in the busy weeks of late 1648. Its news content was not merely a function of its political position.

The quality of news in *Pragmaticus* was, given the conditions of its production, very good.[224] Perhaps the parliament's beagles were not so hot in their pursuit of Nedham as he claimed in print. At the same time Nedham was writing a newsletter to John Lawrans which accompanied and supplemented his printed news: he had to be larger in his particulars when no 'Prag' was 'abroad'. Lawrans transcribed the newsletter and passed it on to Secretary Nicholas, presumably enclosing with it a copy of *Pragmaticus,* and then Nicholas passed it on to a 'freind'.[225] The purge hit Nedham hard, despite his earlier warnings. He began the issue for 12 December in a jubilant mood, and bridled through the week, though his writing remained antagonistic enough. Nedham lucidly pathologized Pride's Purge, making the action seem zealous and unpremeditated:

Wednesday, Decem. 6. The *Saints* being over heated with the former daies work of the *House,* and finding that all went crosse to their wild *Remonstrance.* They sent a paper this day to the Commons, requiring that the *Members Impeached* in the year 1647. and Maior Gen. *Brown,* who (they say invited in the *Scots*) may be secured, and brought to Iustice; and that the *ninety odd* Members, who refused to vote against the late *Scotish* Ingagement, and all those that voted the recalling

[223] *Moderate* 22, [198], 189. The chronicle of kings became a republican genre: e.g. John Hall's *Grounds and Reasons of Monarchy* (Edinburgh, 1651; H346).

[224] Underdown, *Pride's Purge,* 138; Cotton, 310.

[225] Bod.: MS Clarendon 34, ff. 13^{v}, 8^{v}. According to *The Calendar of the Clarendon State Papers,* I, 458, John was probably Edward's son. Nowhere does Nedham's name appear in these letters, but the style and political insight of some of the copied letters, is clearly Nedham's, and in one letter the writer predicts: 'no Prag, wilbe abroad this weeke' (f. 8^{v}). Lawrans is not Nedham himself, and the letters are not in Nedham's hand. In a letter dated 12 Jan. 1648/9, Lawrans observes that he is in danger because the General has issued a proclamation banishing the king's party from the town (ff. 73–4^{v}). Nedham was under threat of arrest long before this, and the proclamation would therefore not have affected him. Moreover Lawrans hints at some treating with the authorities he was doing on behalf of his correspondent: Nedham was hardly in a position to do this.

the Votes of *non-Addresses*, and voted for the *Treaty*, and concurred in yesterdayes *votes*, declaring the Kings *Concessions to be a Ground for the house to proceed upon to the settlement of the Kingdom*, may be immediately suspended the *House*. This paper being delivered in, their *zeale* was so sharp set, that they scorned to stay for an *Answer*, but the *Grandees* immediately sent their *Janisaries*, with a List of those *Members* names which they aimed at; most of which were seized as they were going in, and some pulled out of the *House*, (as Col. *Birch* and Mr *Edw. Stephens*) and carried into the *Queens Court* Prisoners, to the number of 41. persons.[226]

Nedham may have distorted the chronology for polemical purposes: the army council in fact sent their self-justification after the purge. Nedham depersonalizes the army, fashioning a general, a council, and a colonel into a many-headed multitude, the saints, the grandees, and their janissaries. This use of fear is typical of *Pragmaticus*. Nedham pioneered the use of name-calling in royalist journalism, reaching the height of that art.

Elencticus continued to represent a simpler and more staid version of affairs:

For having (betimes this Morning) surrounded the Houses, as the Members came they seized upon and secured the persons of so many of them as they thought favoured not their Designes, and that in a Rude and Ruffianly Manner; without any regard had to the *Age* or *Quality* of the Persons: for they drive them like so many *Swine*, (the *Cavaliers* scarce ever more contemptibly) and Lodged them in *Hell* (perhaps an *Embleme* of their future *Habitation)* where they reviled and insulted over them, not suffering any body to come neare them but by speciall Licence and favour of Col. *Pride*. Their names were these . . .[227]

Wharton's analysis is simple, his objections to the disrespect for age and status are explicit and banal, and consequently his polemic is blunt. Much of the issue was spent moralizing on the fate of 'Rebels', including Hampden, Hotham, and Sir Alexander Carew, who had lost their life in pursuit of their impious cause. Though Wharton repeatedly interjected poetry into the text, his account of the purge was muted and forced in its spiritedness. The purge was a telling moment for royalist journalists. Nedham concluded *Pragmaticus* with a hollow rhyme:

Stand firm, and then down goe their Saintships all:
Pride *and* Rebellion *still doe fore-run a* Fall.[228]

A few weeks later he dropped *Pragmaticus*.[229] The other royalist

[226] *Pragmaticus* 36.37, sig. [Ccc3]; *MTN* 359–64.
[227] *Elencticus* 55, 527. [228] *Pragmaticus* 36.37, sig. [Ccc4v].
[229] See *Pragmaticus (For King Charles II)* 1, 24 Apr. 1649, 370.01/E551(15); Cotton, 311.

newsbook of that week, *Mercurius Impartialis,* did not discuss the event, choosing instead to attack *The Moderate* and the now-defunct *Mercurius Militaris.*[230]

The remaining four newsbooks presented minimal sketches. *Perfect Occurrences* almost rendered the purge invisible. Walker quoted at length the 'Proposals and Desires of His Excellency the Lord Fairfax, and the generall Councell of Officers' and then offered, with no further description, 'A list of severall Members apprehended going to the Parliament, who were kept in Hell this night'.[231] Perhaps Walker was addressing Londoners whom he presumed were already semi-informed. His advertisements for his Hebrew Lectures, delivered on Friday, the same day as *Perfect Occurrences* appeared, suggests this. But by minimizing the description he presented the list as an appendix to the document printed above it, therefore gesturing towards his own approval. The typography sanctioned the authority of the document explaining the motive for the action. Exactly the same format was followed in *A Declaration*; though this newsbook had a different political stance, it was not as coherent and unified as *Perfect Occurrences.* Thomason distinguished the latter by binding it with *A Perfect Diurnall,* separate from other publications, perhaps indicating his respect.[232]

Wednesday's *Perfect Weekly Account* was similarly brief: 'the Members formerly impeached by the Army, with about forty others, were taken into custody: I shall here give you a List of their names.'[233] The list, in three columns, contained only thirty-five names, making prominent its incompleteness.[234] The *Perfect Weekly Account* devoted more of its limited space to provincial news than most other newsbooks, and kept editorial to a minimum.

The *Moderate Intelligencer* was longer than its competitors, though over two-fifths was foreign news; on balance it purveyed less political news than other newsbooks. Despite inaccuracy in the number of imprisoned members, it made the important point that the House had been reduced by a number significantly greater than this:

Certain of the Army appeared at *Westminster* early, who were commanded by Colonel *Pride,* who had a List of Names of Members, whom he was to take into Custody, and not permit to enter the House: Those who came in, after much discourse, agreed not to proceed upon any thing in a Parliamentary way, nor

[230] *Impartialis* 1, 12 Dec. 1648, 333.1/E476(3).
[231] *Perfect Occurrences* 101, 8 Dec. 1648, [755–6], 465.5101/E526(38).
[232] e.g. LT E526.
[233] *PWA* [39], 306.
[234] This does not justify Frank's claim that Border was addressing the 'meaner sort of people': Border claimed to speak to everyone. *Beginnings,* 172.

enter any Order or Vote, untill their Members were at Liberty, who besides those who forbore to come were 34.[235]

The brief report was fitted into the last page of the newsbook, which did not take full advantage of the scoop it had effectively inherited by being the only newsbook to appear on 7 December.

One other English periodical was published this week: the second issue of *Mercurius Catholicus: Communicating his Intelligence from learned Reformed Protestants, to the ignorant and unlearned sort*, containing not news but theological propaganda.[236]

The accounts of Pride's Purge in newsbooks varied for reasons both political and non-political. Even those which were most concerned to impress an interpretation upon the reader conveyed a certain amount of information: in fact some of the most restrained newsbooks were the least adequate. With the exception of the albeit entertaining *Impartialis*, all could have accompanied newsletters, and most probably did.

What is most remarkable is that they were there to comment on the purge at all. Britain had moved a long way from the 1630s and the partial recognition of the king's will that 'none do presume to print or publish any matter of news, relations, histories, or other things in prose or in verse that have reference to matters and affairs of state' without the approval of the secretary to the Privy Council.[237] Anyone who could read could understand in detail the events that led to the king's trial. These circumstances created a broader political nation, and they make it legitimate for historians to refer to 'public opinion'.[238] Newsbooks changed the political culture, influenced the way public men thought and acted, and affected the course of history.

This is not to aver that individual journalists directly persuaded their readers; though there were instances of this. Rather, they influenced perceptions of contemporary events, just as they shaped those events for historiography, presenting the immediate accounts that were later to become the raw material for historians.

Bloody horror at Whitehall

The execution of the king was the most shocking political event of the seventeenth century. Yet it did not have any great immediate impact on

235 *Moderate Intelligencer* 194, 7 Dec. 1648, [1776], 419.194/E475(26). Underdown shows that a greater number removed themselves than were removed by the army; *Pride's Purge*, 152–3.

236 *Catholicus* 2, 295.2/E475(35); date from Thomason.

237 Quoted by Sharpe, *Personal Rule*, 646.

238 Underdown, *Pride's Purge*, 174; Fletcher, *Outbreak of the English Civil War*, esp. chs. 4 and 6.

the newsbooks. Royalists purveyed their sense of outrage, but the decollation had waved the effectual limits of their power before their eyes. If anything there were undertones of disillusionment and mechanical ferocity. They had been representing Charles as a neo-martyr for years. Business remained as usual. Perhaps we should not infer too much from this: only that the literary repercussions of ideological earthquakes can be slow and immensely diffracted.

One innovation which followed the regicide is symbolic of the transformation of, and perhaps damage done to, royalist aesthetics in early 1649. John Crouch's *The Man in the Moon* delineated new directions in reportage, representing the end of the journalism of the 1640s.

April 1649 was not an auspicious time for the début of a new royalist journal, yet it transpired that the stress upon the royalist cause was generically productive. The elegy was the dominant genre in responses to the execution;[239] Crouch broke away sharply from this tendency. He worked together elements of anti-romance, tragi-comedy, ballad, and political and sexual satire. While *Man in the Moon* was generically complex, it was not a sophisticated publication. It relied heavily on prejudices and anti-puritan stereotypes for effect. It collapsed religious toleration with sexual licence, and turned the language of the Englishman's birthright of freedom back on parliament and army as oppressors. Mostly spurious anecdotes of 'rebel' dissolution and humiliation filled its pages, and any news was greatly elaborated upon. It quickly attracted official attention, warrants were issued for the seizure of its author, and its printer, Edward Crouch, was arrested.[240]

The title was taken from the entertainment in *A Midsummer Night's Dream*, signalling a world of disorder temporarily disrupting a more attractive and élite world of normality. When the new moon rises, of course, desires will be satisfied; until then Crouch takes on the role of Starveling in Bottom's play, with his lantern, thorn bush, and dog.[241] Using the figure as more than a metaphor for pure fantasy, its common currency, as in Parker's ballad,[242] Crouch further appropriated dramatic aesthetics as a royalist preserve.[243] He relied heavily on figures of inversion, such as the deployment of a skimmington ride to satirize Fairfax,

239 *Secret Rites*, 184–9; *L&R* 287–94.

240 *CSPD 1649–1650*, 438, 449, 530, 560.; *Man in the Moon* 38, 16 Jan. 1650, 301, 248.38/E589(15). The relationship between the many Crouches is yet to be explicated; *Secret Rites*, 23.

241 *Midsummer Night's Dream* (1967), I. i. 4; V. i. 250–2.

242 See Rollins, *Cavalier and Puritan*, 20–3, 33, 37, 49–51, 160–2; also *Britanicus* 108, 8 Dec. 1645, 957, 286.108/E311(11).

243 See Potter, 'The Plays and the Playwrights, 1642–1660', 263–93; *Secret Rites*, 35–6, 80–5, 90–3; *L&R* 70–92.

stigmatizing his uxorcratic masculinity.[244] His elegies were mock elegies, celebrating the death of regicides and those who had opposed monarchy. 'Heaven is just, we see'; but England was mad. London was inverted to 'Nodnol'; it was a place where royalist newsbooks were hunted down, and the presses authorized instead to print the Koran.[245] These textual representations of rituals of inversion were used entirely for conservative effects.[246] Whether the readers were equally conservative is uncertain. Frank responds with an entirely reasonable prurience, and characterizes it as reactionary and popular.[247]

The Man in the Moon can rightly be called 'popular' in terms of style only. It represents an accessible, unsophisticated commentary on politics. Its pornographic, satirical content was used for political ends.[248] Of course mirth and festivity had long had a political dimension; *The Man in the Moon* is significant because the tropes of inversion and disorder yielded sustained political commentary about monarchy and a free commonwealth.[249] The satire is not just occasional, but outlines a general critique of government.

Crouch made the usual claims to real political influence, gesturing towards his own eloquence:

my Dog is so well flesh'd, that he will make nothing to take the proudest of you all by the *Nose*, and so hold you, till I come with a Hand-saw and Saw off the Horns of your usurped *Power*; and pare your ravening Claws so close, that you shall not have the power to gripe in your devouring tallons one single six pence from a free Commoner; discharging all my murderous pieces against your *new BABEL*, till it tumbles about your eares.[250]

Crouch was, however, preaching to the converted. He mocked the education and the social standing of his enemies, calling them 'illiter-

[244] *Man in the Moon* 40, 31 Jan. 1650, 248.40/E590(12); *Secret Rites*, 35. On skimmingtons see David Underdown, 'The Taming of the Scold', in Anthony Fletcher and John Stevenson, eds., *Order and Disorder in Early-Modern England* (Cambridge, 1985), 116–36.

[245] *Man in the Moon* 40, 315; *Man in the Moon* 1, 16 Apr. 1649, [8], 248.01/E550(26); *Man in the Moon* 7, 30 May 1649, 59, 66, 248.07/E556(32).

[246] Natalie Zemon Davis, *Society and Culture in Early Modern France* (Stanford, Calif., 1975), 124–51; David Underdown, *Revel, Riot and Rebellion: Popular Politics and Culture in England 1603–1660* (1985; Oxford, 1987); Martin Ingram, 'Ridings, Rough Music and Mocking Rhymes in Early Modern England', in Barry Reay, ed., *Popular Culture in Seventeenth-Century England* (New York, 1985), 166–97.

[247] *Beginnings*, 196.

[248] Cf. Robert Darnton, *The Literary Underground of the Old Regime* (Cambridge, Mass., 1982), 199–208.

[249] Cf. Leah S. Marcus, *The Politics of Mirth: Jonson, Herrick, Milton, Marvell and Defence of Old Holiday Partimes* (Chicago, 1986), 1–23; Peter Burke, *Popular Culture in Early Modern Europe* (1978; Aldershot, 1988), 244–86.

[250] *Man in the Moon* '18', 30 Aug. 1649, 156, 248.19/E572(11).

ate'.[251] This suggests that it may not commonly have been read aloud to an audience who could not themselves read. Crouch abused prominent figures in the army and parliament for their low social status, for their having once been, or for being the sons of, tradesmen, pimps, brewers, and draymen. Whether readers in these trades would have been offended we do not know. Would women have been amused by its intense misogyny?[252]

Crouch claimed that he did not hope to make a profit from writing, as he was doing it for the love of the cause, but only desired to pay his printer and supply himself with pens and paper.[253] This, true or not, suggests that print-runs need not have been high, and that extensive demand was not assured. *The Man in the Moon* is supposed to have cost a penny, half the price of other underground newsbooks.[254] It is usually assumed that its readers were the middling sort or their inferiors.[255] Williams writes that its readers were 'lower class', though this reflects his belief that only the lower classes could be interested in uninformative and pornographic journalism.[256] In fact the absence of news from *The Man in the Moon* suggests just the reverse. Would a reader able to afford only one newsbook have purchased this one? The satire in *The Man in the Moon* required that its readers already possessed considerable information; otherwise they would not find it particularly funny or even understand it.

What does this final rhetorical turn reveal about the newsbooks of the 1640s? *The Man in the Moon* went beyond the vitriol of the 1648 mercuries. Crouch was further to stunt the political and swell the pornographic in *Mercurius Democritus* and *Mercurius Fumigosus*.[257] Yet even the extent to which politics are diffracted in *The Man in the Moon* suggests a form of literary escapism. The celebration of the topos of madness was an admission that the royalist grip on history had failed. While Crouch rejoiced that God had taken vengeance on his and the king's enemies, he simultaneously acknowledged that providence also severed Charles's neck. Nedham appears to have felt that his writing was pointless in January 1649; Crouch decided to publicize his impotence.

A few months after the execution, Crouch was already laughing: 'Ha,

[251] *Man in the Moon* 8, 5 June 1649, 67, 248.08/E558(19).

[252] *MTN* 149–51, 138–9; Crouch's misogyny was above ordinary, though see *MTN* 138–9.

[253] *Man in the Moon* 2, 23 Apr. 1649, 10, 248.02/E551(10).

[254] Clyde, 183; *Beginnings*, 196. The sources are not entirely persuasive.

[255] Underdown, '*The Man in the Moon*'.

[256] *History*, 111.

[257] The former appeared between Apr. 1652 and Feb. 1654; the latter between June 1654 and Oct. 1655; N&S 307, 322.

ha, ha . . .'[258] Raising his voice only contributed to the '*new BABEL*': mercury had prevailed. Yet he did it anyway, because the king needed an epitaph. The earnest plain style of 1642, though still upheld in some publications, had capitulated under rhetorical pressure, and paved the way for the new literary cacography.

[258] *Man in the Moon* 4, 7 May 1649, 25, 248.04/E554(4).

4

Paper Bullets: Newsbooks, Pamphlets, and Print Culture

> Mercuries all; for he is reported to have been, besides his going of arrands, to have been the Patron of Eloquence, which is here of lying & of theevery, that is to say Plundering: and to say truth, many Pamphlets there are put forth, which are in nature, though not in expresse termes, very Mercuries.
>
> (*Britanicvs Vapvlans*, 1643[1])

> And they called Barnabas, Jupiter; and Paul, Mercurius, because he was the chief speaker.
>
> (Acts 14: 12)

WHEN the first newspapers appeared their readers did not recognize them. Early readers were sensitive to the innovation which newsbooks represented, but their understanding of them as a distinct form developed gradually. Initially the newsbook emerged, formally, rhetorically and typographically, out of other forms of print; and its reception was partly governed by the same. This fact is dramatized in miniature in a remarkable volume from the library of the antiquary and biographer Anthony Wood, which in his mind pertained to 'writers of Mercuries & Almanacks'.[2] His collocation of pamphlets represents an attempt to present a cross-section through a complex matrix of cultural associations, a kind of ethnographical statement.

To understand the culture of the newsbook, therefore, we must look to its initial dependence on pamphlet culture. This was itself in turmoil in 1641 as the printing industry shifted towards producing short, small books. Many were anonymous; they addressed an expanding audience; their stylistic qualities were rapidly diversifying; and they embraced a broadening range of controversial subjects. None the less the pamphlet

[1] *Britanicvs Vapvlans* 1, [4 Nov. 1643], 1, 29.1/E74(23).

[2] Bod.: Wood 622: inscribed inside the front board. It contains, amongst other things, 'characters' of newsbooks, almanacs, a broadside, pamphlets by Taylor, attacks on Nedham, and the poem *The Great Assises*, discussed below.

was at least sixty years old, and newsbooks relied on its conventions: they used pamphlets as models for their presentational strategies, fancifully piecing their elements together in new ways.[3]

Through the middle years of the 1640s a culture of the newsbook, with its own rhetorical, formal, satirical, and typographical practices, emerged, unfolded, and expanded. It became independent of its sibling. Newsbook writers began to play with the idea of the newsbook as a form. Readers began to recognize the formal rules guiding the newsbook, and were sensitive to their transmutation and to new developments in journalism. The dynamic soon shifted and newsbooks exerted considerable influence on the writing of pamphlets, returning their borrowed strategies transformed and condensed, shaping their tropes, and offering new voices and kenspeckled characters.

This story is best seen through a series of snapshots of this culture in action, the informational structures which inhabited it, the literary games journalists played, of various bullets fired from the presses during the civil war years, and how they were levelled at their targets. This chapter explores the strong metaphors used to describe newsbooks, their relation to pamphlets, and some of the more incisive critiques of the press. These paper bullets show that the newsbook coalesced in relation to other printed forms, and that readers recognized the rules of the form, the commonplaces that surrounded its reception, and understood that these reflected the place of the newsbook in society. They are more coherent than the perceptions of subsequent critics.

The force of eloquence

Thirty-one years after the first appearance of newsbooks, Andrew Marvell, ironically adopting a more-orthodox-than-thou clerical persona, looked back on the civil war and apostrophized type and typography as seditious characters in the state and history: '*O Printing!* how hast thou disturb'd the Peace of Mankind! that Lead, when moulded into Bullets, is not so mortal as when founded into Letters!'[4] The paper bullets trope, the adaptation to modern technologies of the dictum that the pen is mightier than the sword, was not an original one, and writers

[3] The best accounts of 1640s pamphlet culture can be found in *L&R*; Skerpan, *Rhetoric of Politics*; Achinstein, *Milton and the Revolutionary Reader*; Corns, *Uncloistered Virtue*. For the Marprelate controversy, see William Pierce, ed., *The Marprelate Tracts, 1588, 1589* (1911); id., *An Historical Introduction to the Marprelate Tracts* (1908); Donald J. McGinn, *John Penry and the Marprelate Controversy* (New Brunswick, NJ, 1966); Leland H. Carlson, *Martin Marprelate Gentleman: Master Job Throkmorton Laid Open in his Colours* (San Marino, Calif., 1981); Pooley, *English Prose*.

[4] Andrew Marvell, *The Rehearsal Transpros'd*, ed. D. I. B. Smith (Oxford, 1971), 5.

of diverse political persuasions emphasized the role of cheap print in general and newsbooks in particular in precipitating the civil war and inflaming anger and misunderstanding. Edward Cooke thought that the popular press had confused the good people of England with 'strange Perplexing Fears and Jealousies'; Dudley, fourth Baron North recollected that the 'War first began in paper, by Manifestoes and Declarations on both parts'.[5] Bulstrode Whitelocke expressed retrospective surprise at the way 'Paper Combates' had been transformed into a war in the summer of 1642:

It is strange to note, how we have insensibly slid into this beginning of a Civil War, by one unexpected Accident after another, as Waves of the Sea, which have brought us thus far: And we scarce know how, but from Paper Combates, by Declarations, Remonstrances, Protestations, Votes, Messages, Answers and Replies: We are now come to the question of raising Forces, and naming a General and Officers of an Army.[6]

John Nalson wrote that 'the Liberty of the Press' was, with the pulpit, one of the 'Principal Engines of Battery'; 'I know not any one thing that more hurt the late King then the paper Bullets of the Press.'[7] Even the 1648 newsbook *Mercurius Impartialis* admitted:

That the Pulpit and the Presse are in themselves truely Excellent, no man, (not possessed with a spirit of Madnesse) will deny; but that from thence have issued the ruines both of King and people, and his Majesties Subjects beene Poysoned with Principles of Heresie, Schisme, Faction, Sedition, Blasphemy, Apostacie, Rebellion, Treason, Sacriledge, Murther, Rapine, Robbery, and all other the enormous Crimes, and detestable Villanies, with which this Kingdome hath of later times swarmed; sad experience hath given us too perfect a sense.[8]

Such contemporary statements, though hyperbolic, possess an internal logic. The pulpit and the press spread the principles of those sins and crimes which were polemically associated with the civil war. The destructiveness of newsbooks stemmed particularly from their eloquence and their ability to move long distances, to project their disembodied voices, to swarm over and infest the kingdom. Marvell, still ventriloquizing in irony, observed the remarkable powers of the press to find its readers invisibly beyond the reach of censorship, and to address a greater audience than manuscripts or the human voice:

[5] Edward Cooke, *Memorabilia* (1681; C5998), 1; [Dudley, 4th Baron North], *A Narrative of Some Passages* (1670; N1285), 29.

[6] Whitelocke, *Memorials*, 58; cf. BL: Add. MS 37343, ff. 251ᵛ–252.

[7] John Nalson, *An Impartial Collection of the Great Affairs of State*, 2 vols. (1682; N106, 107), ii, sig. Aᵛ, p. 807.

[8] *Impartialis* 1, 12 Dec. 1648, 1, 333.1/E476(3).

'Twas an happy time when all Learning was in Manuscript, and some little Officer . . . did keep the Keys of the Library. . . . There have been wayes found out to banish Ministers, to fine not only the People, but even the Grounds and Fields where they assembled in Conventicles: But no Art yet could prevent these seditious meetings of Letters. Two or three brawny Fellows in a Corner, with meer Ink and Elbow-grease, do more harm than an *hundred Systematical Divines* with their *sweaty Preaching*.[9]

The analogy between newsbooks and preaching was also a prevalent one.

In 1660 Roger L'Estrange compiled an anthology from *Mercurius Politicus* intended to indict Nedham for treason. In the preface he commented: 'It has been made a Question long agoe, whether more mischief then advantage were not occasion'd to the Christian world by the Invention of Typography.'[10] For L'Estrange and others the civil war had finally resolved that question in the affirmative. The mischief perpetrated by the press was frequently figured in terms of violence and military destruction: and newsbooks were always the most extreme example of this general propensity of print. John Cleveland's *Character of Mercurius Politicus* (1650) began: 'The *Mercurius Politicus* is the paper *Militia*, a *Diurnall* Offensive and Defensive.'[11] *The True Character of Mercurius Aulicus* claimed that *Aulicus* did 'the Parliament more hurt then 2000 of the Kings Souldiers'.[12] In the mid-nineteenth century, Eliot Warburton concurred with this estimation of 'the great engine of moral warfare', observing that Charles 'performed his momentous march' to recruit forces 'without artillery, or any other force except this—the mightiest of all'.[13] In a 1644 satire a royalist soldier, commenting on the inaccuracy of *Aulicus*, declares that it 'kills more in a sheet in a week than we can kill in many months in the field'.[14] Propaganda intensified and broadened the conflict, thus multiplying the casualties and shattering the language of political consensus. *A Fresh Whip* opined that Walker's *Perfect Occurrences*, 'and many other scurrillous Pamphlets, have done more mischief in the kingdome then ever all my Lord of *Essex's*, or Sir *Thomas Fairefaxes* whole traine of artillery ever did'.[15] 'Men may be said to shoot from the *Press* as well as from the *Artillery*', wrote Lewis Griffin, in *Essays and Characters* (1661); invectives are warning

[9] Marvell, *Rehearsal Transpros'd*, 4–5.

[10] *Rope for Pol*, 'Advertisement to the Reader'.

[11] John Cleveland, *The Character of Mercurius Politicus* (1650; C2021), 1.

[12] Published 1645, qu. Cotton, 44.

[13] Eliot Warburton, *Memoirs of Prince Rupert and the Cavaliers*, 3 vols. (1849), i. 257.

[14] *The Souldiers' Language* (1644; S4426); qu. Charles Carlton, *Going to the Wars: The Experience of the British Civil Wars, 1638–1651* (1992; 1994), 79. This is a comment on the inaccuracy of *Aulicus*, not its potency, as Carlton implies.

[15] *A Fresh Whip*, 6.

shots, '*Polemicall discourses* are like shooting at a mark, which mark ought to be truth, *Schismatical Pamphlets* are *Granado's*.'[16] Newsbooks mixed all of these modes of writing.

These metaphors are meaningful statements about the transmission of information and the workings of cheap print. Their premisses are worth understanding. Newsbooks were like bullets because they were effective. In 1639 the Earl of Kingston offered Sir Gervase Kingston one of his suits of armour, claiming that despite its age it was superior to 'any of these new which will be unable to resist a paper bullet'.[17] The profound irony lies not only in the confident bluffing of an English aristocrat in the face of a couple of centuries of development in military technology; but also in the real danger inherent in paper bullets. Napoleon, a more experienced soldier with greater weaponry at his command, expressed an antithetical sentiment: 'Four hostile newspapers are more to be dreaded than a hundred thousand bayonets.'[18]

Pulpit and press

The sermon, like the press, was accredited with powers of social control. Charles I informed his son: 'People are governed by the pulpit more than the sword in time of peace.'[19] Thomas Fuller observed that 'those who hold the helm of the pulpit always steer the people's hearts as they please'.[20] Late in December 1641 John Taylor attacked lay-preachers for neglecting their trades and spreading sectarianism; he felt it incongruous and dangerous that such influence should be in the hands and tongues of the socially inferior, who disseminated views antagonistic to the moderate Church.[21]

In 1645 Taylor scornfully linked tub preachers with newsbook writers, as '*Pulpiteers*, and *Pamphleterians*'.[22] When contemporaries compared newsbooks to preached sermons they were making a deliberate connection. After 1660 it might simply be an expression of hostility to two means of communication associated with radicals and regicides, as in Hobbes's *Behemoth*.[23] Yet even with such retrospective examples there is a logic to the commonplace association: 'And undoubtedly the present

[16] L[ewis]. G[riffin]., *Essayes and Characters* (1661; G1982A), sigs. A5^{v}–A6.

[17] *Personal Rule*, 799.

[18] Qu. Stephens, *History of News*, 185.

[19] Christopher Hill, *Society and Puritanism in Pre-revolutionary England* (1964), 39.

[20] Thomas Fuller, *The Church History of Britain*, ed. J. S. Brewer, 6 vols. (Oxford, 1845), iii. 102.

[21] Taylor, *New Preachers, New*, sigs. A3–A3^{v}; id., *Swarme of Sectaries*.

[22] Taylor, *Rebells Anathematized*, 3, 8.

[23] See 290–5, below.

Parliament, Priests, and their Emissaries from their Pulpits and Presses, within these seven last yeares, have added more soules to the number of the damned, then ever the Devill, the Pope, and the subtillest Agents, with their most skilfull and pleasant Rhetorick, were in more then fourescore yeares before ever able to compasse.'[24] In James Howell's *A Trance: Or, Newes from Hell, Brought fresh to Towne By Mercurius Acheronticus*, the young and female voice of sedition which inspired parliamentary rebellion advertised: 'the most advantagious instruments we have used to bring all this about, have been the *Pulpit* and the *Presse*; by these we have diffus'd those surmises and suppositious feares formerly spoken of, to intoxicate the braines of the people.'[25] The pulpit and the press were on the same side and did similar things.

Prior to the appearance of the newsbook the pulpit, along with the stage, was an important medium for the broadcasting of news. This was enhanced by the closure of the theatres.[26] Like the newsbook, and unlike the occasional news pamphlet, the sermon was a periodical. This was underscored when Fast Sermons were introduced as a monthly institution in December 1641.[27] Clarendon wrote with the benefit of hindsight: 'It was an observation in that time, that the first publishing of extraordinary news was from the pulpit; and by the preacher's text, and his manner of discourse upon it, the auditors might judge, and commonly foresaw, what was like to be next done in the Parliament or Council of State.'[28] Confirming Clarendon's opinion, Hugh Trevor-Roper has argued that the Fast Sermons to the Long Parliament were 'a constant sounding-board of parliamentary policy, a regular means of contact with, and propaganda to, the people'.[29] Bishop Gilbert Burnet wrote of the Scottish response to Charles's innovations in church government: 'In their sermons, and chiefly in their prayers, all that passed in the state was canvassed . . . it grew so petulant, that the pulpit was a scene of news and passion.'[30] Taylor claimed regular sermons led to a weekly subsidy for the most anti-malignant of newsbooks. He wrote his *Mercvrivs Aqvaticvs*, he claimed, 'especially because I heard **an assess-**

[24] *Impartialis* 1, 2.
[25] [Howel], *A Trance* (1649; H3120/E526(39)), 9.
[26] Keith Thomas, *Religion and the Decline of Magic: Studies in Popular Beliefs in Sixteenth- and Seventeenth-Century England* (1971; Harmondsworth, 1978), 181; McKenzie, 'The London Book Trade', 1–10; id., '"The Staple of News" and the Late Plays'; Margot Heinemann, *Puritanism and Theatre: Thomas Middleton and Opposition Drama under the Early Stuarts* (1980; Cambridge, 1982), 237–57; Potter, 'The Plays and the Playwrights, 1642–1660', 263–93.
[27] Trevor-Roper, 'Fast Sermons', in *Religion, the Reformation and Social Change*, 306–8.
[28] *History*, iv. 194.
[29] Trevor-Roper, 'Fast Sermons', 342.
[30] Burnet, *History of his Own Time*, 6 vols. (Oxford, 1823), i. 57.

ment of Wit was laid upon the Synod, and every Lecturer, and private conventicler, from Mr *Marshall* at *Margarets* to *Green* the Feltmaker in the Tub, and paid weekly for the continuation of this thing called Mercurius Britanicus'.[31] This indicates that the audiences were assumed to overlap.

In 1645 *Mercurius Anti-Britanicus* outlined a particularly close relationship between *Britanicus* and the pulpit.[32] It identified the groups who were instrumental in overthrowing the king as citizens and lawyers, and, at greater length and yoked together, 'a bold, shamelesse, licentious *Scumme*, and *Rout* of *Writers*', and 'an unstudied, ignorant *Scumme* and *Rout* of now old *New-England* Preachers'. These last, 'as a friend of mine sayes, might very well passe for a *Britannicus* in the *Pulpit*'.[33] The old, New-England preachers include Hugh Peters, who is the companion of *Britanicus* in sedition; 'Mr *Peters*, and *Britanicus* are alike skilled in Hebrew', meaning, ironically, irreligion.[34] In the same year Taylor published a pamphlet-poem entitled *Rebells Anathematized, And Anatomized: Or, A Satyricall Salutation to the Rabble of seditious, pestiferous Pulpit-Praters, with their Brethren the Weekly Libellers, Railers, and Revilers, Mercurius Britannicus, with the rest of that Sathanicall Fraternity.*

Despite the rise of newsbooks, sermons continued to serve as a means of news distribution, especially for the illiterate. Especially in times of heightened soteriological concern, other means of transmitting news could never entirely supersede the sermon. But several criticisms suggest that the pre-eminence of newsbooks caused sermons to be debased by this association. Cleveland wrote mockingly that the *Diurnall* was 'taken for the Pulse of the Body Politique; and the Emperick Divines of the Assembly, those spirituall *Dragooners*, thumbe it accordingly. Indeed it is a pretty *Synopsis*; and those grave *Rabbyes* (though in poynt of *Divinity*) trade in no larger Authors.'[35] One of his animadvertors responded: 'He brands our Assembly of Divines with the reproachfull tearme of Empericks, and twits them for thumbing of *Diurnalls*: I should rather have thought they might have been taunted for thumping of Pulpits then thumbing of *Diurnalls*.'[36] Cleveland's critic missed the point, as Cleveland was suggesting that newsbooks were insufficiently

[31] *Mercvrivs Aqvaticvs*, sig. B2. Blackletter is used here to parody an official publication of parliament.

[32] The style and content of this three-part 1645 serial suggest that it may have been written by John Taylor. The criticisms of newsbooks and preachers are precisely those made in numerous pamphlets by Taylor. This proves nothing, but it is as well to bear in mind.

[33] *Anti-Britanicus* 1 [4 Aug. 1645], 2–3, 267.1/E294(31); *OR* iv. 304–5.

[34] *Anti-Britanicus* 2, [22 Aug. 1645], 22, 267.3/E297(17); *OR* iv. 324.

[35] *Character of a London Diurnall* ([Oxford], 1644[5]; C4659/E268(6)), 1. References are to Bod.: Wood 622; LT has a different edition.

[36] *A Fvll Answer to a Scandalous Pamphlet* (1645; F2340/E277(11)), 3.

serious for theological use, and ultimately that the Assembly were engaged in proselytizing. The gap between the thumping of pulpits and the thumbing of diurnals had dwindled through their realization as propaganda.

There was some overlap between the professions of preacher and journalist.[37] Hugh Peters and Simeon Ashe, both preachers in the parliament's army, experimented with writing newsbooks. The Laudian divine Peter Heylin was the first editor of *Aulicus.* Henry Walker had an extended dual career. In September 1652 Samuel Sheppard, who complained a month earlier of newsbooks 'rayling and praying in one breath',[38] wrote of this '*Hebrew Iron-Monger*' who had become a '*Paradoxical Divine*' that 'You would think (if you heard him preach) that he had his Text from a *Gazet,* you heard so much of a *Curranto.*'[39] Hugh Peters was also said to have taken texts from newsbooks.[40] In 1644 *Aulicus,* commenting on Peters carrying news to parliament from the Earl of Essex, described him as 'that spirituall Newes-monger Master *Peters*'.[41] An earlier *Aulicus* inveighed: 'the Printed Newes-men are this weeke turn'd Preachers, urging Scripture (in place of Newes).'[42]

The Gentle Lash, published in vindication of Daniel Featley, complained how 'the most learned and religious Divines' had been subjected to scandal, slander, and defamation in newsbooks.[43] When newsbooks intervened in religious matters, they were frequently accused of Independent tendencies. This was central to the argument of Clement Walker's *History of Independency* (1648). Walker testified that newsbooks were Cromwellian propaganda, which was 'by many Printed books and papers, spread all *England* over by his *Agitators,* and by some journey-men Priests, (who's *Pulpits* are the best *Juglers Boxes* to deceive the simple)'.[44] Thomas Edwards's *Gangræna* described *Britanicus* as 'a man who hath done' Independents 'many good offices, and cryed up severall of them'.[45] He also praised Presbyterians for abstaining from publishing, whereas the 'Sectaries' insulted them and their petitions, 'branding them in Pulpits, in the weekly News-books, and in their daily

[37] Inappropriately according to Samuel Sheppard, *The Weepers: Or, The bed of Snakes broken* (1652; S3171/E674(34)), 3; LT dated 13 Sept. See also *Berkenhead,* 57 n. 2.

[38] *Mastix* 1, 7.

[39] Sheppard, *The Weepers,* 12.

[40] *Don Pedro de Quixot, or in English the Right Reverend Hugh Peters* (25 July 1660; D1845/669f.25(62)).

[41] *Aulicus* 27, 6 July 1644, 1066, 275.227A/E2(30); *OR* iii. 156.

[42] *Aulicus* 32, 13 Aug. 1643, 438, 275.132, *OR* i. 462. Cf. M. Nedham, *Certain Considerations Tendered in all humility* (1 Aug 1649; N381), 10–11.

[43] *The Gentle Lash, Or the Vindication of Dr Featley* (Jan. 1644; F582), sig. A2.

[44] Clement Walker, *The History of Independency* (1648; W329), 4, 10.

[45] Thomas Edwards, *Gangræna: or A Catalogue and Discovery* (1646; E228), 54–5.

discourses'.[46] Like Featley, to whom he was sympathetic, he saw newsbooks and sermons as means of propaganda, central to the Independent cause.[47] Both 'weekly News Pamphlets' and sermons were being used 'to retard the setling of the Presbyteriall government'.[48] In Edwards's rhetoric pulpit and press become practically synonymous, their association automatic.

Marvell suggested that printing was more potent than preaching, not least because it was possible for the state to control public meetings but not the private encounters between books and their readers.[49] Richard Baxter avouched that 'The writings of Divines are nothing else but a preaching the Gospel to the eye, as the voice preacheth it to the ear.' The voice stirs affections and can be modified according to audience, 'this way the milk cometh warmest from the breast'. But books enable readers to listen to the most able preachers, no matter how distant; books enable readers to choose their subject; books cannot be silenced; books are less expensive to keep than preachers. Books remain at hand when sermons are lost in memory, and they can be consulted at any hour of the day.[50] This explained the power of books. These arguments reveal an uneasiness over the power of eloquence.[51] Newsbooks speak, but they speak in a voice which is not always detectable and none the less flies like a bullet: writing is 'more publick then preaching'.[52]

Despite accusations of mutual infiltration, newsbooks were not preaching the gospel. The analogy between newsbooks and sermons concerned not content but context and form. First, they were perceived to be working in the same interest. They were the main means by which a broader section of the populace was incorporated into political debate: and in the eyes of contemporaries it was this levelling franchise that created the hostility of the masses, which in turn enabled the minority faction in parliament surrounding Pym to start a war against their king. The ignorant multitude were at once being controlled by their betters, and at the same time satisfying the inordinate appetite of their eyes and ears: this slightly contradictory account was held to be true of both newsbooks and sermons.

Secondly, the sermon was a pre-existing model for explaining the eloquent power of newsbooks.[53] Baxter's analysis reveals how the voice

[46] *Gangræna*, 56–7. [47] *Gangræna*, 62. [48] *Gangræna*, 115.

[49] Marvell, *Rehearsal Transpros'd*, 5.

[50] Richard Baxter, *A Christian Directory: Or, A Summ of Practical Theologie and Cases of Conscience* (1673; B1219), 60.

[51] Cf. Abraham Wright, *Five Sermons in Five Several Styles* (1656; W3685), sigs. A3–A3ᵛ.

[52] *CPW* ii. 548.

[53] See Lucasta Miller, 'The Shattered *Violl*: Print and Textuality in the 1640s', in Nigel Smith, ed., *Literature and Censorship*, Essays and Studies², 46 (Cambridge, 1993), 29–32,

was used to explain the way print worked. The metaphor is most familiar from Milton's *Areopagitica*, where print is figured as public speech. While trying to find a way of describing the way newsbooks 'spoke' to their readers, it was to the sermon that some contemporaries turned.

Newsbooks and almanacs

Richard Whitlock described newsbooks as retrospective almanacs.[54] There is much that might be misleading in this, but, like the analogies between newsbooks and bullets and newsbooks and sermons, the point had a significant kernel. According to Samuel Sheppard, newsbooks were 'Prophetical . . . and can as easily and as truely foretel the downfal of Kingdoms, or disquieting and tumults of Nations, as if they were all Gentlemen of *Lilies* Privie Chamber: for since these books were so much in fashion, the reputation of Astrologers is almost utterly decayed.' Sheppard claimed that 'we have jeer'd those Figure-flingers', meaning astrologers, 'into a sensibility of their impudence', but newsbooks had started up in their place instead.[55] Cleveland associated *The Moderate Intelligencer* and *Diurnall* as confederates, with 'the two Empericke Astronomers, *Lillie* and *Booker*' as 'Coadjutors'.[56] Elsewhere Cleveland wrote that a newsbook writer was not a historian: 'Such an Historian would hardly pass Muster with a Scotch Stationer, in a sieve full of Ballads and Almanacks.'[57] *Civicus*, on the other hand, described Lilly as 'Intelligencer of the Starres'.[58] The logical epicentre of the association was that newsbooks and almanacs were both cheap and unrespectable forms of print.

Almanacs and newsbooks did not look very alike. Mid-seventeenth-century almanacs were two-and-a-half-sheet octavos, and were printed in two colours with an illustration. Many almanacs left spaces for the owner to write her or his own notes, observations, and precautions.[59] This sometimes happened with scrivener-produced newsletters, but readers

on speech as a metaphor for print (though I would dissent from her Siebert-based narrative); Achinstein, *Milton and the Revolutionary Reader*, 37–42.

[54] *Zootomia, Or, Observations on the Present Manners of the English* (1654; W2030), 250; cf. *Astrology*, 24.

[55] *Mastix* 1, 4.

[56] *Character of a Moderate Intelligencer*, 4. Lilly and Booker were prominent parliamentarian astrologers: see *Astrology*, *passim*; Patrick Curry, *Prophecy and Power: Astrology in Early Modern England* (Cambridge, 1989), ch. 2.

[57] John Cleveland, *A Character of a Diurnal-Maker* (1654; C4657), 2.

[58] *Civicus* 179, 29 Oct. 1646, 2427–8, 298.179/E359(9).

[59] See e.g. Elias Ashmole's annotated almanacs in the Bodleian.

did not add news to newsbooks, though they might enclose them in letters of news.[60]

Yet Wood collected and bound together a number of attacks on 'writers of Mercuries & Almanacks'. He was probably not the only reader to notice that the three public figures subjected to the greatest number of pamphlet attacks at the Restoration, excluding Cromwell, were representatives of linked arts: Hugh Peters, William Lilly, and Marchamont Nedham.[61] Attacks broached the association. *Mercurius Britanicus His Welcome to Hell* included '*Coelicus*' in a list of offensive newsbooks. *Mercurius Coelicus: Or, A Caveat To all people of the Kingdome, That now have, or shall hereafter happen to reade the counterfeit, and most pernicious Pamphlet written under the name of Naworth: Or, A New Almanacke, And Prognostication For the yeare of our Lord and Saviour 1644*, by the parliamentarian astrologer John Booker, was not a newsbook but an astrological attack on the almanac of the royalist astrologer George Wharton ('Naworth'). The use of 'Mercurius' in the title of an almanac suggests its newsworthiness. Three years later Wharton published *No Merline, nor Mercurie: but a New Almanac*, reinforcing the point.[62] The association was also admitted in Taylor's *No Mercurius Aulicus, But some merry flashes of Intelligence . . . Also the breaking of Booker, the Asse-tronomicall London Figure-flinger.*[63]

The prominent astrologer George Wharton wrote newsbooks, including *Mercurius Elencticus*, one of the malignant trinity of 1647–9. Wharton used *Elencticus* to attack Lilly, and occasionally Booker.[64] In 1648 *Elencticus* exchanged polemical broadsides with John Hall's *Mercurius Britanicus*. Wharton claimed that his enemy Lilly hired Hall to write against him: but Hall may have been motivated by his own interests.[65] The pretended cavalier author of a pamphlet defending Lilly claimed that in a personal meeting Wharton had admitted 'that if he mentioned not *Lilly* in his *Mercuries*, they would not sell'.[66]

This statement, like Sheppard's remark on the decaying reputation of

[60] Ichabod Dawk's *News-letter*, which appeared in 1696 and was produced to look like a script newsletter, did leave space for manuscript additions.

[61] Peters was reported to have been captured with an almanac instead of a Bible in his pocket: *MTN* 466–8.

[62] George Wharton, *No Merline, nor Mercurie* (?York, 1647; A2674). This was declared scandalous: *CJ* v. 72–3.

[63] John Taylor, *No Mercurius Aulicus* (?Oxford, 1644; T498).

[64] e.g. *Elencticus* 27, [201]; *Elencticus* 29, 221; *Elencticus* 3, 19 Nov. 1647, 312.03/ E416(13); *MTN* 139–40; for other uses of astrology, 175, 179, 190, 257–8, 279–80. 4.06, 4.19, 6.01, 6.15, and esp. 4.03.

[65] *Elencticus* 27, 31 May 1648, 206, 312.27/445(23). J. Andrew Mendelsohn, 'Alchemy and Politics in England 1649–1665', *P&P* 135 (1992), 49. Williams believed Wharton's charges against Hall; *History*, 103.

[66] *The Late Storie of Mr. William Lilly* (Jan. 1647[8]; L559), 12.

astrologers, implies that newsbooks and almanacs fought over a shared market. This is also suggested by the newsbook editors and publishers who chose to reproduce prophecies from almanacs.[67] Certainly in 1652 Joshua Childrey complained that newsbooks would limit sales of his superior astrological book:

Had some Mercuries *had so much News to have told the world, three or four quire of Paper would have been too straight a girdle for their Tympany; which disease is grown so much into fashion, that the smalness of my Book tells me, I must expect no other welcome for it into the world but Truth, and no other name but a Trifle.*[68]

Since the advent of the newsbook, he suggested, writers of astrological works received little respect, despite their more economic presentation of news. The small format would, in fact, damn him by association.

Notwithstanding Wharton and Sheppard, the links between almanacs and newsbooks were more rhetorical than economic. There were, of course, a limited number of coins in the hands of their potential readers, but almanacs appeared once a year, and newsbooks once a week. The apparent advantage almanacs had in their print-runs is deceptive. Almanacs were released in editions of 1000s, newsbooks in 100s. There may have been over 13,500 copies for Lilly's 1646 almanac, and twice that number for 1659.[69] No single issue of a newsbook challenged this: though when sales are calculated over a year, many newsbooks had higher totals. Thirteen thousand five hundred equals just over 250 a week, towards the low end of a newsbook edition.[70]

Almanacs transmitted news, but by the time of their annual publication the news had become history. Informed political and military leaders did not generally enclose almanacs in letters to colleagues. Two-page summaries of world history became part of the standard fare for the two-and-a-half-sheet almanac in the early seventeenth century,[71] but during the civil war contemporary events increasingly became an object of focus. 'Naworth' introduced a fifteen-page section of 'Memorable Occurrences since the beginning of this Grand Rebellion' into his 1644 almanac, which prompted Booker to respond with his *Mercurius Coelicus*.[72] Booker accused Naworth of being 'of very neere kindred to

[67] *Perfect Weekly Account*, N&S 533; *Certaine Informations* N&S 36 and *Perfect Occurrences* N&S 465. See *Astrology*, 76; *Beginnings*, 104. See also Cotton, 70. Cotton is surprisingly harsh on William Ingler for doing this.

[68] Joshua Childrey, *Indago Astrologica* (1652; C3873), 4. It was 16pp. long. I owe this reference to Lauren Kassell.

[69] *Astrology*, 76; Curry, *Prophecy and Power*, 21. See also Cyprian Blagden, 'The Distribution of Almanacks in the Second Half of the Seventeenth Century', *Studies in Bibliography*, 11 (1958), 107–16.

[70] See 233–8, below.

[71] *Astrology*, 215.

[72] Naworth, *A New Almanack* (Oxford, 1644; A2673).

Mercurius Aulicus', in a passage which evokes nicely the potential associations between the two forms:

> All that *Infamous Chronology* is nothing else but a *Collection of Untruths,* raked out of the Dunghill of *Mercurius Aulicus* his abominable *lying Legend;* which, like the *Infectious Disease* now raging at *Oxford,* and other the Westerne parts of the Kingdome, had like to have poysoned all the people thereof, had not his *Anti-Mercury,* our freind *Britannicus,* seasonably given them an *Antidote* to purge and cure the *Melancholly* gotten by that *malignant Aulicus.*[73]

Wharton responded in *Mercurio-Cœlico Mastix* that he hoped to see Booker and '*Britannicus*' at the gallows together.[74]

Just as there were mock newsbooks, there were mock almanacs, which, according to Bernard Capp, 'evolved as a branch of royalist journalism'. Unsurprisingly Sheppard contributed to this burlesque literature, which relied on familiar anti-puritan humour and politics.[75] Ridicule of popular astrology was their premiss; in the same way anti-newsbooks challenged not just individual politics but the legitimacy of newsbooks *per se.* The parodies gesture towards the real significance of associations between newsbooks and almanacs: they were both ephemeral, disposable pamphlets with a limited shelf-life. News and astrology were sometimes discredited not for any intrinsic shortcomings, but through their association with the vulgar, who could afford them. News involved the transmission of political arcana, which many feared; likewise, Elias Ashmole claimed that the art of judicial astrology, like alchemy, was essentially secret, and 'not to be reach't by every vulgar Plumet that attempts to found it. Never was any age so pester'd with a multitude of Pretenders.'[76] Both had a serious, disinterested dimension to them,[77] both had a proclivity to be both proscriptive and informative, and both were used as arenas for blatant political polemic.

Bellicose newsbooks and the New Model Army

In 1645 newsbooks reported in great detail on the foundation of the New Model Army, and followed this with keen reporting of its suc-

[73] *Mercurius Cœlicus; Or, A Caveat To all people of the Kingdome* (24 Jan. 1643/4; B37288), sig. A^{v}.

[74] *Mercurio-Cœlico Mastix. Or an Anti-Caveat* (Oxford, 30 Jan. 1643[4]; W1550), 12; see also Taylor, *Rebells Anathematized,* 3.

[75] *Astrology,* 231; Wilson, 'Some English Mock-Prognostications', 6–43; Don Cameron Allen, *The Star-Crossed Renaissance* (Durham, NC, 1941), 190–246.

[76] *Theatrum Chemicum Britannicum* (1652; A3987), qu. Curry, *Prophecy and Power,* 37.

[77] See Curry, *Prophecy and Power,* 8–15.

cesses.[78] They never really grew weary of the 'Arme of flesh' and the arm that was assisted by God.[79] The relationship between newspapers and war hardly needs reiterating. Newsbooks needed heroes. Gustavus Adolphus had featured prominently in corantos. In 1643 and early 1644 Sir William Waller received much attention. 'William the Conqueror' disappeared after the Battle of Cropredy Bridge. With the foundation of the New Model Army Sir Thomas Fairfax was the focus for weekly serials.[80] Cromwell was never really without his publicists. Robert Baillie, one of the Scots commissioners in London, complained in July 1644 that Simeon Ashe was diligent in sending accounts of military success to the press, which ascribed victories to Cromwell rather than his Scottish fellows-in-arms.[81] 'The News-books', wrote Clement Walker, were 'taught to speak no language but Cromwell and his Party; and were mute in such actions as he and they could claim no share in: for which purpose the Presses were narrowly watched.'[82] The official licenser from 11 April 1644 to 9 March 1647 was John Rushworth, secretary to Fairfax and the New Model Army.

The use of military language in newsbooks is too extensive to allow of generalization here, as almost all our language has been taxed by war. In 1653 Richard Flecknoe wrote: 'the Inclination of the *Times* do much confer to the variation of the *Style*: And as in Times of *Peace*, all our *Metaphors* (for example) are deduc'd from peacefull Arts: So in time of *Warre* (we have but too sad experience) our *Language* is all corrupt with military *Tearms*, borrowed from other Nations.'[83] This analysis holds true of newsbooks. Correct military terms, like accurate military news, assisted newsbook editors in promoting their own expertise. Letters from the army, some read in parliament, were a staple part of the newsbook.[84] Some editors had military experience. *A Fresh Whip* mocked Walker's boasts of his prowess, reading the military terms literally.[85]

[78] Ian Gentles, *The New Model Army in England, Ireland and Scotland, 1645–1653* (Oxford, 1992), ch. 1 and notes.

[79] *Scotish Dove* 92, 25 July 1645, 721, 594.092/E293(29); *KWI* 50, 16 Apr. 1644, 403, 214.050/E42(28); *Moderate Intelligencer* 18, 3 July 1645, 419.018/E292(3); *Character of a London Diurnall*, 3. The phrase is from 2 Chr. 32: 8.

[80] *Perfect Passages* 31, 7 May 1645, 248, 523.31/E286(2).

[81] *The Letters and Journals of Robert Baillie . . . 1637–1662*, ed. G. Laing, 3 vols. (Edinburgh, 1841–2), ii. 208–9; cf. Lucy Hutchinson, *Memoirs of the Life of Colonel Hutchinson*, ed. N. H. Keeble (1995), 92–3.

[82] Walker, *History of Independency*, 4.

[83] 'A Discourse of Languages. And particularly of the English Tongue', in *Miscellania. Or, Poems of all sorts, with divers other Pieces* (1653; F1231), 77.

[84] Cf. Cotton, 19.

[85] *A Fresh Whip*, 4.

Metaphors in common use suggest that newsbooks were sometimes seen as being like the army. Sheppard, ever a perspicacious reader, lamented: 'No rest day nor night with these cursed Caterpillers, *Perfect Passages, Weekly Occurrences, Scout, Spye, Politicus, Diurnal*, the devil and his dam. If the States have occasion for Souldiers, they may no doubt press a whole Regiment of these Paper-vermine.'[86] *Mercurius Hibernicus* modestly justified his first appearance: 'the Printer hath seised on me, and now newly pressed me for your service.'[87] Newsbooks were a drain on national resources, like free quarter. *Mercurius Vrbanvs*, who admitted ''tis hard now not to write a Satyr', singled out *Britanicus* for attack, 'Not because he is the best of those peny-worths of paper, but because he sells best, and so is like to doe most hurt to mens Purses, sufficiently drained already.'[88] Newsbooks reported the death of officers somewhat prematurely; Richard Whitlock wrote, 'it is nothing to *kill a man* this *week*, and with *Ink* instead of *Aqua Vitæ* fetch him *alive next*'.[89] Newsbook editors were mocked as armchair-officers.

In 1645 the majority of London newsbooks seemed to swing in favour of the army as it developed a political identity independent of the parliament. *The Moderate Intelligencer*, edited by Dillingham, and in spite of Dillingham's connections with Manchester, was from the start a distinctly pro-army newsbook, with 'millennial visions', though prepared to offer criticism.[90] After the 1648 hostilities, when it swung away from this position, *The Moderate* appeared to occupy the vacuum: and when *The Moderate* became less radical, *Mercurius Militaris* appeared, focusing on the army and perhaps addressing soldiers.[91] *Britaines Remembrancer* had a keen interest in army reform during the spring of 1644.[92] The army's success generated praise from *Scotish Dove, Perfect Passages, Mercurius Civicus, Perfect Occurrences, Weekly Account*, and *Parliaments Post*: 'You shall finde the greatest part of the Modell of our Armies (I say the greatest part, for what composition is there under Heaven, in which there is not some corruptions) to be faithfull temporate, and religious Men. You shall finde the Enemy to worke by perfidiousnesse, cruelty, and profanenesse.'[93] The word 'army' and its derivatives became more common in newsbook titles after 1645, and as

[86] *Mastix* 1, 1–2.

[87] *Mercvrivs Hibernicvs*, p. 1, LT E269(16); see Ch. 1 n. 87, above.

[88] *Mercurius Vrbanvs* 2, 9 Nov. 1643, 9, 29.2/E75(16).

[89] *Zootomia*, 231; cf. *A Fresh Whip*, 5; Cleveland, *Character of a London Diurnall*, 4. Cf. 185–8, above. For premature mock elegies see *MTN* 114–16.

[90] Cotton, 'John Dillingham', 819–20; Gentles, *New Model Army, passim*; qu. from Mark A. Kishlansky, *The Rise of the New Model Army* (Cambridge, 1979), 116.

[91] Gentles, *New Model Army*, 325.

[92] Cotton, 'John Dillingham', 822.

[93] *Parliaments Post* 9, 8 July 1645, 2, 487.09/E292(14).

the New Model Army became a collective hero, its string of victories assisted newsbook editors in their struggle to produce a pamphlet every week.

This affinity enabled elements within the army to use newsbooks to publicize their cause. They were more explicit in this than parliament had been in 1641–2. Walker edited his *Perfect Occurrences* with the assistance of the radical antinomian John Saltmarsh, later Fairfax's personal chaplain, whose wit Taylor mocked in *Mercurius Aquaticus*.[94] In May 1644, just after Rushworth was appointed licenser, Simeon Ashe, a chaplain to the Earl of Manchester, began a serial entitled *A Particular relation of the Severall Removes, Services, and Successes of the Right Honourable the Earl of Manchesters Army*. The possibility of using a newsbook as propaganda must have surfaced more clearly in July 1645 when two serials appeared, both explicitly dedicated to chronicling the New Model Army, and both written by its chaplains.

The first appeared on 9 July, entitled *The Proceedings of the Army under the Command of Sir Thomas Fairfax*. The second issue was entitled *An Exact and Perfect Relation of the Proceedings of the Army under the Command of Sir Thomas Fairfax*, the third *A Continvation of the Proceedings of the Army*. Despite the variations in the title the sequence was numbered, indicating that it was conceived as a newsbook, though initially irregular in periodicity and length. The titles echo parliamentary newsbooks, though it was too early to project the army as a distinct political entity. It was predominantly written in a clear, first-person narrative, 'Sent', as the initial issue advertised, 'from Mr *Bowles* (Chaplain to Sir *Thomas Fairfax*) to a Friend in London'. It incorporated documents and lengthy polemics against the Clubmen. The Presbyterian Edward Bowles tried to evoke the divine thread underlying the actions of the army: 'After that it had pleased God in the midst of our enemies despight and friends despair, to look upon us, and use as Instruments of his Justice upon an enemy fill'd with sin and pride; and of his Mercy to this Nation, in the late Victory at *Nablesby*-Field.'[95] Writing a periodical strengthened the familiar providentialism, as it appeared week after week, reinforcing the progress of the army:

> Thus hath the God of our Salvation protected and prospered us, besotting the enemies old Souldiers, that they should suffer themselves to be engaged contrary to their intentions, and in the midst of their expectation of Supplies to make up a formidable Army, directing us by his good providence, in

[94] N&S 308; Gentles, *New Model Army*, 228–9; see also Gardiner², i. 202; and Brailsford, *Levellers and the English Revolution*, 401–16.

[95] *Proceedings of the Army* [1], 9 July 1645, 3, 565.1/E292(16); published, like *Scots Army Advanced*, by Samuel Gellibrand.

the midst of our irresolutions: His Wisedom was our counsel, his Strength was our Victory; let the praise be his. Our Word was, *God with us*; and he made it good.[96]

The appeals to providence common in newsbooks left their mark on Joshua Sprigge's history of the army, which relied on them as a source.[97]

The second army serial was *Mr. Peters Report from the Army to the Parliament.*[98] This was distinguished by being the only newsbook with its author's name incorporated in the title, though the title varied until it settled as *Heads of Some Notes of the Citie Scout.* It too was slightly irregular, but unlike Bowles, Peters probably did not edit the entire serial. Vigilant of providence, it illustrated that God was on their side.

The delayed final issue in the series has hitherto escaped identification. *M^r. Peters Last Report of the English Wars, Occasioned by the importunity of a Friend Pressing an Answer to Seven Quæres* was printed by 'M. S.' (Matthew Simmons?) for Henry Overton (who had published William Ingler's *Certaine Informations* in 1643–4, and *Weekly Intelligence* in October 1642).[99] The earlier issues were printed by and for Jane Coe (publisher of Walker and Saltmarsh's *Perfect Occurrences*) and Robert Austin (Wither's sometime publisher) variously. It was, Peters claimed, a response to some recent slanderous pamphlets, which explains the gap between it and his earlier reports: its superb rhetoric is a justification of his actions and the actions of the army, once again with a strong providentialist undercurrent.

Like the first newsbooks, like his *Report from the Army*, and like Bowles's *Proceedings of the Army* and its *Continuation*, *M^r. Peters Last Report* had a full title-page, with an ornamental border. This was distinctly unconventional for a 1645 newsbook, and its revival by experienced printers and publishers represents a deliberate attempt to distinguish these serials. The same principle influenced *Melancholicus* in 1647.[100] These pieces of propaganda for the New Model Army should therefore be regarded as a sub-genre unto themselves. This in turn shows that by 1645 a culture of the newsbook had been established, which was well defined, and, like other genres, could be manipulated for effect. The army newsbooks bore a similar relation to the newsbook as a form as the newsbook had to pamphlet literature as a whole.

[96] *Exact and Perfect Relation* 2, 11 July 1645, 7, 565.2/E292(28).

[97] J. Sprigge, *Anglia Rediviva; Englands Recovery: Being the History of the Motions, Actions, and Successes of the Army under the Immediate Conduct of His Excellency Sr Thomas Fairfax* (1647; S5070), sig. A3^v.

[98] On Peters's career as a journalist see Raymond Phineas Stearns, *The Strenuous Puritan: Hugh Peter, 1598–1660* (Urbana, Ill., 1954), 252–83.

[99] *M^r. Peters Last Report* (1646); Bod.: Wood 501(26); Firth e.65(2). Not in Wing or N&S.

[100] Also *Weekly Account*, Jan. 1646: probably distinguishing it for commercial purposes.

Newsbooks and play-pamphlets

Another sub-genre with which the newsbook interacted was the play-pamphlet. This, like the newsbook, was a diffuse genre; and it has been argued that it should be perceived not as a genre in the strict sense but as a mode of discourse containing numerous elements.[101] Yet for our purposes this genre or non-genre shows how tightly the various aspects of writing cheap and largely ephemeral pamphlets were knotted together.

Like newsbooks, play-pamphlets were small quartos between eight and sixteen pages in length. They conveyed a satirico-political message through a dialogue between characters real and imaginary. The genre first became prominent in 1641–2, when it was used to satirize William Laud and Thomas Wentworth, Earl of Strafford.[102] Acerbic comments were also made concerning the desire for news in general. One publication in May 1641, *A Description Of the Passage of Thomas late Earle of Strafford, over the River of Styx*,[103] linked them, as they were indeed linked. One exchange between Strafford and William Noy, Charles's deceased Attorney-General, responsible for conceiving the ship-money scheme, is particularly interesting. Noy, now devising ubiquitous projects in Hell, is eager to hear the news of the world of the living from Strafford:

Noy. I understood indeed that some Priests were severely looked after: that newes I heard from *Mercury*.

Straff. Now you talke of *Mercury*, there is a pretious generation of *Mercury's* above.

Noy. Of *Mercury's*? they are a people never before heard of, a Sect which no age ever understood. I beseech your honour to instruct me who and what they are.

Straff. Why, there are men *Mercury's*, and women *Mercury's*, and boy *Mercury's*; *Mercury's* of all sexes, sorts and sizes; and these are they that carry up and downe their Pasquils, and vent them unto shops.

Noy. How is that taken?

Straff. I know not; but their takings I believe are good enough. But had they carried abroad such ware a yeare agoe, these *Mercury's* had need in earnest to put wings unto their feet to make more haste away.

Noy. They may doe well to read *Lucian*, he will teach their Pamphlets wit and innocence.

Straff. The Divell he will: excuse me, Mr. *Noy*, not too much innocence I beseech

[101] Susan Wiseman, 'News, Pamphlets, Drama: Hybrid Forms and the News in the 1640s', forthcoming; *L&R* 70–92.

[102] See bibliographical appendix to Martin Butler, *Theatre and Crisis 1632–1642* (Cambridge, 1984).

[103] (May 1641; D1166/E156(21)).

> you; but let them write even what they will, the dead bite not, and if they bite not the dead I care not.

Here Strafford refers to hawkers of news pamphlets, already proliferating in mid-1641, owing to the relaxation of press controls sometime since 'a yeare agoe'. Wood dismissed this anonymously written and published pamphlet as 'Nothing but fooleries & rascallitiy';[104] but the author inadvertently anticipated a later generation of mercuries, which would become a fact of life. Contemporaries frequently bound play-pamphlets with newsbooks of parliamentary affairs.

These early play-pamphlets were generally parliamentarian in sympathies. They attacked the king's ministers and advisers, though none were as serious or as challenging as other, directly political pamphlets, such as Henry Parker's *Observations upon some of his Majesties late Answers and Expresses.*[105] The satire of such publications as *The Bishops Potion, Or, A Dialogue betweene the Bishop of Canterbury, and his phisitian* contained little developed political reason.[106] There were also less satirical dialogue-pamphlets, in which news played a role as a subject or a character. They were less theatrical, and did not have the entrances and exits, the multiple scenes, or the vomiting and scatological humour of the anti-Laud pamphlets. 'What newes?' is a frequent refrain in them. In a rare royalist example, a citizen says of London: 'It is newes, to heare good newes there.'[107]

News also appears as an anthropomorphized character in these early dialogue-pamphlets. In Richard Overton's *Articles of High Treason Exhibited against Cheap-Side Crosse. With The last Will and Testament of the said Crosse* (January 1642), Master Newes, 'a Temporiser', announces to Master Papist that Cheapside Cross has been condemned for treason.[108] A dialogue-pamphlet from June 1641, *Old Newes Newly Revived: Or, The discovery of all occurrences happened since the beginning of the Parliament*, consists of 'a short discourse between Mr. Inquisitive, a countrey Gentleman, and Master Intelligencer, a Newes-Monger'.[109] The opposition between the country and London, as the centre of both the news and the production of news, is important to all of these pamphlets, as it

[104] Bod.: Wood 366(11).

[105] Henry Parker, *Observations* (1642; P412). Except, perhaps, *The Anatomy of the Westminster Ivncto . . . by Mercurius Elencticus* (1648; A3062), which mixed serious political content with rhetorical venom.

[106] 1641; B3032. See also *Canterburies Potion* (1641; C460).

[107] *The Last News in London. Or, A Discourse Between a Citizen and a Country-Gentleman, as they did ride betwixt London and Ludlow, October 12. 1642* (1642; L498/E124(11); 25 Oct.), 1.

[108] 1642; O623/E134(23).

[109] 1641; O211/E160(22). Sometimes attributed to Overton (a lot is); Heinemann, *Puritanism and Theatre*, 248.

would be to Restoration drama. *Old Newes Newly Revived* is an informative and didactic dialogue with a satirical edge: it celebrates the fact that Davenant, 'the Queenes Poet', has not, like Sir Francis Windebank and Sir John Suckling, fled the country; he will be eligible for employment writing elegies for the parliament's enemies, including Strafford, Aldermen Abel and Kilvert, and even himself.[110]

In the early 1640s, both the more sober dialogues and the extravagantly satirical play-pamphlets, like newsbooks, tended to ally themselves with the parliament's cause. While an occasional dialogue appeared in the intervening years, the form underwent a revival in late 1647, at about the same time that poetry became an important constituent of mercuries. A transitional state was *Newes From Smith the Oxford Jaylor*, a 1645 mercurial attack on *Aulicus*, in dialogue form.[111] Whereas in the early 1640s play-pamphlets had only loosely been related to newsbooks, in so far as they fulfilled overlapping functions, looked similar, and referred to popular appetites for news, in the late 1640s the play-pamphlet became a dependent form upon the mercury. Mercury figures appeared as characters in them, and authorship was attributed to mercuries. These were frequently not written by the authors of the newsbooks. In December 1647 Nedham responded to one of these play-pamphlets in *Mercurius Pragmaticus*: 'Another *Fellow* sets my name to a *dirty* thing intituled the *Levellers Levell'd* on purpose to make his *Trash* vendible, and feede himselfe upon another mans *reputation*: But if I have any more of this doings, out come their *names*, and so I shall deliver them into the hands of the *Tormentors* at *Westminster*.'[112] The mercury was a public figure: its name could sell books, and, more importantly, it had a literary and stylistic identity, an influential public voice, which others could borrow and wear like a mask.[113]

These later play-pamphlets were ardently royalist. *Welcome, most welcome Newes. Mercurius Retrogradus, (One of the Fraternity)*, which Thomason dated 15 October 1647, is a dialogue between *Retrogradus, Aulicus, Britanicus, Aquaticus, Melancholicus, Morbicus*, and '*Moderator*' (presumably *The Moderate Intelligencer*). The villain of the piece is *Britanicus*, guilty of 'that unpardonable crime', his Hue and Cry, for which God, unlike parliament, has not pardoned him. For about a month Nedham had been writing *Mercurius Pragmaticus*, so it is clear that Charles had also pardoned him; but *Britanicus* has a social identity, independent of its author Nedham. *Britanicus* is somewhat prematurely described as 'King-murdering': presumably *Retrogradus* refers to *Britanicus* as a

110 *Old Newes Newly Revived*, sigs. A3–A4.
111 *Newes from Smith* (5 Feb. 1644[5], S4264).
112 *Pragmaticus* 12, 7 Dec. 1647, sig. M^v, 369.112/419(12).
113 See *MTN* 20–1.

desacralizing power, implicated in the political developments which were to lead to the execution of the king.[114] *Welcome, most welcome Newes* claims the imprimatur of Gilbert Mabbott, which does not appear in the Stationers' register and is probably spurious, but it may indicate that the publication was regarded as mostly harmless.

It did precede, however, a pack of more aggressive, fugitive play-pamphlets. These included: *The Levellers levell'd, or, The Independents Conspiracie to root out Monarchie. An Interlude: Written by Mercurius Pragmaticus* (3 December 1647);[115] *Craftie Cromwell: Or, Oliver ordering our New State. A Tragi-Comedie. . . . Written by Mercurius Melancholicus* (10 February 1648);[116] *The Second part of Crafty Crvmwell. Or Olivėr in his glory as king . . . Written by Mercurius Pragmaticus* (?February 1648);[117] *Mistris Parliament Brought to Bed of a Monstrous Childe of Reformation . . . By Mercurius Melancholicus* (29 April 1648);[118] *Mistris Parliament Presented in her Bed, after the sore travaile and hard labour which she endured last week, in the Birth of her Monstrous Off-spring, the Childe of Deformation. . . . By Mercurius Melancholicus* (10 May 1648);[119] *Ding Dong, or Sr. Pitifull Parliament, On his Death-Bed. . . . By Mercurius Melancholicus* (10 May 1648);[120] *The Devill, and the Parliament; Or, The Parliament and the Devill. A Contestation between them for the precedencie* (18 May 1648);[121] *Mistris Parliament Her Gossipping. . . . By Mercurius Melancholicus* (22 May 1648);[122] *Mrs. Parliament Her Invitation of Mrs. London, To a Thanksgiving Dinner,* 'By Mercurius Melancholicus' (29 May 1648);[123] *The Kentish Fayre. Or, The Parliament sold to their best worth* (8 June 1648);[124] *The Cuckoos Nest at Westminster . . . By Mercurius Melancholicus* (15 June 1648);[125] These were followed by two in 1649, probably by John Crouch: *A Tragi-Comedy, called New-Market-Fayre, Or a Parliament Out-Cry: of State-Commodities Set to Sale,* by 'The Man in the Moon' (15 June 1649); and *The Second Part of the Tragi-Comedy called New-Market Fayre, Or Mrs. Parliaments New Figaryes . . . Written by the Man in the Moon* (16 July 1649).[126]

[114] *Welcome, most welcome Newes* (1647; W1259/E411(2)).

[115] 1647; N394/E419(4). All dates in this paragraph, except otherwise stated, from LT.

[116] 1648; C6772/E426(17).

[117] 1648; S2294. This probably dates, like its predecessor, from Feb. as it refers to events (the trial and execution of Captain Burley) which happened in late Jan. as recent.

[118] 1648; M2281/E437(24).

[119] 1648; M2284/E441(21).

[120] 1648; D1495/E441(20).

[121] 1648; D1216/E443(18).

[122] 1648; M2282/E443(28).

[123] 1648; M2283/E446(7); attribution in half-title, 1.

[124] ?London, 1648; K324/E446(21); it gives a probably false Rochester imprint.

[125] 1648; C7459/E447(19).

[126] T2018/E560(9); and S2318/E565(6) respectively. The attribution is made in the second part, and in a 1661 reprint by Edward Crouch, probable printer of *The Man in the Moon* and possibly brother to John; see Frank, *Beginning,* 203.

The play-pamphlets authored by royalist mercuries were an unstable composite genre, mixing elements of drama, reportage, satire, and prose polemic. They sucked in diverse aspects of print culture and spat them out again. From newsbooks they borrowed authorial pseudonyms and characters. Some parodied imprints: *New-Market-Fayre* was 'Printed at *you may goe look*'. The *Mistris Parliament* pamphlets were 'Printed in the yeer of the Downfall of the Sectaries' or 'Printed in the Yeer of the Saints fear'. A newsbook of June 1648, *The Parliaments Scrich-Owle*, claimed likewise: 'Printed in the first year of the decease of King *Oliver* 1648.'[127] Martin Marprelate had, out of necessity, satirized the conventions of typography with false locatives in 1588; the tradition was revived in 1645 by Richard Overton, in the guise of Martin Mar-priest.[128] The practice was soon dominated by newsbooks, which the mercurial play-pamphlets imitated. This exchange dramatizes the pattern of borrowing and revitalizing which newsbooks repeatedly played through in relation to pamphlet culture.

The main purpose of play-pamphlets was fruit-throwing. The hybrid genre was aggressive, and the attribution to a mercury allowed vicious and outrageous politico-sexual satire. Since this was evidently a recognizable opportunity for licence, it should be regarded as a form of tolerated misbehaviour. This does not mean that the authorities condoned 'Pragmaticus' and 'Melancholicus' or were content to let them continue their slanderous practices. Rather, it indicates that readers learned to anticipate the content of these publications and neither responded with outrage nor took many of the accusations seriously. The scurrilous satire of Crouch's *Man in the Moon* did not confound but fulfilled the expectations of readers.

The 1641 satires of Laud deployed images of imprisonment and displays of bodily functions: in *The Bishops Potion*, Laud vomits a series of books and papers symbolic of his malpractices in the 1630s.[129] This tradition was continued and broadened in the 1647–9 period where sexual intercourse, involving the wives of Cromwell and Fairfax, impotence, child-birth, vomiting of black bile, blood, and gold, drunkenness, the beshitten breeches of Alderman Atkins, and death were common elements. All of these elements were an extension, often into visual terms, of the transgressive, corporeal, and scatological language of the mercury.

[127] *Parliaments Scrich-Owle* 1, ?29 June 1648, 489.1/E450(5).

[128] *Marprelate Tracts*, ed. Pierce, 15; [Richard Overton], *The Araignement of Mr. Persecution* (1645; O620); Heinemann, *Puritanism and Theatre*, 243–51; Nigel Smith, 'Richard Overton's Marpriest Tracts: Towards a History of Leveller Style', *Prose Studies*, 9 (1986), 39–66; Pooley, *English Prose*, 159–60.

[129] *Bishops Potion*, 2–3. See also *A new Play Called Canterbury His Change of Diot* (1641; N702/E177(8)), LT dated Nov.

Play-pamphlets were to some extent a continuation of pre-war theatre, rechannelled when the theatres were closed.[130] The connection can be made with journalism and pamphleteering in general; for instance in the writing of John Harris, who had been an actor before the war, and whose journalism contains echoes of the drama of Shakespeare and Jonson.[131] A satirical 1643 pamphlet entitled *The Actors Remonstrance, Or Complaint: For The silencing their profession, and banishment from their severall Play-houses* reinforces this case. The context resists a literal reading, but some of the underlying assumptions stand none the less:

For some of our ablest ordinarie Poets, instead of their annuall stipends and beneficiall second-dayes, being for meere necessitie compelled to get a living by writing contemptible penny-pamphlets in which they have not so much as poetical licence to use any attribute of their profession; but that of *Quid libet audendi?* and faining miraculous stories, and relations of unheard of battels.

This lamentation echoes non-satirical complaints over the decay in trade familiar from 1641–3. But the claims that the stage has been reformed, and the allusions to decline in the associated trades of brewing and tobacco-selling, reveal a critical and comic agenda. This is reinforced by an appeal to the court of Apollo, in the tradition of Trajano Boccalini's *De' ragguagli di Parnasso.*[132] Journalism is described as a more fictitious means of representing reality than the stage. *The Actors Remonstrance* expresses concern for the career prospects of out-of-work actors; 'Nay, it is to be feared, that shortly some of them; (if they have not been enforced to do it already) will be encited to enter themselves into *Martin Parkers* societie, and write ballads. And what a shame this is, great *Phœbus*, and you sacred Sisters; for your owne Priests thus to be degraded of their ancient dignities.'[133] Ballads are a more debased and more inaccurate literary form than newsbooks, a further step down from the stage on the ladder of prestige.

The continuity was accented by contemporaries. Attacking newsbooks in 1644, Cleveland commented on the theatricality of parliamentary proceedings as reported in the diurnals: 'since Stages were voted downe, the onely Play-house is at *Westminster.*'[134] Samuel Sheppard's *The Committee-Man Curried* (1647) advertised itself as a near-alternative to the theatre, 'Since it is held a crime, that on the Stage I

[130] Butler, *Theatre and Crisis*, 228–250; Heinemann, *Puritanism and Theatre*, 239–57; Potter, 'The Plays and the Playwrights, 1642–1660', 280–93; *L&R*, 72.

[131] Heinemann, *Puritanism and Theatre*, 252–5; Sirluck, 'Shakespeare and Jonson', 38–99; also *The Royall Diurnall (for King Charls the II.)* 1, 25 Feb. 1650, sig. A^v, 587.1/E594(6).

[132] See 212–13, below.

[133] *The Actors Remonstrance* (24 Jan. 1642; A454/E86(8)), 7.

[134] Cleveland, *Character of a London Diurnall*, 2.

Wit should present itself'.[135] This and its sequel, *The Second Part of the Committee Man Curried* (1647), were plays of sexual intrigue and cavalier mock heroism which anticipated Restoration drama. Sheppard's politicized invocation of 'Wit' anticipated the elaboration of it in Davenant's *Preface to Gondibert*: and its subsequent centrality to Restoration literary theory.[136] The subtitle, 'A Comedy presented to the view of all Men', toyed with the paradox, enabled by publication, of a play that was open to a universal audience.

The prologue to *Craftie Cromwell* stated the continuity clearly:

> An Ordinance from out pretended State,
> Sowes up the Players mouths, they must not prate
> Like Parrats what they're taught upon the Stage,
> Yet we may Print the Errors of the Age:
> All their projections cannot hinder so,
> But if we write, the Presses needs must goe.
> That, that alone, heales our dejected Sense,
> We can divulge our pen'd Intelligence:
> Slight is our veine, not *Clio's* ayd we crave,
> If *THALIA* smile, we our sole wishes have:
> Smooth *PLAUTUS, ARISTOPHANES* his veine
> We now affect, not *SOPHOCLES* high streine:
> Yet thus we differ, they for mirth were fixt,
> But we have *Joy* and *Dolor*, both commixt.[137]

This gestures nicely to some of the continuities between newsbooks and theatre, to the role of the journalist as public rhetor, as 'the abstracts and brief chronicles of the time'.[138] It is questionable, however, whether the pre-civil war stage could or would have accommodated the political content of many of these pamphlets.[139] The perverse irony of the prologue is that the fictions which had once been displayed on the stage in order to expose and hence to criticize the 'Errors of the Age' have been replaced by news reports. This is the madness of the times, both tragic and comic. In the words of *Moderate Intelligencer*: 'The Ordinance for suppressing of Stage Plays, was concurred with by the Lords, there's an end of those Gamesters, there's Tragedies (though not Comedies) enough besides in *England* and *Ireland*.'[140] The same point was made by a number of newsbooks written in dialogue form: the generic hybridity reflected the perversity of the times. This also evoked the emphasis and

[135] Samuel Sheppard, *The Committee-Man Curried* (1647; S3160), sig. A^v.
[136] Zwicker, *Lines of Authority*, 17–36.
[137] *Craftie Cromwell*, prologue, sig. A^v.
[138] *Hamlet*, II. ii.
[139] Cf. Orchard, 'Literary Theory', 12–13.
[140] *Moderate Intelligencer* 136, 28 Oct. 1647, 1334, 419.136/E412(2).

authority of a speaking voice, which could be particularly useful for abuse and insults invigorated by oral registers.[141]

Several commentators suggest that the play-pamphlets were performed; and while this is plausible no substantive evidence has been presented for actual staging. While any pamphlet might have been read aloud, the vomiting of books would have been a more demanding scene for a tavern performance. The common use of woodblock illustrations in these pamphlets therefore works against the performance thesis: they were a substitute rather than an aid to it. The dramatic structure, the revelation of plot, and arrangement into scenes is generally very weak, though other elements, the rake characters, sexual innuendo, the writing of politics in terms of style, perhaps the triumph of wit, are antecedents of Restoration comedy.

The dramatic form affected familiarity and rambunctiousness in order to address a wide audience.[142] Pamphleteers summoned up borrowed costumes and speech, but this does not mean that there was substantial functional continuity. The stage referred to in the prologue (equivalent to the newsbook's title-page poem) to *The Second Part of the Tragi-Comedy called New-Market Fayre* is metaphorical: 'Which cannot chuse but make proud *rebels* rage, | To see themselves thus acted on the Stage.'[143] This creates a textual stage, embracing a performance of language and political satire rather than proxemics and embodied speech. Singing frequently appears in these plays, signifying not so much a dramatic technique employed to stir or manipulate the audience's attention as a different register of discourse.[144] It bears the same relation to the pamphlet as poetry bears to newsbooks. In *The Levellers levell'd* the character 'Pragmaticus' speaks in verse, indicating a different kind of speech, suggesting the function of a narrator, and endowing him with greater authority. It is the function of the chorus, which appears in more traditional form in *Craftie Cromwell.* Hence a stage technique has acquired a new meaning in the context of a play-pamphlet. To infer that this gestured towards actual performance may be a misreading.[145]

The 1661 reprint of *New-Market-Fayre* advertised that it was 'reprinted

[141] *Parliament-Kite* (1648), N&S 483; *A New Mercury* (9 Sept. 1644; N670/E8(17)); *Mercurivs Honestus* 1–2, 19 and 25 May 1648, 331–2/E443(23) and E444(8); *Wandering Whore* (1660), N&S 668.1–6.

[142] Butler appears to be unsure about their performance: he claims that almost all are 'conceivably performable', but later adds the qualification 'even if only a proportion of them are stageable'; *Theatre and Crisis*, 237, 239, 247.

[143] *Second Part of . . . New-Market Fayre*, 1.

[144] Cf. the symbolic 'Confused Musick' in *The Levellers levell'd*, 2.

[145] Some consumers expressed a preference for printed plays; see the prefatory poems to Humphrey Moseley's 1647 Beaumont and Fletcher folio.

at the request of some young Gentlemen, to *Act* in *Christmas Holy-dayes*'. The original conspicuously did not. *The Second part of Crafty Crvmwell* recommended that the reader live 'to see this plaid another day', projecting performance as something that would happen in an improved future.[146] The prologue to *The Levellers levell'd*, 'Spoken by *Mercurius Pragmaticus*', claims that he will

> on the Stage
> Present to view the Monsters of the Age,
> These sonnes of Belial, you must onely read;
> And yet this Play was acted once indeed.[147]

The play has been acted in reality: the honest journalist has been forced to become the tragi-comic playwright. The machinations of 'John [Lilburne] of London' are best exposed in dramatic form because the actors manifest themselves in their own words and deeds, are condemned out of their own mouths, and are seen to lose at the end: this, like many other royalist play-pamphlets, ends in an extravagant fantasy of wish-fulfilment with the providential and imminent return of the king. Straightforward journalism could only offer promises and prophecy. Attenuating the possibility of physical performance, and instead emphasizing the play-pamphlet as a form of discursive performance, brings them closer to newsbooks. This is why their authors cast mercury figures in such important roles. The play-pamphlets were not of course periodicals, though some appeared in several parts. With hindsight, the 1661 reprint of *New-Market-Fayre* promised a second part the next week.[148] *The Second part of Crafty Crvmwell* claimed to be by 'Pragmaticus', whereas the first attributed itself to 'Melancholicus'. Evidently this assumed a form of continuity which was not authorial: a shared cause, a shared language. *Mistris Parliament Presented in her Bed* was clearly a sequel to *Mistris Parliament Brought to Bed*; the child of reformation had been born a child of deformation. Some of the play-pamphlets thus hinted at seriality.

The play-pamphlets were also, like newsbooks, topical and sometimes informative. *The Second Part of . . . New-Market Fayre* was concerned with Cromwell's preparation for Ireland; *The Second part of Crafty Crvmwell* with the trial of Captain Burley. *The Levellers levell'd* included a story involving Lilly which had appeared in the newsbooks two weeks earlier.[149] *Ding Dong, or S^r. Pitifull Parliament*, which appeared in early May 1648, reported on the rebellions of Colonels Poyer and Powell, which

146 *The Second part of Crafty Crvmwell*, prologue, 2.

147 *The Levellers levell'd*, sig. A^v.

148 *New-Market-Fayre*, 8.

149 *Mercurius Elencticus* 3, 19 Nov. 1647, 312.03/E416(13); *MTN* 139–40. See also *The Late Storie of Mr. William Lilly* (Jan. 1647[8]; L559).

happened in the last week of February. These play-pamphlets do not generally require detailed background knowledge, but fulfil a news-function. This is journalism and effective reporting as well as political satire and wish-fulfilment.

The Great Assises: *newsbooks on trial*

The most perceptive comments on the style and internal logic of newsbooks have been made not by modern critics but by relatively hostile contemporaries, whose criticisms were sometimes informed. By 1645 the pamphlet literature around newsbooks shows that some readers understood the form and its relation to society. Cleveland's *Character of a London Diurnall* and the numerous responses to it recognized and mapped out a framework in which newsbooks were to be discussed.[150] Several attacks on *Britanicus* were published, revealing the public recognition that parliament's paper bullet had triumphed over *Aulicus.* 'I see by your printed books that you have some men can do as much for our victories as *Aulicus* can do for his Majesty,' wrote Sir Samuel Luke to his father in May.[151]

On 11 February 1645 the anonymous poem *The Great Assises Holden in Parnassus* appeared. Following the erroneous attribution to the poet and pamphleteer George Wither,[152] Joseph Frank describes it as 'generalized' and representing 'Wither at his verbose and pompous worst'.[153] Nothing could be further from the truth. *The Great Assises* was a sophisticated text, which revealed a sensitivity to and a considerable knowledge of the London bookseller's shelves. It acknowledged that newsbooks were a fact of literary and political life, and its criticisms were of a complex nature.

The Great Assises, perhaps inevitably, did repeat the formulaic and commonplace accusation, which its readers would have anticipated, that newsbooks were replete with lies. The author (or one of them) of *The Gentle Lash* wrote that the 'nature and property' of diurnals 'is to

[150] LT, E268(6) dated Feb. The first published notification was on 10 Feb.; *Britanicus* 69, 10 Feb. 1645, [548], 286.069/E269(6).

[151] *The Letter Books of Sir Samuel Luke 1644–5*, ed. H. G. Tibbutt (HMSO, 1963), 268.

[152] Attribution made by Thomas Barlow, Bodleian librarian between 1652 and 1660 (Bod.: Linc. c.14.7, title-page). Alexander Dalrymple also made the attribution in his edition, *Extracts from Juvenilia or Poems* (1785), 72, though it is not clear whether he was following Barlow. Wing follows; W3160. Internal evidence militates very strongly against Wither's responsibility.

[153] Frank, *Cromwell's Press Agent,* 24; cf. Wedgwood's simplistic and literal interpretation of it in *Poetry and Politics,* 72–3. Wedgwood sees it as Wither's 'cry of rage' against the damage done to verse and prose by the printing press. For a more recent reading see Achinstein, *Milton and the Revolutionary Reader,* 76–7.

Lye': 'I feare it goes against your consciences to print a truth.'[154] Cleveland accused London diurnals of writing 'the *Roundheads* Legend, the Rebels Romance', tall stories of inaccurately reported deaths: 'Such, and so empty, are the Triumphs of a *Diurnall*: but so many impostumated Fancies, so many Bladders of their owne Blowing.'[155] A response to Cleveland wrote in return that *Aulicus* 'for want of truth and honesty in stead of a History presents to the Reader a Legend of lies'.[156] Probably attacking the *Perfect Diurnall* one anti-newsbook observed: 'sure however Poets have got an ill name, I had rather beleeve in the supplement of *Lucan*, then the relation of the battell at *Newbury*.'[157] This was, strangely, an allusion to an erudite and literary work: Thomas May's *A Continuation of Lucan's Historicall Poem till the Death of Julius Cæsar*.[158] The second issue of *Englands Remembrancer* preached against the 'lying relations' of 'the weekly Pamphleters'.[159] The editor of *Perfect Occurrences* was, according to *A Fresh Whip*, 'ever a favourer of Lyes'.[160] A 1644 broadsheet, *The Two Incomparable Generalissimo's of the world, with their Armies briefly described and embattailed, visibly opposing each other*, noted that the Devil, the 'Generall of the Church Malignant', 'sends abroad his nimble *Mercuries*, | Intelligencers, Scouts, and *Aulick* lyes.'[161] According to Taylor, himself not averse to relating the improbable or apocryphal, *The Scout*, *The Scotish Dove*, and the *Diurnall* 'madly strive the Truth to overturne'.[162] In 1652 Samuel Sheppard, with equally dubious credentials, exclaimed: 'Sure they pretend a priviledge to lye, from the very name: nor could they justly style themselves *Mercuries*, unless they did sometimes start notoriously aside from the truth.'[163] The same had been said of corantos: in 1639 John Dillingham had written to Lord Montagu claiming that one of the ways his newsletters differed from the printed versions was that 'they print all, and ours seldome prouves false'.[164] Attacking Henry Walker, the author (possibly Taylor) of *A Recommendation to Mercurius Morbicus Together with a fair Character upon his worth*

[154] *Gentle Lash*, sigs. A2v, '*'. The latter accusation is specifically against *The Continuation*. The pamphlet was probably written by Featley, though not the lashing introduction.

[155] Cleveland, *Character of a London Diurnall*, 3, 6.

[156] *The Oxford Character Of the London Diurnall Examined and Answered* (1645; O851/E274(32)), 2.

[157] *Britanicvs Vapvlans* 1, 2.

[158] (1630; *STC* 17711); 2nd edn. in 1633.

[159] *Englands Remembrancer* 2, [11 Feb.] 1647, 2, 126.2/E375(9).

[160] *A Fresh Whip*, 5.

[161] May 1644, attributed to George Wither, probably printed by Gilbert White; W3204B/669f.10(5).

[162] Taylor, *Rebells Anathematized*, 3.

[163] *Mercurius Mastix* 1.

[164] Cotton, 83: quoting Beaulieu MSS, *Papers and Letters*, i, f. 54, 14 Jan. 1639. Cf. Brathwaite and Lupton, *MTN* 12.

wrote: 'no News stirring but what passes by his doore; and be it true or false, good or bad, all's one to him, he puts it off, though at second or third hand, for pure Orthodox.'[165] These criticisms were reiterated in invectives against individual authors and newsbooks in general.

The Great Assises at certain points perpetuated this convention, indicting the mercenaries 'Who weekly utter, slanders, libells, lies, | Under the name of specious novelties'.[166] The author punned on specious, meaning both attractive and calculated to appear attractive though in reality not so. A specious novelty would, paradoxically, actually be stale. Other contemporary uses of the term associate it with the 'popular', perhaps implicit in this case.[167] Apollo, the monarch of Parnassus, observes that 'truths now for imperfections passe'; the '*Writer of Occurrences*', possibly Henry Walker, is accused of having 'disguis'd falsehood by the name | Of *Truth*' and of deceiving his readers with lies; the *London Post* writes 'no newes, but *Romants*', and contrives and forges his letters of intelligence; the *Kingdomes Weekly Intelligencer* likewise 'for lucres sake | Did false intelligence devise'; Border's *Weekly Account* practises the 'art of lying'; and in *Perfect Passages* there are 'many stories' which have 'injur'd Truth'.[168] *Perfect Passages* responded to *The Great Assises*: 'truly his stories are very vaine, even as vaine as *Aulicus* his stories, and to as little purpose.'[169] Despite these formulae, *The Great Assises* is not a simple restatement of dubious platitudes; its observations are more specific. It is an insightful work of cultural criticism.

The idea for the trial was derived from Trajano Boccalini's *De' ragguagli di Parnasso* (1612). In 1622 a selection from this was published in English, translated by Thomas Scott, as *Newes from Pernassus. The Politicall Touchstone, Taken from Mount Pernassus: Whereon the Governments of the greatest Monarchies of the World are touched.* The work was translated in its entirety by Scott, John Florio, and William Vaughan in 1626 as *The New-found Politicke.*[170] It consists of a series of newsletters from Parnassus, in which many near-contemporary European politicians and philosophers are satirized from a Tacitist position: sections of

[165] 1647; T502, 6. Attribution in Wing, accepted by Cotton.

[166] *Great Assises*, 2.

[167] e.g., in July 1645, the Westminster Assembly expressed a fear of radical Arminianism, through which 'Multitudes' would 'make Use of the specious Name of Liberty for a Cloak of Naughtiness'; *LJ* vii. 505–6. Milton used the word similarly, notably in *Eikonoklastes*; *CPW* i. 872; iii. 360, 388, 418, 472, 507, 525; also *Paradise Regained* 2.392; *Paradise Lost* 2.484 and 9.361; *The Complete Poetry of John Milton*, ed. John T. Shawcross (New York, 1971).

[168] *Great Assises*, 14, 18, 24, 25, 27.

[169] *Perfect Passages* 17, 19 Feb. 1645, 130, 523.17/E270(5).

[170] See William F. Marquardt, 'The First English Translators of Trajano Boccalini's *Ragguagli di Parnaso*: A Study of Literary Relationships', *Huntington Library Quarterly*, 15 (1951), 1–19.

it were conceived as part of a longer series of commentaries on Tacitus.[171]

The most relevant section from the perspective of *The Great Assises* is a report of an 'admirable Custome' Apollo has introduced into Parnassus, the court of Europe, in order to ensure the continuing upright government of the European states:

That euerie yeare, the names of the chiefest Potentates of the earth, written vpon litle schedules, should be put into an Vrne, and then being drawen foorth one by one, the publicke Censor of Politicall matters should (in the presence of the sacred Colledge of the Learned) record the disorders, which he had obserued in the gouernment of their States; whereupon those Princes were bound either incontinently with satisfying reasons to defend such things as were obiected against them, or els within a Moneth to reforme them.[172]

The Great Assises differs from this model in that the officials and jurors by whom the newsbooks are tried are not their fellow newsbooks, or even disinterested officials, but poets and men of letters: Francis Bacon is the Chancellor, Joseph Scaliger is the Censor (replacing Baldasar Castiglione in Boccalini's version), and the jurors include George Wither, Thomas Carew, Thomas May, William Davenant, Joshua Sylvester, George Sandys, Michael Drayton, Francis Beaumont, John Fletcher, Thomas Heywood, William Shakespeare, and Philip Massinger; 'fat' Ben Jonson is the jailer. Jonson later appeared in a similar role, though with a touch of the ventriloquist's irony, as an arbiter and judge in Marvell's poem 'Tom May's Death'. Marvell was probably not in the country when *The Great Assises* was published, however, and the coincidence is possibly just a testimony to Jonson's enduring reputation as a critic. The court of Apollo is a roll-call of the European intellectual renaissance: Philip Sidney, Guillaume Budé, 'Picvs, *Earle of* Mirandula',[173] Erasmus of Rotterdam, Justus Lipsius, William Barclay, Jean Bodin, Isaac Casaubon, John Selden, Hugo Grotius, Conrad Vorstius, Agostino Mascardi. Like its forebear, *The Great Assises* has a markedly Tacitist cast.

While the author establishes these English and Continental figures on one side of the line that divides élite culture from the vulgar (overlooking the fact that Wither had written at least one newsbook[174]), he simultaneously questions the objective viewpoint of the jurors. Thus they too are seen to be motivated by self-interest. John Taylor, the 'Cryer' of the court, was the author of pseudo-newsbooks and vitupera-

[171] See Tuck, *Philosophy and Government*, 101–3.

[172] *Newes from Pernassus* (Helicon [i.e. Holland], 1622; *STC* 22080), 57.

[173] A title evidently derived from Sir Thomas More's biography.

[174] George Wither, *Mercurius Rusticus: Or, A Countrey Messenger* (Oct. 26, 1643; W3171); see *MTN* 101.

tive attacks on them. The contest then, as the contrast with *Newes from Pernassus* makes clear, reveals the clash of interests between twelve poets and twelve newsbooks, and thus admits fundamental similarities between the two.

The initial charge that the Censor makes against newsbooks is that they 'disturbe' Apollo's government: typography is a powerful engine unknown to 'our forefathers' and we must be careful that 'the literary Presse' does not have unwanted side-effects. Accordingly the usual suspects are rounded up (literally, by Torquato Tasso and his cavalry) and placed in the dock. The newsbooks are accused, not their authors: this relies on the convention of using them as independent figures in all kinds of pamphlet literature, particularly play-pamphlets. What follows is a kind of Battle of the Books, presided over by Apollo, in whose state the 'instrument of Art' is ideally produced by motives other than 'Interest'.[175] This term, central to the writings of the Florentines Niccolò Machiavelli and Francesco Guicciardini, and Henri, Duc de Rohan, was frequently invoked to abuse newsbooks, and was later turned to great effect by Marchamont Nedham.[176] Apollo sits above all the mudslinging, at the top of the hierarchy of genres; his name is correspondingly distinguished from all others in the *dramatis personæ*, at the head of the page, in a border. In the drama literary relations are strained: when Tasso is appointed Lieutenant-General of all Italian poets, Dante, Petrarch, and Ariosto look on with discontent and jealousy.[177] Apollo is called upon to speak in justification of the literary figures, who are generally over-passionate and incompetent in their own defence.

Mercurius Britanicus is first in the dock, charged with writing scandalously and in contempt of the dignity of Apollo, and with infusing his ink with poisonous mercury. In response *Britanicus* asks for the names of the judges, and hearing them objects against Wither on the grounds:

> That *Withers* was a cruell Satyrist;
> And guilty of the same offence and crime,
> Whereof hee was accused at this time.

This inflames Wither's choler, but when calmed he is able to legitimize his own satire: 'his impartiall pen | Did rather grosse abuses taxe, then men.' He had also already suffered for his own transgressions.[178] This last point ensures that *Britanicus*' accusation sticks. Not yet satisfied *Britanicus* then turns on Sandys and Sylvester who are, he claims, not poets but 'meer Rhymers', being translators.[179] 'Poems lose by their

[175] *Great Assises*, 2, l. 12.
[176] See J. A. W. Gunn, *Politics and the Public Interest in the Seventeenth Century* (1969).
[177] *Great Assises*, 5, ll. 4–16.
[178] *Great Assises*, 9, ll. 14–16.
[179] *Great Assises*, 10, l. 7. Macdonald gives 'meet', misreading Bod.: Wood 622(12).

translation' their initial lustre, therefore these two are not artists but artisans, appealing to 'vulgar wits' in 'vulgar language', and are accordingly unfit to sit in judgement on him. This is not simply a reversal of the charge: it is a repudiation of the charge in a style typical of *Britanicus* (though *Britanicus'* actual response was somewhat different). Overcome by the eloquence of *Britanicus* the translators are dumb and Apollo must step in to defend them, by claiming that they are suitable for women readers.

But the point has been made. Within the text *Britanicus* is allowed to speak for himself, with a swagger not unlike his own, and thus his objection acquires a legitimacy, despite the eventual judgement and sentence. *Britanicus* is reprieved at the very end of the poem. The real *Mercurius Britanicus* was not satisfied with this account. He objected to the accusations against himself and Wither, claiming that *The Great Assises* was a malignant partner to Cleveland's *Character of a London Diurnall*.[180] *Perfect Passages* and *The Scotish Dove* agreed with this characterization.[181] Nedham wrote that the pamphlet was specifically directed against him, and that the charges against *Aulicus* were 'but a little by the *by* to dresse out the plot', inserted purely to conceal the political partisanship. He protested that his lashing pen was as justified as Wither's.

When *Aulicus* is brought before the court (something Nedham had recommended in *Britanicus* a week earlier[182]) he objects that May had conceived some 'private spite' against him, and, furthermore, that 'hee was guilty of ingratitude'. Whatever the validity of the latter claim, which literary historians have gullibly accepted as true,[183] the former seems probable, particularly if May had authored *The Character of a Right Malignant*, which appeared only days earlier.[184]

The Parliament Scout had appeared on the shelves of booksellers for the very last time twelve days before *The Great Assises* was published.[185] The *Scout*'s claim that he deserves to be tried fairly, by the detective senses of twelve noses as well as by twelve mouths, and therefore Davenant, with his notoriously minute organ, has no place in the jury is, of course, straightforward buffoonery. But the charge against the *Scout*, that he had strayed 'Into some matters farre beyond his way', is underpinned by well-defined conceptions about the nature of newsbooks as a

[180] *Britanicus* 70, 17 Feb. 1645, sig. Bbbb3^v, 286.070/E269(25).

[181] *Perfect Passages* 17, 130–1; *Scotish Dove* 70, 14–21 Feb. 1645, 548, 594.070/E270(11).

[182] *Britanicus* 69, 541.

[183] See Norbrook, 'Lucan, Thomas May, and the Creation of a Republican Literary Culture'. In *Britanicus* 70, Nedham took exception to this charge.

[184] 1645; M1400/E27(3), LT dated 1 Feb.

[185] On 30 Jan. 1645, the Lords sent for the printer and author, and ordered the seizure of the copies; *LJ* vii. 164–5.

literary form. The *Scout* is accused, not for the first time, of indiscretion: he

> Had toss'd and tax'd high actions in a sheet: . . .
> And that he had presum'd likewise to mixe
> With his Avisoes sweet, soure politicks,
> Dispersing weekly maximes of State,
> As if he chiefly at the helme had sate: . . .
> And that he with his mercenary hand,
> Had touch'd affaires of weight not to be scann'd
> By such as hee: thus was the *Scout* indicted.[186]

The *Scout*'s feeble defence, that he should not be punished for errors stemming from a lack of attentiveness, is perhaps a little harsh on Dillingham, its editor. Nevertheless, the previous month Dillingham had pleaded for clemency before the Lords for defamation of the Earl of Essex.[187] *The Great Assises* may specifically refer to this incident. In a sense the *Scout* makes the only defence he can: it is true that Dillingham chose to comment on affairs of state, and risked the common prejudice that this was properly beyond the reach of the newsbook-reading public. An 'aviso' carries overtones of foreign news, though not restricted to it. This is perceived as legitimate fare for newsbooks: popular political commentary was the worst fear of those who were nervous about newsbooks. They should not be mixed. The criticism is not that this newsbook is untrue or inaccurate. The *Scout* was guilty of political and literary inappropriateness; it had broken the hierarchy of genres. Two months later the author of *A Fvll Answer to a Scandalous Pamphlet, Intituled, A Character of a London Diurnall* observed, 'I find in *Diurnals* no such politique maximes, as be in *Tacitus* his *Annals*'.[188] He had looked rather less closely at the diurnals than the author of *The Great Assises.*

Mercurius Civicus is mocked for his poor resemblances of newsworthy figures in woodblock on the title-page.[189] His fondness for news from the Continent is also observed. In defence, the friends of *Civicus* attempt to bribe the judge with sack and sugar loaves, suggesting the financial interest and weight of wealthy Presbyterian citizens, the supposed readership of *Civicus.*[190] The writer of *Perfect Occurrences* is also characterized with ungenerous accuracy:

> He had his readers rob'd of their beleife,
> And of their wit, and judgment them bereav'd,

[186] *Great Assises,* 15, ll. 12–27.
[187] See *LJ* vii. 164; *Beginnings,* 90; Cotton, 98–100; see 39, above.
[188] *A Fvll Answer,* 2.
[189] *Great Assises,* 16, ll. 26–30.
[190] *Great Assises,* 17, ll. 19–26. For the Presbyterian readership see Frank, *Beginnings,* 44–5.

That willingly, were with his lies deceiv'd:
But if some truths (by chance) he utter'd had,
These were in such a tedious language clad,
That many actors of renowned jests,
Depriv'd were of their honour'd interests,
By his inglorious penne.[191]

This summarizes the underlying argument of the *Great Assises* in epitome: questionable reporting is a concern, but the real engagement is with elements of style. The language is inappropriate to the matter. The unelevated, homely style of Henry Walker's *Occurrences* was sometimes ill at ease, with serious news nested between wonder stories; though this did not stop William Dugdale from using it for his *Short View of the Late Troubles.*[192] Walker addressed a broad reading public and was apparently successful at communicating his sometimes radical view of events to his audience. His Independent views may well have resulted in his 'radical' prose style: *The Great Assises* accuses him of social levelling by compiling lists of soldiers with insufficient respect for rank.[193]

In *The Great Assises*, the writer of *Occurrences* strikes back at his accusers, berating Carew for obscenity. In 1640 Carew's libertine poetry, published posthumously that year, had been named in a petition to the Long Parliament as a grievance of the kingdom.[194] Apollo accepts *Occurrences*' criticism, on the principle that the greater arts should set an example for the lesser, but excuses Carew because his later, chaster poems make amends for the fault. Apollo lamely blames the readers who enjoy lascivious verse, begging the question why this argument was never used in defence of newsbooks.[195] *A Perfect Diurnall* is accused of mixing facts with fiction:

That hee had wrong'd th'*Athenian Novelists*,
By selling them meere aire, in stead of Sack,
And puffes of wind, for strong Frontigniac:
For empty bottles hee was wont to mixe
Among full flasques.[196]

The modest *Perfect Diurnall* disdains to question Taylor's imputation of imperfection; this has a ring of truth for a newsbook more concerned with diligent and passive parliamentary reporting than vituperation.

The tail-enders are dismissed with greater brevity and more obvious charges. Accusations of lying and greed are made against *London Post*,

191 *Great Assises*, 18, l. 19–19, l. 1.

192 William Dugdale, *Short View of the Late Troubles* (1681; D2492); see Ch. 6, below.

193 *Great Assises*, 19, ll. 9–16.

194 David Norbrook, *Poetry and Politics in the English Renaissance* (1984), 225; J. E. Ruoff, 'Thomas Carew's Early Reputation', *Notes and Queries*, 202 (1957), 61–2.

195 *Great Assises*, 22, ll. 7–10.

196 *Great Assises*, 14, ll. 17–21.

Kingdomes Weekly Intelligencer, Weekly Account, and *Perfect Passages*, though not *The Spye*. The incisive use of stylistic criticism continues, however: *Scotish Dove* 'did Laconick brevity detest', and prefers to preach rather than report; *The Spye* 'Forbidden objects had presum'd to see'.[197] In self-defence the *Spye* attacks Drayton, claiming that his *Poly-Olbion* is 'a rude Embrion of wit', a phrase which might have been applied to a newsbook. Apollo is forced to resort to some transparently opportunistic efforts at literary criticism in defence of Drayton, extolling the virtues of his use of various genres.

The London Post is arraigned for using the 'language gay' of *Euphues* and *Arcadia*, more appropriate to romance than to news-writing. The real *London Post* responded with another piece of literary criticism, claiming that the *Arcadia* deserved better than to be set alongside both *Euphues* and his own humble journalism:

I (who onely live to serve you) having no Jurie but what malice and madnesse had impannelled was brought in print (amongst some of my Companions) to the Assizes of *Parnassus*, and proclaimed a Rebell unto Truth, A Felon who had robbed the *Arcadia*, and another honest man, so miserably poore himselfe that, in earnest, I am almost ashamed to name him. His name (if I hit it right) is *Euphues*, the very same *Euphues* whom I (professe) I never looked on but presently with neglect if not with Indignation I flunge him by. There is no man of so thick, so churlish an understanding or so little indebted to the Muses or the Graces that doth not honour the *Arcadia*, but how much the beauty and the Acutenesse of *Sidneys* stile, How farre his numbers and his measures doe exceede the rudenes of my Accents, How different my Expressions are from his, I doe leave unto those to judge who are able to discerne me and absolve me.

He admits that he is flattered, and claims that the author of *The Great Assises* was at a loss to find any criticism of the *Post* yet felt it necessary to include him in the trial. Because, he writes, in typically mock-self-deprecating terms, 'this is indeed enough to legitimate a Pamphlet', he moves 'to the cleering the Author of this laughing and lashing Satyre':

I have read the Satyre againe and againe, and if I have any knowledge in the Art of Poetry (as my best friends perswade me that I have too much) I must acknowledge, that it is one of the most laboured Pieces that I have seen in Print since the Wars began, full of Witt, & Art, and Learning. Yet it is not without some egregious Solæcismes, and (without any relation to my self at all) I could wish that it never had been extant.[198]

These literary aspirations reveal just how pretended the *Post*'s rhetorical self-deprecation was. The same aspirations suggest why the insightful

[197] *Great Assises*, 22, 24, 28.
[198] *London Post* 24, 18 Feb. 1645, 3, 233.124/E270(2).

author of *The Great Assises* chose mockingly to place the *Post* in the company of Sidney and Lyly; and the *Post* fell to the bait.

The author of *The Great Assises* was not purely sympathetic to newsbooks. But she or he recognized that they constituted a literary form, and that they might have coherent responses to their detractors. None could be accused of libertinism, at least in 1645, and the author may even have noticed a distinctly respectable, 'puritan' streak. *The Kingdomes Weekly Intelligencer* attacks playwrights and the stage, invoking the authority of Plato. Apollo's response is that the complaint is not made 'for vertue's sake, | Or true affection to the Common-weale', otherwise it would be accepted.[199] The author had also read a considerable number of newsbooks, enough to recognize and distinguish between different stylistic tendencies. The assize is not simply a kangaroo court. Unlike unqualified attacks, *The Great Assises* contains informed, considered analyses, and its very existence shows how newsbooks had emerged as central to reading life in 1645.

In Boccalini's *Ragguagli* Apollo arraigns Lipsius for his edition of Tacitus, which has put Tacitus into the hands of the multitude, so 'that euen Shop-keepers . . . shew not themselues more cunning in any profession than of State policy'.[200] This tongue-in-cheek representation of the anti-Tacitist reaction was ironically re-enacted in 1627 when the Venetian Council of Ten refused publication to Boccalini's commentaries on Tacitus. Like the *Scout*, there was too much *ragion di stato* in them.[201] In 1654 Richard Whitlock complained about shopkeepers reading newsbooks. He added, with unintentional irony:

> What Pamphlets the World in these latter times hath swarmed with, the studious *Shop-keeper* knoweth, who spendeth no small time at the *Bulk* in *reading*, and *censuring modern controversies*, or *News:* & will be readier to tell you *what the times lack*, than *to ask what you lack*. We live in an Age wherein never was lesse *Quarter* given to *Paper*: should *Boccalines* Parliament of *Parnassus* be called among us, I feare our Shops would be filled with printed wast Paper, condemned to *Tobacco*, *Fruit*, &c.[202]

Whitlock was apparently unaware of the different verdict in *The Great Assises*. Cleveland, in *The Character of Mercurius Politicus*, proffered a suggestion for the punishment of Nedham: '*Boccalini*, that innocent Moralizer, yet for writing somewhat too freely for those that were partiall, was thrown into the Canal at *Venice*, and there drown'd: It is time that we had our State-scold to the Ducking-stool.'[203] Thc parallels

199 *Great Assises*, 25, l. 15–26, l. 19.

200 *The New-found Politicke* (1626; *STC* 3185), 20.

201 See Alan T. Bradford, 'Stuart Absolutism and the "Utility" of Tacitus', *Huntington Library Quarterly*, 45 (1983), 135–6; Tuck, *Philosophy and Government*, 101.

202 *Zootomia*, 229.

203 *Character of Mercurius Politicus* (1660; C2021), 8.

are instructive: newsbooks are placed within an intellectual context, though their position there is disputed. The contrast is also instructive: the author of *The Great Assises* was more sympathetic to Boccalini's republicanism and populism than he or she admitted.

Who was the author? The attribution to Wither waxes and wanes, and is certainly false, on the grounds of style.[204] The poem's political allegiances are difficult to establish. The identity of Apollo might be a key. May appears to have committed his 'ingratitude' to Apollo, suggesting that Apollo is Charles. Apollo is also stated to have granted a patent to the *Parliament Scout*, which would equate him with parliament: the *Scout* was the first newsbook licensed after the June 1643 Ordinance, and Dillingham was immediately accused of enjoying a monopoly.[205] This allusion indicates the depth of the author's expertise. *Perfect Passages*, in its response to the attack, equated Apollo with the licenser (at the time this was the positively non-royalist Rushworth), yet regarded it as a cavalier poem.[206] Apollo remains slippery and ambiguous, and consistently signifies only a literary authority; the poem begins with Scaliger warning Apollo of the dangerous potency of typography: 'This instrument of Art, is now possest | By some, who have in Art no interest.'[207] The author is even-handed: both royalists and parliamentarians stand in the dock and jury-box, and no one is excepted on political grounds. *Aulicus* and *Britanicus* are allowed to continue their war. *Aulicus* perhaps receives a harsher punishment (Nedham would have disagreed): but the parable of the Cranes and the Pygmies (mentioned during the sentencing at the end of the poem) apparently favours the latter, who are described as 'Cavaliers'.[208] Jonson's masque *Pleasure Reconciled to Virtue* contains an antimasque of dancing pygmies. It may be fanciful to infer a covert reference to this, but the antimasque is interrupted by the arrival of Mercury.[209] *The Great Assises*, moreover, does explore the relationship between pleasure and virtue, albeit in a context very different from the masque. The absence of obvious partisanship erases an embittered and committed royalist, such as Taylor or Cleveland, from a list of potential authors: we are left with a moderate royalist or Presbyterian (despite the punishment of exile in Scotland).

The position could perhaps be summarized as a 'right Malignant',

[204] Bod.: Linc. c.14.7; Macdonald, *Great Assises*, p. v; it was rejected in F. W. Bateson, ed., *Cambridge Bibliography of English Literature*, vol. i: *600–1600* (Cambridge, 1940), 448; then accepted in George Watson, ed., *New Cambridge Bibliography of English Literature*, vol. i: *600–1600* (Cambridge, 1974), 1192, 2089.

[205] Cotton, 'John Dillingham', 817.

[206] *Perfect Passages* 17, 130.

[207] *Great Assises*, 2, ll. 7–8.

[208] *Great Assises*, 34, l. 4.

[209] *Ben Jonson*, vii. 485.

after *The Character of a Right Malignant*, published on 1 February 1645. This should be understood not as an attack on royalists but on moderates, who are regarded as crypto-royalists. The 'malignant' is a hypocrite who professes allegiance to the parliamentarian cause yet always criticizes it. He loves a parliament in so far as it claims no power; he is opposed to slavery but favours absolute monarchy. May seizes upon some of the contradictions in the soft-royalist position to challenge inconstant and ambivalent Londoners. The objects of May's attack would no doubt have regarded themselves more favourably.

The aúthor of *The Great Assises* was 'an *Oxonian* living here among us' suggested *Scotish Dove*.[210] This would certainly have facilitated his familiarity with so many newsbooks. Several newsbooks were outraged that Edward Husbands, who printed the *Great Assises*, had formerly been printer to the House of Commons.[211] None of the responses to the pamphlet in newsbooks suggest any knowledge of the author's identity, and hence with confidence I must leave it attributed to anon.

Character of a London Diurnall

Another controversy sparking insights into the culture of the newsbook occurred in the early months of 1645. This was precipitated by Cleveland's *Character of a London Diurnall*, published in Oxford anonymously and without a colophon, probably in February 1645.[212] Over the next eleven weeks three pamphlets were released in response, gradually increasing in length and detail: *A Character of the New Oxford Libeller* on 11 February; *The Oxford Character of the London Diurnall* on 31 March; and *A Fvll Answer to a Scandalous Pamphlet, Intituled, A Character of a London Diurnall* on 10 April. In addition to these many newsbooks elected to defend themselves. The exchange reveals something of the contemporary perceptions of newsbooks.

Cleveland was attacking, under the name of *Diurnall*, all London newsbooks; the descendants of *Gallobelgicus*, including '*Scoticus*' (*Scotish Dove*), *Civicus*, and *Britannicus* (*sic*). Cleveland identified the *Perfect Diurnall*, by Pecke, Coles, and Blaicklocke, through the woodblock on its title-page: 'In the Frontispice of the old *Beldame Diurnall*, like the Contents of the Chapter, sits the House of Commons, judging the twelve Tribes of *Israel*.'[213] In contrast to *The Great Assises*, Cleveland feminized diurnals: and in return one critic accused him of writing for

[210] *Scotish Dove* 70, 548.
[211] *Britanicus* 70, sig. Bbbb3^{v}; *Perfect Passages* 17, 131; *Scotish Dove* 70, 547.
[212] See n. 150, above.
[213] *Character of a London Diurnall*, 1.

the favours of ladies.[214] The 'old *Beldame Diurnall*', however, provoked another response: the author of *The Oxford Character*, restoring the *Perfect Diurnall* to its masculinity, expanded the charge of seniority: 'And yet our Journall is elder brother unto *Aulicus* by much, who I beleeve was begotten at *Oxford* (though illegitimately) in envy of ours at *London* of honest parentage.'[215] There was some historical truth in this description.

Cleveland accuses newsbooks of simply reporting lies. The mode of misrepresentation which he attributes to them is a form of pure fictionality. The *Diurnall* reports the 'still-borne' Acts and ordinances of parliament, and is thus 'like the old *Sexton*, who swore his clock went true, whatever the Sunne said to the contrary'. *Diurnalls* devise plots by absurdly over-reading ordinary actions, and thus Quixotically joust 'with the Windmills of their owne Heads'. They are romances, 'Stories of a larger size, then the Eares of their Sect'. They report deaths of royalist commanders repeatedly and without foundation; 'these Artificers of Death can kill the Man, without wounding the Body, like lightning, that melts the Sword, and never singes the Scabbard.'[216] Cleveland's examples are inventive rather than informative; he is not interested in how or why these misrepresentations arrive at the press. *A Character of the New Oxford Libeller* observed that Cleveland used 'religious Epithites' for humour and not for understanding: the same was true of his comments on newsbooks.[217]

Cleveland's pamphlet is a character-sketch, a hostile *blazon* of the parts of a London *Diurnall*. Yet in truth, the *Diurnall* is a substitute victim for the military leadership, and specifically Cromwell:

> But the *Diurnall* is weary of the Arme of flesh, and now begins an *Hosanna* to *Cromwell*, . . .
>
> This is he, that hath put out one of the Kingdomes eyes, by clouding our Mother Vniversity, and (if the Scotch-mist further prevaile) will extinguish this other: . . . Barbarous Rebell! who will be reveng'd upon all Learning, because his Treason is beyond the Mercy of the Book.
>
> The *Diurnall* as yet hath not talk't much of his Victories; but there is the more behind: For the Knight must always beat the Gyant; That's resolv'd.[218]

The *Diurnall* is not given a rounded character: it is attacked for inflating the 'Victories of the Rebels'. Cleveland's representation of newsbooks, unlike that in *The Great Assises*, is neither accurate nor closely observed.

[214] *A Character of the New Oxford Libeller* (1645; C2026/E269(7)), 2, 6.

[215] *Oxford Character*, 1; cf. Ch. 1 n. 14, above.

[216] *Character of a London Diurnall*, 1–4.

[217] *Character of the New Oxford Libeller*, 2.

[218] *Character of a London Diurnall*, 4, 5–6; the middle paragraph echoes the attack on John Hall in *Elencticus* 27, 205–6.

The *Diurnall* he attacks is a hybrid of the characteristics of London newsbooks; in fact it was *Kingdomes Weekly Intelligencer* which had alluded to the Arm of Flesh in a pious, providential editorial in 1644.[219]

The Oxford Character Of the London Diurnall objected to the distance Cleveland had placed between diurnals and annals: 'Surely he meaneth our Journall is a little Annall, or such like: If he had Latine enough, he would call the childe with which he laboureth, if he could speak, *Ephemeris*, or *A Diary*; and such a body is big enough for a conception of six dayes.'[220] This common sense is entirely sound. Newsbooks constituted fairly substantial histories, so to mock them for their diminutive stature was simply wrong-headed. Cleveland had not seen Thomason's collection of newsbooks. The author of *The Oxford Character* says that Cleveland is playing a game of mere terminology. Denigrating newsbooks in relation to histories relies on a matter of scale, which is not sufficient to undermine newsbooks when there are terms for smaller histories. *The Oxford Character* successfully pushes aside the issue of the truth, whether contained in folio or small quarto, adding, quite reasonably: 'it is no dishonour *to comprehend an Iliad in a Nut-shell*, a great matter in a little space.'

A Fvll Answer to a Scandalous Pamphlet also adopted a moderate position, noting that although newsbooks lacked Tacitist maxims and were not 'so authentique as *Livies Decades*; yet experience shewes, that they usually render so much truth, as will make the most clamorous Malignant as silent as a *Seriphian* frog, and appeare with a face as ill as his heart'.[221] Cleveland's animadvertors took the *blazon* seriously, sacrificing humour to analysis and thus losing the debate: but in doing so they showed how subsidiary the issue of truth was in Cleveland's thesis. What was at stake was the success of the parliament's cause and the reputation of the army leaders, not the value of newsbooks.

Nedham recognized this, and responded in kind. He noted the appearance of the *Character* in *Britanicus* on 10 February and deferred his response to the next issue. On 17 February he named Cleveland as the author and accurately characterized his strategy: 'Under the name of *Diurnall* he pretends to *fling* at our *Pamphlets* here, but aimes altogether at some principall *Members* and *Commanders*; and therefore I shall *tracke* him in his own way.'[222] Nedham's rhetoric was more outrageously abusive than Cleveland's:

> A *whelp* of the same *litter* with *Aulicus*, *Cousin Germans* by the two *blind Sisters*; things halfe made up between *Syllogisme* and *Sophistry*, reason and treason; the one learned to *lappe* the rudiments of *Logicke* and Popery in *Oxford*, the other

[219] *KWI* 50, 16 Apr. 1644, 403, 214.050/E42(28).

[220] *Oxford Character*, 3. [221] *Fvll Answer*, 2. [222] *Britanicus* 70, 550.

was bred up among the blessed sons of *Cham*; whose footsteps he followes close: for he of old discovered the *nakednesse* of his *Father*, and this does the like to his *Mother-Vniversity*.[223]

Having blighted Cleveland's credentials, and claimed that *The Character* was undergoing accelerated price deflation, just as *Perfect Passages* claimed that *The Great Assises* was selling poorly,[224] Nedham proceeded to rewrite the *Character* phrase for phrase, translating it into a parliamentarian text. This was a mercilessly laboured response, with not entirely funny results. But it did amount to a manifesto, a declaration of war on all uses of language and on every point of interpretation, including that of the origins of newsbooks.

Three weeks later *Britanicus* responded to criticisms in *Aulicus* with an even more explicit reduction of the issues of the war to issues of language. Having declared that the royalist cause was only still in existence because *Aulicus* deceived the kingdom 'with *lies* and *slanders*, instead of *intelligence*', *Britanicus* produced the final, unassailable repudiation of the standing joke about the 'misspelling' of its name:

But thou art mistaken; we doe not *write*, nor read here, as you doe at *Oxford*: they are not able to spell one word true there; for they *spell* the Parliament *Rebels*; Popery, the *Protestant Religion*; Idolatrie and Superstition, *Decencie*; Episcopacie, *Iure Divina*; Reformation, *Schisme*, &c. and many such strange kind of *spellings*: Doe you thinke then, that *Britanicus* will *spell* his own name, as *Aulicus* would have him? That were a *Iest* indeed. It is sufficient, that *Britanicus* hath taught the People to *spell* the truth of their Plots, and ungodly designes at *Oxford*; to spell the names of the *Evill Councellours*, and *Incendiaries*; and to spell the meaning of *Prelacie*, and King *Charles* his (I mean *Canterbury's*) Protestant Religion, and the Truth of the late *Mock-Treaty*. And hereafter, whatsoever they doe, I shall be able to *spell* it so plainly, that those which run, may read.[225]

Language conceals, covers, and renders the odious superficially acceptable; it also uncovers, educates, demystifies, and enlightens: signification is both means and end, a prize worth fighting over. According to *Britanicus* the war was a war of words: the future of the three kingdoms could be suspended upon an '&c.'

The grounds for the condemnation of newsbooks were more complex than mere lying, a formula employed to displace more important issues. *Britanicvs Vapvlans*, who thought Mercury the patron of eloquence and of lying, complained that it was not becoming for the 'mongrel' *Britanicus* to be witty, because his party was dull, phlegmatic, and melancholy: 'Shall we have a new prodigy more? wit in a Round-

[223] *Britanicus* 70, 549–50.

[224] *Perfect Passages* 17, 130.

[225] *Britanicus* 73, 10 Mar. 1645, 587, 286.073/E271(21); Elencticus 2, 8 May 1648, 10, 316.02/E554(10), borrowed the joke: 'An Act (forsooth) was this day read . . .'

head, as monstrous as the title of the Play, Wit in a Constable . . . ?' The pamphlet speculates that *Britanicus* must have been fathered by a cavalier, not by a plain-speaking parliamentarian.[226] The style of *Britanicus* is insufficiently salty, *Vapvlans* claims, and with an informed and considered argument allows that there is something meritorious waiting to be amended by the addition of salt (and royalism). A grudging respect inhabits the invective.

The Great Assises is concerned with the proper use of language; Cleveland with the support for the army and the political reach of the fourth estate. On paper the war could be fought over questions of style. Genre, effectiveness, and eloquence are the real interests of these pamphlets. Contemporaries had learned to acknowledge all of these when they read a newsbook; newsbooks were fully integrated into the dense life of mid-seventeenth-century print culture. It is worth recalling this when we read twentieth-century comments on their shortcomings.

What next? the anti-mercury or newsbook turned upside down

One of the few opinions which most writers in the middle decades of the seventeenth century shared was that the world was glutted with books. Writers apologized for contributing to this bibliorrhoea, pleading special circumstances: because they wrote truth, because they were honest, because they started before the war began, because friends asked them to.[227] This paradoxical stance, words condemning an excess of words, justified and perhaps led to the tradition of the anti-mercury. The anti-mercury was a newsbook which contained little or no news and criticized the very existence of newsbooks. This kind of vituperative inversion was central to the world of pamphlets: there had already been mock romances, anti-almanacs, and other satirical forms which undermined the truth or value of the genre they purported to represent.[228] Related to these, the anti-mercury was a particularly energetic literary form which had quite a specific significance.

Initially, anti-mercuries attacked individual mercuries; many newsbooks did this, but some were primarily dedicated to the repudiation and refutation of the enemy. The anti-mercury was conceived as an act of literary inversion. This indicates just how recognizable the newsbook was as a distinct form: it was inverted with confidence. Hence

[226] *Britanicvs Vapvlans* 1, 2–3, 4.

[227] Sheppard, *The Weepers*, sig. A2; parliamentary speeches, e.g. *The Speech Of Mr Plydell* (1641; P2658C); Thomas Fuller, *The Holy State* (Cambridge, 1642; F2443), sig. A2; [North], *A Narrative*, sigs. A4–A4v.

[228] *L&R* 233–49 and *passim*; see n. 75, above.

in August 1645 appeared *Mercurius Anti-Britanicus*; in September 1647 *Mercurius Anti-Melanchollicus*; in October 1647 *Mercurius Anti-Pragmaticus;* and these culminated in September 1648 with *Mercurius Anti-Mercurius.*[229] They were formally very much like other mercuries, the differences being the configuration and concentration of satire. *Anti-Britanicus* followed a tradition of royalist burlesque, resembling closely Taylor's attacks on tub preachers etc. Like others, it relied heavily on animadversion; *Anti-Pragmaticus* promised to 'trace' *Pragmaticus* page by page.[230] Taylor's *Mercurius Aquaticus* took this to extremes, reprinting an entire issue of *Britanicus* in order to contradict it in extensive detail.[231]

Anti-mercuries offered news at the same time as they dismissed the value of news and criticized those who appeared to be interested in it. Hence *Anti-Melanchollicus*: 'it is now grown in fashion to *new-vamp* old *Declarations, Letters*, and other *Newses* by *Luke Ha-run-ly*. I could even almost find it in my heart to new-vamp yee some old newes of him.'[232] In November 1643 *Mercurius Populi*, itself containing little that was newsworthy, harangued the reader; 'if ye heare no more of me for longer time, I pray faile not to peruse this till ye doe; as yee may make it yours rather by reading, then only by buying; for it is one of your usuall faults to hearken more after newes and new books, then to make a profitable use of the ould.'[233] The news in *Anti-Pragmaticus* consisted of counter-examples to arguments in *Pragmaticus* as much as original news. It supplemented, rather than replaced, a reading of *Pragmaticus*, which was an informative organ. It was an antidote, counteracting lies:

> have amongst you my royal Roisters. *Pragmaticus, Melancholicus*, and the rest of the malignant Paper-spoilers, must not go on without controule, what a president will it be for the after-Ages to read their shamelesse lies fatherd upon the Fathers Conscript of this Kingdome, and find no one recorded, furnished with so much gall, as to returne them lash for lash.[234]

More informatively, *Anti-Pragmaticus* illuminated the close relationship between *Pragmaticus* (meaning Nedham) and the Leveller John Lilburne, suggesting that mutual opposition to parliament had pushed them into an uneasy alliance which involved co-authoring pamphlets.[235]

[229] N&S serials 267, 268, 270, 269, respectively.

[230] *Anti-Pragmaticus* 4, 11 Nov. 1647, 2, 270.04/E414(2).

[231] This presumably decreased the demand for the original text, mounting a financial as well as a verbal challenge. The text was compressed into six pages.

[232] *Anti-Melanchollicus* 1, 24 Sept. 1647, 2, 268.1/E408(9).

[233] *Mercurius Populi* 1, Nov. 1647, 8, 364.1/E413(14).

[234] *Anti-Pragmaticus* 4, 1–2. Possibly referring to Nedham's pragmatical catch-phrase 'Nemo me impune lacessit.'

[235] This seems plausible. Two years earlier Nedham had published Lilburne's *An answer, to nine arguments: written by T. B. Written long since by J. Lilburne: now publ. by a well*

Such politically astute commentaries were news in a highly complex form.[236]

Anti-Pragmaticus repeatedly highlighted the relationship between mercuries and romance. In this equation 'romance' meant purely fictitious, though also hinting at heroic and deceptive tales written to satisfy the imagination of women. So *Anti-Pragmaticus* wrote on the return of *Pragmaticus* after a period of absence:

> the Cavalierish shee-Firkers, those rampant Girles, began to bemoane his absence in more tears, then if their deare Amadis or red-rose Knight were called in, and they enjoyned on penalty of being forced to be conventives, not to read them: the Twibill Knights, the Quixots of the Royall Party, began to bewaile the silence of their Oracle, imagining their *Apollo* had left *Delphos*.[237]

Hall's *Britanicus* mocked *Elencticus*: ''Tis a pitty so much fine invention was awanting while *Knight-Errantry* was on foot, for then we had more Gigantick lyes then ever we can hope for, unlesse from this pen, which like *Ajax Mastigophorus*, makes these ordinary mistakes of Sheep and Armies, Bel-weathers and Captains.'[238] *Britanicus* mocked the industrious romancing of royalist journalism, 'which while they think they attempt great castles, will (by a piece of moralized Knight-Errantry) be found some little encounter with a Windemill'. Likewise the clergy were '*Don Quixots* of Religion'.[239] Hall himself wrote a romance, 'such, as, had it been finished, might have raised envie in the famous Romanticist Monsieur *De Scudery*', which is now lost.[240] When accusing other newsbooks of fictitiousness he repeatedly used romance imagery, invoking particularly Quixote's distorted vision.[241] This was in the tradition of

willer (1645; L2081). Nedham's politics went in and out of phase with Lilburne's as his comments on the Levellers in *Pragmaticus* make clear.

[236] 'This fellow *Lilburne* hath taken [Prag] to be his Assistant: and I now believe the wit of these two Juglers compiled the late printed Pamphlet entituled Juglers discovered', *Anti-Pragmaticus* 1, 19 Oct. 1647, 2–3, qu. 3, 270.01/E411(10); '*Pragmaticus* and *Lilburne* (of late friends) were greatly fallen out about the matter of Libertie, the one proclaiming all power inherently in the King, the other all Authoritie and Jurisdiction to be in the people, but his Excellency to make them friends hath taken a verie judicious course, by making his violent Adjutators know that the power is in neither, but at present in his and the Parliaments hands, and hath so crushed the Adjutators that they will never be able to look up againe.' *Anti-Pragmaticus* 6, 3–4; see also *Anti-Pragmaticus* 3, 4 Nov. 1647, 7, 270.03/E412(27); *Anti-Pragmaticus* 4, 2.

[237] *Anti-Pragmaticus* 2, 28 Oct. 1647, 1–2, 270.02/E412(5).

[238] *Britanicus* 2, 25 May 1648, 12, 282.02/E444(7).

[239] *Britanicus* 13, 16 Aug. 1648, 98, 282.13/E459(6); *Britanicus* 2, 16.

[240] John Davies's biography, prefaced to Hall, *Hierocles*, sig. b2.

[241] *Britanicus* 3, 30 May 1648, 19, 282.03/E445(14); *Britanicus* 5, 13 June 1648, 37, 282.05/E447(9); *Britanicus* 6, 21 June 1648, 43, 282.06/E449(5); cf. *Anti-Mercurius* 2, 2 Oct. 1648, 5, 269.2/E465(11); *Melancholicus* 51, 14 Aug. 1648, sig. Gg^{v}, 344.51B/E458(10).

Nedham's *Britanicus*.[242] Taylor also used romance as a synonym for fictitiousness.[243] Other writers, including Restoration historians, threw accusations involving jousting at windmills and writing romance.[244]

In September 1648 the aptly titled *Mercurius Anti-Mercurius* combined the scatological images of Lucianic satire with stylistic criticism of various serials. News is fashioned 'to gull the credulous world', a form of jeering, railing excrement, written by 'the excrements of humanity'. *Anti-Mercurius* contained no news.[245] Far from being paradoxical, the choice of form was logical: the mercury was the only literary form low enough to do justice to the mercury.[246] Criticism in more elevated genres could damage the prestige of those genres or even their authors. *Britanicus* made the point with profound irony in responding to criticisms made by Daniel Featley:

> Oh! he doth so declaime against me for discovering some secrets in the Chancellours Chamber, and in the *Cathedrall Service*, but well, how many *Plots* have there been against *Britannicus*? how many *Pens* entred into a Confederacy? the Pen of *Urbanus*, and *Aquaticus*, with a Regiment of Quils more in a Garrison at *Oxford*, and now Doctor *Featlies* Folio, a most *serious, grave*, and *Elaborate, I know not what*, strange! that a Doctor with so many testimonies behinde him of his sufficiency should so puzzle his learning against this one sheet, and write a volume of eighteen pence against a Penny worth of Paper, and goe trouble his Logicke, his Divinity, and Schoole Divinity, his Philosophy, and Astronomy, to write against my *Mercury*; but I pray observe, how handsomely Master Rogers Letter, and the Doctors book agreed to come out at one time, excellent! . . . your Nemesis of Pamphlet of a dozen sheets is only calculated for *Oxford* and *Cambridge*.[247]

Featley's erudition and extensive quotation were inappropriate to the context of criticizing a newsbook. So was a multi-sheet folio format, costing eighteen times as much as the object of his criticism. The rebuttal addressed a limited audience. Nathaniel Rogers's *Letter, Discovering The Cause of Gods continuing wrath*, its author's sole published work, was an earnest, Calvinist treatise, arguing that parliament's guilt in not proceeding to religious reformation at an earlier date was the cause of

242 *Britanicus* 115, 26 Jan. 1646, 1012, 286.115/E318(8): 'as if [*Academicus*] had ravisht a *fragment* out of *Amadis, Poggius* or *Æsop*.'

243 Capp, *World of John Taylor*, 179, 186–7.

244 e.g. Nalson, *Impartial Collection*, i, p. i. See also *MTN* 57–8; Cleveland, *Character of a London Diurnall*, 3; *Mercurius Aulicus Againe* 10–12, 10 Apr. 1648, sig. K^v, 273.10A/E436(16).

245 *Anti-Mercurius* [1], sigs. A^v, A4.

246 The second issue was a different kind of text with overtly parliamentarian politics. The first issue had expressed opposition to all forms of partisanship. They probably had different authors, and whoever took up the pen for the second issue made no effort to assume the mercury's original voice.

247 *Britanicus* 47, 19 Aug. 1644, 367–8, 286.047/E6(26).

present hindrances. A late digression criticized *Britanicus* for the 'Scornefull dishonour' it showed to 'the Lords Annointed'.[248] This passage did indeed commit a mild breach of decorum. By emphasizing the evident inferiority of *Britanicus,* Nedham was of course underscoring the superiority of his arguments. He made the same point by claiming that *Aulicus* was produced by a troop of writers against his lone pen.[249] It seems that Nedham could not lose.

A few weeks after *Anti-Mercurius,* a different anti-mercurial direction was taken by *Martin Nonsence, His Collections which he saw with his Brains, and heard with his Eyes, of the witty follies; peaceably fought for, in this poore flourishing Kingdome of England.* The title may well have gestured to Martin Marprelate, and his revival as 'Martin Mar-priest'.[250] *Martin Nonsence* was, however, a loosely royalist newsbook mixing news and documents with a thoroughly ironic narrative. It inverted its world, and the admixture of reality and calculatedly perverse interpretations resists the reader's attempt to turn the world the right way up.[251] Other anti-mercuries were content to represent the inverted as self-evidently inverted. *Martin* began, quite truthfully, 'If you do not find me altogether nonsence, then you cannot understand me.'[252]

By the end of the decade the glut had begun to eat itself, revelling in paradoxical shouting about too much noise, in the schizophrenia of too many mixed metaphors. The representation of writing as a form of excreting or vomiting was repeatedly employed to suggest that writing was an epidemic of pointlessness and virulence: 'Every Jack-sprat that hath but a pen in his ink-horn is ready to gather up the Excrements of the Kingdom, purgd forth by the glister of distraction.'[253] All forms of publication, all modes of writing, no matter how elevated, were in danger of being sucked into this logo-phthisis. In September 1652 Samuel Sheppard, who had abandoned his epic romance *The Faerie King,* defended a polemical publication:

> If any *Simplician* take exceptions, let him turn the Buckle of his Girdle; he that manifests distemper at the perusall of these Sheets, must of necessity be a Knave or Foole, or both: If any man deny me the liberty of speaking Truth, I will take

[248] Nathaniel Rogers, *A Letter, Discovering The Cause of Gods continuing wrath against the Nation* (1644; R1821), 9.

[249] For example *Britanicus* 6, 3 Oct. 1643, 41, 286.006/E69(19); *Britanicus* 17, 21 Dec. 1643, 131, 286.017/E79(2); *Britanicus* 23, 177, 286.023B; *Britanicus* 25, 6 Mar. 1644, 194, 286.025/E35(28).

[250] See nn. 3, 128, above.

[251] Cf. Davis, *Society and Culture in Early Modern France,* 124–51; Stuart Clark, 'Inversion, Misrule and the Meaning of Witchcraft', *P&P* 87 (1980), 98–127.

[252] *Martin Nonsence,* 'Numb.' [*sic*], 27 Nov. 1648, 1, 252.1/E526(33).

[253] *Anti-Mercurius* [1], sigs. A–A^{v}; Benne Klaas Faber, 'The Poetics of Subversion and Conservatism: Popular Satire, c.1640–c.1649', D.Phil. thesis (Oxford, 1992), 192.

it I say, I will take it: I am an Independent, I feare not: Some I doubt not so much do doat upon a dirty *Diurnall*, a *Weekly Accompt*, or a ridiculous nonsensical *Mercury*, that they will condemne me to no worse Pennance than to bathe in blew Flames, for presuming to bid Defiance to so reverend a Rabble——pew——mew——vew——A Degenerate, besotted, insaniated, ignorant People, a Monster onely fit to feed on such Raffe and Garbage.[254]

The confusion of Babel followed on from this 'liberty of speaking Truth'; Sheppard, ideologically antithetical and after eight more years of cacophony, disagreed with Milton's view in *Areopagitica* that 'that which purifies us is triall, and triall is by what is contrary'.[255] Sheppard envisaged a Gresham's law of books, in which bad drove out good. Readers could not distinguish between good writing and wasted ink. Sheppard expostulated:

he that writes in *London*, must resolve to please Cuckolds and fools; and there least Sense goes farthest. *Midas* his ears are frequent in the City: and if it should chance that *Ben Iohnson* and Master *Taylor* should stand in competition before the Plum-pudding eaters in *London*, its not questionable who should carry the commendation. Stupid dull animals they are: nothing pleases their palates, but what runs thick and muddie, like the brains from which it issues. . . . Yet will these Infidels confidently give up their judgement of all books, (though the devil a one they understand) and scan every one of them severally, you would believe, with as great maturity of judgement, as if *Scaliger's* Ghost were once more returned, and entered into their bodies: and be sure they dislike that most, which they least understand; which is commonly the best of the whole Piece.[256]

In a sense *The Great Assises* made a similar point, though with more tolerance and subtlety. In the anti-mercuries and the attacks on newsbooks alike, the collapsing of fine aesthetics with poor (or their inversion) is associated with the author's pretended indifference to the distinction between truth and falsehood. In the internal logic of the anti-mercury these values no longer hold. The world, according to *Mercurius Anti-Mercurius*, is 'bewitched'.[257] Sheppard avers that mercuries, by definition, lie. He writes this in a mercury; *Mercurius Mastix*, Numb. 1, 20–7 August 1652.[258]

This is more than simply revelling in the nonsensical. Though Sheppard spoke contemptuously of their being 'famous for a whole week', newsbooks were, by 1652, there to stay. Sheppard knew this. To write an anti-mercury like *Mercurius Mastix* was to concede defeat. It

[254] Sheppard, *The Weepers*, sigs. A2–A2^{v}.
[255] *CPW* ii. 515.
[256] *Mastix* 1, 6–7.
[257] *Anti-Mercurius* [1], sig. A.
[258] *Mastix* 1, 2–3: a second issue might have been illogical.

began with an aggressive *blazon*, a poem which threatened violently to dissect the mercuries; Sheppard did not criticize from a removed standpoint of superiority, but engaged tooth and claw.[259] Because the newsbook had in fact won the paper war there had to be satires of it, and these satires accordingly acknowledged its authority and importance. The topoi of Hell and Charon's ferry, frequent in attacks on newsbooks, also exploited the entertaining and educative possibilities of a world turned upside down.

In these literary games, the descent into cultural chaos was temporary, and emergence out of it led more or less into the world of light and truth. The vituperation was ultimately celebratory, and the act of criticism was simultaneously one of recognition. The culture of the newsbook, which reveals writer-readers who were at once well informed of the rules of the genre, sensitive to the means of representation, and eager to derogate and mock the newsbook and its audience in cheap print, is nothing other than a celebration of the social significance of the men, and perhaps women, who worked late nights on Grub Street.

[259] *Mastix* 1, 6, 1; 'Ye mungrel Mercuries that flie | Like dust about the streets, | With borrow'd wit, and tales on trust, | Trust up in single sheets. || I'll whip you all and make your hides | Look in a diff'rent weed: | I'll rend and tear your paper-sides, | And jerk you till you bleed . . .'

5

Newsbooks, their Distribution, and their Readers

From *Bristol*, thus,
Dear Sir, I wonder where you are, that I receive no account in these perilous times of the series of affairs; I must needs tell you that I very much want it in this dark angle.

(*Mercurius Militaris*, Oct. 1648[1])

Excester Decemb. 12. 1648. The well affected in these parts thirst after intelligence from *London*, looking for a settlement of the distractions of this Kingdom.

(*Perfect Weekly Account*, Dec. 1648[2])

For Books are not absolutely dead things, but doe contain a potencie of life in them to be as active as that soule was whose progeny they are.

(J. M., *Areopagitica*, Nov. 1644[3])

WHO read newsbooks, why, and what did they think of them? These are questions of fundamental importance.[4] They change how we read newsbooks; and like many essential questions, answering them is a bedevilled process, requiring the use of eclectic forms of evidence. Two accounts of the 'new bibliography' remind us why and how we do this. D. F. McKenzie defines bibliography as the study of texts 'as recorded forms, and the processes of their transmission, including their production and reception'.[5] Roger Chartier writes:

To consider reading to be a concrete act requires holding any process of the construction of meaning (hence, of interpretation) as situated at the crossroads between readers endowed with specific competences, identified by their

[1] *Militaris* 3, 31 Oct. 1648, 21, 346.3/E469(10*).
[2] *PWA* [40], 20 Dec. 1648, 313, 533.40/E477(13).
[3] *CPW* ii. 492.
[4] A history of reading is needed; Darnton, 'History of Reading', *passim*.
[5] McKenzie, *Bibliography and the Sociology of Texts*, 4.

positions and dispositions and characterized by their practice of reading, and texts whose meaning is always dependent on their particular discursive and formal mechanisms—in the case of printed texts we might call them 'typographical' (in a broad sense of the adjective).[6]

We can only understand how the newsbook worked in its culture by specific analyses of human interaction and agency, as manifested in the texts themselves, typographical practices, and individual responses. And only by using newsbooks both as material artefacts and as symbolic maps of determinations and influences can their history be written. The rhetorical, generic, and formal qualities of newsbooks have been described above: it is now time to substantiate their relationship with their readers.

Time, profit, and print-runs

The sizes of editions of newsbooks partly determined the size of their readership, and affect our perceptions of their importance. Commentators usually estimate an average from 250 or 500 copies up to 1,000, sometimes stretching this considerably for *Aulicus*. The larger a print-run the higher circulation a text was likely to have, leading to greater opportunities for influence. It is a question which all historians coming across this material ask, yet there are no conclusive answers.

Cotton argues that print-runs for newsbooks varied from 250 to 850, with a few reaching 1,000.[7] He arrives at these figures from entirely reasonable considerations of necessary profit and typesetting speed. Frank recommends 500 copies as a general minimum, 200 as the absolute minimum, using what he confesses is 'semicircumstantial evidence'.[8] Two hundred and fifty copies was the incremental unit for print-runs, and would normally be regarded as an exceptionally low figure.[9] None of these figures is, on the surface, unreasonable.

Cotton records that in 1642 Robert White (a printer of newsbooks) charged 18*s.* for printing three reams (1,500 sheets) of a quarto pamphlet.[10] At 0.144 pence per sheet this seems improbably

[6] Chartier, *Cultural History*, 12.

[7] Cotton, 8, 10, 12.

[8] *Beginnings*, 57, 314 n. 54.

[9] The Stationers' Company Ordinance of 1637 established maximum editions of 5,000 for a nonpareil, 3,000 for a brevier (6,000 with permission), and 1,500/2,000 (3,000 with permission) for other books. Such limitations would not have held in the 1640s. Philip Gaskell, *A New Introduction to Bibliography* (1972; Oxford, 1985), 160–3; McKenzie, 'Printers of the Mind', 59; Blagden, 'Distribution of Almanacks', 107–16.

[10] Cotton, 8; *CJ* ii. 612, 613, 615. Cotton had to speculate about the length of the book because he could not identify it. He was correct to guess that it was a single-sheet

low.[11] Let us, however, examine this figure for a moment. Given that paper constituted the largest element, about three-quarters, in the cost of book production, it is not unreasonable that Cotton concludes that 'it seems unlikely that 250 newsbooks would cost more than half that sum'.[12] It is possible that 250 newsbooks would cost less than half of this 18*s*. But even at 9*s*., that would leave, if the newsbooks were sold for a penny each, 11*s*. 10*d*. to divide between the newsbook editor and publisher and/or hawker or mercury woman.[13] This is a reasonable sum: and in a time of economic depression, such as most of the 1640s, is it possible that entrepreneurs would have satisfied themselves with smaller sums? With the progressive use of advertising through the 1650s, this figure would have been increased, allowing greater profit or increased flexibility in printing small numbers. From these figures 250 copies appears to be a plausible minimum.

An alternative means of estimating edition size is the time taken to compose and print. Cotton argues, using as a model the first Shakespeare folio, that composing the two formes of a sheet would have taken twenty-eight hours, the same time as for Shakespeare, 'for though no doubt the quality of the type-setting was a good deal lower, the quantity was much greater'.[14] The argument then hinges on how much time was left to print. Cotton argues that both formes were set at the same time, because most newsbooks regularly reported on page 7 events that happened the previous day. Both sides of the sheet would therefore have been printed at the last moment. This leaves, according to Cotton, perhaps ten hours to print (the morning and early afternoon on the day of publication); and he infers from this a maximum print-run of 850. He concludes that 'there is little evidence that any newsbook found this technical limit an encumbrance'.[15] Yet the silence of absent evidence is far from conclusive.

Cotton's whole picture should be questioned. Printing speeds may be relatively inflexible, though more recent commentators have worked with an average of 250 impressions per hour, which is high but by no means implausible.[16] This would result in a maximum of 1,250

quarto; the book was Roger Pike, *A True Relation of the Proceedings of the Scots and English Forces in the North of Ireland*, published by Francis Coles and Thomas Bates (8 June 1642; P2224). It reasonably compares with the amount of work involved in a newsbook.

[11] Cf. Johnson, 'Notes on English Retail Book-Prices', 83–112; Gaskell, *New Introduction to Bibliography*, 178.

[12] Gaskell, *New Introduction to Bibliography*, 177; Cotton, 8.

[13] For the price of a penny see Plomer, '"Mercurius Civicus"', 184–207. Many newsbooks are referred to as costing a penny.

[14] Cotton, 9–10; Charlton Hinman, *The Printing and Proof-Reading of the First Folio of Shakespeare*, 2 vols. (Oxford, 1963), i. 45–6.

[15] Cotton, 10.

[16] Hinman, *Printing and Proof-Reading*, i. 39–47; McKenzie, 'Printers of the Mind', 8.

newsbooks printed in those ten hours. Composition speeds, however, varied greatly: up to a factor of four, depending on age, experience, and labour conditions.[17] While it is simple to reconstruct printing procedures, the actual quotidian practices are infinitely complex. Twenty-eight hours seems a significant overestimate of the composition time of a newsbook; possibly by a factor of two or more. All commentators emphasize that the standard figure of 1,000 'ens' per hour varied enormously.[18] Another problem lies in the variation between newsbooks; there was no such thing as an average newsbook. A copy of *A Perfect Diurnall* from the mid-1640s could have two or three times as much type as an early 1642 newsbook, with a full title-page with a blank verso, and lots of white space in the text. There were dense and sparse texts, but it would be foolish to infer too much from these typographical variations. Most newsbooks, moreover, seem to have been set very quickly, judging by the high incidence of severe typographical errors, even in titles set in very large type. It is possible that they were not read in proof.[19] *Civicus* states that the copy for *The Kingdomes Weekly Intelligencer* was sent in overnight, which would have necessitated extraordinarily swift work.[20] If we were to take the figure of fourteen hours' composition (as reasonable as twenty-eight hours), and add the remaining fourteen hours to the ten Cotton suggests, we could leave Cotton's other figures intact and calculate a figure of 2,040 copies printed in twenty-four hours. If we were to take the figure of 250 impressions per hour, we could assume 3,000 copies could be printed. This is not to suggest that this was actually the case, but that technically it could have been. If any one of Cotton's figures is inaccurate, radically different conclusions can be deduced.

There are other question marks which should be appended to these figures. Cotton is right that some newsbooks had recent news on page 7;[21] yet others did not. Some, significantly, squeezed large quantities of unexpected news onto page 8 by dramatically reducing type size. No experienced printer would have divided text between pages so unevenly without constraining circumstances. In such cases it is evident that the first forme was composed long before the end of the printing-week. For every example Cotton gives of a newsbook with recent news on the penultimate page, there are examples of other issues of the same serial

[17] Gaskell, *New Introduction to Bibliography*, 54–6.

[18] Gaskell, *New Introduction to Bibliography*, 54–5; McKenzie, 'Printers of the Mind', 10–11.

[19] McKenzie expresses suspicion of arguments about proof-reading, observing that they escape even experienced printers' eyes; 'Printers of the Mind', 43–6. Nevertheless even if newsbooks were proof-read, it was done less thoroughly than in most texts.

[20] *Civicus* 179, 29 Oct. 1646, 2427–8, 298.179/E359(9).

[21] Cotton, 12–13.

in which type has been squeezed onto the final page. This suggests that practices varied from week to week.[22] Some newsbooks presented completely contradictory news on consecutive pages. The most probable explanation for this is that the earlier, inaccurate news was already set, otherwise an editor could simply have deleted it.[23] It is even possible that all but the final page was set a day in advance (or all but the two final pages two days in advance). The issue of *Perfect Weekly Account* which appeared on 14 February 1649 contained an imprimatur dated 12 February. Yet it contained news of 13 February. The final item concluded; 'but the matter holding debate untill the day drew to a period, unto which this sheets intelligence is confined, I am necessitated to conclude here, with a promise, to give further satisfaction here in the next Week.'[24] This is incommensurate with Cotton's argument. The production of newsbooks was very flexible. Practices were lax, and publishers, printers, and authors learned to improvise.

Cotton rightly points out that multiple editions need not indicate greater print-runs. Yet they might. There are for instance at least three settings of the issue of *A Perfect Diurnall* describing Laud's execution.[25] Cotton argues that *Perfect Diurnall*, being produced on Mondays, had to be set quickly, so, rather uneconomically, two printers were used.[26] Yet it is not clear that printers honoured the Sabbath; certainly parliament and press accused them of ignoring it.[27] Moreover they need not have transgressed for long to compose the last page or two, as Sunday news rarely featured in Monday newsbooks. So printing flexibility or high print-runs can be deduced from double and triple editions. Prolific counterfeit serials show that some booksellers, printers, and/or editors felt that the market was sufficiently bountiful for it to be subdivided.

Other factors make the overall picture more complex. The possibility of concurrent printing makes any argument based on simple economic units tenuous.[28] Profit should not necessarily be calculated according to the economics of a particular publication; the overall performance of

[22] Cotton's examples are given here in parentheses, followed by my counter-examples: *Civicus* (154), 137; *Perfect Diurnall* (235), 16; *KWI* (123), 172; *Weekly Account* (3), 35; *Diary* (83), 2 (6 Feb. 1646). See also Nelson and Seccombe, *Periodical Publications*, 42–3.

[23] The term 'front page news' would have made no sense in the 1640s.

[24] *PWA* [48], 14 Jan. 1649, 388, 533.48/E543(2).

[25] Compare LT copy with two at Bod.; see N&S pp. 615–18.

[26] Cotton, 11–12; but see Nelson and Seccombe, *Periodical Publications*, 44–52.

[27] BL: Harl. 163, f. 52^{v}; *A Fresh Whip*, 3: 'And so by this means making the poor workmen stand still for their labour, and that which he should do on Saturday, he must do on Sunday.'

[28] McKenzie, 'Printers of the Mind', 16.

the printing house was what mattered.[29] Close collaboration between printer, publisher, bookseller, and editor could reduce the costs of any one party. When doing job-work for a publisher/bookseller fewer risks were involved for the printer, who might lower his profit margin accordingly.[30] Such collaboration existed between the publishing groups around newsbooks.[31] Each group produced a number of serials on a weekly basis, and the establishment of paths of distribution and the guarantee of a certain regular clientele could have reduced costs and risks.

This is not to argue that all newsbooks were printed in very large editions, but that the accepted loose estimates are plucked from uncertainties. Printing was a very much more flexible procedure than our understanding of procedure and empirical data allow. Newsbooks were cheap, slipshod, and probably profitable, and their printing was even more improvisatory and flexible than that of more prestigious texts. If any of the above figures are teased to entirely possible extremes we can produce conclusions of such variance that calculations are more or less useless. Hence 250 should not be accepted as an unbreachable minimum and 1,000 would be conservative as a maximum. Estimations of the print-runs of corantos (250 to 850) might equally be conservative.[32] *Mercurius Elencticus* suggested that the third issue of Hall's *Britanicus* was printed in an issue of 200.[33] This figure may be meant to appear either ridiculous and impossibly small or ridiculously small and plausible.

Cotton concludes, 'A circulation of 850 copies to 1,000 copies seems miserably small' when compared to other pamphlets; 'newsbooks were only current for a few hours, unless they were prized for something other than their news content, and had to be sold before the next day's crop appeared on the stalls.'[34] This sentiment wrongly depreciates books with considerable long-term influence. Newsbooks were read days later in the provinces, months later in America, years later by writers of memoirs, and centuries later by historians. Contemporaries

[29] McKenzie, 'Printers of the Mind', 17–18.

[30] Gaskell, *New Introduction to Bibliography*, 178; Johnson, 'Notes on English Retail Book-Prices', *passim*. Printers would normally mark up their costs by 100%, but in a co-operative relationship with a bookseller/publisher, as was generally the case with newsbooks, this could have been reduced.

[31] Cotton, 17–19.

[32] Frearson, 'London Corantos in the 1620s', 5–6; cf. Dahl, 22.

[33] *Elencticus* 29, 14 June 1648, 222, 312.29/E447(11). See 63, above.

[34] Cotton, 13. In fact, the *circulation* would have been higher as many copies had more than one reader. The figure which Cotton uses for comparison is entirely unreliable: he cites 400,000–500,000 (*sic*) mentioned in one of John Taylor's satires.

read them for other reasons than the desire for a quick news-fix. The pessimistic view is unrealistic.

The marketplace: physical distribution and literacy

The audience of newsbooks was partly determined by the constraints of distribution. In London newsbooks could easily be purchased from booksellers, based in the city or at stalls around St Paul's, or from hawkers and mercury women who sold them on the streets.[35] Once acquired, they were frequently distributed to the provinces, where they found an even larger audience. London was of course an important centre for printing and the development of literacy, and literacy was concentrated in the capital; but at least 30 per cent of men nationwide were literate, hardly a negligible figure. Paths of distribution for books were already established in the 1620s, and the introduction of a public postal service in 1635 further improved the networks.[36]

Carriers and the post were the two main means of distributing printed texts in the provinces. Chapmen and women also played a part in the movement of newsbooks, though the size of that part is uncertain.[37] Armies also transmitted them, not as a service but as an incidental effect of moving around the country.[38] Carriers could supply provincial booksellers, or take books to individuals, sometimes directly from publishers, sometimes from London readers who passed them on with correspondence. Pamphlets and newsbooks were not individually significant or valuable enough to be inventoried in detail, hence we do not find them listed in holdings of booksellers.[39] The same is the case with library lists and testament inventories.[40] Yet there is plenty of evidence that newsbooks were purchased and distributed.

[35] Freist, 'The World is Ruled and Governed by Opinion', 84–110.

[36] Frearson, 'London Corantos in the 1620s', 6–15, 20.

[37] On pedlars, hawkers, and chapmen see Spufford, *Small Books and Pleasant Histories*, 111–26; Watt, *Cheap Print and Popular Piety*, 23–30 and index, 'chapmen'.

[38] Gentles, *New Model Army*, 325.

[39] But see *STC* iii. 207–15 for a convenient summary of provincial booksellers and printers named in imprints of pre-1641 texts. Provincial booksellers could have very large stock, however, and newsbooks constituted a part of it; T. S. Willan, *The Inland Trade: Studies in English Internal Trade in the Sixteenth and Seventeenth Centuries* (Manchester, 1976), 60–2.

[40] The Earl of Essex possessed newsbooks, but a 1646 inventory of his library did not identify any, though it did have a volume of 'speeches in this present Parl*iament*'; see Vernon F. Snow, 'An Inventory of the Lord General's Library, 1646', *Library*^{3}, 21 (1966), 115–23. Essex either did not list them, did not keep them, or kept them elsewhere. Interestingly he possessed an item described as 'Apollo's Pernassus' (131), which presumably refers to *The Great Assises*.

Highways spread out in all directions from London, the centre of the web, though not all were in a good state of repair in 1640. Carriers weekly left London to travel to many parts of the country. The poet, pamphleteer, and sometimes journalist John Taylor published in 1637 *The Carriers Cosmographie*, a manual facilitating the use of carriers, indicating their destination and time and place of departure; another edition appeared around 1642.[41] Even Taylor, not given to modesty, admitted that his information was patchy, so his guide can serve as a pessimistic picture of the minimum services available. Though not comprehensive it is none the less extensive. Taylor identified carriers conveying goods to most parts of England, and indicated how packages could be then forwarded to Scotland and Wales. Ireland obviously represented different circumstances, and it is difficult to gauge in what quantities books were distributed there in the 1640s. The areas immediately surrounding London were predictably best served, but Taylor also indicated local concentrations in Yorkshire, Sussex, Kent, and Buckinghamshire. The relative quantities should perhaps be disregarded, but Taylor does show that there were means of distributing books, and that these means were relatively easy to access.[42]

Cheaper than carriers, however, was the postal service, though this suffered from some internal confusion in the 1640s and 1650s, not least because of competition from independent carriers. In 1642 there was also competition between members of the Lords and Commons for the lucrative control of the letter office. The post played a role in propaganda exercises during the civil war, with the court at Oxford and the Committee of Both Kingdoms struggling to control it.[43] The post was both swifter and cheaper than carriers, though less flexible. It left London on Tuesdays, and carried a single letter up to 80 miles for 2*d.*, up to 140 miles for 4*d.*, and more than 140 miles for 6*d.* Postage to Scotland was 8*d.* Despite its problems the service generally improved: an additional post was established in March 1649 to run on Saturdays. In 1649 the Common Council introduced a post to Scotland of their own, not satisfied with existing services. Prices were reduced in 1650; up to 80 miles from London for 2*d.*, 3*d.* to remote parts of England and Wales, 4*d.* to Scotland, and 6*d.* to Ireland, this last indicating an improvement in the Anglo-Irish book trade following

41 *A Brief Director* (?1642; Wing T434aA).

42 John Taylor, *The Carriers Cosmographie* (1637; *STC* 23740); the tract was written in order to facilitate access, organized as a reference work, with destinations in alphabetical order. It did, however, rely on some geographical knowledge. *Civicus* 6, 16 June 1643, 298.006/E106(13) refers to carriers transporting paper to Oxford for *Aulicus*. See also Frearson, 'London Corantos in the 1620s', 13–15.

43 Stone, *Inland Posts*, 94–9.

Cromwell's solution to the 'Irish problem'. A further post was introduced in 1654.[44]

Speeds were limited, however. Carriers travelled at between 20 and 24 old English miles per day; whereas the post nominally travelled at 7 miles per hour in summer, down to 5 in winter.[45] John Rushworth was celebrated as 'o^{r} nimble Mercury Mr Rushforth', because of the speed at which he travelled between London and York, taking only twenty-four hours for the journey.[46] Other mercuries were less punctual, and news could be days in arriving or in being confirmed by printed materials.

Yet newsbooks did reach diverse destinations ultimately. The most useful source for informative references is correspondence, and while there is an unsurprising concentration of references around London, where literacy was highest for both men and women and where most printers were based,[47] there is none the less much information about provincial readers. From London newsbooks moved outwards: the commissioner Robert Baillie sent them to Scotland; Edmund Warcupp received them in the Isle of Wight; they reached every county of England; some made it into the dark corners of Wales; and some were sent to the court in exile in Paris. Baron North looked back in 1670 and commented on the effectiveness of newsbooks in reaching the provinces; country parsons were conventionally satirized for reading London publications.[48] The south-east was on the whole probably better informed, as Henry Oxinden recognized in November 1641 when he wrote from Deane, near Leeds, to his eponymous kinsman at Barham: 'Wee live heere in the west, and our newes doth much resemble our Situation; you live in the East and South of occurrencies, and therefore in vaine and absurd were itt for mee to make a retrograde of knowledge praeposest. . . . Pray lett mee heere some newes from you.'[49] In contrast Captain Anthony Willoughby wrote from York or Oxford to Henry Mulliner at Cambridge in January 1643, saying, 'I have not need to write London news, though our intelligence even of their actions is not inferior to yours.'[50] Little can be gleaned from analysing the geographi-

[44] Herbert Joyce, *The History of the Post Office: From its Establishment down to 1836* (1893), 15–32; Robinson, *The British Post Office*, 23–47; *Beginnings*, see index, 'Posts'.

[45] Old miles were between a quarter and a half greater than modern miles; Frearson, 'London Corantos in the 1620s', 9; Robinson, *British Post Office*, 15; Joyce, *History of the Post Office*, 19.

[46] Bod.: MS Tanner 63, f. 43; MS Wood F39, f. 384.

[47] David Cressy, *Literacy and the Social Order: Reading and Writing in Tudor and Stuart England* (Cambridge, 1980), 72–4, 128–9, and *passim*.

[48] North, *A Narrative*, 15, 37; *Ben Jonson*, vi. 293–4; cf. *Mastix* 1, 3.

[49] *The Oxinden Letters 1607–1642*, ed. Dorothy Gardiner (1933), 257–8.

[50] *HMC: Fourteenth Report . . . The Manuscripts of His Grace the Duke of Portland* (London: HMSO, 1891), i. 86.

cal distribution of references to newsbooks in correspondence, as they may have survived unevenly, but they do provide information about the extent of movement, and firmly establish provincial access to the newsbook.

It was perhaps in order to overcome time delays that Edinburgh editions of some newsbooks were established, including *Heads of Severall Proceedings*, *Diurnall Occurrences*, and *Mercurius Politicus*, initially printed at Leith.[51] Provincial printing is, however, an effect and not a cause of provincial distribution networks.[52] Newsbooks travelled into Scotland, created a market, and then persuaded local publishers that that market could more effectively be exploited by local editions.

The marketplace: literacy and identifying readers

The limits of readership were partly determined by literacy. David Cressy's analysis of signatures suggests that in the 1640s male literacy was 30 per cent nationally, and about 70 to 80 per cent in London; and for women about 10 per cent nationally, perhaps 15 to 20 per cent in London. These figures should be treated with caution, as minima.[53] The age at which children left school frequently lay between the ages at which they learned to read and to write. Their ability to write or sign their name is thus a poor indicator of the ability to read. Those provincial labourers who could read were interested in political and religious controversy, and they served as a bridge to a surrounding group of non-reading fellow-workers. Using evidence from the 1690s Margaret Spufford has identified a disproportionate number of women, wives of day-labourers and small craftsmen, who taught reading but who could not themselves write.[54] There may well have been pockets of unusually high literacy, for instance among the godly.[55] Peter Clark's study of book ownership in Kent shows a large increase in book ownership in

[51] See N&S 182, 97, 98, and 362.

[52] John Feather, 'The Country Trade in Books', in Myers and Harris, eds., *Spreading the Word*, 165–72.

[53] Cressy, *Literacy and the Social Order*, chs. 4, 6, and 7; Keith Thomas, 'The Meaning of Literacy in Early Modern England', in Gerd Baumann, ed., *The Written Word: Literacy in Transition* (Oxford, 1986), 97–131, challenges the methodological basis of Cressy's figures.

[54] Margaret Spufford, 'First Steps in Literacy: The Reading and Writing Experiences of the Humblest Seventeenth-Century Spiritual Autobiographers', *Social History*, 4 (1979), 407–35. On the lower and middling sorts' active interest in national politics, see Derek Hirst, *The Representative of the People? Voters and Voting in England under the Early Stuarts* (Cambridge, 1975), *passim*.

[55] John Morgan, *Godly Learning: Puritan Attitudes towards Reason, Learning, and Education, 1560–1640* (Cambridge, 1986), 159–69.

the early seventeenth century, assisted by provincial booksellers and distribution and by the second-hand book trade. This is probably true of other regions. With this kind of qualitative evidence, a picture of much more widespread dissemination of printed material emerges.[56]

There was a large potential audience for newsbooks which apparently has been overlooked. It may have contained a high percentage of women, though no newsbooks specifically addressed women readers (as some specified country readers). Some seventeenth-century fiction implied a female audience; the civil war newsbook seems to have had no equivalent.[57] Yet Cressy depicts too sharp a boundary between the ability and inability to read.[58] Between those who could sign their names and those who could not read were further distinctions. Not all those who could read could read handwritten script. A significant number of people who could read could only read print.[59] Court cases concerning libellous ballads and rhymes reveal evidence of readers who could 'neither write, nor read written hand', but who read 'print hand'.[60] Newsbooks did not have to wait until the eighteenth century to 'become a regular feature of life'.[61] This structure of literacy shows how significant the newsbook could be to this group of people who found only print manageable. For this audience the periodical newsbook was an important invention. Historians who emphasize the superior quality of newsletters, owing to their élite audience, entirely overlook a readership who were just as rational and intelligent, and almost as educated as their peers.

The individual readers who can be named do not necessarily represent the greater part of the readership. A large number of the poorer sort may have been dramatically affected, while leaving only fragmentary traces. An officer reading to his soldiers represents many men, some unable to read, sharing access to a pamphlet, and a single refer-

[56] Peter Clark, 'The Ownership of Books in England, 1560–1640: The Example of Some Kentish Townsfolk', in Lawrence Stone, ed., *Schooling and Society: Studies in the History of Education* (Baltimore, 1976), 95–111; Cressy, *Literacy and the Social Order*, 46-52; Watt, *Cheap Print and Popular Piety*, 328–31; Spufford, *Small Books and Pleasant Histories*; Wrightson, *English Society 1580–1680*, 187–91, 194–9; Wyn Ford, 'The Problem of Literacy in Early Modern England', *History*, 78 (1993), 22–37.

[57] Salzman, *English Prose Fiction 1558–1700*, 6, 11, 177–8. See also Ros Ballaster, *Seductive Forms: Women's Amatory Fiction from 1684 to 1740* (Oxford, 1992); for a complex analysis of women's place as readers of romance see Lorna Hutson, *The Usurer's Daughter: Male Friendship and Fictions of Women in Sixteenth-Century England* (1994).

[58] Cf. Ford, 'Problem of Literacy' on the complex structure of literacy.

[59] Thomas, 'Meaning of Literacy', 99–103.

[60] Adam Fox, 'Ballads, Libels and Popular Ridicule in Jacobean England', *P&P* 145 (1995), 47–83, qu. 60.

[61] Thomas, 'Meaning of Literacy', 113; contrast id., *Religion and the Decline of Magic*, 778–9.

ence hints at many others.[62] This sharing of texts further establishes the potential reach of cheap publications.

Statements about the readers of newsbooks are often deduced from internal evidence. Newsbooks are sometimes cited as evidence of specific public opinions.[63] We should pause before accepting such illation. Inferences about readership should not be made on grounds of style in the absence of other, correlating evidence. Readers need not have shared the political or religious stance of the newsbooks they read. Sir Samuel Luke, parliamentarian governor of Reading, on whom Samuel Butler's Hudibras was supposedly based, was particularly interested in *Mercurius Aulicus*. The royalists Edward Rainbowe and the Lord Keeper of Oxford read *Moderate Intelligencer*.[64] London correspondents writing to the provinces enclosed newsletters and pamphlets representing quite different opinions.[65] It is possible that in some cases this was because of the difficulties involved in finding newsbooks; an excess of demand over supply would oblige purchasers to make compromises.

Is there any real evidence that anyone, other than other pamphleteers and writers, attended to newsbooks? According to many writers, particularly after the Restoration, Marchamont Nedham was exceptional, wreaking incalculable damage while plying his trade. But this kind of evidence may mislead. Secretary of State Sir Edward Nicholas referred Edward Hyde to *The Faithfull Scout* as an 'excellent author', a commendation seriously at odds with most royalist accounts of newsbooks.[66] Readers of newsbooks who referred to them in printed texts are not far to seek. There are however various other sources which can be used to draw an impressionistic picture of the broader readership of newsbooks.

Newsbooks were frequently mentioned in gentry correspondence in the 1640s. Most allusions to them were ambivalent, and merely mentioned the fact that one had been enclosed.[67] The fact of sending one was an implicit recommendation of sorts, rather at odds with the published attacks on newsbooks. Poets read newsbooks; would-be historians read them; members of parliament read them; lawyers, merchants, and

[62] C. H. Firth, ed., *The Clarke Papers*, 4 vols. (1891–1901), iv. 231; Roger Chartier, 'Leisure and Sociability: Reading Aloud in Modern Europe', trans. Carol Mossman, in Susan Zimmerman and Ronald F. E. Weissman, eds., *Urban Life in the Renaissance* (Newark, NJ, 1989), 103–20; id., *Cultural Uses of Print*, 152–5.

[63] B. S. Manning, 'Neutrals and Neutralism in the English Civil War 1642–1646', D. Phil. thesis (Oxford, 1957), 405–8; cf. Gardiner², i. 296.

[64] *Letter Books of Sir Samuel Luke*, *passim*; Bod.: MS Tanner 60, f. 354; Frederick John Varley, *The Siege of Oxford* (1931), 147.

[65] Morrill, *Revolt of the Provinces*, 35; id., *Cheshire 1630–1660* (Oxford, 1974), 39–45.

[66] *Calendar of the Clarendon State Papers*, vol. ii, ed. Revd W. Dunn Macray (Oxford, 1869), 231.

[67] Cf. Morrill, *Revolt of the Provinces*, 22, 35.

those involved in trade read them; the General Assembly in Scotland read them; but most readers were none of these, and read them because they were interested in current affairs. This suggests that newsbook writers, while they may have overestimated their own importance, did not found their claims on castles in the air.

Readers of newsbooks

People of all literate classes, from Nehemiah Wallington and John Rous to the Earl of Essex and Charles II, read newsbooks. Some who were fortunate in being able to read were excited by newsbooks, notably the puritan artisan Wallington.[68] There are some of whom we know little more than a name: the Mr Prattes in Hockwold, Norfolk, who owned a copy of *Speciall Passages* for the week 8–15 November 1642. Some readers left no trace of their circumstances, only their name: Isaac Appleton, Robert Bridges, Colonel John Harrington, William Catherens and Edward Pitt, John Howle, and, perhaps, Thomas Millie.[69] There are even more insubstantial figures who left marks upon newsbooks. We know next to nothing about those who were part of the illiterate majority but had newsbooks read to them, or were indirect beneficiaries of the greater dissemination of news. Of course news continued to be transmitted orally,[70] but newsbooks affected this process: Thomas Fuller suggested that the men of the civil war armies were for the most part illiterate, but they did have newsbooks read to them by their officers.[71] Ralph Josselin heard on 31 January 1649 that the king

[68] For the structure of illiteracy see Cressy, who notes, however, that turners were less likely to be illiterate than ordinary carpenters. *Literacy and the Social Order*, 136.

[69] *Diary of John Rous*, 127; Bod.: MS Tanner 40, f. 354; GCRO: D/DF F/243^v and F/245: see also acknowledgment on F/244. BL: Add. MS 46375 is a volume of newsbooks, bound sometime after 1720, f. 5^v with the inscription: 'These papers were collected by John Harrington Esqr of Kelston, Colonel in his Majesty's Army. 1644.' This identification of 'Harrington' as a royalist is probably wrong. A John Harington of Kelston attended upon the king at Holmby and Newcastle upon Tyne as a parliamentary commissioner; *The Political Works of James Harrington*, ed. J. G. A. Pocock (Cambridge, 1977), 2–3; *The Diary of John Harington, M.P., 1646–53*, ed. Margaret F. Stieg, Somerset Record Society, 74 (1977). The newsbooks are mostly from the 1640s, with four from 1650–2, and two post-Restoration items. These are not catalogued in N&S; see J. Raymond, 'Some Corrections and Additions to *British Newspapers and Periodicals 1641–1700: A Short-Title Catalogue*', *Notes and Queries*, 240 (1995), 451–3. BL: Add. MS 29974, f. 338; Folger: M1768.49, a copy of *Pragmaticus*. Howle wrote his name in this several times: his marginalia were subsequently cropped. Folger: M1766.5[/4], a copy of *Melancholicus*. This hand may not be exactly contemporary.

[70] Levy, 'How Information Spread among the Gentry', 11–34.

[71] *Mixt Contemplations in Better Times* (1660; F2451), ii. 26; Firth, ed., *Clarke Papers*, iv. 231. This is a single incident, which caused some controversy, but Captain Newman refers to reading to the soldiers as if it were a normal practice.

had been executed, but qualified the report as 'uncertaine'; four days later he had rather more definite information, alluding to 'passages' which came from one of the newsbook accounts.[72] These he discussed with others. Newsbooks facilitated the oral transmission of news.[73]

Some readers thought newsbooks worthy of inclusion in their diaries, personal journals, or notebooks. The Earl of Leicester transcribed numerous passages, frequently expressing distaste.[74] The republican Edmund Ludlow transcribed newsbooks into his autobiographical manuscript, which he had reputedly told Thomas Blood was 'true as the Gospell'.[75] Wallington also thought extracts from the 'little pamphlets of weekly news' worthy of inclusion in his notebooks, addressed to posterity.[76] The barber Thomas Rugg entitled his manuscript of historical memoirs 'Mercurius Politicus Redivivus, or a Colection of the Most Materiall Transactions in Publick Affaires since Anno Domini 1659'. Into it he transcribed passages from *Politicus, Publick Intelligencer, Mercurius Publicus,* and other, later newsbooks. He even referred to Nedham's discharge and replacement by Giles Dury and Henry Muddiman in 1660.[77]

Wallington and Rous were a little obsessed with news: Wallington bought newsbooks against his expressed will. He refers to over three hundred printed items in his journal, copying out stories which interested him: of floods of petitions and repeated royalist plundering and cruelty.[78] In 1642 the reluctant Rous exclaimed in his diary: 'The many occurrences about the Parliament businesses, the differences between the King's Majestie and them, theire Petitions, his answers (supposed or otherwise), the affairs of Ireland, &c. are extant in multitudes of bookes and papers (unto which God in mercy put an end!) but the newes of Suffolke in Bartholomewe weeke I here set downe briefly.'[79] Elsewhere he referred suspiciously to the truth of books, but this did not stop his

[72] *The Diary of Ralph Josselin 1616–1683*, ed. Alan Macfarlane (1976), 155. For these accounts, see *MTN*, ch. 5.

[73] Levy, 'How Information Spread among the Gentry', 20–5, 34. Ong, Goody, and Eisenstein likewise argue that the influence of print on a society affects even those members of the society who cannot read. Walter J. Ong, 'Writing is a Technology that Restructures Thought', in Baumann, ed., *The Written Word*, 23–50; see also Ch. 2 n. 92 above.

[74] *Sydney Papers*, ed. Blencowe, *passim.*

[75] Qu. in Edmund Ludlow, *A Voyce from the Watch Tower*, ed. A. B. Worden, Camden Society^4, 21 (1978), 14; for Ludlow's use of newsbooks, see 13–17.

[76] Seaver, *Wallington's World*, 156–7.

[77] Thomas Rugg, *The Diurnal of Thomas Rugg 1659–1661*, ed. William L. Sachse, Camden Society^3, 91 (1961), pp. xi, xiii, 1, 40, 47; *MTN* 379.

[78] BL: Add. MS 21935; Wallington, *Historical Notices*, i. 142–308 and ii, *passim.*

[79] *Diary of John Rous*, 121. For more on Rous and his interest in news, see Cogswell, 'The Politics of Propaganda'; and Cust, 'News and Politics'.

excitement at the sight of Mr Prattes's *Speciall Passages*, nor did it stop him from recording the news therein contained at length in his diary.[80] Both Rous and Wallington read the serious newsbooks of the early 1640s, though Wallington also satisfied a strong taste for providential wonder stories.

Other godly men who expressed an interest in news included the Quaker George Fox and Richard Baxter.[81] In 1659 Baxter referred to *Publick Intelligencer* as a reliable source.[82] Samuel Jeake the elder possessed a number of newsbooks amongst his considerable library.[83] In his earlier years John Bunyan valued not the Bible or the sermons of preachers:

> the Scriptures thought I, what are they? a dead letter, a little ink and paper, of three or four shillings price. Alas, what is the Scripture, give me a Ballad, a Newsbook, *George* on horseback, or *Bevis* of *Southhampton*, give me some book that teaches curious arts, that tells of old fables; but for the holy Scriptures I cared not.[84]

Bunyan famously found God and renounced penny-sheet frivolity. His objection to newsbooks on spiritual grounds can be compared with Dorothy Shawe, wife of John Shawe, the puritan divine. John wrote in his memoir of her, 'When any Diurnals, weekly, were brought to the house, she would say, let me hear so far as concerns the Church, and Cause of God: for other things, I let them passe; she was no *Athenian*, like them *Act.* 17. but with *Nehemiah*, enquired much how it went with *Jerusalem* and the Church, *Nehem.* 1.2.'[85] This recognized that a weekly newsbook did carry accurate information about the progress of the Church in the world which did not go against the conscience even of a saint, male or female.

Politically prominent readers thought likewise. In March 1651 Edward Nicholas recommended to the Earl of Norwich that he read *Politicus*, adding, 'observe how soon those in England have all the news of the Louvre'.[86] In 1647 Nicholas had been offered, along with some more elevated books, 'Londons Accompt (a thing weakly done)'.[87] No

[80] *Diary of John Rous*, 122, 127–9.

[81] *The Journal of George Fox*, ed. Nigel Smith (forthcoming); *Autobiography of Richard Baxter*, ed. J. M. Lloyd Thomas (1925), 49.

[82] Baxter, *A Holy Commonwealth*, ed. William Lamont (1659; Cambridge, 1994), 4.

[83] I am grateful to Giles Mandelbrote and Nigel Smith for this information from their forthcoming account of his library.

[84] *A Few Sighs from Hell* (1658), in *The Miscellaneous Works of John Bunyan*, vol. i, ed. T.L. Underwood with the assistance of Roger Sharrock (Oxford, 1980), 333.

[85] John Shawe, *Mistris Shawe's Tomb-Stone. Or, The Saints Remaines* (1658; S3029), 17. Athens was a 'city wholly given to idolatry', Acts 17:16.

[86] *The Nicholas Papers: Correspondence of Sir Edward Nicholas, Secretary of State*, ed. George F. Warner, vol. i, Camden Society[2], 40 (1886), 225.

[87] *Nicholas Papers*, 81.

orthographical pun was intended here: *Weekly Account* communicated serviceable news. This could be supplemented up to the day the newsbook was sent. Sidney Bere wrote to Sir John Pennington on Thursday 16 December 1641: 'For the proceedings of the Parliament you have them here inclosed until Monday, which day there happened . . .' He enclosed *The Diurnall: Or, the Heads of all the Proceedings in Parliament* for the week 6–13 December.[88]

Sir Samuel Luke sent copies of newsbooks, preponderantly *Aulicus*, to many correspondents, including his father Sir Oliver Luke, the Earl of Essex, Captain Henry Andrews, Sir John Norwich, Sir Edward Ayscough, a Dr Strogall, Thomas Bristow, and John, Lord Robartes.[89] In return he received them, when at Newport Pagnell, from Samuel Bedford at Reading. One of Bedford's letters, interestingly, suggested that he had difficulty in acquiring sufficient numbers of London diurnals.[90]

One incident shows that newsbooks travelled into north Wales, at least in the hands of the New Model Army. It also suggests their instrumental force. On 30 August 1646 Colonel William Salesbury rejected Colonel Thomas Mytton's summons for the surrender of Denbigh Castle, except on the terms that he could contact the king for permission. The postscript to his letter read: 'I doe returne, per this Drume, Sir John Trevour's letter and the Diurnall.'[91] Mytton appears to have included a newsbook in order to represent to Salesbury just how desperate his condition was. Denbigh was surrendered on 26 October.

Newsbooks were read on the Continent. In August 1648 Arnold Boate wrote from Paris to Samuel Hartlib enclosing details of Balthasar Gerbier's projected English academy, requesting that if Hartlib was not interested they be forwarded to the editor of *Moderate Intelligencer*. Two months later Gerbier himself wrote requesting that another 'weekly intelligence' advertise his plans. Hartlib noticed a scheme in *Perfect Proceedings* in 1655 for an office of addresses not unlike his earlier ones; evidently he read more than one newsbook.[92]

Royalists in exile were forced to rely on newsbooks, however unwillingly. In 1649 *Kingdomes Weekly Intelligencer* reported that Prince Charles garnered his news from English newsbooks.[93] The same year the prince

[88] *CSPD 1641–1643*, 201; *The Diurnall*, 109.1; the only newsbook available that week.

[89] *Letter Books of Sir Samuel Luke*, 23, 57–8, 78, 96–7, 117, 239, 240, 254, 254–5, 255, 259, 268, 310, 322, 329, 330.

[90] *Letter Books of Sir Samuel Luke*, 423, 428.

[91] Qu. Norman Tucker, *North Wales in the Civil War* (Wrexham, 1992), 120.

[92] Turnbull, *Hartlib, Dury and Comenius*, 57–8, 86. See also Solomon, *Public Welfare, Science, and Propaganda*, 94; Hartlib, *A further Discoverie of the Office of Pvblick Addresse for Accommodations* (1648; H987); Webster, *Samuel Hartlib and the Advancement of Learning*, 19, 42.

[93] *KWI* 321, 24 July 1649, 1440, 214.321/E565(25); *KWI* 328, 11 Sept. 1649, 1496, 214.328/E573(10).

apparently sent to England an 'intelligencer' with instructions to send him pamphlets weekly, to inform him of proceedings in parliament and the Council of State.[94] More revealingly, he wrote to royalists in Scotland noting that he knew little of what was done, 'save that of which the London prints' informed him.[95] The term 'London prints' highlights some of the problems in identifying what denotes a newsbook and what a pamphlet or unprinted newsletter. Where several references occur, it is possible to detect a pattern and identify the nature of the publication to which a reference is made. In Luke's letters, for instance, a 'paper of news' refers to a manuscript.[96]

A reference to a particular document could be to a separate pamphlet or to the text as reproduced in a newsbook. If a pamphlet was sent in order to convey general news, or particularly the week's news, it was almost certainly a newsbook. When J. Powell wrote from Westminster to Edmund Warcupp at the Isle of Wight on 15 November 1648, adding 'for other Newes I referre yo^w^ to the inclosed', the enclosed was probably a newsbook, though it may have been a more exclusive manuscript.[97] When James Waynwright wrote in May 1654 to Richard Bradshaw, the Lord Resident for the State of England in Hamburg, stating after his news, 'I noe not ells but refer you to the booke for more p'ticular things', he probably referred to *Politicus*.[98] John Thurloe wrote from Whitehall to John Pell in Zurich on 7 February 1655 that 'Wee have lately had lett^rs^. from Jamaica, the truth of what they conteyne, you will finde in the enclosed print I therfore shall add noe more.'[99] This might be ambiguous were it not for a faint impression of the title of *Mercurius Politicus* visible over the text of the letter. This unexpected piece of evidence shows that the newsbook was folded first along the horizontal axis and then along a central vertical axis before being wrapped up in the letter. In 1662 John Beale, writing to Henry Oldenburg, implied that the enclosure of newsbooks in correspondence as an easy alternative to writing at length had become the norm: 'I have long mervayled, that you never condescend to use the Mercuryes for communications. Tis ye expedient of late dayes.'[100]

Even the most highly informed correspondents resorted to newsbooks, repeatedly acknowledging that they were adequate. Edward Rainbowe, Master of Magdalene College, Cambridge, wrote to Isaac

94 *CSPD 1649–1650*, 355–6. 95 *Clarendon State Papers*, ii. 409–10.

96 *Letter Books of Sir Samuel Luke*, 271. 97 Bod.: MS Rawl. Letters 47, f. 60.

98 *The Farington Papers*, ed. Susan Maria Ffarington, Chetham Society, 39 (1856), 175; he had been with John Bradshaw that day.

99 BL: Lansdowne MS 753, f. 6^v^.

100 *The Correspondence of Henry Oldenburg*, ed. and trans. A. Rupert Hall and Marie Boas Hall, vol. i: *1641–1662*, with the collaboration of Eberhard Reichmann (Madison: 1965), 481.

Appleton that he had 'obstinately resolved not to spot my paper with newes, whilst the pennyworth from the presse may out-doe me'.[101] William Catherens wrote to Edward Pitt, probably referring to newsbooks, 'the inclosed doe give more satisfaction then my Penn is able to performe therefore I desiste from writing particulars'.[102] Samuel Trotman wrote from London to his brother Edmund Warcupp on 14 November 1648: 'Such newes as is here yow may vnderstand by the inclosed.'[103] Warcupp was secretary to the parliamentary commissioners, then treating with the king. Robert Baillie wrote to one correspondent in Glasgow: 'For publick news that any man may see, I have sent yow the printed papers, to spare my writing.' Baillie also, significantly, enclosed newsbooks in his public letters to the General Assembly in Scotland through 1644 and occasionally in 1645: 'our affaires here goes as yow may see in the two inclosed Diurnalls, and business abroad as yow have in the paper.' He mentions 'printed papers', sending as many as six, perhaps not all newsbooks, at a time. He refers to a manuscript 'paper' of foreign news as 'wryte' or 'in wryte', perhaps illuminating common terminology.[104]

Henry Oxinden of Deane also used the newsbook as a labour-saving device, at a very early stage in its development, when he wrote to Henry Oxinden of Barham on 27 January 1642, 'I need nott bee tedious in relating how things have past of late; the petitions, diurnall, and pym's Speech, which I have prayd my father to send you, will save mee that labour.'[105] The next month he wrote, 'As for the State affaires, they have little varied for the better since I last wrott to you; you shall receive a booke that will better satisfie you then I of the parlment's desires and the King's answers.'[106] This almost certainly referred to a newsbook. Five years later, when the rhetoric of newsbooks had settled, Oxinden was saying the same thing: 'I can write you noe newes but what the diurnalls have.'[107] From London Thomas Barrow wrote to Oxinden of Barham: 'Concerning newes nott in printt, here is litle.'[108] John Rushworth was extremely well informed on certain subjects, being secretary to Sir Thomas Fairfax and the signatory to many letters appearing in newsbooks in the 1640s, yet he collected newsbooks, and read them

[101] Bod.: MS Tanner 60, f. 354. [102] BL: Add. MS 29974, f. 338.

[103] Bod.: MS Rawl. Letters 47, f. 56.

[104] *Letters and Journals of Robert Baillie*, ii. 171, 182, 195, 220, 231, 243, 246, 289, 324, 369.

[105] *Oxinden Letters*, 271.

[106] *Oxinden Letters*, 285; BL: Add. MS 28000, f. 48.

[107] *The Oxinden and Peyton Letters 1642–1670*, ed. Dorothy Gardiner (1937), 97. In Nov. 1651 Oxinden passed on news to his wife which he specified was not in a diurnal: ibid. 163.

[108] Dated 3 July 1642, *Oxinden Letters*, 310.

carefully. William Clarke, assistant to Rushworth, received newsletters from London as often as every day, and his correspondence gives the impression of a man who had no need for slightly belated and limited printed news, yet he collected a remarkable number of newsbooks.[109] He may have been interested in them as publications rather than for the news they contained, or he may have had a historiographical project in mind, as Rushworth did.[110] Collections of newsbooks became especially useful after the Restoration. Repositories of newsbooks were sought after, and their fame travelled. As late as 1671 Edmund Waller wrote to an unidentified correspondent requesting, 'you will bee pleased to lett me know the name of that person and where he dwells who kept the diurnalls and newsbooks and speeches & other papers that belonged to the long parlament Especially in the years 43 and 44 in the knolledge whereof I am att present very much concerne<d>'.[111]

There is some evidence of women reading newsbooks. Women certainly printed them, including Elizabeth Alsop, Mary Constable, Jane Coe, and Sarah Griffin, though no woman is known to have written a pre-1660 newsbook. Women, lower-class 'mercury women', were said to have sold them.[112] But the evidence for readers is thinner. Brilliana, Lady Harley, like her husband and son, read newsbooks; as did Dorothy Osborne, though she claimed to have done so only out of boredom.[113] Edward Dering sent letters enclosing pamphlets of parliamentary and London 'intelligence' to his wife from January 1642 onwards.[114] Oxinden requested from Elizabeth Dallison 'such pamphlets as are come out this weeke'. His phrasing suggests that he recognized the periodicity of newsbooks as early as December 1641. In his thanks he commented that the books 'at these times stand mee good sted'.[115] Henry's wife Katherine also read newsbooks, even in May 1648, when they were at their vituperative apogee. Her husband, perhaps flattering himself, implied that she would, or should, prefer hand-prepared news, but the newsbooks were adequate: 'I am in hast and can not write so

[109] See e.g., Clarke MSS 41 and 110, dating from 1647. His newsbooks are in the Worcester College Library.

[110] A practice Sheppard condemned: *Mastix* 1, 3–4.

[111] BL: Add. MS 30262, f. 88. Reproduced in *English Literary Autographs 1550–1650*, part II, selected and edited by W. W. Gregg in collaboration with J. P. Gilson, Hilary Jenkinson, R. B. McKerrow, and A. W. Pollard (Oxford, 1928), plate 54. The information probably related to his activities as an MP.

[112] This is implied by a diversity of pamphlet literature; cf. Freist, 'The World is Ruled and Governed by Opinion', 82.

[113] *Letters of the Lady Brilliana Harley*, ed. Thomas Taylor Lewis, Camden Society, 58 (1854); *Letters of Dorothy Osborne to William Temple*, ed. G. C. Moore Smith (Oxford, 1928), 76.

[114] Larking, ed., *Proceedings Principally in the County of Kent*, 69.

[115] *Oxinden Letters*, 264, 267, 292–3; cf. *Oxinden and Peyton Letters*, 3.

much to thee as I would in regard of busines. I therfore refer thee to the bookes.'[116] Evidence for female readers is sparse because of lower female literacy rates, particularly for writing literacy.[117] When women readers are recovered, they are frequently amongst the most eager to receive newsbooks.[118]

Though not eager, Lucy Hutchinson read them with her very shrewd eye, suspicious of their power to misattribute the credit of military victories. The parliamentarian general Sir John Gell, according to Hutchinson,

> kept the diurnal makers in pension, so that whatever was done in any of the neighbouring counties against the enemy was ascribed to him; and he hath indirectly purchased himself a name in story which he never merited . . . that which made his courage the more doubted was the care he took, and expense he was at, to get it weekly mentioned in the diurnals, so that when they had nothing else to renown him for, they once put in that the troops of that valiant commander, Sir John Gell, took a dragoon with a plush doublet. Mr Hutchinson, on the other side, that did well for virtue's sake and not for the vainglory of it, never would give anything to buy the flatteries of those scribblers; and when one of them had once, while he was in town, made mention of something done at Nottingham, with falsehood, and had given Gell the glory of an action wherein he was not concerned, Mr Hutchinson rebuked him for it, whereupon the man begged his pardon, and told him he would write as much for him the next week; but Mr Hutchinson told him he scorned his mercenary pen, only warned not to dare to lie in any of his concernments, whereupon the fellow was awed, and he had not more abuse of that kind.[119]

Hutchinson is a reliable and informed commentator, and the anecdote of the venal journalist, perhaps Henry Walker, who, like Gell, came from Derbyshire, rings true.[120]

Newsbooks even circulated in America. Many of the colonists still maintained close ties with Britain and with occurrences there. During the wars the British, including Herbert Pelham, Stephen Winthrop, Brampton Gurdon, and Ralph Josselin, and many former New Englanders in Britain, sent letters and newsbooks back across the Atlantic, just as metropolitan agents conveyed similar materials to the prov-

[116] *Oxinden and Peyton Letters*, 138; cf. 141: 'I know no newes but what I have sent.'

[117] Cressy, *Literacy and the Social Order*, 119–21, 144–5, and *passim*.

[118] In 1631 Sir Francis Harris wrote to Lady Joan Barrington: 'I have sent you madam (because I harde yow once saye yow loves forryne newes) a new boke, and could Mr Scott have stayed but an ower longer yow had received likewise the weekely currant.' Several other correspondents sent Lady Barrington corantos. *Barrington Family Letters 1628–1632*, ed. Arthur Searle, Camden Society[4], 28 (1983), 206–7; see also 201, 215, 218, 222–4, 227.

[119] Hutchinson, *Memoirs*, 92–3.

[120] Cotton, 228–30.

inces.[121] According to Cressy, 'an enviable selection of printed gazettes and mercuries circulated in new England'; though Carolyn Nelson adds that these were selected partly by 'the vicissitudes of war and weather'.[122] They did not arrive on a regular or frequent basis, but in clusters. Though out of date (the average crossing took eight weeks) they were still avidly received, indicating that interest in newsbooks frequently survived the week of their publication. John Winthrop reported to John Jr. in November 1648 and February 1649 that he had received thirteen newsbooks from England; on another occasion he mentioned an intercepted letter found among 'a bundle of Newes Books'. William Pynchon wrote to Winthrop in March 1644 that he had recently received seven or eight 'bookes of records'. In late 1643 or early 1644 the regicide William Goffe received a letter mentioning '5 Diurnalls, wherin theire was little more than forraign Newes'.[123] This trade which picked up in the early 1640s continued until the importation of journals was replaced by the importation of journalists, and the *Boston News-Letter* (1705) displaced the *London Gazette*.[124]

Newsbooks also moved around the colonies. Cressy depicts a very active community, 'especially among the governing elite' who had a political as well as religious investment in the war and who retained membership in a British 'political "county community"'. . . . The Winthrops, Pynchons, Winslows, Dudleys, and Hayneses shared in a network of information stretching from northern Massachusetts to the western frontier, and from Plymouth Colony to southern Connecticut, with outliers in Newfoundland, Virginia, Bermuda and the Caribbean.'[125] Naturally newsbooks could travel no faster than passengers, and most colonists probably received news of Britain by word of mouth. Nelson argues that Cressy overstates the numerousness and usefulness of newsbooks in New England: 'If one takes into account every mention of news in the correspondence, printed serials get short shrift. Allusions to printed news are more often to news *not* sent, newsbooks lost, or lent out and never returned.'[126] The last instance perhaps indicates higher, rather than lower, circulation. But even the identification of absent

[121] David Cressy, *Coming Over: Migration and Communication between England and New England in the Seventeenth Century* (Cambridge, 1987), 235–62.

[122] Cressy, *Coming Over*, 246; C. Nelson, 'American Readership of Early British Serials', in Myers and Harris, eds., *Serials and their Readers*, 27–44, qu. 29.

[123] Nelson, 'American Readership', 28–9; Cressy, *Coming Over*, 246–7.

[124] On the reprinting of English pamphlets and newsbooks in America, beginning in 1645, see M. A. Shaaber, 'Some Forerunners of the Newspaper in America', *Journalism Quarterly*, 11 (1934), 339–47.

[125] Cressy, *Coming Over*, 241, 247; also sharing were Theophilus Eaton and John Davenport.

[126] Nelson, 'American Readership', 31.

newsbooks may hint at their less exceptional presence, not mentioned in the majority of cases when they arrived. Once again the fragmentary evidence prevents us from developing a focused picture. Newsbooks were detached from the letters which they accompanied, and have been lost with time; in one sense their absence is an indication of their appeal.[127]

In conclusion: the readership of newsbooks was socially and geographically diverse, as diverse as any and probably all other publications. Private correspondence corrects the distorted view that has arisen from the use of printed sources. Despite their reputation for purveying untruths, newsbooks were viewed as a staple diet of information. The kind of criticisms levelled at newsbooks could be directed at other things. Richard Whitlock, worried about the influence of popular print, wrote:

> Such is the fate of Books, of all other Ware, the *courser* the Ware, the more the *Seller* getteth by it; examine the truth of it at *Stationers Hall*, & it will too truly appeare in these latter times, the *Book-seller* hath got *most* by those Bookes, the *Buyer* hath *got least*, being not only the Luck of *Rablais* his Book-seller, that was a looser by his Book of *Sence* and *Judgement*, but abundantly repaired by that *Ingenuous Nothing*, the Life of *Gargantua*, and *Pantagruel*. What Age ever brought forth more, or bought more *Printed Wast Papers?*[128]

Readers can make up their own minds, and not be impaired in judgement.

Naming your poison

A reader's choice of which newsbook to purchase or read probably depended to a great extent on availability. It is impossible to gauge just how popular individual titles were. Claims for the readership of *Aulicus* have been based only minimally upon contemporary references to it.[129] Allusions to it in correspondence may be unrepresentatively numerous, because of its prominence, as the unique malignant between 1643 and 1645, as much as the size of its readership or its intrinsic merit.

Sir Samuel Luke single-handedly ensured that *Aulicus* was widely

[127] Some, though remarkably few, survive in the collections of American libraries. See, for instance, the newsbooks which belonged to William Penn, now in the Library Company of Philadelphia: Per M80. The library of William Byrd, who began collecting in the later 17th cent., contains two volumes of L'Estrange's *Observator*. Nelson, 'American Readership', 41–2.

[128] *Zootomia*, 233–4.

[129] Beginnings, 7; id., *Cromwell's Press Agent*, 1, 31 n. 3; Malcolm, *Caesar's Due*, 126; Cotton, 37; *Berkenhead*, 49–52; Thomas does identify readers.

distributed, but he did not wholeheartedly endorse its exhaustiveness and accuracy; he referred oxymoronically in one letter to 'one of *Aulicus*' truths'.[130] *Aulicus* should be compared 'with your other intelligence at London'.[131] He could also be facetious, such as when he wrote to Dr Strogall: 'That your multiplicity of business may not make you forget your Summer's march accept of *Aulicus* to put you in mind of it.'[132] Luke appears to have been an informed commentator on the subject. He requested 'the printed Diurnalls' from his father, and in return commended *Mercurius Hibernicus* to him; he also passed on a *Perfect Passages.*[133] He mentioned 'the London pamphlets' to Oliver Cromwell, implying that the latter was equally familiar with the newsbook scene. He could be sceptical of the propaganda of his own side, as suggested when he wrote to his father, 'I fear the Cavaliers have had good success which makes your Diurnalls so silent at London.'[134] Luke mentioned *Aulicus* so frequently because it represented the enemy. When he wrote on 26 June 1645 that it had ceased publication since the Battle of Naseby he effectively equated the pamphlet war with the one he was fighting; when Henry Connington told Luke in December 1643 that 'Aulicus lyes a dying' he did not mean just the newsbook.[135]

Aulicus was distinguished by being the only newsbook named in Rushworth's *Historical Collections*, a work which relied extensively on newsbooks, but this may have been deliberately and blamelessly to reveal its inaccuracies.[136] Richard Baxter, on the other hand, was surprised to find that the enemy propaganda could be accurate:

> when the court news-book told the world of the swarms of Anabaptists in our armies, we thought it had been a mere lie, because it was not so with us nor in any of the garrison or county forces about us. But when I came to the army among Cromwell's soldiers I found a new face of things which I never dreamt of. I heard the plotting heads very hot upon that which intimated their intention to subvert both Church and State.[137]

Baillie drew a clear distinction between informative and polemical newsbooks, and could be bluntly dismissive: 'For publick news that any may see, I have sent yow the printed papers, to spare my writing: the most in the Diurnall and Intelligencer are true; Aulicus and

130 *Letter Books of Sir Samuel Luke*, 322.

131 To Earl of Essex, *Letter Books of Sir Samuel Luke*, 322.

132 *Letter Books of Sir Samuel Luke*, 330.

133 *Letter Books of Sir Samuel Luke*, 35–6, 117, 60; second letter dated 26 Dec. 1644.

134 *Letter Books of Sir Samuel Luke*, 260, 252.

135 *Letter Books of Sir Samuel Luke*, 329; for Connington see *Journal of Sir Samuel Luke*, ed. I. G. Philip, 3 vols. Oxfordshire Record Society, 29, 31, 33 (1950–3), 221.

136 *HC*^{3} ii. 723–9; cf. 376.

137 *Autobiography of Richard Baxter*, 49; cf. 215.

Britannicus are for jests only, and not worth the reading.'[138] He probably sent copies of both anyway. Most of these examples show that *Aulicus* was perceived as much as a paper bullet as a work of useful journalism.

Newsletters to Edward Hyde in 1647 and 1648 alluded to news in mainly royalist mercuries, and one mentioned an enclosed copy of *Pragmaticus*.[139] This was not necessarily just for news content: presumably he found it entertaining. One term which recurs in allusions is 'Diurnall'. Given that the term, like 'Mercury', is generic, its significance in correspondence is ambiguous. Frequently, however, it refers to Pecke's *Perfect Diurnall*, which had relatively exclusive propriety over the word from 1644 through to 1649.[140] Secretary Nicholas sent extracts from it to the Marquess of Ormonde in 1648.[141]

The Moderate Intelligencer also received considerable attention. Baillie condemned it, as did Thomas Edwards, Edward Rainbowe, and Isaac Appleton. It also received, as we shall see, a close reading from an anonymous reader now evident in the New York Public Library (hereafter NYPL) holdings. Its report of the imprisoned king in 1646 made the Lord Keeper of Oxford cry.[142] This newsbook, though widely perceived as destructive and subversive, never received the superlative accolade the Earl of Leicester afforded to *The Moderate*:

> An author, that writes allwayes for the Levellers, as it hath appeared often, but at no time more than this; wherein he endeavours to invite the people to overthrow all propriety, as the original cause of sin; and by that to destroy all government, magistracy, honesty, civility, and humanity. It passeth every week for one of the Parlement's writers, and it is a wonder that it hath bin so long suffered; there being allmost every weeke, such passages like this allmost in it; and such as would not be permitted in any Christian State, nor even amongst the Heathen.[143]

The Moderate did not destroy humanity, however, nor did the earl cease to refer to it. Despite his expressions of outrage he evidently enjoyed reading it. He regularly read *Perfect Diurnall* and *Perfect Occurrences*, and his journal also refers to *The Moderate Intelligencer*, *Mercurius Politicus*, and *Severall Proceedings*. He even once experimented with *Pragmaticus*. He was more at home with less polemical newsbooks, however, and he respected them sufficiently to transcribe their contents into his journal.

[138] *Letters and Journals of Robert Baillie*, ii. 171.

[139] *Clarendon State Papers*, i. 404, 415, 419.

[140] N&S 504, effectively continued as 503.

[141] Thomas Carte, ed., *A Collection of Original Letters and Papers Concerning the Affairs of England From the Year 1641 to 1660*, 2 vols. (1739), i. 168 and following.

[142] Varley, *Siege of Oxford*, 147.

[143] *Sydney Papers*, ed. Blencowe, 79.

He noted that the *Diurnall* and *Politicus* were 'printed . . . with license, so as the truth thereof is not doubted'.[144]

Numerous allusions to *Mercurius Politicus* distinguish it as a different kind of publishing phenomenon; a list of its readers would begin with Charles II, George Green, Edward Hyde, Edward Nicholas, Thomas Rugg, John Pell, Samuel Hartlib, John Dury, Balthasar Gerbier, John Thurloe, Samuel Morland, Henry Oldenburg, and Dr John Worthington, to name a few.[145]

Testimonies of the present

Though in January 1642 the poor of London could barely afford bread, some readers decided not only to purchase but to collect newsbooks. The case of Nehemiah Wallington is well documented. George Thomason continued to purchase pamphlets, and notably the newfangled newsbooks, in large numbers, constructing a monumental collection charting the textual life of London for twenty years. John Rushworth and William Clarke acquired substantial collections, as did the original owner of the set of *Mercurius Aulicus* which Thomas Turner later acquired.[146] The Earl of Leicester referred to extensive holdings in his journal.[147] Newsbooks survive in greater numbers than corantos. Most purchasers of newsbooks passed them on to other readers, who forwarded them in turn.[148] Making a collection depended upon both available resources and a selfish desire to keep them for reference. This spirit of collection represents a sensitivity to political events and a feeling for the historicity of the times, to which newsbooks contributed.

It is difficult to reconstruct the remote motivation for these impulses. The source of Turner's collection may have foreseen that a complete set of the royalist newsbook would be valuable when the war was over and king restored, and was therefore making a shrewd investment. Rushworth was later to use his newsbooks as a source for his *Historical Collections*, but this was not necessarily his only motivation in the early

[144] *Sydney Papers*, ed. Blencowe, 3–4, 12, 39, 44, 47, 68–9, 75, 77, 79, 81, 82, 91, 93, 106, 112, 115, 119, 128, 136, 149, 155. Leicester referred to *Severall Proceedings* as 'Generall Proceedings', attributing it to Scobell at one point, though later just describing it as licensed by him.

[145] See my forthcoming study of Milton, Nedham, and *Politicus*.

[146] Peter Thomas, ed., *OR* i. 8. Turner was too young to have bought them himself: either he was given them by his father or he purchased them from an unknown source at a later date.

[147] *Sydney Papers*, ed. Blencowe, 37.

[148] Newsbooks sent through the post were usually separated from the accompanying letters; Nelson, 'American Readership', 27–8.

1640s. Wallington sometimes lamented the expense he laid out on the 'little pamphlets of weekly news about my house' which 'were so many thieves that had stolen away my money before I was aware of them'.[149]

Lois Spencer describes Thomason as a 'born Collector', and notes that he differed from his friend Rushworth in that while the latter pursued the 'factual and relevant', Thomason 'sought out everything . . . he seeks only to provide material which posterity itself must sift'.[150] Yet Thomason was not free from politics, as he sought some publications, including anti-Cromwell libels, with greater eagerness than others. In 1647 the king famously requested the loan of a particular pamphlet from Thomason, who responded, 'if I should . . . loose it, presuming that when his Matie had done with it, that little account would be made of it, and so I should loose by that losse a limbe of my Collection, which I should be very loth to do, well knowing it would be impossible to supplie it.' Charles eventually secured the loan, and when fleeing to the Isle of Wight dropped it in the dirt, but charged two servants to retrieve it. Thomason's post-Restoration note remarks that this volume 'hath the marke of honor upon it, which no other in my Collection hath'.[151] The same year saw his conversion to a soft-royalism.[152] After 1647 the collection was conceived of as a historical testimony to the misbehaviour of the governors, indicting them of victimizing the king; hence his increasing interest in forbidden material. Such was clearly not the case for the first chronological third of Thomason's tracts, before he invested in such a large number of anti-Independent publications. His outstanding resources of 1640s tracts document the rebellion in Ireland, the Grand Remonstrance, the misdeeds of the king, and the happy settlement that the parliament was surely to bring. His friendships with Rushworth and with Milton, who gave him his more inoffensive tracts in the 1640s, dated from this period; and these friendships survived until that curious Restoration intersection whereby Rushworth became a trustee of Thomason's collection, and Thomason published the first volume of Rushworth's *Historical Collections.*

Thomason's tracts later became known as the 'King's Pamphlets'.[153]

[149] Seaver, *Wallington's World*, 156.

[150] Spencer, 'Politics of George Thomason', 24–5; 'Professional and Literary Connections of George Thomason'; *DNB* entries for Rushworth and Thomason; also the articles by Greenberg and Mendle cited in Introduction, n. 61, above.

[151] Spencer, 'Politics of George Thomason', 13.

[152] Sometimes mistakenly backdated to 1641. Fortescue, preface, *Catalogue to the Thomason Tracts*, i, pp. xiv–xv.

[153] The 'King' refers to George III. It was erroneously rumoured that they were collected at Charles I's request; Carlyle, ed., *Cromwell's Letters and Speeches*, i. 97.

In his later years, when 'dryasdust' Rushworth was drowning his memories and the cold in brandy, Thomason was turning them into a commodity. Yet Thomason was not in the early 1640s motivated by royalism or economics, he was more interested in the exhaustive nature of his collection.[154] Six weeks in prison did not affect his purchasing.[155]

We can speculate: in the face of what might have been the oncoming millennium, the purpose for which collectors pursued their objects was not as mundane as money. They may have gathered the ephemeral fragments of their culture as a witness and testimony to God, for when the kingdom of God came on earth, mortal time would at last be subjected to hermeneutical scrutiny. They regarded financial considerations less than they counted the days which one by one would bring his glorious kingdom. Each documented event encoded the Providence of God's journey hither.[156] When the latter days came the narrative would all make sense as a part of God's eternal plan. Wallington thought that when he came to 'give account before God . . . how I have improved and laid out every penny', his journal would legitimize him by enabling 'the generation to come' to 'see what God hath done'. His collections were for himself, for God, and for his descendants.[157] These were active readers, creatively producing meanings diffracted through the surface of the text, 'poets of their own affairs'.[158]

How were newsbooks read?

The patterns in which newsbooks were read are an enigma. They were sometimes read for the pleasure of their untruths; they were read for

[154] He gave a hostage to fortune in the 20 Jan. 1665 codicil to his will: 'Now not knowing how my estate may fall out after my death according to my Will lately made in case it shall fall short, Then I doe give to my two deare children, my daughter Grace Thomason and my sonne Thomas Thomason That full summe of money that my collection of Pamphletts shal be sold for to bee equally divided betwixt them both for their advancement.' *Catalogue to the Thomason Tracts*, i, pp. xii–xiii. After the Restoration the collection, in the process of this commercial exchange, became a commodity, stunted in imagination, like his son's name.

[155] Spencer, 'The Politics of George Thomason', 20.

[156] Millenarian responses to the civil war have been well documented: William M. Lamont, *Godly Rule: Politics and Religion, 1603–1660* (1969); B. S. Capp, *The Fifth Monarchy Men: A Study in Seventeenth-Century English Millenarianism* (1972); J. F. McGregor and B. Reay, eds., *Radical Religion in the English Revolution* (Oxford, 1984); Nigel Smith, *Perfection Proclaimed: Language and English Radical Religion 1640–1660* (Oxford, 1989). One American reader of newsbooks wrote to another, on hearing of the Solemn League and Covenant, of the overthrow of Antichrist and the coming Armageddon. Cressy, *Coming Over*, 247. This is the kind of response I mean.

[157] Seaver, *Wallington's World*, 156–7.

[158] De Certeau, *Practice of Everyday Life*, 34, 165–76.

the basically true news they contained, whatever their Information or Intelligence. There were engaged ways of reading. Sir John Meldrum took censure to heart. In October 1644 the Committee of Both Kingdoms thanked Meldrum for his good service, adding, 'Sir Wm Brereton in his letter has attributed to you your due honour, and we earnestly desire you not to think of what is in printed diurnals or such books. The authors of them take too much liberty to themselves, but which for the present is not to be remedied.'[159] This concern can be juxtaposed with the experience of Dorothy Osborne, who was convinced that newsbooks were entirely unreliable, but who recorded on one day in 1653: 'I know not how I stumbled upon a new's book this week, and for want of something Else to doe read it. it mentions my L. L[i's] Embassage againe, is there any such thing towards? I mett with something else in't, that may concerne any body that has a minde to marry.'[160] The boredom was probably a feigned excuse. She encountered some information of significance to her, involving her suitor, Lord Lisle, and Commonwealth marriage legislation. News that concerned anyone who intended to marry had an immensely broad potential audience. This did not make her any more reflexive about the nature of newsbooks.

Brereton's and Osborne's very different attitudes share the supposition that newsbooks were first disposable and secondly instruments of communication. This is characteristic of the majority of readers, who could divorce the content from the form, and damn newsbooks for being newsbooks. For more positive information about how they were read it is necessary to work with marginalia and tendentious evidence such as their influence on poetry and other forms of writing, and their significance to contemporary historians.

D. F. McKenzie has argued that the history of reception of printed texts should include 'a history of misreadings'.[161] While McKenzie means textual misreadings, it is worth considering the significance of the misinterpretations imposed upon texts. The act of reception investigated below is the association drawn by some contemporaries between Independency and newsbooks. At several points in the 1640s, notably in 1643 and in 1647–8, most newsbooks wrote in favour of the Presbyterian cause, yet accusations of interest usually associated them with Independency. This charge constitutes a misinterpretation which helps us to understand the texts and the active nature of reading in the mid-seventeenth century.

The term 'Independency' is not without its problems. From its earliest days its use was politically contested in newsbooks. Henry Walker

159 *CSPD 1644–1645*, 24.

160 *Letters of Dorothy Osborne*, 76; to Sir William Temple, 20 Aug.

161 McKenzie, *Bibliography and the Sociology of Texts*, 4, 16.

gave the terms 'Presbyterian' and 'Independent' political overtones in *Perfect Occurrences* in December 1644; in 1645, in his *Parliament Scout*, John Dillingham, concerned to promote unity, denied that they were relevant.[162] The terms have been retained by historians to indicate political groups as well as religious ones, and these groups did not necessarily correspond.[163] It is necessary to keep this distinction in mind when considering the connections hostile writers made between Independency and newsbooks.

Some of the army newsbooks were Independent in tone. Ashe and Bowles were Presbyterians, Peters and Saltmarsh Independents, but the New Model Army had a distinct Independent hue, which intensified with time. From the outbreak of the war royalist writers had accused the parliamentarian army of sectarianism, claiming that it was composed of Brownists, anabaptists, and atheists.[164] This was not true, any more than claims that the New Model army was thoroughly sectarian from the outset. Preaching, including lay preaching, central to the culture of the 'praying Army', encouraged the spread of religious toleration through the rank and file.[165] *Moderate Intelligencer* expressed a hope that the army would destroy Antichrist and be the instrument of religious reformation.[166] Newsbooks were associated with the interest of the army in 1645–6, thus it is not surprising that their enemies should also condemn them for religious Independency. The reason why the association stuck is not as straightforward, however: *Moderate Intelligencer* later passed through a royalist phase, and was temporarily banned for this in September 1648.[167]

Through 1644 Robert Baillie (Milton's 'Scotch what d'ye call') regularly sent newsbooks with his public letters to the General Assembly in Scotland. In the spring and summer of 1645 he refrained. On 25 April he wrote to William Spang at The Hague complaining that 'Their new-modelled Armie consists, for the most [part] of raw, unexperienced, pressed sojours', and that many of the officers 'are sectaries, or their confident friends'. He qualified the accusations of sectarianism, suggesting that they had been overstated and that the army was essentially obedient to the parliament.[168] He had already complained, in July 1644,

162 Cotton, 'John Dillingham', 827–8.

163 See J. H. Hexter, 'The Problem of the Presbyterian Independents', in *Reappraisals in History* (1961), 163–84; Ashton, *English Civil War*, 336; Underdown, *Pride's Purge*, 18.

164 e.g. *MTN* 71–3.

165 See Kishlansky, *Rise of the New Model Army*, and Gentles's revision of his argument in *New Model Army*, esp. ch. 4; for 'praying Army', *England's Remembrancer* (1646), qu. Gentles, *New Model Army*, 94.

166 *Moderate Intelligencer* 16, 19 June 1645, 125, 419.016/E288(37).

167 *LJ* x. 508; *Beginnings*, 152–3; Brailsford, *Levellers and the English Revolution*, 402–3; Cotton, 267–70; id., 'John Dillingham'; Underdown, *Pride's Purge*, 96.

168 *Letters and Journals of Robert Baillie*, ii. 265.

that the press, with the assistance of Ashe, had praised Cromwell to the detriment of Scottish officers. Baillie continued to send the occasional diurnal north even after the appearance of Thomas Edwards's *Gangræna* in February 1646, for which Baillie showed great enthusiasm.[169]

Edwards (Milton's 'shallow Edwards'[170]) described *Moderate Intelligencer* as 'the great Historian and Chronicler of the sectaries . . . who writes their lives and deaths, and trumpets forth their victories and praises so immoderately as if they did all'.[171] He used newsbooks as sources for accounts of sectarian behaviour. John Goodwin accused Edwards of 'drinking in with so much greedinesse, all, and all manner of reports, that are brought into him, whether with ground or without', and it is true that some of Edwards's reports echo the sensationalism of some newsbooks.[172]

Edward Rainbowe, who recognized the value of newsbooks in his correspondence, construed *Moderate Intelligencer* similarly. On 1 January 1646 he wrote to Isaac Appleton complaining of the danger of being inundated by a torrent of sectarian lay-preachers, and added:

> If you observed the moderat intelligencer, wch ended at Decemb: 25. in his beginning, he insinuats a way for guifted men to be sent preachers into ye North although they be not ordayned ministers; some imagine for this reason, that in regard trading is now decayed and some of the best Livings (and he desires not the worst onely for them) might supply their wants . . .[173]

Rainbowe approved of the General Assembly in Scotland's stance against toleration.

Edwards drew lengthy parallels between sectaries and malignants as enemies of Presbyterianism. In doing so, like Baillie, he manipulated the arch-enemies, *Britanicus* and the 'grand Malignant' *Aulicus*, into improbable associates. He suggested that the latter would be pleased by sectarian arguments against Presbyterianism, and that there were some 'Malignant Ministers, and others of note who are for Independency against Presbytery; but this is now so commonly known, that *Britanicus*, a man who hath done them [Independents] many good offices, and cryed up severall of them, confesses in one of his Pamphlets about a fortnight since, that the Malignants are turned Independents'.[174] *Britanicus* had indeed written something like this, but that is hardly what

[169] *Letters and Journals of Robert Baillie*, ii. 352, 358–9, 416.

[170] Both Baillie and Edwards in 'On the Forcers of Conscience' (1647), *Complete Poetry of John Milton*, 211–12.

[171] *Gangræna*, 11.

[172] John Goodwin, *Cretensis* (1646; G1161), 19; e.g. the monstrous birth story in *The Second Part of Gangræna* (1646; E234), 4–6.

[173] Bod.: MS Tanner 60, f. 354.

[174] *Gangræna*, 52, 54–5.

he intended by it. Edwards contrasted the meek and respectful bearing of Presbyterians, 'the greatest part of both Kingdoms', with the sectaries who made as much noise as possible with pulpits and newsbooks.[175] He may have had in mind the involvement of Peters, 'Soliciter Generall for the Sectaries',[176] and Saltmarsh with newsbooks in 1645. Edwards associated newsbooks with the army sectaries against parliament as well as the Presbyterians. Sectaries formed only a fifth or sixth of the army, though they acted as if the whole of the army were so inclined.[177] The first of Edwards's twenty-eight characterizations of the practices of the sectaries echoed Baillie's complaint (and perhaps Lucy Hutchinson's) of the partisanship of the press; 'They use to ascribe and attribute all the successe of things, all thats done in field, at leagures, all victories, brave actions to their party, crying them up in Pulpits, News-books, conferences, calling them the saviours of the Kingdoms.' And in point nineteen: 'they have got most of the weekly writers of News to plead their cause, commend their persons, cry up their actions.'[178] Just as Edwards made homogeneous extremely diverse beliefs and practices, under the amorphous headings 'Sectarian' and 'Independent', he treated newsbooks as an unredeemed, uniform phenomenon, conflating *Britanicus* and *Moderate Intelligencer* and barely distinguishing *Aulicus* from these two. All were complicit in spreading 'Errors, Heresies, Blasphemies'.[179] The enemy within was more perilous than the cavaliers.

Edwards argued that the relationship between sectaries and newsbook writers was consolidated by money. The suggestion of party subsidization has interesting implications for the economics of newsbooks: they could be sold in greater numbers at a lower price. This passage, discussing the reception of a petition, reveals the conventional perception that newsbooks are the quintessence of 'pamphlets':

> Many also of the Pamphleteers (who I think are the pensioners of that party [sectaries], and I am sure one of them being lately tryed to insert into his weekly Newes the petition presented at the choice of the new Common-councel, confessed ingenuously he could not, for he was ingaged to the other side,) branded this Petition, *The Perfect Passages,* as *promoted by persons ill-affected, invented by the Lord* Digby, *to make fractions in our Army, a very dangerous Petition, and if any be not of this minde, if they will but repaire to Mr.* Burroughes *or any well-affected Minister they may be further satisfied.* The Moderate Intelligencer as voted to be *false, scandalous, and that a Commitee should inquire out the Author to be punished*; besides he makes it to be a quarrelling with our friends, and making enemies of

[175] *Gangræna*, 56–7. [176] *Gangræna*, 98.
[177] *Gangræna*, 60 and marginal note.
[178] *Gangræna*, 62, 69–70.
[179] *Gangræna*, 148.

them, and unseasonable; so also the *Perfect Occurrences* of that week, with others of them had a fling at this Petition and the Petitioners.[180]

Clement Walker, for whom newsbooks were Cromwellian partisans, described *The Moderate* as 'one of the raling Pen-men of the Faction who hath a large share in the 500. or 600. a year allowed to these Pamphletires, for divulging State-lies and Slanders amongst the People'.[181] These statements are intended to discredit enemy propaganda, but they may also indicate an underground economy of secret patronage.

Edwards, Walker, and Baillie suggest that Presbyterians, despite the efforts of George Smith, who was silenced in September 1646,[182] perceived newsbooks as their enemies. *Englands Remembrancer* in February 1647 confirmed that newsbooks were associated with sectarianism as a homogeneous group, despite quite different individual styles and intentions: 'Another sort of men he imployeth, which justifie the wicked for reward, and take away the righteousnesse of the righteous from him (ISA. 5. 23.) These are the weekly Pamphleters, who make it their trade to call evill good, and good evill; and to deceive the Kingdom with lying relations.'[183] 'All sort of Independent Sectaries' (a collocation that would have gratified Edwards) spread England over with 'Schism, Heresie, Error, and Blasphemy' using these means.[184] Newsbooks physically transmitted sedition and Independency; as did the army, in the accounts of Edwards and Walker. This was not an entirely fair interpretation, but this convergence of a series of perceptions reveals that the content and actual politics of newsbooks could be overshadowed by a stereotype of what they were supposed to do. A 'misreading' perhaps, but a potent one, not least because it constitutes a serious effort to construe the meaning of a text, as well as its social significance.

Readers read critically, and with intelligence, sometimes comparing newsbooks and thereby resolving uncertainties or inaccuracies. *Scotish Dove* suggested that readers commonly bought more than one newsbook.[185] In 1651 Clement Barksdale wrote:

> As the *Armies* did against each other fight;
> Even so doe our moderne *Historians* write:

[180] *Gangræna*, 110–11; marginal notes: '*Vide* Perfect Passages, Numb. 48. from *September* 17. to 23.' and '*Vide* Moderate Intelligencer, Numb. 30. from *September* 18. to 25.'

[181] *The Compleat History of Independencie* (1661; W324), part II, 24n.; cf. Hutchinson, 251, above.

[182] *LJ* viii. 498, 504.

[183] *Englands Remembrancer Of Londons Integrity* 2, [11 Feb.] 1647, 10, 126.2/E375(9).

[184] *Englands Remembrancer* 2, 15, 10.

[185] *Scotish Dove* 74, 21 Mar. 1645, 584, 594.074/E274(17).

Each for his *side*. The *Stationer* says, *Buy both*:
Compare them, and you may *pick* out the Truth.[186]

The modern historians included newsbook writers. One reader who actively compared several accounts and recorded his conclusions was the Earl of Leicester, who wrote in his journal:

The 23d *August* [1649]. Cromwell, Lord Lieutenant of Irland, by commission of the Parlement, after his landing at Dublin with his forces, and those which Ireton brought thither some few dayes after him, set forth a proclamation, which is in the Perfect Diurnall, from the 27th *August* to the 3d *September*, wherein he useth the termes of 'we,' 'us,' and 'our,' in the plural number; and though in the sayd Diurnall it be sett down, that he subscribed his name O. Cromwell, yet others say, that he wrote his name above, as King use to do to theyr subjects, and as other Chiefe Governors of Irland have formerly don. And the pamphlet called the Moderate impartially communicating, &c. who is a friend to the Levellers, and not to Cromwell, (at the least he seemeth so,) from the 28th *August* to the 4th *September*, sayth, 'A Proclamation coming forth superscribed, and not subscribed, with the Chiefe Governor of Irland's name, and running in a royal language of "we," which therefore many do not believe reall, or if so, then the printer mistaken, I here insert at large: "By the Lord Lieutenant O. Cromwell" above, and then followeth the proclamation, and at the end, "Given at the Castle of Dublin this twenty-third of *August*, 1694."' It falls out, that by such a signing of a name in Irland, with O, (which there is for Oliver,) it may be taken for the note of excellency, or chiefe of the family, as O Neale, O Bryan, O Connor, &c. and so O Cromwell.[187]

Leicester compared the two newsbooks, resolved what he believed to be the case, that the proclamation was headed 'O. Cromwell', and then explained the partial misinterpretation in other newsbooks. He also satisfied himself that Cromwell was now using the royal 'we', and found a discomforting amusement.

Traces of readings

Reading does take some measures against the erosion of time, providing evidence for the way in which newsbooks were read, in marginalia.[188] Marginalia consist of different, spontaneous, or considered reactions; immediate responses, deliberate animadversion, and markers, including corrections to the text for future readings and readers. It is not

[186] [Clement Barksdale], *Nympha Libethris: Or the Cotswold Muse* (1651; B804), 43.

[187] *Sydney Papers*, ed. Blencowe, 88–9; elsewhere (p. 93) he noted darkly that *The Moderate* frequently wrote favourably of Catholics.

[188] On which, see H. J. Jackson, 'Writing in Books and Other Marginal Activities', *University of Toronto Quarterly*, 62 (1992/3), 217–31.

particularly common in newsbooks, perhaps suggesting that they were regarded as being relevant only for a single reading. The same is true of all civil war pamphlet literature. There are exceptions: John Rushworth left some important marginalia; and a particularly interesting set of annotations survives in NYPL. There are also other, scattered instances.

Most traces of reading are simply marks. The underlining of words or phrases is the most common.[189] Sometimes small crosses were put in the margin.[190] One not uncommon mark is a small hand pointing to a place of interest thus: ☞.[191] This may be characteristic of later readers. Some habitually corrected spellings, particularly the NYPL reader, who obsessively deleted unnecessary 'e's and 'k's at the end of words, but also inserted letters where they were missing.[192] The same reader made some corrections to copies of *Moderate Intelligencer*, inserting 'so' in the phrase 'Sir, I do [^] much confide', apparently on the grounds of personal taste. Finding the phrase 'it was resolved to cause all the Army [^] towards the sea', he or she added the elided verb 'march'.[193] The emendations suggest the habits of a tidying mind as much as the desire to facilitate reading or rereading or the intent to construct a history using these passages at some future date. Some more temperate literal corrections were made by a reader of Cooke's *Perfect Diurnall*.[194] Rushworth changed the original spellings when he transcribed passages from newsbooks for his *Historical Collections*, and some of these emendations he had earlier marked in his copies.[195]

These marks are indicative only of someone reading closely; others indicate someone reading systematically, which in turn underscores the serious nature of newsbooks to some readers. Some evidence must be handled tentatively. The fact that Thomason carefully wrote on all the title-pages in his collection the date on which he purchased them, or some date relating to the contents of the publication, does not mean he read them. The same is not true, however, of the NYPL reader, who made a series of marks which function as apparatus for the reader. She or he boxed off all the names and dates indicating the origin of news

[189] e.g. Library of Congress: DA411.M6; a volume of *Politicus*, especially 7336–43 and the heavily marked list on 7231–38.

[190] e.g. University of Pennsylvania copy of *Britanicus* 106, 942. These are probably contemporary: as with any simple mark, the probability stands in favour of an early reader, though this judgement cannot be made with any certainty. See also *Publick Intelligencer* 1, 18 in NYPL.

[191] e.g. Library Company of Philadelphia: KD*36.i–iii; KD*361, four various volumes. These may have been drawn by Henry Physick or his father Edmund in the late 17th or early 18th cents.

[192] NYPL: *Publick Intelligencer* 2, 21–3, 29; 575.002/E589(4).

[193] NYPL: *Moderate Intelligencer* 76, 419.076/E350(21).

[194] Folger: P1486.62, *Perfect Diurnall* 9, 4, 5; 510.9/E202(34).

[195] Bod.: Arch. H e. 108, 109.

items, and enclosed the headings for lists in boxes, more clearly to identify them. The same reader noticed when *Moderate Intelligencer* skipped a week in the summer of 1647, writing on the cover of her or his copy of issue 124: 'Noe more wr[it]ten till Aug. 5', which was correct.[196] Rushworth had been similarly observant when newsbooks disappeared in April 1642.[197] In her or his volume of *Moderate Intelligencer* the NYPL reader marked '8 weeks' on the top of the front page of every eighth issue. A reader of *Politicus*, whose volumes survive at the Library of Congress, amended dates, and, more interestingly, indexed the contents of some issues.[198] A reader of a copy of *Perfect Diurnall* from 1643 marked his or her own description of the pertinent contents just below the title: 'The relation of the deth of the Lord Brookes.'[199] These annotations, taken as a whole, suggest the concentration and seriousness with which some readers consulted and interacted with newsbooks.

The fact that a reader could find room to place such a marker indicates that newsbooks participated in the triumph of white space over black, the fragmenting of the page to assist reading. Such 'breathing space' enabled a broader audience to access the text, particularly through the use of small units with distinct headings.[200] Newsbooks were particularly suited to this partitioning because they were broken down into reports by day and by place of origin. The great flow of news in the mid-seventeenth century was served up, as Cleveland wrote, in 'sippets'.[201] This was an important printing-house technique for cheap books, as readers with only basic literacy skills relied on a segmented text with frequent signposts.[202] Many practices remained haphazard and conventional; yet the foregrounding of typographical elements like numbered issues and pages, breaks in the text, and short, summarial headlines was encouraged by the widespread dissemination of the printed word by the hand press and movable type, not because of the systematic structure of the printer's workshop, but because of the practical need to be understood.[203] As an incidental consequence, residual space in newsbooks could be used to introduce personal comments, indices, and reading markers; the NYPL reader of *Moderate Intelligencer* evidently thought that the systematization had not proceeded far enough.

[196] NYPL: *Moderate Intelligencer* 124, 29 July 1647.

[197] Bod.: Arch. H e. 108, f. 143ᵛ.

[198] Library of Congress: A411.M6. The first three volumes, like other material there, are not in N&S. For indexing, see e.g. *Politicus* 285, 5573.

[199] Bod.: Hope adds. 1128(15); *Perfect Diurnall* 38, 6 Mar. 1642[3], 513.38A.

[200] Chartier, *Order of Books*, 11.

[201] Cleveland, *Character of a London Diurnall*, 1.

[202] Chartier, *Cultural Uses of Print*, 249.

[203] See Ch. 1 n. 11, above.

Other private readers reacted with passion: one reader of a *Perfect Diurnall* wrote 'false' against the several clauses of a Worcester County declaration printed therein;[204] another took exception to the exclusion, in the description of an execution, of the condemned man's last words, noting, 'what he spake was disliked & soe not printed'.[205] The NYPL reader of *Moderate Intelligencer* underlined the phrase 'but that we see so many rocks, as are able to split the Royall Soveraign' and added in the margin, 'and s<o> did'.[206] This reveals at least one retrospective reading. One reader of a 1643 *Aulicus* underlined in the text the name of a Mr Jones and annotated the margin: 'made a Judge 1646'. This was the only mark she or he made in a complete volume of the first year.[207] On a copy of *Perfect Diurnall* which reported that the judges would sit in the King's Bench, one reader noted, 'The Judges doth not sett this pnt monday as is here sett forth'.[208] William Lilly regularly purchased *Elencticus* and left marks, perhaps anticipating a response.[209]

The marginalia of John Rushworth are exceptionally interesting, because they reveal the several layers of his reading, each accumulating until his final verdict. Like other readers, Rushworth made hasty marks on his first, immediate reading, and then in retrospect elaborated upon them, preparing for his future work. Rushworth inscribed comments in the margin, he underlined phrases, particularly the names of persons and places, he noted important developments, preparing to return to them. In the endpapers to one volume of newsbooks Rushworth wrote: '20 Jan: 42/3 Citizens Imprisond for not paying assessm[en]ts—201.'[210] He also annotated them in shorthand, usually noting 'book' or 'observe for book', though occasionally using such evocative terms as 'fears'. He highlighted the proximity between his volumes of newsbooks and his projected history of the civil war by writing 'Historical Collections' on the spines.

Rushworth occasionally underlined descriptions which emphasized opinion and subjective response. 'Goring is afraid himselfe,' he underscored, and 'he hath delivered such things of their [the Irish] speeches and actions while he was prisoner with them as it makes

204 Bod.: Hope adds 1128(41); *Perfect Diurnall* 85, 17 Mar. 1644[5], 504.085/E258(36). Possibly the same reader as n. 199 above.

205 Bod.: Vet.A3 d.15; *Perfect Diurnall* 324, 2825, 22 July 1650, 506A.324/E778(1).

206 NYPL: *Moderate Intelligencer* 54, 19 Mar. 1646, 339, 419.054/E328(21). The 'o' has been cropped.

207 Private copy, in a contemporary Oxford binding. *Aulicus* 32, 12 Aug. 1643, 435, 275.132/E65(26#).

208 Bod.: Hope adds 1128(14); *Perfect Diurnall* 19, 24 Oct. 1642, sig. T4, 519.19A/E240(46). Cf. nn. 199, 204, above.

209 See Bod.: [MS] Ashmole 720.

210 Bod.: Arch. H e. 109.

me tremble to thinke upon'. And, 'Thus much I gather, that although great and strange words are uttered about the generall differences in England, yet the Souldiers hatred to the Irish is uncontrollable, and will never be appeased.'[211] The NYPL reader exhibited similar interests, marking, for instance, 'as gallant a man as ever fought' and 'the most incomparable strength in England'.[212] These readers' observations of such phrases, some of which are the newsbook editor's own intervention, indicates that it was not only for the intelligence that contemporaries read newsbooks.

From these shadowy glimpses, a significant picture emerges. Some readers of newsbooks were far from the gullible, passive victims guided by their appetites described by some of their proud contemporaries and a few later historians. The involvement of persistent readers must change the way we perceive not only these readers but the newsbooks themselves.

[211] Bod.: Arch. H e. 109: *Speciall Passages* 2, 9; *Speciall Passages* 13, 114.
[212] NYPL: *Moderate Intelligencer* 53, 338; *Moderate Intelligencer* 76, 610.

6

The Crisis of Eloquence: Newsbooks and Historiography

> *History* (saith Cicero, *is the witnesse of the times, the life of memory, and light of verity:* I have therfore undertaken to testifie that, whereof I was an eye-witnesse, and to give light unto the truth of all the following passages, which otherwise might be obscured or prejudiced, by the exception of the first, and none of the truest Newes.
> (*A Iovrnall, Or a true and exact Relation of Each dayes passage,* 1644[1])

HISTORIANS of the civil wars faced what they felt to be a new problem. In 1642, gesturing to the lack of control over the presses, Thomas Fuller lamented that 'the Pamphlets of this age may passe for Records with the next (because publickly uncontrolled) and what we laugh at, our children may believe'. He was one of many who emphasized the novelty of pamphlet wars; 'who is not sensible with sorrow of the distractions of this age? To write books therefore may seem unseasonable, especially in a time wherein the *Presse,* like an unruly horse, hath cast off his bridle of being *Licensed,* and some serious books, which dare flie abroad, are hooted at by a flock of Pamphlets.'[2] Fuller excused himself because he had begun his own project, *The Holy State,* before the potential aggression of movable type was unleashed. Years later, responding to an attack by Peter Heylin, Fuller appealed to a notion of a pre-Babel mankind:

> Happy those *English Historians* who wrote some *Sixty years since,* before our *Civil Distempers* were born or conceived . . . I mean, before *Mens latent Animosities* broke out into *open Hostility;* seeing then there was a generall *right understanding* betwixt all the Nation.
>
> But alas! Such as wrote *in* or *since* our *Civil Wars,* are seldome apprehended *truely* and *candidly,* save of such of their owne *perswasion,* whilest others *doe not* (or what is worse *will not*) understand them aright.[3]

1 *A Iovrnall* (1644; J1113/E8(4)), 1.

2 Thomas Fuller, *The Holy State* (Cambridge, 1642; F2443), 201, sig. A2.

3 Peter Heylin, *Examen Historicum: Or A Discovery and Examination Of The Mistakes, Falsities, and Defects In some Modern Histories* (1659; H1706); Thomas Fuller, *Appeal of Iniured Innocence* (1659; F2410), 1.

Newsbooks were the quintessence of this new Babel, poisoning testimony, vitiating the building-blocks of history, and thereby deceiving posterity.

Fallen speech and cheap history

The problem involved speech and authority. With printed speeches, pamphlets, and particularly newsbooks, it was never clear who was saying what to whom, nor what the precise context and language were. This troubled John Rushworth, when he wrote the preface to his *Historical Collections*, at some point in the 1650s. He planned his history, 'whilst things were fresh in memory', as a set of semi-mediated documents by means of which a reader could furnish a narrative. Caution was necessary precisely because of the fabulous number of printed pamphlets which flew from the uncontrolled presses:

> Hereafter they will hear, that every man almost in this Generation durst fight for what either was, or pretended to be Truth: They should also know that some durst write the Truth; whilst other mens Fancies were more busie then their hands, forging Relations, building and battering Castles in the Air; publishing Speeches as spoken in Parliament, which were never spoken there; printing Declarations, which were never passed; relating Battels which were never fought, and Victories which were never obtained; dispersing Letters, which were never writ by the Authors; together with many such Contrivances, to abet a Party or Interest. *Pudet hæc opprobria.* Such practices, and the experience I had thereof, and the impossibility for any man in After-ages to ground a true History, by relying on the printed Pamphlets in our days, which passed the Press whilst it was without control, obliged me to all the pains and charge I have been at for many years together, to make a Great *Collection*; and whilst things were fresh in memory, to separate Truth from Falshood, things real from things fictitious or imaginary.[4]

Rushworth had been licenser of the press between 11 April 1644 and 9 March 1647, so he was well informed of the limited powers of the willing censor. The danger was that the uninformed historian, while fighting for truth, would be deceived by the falsifying imagination of propagandists.[5] Writing in the late nineteenth century on the recent forgery of a newsbook entitled *The English Mercurie*, James Grant observed that if the iniquitous deception had not been unveiled, 'an historical mis-statement might have been everywhere, and by everybody, implicitly believed till the end of time'.[6] This fear was two centuries old. Gilbert Burnet wrote that 'History is a sort of Trade in which false Coyn

[4] *HC*[1] i, preface, sigs. b[v]–b2. [5] *HC*[1] i, b2.
[6] Grant, *Newspaper Press*, i. 11–15.

and false Weights are more Criminal than in other Matters; because the Errour may go further and run longer'.[7] Rushworth hoped 'I may but prove an ordinary Instrument to undeceive those that come after us'; Clarendon wrote in order 'That posterity may not be deceived by the prosperous wickedness of these times'.[8] After the Restoration Richard Atkyns opined: 'Historians must of necessity take many things upon trust, they cannot with their own but with the Eyes of others see what things were done before they themselves were.'[9]

'Paper Combates & replies'[10] led to the spilling of blood, and then these paper bullets landed on historians' desks. The consensual gestures which characterized the method and rhetoric of pre-civil war historiography were chased off.[11] Pre-war writers were cautious of producing narratives which either too obviously reflected upon, or were chronologically too close to, the present, not wishing their teeth struck out by the heels of time, as Raleigh famously put it.[12] Ideology certainly played a part, as it did in the humanist endeavour to publish classical texts, but had none of the explicit factional allegiances it later acquired.[13] The most prominent conflict, at least since Polydore Vergil's debunking of Geoffrey of Monmouth,[14] arose over John Selden's *Historie of Tythes* (1618), which touched upon contemporary concerns easily translated to the tendentiousness of ideology. Richard Montagu questioned whether Selden was writing history at all: 'A meere narration is a plaine relation, nothing else. History disputeth not pro or con, concludeth what should be, or not be: censureth not what was well done, or done amisse: but proposeth accidents and occurrences as they fall out: examples and precedents unto posterity.'[15]

Antiquarians like Selden and William Camden faced forged docu-

7 Gilbert Burnet, *Reflections on Mr. Varillas's History* (Amsterdam, 1686; B5852), 16.

8 *HC*[1] i, b; Clarendon, *History*, i. 1.

9 Richard Atkyns, *The Original and Growth of Printing: Collected out of History, and the Records of this Kingdome* (?1660; 1664; A4195), 3.

10 Whitelocke; BL: Add. MS 37343, ff. 251^{v}–252.

11 D. R. Woolf, *The Idea of History in Early Stuart England: Erudition, Ideology, and 'The Light of Truth' from the Accession of James I to the Civil War* (Toronto, 1990); Antonia Gransden, *Historical Writing in England*, vol. ii: *C. 1307 to the Early Sixteenth Century* (1982), esp. 454–79.

12 Sir Walter Raleigh, *The History of the World* (1614; *STC* 20637), sig. E4.

13 Woolf, *Idea of History*, 3–44, 243–65; Tuck, *Philosophy and Government*, 65–119; Bradford, 'Stuart Absolutism and the "Utility" of Tacitus'; David Womersley, 'Sir Henry Savile's Translation of Tacitus and the Political Interpretation of Elizabethan Texts', *Review of English Studies*[2], 42 (1991), 313–42.

14 Gransden, *English Historical Writing*, ii. 430–43.

15 Qu. Woolf, *Idea of History*, 233. There was also the case of Isaac Dorislaus, for which I have insufficient space; Kevin Sharpe, 'The Foundation of the Chairs of History at Oxford and Cambridge: An Episode in Jacobean Politics', in *Politics and Ideas*, 207–30.

ments and were sceptical.[16] The dilemma was different for civil war historians: their documents were not inauthentic but polemical, the very information they offered was not extricable from their committedness. Paper bullets led to the war, and for decades after the Restoration, the civil war was fought over and over again in all genres of writing. Historians turned to the classics for assistance, but the tens of thousands of pamphlets published in England between 1640 and 1660 were unknown to Polybius, Tacitus, Sallust, Herodotus, Pliny, and Livy, who could offer no assistance on the troublesomeness of the newsbook. Autolycus and his Pasquils were never as pervasive. *Pharsalia* was a fine means of exposition for a republican interpreting or commenting on the events of 1637–42, but it would not serve as a model for correct historical investigation. From the epistemological ravages of pamphlet wars the ancients had been felicitously sheltered. The moderns faced the danger of becoming Quixotes, jousting with the windmills of postlapsarian testimony.

Rushworth claimed that the speeches in his account of proceedings in parliament offered 'not onely great wit and wisdom, but choice Eloquence, and excellent Orators, *Diggs, Wentworth, Phillips, Elliot, Glanvile,* and others not much inferiour to the Roman *Demagogue*'.[17] In both classical and British histories fictional speeches had conventionally been introduced to invoke the eloquence of the protagonists. Yet a sceptical approach, combined with the fact that many of the speakers were still alive, made this impermissible.[18] Rushworth complained of speeches which were never spoken, not fictional but inaccurate and deceptive; the authority of the spoken voice had disappeared and been replaced by the unreliability of printed texts. Yet John Nalson accused Rushworth of concealing the prejudice of Edward Coke in a speech from the 1628 parliament, quoting Francis Bacon on Coke's character to confirm the point.[19] Although Bacon lived in a time when, according to Nalson, Presbyterians, papists, and anabaptists were plotting to overthrow the Church of England,[20] it was before sedition had become general, before the creation of a mass industry which laboured artfully to calumniate and libel the king and his faithful. Bacon was beyond

[16] Woolf, *Idea of History*, 116–24, 200–42; David Sandler Berkowitz, *John Selden's Formative Years: Politics and Society in Early Seventeenth-Century England* (1988); Sharpe, *Sir Robert Cotton*, 17–47.

[17] *HC*[1] i, b3[v].

[18] See Richard H. Popkin, *The History of Scepticism from Erasmus to Descartes* (Assen, 1960). Though modelling himself on Polybius and Tacitus, Camden eschewed fictional speeches in his *Annales*.

[19] Nalson, *Impartial Collection*, i, pp. xxvi–xxvii.

[20] Agreeing with William Dugdale, *A Short View of the Late Troubles in England* (Oxford, 1681; D2492).

impeachment; not so Rushworth's sources.[21] The problem was much more complicated than the metaphor of Babel allows. For historians of the civil war there were no universally agreed stamps of authenticity and authority; even the king's Great Seal had been multiplied. The raucous catcalls of the textual marketplace, silently fired from the presses, hardly seemed points of origin for permanent, didactic truths.

By the time anyone settled down to write the history of the civil war the newsbook had become a dominant literary form and had infected the whole kingdom of poetry and prose. Thomas Edwards saw himself not as a representative of a prevailing orthodoxy, but as a victim, preaching from the peripheries in an age of darkness:

> These Errors, Heresies, Blasphemies, are not onely vented in a corner, in secret close chambers, with doors double locked, among two or three, that few or none heare or know of them, or in some private village and remote dark corner of this Kingdom, that a man must dig through a wall to see and hear them . . . but in Houses that stand open for all, where many hundreds come and in the Metrapolis of the Kingdom, *London*, and that in the heart of the City; so that they are not preached with us in the ear, but on the house-top, we declare our errours, as *Sodom*, and are not ashamed: yea, abominable errours are Printed, the Books sold up and down in *Westminster-Hall*, *London*, and dispersed in all places; yea, given into the hands of Parliament men in *Westminster-Hall*, and daring at the Parliament doors, to disperse Books written in the defence of such and such errours.[22]

By a twisted development the advocate of truth was forced to spend much ink outlining heresy and perniciousness. Historians had a new role as venders of falsehood. Accordingly Edwards vindicated himself from the possible charge of being a Ham out to uncover his fatherland's nakedness, on the grounds that it had been purveyed around the corners of the land in the form of cheap pornography.[23]

John Hall and the Crisis of Eloquence

The republican John Hall was sensitive to the problems of print. In 1645 he grumbled, following Bacon as usual, that the times gave birth to few impressive history works: "Tis lamentable wee in such a fruitfull age of Books & haruest of historians should haue so few good ones; eyther they swell into monstrous volumes, able to weary the eye in reading, hand in turning, memory in receauing, & most commonly

[21] Nalson, *Impartial Collection*, i, pp. vii–xxxvi. Bacon and Coke, however, had been rival suitors for both the Attorney-Generalship and the hand of Lady Elizabeth Hatton.

[22] Edwards, *Gangræna*, 148–9.

[23] May rejected Statius' injunction to silence in a comparable instance; *History*, i. 15.

fraught wth Impertinent & lying Legends.'[24] Hall's early historiographical tract, 'A Method of History', like Deggory Whear's *De ratione & methodo legendi historias dissertatio*, was an outline of an education in history, mainly devoted to discussing a classical canon.[25] He did not wish to trip on the heels of time, and politicly avoided a history covering the post-Elizabethan period. Hall's circumspection might have been a concession to the addressee of the treatise, probably Thomas Stanley, to whom he dedicated his 1646 *Poems*.[26] These showed a greater interest in self-presentation than in writing for a cause, and in 1645 his credentials as a republican were ambiguous. He recommended a variety of authors, including Gaius Velleius Paterculus, who was frowned on by Tacitists for his deceptive, florid prose.[27] In his 1655 preface to Drummond's *The History of Scotland* Hall even admired the use of fictional speeches, '*since* Livys *time . . . never accounted Crime in an* Historian'.[28] He none the less insisted on the importance of 'Politick Observacons' in History.[29] His friend John Davies of Kidwelly claimed that Hall's principles were already 'anti-monarchicall' even at this early stage, and Hall's appeal to classical precedent gave authority to the parliament's cause.[30] For Hobbes, Hall was one of the young University men who had been seduced by the eloquence of the Greeks and Romans.[31]

Hall's translation of Longinus, *Peri hypsous Or Dionysius Longinus of the Height of Eloquence* (1652), sought to establish a language for heroic republicanism. He summed up a challenge made to the power of the voice, describing a change from the structure of political decision-making to be found in ancient Greece:

[24] John Hall, 'A Method of History', Bod.: MS Rawl. D.152, f. 14^v^. Cf. Bacon, *Advancement of Learning*, 73.

[25] The proposals for a history syllabus in Hall's *An Humble Motion to the Parliament of England Concerning the Advancement of Learning* (1650; H250) corresponded with 'A Method of History'. Whear, *De ratione & methodo legendi historias dissertatio* (1623; *STC* 25325), reprinted in 1625 and 1637.

[26] Reprinted in *Minor Poets of the Caroline Period*, ed. George Saintsbury, 3 vols. (Oxford, 1905–21), ii. 175–225.

[27] See Woolf, *Idea of History*, 142; and Bradford, 'Stuart Absolutism and the "Utility" of Tacitus'.

[28] Hall's preface to William Drummond, *The History of Scotland* (1655; D2196), sigs. [A2–A2^v^].

[29] Hall, 'Method of History', ff. 4^v^, 5.

[30] Hall, *Hierocles*, sig. b3^v^; on Hall see John W. Pendleton, 'The Prose Works of John Hall of Durham', B.Litt. thesis (Oxford, 1934); John Burnham Shaw, 'The Life and Works of John Hall of Durham', Johns Hopkins University Ph.D. thesis (Baltimore, 1952); Melvin Hill, 'The Poetry of John Hall (1627–1656)', Columbia University Ph.D. thesis (New York, 1963/4).

[31] *AO* ii. 457–60.

> *In* Senates *and* Harangues *to the people length was necessary, for the same men acted both parts, (and that in a single Citie) & that which was necessary to gain the people, degenerated in time to be in fashion in counsel, so that this was play'd for a* prize, *and was held so far unnecessary, that as if the best Masters had not been enough, it was the care of parents themselves to instruct their children, who seeing it the readiest way of advancement, were not like to be wanting in emulation and indeavour, whereas now the* Scene *is changed, and (in Civil matters) we are to speak to the* few *and not the* many: *For as the corruption of time hath diseas'd most Governments into* Monarchies, *so the least of these few populacies now in being, is too great to be included in the same walls, or brought to the hearing of one voice (long studied Orations being become uselesse) and therefore as men now endeavour to summe up their Notions, and draw them into a sharp angle, expecting reason should overcome, so in the management and conueiance of that reason, there must be needfull so many artifices, charms, masteries, and such subtle conducts, that without them a man cannot so well obtain his end, and a man of skill that brings not so much force of reason may easily avoid them.*[32]

Hall's realpolitik is insightful. A change in the state means that eloquence is now transmitted via a disembodied medium, and length and reason in eloquence have both been sacrificed to brief and effective, perhaps machiavellian, persuasion. His phrase for the structure of communication, the moment in which political motions are decided, is 'the *Crisis* of eloquence'.[33]

Hall's perception of this altered crisis of eloquence was filtered through his experience as a writer of newsbooks and pamphlets. He enjoined those who studied history to 'Bee not a stranger at home', and he was not.[34] Eloquence was 'A way of speech prevailing over those whom we designe it prevail'; its meridian required an understanding not only of one's own passions but of science, prudences, and history.[35] This crisis of eloquence will serve as a model for the crisis which faced historians upon the appearance of the weekly newsbook.

Some, like Hall, recognized the change enforced when the classical oration was replaced by the textual Billingsgate, the booksellers' Tower of Babel. No one wrote a historical sociology of the newsbook, but some allowed that paper bullets intervened in history. Rushworth reprinted from *Aulicus* a lengthy account of the second Battle of Newbury, acknowledging his source. This followed a number of more trustworthy reports, drawing attention to the amusing excesses and evasions of the newsbook version, which turned the ambiguous military encounter into

[32] *Peri hypsous Or Dionysius Longinus of the Height of Eloquence* (1652; L2999), sigs. A7v–B; on this see David Norbrook, 'Marvell's "Horatian Ode" and the Politics of Genre', in Thomas Healy and Jonathan Sawday, eds., *Literature and the English Civil War* (Cambridge, 1990), 155–8; Patterson, *Reading between the Lines*, 256–72.

[33] *Peri hypsous*, sig. A7v.

[34] Hall, 'Method of History', f. 16v.

[35] *Peri hypsous*, sig. Bv.

an unqualified triumph. This re-presentation, in the disingenuous guise of a presentation of a different point of view, was a representation of the extremities of royalist propaganda in 1644.[36]

It was possible for historians to avoid cheap print altogether, but most historians felt reluctance, not revulsion. If, as Cleveland put it, newsbooks were 'the Embrio of History slinckt before Maturity',[37] then newsbooks were history in an embryonic fashion, and consequently could be cultivated into more mature studies by the intervention of a careful historian.

Pennyworths of history

Criticisms of newsbooks, which, like newsbooks themselves, were often very repetitive, focused on six more or less equally important attributes: first, the inferior typography and diminutive stature of newsbooks; secondly, the grand untruths they told; thirdly, the greed of their writers, printers, and publishers; fourthly, the vulgarity of their readers, who were accordingly prone to believing the lies they read (which, in the case of provincial readers, was only to furnish them material with which to gossip with the local vicar on Sundays); fifthly, the disruptive effect they had not only on relations between the king and parliament, but on society in general (they were said to have done more damage than the armies of Essex and Fairfax);[38] and lastly, their poor literary qualities.

One consequence of the fact that newsbooks were small and inverted all known truths and social decencies was that they were not history. Any reader of mid-seventeenth-century pamphlets probably would have known this. History was serious, substantial, and, above all, true. Newsbooks were not. Cleveland elaborated an interesting antithesis between newsbooks and history:

A *Diurnall* is a puny Chronicle, scarce pin feather'd with the wings of time: It is an History in *Sippets*; the English *Iliads* in a Nut-shell; the *Apocryphal* Parliaments book of *Maccabees* in single sheets. It would tyre a Welch pedigree, to reckon how many aps 'tis remov'd from an Annal . . . the *Quixotes* of this Age

[36] *HC*³ ii. 723–9. See also Gardiner², ii. 48–58. Gardiner avoids mentioning *Aulicus*, fulfilling Rushworth's intentions. Rushworth made a much less weighted juxtaposition of the Battle of Edgehill, 'where the Victory being Challeng'd by either Party, and very differently related, I shall, to avoid the imputation of Partiality, give you the Narratives thereof, as they were then publisht on either side by Authority'. *HC*³ ii. 33. He may have alluded to *Aulicus* when he noted that when John Pym died, 'it was reported by some'; *HC*³ ii. 376. He also mentioned *Aulicus* and Berkenhead in a case of mistaken identity during Laud's trial, *HC*³ ii. 832.

[37] Cleveland, *Character of a Diurnal-Maker*, 3.

[38] *A Fresh Whip*, 6.

fight with the Windmills of their owne Heads; quell Monsters of their owne Creation; make Plots, and then discover them.[39]

Rushworth used this same image of jousting with windmills to describe the effect of the pamphlet wars on the historian's grasp of truth. In a later pamphlet Cleveland fiercely denied the role of the newsbook in the composition of history while at the same time admitting that there was a microscopic resemblance between the two. A newsbook was 'the Embrio of History'; to call a newsbook-writer a historian

is to Knight a Man-drake; 'tis to view him through a Perspective, and by that glass *Hyperbole*, to give the reputation of an Ingineer to a Maker of Mouse-traps: Such an Historian would hardly pass Muster with a Scotch Stationer, in a sieve full of Ballads and Almanacks . . . The most crampt Compendium that the Age hath seen, since all Learning was torne into ends, out-strips him by the head . . . When those weekly Fragments shall pass for History, let the Poor mans box be entitled an Exchequer, and the Alms-Basket a Magazine . . . A Marginal Note of *William Prins*, would serve for a winding-sheet.[40]

A writer of diurnals was 'the Antimask of an Historian', creating an inverted world of disorder and chaos which turned topsy-turvy the serious values of proper history. 'The word Historian,' wrote Cleveland,

imports a sage and solemn Author, one that curles his brow with a sullen Gravity, like a bull-neck'd Presbyter, since the Army got him off his jurisdiction, who Presbyter like, sweeps his brest with a reverend beard, full of native moss-Troopers; not such a squealing Scribe as this that is troubled with the Rickets, and makes penny-worths of History.[41]

While Cleveland had little positive to say about the historian, the newsbook writer was worse: whereas the historian produced only a partial image of reality, the newsbook writer produced a perverted distortion of that image.

Of course size was not everything. Popular brief histories, or 'marrows', included the Roman history of Florus, and Heath's *Brief Chronicle of the Late Intestine War*, which was described as 'the English Iliads in a nut-shel, being comprized in such an Epitomy and Abridgement; yet with so much perspecuity, faithfulness and truth, as would be allowance enough for a reasonable volumn'.[42] Another royalist, George Wharton, thought this a good analogy, and called his abbreviated history *Eng-*

[39] Cleveland, *Character of a London Diurnall*, 1, 3; Cleveland alluded to 'Maccabees' and Don Quixote in 'Smectymnuus, or the Club-Divines', ll. 14, 19. *The Poems of John Cleveland*, eds. B. Morris and E. Wittington (Oxford, 1967), 23.

[40] Cleveland, *Character of a Diurnal-Maker*, 2.

[41] Cleveland, *Character of a Diurnal-Maker*, 6, 5.

[42] *Brief Chronicle of all the Chief Actions so fatally Falling out in these three Kingdoms* (1662; H1318).

land's Iliads in a Nut-Shell.[43] Likewise Bruno Ryves appended to the 1647 single-volume collection of his *Mercurius Rusticus* a similar summary entitled *Micro-Chronicon.*[44] An advertisement for *The Historians Guide: Or, Englands Remembrancer* (1679) suggested that a brief amalgamation of diverse sources could be accurate: 'Altho you have but a little Book, yet you have a great deal of Truth and History, it being the fruit of many mens Labour.'[45] Despite concessions to brevity, the prejudices against newsbooks remained vociferous.

Samuel Sheppard agreed with Cleveland that there could be no beneficial relationship between newsbooks and history. In *Mercurius Mastix*, perhaps aware that Rushworth, Thomason, and William Clarke were collecting newsbooks and pamphlets, Sheppard wrote:

> I cannot chuse but wonder at the wisdom of those who preserve these notorious untruths, and put them all upon a File, as if they meant to extract a Chronicle out of them, or convince any that should gainsay them, by a testimony in Print; which is no doubt, as authentick as *Lucian's* true Histories or our modern Legend of Captain *Jones.*[46]

Captain Jones was an interesting analogue for a newsbook. David Lloyd's popular poem narrating the adventures of the Welsh Elizabethan hero and his cowardly sidekick Reymond went through several editions after its original publication in 1631. Each new edition adjusted it to fit the times. Marvell referred to the legend as a model for the distorting of history.[47] The 1648 edition recommended itself to the heroes of Newbury and Edgehill, suggesting that they might want to avoid the excesses of Jones and his self-aggrandizing inventiveness. The second part of the 1648 edition began:

> Will nothing please the taste of these rough times
> But rue and wormwood stuf't in prose or rimes?
> No verse to make our poets Laureate
> But smart Iambicks lashing King or State?
> Must all turne Mercuries, these times to fit
> By poisoning fame with their quick-silver wit?

[43] (Oxford, 1645; Wing W1544). Wood, in Bod.: Wood 207, ascribes the pamphlet to Wharton.

[44] Ryves, *Mercurius Rusticus*, and *Micro-Chronicon: Or, A briefe Chronology* (Oxford, 1647; R2447 and R2451).

[45] 1679; Wing H2094B, sig. A2v; originally published in 1676, H2094A. This was another plain-style history, merely listing events.

[46] *Mastix* 1, 3–4. Sheppard unconventionally attributes original and prime blame to the newsbook writer, who exploits the printer or stationer, who exploits the hawker, who in turn exploits everyone.

[47] Marvell, *Rehearsal Transpros'd*, 12.

> That name that's got by some notorious ill,
> And merits Gives, is hatefull to our quill.[48]

The Legend is a mock-heroic poem, beginning with an echo of Virgil, replete with indecorous rhymes and images, a precursor to Butler's *Hudibras.* Sheppard's allusion is particularly curious because Jones and his crew survive the perils of a terrible desert called 'Asdriasdust', which was Thomas Carlyle's epithet for Rushworth and for civil war newsbooks and pamphlets in general.[49]

The fact that Jones tells lies is fundamental to the genre. The mock-heroic is a critical debasement of the heroic; the genre lies and exaggerates as pathologically as Jones himself. It would be pointless trying to reconstruct historical truth from it, because it is by definition an attack on serious truth. As Jones's epitaph declares:

> *Tread softly (mortals) ore the bones*
> *Of the worlds wonder Captaine* Jones:
> *Who told his glorious deeds to many,*
> *But never was believ'd of any:*
> *Posterity let this suffice,*
> *He swore all's true, yet here he lyes.*[50]

In a similar vein *Anti-Pragmaticus* attacked Nedham's *Pragmaticus* for imitating *Aulicus* in retelling 'light skirmishes and triviall Victories, in as high Language as Homer the Acts of Achilles'.[51] Not only historical truth but the elevated language and hexameters of heroic epic were debarred to the newsbook. The premiss that newsbooks were a debased, delusive genre was not exclusively royalist. George Wither, making his preliminary excuses in his first and only newsbook, remarked that 'all Mercuries having the Planet *Mercurie* predominant at their Nativities, cannot but retaine a twang of Lying', and that his 'Cousin-Mercuries' vended only 'down-right Lies'.[52]

These few examples are representative of many. The point is that while their critics recognized that newsbooks in some way pertained to history in a microscopic, embryonic, synoptic fashion, there remained a consensus that the contents of newsbooks were either pure fabrications, or so depraved that they could not be safely used by any conscientious historian. At the most fundamental, indivisible, atomic level they were corrupt and distorted. The use of newsbooks in writing a history was synonymous with laziness, unoriginality, and fictitiousness.

[48] David Lloyd, *The Legend of Captaine Iones: Continued From his first part to his end* [the second part] (1648; L2630), 1.

[49] Carlyle, ed., *Cromwell's Letters and Speeches,* i. 1–10.

[50] Lloyd, *Legend of Captain Jones,* sig. F4.

[51] *Anti-Pragmaticus* 1, 19 Oct. 1647, '5', 270.01/E411(10).

[52] Wither, *Mercurius Rusticus,* 1.

This would seem to make the issue clear. If you were a historian you used other, respectable printed texts, preferably manuscripts, perhaps personal experience, or nothing. End of issue: consign newsbooks to the privy or to wrapping fish.

Newsbooks into history: Sprigge, Heath, Dugdale, and so on

The practice was considerably different from the theory. It is, as ever, necessary to hear the polemic in these assaults. The accusations which equate newsbooks with fiction and romance should not be read literally. Despite their reputation, many authors did use newsbooks for non-scatological purposes, including the writing of histories of the civil wars. As historians commented in their prefaces, time could be the mother of falsehood as well as of truth,[53] and even for those who were in the right place at the right time, in so far as this was possible, and who remembered their personal experience of events, other evidence was required for the sake of accuracy, if only in order to corroborate dates. In the absence of widely available and accepted sources of historical truth this could result in a compromise of the rhetoric of scepticism. Between 1649 and 1701 many histories of the civil war were published. They flourished in the early 1680s, when the Popish Plot was interpreted through the experiences of 1637–42, and seen by some as a repetition of the events which led to the war.[54] These volumes were followed by a spate of memoirs of leading figures during the war years, published in the 1690s, by, amongst others, the Calves-head fraternity, a group of republicans hoping to influence a new political climate.[55] These historians turned to newsbooks in order to inform their accounts of the past.

This is unsurprising. The dichotomy between fair speech and reality arises from the political polemics which both obfuscated and revealed the social function of newsbooks. If Nedham was right in arguing that *Interest will not Lie* (1659), then the disparity between words and practice reveals the political importance, to some writers, of suppressing the sociological reality of newsbooks.[56] The same can be inferred from the unforgiving criticisms levelled at the use of newsbooks in writing

[53] Raleigh, *History of the World* (1614), sig. E4; [James Heath], *A Brief Chronicle Of the Late Intestine War In The Three Kingdoms* (1663; H1319), sig. [A6]; Nalson, *Impartial Collection*, i. 1; Shirley, biographical preface to Raleigh, *History of the World* (1665; R164), 1.

[54] Scott, *Algernon Sidney and the Restoration Crisis, 1677–1683*.

[55] See Worden's introduction to Ludlow, *Voyce from the Watch Tower*, 17–31.

[56] Marchamont Nedham, *Interest will not Lie* (1659; N392). On the language of the new, Tacitist humanism, see Tuck, *Philosophy and Government*, 222–3; and Gunn, *Politics and the Public Interest*.

histories. What is really at stake is the public availability of newsbooks. Newsbooks were the troubled conscience of historiography, its first draft; without news there can be very little history.

Joshua Sprigge, a chaplain in the New Model Army and its historian, thought that the best kind of History was pure Truth, a story not '*adorned* with such *Artificial* stuffe of *feigned* speeches, *Prosopepeia's*, and *Epistrophe's, &c.*'[57] In the dedication of his *Anglia Rediviva* (1647) to William Lenthal, Sprigge excused himself and his work by clearly differentiating between the falsehoods purveyed by language and the truth implicit in a candid account of actions which are themselves a representation of the will of God; 'what is wanting in it of *Elegancie* of Phrase, hath been endeavoured to be supplied in the *truth* of the Relation: And next to that, a good proportion of my care hath been to carry it without *distastefull reflection* . . . you will easily discern a thread of *Divinity*.'[58] The rejection of distasteful reflections anticipated Rushworth's practice. The critique of artificial language was not uncommon. Thomas May likewise expressed a dedication to the Rule of Truth, repudiating those who have 'dressed Truth in such improper Vestments, as if they brought her forth to act the same part that falshood would; and taught her by Rhetoricall disguises, partiall concealements; and invective expressions, instead of informing, to seduce a Reader, and carry the judgement of Posterity after that Byas which themselves have made'.[59] In spite of his commitment to truths expressed in plain language, and though he had been an eye-witness to many of the events described, Sprigge, like May, relied heavily on newsbooks. C. H. Firth commended *Anglia Rediviva* but added in qualification that it was 'throughout based on the pamphlets and newspapers of the period, and contains very little information which can be regarded as embodying the author's own recollections'.[60]

One of the most popular Restoration histories of the civil war was James Heath's *A Brief Chronicle of all the Chief Actions so fatally Falling out in these three Kingdoms*, first published in 1662, then reprinted in a greatly enlarged edition the next year as *A Brief Chronicle Of the Late Intestine War In The Three Kingdoms*. Though Heath died in 1664, further extended editions were published, as *Englands Chronicle*, in 1689, 1691, and 1699.[61] The title 'Chronicle' was carefully chosen, Heath wrote, 'which name it onely pretends to, as a Journal or Day Book of time'.[62] To

57 Sprigge, *Anglia Rediviva*, sig. *B3. 58 Sprigge, *Anglia Rediviva*, sig. A3v.

59 May, *History*, sigs. A3–A3v.

60 *DNB*. Wood dismissed the work in his customary way. He also mentioned a rumour that Nathaniel Fiennes had a large hand in its construction. Like Wood, I have been unable to verify this rumour. *AO* iv. 136.

61 Wing H1318–1326A. 62 *Brief Chronicle* (1663), preface, sig. [A7].

this purpose newsbooks were germane. Heath did not acknowledge the newsbooks he used, which lie underneath the surface of his text. Even those passages most closely derived from periodicals are smothered with a thick layer of royalist rhetoric. The plain narration of some 1640s newsbooks was not commensurate with a 'modest and plain meaning History' in 1662 or 1663, and there was, despite the familiar adage in the preface, little chance of Heath tripping on the heels of time.[63] The passages most closely derived from newsbooks were immediately prior to the Restoration, when the original texts expressed views broadly close to Heath's own.[64] Despite their political differences, some passages were based on May's narrative.[65] Wood, though a general misanthrope, had no particular grudge against Heath, but noted he 'wanted a head for a Chronologer', and relied on 'news-books', thus perpetuating their errors. He also scornfully noted that John Phillips's 1676 continuation of Heath was 'mostly made up from *Gazetts*'. The criticisms were not entirely without foundation.[66]

In the preface to his *Short View of the Late Troubles* (1681), William Dugdale admitted in an exceptionally casual fashion that 'What falleth within my own cognisance, I deliver with mine own words: what is beyond my knowledge, in the words of Authors; most of which I have quoted; the rest being taken from the common Mercuries, and other public licensed Narratives of the chiefest occurrences in those times.'[67] Throughout the margins of his work Dugdale referenced numerous newsbooks by name. The specification of licensed newsbooks was an unusual qualification; though it emphasized that Dugdale did not use the most scurrilous newsbooks, it occluded his enmity to those who had the power to license in the 1640s. In truth his claim that all of his sources were licensed was an exaggeration. Dugdale did not admit authorship of his history, and Thomas Dixon privately speculated that this was because he 'displays the Presbyterians to the life', a sensitive issue in 1681.[68] Dugdale had not originally intended to publish his book, and may have been persuaded to by the events surrounding the Popish Plot.[69] Like Nalson and others he connected the origins of the

[63] *Brief Chronicle* (1663), sig. [A6].

[64] *Brief Chronicle* (1662), 64–5; *MTN*, ch. 10. Also particularly evident in the account of the trial of the king.

[65] e.g. *Brief Chronicle* (1662), 9–10.

[66] *AO* iii. 664. Here Wood does not consider putting England's Iliads in a nutshell to be a historiographical heresy—provided the names and dates were right.

[67] Dugdale, *Short View*, following sig. A2^{v}. Note the opposition between newsbooks and authored texts.

[68] Letter from Dixon to D[aniel]. F[leming]., 16 Mar. 1681; *HMC: Twelfth Report . . . The Manuscripts of S. H. Le Fleming* (HMSO, 1890), 180.

[69] Royce MacGillivray, *Restoration Historians and the English Civil War* (The Hague, 1974), 55.

war with the infestation of the kingdoms by a 'viperous brood', in part denoting a plague of German anabaptists.[70] This had been a common theme at least since the publication in 1642 of a volume entitled *A Short History of the Anabaptists of High and Low Germany*.[71] Wood's biography of Dugdale expressed resentment for the way he had padded out his text, and 'made the book a folio, which otherwise might have been made an ordinary quarto'.[72] Wood did not make specific complaints about Dugdale's sources (which included the royalist bogy Rushworth), but implied that folio format was an unwarranted aspiration for newsbooks. Wood was particular about historical method: he also criticized William Sanderson (for whom James Heath wrote an elegy[73]) for using newsbooks in his *A Compleat History of the Life and Raigne of King Charles*, published in 1658. This was in spite of the fact that Sanderson could claim to be '*an* Eye *and* Ear *witness*' to the events at court.[74]

John Vicars was further prey for Wood. His *Magnalia Dei Anglicana. Or, Englands Parliamentary-Chronicle* was published in four parts between 1642 and 1646, with titles indicating the providential underpinnings of the narrative.[75] Vicars said his method had been to 'set down and insert nothing, but what I partly knew, and partly, on most probable Conjectures conceived, and with my utmost industry and endeavour diligently enquired after and found to be really true and authentick'.[76] This was a written history, not just a brief, compiled chronology; and despite Vicars's warning about his sources he resorted to newsbooks. They were detailed, easily available, and contained documents which *Magnalia Dei Anglicana* represented. Sometimes newsbooks assisted not only as a source for names and dates: the graphic story of Prince Rupert's siege of the house of one Mr Purefrey (or Purefoy), in which a handful of men held off a royalist troop while the women of the household melted down pewter to make more bullets, was taken directly from *Speciall Passages and certain Informations*.[77]

70 *Short View*, sig. A2; see also 1–9.

71 (1642; S3597); this had an allegorical relevance. The anonymous reader of the Bodleian copy (Pamph D.53(5)) underlined some of the key actions, beliefs, and dangers of the anabaptists which were probably perceived to relate to the present.

72 *Fasti Oxonienses*, ed. Philip Bliss, 3rd edn. (1815), ii. 27.

73 *An Elegy On the Much lamented Death of Dr Sanderson* (1662), not in Wing.

74 The phrase is from James Howell's address to Sanderson, in Sanderson's *A Compleat History of the Life and Raigne of King Charles From His Cradle to his Grave* (1658; S646), sig. A2; MacGillivray, *Restoration Historians*, 11–12.

75 John Vicars, *The Burning-bush not Consumed* (1641[2]; V295); *God in the Mount. Or, Englands Remembrancer* (1641[2]; V307); *Jehovah-Jireh. God in the Mount. Or Englands Parliamentarie-Chronicle* (1644; V313); *Gods Arke Overtopping the Worlds Waves* (1646; V309); *Magnalia Dei Anglicana* (1646; V319). See also Vicars, *A Summarie, or Short Survey of the Annalls* (1646; V330); *A Sight of ye Transactions* (1646; V327); *All the memorable and wonder-strikinge Parliamentary Mercies* (1642; A944/E116(49)).

76 *Jehovah-Jireh*, sig. A4.

77 *Special Passages* 4, 6 Sept. 1642, 605.04/E115(21); *MTN* 87–8.

Wood recorded that Vicars 'did affright many of the weaker sort and others from having any agreement with the king's party, by continually inculcating into their heads strange stories of God's wrath against the cavaliers'. Newsbooks promoted a similar providentialism. According to Wood, Vicars 'was esteemed by some, especially the puritannical party (of which number he was a zealous brother) a tolerable poet, but by the royalists not, because *he was inspired with ale or viler liquours*'.[78] The accusation of fictitiousness combined with drunkenness was paralleled in two other parliamentary historians: May and Rushworth.

Decades earlier Sir Philip Sidney had written that the historian was 'laden with mouse-eaten records' and was 'better acquainted with a thousand years ago than with the present age'.[79] As historians increasingly emphasized the importance of historical documentation, its grounds were being populated by many eloquent and disembodied texts, themselves part of the turmoil. Historians were not meant to use newsbooks, but they did; to chronicles and annals alike, as Sprigge, Dugdale, Heath, Sanderson, Vicars, and others recognized, newsbooks were extremely useful. They even insinuated their way into memoirs. Sir Philip Warwick resisted the temptation, preferring to stick with 'a fraile memory and some old ill-digested notes', as a consequence of which the times and places of his narration, he admitted, 'shall not be exact'.[80] So much for the reliable, unpublished testimony of eye-witnesses.

Facing up to the facts: Thomas May

The historiographical crisis facing writers of the 1640s who were forced to contend with pamphlet wars and weekly pennyworths of history was dramatized in miniature in the career of Thomas May. May had displayed his poetic and historical skills in translating Lucan's *Pharsalia* and subsequently writing a continuation of the same. In July 1642 he deployed many precedents in a historico-political argument that parliaments had always been beneficial to princes and to peoples.[81] He also wrote poems on the reigns of Edward III and Henry II (1635 and 1638). In mature years, having sided with the Commonwealth, he became an apologist for and then historian of the Long Parliament. After his

[78] *AO* iii. 308–12.

[79] 'A Defence of Poetry', in *Miscellaneous Prose of Sir Philip Sidney*, ed. Katherine Duncan-Jones and Jan Van Dorsten (Oxford, 1973), 83.

[80] Warwick, *Memoires*, 207. See e.g. his confused narration of the Hothams' execution, 209, and compare with *MTN* 299–303. R. B. Wernham, 'The Public Records in the Sixteenth and Seventeenth Centuries', in Levi Fox, ed., *English Historical Scholarship in the Sixteenth and Seventeenth Centuries* (1956), 11–30; Woolf, *Idea of History*, 1–36.

[81] May, *A Discovrse Concerning the Svccesse of Former Parliaments* (1642; M1404).

death, according to Marvell, in the most used and least reliable source for May's life, Ben Jonson dispelled him from Elysium with these words:

> Far from these blessed shades tread back agen
> Most servil' wit, and Mercenary Pen.
> *Polydore, Lucan, Allan, Vandale, Goth,*
> Malignant Poet and Historian both,
> Go seek the novice Statesmen, and obtrude
> On them some Romane cast similitude.[82]

The accusation of greed was merely formulaic, a conventional piece of propaganda against a parliamentarian propagandist, like the accusation of insobriety. The allusion to classical analogues involved a more original perspective on May's methodology.

In the dedicatory epistle to his translation of *Pharsalia* (1627), May remarked that 'the History of it, is the greatest of Histories, the affairs of *Rome*, whose transcendent greatness will admit of no comparison with other *states* either before, or after it'.[83] Twenty years later, when he wrote his history of the Long Parliament, he proceeded to draw comparisons between this period, incomparable in greatness, and the present.

May began by reflecting on the sea-changes historiography had undergone, and looked back on a golden age before faction and dissent had made writing contentious. He characteristically cited a classical precedent for this:

> I cannot therefore be so stupid, as not at all to be sensible of the taske imposed on me, or the great envy which attends it; which other men who have written Histories, upon farre lesse occasion have discoursed of at large in their Prefaces. And *Tacitus* himselfe, complaining of those ill times which were the unhappy subject of his Annals, though he wrote not in the time of the same Princes, under whom those things were acted; yet because the families of many men, who had then been ignominious, were yet in being, could not but discourse how much happier those Writers were, who had taken more ancient and prosperous times for their Argument; such as he there expresses, in which the great and glorious actions of the old Romans, their honourable Atchievements, and exemplary Vertues are recorded.[84]

[82] Andrew Marvell, 'Tom May's Death', in *Poems and Letters of Andrew Marvell*, ed. H. M. Margoliouth, rev. Pierre Legois and E. E. Duncan Jones, 2 vols. (Oxford, 1971), i. 94–7, ll. 39–44. Cf. ll. 53–4: 'And who by *Romes* example *England* lay, | Those but to *Lucan* do continue *May*.' May cited Polydore Vergil in *A Discovrse*, 5. John M. Wallace was too busy defending Marvell to question the evaluation of May in these lines; *Destiny his Choice: The Loyalism of Andrew Marvell* (1968; Cambridge, 1980), 104. For a long-overdue reassessment of May see Norbrook, 'Lucan, Thomas May, and the Formation of a Republican Literary Culture'.

[83] May, *Lucan's Pharsalia: or The Civil-Warres of Rome* (1627; *STC* 16887), sigs. A2^{v}–A3. The first three of the ten books had been published in 1626 under the same title, *STC* 16886.

[84] May, *History*, i, sigs. A4–A4^{v}.

May nevertheless emphasized that the extent of this conflict was a modern problem. Later he commented that 'The fears and jealousies that now reigned', in December 1641, 'were of a sadder nature then the fears of any former times had been'.[85]

May professed to follow the single rule of truth, while also admitting that there were formal provisions required of him, because 'The use of History, and the just Rules for composure of it, have been so well and fully described heretofore by judicious Writers'.[86] Accordingly, in the first book of the *History,* he alluded to Tacitus, Seneca, and others, comparing events from their narratives with moments in recent British history. By doing this he introduced authority for the moral judgements he wished to pass. For instance, on the appropriateness of representing the sins and unhappiness of the times:

> The Heathen Historians do well instruct us in that point of piety; who never almost describe any Civill Warre, or publike affliction, without relating at the beginning, how vitious and corrupted their State was at that time grown; how faulty both the Rulers and People were, and how fit to be punished, either by themselves or others. Nor doe any of the Roman Poets undertake to write of that great and miserable Civill Warre, which destroyed the present State, and enslaved posterity; without first making a large enumeration of such causes; how wicked the manners of *Rome* were growne, how the chiefe Rulers were given to avarice and oppression, and the whole State drowned in luxury, lusts and riot, as you may see upon that subject in two the most elegant of them. And shall we Christians, who adore the true God, and live under the Gospell-light, not be sensible under so heavy a judgement of our owne offences.
>
> To begin with the faults of the higher powers, and their illegall oppression of the people, during these eight or nine yeers, in which Parliaments were denyed to *England*...[87]

It was perhaps inevitable that a classicist like May would call upon his predecessors in a period of opposition. During the personal rule the ancients were mouthpieces through which a silenced republicanism could be spoken; the 1640s largely relinquished the necessity for doublespeak, even for polite discourse. In this context May could make explicit comparisons between Lucan's Curio, Appianus' Sylla, and Sir Thomas Wentworth.[88]

[85] May, *History,* ii. 19. On the importance of Tacitus to 17th-cent. historiography, see Macdonald, 'Another Aspect of Seventeenth-Century Prose'. On the popularity of Tacitus see Peter Burke, 'A Survey of the Popularity of Ancient Historians', *History and Theory,* 5 (1966), 135–52.

[86] May, *History,* i, sig. A3.

[87] May, *History,* i. 15–16.

[88] May, *History,* i. 10, 95; cf. John Toland, ed., *Memoirs of Edmund Ludlow Esq.* (?London, 1698; L3460), i, p. iii; Frankland, *The Annals of King James and King Charles the First* (1681; F2078), preface; Clarendon, *History,* i. 95, 96, ii. 36, etc.

Like John Hall, May was sensitive to the need for a language of heroic republicanism. He perceived the usefulness of the classics in stating the parliament's case, and the Roman war of liberty against tyranny was never far from his mind.[89] The tripartite structure of *The History of the Parliament*, however, suggests that May found analogies problematic. The three books of the *History* have different atmospheres, and May's initial intention of saturating his history in precedent did not hold out for long. In the second book, which began with the meeting of the parliament on 3 November 1640, May faced up to the pamphlet war, from which he was obliged to draw his facts, and which was itself one of the historical facts he was obliged to describe. The atmosphere of fear and jealousy changed his method. Hall observed that some of the ancient authors' advice on the use of 'engines' had been 'Cashier'd by the use of Gunnes'.[90] May likewise found that paper bullets occluded classical precedent, and accordingly the ancients disappeared from the second book of his history.

This dramatizes one historiographical response to the rise of the newsbook and the repudiation of the oration which guided classical histories. Instead of the certainties of orations, the reader was required to deal with documents. The ideal behind an oration was a speech act with a known authorship, a reliable, because legitimately fictional, text, and an authorial presence. A document was either public or private, the former frequently a printed text or pamphlet with less authorial 'presence' than a manuscript. Pamphlets were speech acts with doubtful or collective authorship, questionable accuracy, seditious intent, and no vocal guarantee. In the new environment of proliferating documents, not only orations but classical allusions in general were overshadowed and replaced by free-floating texts which were the new atoms of a narrative. May was forced to incorporate the paper war of the early 1640s.

May was conscious of the significance of this necessity. Like Bulstrode Whitelocke, he observed how strange it was that the king, facing only 'such bootlesse opposition as Pen and Paper', managed to pursue his business until the whole kingdom was involved in a war. At the transitional point in his narrative May announced with much gravity, 'now the fatal time was come, when those long and tedious Paper-conflicts of Declarations, Petitions, and Proclamations, were turned into actual and bloody Wars, and the Pens seconded by drawn swords'.[91] May made the necessary compromises and reproduced the paper wars at the level of form in his own text. It is therefore fitting that he used newsbooks.

89 May, *History*, i. 30.

90 Hall, 'Method of History', f. 8v.

91 May, *History*, ii. 45, 96; cf. Whitelocke, 186, above.

Although certain phrases remained intact, May did not reproduce these sources unaltered, as Rushworth was later to do. He used newsbooks to construct a narrative of events, and, along with other cheap pamphlets, as a source for the petitions and declarations which he reproduced verbatim. May's sonorous prose required a considerable reworking of the dry style of early newsbooks. *Diurnall Occurrences in Parliament* described the king's entry into the House of Commons on 4 January 1642:

> Presently after this the King came to Westminster, guarded with two or three hundred Cavaleirs, which were that day feasted at Court, his Guard of yeomandry, Gent. Pencioners, his Serieants at Armes, and divers others.
>
> All of them placing a Court of Guard along Westminster Hall to the House of Commons doore, whilst his Maiestie went into the House.
>
> At which the House being much amazed to see his Maiesty, who had never before been at their House, and having no notice of his comming.
>
> His Maiesty placing himselfe in the Speakers Chayr, Told them he came to demand those men of them which he had sent for the day before; but none of them being there, hee told them he expected they should send them to him so soone as they returned thither; and so left the House and went back to White-Hall guarded as before.[92]

The event was reported in *Divrnall Occurrences: Or The Heads of Severall Proceedings* thus:

> About two of the clock his Majesty came into the House of Commons, and the Speaker rising out of his place, he sate therein, and demanding of his Prisoners Mr. *Pym*, &c. who were not there to be found hee made a short Speech, commanding the House to send them to him, so soone as they came, otherwise he would take them where he found them, and wished them to proceed in their affayres, without any feare of his concordancy with them to all their just requests or words to that effect.[93]

May reworked these and other basic sources into a more orthodox mode of historical narrative:

> The next day after that the King had thus answered the Petition of the House, being the fourth of *January* 1641 he gave unhappily a just occasion for all men to think that their fears and jealousies were not causelesse. For upon that day the King came to the Parliament in Person, attended with a great number of Gentlemen, Souldiers, and others armed with Swords and Pistols to the number of about three hundred, who came up to the very door of the House of Commons, and placed themselves there, and in all passages neer unto it: The King in Person entered the House of Commons, and demanded five Members of that House to be delivered to him.[94]

[92] *Diurnall Occurrences*, 10 Jan. 1641[2], 2–3, 97.2/E201(6); *MTN* 38–41.

[93] *Divrnall Occurrences*, 10 Jan. 1641[2], sig. A3, 181.106/E201(7).

[94] May, *History*, ii. 21.

May rationalized the detail of geography, carefully placing the soldiers outside Westminster, emphasizing the physical dangers they represented. He then underplayed some of the drama inside the House, not locating the Speaker's chair, removing the hubristic as well as the heroic elements of the king's action. This can be compared with the corresponding passage in *A Breviary of the History Of the Parliament of England* (1650), originally written in Latin to justify the regicide to a European audience, and 'for the generall good translated' into English.[95] The translation gives a greater sense of compression than its 1647 predecessor:

Three daies after the Proclamation against those Irish Rebels, being the fourth of *Ianuary*, the King, attended with about three hundred Armed Gentlemen, came to *Westminster*, and entring in Person into the House of Commons, and seating himself in the Speakers chair, demanded five Members of that House to be delivered to him, Mr. *Hollis*, Sir *Arthur Haslerig*, Mr. *Pim*, Mr. *Hamden*, and Mr. *Strode*.[96]

The number of men and the Speaker's chair are specified, the door omitted. The newsbooks provided a ragbag of detail which could selectively be used. May's rich prose worked against the corruption of newsbook style, but infection by sources was more difficult to overcome when reproducing the Grand Remonstrance or the 'heads' of any other document. The same was also true for May's account of the cruelties of the rebellious Irish. Lacking objective or privileged sources, he derived those stories from pamphlets and newsbooks, and inherited the anxious credulity of the latter.[97]

When May turned to the third part of his history, and narrated the progress of the gunpowder war from late 1642 onwards, the changed times were once again reflected in a change of style. It was no longer necessary to reproduce documents to the same extent, though pamphlets and newsbooks remained the dominant source. Classical citations reappeared, but curiously they no longer confirmed moral judgements passed upon individual protagonists; instead they positioned the veracity of sources. Dion Cassius was invoked as 'a Writer of as little bias, in the opinion of all Criticks, as any among the Antients'; and when May related the first Battle of Newbury, he was obliged, in the absence of alternatives, to present the narrative of a parliamentary colonel, justifying this by noting: 'since JULIUS CÆSAR is acknowledged to have written his owne Commentaries, not onely of the *Gallike* but Civill Warre, with so much cleare integrity, that his Enemies had nothing to blame in it.'[98] The third and last book concluded with this

[95] May, *Breviary of the History of Parliament* (1650; M1395), title-page.
[96] May, *Breviary*, 43–4.
[97] May, *History*, ii. 13–14.
[98] May, *History*, iii. 30, 108.

relation. The *Breviary*, on the other hand, ended with the petitions which demanded that the king should along with other offenders be brought to trial.[99]

What we find in May's *History* is therefore a critical recognition of the shifting basis of historiography in a culture where cheap print had to function as one of the historian's primary sources. The historian was obliged to reproduce documents which the reader had to interpret for him- or herself, and to reproduce the content of newsbooks in a more elevated language. The fallen speech of the newsbook had undermined the relative certainties of an earlier world.

Not facing up to the facts: Thomas Hobbes

During the late 1660s Thomas Hobbes, concerned with the question of religious toleration, wrote a history of the origins and progress of the civil war and Interregnum. It argued that the war was occasioned by Presbyterian clergy struggling to gain control over the people against the prerogative of the king.[100] The prime means by which the clergy sought to dominate the people was speech. Hobbes was nervous about the power of eloquence, and attacked it as a form of passion which distorted the meaning of words.[101] He did not concede the historiographical transformation which had occurred to Hall and May, but structured his exposition of the civil war, *Behemoth or the Long Parliament*, as a dialogue, despite the recent corruption of that genre by the play-pamphlet. The progression of the argument is more Platonic than Ciceronian, transmitting truth through logic rather than through rhetoric.

Hobbes's dialogue is a didactic exchange between *A*, an eye-witness to the civil war, and *B*, a willing and younger student, who did not see so well the 'highest of time' between 1640 and 1660, and, consequently, was not subjected to the glistering words of the Devil. It is divided into four parts: in the first the interlocutors discuss politics, opinion, and human psychology, the long-term causes of the war; the second covers the emerging opposition between king and parliament, including the documents sent out into a sphere of public opinion already poisoned by propaganda and by too much undirected education; the third charts the civil war and the personal treaty, ending with the execution of the king; and the fourth outlines the days of 'the Rump', then hurries

[99] May, *Breviary*, 216.

[100] Tuck, *Philosophy and Government*, 343; contrast MacGillivray, *Restoration Historians*, 62–82.

[101] *Behemoth*, 8–9; *Leviathan*, ch. 4.

cursorily through the Protectorate to the Restoration. Hobbes ended not with the Declaration of Breda or the arrival of Charles Stuart in London, but with a brief paean to General George Monck.

Hobbes's concern was not antiquarian; he rationalized existing material in order to provide a logical account of how the war and the regicide happened.[102] His two main questions were the same as most historians': how did speeches and paper bullets turn to lead bullets, and how did the people let a deranged minority decapitate their king? There was no original material in *Behemoth.* In the 1640s he was on the Continent, and the 1650s, which he experienced personally, he represented without detail. This was not the point of Hobbes's account. In the manuscript dedication, Hobbes alludes to the familiar didactic purpose of history: 'There can be nothing more instructive towards loyalty and justice than will be the memory, while it lasts, of that war.'[103] But Hobbes had no pretence to impartiality, he neither left the reader floundering in a night of conjectures, nor took her or him on a guided tour through the relevant documents. There was no careful negotiation of sources, balancing scepticism and dependency. Hobbes simply abstracted the meaning. In this respect *Behemoth* was quite unlike the histories of the civil war by May, Hall, Rushworth, Nalson, Frankland, Burnet, Sprigge, Fuller, Heylin, Sanderson, Dugdale, or any of the writers of memoirs.

The answer to the big questions was the same: eloquence. People were persuaded with 'words not intelligible'. Interlocutor *A* asks: 'What account can be given of actions that proceed not from reason, but spite and such-like passions?' In *Behemoth* the perpetrators of the revolution are not rational because of their erroneous conception of Church and State; they break the contractual relationship with their sovereign in an attempt to establish an independent authority for the Church. Within this scope of irrationality, they act with forethought, possessed of greater policy than their victims. They were wise, at least in craft, and seemed to have decided, prior to Hobbes's narrative, to make war upon the king. They were enabled to do so through oratory and deliberation. Such men produced 'distinctions that signify nothing but serve only to astonish the multitude of ordinary men'.[104] Just as the English Bible dissolved scriptural authority, so that 'every man, nay, every boy and wench, that could read English, thought they spoke with God Almighty, and understood what he said', sermons produced popular politics.[105]

[102] This is a matter of intention, and so Philip Styles is wrong to claim that Hobbes had an 'entirely unhistorical mind'; 'Politics and Historical Research in the Early Seventeenth Century', in Fox, ed., *English Historical Scholarship*, 72.

[103] *Behemoth*, p. v.

[104] *Behemoth*, 164, 169, 38, 35.

[105] *Behemoth*, 21, cf. 10.

Hobbes vividly described the orator in action, emphasizing the importance of his bodily presence and gestures:

for the manner of their preaching; they so framed their countenance and gesture at their entrance into the pulpit, and their pronunciation both in their prayer and sermon, and used the Scripture phrase (whether understood by the people or not), as that no tragedian in the world could have acted the part of a right godly man better than these did; insomuch as a man unacquainted with such art, could never suspect any ambitious plot in them to raise sedition against the state, as they then had designed; or doubt that the vehemence of their voice (for the same words with the usual pronunciation had been of little force) and forcedness of their gesture and looks, could arise from anything else but zeal to the service of God.[106]

The portrait resembles a description of Hugh Peters extemporizing in the pulpit.[107]

The faith of the 'common people' was hard to achieve. The law should have been clear and sufficient, 'religion in itself admits no controversy'; but some men claimed to have greater insight into Scripture than others.[108] These men went 'preaching in most of the market-towns of England' and undermined the goodwill of the kingdom because 'it is impossible that the multitude should ever learn their duty, but from the pulpit and upon holidays' and because 'there can hardly arise a long or dangerous rebellion, that has not some such overgrown city, with an army or two in its belly to foment it'.[109] Unlike Milton, who thought that too many of the contemporary sermons were tedious,[110] Hobbes, like Clarendon, considered preaching to the urban poor, 'the first encouragers of rebellion',[111] effective propaganda.

Despite the force he attributes to eloquence, Hobbes does not mention newsbooks. Sermons figure proudly in *Behemoth*, but pamphlets, even printed sermons, appear only as weakened incarnations of other phenomena.[112] This is doubly curious because Hobbes spent the 1640s in France, and while he certainly had access to English publications there, he heard no London sermons.[113] It is triply curious in the light of another history which had a significant, hitherto unacknowledged, influence on *Behemoth*.

James Howell's *The Tru Informer* (1643), written in the Fleet prison, is a dialogue between Patricius, an Englishman, and Peregrin, a foreigner

[106] *Behemoth*, 24; describing an Elizabethan Presbyterian, but the earlier fanatic orators blurred into those of the 1640s.

[107] *Pragmaticus* 39, 26 Dec. 1648, 369.239A/E477(30); and the literature of 1660 in general.

[108] *Behemoth*, 115, 90, 52–5.

[109] *Behemoth*, 24, 39, 126.

[110] *CPW* ii. 406.

[111] *Behemoth*, 126. Cf. Clarendon, *History*, iii. 37.

[112] e.g. *Behemoth*, 47, 36.

[113] See 247–8, above.

largely ignorant of the circumstances of the war. Patricius, playing the role of Hobbes's *A*, emphasizes the wealth and commerce of pre-war Britain, and suggests that some times naturally bring peace, and others 'ugly mishapen clouds of jealousies, fears, and discontentments'.[114] Yet Patricius' analysis in the main belies this meteorological metaphor and anticipates Hobbes: a group of 'Viper-like' men, 'politicians' and puritans, closely associated with the Scots, stir up the people against their rightful monarch. They do this by creating groundless fears. London, as Hobbes had argued, was in part to blame; it was too big for the country.[115] The people were predisposed to oppose Church and monarch, with the singular failing that 'They are great listners after any Court-news'.[116] The means used to seduce their loyalty was, as in *Behemoth*, eloquence. The pulpits in Scotland were particularly to blame, but also preachers returned from New England, 'to *poison* the hearts of the Londoners, to puzzle their intellectuals, and to intoxicate their brains by their *powerfull gifts*'. Peregrin observes, in a voice close to Hobbes, that there has been 'a total Eclipse of reason' amongst the English. This is part of a plot to introduce Presbyterianism.[117]

On the power of cheap print Patricius speaks with even greater vividness:

> Nor did the *Pulpit* only help to kindle this fire, but the *Presse* also did contribute much stubble; What base scurrilous Pamphlets were cryed up and down the streets, and dispersed in the Countrey? What palpable and horrid *lies* were daily printed? How they multiplied in every corner in such plenty, that one might say ther was a *superfœtation* of lies, which continue unto this day? . . . and though the Authors of them were worthlesse and mean futilous persons, yet the reports themselves had that credit as to be entertain'd and canvas'd in the High Court of Parliament. But these false rumors produc'd one politick effect (and it was the end indeed for which they were dispers'd) they did intimidat and fill the peoples hearts with *fears*, and dispose of them to up-roars and so to part with money.

Thus the parliament's army was funded.[118] Howell's writings reveal that he was familiar with Venetian *gazetta* prior to the war, and with newsbooks in the 1640s.[119]

The similarities in form and content between *The Tru Informer* and *Behemoth* suggest that the former was a model for the latter. Yet on the role of the press they differ. *Behemoth* also contrasts with a treatise

[114] Howell, *The Tru Informer* in *Divers Historical Discourses*, 10.
[115] *Tru Informer*, 33.
[116] *Tru Informer*, 15, 11–12.
[117] *Tru Informer*, 16, 48–54; see also 121–2, 126, above.
[118] *Tru Informer*, 49–50.
[119] Howell, *Epistolæ Ho Elianæ* (1645; H3071), e.g. § 5, p. 3; [id.], *Mercurius Hibernicus* (Bristol, 1644; H3093); [Howell], *A Trance*.

written by Hobbes's former patron, the Earl of Newcastle, which emphasized the role of newsbooks in generating popular participation in politics.[120] Hobbes's position was anomalous, and needs to be explained.

Hobbes was critical of the propaganda exercises of Colepeper, Hyde, and Lucius, Viscount Falkland, arguing that engaging in a 'paper war' had done the king's cause no good, and would continue to do none, 'for the common people, whose hands were to decide the controversy, understood not the reasons of either party'. *B* understands that in this case 'papers and declarations must be useless'.[121] Readers, as Thomas Fuller complained, could construe interpretations against the writers' intentions, and stick to their own persuasion.[122] Sir Philip Warwick followed Hobbes, and complained of the excess of wit and eloquence in royalist propaganda of the early 1640s, which would ultimately make their readers more froward than compliant. He added: 'Mr. Hobbes hath made a reflexion on this in his late book of the Civil warrs.'[123] Allegiance to the king should not have been a case needing persuasion.

Why did Hobbes overlook the newsbook as a disseminator of subversion? No doubt in part because, as one of his mouthpieces claimed, 'the people either understand not, or will not trouble themselves with controversies in writing'.[124] There may have been another reason. Sitting in France, contemplating the downfall of the three kingdoms, Hobbes tried to follow the reasons and causes of the tragedy. Why had the people been so fickle and irrational? He read the pamphlets and newsbooks, and they offered no answers; they were too ineloquent to prompt disobedience. So he chose to blame the spoken word, a spoken word quite inaudible to him, for providing the infrastructure by which the ignorant could overthrow their rightful master. Newsbooks and pamphlets, out of context, were simply not potent enough to provoke a revolution.

You had to be there really. Hobbes's silence confirmed that newsbooks were not inherently powerful, but as thin as the paper they were printed on. Instead of documents, Hobbes presented two voices: their presence, not identical with their author's, gives breath and authority to the words. Hobbes thereby excluded the problem of disembodied texts, not only removing them as sources of evidence by presenting a speaker who claims direct experience, but ignoring that historiography had perforce been changed by them. *A* was a recension

[120] See 96–7, above. Contrast MacGillivray, *Restoration Historians*, 66. Charles II read and refused publication to *Behemoth*; Tuck, *Philosophy and Government*, 341.

[121] *Behemoth*, 115, 125.

[122] *Appeal of Iniured Innocence*, 1; see 269, above.

[123] Warwick, *Memoires*, 197.

[124] *Behemoth*, 125.

of the authoritative rhetor of Livian and Thucydidean history. Hobbes positioned himself as a Canute facing the tide of history, ignoring the epistemological crisis of print.

Hobbes admitted that his contribution was purely interpretative. In the Dedication to Arlington, unprinted until 1889, Hobbes remarked without any apparent guard that 'The two last' dialogues 'are a very short epitome of the war itself, drawn out of Mr. Heath's chronicle'.[125] This single acknowledgement of source, proudly on the entrance to his book, is revealing. The main source for Heath's *Brief Chronicle*, and therefore Hobbes's source by one remove, was the baneful antithesis of reliable history. As Wood wrote, 'this *Chronicle* being mostly compiled from lying pamphlets, and all sorts of news-books, there are innumerable errors therein, especially as to name and time, things chiefly required in history'.[126] Despite Hobbes's efforts, newsbooks crept into *Behemoth* anyway. He could not be Thucydides.

'O^r nimble Mercury Mr Rushforth'

On 12 May 1690 John Rushworth passed from this life. 'He had forgot his children before he died', noted John Aubrey with understated grief.[127]

His death caused few tremors. He had disappeared from public life completely over the preceding ten years, the last few of which had been spent in prison for debt at the King's Bench, Southwark. Aubrey records that in his last years he had entered his second childhood. Accordingly he left his four daughters to fend for themselves. His daughters were 'virtuous woemen' according to Aubrey, with 'the education of gentlewomen' according to Katherine Rushworth,[128] which made their inherited poverty the harder to bear. Aubrey visited Rushworth, and a few patrons made gifts to this remnant of history, but otherwise his separation from the world was almost complete, except for the major project of his dying years: his *Historical Collections*, a massive documentation of the years 1618 to 1649, published in four parts in 1659, 1680, 1691, 1701. As these dates suggest, Rushworth's death did not retard the publication of his work, but probably speeded it up: the Third Part, published eighteen months after his death, had lain in manuscript for almost ten years.

[125] By the time *Behemoth* was printed, in an unofficial edition, Hobbes was almost dead and Arlington, co-manager of Charles II's mistresses, had fallen from grace. The dedication first appeared in Tönnies' edition.

[126] *AO* iii. 664.

[127] Aubrey to Wood, 5 July 1690; Bod.: MS Wood F39, f. 405.

[128] Katherine Rushworth to the Earl of Newcastle, *HMC: Portland*, ii. 164–5.

John Rushworth has never received a substantial study.[129] Yet his *Historical Collections* has been as influential, though in a different way, as Clarendon's *History of the Rebellion.* His use of newsbooks ensured that they would influence future historiography. Despite the patina which his last years left over his earlier career, Rushworth was, like Clarendon, a participant in as well as an observer of events. His role was always as a collector and communicator of information. This fascination was marked at an early age, and the inception of his collecting pre-dated his career as a solicitor.[130] Sir Edmund Moundeford described Rushworth, who was his source of news from the north, as 'o^r^ nimble Mercury Mr Rushforth'.[131] In the 1630s, then in his twenties, Rushworth began to document the 'interval of Parliament', even before formulating an intention to compose a history from this raw material. He drew attention to this in his elegant preface: 'I did personally attend and observe all Occurrences of moment during the Eleven years Interval of Parliament, in the *Star-Chamber, Court of Honour,* and *Exchequer-Chamber,* when all the Judges of *England* met there upon extraordinary Cases; at the Council Table, when great Causes were heard before the King and Council.' On the calling of the Short Parliament his involvement increased:

> For I began early to take in *Characters,* Speeches and Passages at Conferences in Parliament, and from the Kings own mouth, when he spake to both the Houses; and have been upon the Stage continually, and an Eye and Ear-witness of the greatest Transactions; imployed as an Agent in, and intrusted with Affairs of weightiest concernment; Privy also both to the Debates in Parliament, and to the most secret Results of Councils of War, in times of Action.[132]

When newsbooks appeared, he accordingly purchased them.

From December 1641 he usually bought one newsbook a week, not always from the same publisher, and formed an impressive collection.[133] When Blunden started producing newsbooks, Rushworth diligently collected them; and when he bound them and tried to pull together the information they contained, he marked 'Blunden's passages Begin now' at the top of the page.[134] On these newsbooks Rushworth made mar-

[129] For biographical accounts, see Rushworth's own, in Bod.: MS Wood F39, ff. 383–4^v^; reprinted in Aubrey, *Brief Lives,* ed. Andrew Clark, 2 vols. (Oxford, 1898), ii. 207–9; Firth in *DNB*; Gillian Hampson in Basil Duke Henning, ed., *The House of Commons 1660–1690,* 3 vols. (1983), iii. 357–9; Ruth Spalding, *Contemporaries of Bulstrode Whitelocke 1605–1675* (Oxford, 1990), 291–2.

[130] Wood followed Aubrey in describing him as 83 or 84 at his death in 1690; see Bod.: MS Wood F39, f. 405. But Rushworth claimed to be 63 in 1675. *HMC: Portland,* ii. 151.

[131] Letter to Sir John Potts, 7 June 1642; Bod.: MS Tanner 63, f. 43.

[132] *HC*^1^, sigs. b4, b^v^.

[133] See Bod.: Arch. H e. 108, 109.

[134] Bod.: Arch. H e. 108, f. 43; *A Trve Diurnall,* 17 Jan. 1641[2], 623.01A.

ginal notes and underscored passages with which he intended to inform his history. Frequent shorthand comments in the margins denoted 'observe' or 'an observacion' or 'boke' or even 'observe for boke'. While collecting these newsbooks he was attending parliament, to which he had been appointed clerk-assistant on 25 April 1640, and, later, riding to York and Oxford as a messenger for the parliament. He was duly praised in some newsbooks, which he proudly marked.

Rushworth was appointed licenser of the press on 11 April 1644, a post he retained until March 1647, when the army took over responsibility.[135] With the formation of the New Model Army, he became secretary to Sir Thomas Fairfax, a distant kinsman.[136] After he had delivered Fairfax's resignation to parliament, Rushworth continued for a while under Cromwell, then resigned his post in order to become a supplier of intelligence to the Council of State, and a member of several committees. In the later 1650s Rushworth seems to have been remotely involved in royalist plotting, though his actual role amounted to little more than facilitating Lord Mordaunt's access to information concerning Fairfax and Monck. After the convention parliament of 1660, Rushworth began to recede from public life, working as an agent for Berwick, his old constituency, and for the Massachusetts colony. He represented Berwick again in 1679 and 1681, just after the publication of the Second Part of his *Collections*. Some time before 1687 his poverty led to imprisonment. Contemporary hints that he had embezzled great sums of money during his years of influence may be belied by this fact. Marvell commented that Rushworth was a man 'I thinke of much honesty', and specified him as a 'Friend' as opposed to an 'acquaintance'.

In the same letter of 1674, Marvell expressed a desire to 'discourse' over a legal problem 'very plainly with Mr Rushworth over a pint of wine and I will do soe and that ere long'.[137] In doing so Marvell left something of a hostage to fortune.[138] Rushworth's last years were said to be tainted by senility, developed from excessive, depressive drinking. Wood wrote: 'he spent the six last years (or thereabouts) of his life in the prison called the King's bench in Southwark, where being reduced to his second childship, for his memory was quite decayed by taking too much

[135] *CJ* iii. 457; v. 109; Siebert, 207–12.

[136] Rushworth to Wood, 21 July 1687; Bod.: MS Wood F39, f. 3.

[137] Marvell to Sir Henry Thompson, 19 Dec. 1674; *Poems and Letters of Andrew Marvell*, ii. 335. The acquaintance Marvell distinguished from Rushworth in this letter was Samuel Hartlib (Jr.), 'a man of some ingenuity'. Whitelocke also consulted Rushworth for legal advice concerning his son's lawsuit and financial difficulties; *Diary of Bulstrode Whitelocke 1605–1675*, ed. Ruth Spalding (Oxford, 1990), 777–8, 783; 5 Sept. and 7 Nov. 1671.

[138] A phrase from Lucan via Bacon.

brandy to keep up his spirits, he quietly gave up the ghost in his lodging in a certain alley there, called Rules Court.'[139] Wood overlooked Aubrey's private comment of two years earlier that 'His landlady wiped his nose like a child.'[140] The charge of drunkenness echoed the received image of other parliamentarian historians, including Thomas May and John Vicars. These images of Rushworth's latter days overwhelmed much of the picture left by earlier biographical information. He has become a passive figure, symbolic of the experience of defeat. His *Historical Collections* have been interpreted likewise; as a methodologically passive, occasionally deceptive text, biased yet without clear political ideals. The image of Rushworth feeds this interpretation, and a quietist reading of the *Collections* encourages us to infer a man with his spirits broken, conforming to the restrictions of Restoration England.

An examination of Rushworth's professed methodology and his practised method suggest the ease with which this crude reading has been enforced upon a subtle text. Rushworth's implied or ideal reader actively forged her or his own interpretation. Rushworth used his own experience 'to separate Truth from Falshood', but after this necessary mediation the reader was her or his own guide through the complex political and legal issues of 1618 to 1649, with only transcriptions of speeches, printed documents, and a sparse narrative to illuminate the way. In the preface Rushworth claimed there was neither vinegar nor gall infused in his ink.[141] To Wood he claimed that his method was original: 'I gave ye first President of my method in writing & declaring onely matter of fact in Order of time without observation or Reflection.'[142] He repeated the last phrase in a letter to Grimston,[143] and it appeared in advertisements for the *Collections*.[144]

One of Rushworth's fiercest critics, the arch-Tory Anglican clergyman John Nalson, was stung by this rhetoric of impartiality. In the introduction to his *Impartial Collection*, the title of which was framed to reflect on Rushworth's, Nalson wrote:

> I must confess, in the following Discourse I have not tied my self strictly to the Rules of a Bare Collector, but indulged myself in the Liberty of an Historian, to tie up the loose and scattered Papers with the Circumstances, Causes, and Consequences of them . . . whatever Opinion I may fall under, the dissatisfaction which I have met with my self in Reading such naked and bare Relations

[139] *AO* iv. 280–4, qu. 284. [140] Bod.: MS Wood F39, f. 386^v^.

[141] *HC*^1^, sig. b2^v^. [142] Bod.: MS Wood F39, f. 383.

[143] 7 May 1681; printed in *Notes and Queries*^6^, 5 (1882), 325; *HMC: Report on the Manuscripts of the Earl of Verulam* (HMSO, 1906), 82.

[144] Rushworth, *The Tryal of Thomas Earl of Strafford* (1680; R2333), preface; *Short memorials of Thomas Lord Fairfax* (1699; F235), sigs. K3–K4.

of matters of Fact, would not permit me to fall into that, which I condemned as an Error in others; and having found it a sensible disappointment to be left groping in the dark and unpleasant Night of Conjectures, I could not but in Charity lend the Reader all the Light I could possibly furnish him with.[145]

Nalson used the example of John Bastwick, whose encounters with Star Chamber should not, in his view, have been mentioned without qualifications observing what an odious character he was. Rushworth's failings consisted not only in the inaccuracies which Nalson outlined at length, but in the absence of the moral judgements, condemnations and affirmations, which were necessary for impartiality.

More recently, Kevin Sharpe has sided with Nalson on the issue of Rushworth's representation of Star Chamber, arguing that the 'seemingly innocent collections of texts' by Rushworth and his antagonist Nalson 'constructed a narrative and imposed a thesis by selection, ordering and gloss—and even invention'.[146] In Rushworth's depiction of Star Chamber, he 'weaves the most contentious and political cases into a narrative', leaving the more typical for an appendix.[147] It is, however, necessary to distinguish between the ways Rushworth and Nalson politicized their texts. Rushworth juxtaposed texts; it was predominantly his selectivity that was ideological. Nalson was blunt about his politics; he did not tie himself to 'the Rules of a Bare Collector', leaving his readers 'groping in the dark and unpleasant Night of Conjectures', but took the historian's liberty of drawing inferences and causes. He legitimized his interpolations thus: 'I shall attempt no other Justification of them than their conformity to Truth, from which if any of them be found to straggle or deviate, my own hand shall be ready to throw the first stone at such Adulterations of Truth and History.'[148] Nalson's frontispiece was an attractive symbolic representation of a Janus-faced puritan, his cloven hoof on the Bible, preaching at a tearful 'Britania'; Rushworth's a clumsy allegory of the events that led to the civil war.[149] These two ways of guiding a reader should not be confused.

Nalson's criticisms focused on the ideological bias implicit in Rushworth's abridgements, inaccurate transcriptions, uneven weight given to opposed parties, and uncited sources. Nalson wrote to Archbishop William Sancroft that Rushworth 'has had very ill fortune sure, to meet with ill materials, but he is much more unhappy in so malitiously putting them together; by his abridgments &c, as wholy leaving out in most places, what may give any reputation to the Govern-

[145] Nalson, *Impartial Collection*, i, p. ii.
[146] *Personal Rule*, p. xx.
[147] *Personal Rule*, 666 and n. 159; also 670.
[148] Nalson, *Impartial Collection*, i, p. ii.
[149] Nalson's is reproduced in *Personal Rule*, p. xxi.

ment, or the Kings then Reigning'.[150] According to Nalson, Rushworth intermingled his personal inclinations, his allegiance to party, and 'in the whole proves himself a better Advocate than an Historian, writing with such a strong byass of Partiality'.[151]

Restoration England did not welcome Rushworth. In the preface to *Annals of King James and King Charles the First Both of Happy Memory* (1681), the corrupt[152] Thomas Frankland criticized Rushworth's honesty. Frankland argued that in the modern world, unfortunate as the fact might be, the historian was obliged to provide evaluative commentary.

> I am very sorry that the necessity of this Province wherein I am engaged, should extort from me any *Reflections* or *Observations* upon either Party; but Truth must and ought to be spoke by an *Historian*, or else he cannot truly be called such: It would not (I think) become any ingenuous Person to say he will not in his History reflect upon any Party, and yet throughout the whole Contexture thereof to do it.[153]

One contemporary reader wrote in the margin: 'R____th'.[154] Frankland proceeded to condemn Rushworth directly, like Nalson, first legitimizing his own political views, then criticizing Rushworth in relation to apparently objective, methodological criteria. In 1683, in his life of Plutarch, John Dryden attacked bigoted, sectarian writers who obscured truth, who were 'not Historians of an Action, but Lawyers of a party'. He added:

> in the front of their Histories, there ought to be written the Prologue of a pleading, *I am for the Plaintiff*, or *I am for the Defendant.* We have already seen large Volumes of State Collections, and Church Legends, stuff'd with detected forgeries in some parts, and gaping with omissions of truth in others: Not penn'd I suppose with so vain a hope as to cheat Posterity, but to advance some design in the present Age.[155]

A contemporary would have recognized this as an attack on Rushworth, and probably Thomas Fuller. Dryden praised Thucydides for writing history with ornaments and sententiae, rather than mere annals; history should be active and Rushworth appeared somewhat passive.[156]

Nalson glossed Rushworth's citation of the '*French Mercury*':

[150] Bod.: MS Tanner 32, f. 65; Nalson to Sancroft, 9 June 1684.
[151] Nalson, *Impartial Collection*, i, p. vi.
[152] MacGillivray, *Restoration Historians*, 58.
[153] Frankland, *Annals*, sig. a.
[154] Copy in the Hayden Library at Arizona State University, Tempe, Ariz.
[155] *The Works of John Dryden*, vol. xvii, ed. Samuel Holt Monk (Berkeley, 1971), 235–6.
[156] Cf. Earl Miner, 'Milton and the Histories', in Sharpe and Zwicker, eds., *Politics of Discourse*, 183–4.

if the Mercury *Francois* be his Author, his Reputation is far less, being of the same standard and Reputation with our Courants, Domesticks and Mercuries, who pick up materials to stuff a page at all adventure, and can be supposed to have as little knowledg of the secret Affairs of Princes, as they have occasion of Conversation or Intimacy with them or their Cabinet Councels.[157]

Nalson implied that true history was occluded from common sight, taking place in closed rooms, amongst men whose councils and decisions determined the future. This exclusive mode of history was one which Rushworth acknowledged, while none the less advocating his own method as a viable alternative:

I have chosen to be a Collector of Matters of Fact, *rather than to write in the usual form of* Historians, *to pretend to have seen in the dark Closets of* States-Men *and* Church-Mens *Minds, and to have viewed and measured the first Models by which they wrought. In such an Attempt I might have bin a false Guide to my* Country-Men *against my will, and had assumed to my self to be wiser than they.*[158]

Whereas Rushworth admitted the right of his readers to draw their own conclusions,[159] Nalson argued that historical judgement, like political judgement, was accessible neither to common people nor to the cheap publications which they read. Numerous writers emphasized this private dimension central to history.[160] If history by definition predominantly included the private thoughts and words of its few protagonists, then newsbooks, as a very public form of document, were precisely what history could be defined against.

Rapin de Thoyras, a French contemporary observer, positioned outside the struggle of British domestic politics, though a sympathetic historian of the Whig party, responded to this public exchange. Rapin wrote that with Rushworth's *Collections* 'every man is free to make what use of them he thinks fit, according to his own principles'.[161] It was not 'a regular History', in the form of a narration, but afforded the materi-

[157] Nalson, *Impartial Collection*, i, p. liv.

[158] *HC*² i, sig. A.

[159] 'It will be the *Reader's* part to call them all into Judgment, to Try, Condemn, or Acquit them, according to their severall Merits; it belongs to him, by forming Inductions from the particular Facts, to enable himself to understand the Designs then managed, and the Methods propounded to effect them.' *HC*² i, sig. Aᵛ.

[160] Frankland, *Annals*, sig. b2; Hall, 'Method of History', ff. 16ᵛ–17; Shirley, preface to Raleigh, *History of the World* (1665), 1; Burnet, *History of his Own Time*, i. 4; Sir Henry Spelman, *Of Parliaments* in *Reliquiæ Spelmannianæ* (Oxford, 1698; S4930), 57; Whitelocke, *Memorials*, sig. A2ᵛ.

[161] P. A. Rapin de Thoyras, *The History of England*, trans. N. Tindal, 2nd edn., 2 vols. (1732–3), ii. 347. This corresponds to Rushworth's declared intentions. For Rapin's history of the Whigs, see *Dissertation sur les Whigs & les Torys*, trans. Ozell (1717). Rapin used the terms 'Whigs' and 'Torys' for the reign of Charles II, though expressing caution about their date of origin.

als to compose one. After noting the general outcry by Tory writers against Rushworth, Rapin dissected Nalson's particular objections, admitted that those of them which were not based on probability represented a certain element of truth, and then concluded that they made very little difference. Rushworth had certainly aimed by publishing his collections 'to disparage the King's conduct, and favour the Parliament's cause', but this did not mean that they could not safely be used, or that they were false. In spite of the slurs cast upon the reputation of the *Collections*, according to Rapin, even those historians most devoted to Charles I 'have been forced to make use of these Papers'[162] because the materials were indispensable. Despite 'many exclamations against *Rushworth's* concealments and omissions',[163] his contemporary opponents succeeded in producing few documents that were not in his *Collections.* Rapin was generously praised by Voltaire for his rationalism and objectivity.[164]

Rewriting newsbooks

The Second Part of *Collections* concluded with some speeches from the early days of the Long Parliament, followed by an appendix extensively recording cases in Star Chamber in the 1630s. The latter contrasted with the two particular cases which Rushworth foregrounded. Rushworth was no revisionist; his was an implied narrative of competing ideas of liberty and political right. But the Long Parliament speeches, 'huddled up' into the close of the text 'fearing then alsoe an interruption of the presse',[165] were anomalous in the context of the broader narrative, and expose the undercurrents of Rushworth's intentions.

Some of the passages were censored. Rushworth wrote on 6 September 1677 to Thomas Thynne, MP for Drayton, thanking him for a 'kind Remembrance', and continuing:

Mr. Secretary who delivered mee all my papers back again, excepted against nothing but some passages in the beginning of the Parlament the 3[d] of Novemb[er] 1640, not but that he knew the passages mentioned were spoken by the Lord Digby, Lo: ffaulkland, Culpeper Hide &c. Some reflecting upon the Bishops, others upon the Judges, others upon Projects &c. Yet saith he if I Licence the same I allow of these Passages that reflect on them, and in respect that throughout my History, which he hath perused there is no passage of

[162] Rapin, *History of England*, ii. 347.

[163] Rapin, *History of England*, ii. 347.

[164] On Rapin see Hugh Trevor-Roper, 'Our First Whig Historian: Paul de Rapin-Thoyras', in *From Counter-Reformation to Glorious Revolution* (1992), 249–66; *Nouvelle Biographie générale* (Paris, 1862), xli. 653–4.

[165] Rushworth to Sir Harbottle Grimston, 7 May 1681; see n. 143, above.

Reflection he would observe the same Rule throughout Hereupon I closed with Mr Secretary. ~~And~~ ^that^ I will not make any mention of these or any other passages in that Parlament which begun the 3^{d}. of Novemb^{er} 1640 but break of just before the meeting thereof and so confine my selfe to a Narration of Proceedings during 11 years interval of Parlament. Onely Mr Secretary desires of me before he gives a Licence, a Coppy fairely written of ye Second part, to remain by him to the end that he may see whether the Coppy that goes to the press doth ^not^ differ from the Coppy remaining with him, which will be some charge & protracting of time before the Book can come out, and it is but reason I should gratify his dersire therein.[166]

The rest of the letter contained news. Rushworth's *Collections* were controversial, though the licenser seems to have deliberated about his objections, and, unusually, read the manuscript carefully. Yet in the event Rushworth did not break off just before the meeting of the Long Parliament. In 1681 the press was somewhat freer for such Whiggish politics than in 1677, though this was not to be the case for long.[167] The published text concluded with a section of speeches fitting Rushworth's description. It consisted of thirty-four speeches, each identified by its speaker and distinguished by concise, evocative headings. These formed not a narrative but an impressionistic guide to the key issues of the early days of the parliament of 3 November 1640. Apart from the king's opening speech, none of the items was dated.

Rushworth attended many of the sessions and heard the speeches in person, but the texts he reproduced derived neither from memory nor from shorthand notes. When he was appointed clerk-assistant to the Short Parliament, he had been forbidden to take notes of proceedings.[168] When he famously took down the king's words on 4 January 1642, he boldly chose to overlook the ruling on account of the momentousness of the occasion. For the brief picture of the early Long Parliament at the close of the Second Part, Rushworth used a limited number of easily available printed sources. Twenty-seven of the thirty-four speeches appeared in William Cook's large pre-newsbook volume *Speeches and Passages of this Great and Happy Parliament From the third of November, 1640, to this instant June, 1641*. Another two were available in the sequel volume *The Diurnall Occurrences, Or Dayly Proceedings of this Great and Happy Parliament*, or as separates.[169]

166 BL: Add. MS 32095, f. 36; 8 Sept. 1677. There is an inaccurately printed notice in *HMC: Fifth Report, Appendix* (HMSO, 1876), 317–18; also 26, 34, 147, 185. Rushworth still had plenty of contact with London and information distribution in general. The retention of a copy by the licenser was standard procedure.

167 For recent accounts of the changing political context see Scott, *Algernon Sidney and the Restoration Crisis, 1677–1683*, and Tim Harris, *Politics under the Later Stuarts: Party Conflict in a Divided Society 1660–1715* (1993), 80–109.

168 *CJ* ii. 12, 42.

169 See 106–8, above.

Of the remaining five speeches, three by Hyde were available in a single pamphlet; the others, by Falkland and William Pleydel, as separates.[170] Rushworth paraphrased certain passages, changed spellings, removed clauses and interjections. He omitted one section spoken by Digby, on 19 January 1641, which viciously attacked Wentworth.[171]

Most significant about the transmission of the texts of these speeches into the *Historical Collections* was that not only did Rushworth omit parts of speeches and précis them; he even broke them down into smaller fragments and reproduced them separately, with different headings, according to the political current he wished to underscore. Thus six speeches of Benjamin Rudyerd all corresponded to a single speech as presented in *Speeches and Passages.*[172] This illustrates precisely the kind of ideological weighting which characterized the *Historical Collections.* The particular documents were selected according to their content and arranged to constitute a considered argument, with no respect for chronological sequence.

Rushworth concluded his Third Part, in a voice from the grave:

Thus have I (as the best Legacy my dying Years could bequeath Posterity) endeavoured to give a true Impartial Deduction of Memorable Occurrences, Civil and Military, within these Kingdoms of Great Brittain *and* Ireland*; As in my First Volumne from the Year* 1618 *to* 1629. *And in my Second, thence to the Year* 1640. *so in this my Third Part, from the first Convention of the Parliament Assembled* November 3. 1640. *to the end of the Year* 1644. (English *Account.) At and about which time the two Houses at* Westminster *Forming a New Model of their Army, there appeared thenceforwards a New Scene (though still the same Tragedy) of Affairs. The reporting the Particulars whereof in the same manner, I am necessitated (this Volumne swelling so much, and yet not to be Lessened without publick Injury) to refer to a Fourth Part; which shall (God willing) Continue the like Remarkable COLLECTIONS to that fatal period of the Life and Reign of King* Charles *the First,* January 30th. 1648/9.

FINIS.[173]

It was not until the Third Part of his *Collections* that Rushworth arrived at November 1641 and was thus able to use newsbooks. By the time of its publication in 1691, however, he was dead, the revolution of 1688 had blunted its most contentious edges, and thus the scope for fierce reprisals was limited. The publisher of the Third Part summarized the effect of Rushworth's method:

170 *Mr. Edward Hyde's Speech at a Conference betweene both Houses, on Tuesday the 6th of July, 1641* (C4426); Hyde's speeches in *HC*² ii. 1340, 1353, 1360–2. *The Speech of Mr Plydell* (1641/2; P2658C) corresponds to *HC*² ii. 1363. Falkland, *A Speech Made to the Hovse of Commons Concerning Episcopacy By the Lord Viscount Faulkeland,* printed for Thomas Walkely (1642; F324) corresponds to *HC*² ii. 1351.

171 *HC*² ii. 1356; corresponding to *Speeches and Passages,* 17–18.

172 *HC*² ii. 1341, 1346, 1349, 1351–2, 1355, 1358; *Speeches and Passages,* 103–9.

173 *HC*³ ii. 988.

The Reasons of both Sides for betaking themselves to Arms, and their several Justifications, are delivered in their own Words, expressed in their Declarations, Remonstrances, Petitions, Addresses, *and their* Answers. *Actions in the Field are related from Letters of Persons concerned in the Actions themselves, or from such Prints as were then published, and not in the least suspected of Falshood. And wherever the Contending Parties gave out different Relations, those different Relations are published at large in their own words.*[174]

The extensive re-presentation of the documents of the opposed sides as a means of narrating the civil war was not a purely impartial technique, and was a long way from antiquarianism.[175] It implied a certain version of events, placing an emphasis on communication and psychology. It suggested that the writers of such documents expressed their motivation, and that their readers understood the intent, explicit or half-concealed, behind their communications, and responded to it. The presence of 'fears and jealousies' in Rushworth's version of events did not preclude a rational process, as it would have for Hobbes, who argued that emotions clouded the mind. Rushworth's use of documents, including newsbooks, created an atmospheric history, with some excellent anecdotes. Yet there was no room for 'Character' in *Historical Collections*, only characters implied by speeches and deeds. This is where Gardiner diverged, who in many respects diligently followed Rushworth's lead.

It was at the level of narrative that the ingress of newsbooks was most significant. Some of Rushworth's documents were obtained from newsbooks, most were available as separates. Rushworth consulted his newsbooks for facts, dates, and names, and for turns of phrase. For instance, in the margins of a December 1641 issue of *Divrnall Occvrrences*, Rushworth wrote 'Ballfore', echoing the text, in which the same was spelt 'Bellfore'.[176] In *Historical Collections*, the description of William Balfore's appearance before the Commons was basically a compression of three separate passages in Butter's newsbooks, the form of which was constricted because it was written as the discrete events happened.[177]

The revisions which newsbooks underwent in Rushworth's writing reveal his visions of narrative and prose. In January, Blunden's *Trve Diurnall* reported:

Information was given to the House, that *Theophilus Calthrop* and seconded by some Knights and Gentlemen from about *Kingston*, that *Lunsford* with divers other Commanders that were imployed in the North, wherewith the Lord

[174] *HC*[3] i. 'To The Reader'. [175] Woolf, *Idea of History*, 256.

[176] Bod.: Arch. H e. 108, f. 6. *Divrnall Occvrrences*, 27 Dec. 1641, 181.104B; he also introduced Henry Walker's forename, not in the newsbook.

[177] *HC*[3] i. 459.

George Digby joyned himself, were assembled in warlike manner to the terror of the Countrey. Whereupon it was voted . . .[178]

The same event appeared, after reworking, thus:

Information was given to the House of Commons, That the Lord *Digby* with Colonel *Lunsford* and other disbanded Officers and Reformado's have with Troops of Horse appeared in a warlike manner at *Kingston* in *Surrey*, where the Magazine of Arms for that part of the County lies, to the terror of his Majesty's Subjects, and that 'tis given out, They were to go to *Portsmouth.*[179]

The opening phrase, the 'warlike manner', and 'to the terror of' confirm that Rushworth observed this passage: his version might well have been composed with no other source, apart from his own memory. Rushworth removed the syntactical glitch from the newsbook, and introduced a pleasing riff of sequential clauses which, if anything, increased the drama and terror. In the margin of the newsbook he noted, in shorthand, 'fears'.[180]

In some cases there was substantial rewriting, and in others newsbooks were incorporated with little revision. An intermediate case is a description of the Bishop of Lincoln being swamped by citizens protesting against Colonel Thomas Lunsford's appointment as Keeper of the Tower. The story appeared in *Diurnall Occurrences* in January:

This day a great company of Citizens attending about the Parliament, for answer to their Petition against Colonell *Lunsford*, as also to desire answer of their Petition against Bishops, crying out, *No Bishops, No Bishops:* the Bishop of Lincoln (now Bishop of York) comming along with the Earle of Dover towards the Lords house, observing a young youth in the company to cry out against Bishops, all the rest of the Citizens being silent, stept from the Earl of Dover, and laid hands on him: Which the Citizens observing, with-held the youth from him, and about an hundred of them comming about the Bishop, hem'd him in that he could not stirre; and then all of them with a loud voice cryed out, *No Bishops, No Bishops*; and presently after let him go. There were also three or four Gentlemen walking among the Citizens, and hearing them crying out against the Bishops, one of them in a desperate humour drew his sword, desiring the other Gentlemen to assist him, and he would cut the throats of them that cryed out against the Bishops; but they refusing, he in two severall places drew upon the Citizens; upon which he was apprehended by them, and brought before the House of Commons, and committed to prison.[181]

Alongside this passage Rushworth wrote 'Dauy Hide'. He also wrote 'Sr John Biron' opposite Lunsford's name and underlined the fact that the

[178] *Trve Diurnall*, 17 Jan. 1641[2], 4, 623.01A.

[179] *HC*[3] i. '469' [495].

[180] Bod.: Arch. H e. 108, f. 44[v]. *Trve Diurnall*, 17 Jan. 1641[2].

[181] *Diurnall Occurrences in Parliament*, 2 Jan., 1641[2], 97.1. The event occurred on Monday 27 Dec.; Bod.: Arch. H e. 108, f. 24[v].

Bishop of Lincoln had become Bishop of York. The unevenness of the incorporation of this information into *Historical Collections* suggests that the marginalia were dated nearer to 1641 than to 1680.[182] This is the corresponding event in *Historical Collections*:

It not being yet known that the King had removed *Lunsford*, the Citizens that Petitioned against him, attended at *Westminster*, as also did the Apprentices for an Answer to their before recited Petition, so that there was a great and unusual Concourse of People at and about *Westminster* many of them crying out *No Bishops! No Bishops!* And the Bishop of *Lincoln* coming along with the Earl of *Dover* towards the House of Peers, observing a Youth to cry out against the Bishops, the rest of the Citizens being Silent, stept from the Earl of *Dover*, and laid hands on him; whereupon the Citizens with-held the Youth from him, and about one hundred of them, coming about his Lordship *hem'd him in*, that he could not stir; and then all of them with a loud Voice cry'd out, *No Bishops*! and so let his Lordship the Bishop go; but there being three or four Gentlemen walking near, one of them named *David Hide* a Reformado in the late Army against the *Scots*, and now appointed to go in some command into *Ireland*, began to bussle and said he would cut the Throat of those *Round headed Dogs that bawled against Bishops* (which passionate Expressions of his, as far as I could ever learn, was the first miniting of that Term or Compellation of *Round-heads*, which afterwards grew so general) and saying so, drew his Sword, and desired the other Gentlemen to second him; but they refusing, he was apprehended by the Citizens, and brought before the House of Commons and committed, and afterwards cashiered from all Imployment into *Ireland*.[183]

In the margins of *Diurnall Occurrences*, Rushworth also wrote, in shorthand, 'book'.[184] He transcribed some elements closely: the youth crying out against bishops, the silence of the rest of the citizens, and the hundred citizens hemming him in and crying out against bishops are obvious. Rushworth took out excess words in order to sharpen the prose; including the 'young' qualifying the youth and the 'all' qualifying the rest of the citizens. Rushworth also rationalized the text. Hide's name was revealed in a later newsbook, and Rushworth must have turned back the pages to inscribe it.[185] He removed the intemperate phrases 'in a desperate humour' and 'he would cut the throats of them', perhaps because they were too partial. He added additional information, such as the comment on the appearance of the 'Term or Compellation of *Round-heads*', unavailable to the newsbook writer. He

[182] On Blunden's *Speciall Passages* 12, 1 Nov. 1642, 103, 605.12/E126(1), in Bod.: Arch. H e. 108, Rushwoth wrote 'Contract this.—'; he did not, and much of his marginalia suggests that he could not include all the information he wanted to.

[183] *HC*[3] i. 463–4.

[184] Bod.: Arch. H e. 108, f. 24[v].

[185] Hide reappeared in *HC*[3] i. 482, represented as a stereotypical cavalier: swearing, making threats, using abusive language, and waving his pistol around.

introduced a repetition of 'Lordship', emphasizing respect. Otherwise the texts were very similar. Rushworth realized what has subsequently been obscured: that newsbooks were histories. There is no simple distinction between contemporary printed reports and later, more developed histories.[186] Rushworth had a very modern sense of the relation of history to its sources.

Rushworth borrowed verbatim from Sprigge's *Anglia Rediviva* (1647), itself dependent on newsbooks, and from the 1641 volume *Diurnall Occurrences*. In the Fourth Part, published in 1701, shortly after the numerous memoirs of the late 1690s, he took this to new extremes. For the years 1647–8, Rushworth incorporated extensive, unaltered passages from Pecke's *Perfect Diurnall of Some Passages in Parliament*. He chose this newsbook presumably because of its longevity and seriousness, perhaps because he had worked with Pecke.[187] The later passages of the first volume of the Fourth Part were remarkably literal transcriptions. Rushworth made little or no effort to conceal the origins of his text. Sometimes he changed the original text but left inappropriate markers intact. This passage is from *Perfect Diurnall*:

The great expectation of the Kingdome now is concerning the Army, we will therefore begin this week with the News from thence, and hope to give you Accompt of the grand transactions, & daily proceedings there, the better to satisfie the Kingdome and shew the vanity (but Machavilian policie) of those groundless stories (to say no worse) this week hath brought forth concerning them, And first from *Edmunds Bury* the Generalls Head Quarters we had this day Inteligence to this purpose, His Excellency having thought it requisite for the better knowledge of the temper of the Souldiers (in relation to disbanding) to call a Councell of War at *Bury*: Accordingly the Officers met there on, Saterday last [about 200. in all] the Generall first communicated unto them the Votes of both houses concerning the time of disbanding severall Regiments. And having advised them to a compliance with the order of Parliament, and used severall perswasions thereunto.

The Councell of war first had a presentation . . .[188]

This then appeared in *Historical Collections* thus:

The great *expectation of the Kingdom* now is concerning the Army; from whence Intelligence comes to this purpose: And first from St. *Edmunds-Bury*, the General's Head-Quarters, we had this day Intelligence to this purpose; His Excellency having thought it requisite, for the better knowledge of the Temper of the Soldiers, in relation to disbanding, to call a Council of War at *Bury*; accordingly

186 MacGillivray, *Restoration Historians*, 15.

187 The nearest rival was *Perfect Occurrences*; *A Fresh Whip* identified the latter as being 'compacted' with 'a great deale more pains', 4–5. Perhaps religion was also an important issue.

188 *Perfect Diurnall* 201, 7 June 1647, 1607, 504.201/E515(17).

the Officers met there on *Saturday*, about 200 in all. The General first communicated unto them the Votes of both Houses concerning *the Time* of disbanding several Regiments; and having advised them to a compliance with the Order of Parliament, and used several Perswasion thereunto,

The Council of War first had a Presentation . . .[189]

Rushworth politicly deleted the reference to machiavellian policy, but left in the contemporary asides, though detrimental to his prose.

In the second volume of the Fourth Part there was very little not taken from *Perfect Diurnall*. Here newsbooks, with some sleight of hand, became history; without warning Rushworth presented his readers with unreconstructed newsbooks. Yet newsbooks were not quite exactly history, and the seams between a weekly publication and a folio history, published fifty years later, abounded:

An Ordinance this day passed both Houses against *Clipped Silver*; the Business so generally concerning the whole Kingdom, we will give you the Ordinance . . .

There was also something Published in one of the Weekly Sheets not long since . . .

Amongst the Letters this Week from beyond Sea, we cannot but take Notice of one telling strange Stories in Relation to the Affairs of this Kingdom; and 'tis worth the observing what Credit such Fictions gain abroad. The Letter runs thus . . .

There is this present *Monday a new Bible in* 12° published, very useful for all sorts of People, being of a larger Character than any yet printed; and to be sold by *John Partridge*.[190]

The verbatim inclusion was a marginal case, an exception to the general practice of historians. What is most remarkable is that it advanced a version of history which was not particularly disturbing. Rushworth's *Collections* have been widely used.

One seam in *Historical Collections* is exceptionally startling. The entry is dated 26 July 1648, and is taken from *Perfect Diurnall*. What begins as an editorial intervention, a careful political allegory, in which the army supplants parliament as the chief physician to the kingdom, silently metamorphoses into a contribution to medicine. Perhaps if the reader of *Historical Collections* had developed pleurisy by the seventh volume it might have served as a welcome relief; and likewise to the reader of the present volume. Its inclusion by Rushworth seemed to be a simple matter of fact, a consequence of the direct transcription of newsbooks into history. Yet its function in both texts, the deliberation behind its composition, is an entanglement I leave the present reader to unravel or cut.

[189] *HC*[4] i. 497. [190] *HC*[4] ii. 801, 1012, 1014, 1112.

Amidst these times of killing and destroying, it is a work of Charity to Save such as may be Saved. To this end a Medicine is offered, by which many Lives have been Saved, and in so dangerous a Case, that it hath been often left by Physitians as desperate, and by one of the greatest of Physitians in this Kingdom, hath been thought remediless, but only by cutting a hole in the Breast, so that both Pain and Danger is here prevented by an easie Remedy.

When the Plurisie is past the time of Bloud letting, take an Apple and cut away the top of it to make a Cover, then pick out the Core, and fill the empty room with the white of Frankinsence, then lay on the Cover, and Roast it, when it is soft bruise and mix it all together, then put so much Sugar to it as will make it savory; let the sick Person eat it, and it fails not to Cure: If need be, it may be taken more than once.[191]

The transformation in May's *History of Parliament*, the accidental inclusion of newsbooks in Hobbes's *Behemoth*, and the transferral of newsbooks into pure history in Rushworth's *Historical Collections* have a single conclusion: the rhetoric which dismissed newsbooks as a perversion of true and proper history was a strained, unrealizable one. The distinction between newsbooks and history was not an absolute epistemological, hermeneutical, and ontological divide. There were differences in length, one was prone to contain more public information, another more private information, and so on; but the real difference was a matter of genre. And the rules of genre were never hard and fast, nor solid and defined for any more than a week.

Some just proportions

John Rushworth, 'or nimble Mercury', should not be understood solely as a metaphor. His case reveals the literal and material inclusion and the historical transmission of newsbooks as part of our acculturated versions of the past. My argument is not simply that our tall, sublime, classical bodies are only giants because they stand on the shoulders of the invisible, grotesque multitude.[192] It is, first, that seventeenth-century criticisms of newsbooks were part of the game, or war, of genres. Their literal, unmediated interpretation by modern historians is naïve and misleading. Furthermore, narratives of the 1640s are, perhaps irrevocably, informed by newsbooks; not only in terms of fact and detail, but through the construction of narrative. The first narratives of the events of the civil war appeared on the pages of weekly serials. These could not

[191] *HC*[4] ii. 1205. The marginal notes to each paragraph were: 'Medicine offered in desperate cases' and 'Another in the case of a Pleurisie' respectively. The passage was taken from *A Perfect Diurnall* 261, 31 July 1648, 3002 [2102], 504.261/E525(10).

[192] Apologies to Mikhail Bakhtin, *Rabelais and his World*, trans. Hélène Iswolsky (Bloomington, Ind., 1984).

be, and were not, ignored: from this point there was no turning back. History was committed to the newsbooks' points of view.

Newsbooks were bigger than they looked. Rushworth transprosed thirty-two small-quarto pages of newsbooks, minus four half-titles, to about twenty-nine folio pages. Cramped type and narrow margins meant detail. Newsbooks could represent an extremity of completeness which was not available to a historian. A glance at the collections of Thomason or Wood suggests a Parnassus of information and detail.

The Parnassus could not be scaled by a single historian. Burnet left aside the history of the wars, referring the reader to Rushworth and Clarendon, and, for the trial of the king, 'to common historians', perhaps meaning newsbooks.[193] It was accepted that historians who were not eye-witnesses would borrow.[194] Historians attempted to distinguish between a history and a newsbook with a concept of just proportion. May remarked of the quotidian business of July 1641 that 'it were an endlesse, and indeed an improper thing for an Historian to describe them all'. Hall criticized summarial overviews: 'Epitome's being the greatest Enemyes to Historyes, because them seeme frinds under which colour they suck the marrow out of them, & have caus'd the destruction of many excellent Volumes.' In *Ephemeris Parliamentaria* (1654), Fuller suggested that it would disadvantage the essentials if he were diligently to represent the minutiae of every speech in the 1628 parliament.[195] In the preface to *Cosmographie* (1652), Peter Heylin expressed a hope that the reader would not 'think himself unsatisfied in his expectation if he find not here the situation and affairs of each Town of War, or the Quartering place of every Company or Troop of Souldiers, which are presented to him in the Weekly-News-Books'.[196] Yet *Cosmographie* was a substantial volume of over a thousand pages.

So historians did not describe everything; they left this task to others and themselves pruned a narrative according to their intent. Frankland, having criticized Rushworth for naïvety in his use of sources, proceeded to apologize:

our Reader, I presume, will excuse us, if we do not here pretend to mention every minute Affair or inconsiderable passage which happened in the Times, whereof we have in these *Annals* discoursed, such are the Mutinies of disorderly Souldiers in their Marches, Orders of the Justices to suppress their Insolencies at their Sessions of the Peace, the Books for disciplining the Souldiers, by Authority made publick, or any other such like of less import, which perhaps to

[193] Burnet, *History of his Own Time*, i. 56, 79.

[194] Fuller, *Appeal of Iniured Innocence*, 8; Hall, 'A Method of History', ff. 14–14^{v}.

[195] May, *History*, i. '106' [i.e. 111]; Hall, 'Method of History', f. 15; Fuller, *Ephemeris Parliamentaria* (1654; F2422), preface.

[196] Peter Heylin, *Cosmographie In Four Books* (1652; H1689), sig. A5.

some men may commend an Authors industry, with the hazard of his Prudence or Discretion; such then as these we have omitted, remembring the Remarque of the *Historian* hereupon, *that they are the proper Subject for a Diurnal, rather than an History. Nerone secundo Lucio Pisone, Coss. pauca memoria digna evenere, nisi cui libeat laudandis fundamentis & trabibus volumina implere, cum ex dignitate populi Rom. repertum sit, res illustres* Annalibus, *talia* Diurnis *Urbis actis mandare.*[197]

Tacitus was not aware of the newsbook, but this passage (*Annals*, 13. 311), translated into Frankland's text, accommodated a modern meaning of the word 'Diurnal'. Frankland's translation of 'Diurnis' as 'Diurnal' made this clear. Indeed, accounts of mutinous soldiers, statutes for their conduct, and so on were the raw material of diurnals and newsbooks. In this analysis newsbooks were granted a completeness which, because of the necessary confines of publishing economics, eluded histories.

Newsbooks, by crooked ways or direct, became part of the received knowledge about the seventeenth century. To avoid them is to vitiate the concept of culture. Newsbooks made the history of the civil war, influenced society, and shaped the course of events. Then they made historiography, furnishing a language with which to describe history ('diurnal occurrences', an 'exact journal', a 'perfect diurnal') and establishing the content of that history.[198] The distinction between histories and newsbooks must be drawn with more care than hitherto, with a focus on language and the slight scars that resulted when a newsbook was grafted onto a history. Pronouns and tense were only the deceptive surface of these languages: scratch away these mere syntactical problems and we find that the intent and constitution of the supposedly different forms were connatural, and deeply embedded in one another. I repeat: there was very little history without newsbooks.

This simple proposition requires extensive exposition after hundreds of years in which newsbooks have been incorporated to the point of invisibility, just as the processes of mass media have become too ever-present to be seen by the naked eye. By the late 1640s Sir John

[197] Frankland, *Annals*, preface, sig. B2^{v}. On this use of the word 'Annals', see also Warwick, *Memoires*, sig. A4^{v}; contrast Raleigh, *History of the World* (1614), 'To The Reader', preceding chronological table; Raleigh distinguishes annals from general histories which 'yearly set downe all Occurrences not cohærent'. General history is equivalent to Frankland's 'Diurnall'. The term 'Diurnis' echoed the *Acta Diurna* of Imperial Rome.

[198] Also, *Modern History, Or, A Monethly Account Of all Considerable Occurrences, Civil, Ecclesiastical, and Military*, Oct. 1687; N&S 429. The recurrent title *Historical Collections* suggests the fragmentary, diverse, and journalistic format of newsbooks; see, in addition to Rushworth, Heywood Townshend, *Historical Collections: or, An exact Account of the Proceedings of the Four last Parliaments of Q. Elizabeth Of Famous Memory* (1680; T1991); *The Connexion Being Choice Collections* (1681; C5882), documenting the rule of James I; also Edward Cooke, *Memorabilia: Or, the most Remarkable Passages and Counsels Collected out of the several Declarations and Speeches* (1681; C5998).

Berkenhead, editor of the enviably successful *Mercurius Aulicus*, looked longingly back upon a world before newsbooks. Roger L'Estrange did the same in the first issue of *The Intelligencer* in 1663.[199] These were not necessarily heartfelt expressions of nostalgia; this was a generic position, a commonplace piece of playful self-effacement prior to writing on. But soon even this cursory renunciation was redundant, beyond the horizons of imagination, or even plain sense.

In late November 1641 John Thomas was certainly unaware of the turmoil into which he was about to throw the world. The manuscript was, after all, one of a long sequence. Yet committed to type it was changed, and a functional, sober text was slowly transformed into vociferous, instrumental satire, fraught with the power to open and close politics, the power to inculcate virtue; even if it did not always look that way. This crisis of eloquence crept on the modern world unawares.

[199] *Berkenhead*, 67; *Intelligencer* 1, 31 Aug. 1663, 1, 201.1001.

Appendix
'Diurnall Occurrences' from Manuscript to Print

THE following pages contain the texts of BL: Add. MS 33468, ff. 71–81^{v}, a 'Diurnall Occurrences' manuscript for the week 22–9 November 1641, and *Heads of Severall Proceedings*.

In three places I have corrected the text of the newsbook, where it is clear that a letter has been inverted or misplaced in the case of type. I have, however, assumed conventional pagination, beginning with [1] for the title-page. The pagination in the original is highly erratic: [none], 1, 2, 5, 4, 5, 6, 8. The only signature appears on the verso of the title-page (where the text begins), which is labelled, improbably, 'A2'.

For the manuscript I have expanded contractions, indicating this with underlining. A line *above* the letters denotes a fairly arbitrary contraction, usually in the form of a line curling up from an 'n' ending the word. ⟨. . .⟩ indicates a deletion. In the manuscript, the days of the week are indented into the margin, as a form of section heading.

Add MS 33468

[f. 71]
Diurnall Occurences
or
The heads of proceedings in Parlam^{t} from the 22th of november to the 29th 1641

———

Monday
The 22th In the morneing the howse of Comons they rec^{d} letters from Ireland intimateing that there troubles are soe greate that they haue scarce time day or night to write [71^{v}]

That the Rebbells doe much increase & press heard towards dubline wch put the Kingdome into great feare being scearce able to Resist them./

That they want money to pay the souldiers allreadie entertayned

That the Rebells doe expect Armes & supplye from forraigne parts both from England ffrance & Spaine

That sending to [72] the Rebells to demand the cause of takeing up Armes they retourned a Remonstrance y^{t} it was to maintaine the Kings Prerogatiue And the freedome of conscience in the exercise of there owne religion wch if they haue by Act of Parlam^{t} confirmed they will lay downe theire Armes & make restitucōn for the harmes done by them/

That the Gouernors retourned an answer to there remonstrance that if they [72^{v}] would lay downe there Armes and repayre to there owne dwellings they should haue pardon

And that they would vse meanes to the Parlam^t for the satisfacõn of there demands

Upon this l_ett_er there was a conference wth the Lords for the raising 50000^£ more to y^t allreadie lent as is desired by the l_ett_er

Allsoe the examinacõn of Sergiant Maior Shelley [73] taken in Ireland ag^t Sr Henery Beningfeild was then read that he beinge at his howse in Norfolke about Aprill last The said Sr Henery asked him how the Armie stood in Ireland And if there were any good huntinge & hawking he would goe ouer But now he would stay for that before the next Christmas there would come the greatest troubles in England & Ireland [73^v] y^t haue happened these 100 yeares

After this in the howse of Comons they read the remonstrance or declaracõn of the Kingdome and how farr the greiuances of the Kingdome haue bine reduced by this Parlam^t

There was a great debate about diuers clauses in it & it was first put to the Question whether these clauses wherein the B^pps [74] are counted Malignant p_er_sons to the wellfare & peace of this Kingdome in the p_ar_ticulers named, or should be altered

And the howse beinge diuided it was caried by the Maior p_ar_t that it should soe stand

Afterward the howse was twice diuided vpon the question for the passinge the said Remonstrance wth out any alteracõn for publish ing & the Maior p_ar_t caried it ⟨for⟩ in both, there being great [74^v] opposicõn & debate one both sides

Then Mr Peard moued to haue the Remonstrance printed

Mr Palmer p_re_sent he stood vp and p_ro_ferred 3 times to make a p_ro_testacõn in the behalfe of himselfe and the rest of that p_ar_t ag^t the Vote of the house as was conceiued for the publish ing of the same

p_re_sentlie heere vpon the howse rose haueing sate in debate vpon this busines [75] till after 2 of the clocke in the morneing the traynd bonds attending the howse all that time/

Tuesday

in the afternoone the howse againe meeting p_er_fected 3 bills & sent them vp to the lords

One ag^t p_ro_teccons y^t noe parlam^t man should protect his serv^t or any other man nor his own p_er_son from paying of lawfull debtes wch bill to be recalled at the pleasure of the howse [75^v]

An other agt one Ieames that stabed Iustice Heyward that he shall forfeit all his meanes for 7 yeares to the Iustice being neere worth 200^£ p_er_añn Loose his right hand and haue p_er_petuall imprisonm^t

And the other for S^r ffrancis Pophum for the passing of lands

The rest of the day was spent in debate of an order for the councell of warr [76] touching the proporcõn of p_ro_uision to be allowed the souldiers

Wensday

This morneing the howse sate in debate of Mr Palmers offence ag^t the remonstrance And there was a great controu_er_sie whether he spake ag^t the vote of the howse for the publishing the remonstrance for the printing of it being generally concluded it was ag^t the vote of the howse And it was moued for his punnishm^t [76^v]

1) That he should be called to the Barr/
2) Comitted to the Tower
3) To be expelled the howse
4) disabled for euer being a parlam^t man or for sitting in any place of Iudicature

In this the howse could not agree but it was put to the question and caried soe y^t he should be called to the Barr to answer for himselfe

Wherevpon he comeing to the Barr said he [77] was sencible of his misfortune to speake at y^t time yet it was farr from his intencōn to raise a tumult as was conceiued for y^t he spake or intended any thing ag^t the vote of the howse but only ag^t the printing of the same

This debate held the howse all the day there being great opposicōn & debate about it, This day Sr John Littel a recusant was brought to the [77^v] howse and comitted to safe Custodie till further leasure for his examinacōn

Alsoe some Irish men y^t lately came over was taken & brought to the Gatehowse till further leasure to examine them

Thirsday
morneing they againe sate in debate about Mr Pamer & it was put to the question and agreed vpon y^t he should be sent to the Tower

Then there was a [78] a bill read drawen vp ag^t recusants wch was conceiued dangerous or beareing anie office in the Kingdome

Whose names were drawen vp by the Comittee the ⟨next⟩ last weeke wch was once read And they allsoe then allsoe read a new bill for subsidies

This day the howse herd the report from the Comittee conc<u>ern</u>ing the Irish men lately comitted vpon wch they were discharged only [78^v] Captaine English At whose howse where they lodged when they first came over vpon some p<u>er</u>emptorie speeches to the Comittee appointed to examine him Ordered that he should be examined before the lord chiefe Iustice And y^t good bayle should be taken for his fourth comeinge

This day his Matie retourned from Scotland & was rec^d by the Cittizens in great state/

[79] ffriday
They drew vp anew bill for Tunnadge & poundage for his Matie to the 1° ffeb̄ next

This day allsoe vpon reading the Bill conc<u>ern</u>inge the wine busines in the lords howse they referred it to a Comittee in the painted Chamb<u>er</u> one Tuesdaie next & the Masters and Wardens of the Vintnes companie should then attend to make there defence

This day his Matie [79^v] was expected at the lords howse & p<u>re</u>paracōn made for his Comeing But by reason the Queene goeing to Hampton Court refuse ing to stay at White hall vpon some discontentm^t conceiued to be taken ag^t the Cittie at her Mothers departure his Matie came not as was expected but went to the Queene & is expected at the howse vpon Tuesdaie next

[80] Satterday
there was a Compl<u>ain</u>t made in the howse ag^t one that should informe the Lords that the Comons disliked of the entertaynem^t y^t the Cittie gaue the Kinge vpon wch a warrant was sent to bring him before the howse

Then they againe read the bill of Tunnadge & poundage And the Bill ag[t] recusants & sent it vp to the lords desireing there might be acourse taken of them/ [80v]

Then they read the bill of Tunnadge & poundage the 3[d] time & made it readie for the lords

Then they drew vp a peticōn to his Ma[tie] desireing his assent for the pubblishing the remonstance

They then ordered y[t] the Coppie of the Remonstrance should be ānex to the peticōn & another Coppie to be sent to the lords to the same purpose

And at night there [81] was aconference wth the lords At w[ch] the lords declared that his Ma[tie] had discharged the trayned bands from there daylie attendance for that it would cause Iealosies & feared in the Kingdome

But if it should be thought fitt he was willing it should be continewed for certayne dayes

Where vpon the Commons moued the lords to Ioyne wth them & peticōn [81v] his Ma[tie] for there continewinge & that in the meane time they would consider of it/

This euening the Cittizens of London vnder standing y[t] the trayned bands was discharged came agreat companie of them and voluntarily proffered the Comons to attend daylie and guard the Parlam[t] if it should be desired

ffinis

[1]

The Heads of Severall Proceedings in this Present Parliament

from the 22 of *November*, to the 29. 1641.

Wherein is contained the substance of severall Letters sent from *Ireland*, shewing what distresse and misery they are in With divers other Passages of moment touching the Affaires of the Kingdomes.

[2] Monday in the House of Commons they received letters from *Ireland*, intimating that theire troubles are so great, that they have scarce time eyther day or night to write That the Rebells doe much increase and presse hard toward *Dublin*, which putteth the Kingdom into great feare being scarce able to resist them. That they want mony to pay their Souldiers already entertained.

That the Rebels doe expect Armes and supply from forraine parts, both from *England*, *France*, and *Spaine*.

That sending to the Rebels to demande the cause of theire taking up of Armes, they returne a remonstrance that it is to maintaine the Kinges prerogative and the freedome of Conscience, in the exercising of religion, which if they may have confermed [3] by Acte of Parliament they will lay downe theire Armes, and make restitution for the harmes done by them.

That the Governours returned answere to theire Remonstrance, that if they would lay downe theire Armes and repaire to theire owne dwellings, they should have pardon and that they would bee a meanes to the Parliament for the satisfaction of theire demandes.

Vpon this letter there was a conference with the Lords for the leavying of

50000. pound more to that which is sent according as it is directed in the letter.

Also the examination of Sergeant Majour Shelley taken in Ireland against Sir *Henery Beddingfield* was then read. That he being at his house in Norfolke about Aprill last, the said Sir Henery asking how the Army stood in Ireland: and if there were good hawking and hunting there, he intended to goe over: but now hee would stay, for that before the next Christmas there would come the greatest troubls upon England and Ireland that have hapned these 100. Yeares.

After this, in the house of Commons they read the declaration of the State of the Kingdom; and how farre the grievances had beene reduced by this Parliament.

there was a great debate about divers clauses in it, and it was first put to the question that those clauses wherein the Bishops are tearmed malignant persons to the well-farre, and peace of this [4] Kingdome in the particulars named should be altered, and the house being divided it was carried by the Majors part that it should so stand.

Afterwards the house was twice divided upon the question for the passing of the said Remonstrance without any alteration, and for the publishing thereof, and the greater part carried it, in both there being great oppositions, and debate about it.

Then *Master Peard* moved to have the remonstrance printed.

Master Palmer, presently standing up, offered eight times to make a certificate in the behalfe of himselfe, and the rest of that part; against the vote of the house, as was conceived for the publishing of the same, Presently thereupon the house rose having sate in debate about it, till three of the clocke in the morning, the trayned Bond attending the House all that time.

Tuesday, in the afternoone, the house againe meeting, preferred three Bills, and sent them up to the Lords, one against protections, that no Parliament man should protect his servant or any other, nor his owne person from the payment of his lawfull debts, which Bill is to bee recalled at the pleasure of the house.

Another against one *Iames* who stabbed Iustice *Heywod* that hee should forfeete, all his meanes for seuen yeares to Iustice *Heywood* haue his right hand cutt of, and perpetuall imprisonmente.

And the other for Sir *Francis Popham* for the passing of Land. [5]

The rest of this day was spent in debate of an order from the Covncell of Warre tovching the proporsion of Annuncion for this expedition.

This day a Report made to the house of certain Irish lately come over, and lying in Rosemary-laine, who were suspected to be dangerous persons, it was presently ordered, that a search should be made in the said house, & to bring such persons as they found there to the house.

Wednesday morning, the house sate in debate about *Master Palmers* offence against the remonstrance, and there was a great conference, whither he spake against the vote of the house for publishing, or against the printing thereof; it being generally concluded that he spake against the vote of the house, and it was moved for his punishment.

First, that he should be called to the barre.

Secondly, committed to the Tower.

Thirdly, that hee should be expelled the house.

Fourthly, that he should be disabled for ever being a Parliament man, or to sit in any place of judicature; in this the house could not agree, but it was put to the question, and carried so, that he should be called to the bar to answere for himselfe, whereupon coming to the barre he said, that he was sensible of his misfortune to speake at that time: yet it was farre from his intentions to raise a muteny, or that he spake or intended any thing against the vote of the house, but onely against the printing of the same.

This debate held the house all that day, being great oppositions and debate about it. [6]

Also there were Irish men lately come over and brought to the gate-house till further leisure to examine them.

Thursday, morning they againe fell into debate about *Master Palmer,* and it was put to the question and agreed upon that he should be sent to the Tower.

This day the King came to *London,* with the Queene and Prince; and was met, and brought into the City, by most of the Nobility, the Lord Majore Aldermen, and companies of *London* in great state and triumph, and was feasted by the City in Guild hall, and afterward conducted by them to White-Hall, & the City presented his Majesty with a gift of 20000. pounds put into a great cup of gold, 5000.l. to the Queene in a golden Basen, which in all amounted to 30000 Vpon this the King made the Lord Major a Knight Barronet, and the recorder a Knight.

This day the house received the report of the committe concerning the Irish lately committed, whereupon they were discharged, onely Captaine *English,* at whose house they lodged when they first came over about some perumptory speeches to the committe appointed to examine him.

Ordered that hee should bee examined before the Lord chife Iustice, and that good bayle should bee taken for his forth comming.

Fryday they drew up another bill for Tunnage and poundage to his Majestie to the first of Februarie next.

This day also reading the bill for the maine businesse in the Lords house, they referred it to [7] a committee in the painted Chamber: the next Thursday following. And that the Masters and Wardens of the Vintners Company should attend to make theire defence.

This day his Majestie was expected at the Lords house, but came not by reason of his going to Hampton Court to the Queene, but sent a message to the Lords that hee thought fit that the Trained band should bee discharged from theire dayly attendance for that it would cause Ielowsies and feares in the kingdom, the Lords acquainting the house of Commons therewith, whence upon they returned a message, desiring the Lords would joyne with them in peticioning his Majestie they might bee deferred till the affaires of the kingdom were better setled: whereupon the Lords accordingly sent the Earle of Warricke and Bristoll to move his Majestie therein.

Satturday there was a complaint made in the house to the Lords, against one that should enforme the Lords that the Commons disliked the entertainement the Commons gave to the King vpon which a warrant was sent to bringe him before the house, they then againe reade, and voted the Bill against Recusants and sent it to the Lords desireing theire might bee care taken of them. Allso they read and voted the Bill of Tunnage and poundage the second and third time.

After that they drew up a peticion to his Majestie desiring his assent for the publishing of the Remonstrance and the annexed Coppy of the remonstrance to the petition [8]

Also they ordered to send another Coppie thereof to the Lords to the same purpose.

This evening the Lords being returned from his Majesty, brought word that he was pleased, that the trained band should continue foure or eight dayes longer, and that he intended to bee there the Tuesday following, upon which there was a conference with the Commons, and it was then moved that the Lords should joyne with them in drawing up a petition to his Majesty to give reasons for the longer continuance of the trained band.

This evening the Citizens of London understanding that the trained band was discharged, came a great company of them volluntariy, profering the commons to attend dayly the Parliament, if they should be desired.

Bibliography

The bibliography is divided into eight sections: general manuscripts; a chronological list of 'Diurnall Occurrences' manuscripts; newsbooks; *STC* publications; Wing publications; post-1700 primary sources; theses; and secondary sources.

MANUSCRIPTS

Bodleian Library, Oxford:
MS Clarendon 34.
MS Rawl. Letters 47.
MS Rawl. D.152: John Hall, 'A Method of History'.
MS Tanner 66–59.
MS Tanner 32.
MS Tanner 40.
MS Wood F39.

Bodleian Adversaria:
[MS] Ashmole 720.
Arch. H e.108.
Arch. H e.109.
Hope Adds. 1136.
Hope Adds. 1128.
Linc. c.14.7.
Pamph. D.53.
Vet. A3 d.15.
Wood 207.
Wood 366.
Wood 373.
Wood 501.
Wood 622.
Wood 657.

British Library:
Add. MS 4295.
Add. MS 6521.
Add. MS 21935.
Add. MS 25303. (ff. 183^{v}–184: 'A Character of a London Scriuenor').
Add. MS 28000.
Add. MS 29974.
Add. MS 30262.

Add. MS 32095.
Add. MS 33468.
Add. MS 34485.
Add. MS 36828.
Add. MS 36829.
Add. MS 37343.
Add. MS 46375 (volume of newsbooks).
Harl. MS 163.
Harl. MS 389.
Harl. MS 4262.
Lansdowne MS 20.
Lansdowne MS 753.
Lansdowne MS 1232.
Loan MS 331.
Sloane MS 1467.
Sloane MS 3065.
Sloane MS 3317.
Stowe MS 361.

Durham University Library:
Mickleton & Spearman MS 26.
Mickleton & Spearman MS 30.
MS Cosin Letter Book 1A.

Glamorgan County Record Office:
D/DF F/241.
D/DF F/242.
D/DF F/243.
D/DF F/244.
D/DF F/245.

Public Record Office:
SP 16/450/94.
SP 16/452/30.
SP 16/483/29.
SP 16/483/54.
SP 16/483/99.
SP 16/484/26.
SP 16/485/52.
SP 16/485/56.
SP 16/485/64.
SP 16/485/66.
SP 16/485/67.
SP 16/485/72.
SP 16/486/61.
SP 16/486/63.
SP 16/486/69.

SP 16/486/90.
SP 16/486/92.
SP 16/486/93.
SP 16/486/102.
SP 16/489/3.
SP 16/493/62.
30/53/12.

Worcester College, Oxford:
Clarke MS 41.
Clarke MS 110.
MS 5.20.

'DIURNALL OCCURRENCES' MANUSCRIPTS

For the Cholmondeley MSS, see *HMC: Fifth Report, Part I* (London: HMSO, 1876), 355. For Phillips MS2393, II at the National Library of Scotland, and the Petyt MSS at the Inner Temple, see *Journal of Sir Simonds D'Ewes*, ed. W. H. Coates (New Haven, 1942), 403–4.

25 Feb.–6 Mar.	Lansdowne MS 1232, p. 290.
15–22 Mar.	Tanner MS 65, f. 285.
22–9 Mar.	Lansdowne MS 1232, p. 296.
12–19 Apr.	Tanner MS 66, f. 61.
31 May–6 June	Stowe MS 361, f. 94.
	BL: Sloane MS 3065, f. 7.
28 June–5 July	Stowe MS 361, f. 96.
26 July–2 Aug.	Tanner MS 66, f. 113.
9–16 Aug.	PRO: SP 16/483/29.
16–23 Aug.	PRO: SP 16/483/54.
30 Aug.–5 Sept.	PRO: SP 16/483/99.
1–8 Sept.	Cholmondeley MSS.
6–10 Sept.	BL: Add. MS 33468, f. 33.
6–18 Sept.	Lansdowne MS 1232, p. 324.
11–18 Sept.	PRO: SP 16/484/26.
9 Sept.–20 Oct.	Phillips MS, 421–2.
20–5 Oct.	BL: Add. MS 34485, f. 78.
	Phillips MS, 153–76.
25 Oct.–1 Nov.	BL: Add. MS 33468, f. 35.
	Phillips MS, 489–514.
1–8 Nov.	BL: Add. MS 33468, f. 41.
	Phillips MS, 525–49.
	Petyt 538.20, p. 531.
8–15 Nov.	PRO: SP 16/485/66.
	BL: Add. MS 34485, f. 91.
	Phillips MS, 129–49.
	Worcester Coll. MS 5.20.

15–22 Nov. BL: Add. MS 33468, f. 56.
Phillips MS, 51–71.
22–9 Nov. Add. MS 33468, f. 71.
Phillips MS, 353–65.
29 Nov.–4 Dec. Phillips MS, 269–80.

BIBLIOGRAPHY OF ENGLISH NEWSBOOKS 1641–1649

Format: N&S number; short title; period of publication. An asterisk (*) indicates that some issues of the serial may be missing. Some changes in titles are indicated. Post-1649 items which are quoted in the text are also included.

14.1–2 Anti-Aulicus (Feb. 1644).
15.1 An antidote against the malignant influence of Mercurius (surnamed) Aulicus (Sept. 1643).
18.1–5 The armies modest intelligencer/armies weekly intelligencer (Jan.–Feb. 1649).
19.1 Armies painfull-messenger (Aug. 1649).
20.1 The armies post (July 1647).
26.1–2 Book without a title (June 1649).
27.01–57 Briefe relation of some affairs (Oct. 1649–Oct. 1650).
28.1–3 Britaines remembrancer (Mar.–Apr. 1644).
29.1–2 Britanicvs vapvlans/Mercurivs vrbanvs (Nov. 1643).
36.01–57 Certaine informations (Jan. 1643–Feb. 1644).
37.1 Certaine speciall and remarkable passages (Oct. 1642).
41.1 Chiefe heads of each dayes proceedings (May 1644).
45.01–11 Citties weekly post (Dec. 1645–Mar. 1646).
48.1–3 Colchester Spie (Aug. 1648).
52.1–5 Compleate intelligencer and resolver (Nov. 1643).
54.01–53 A continvation of certain speciall and remarkable passages (Oct. 1642–June 1643).
55.1 A continuation of certaine speciall and remarkable passages (Oct. 1642).
56.15 A continvation of certain speciall and remarkable passages (Oct. 1642).
57.1–3 A continuation of certaine speciall and remarkable passages (Nov. 1642).
58.1 A continuation of certaine speciall and remarkable passages (Nov. 1642).
59.01–20 A continuation of certaine speciall and remarkable passages (Dec. 1643–May 1644).
60.1–4 A continuation of certaine speciall and remarkable passages (July–Aug. 1644).
61.01–24 A continuation of certaine speciall an [*sic*] remarkable passages (Sept. 1645–Mar. 1646).

62.01–13 A continuation of certaine speciall and remarkable passages (June–Sept. 1647).

62A.1 A continvation of our weekly intelligence (12 Sept. 1642).

63.1 A continuation of the diurnall passages in Ireland (Feb. 1642).

64.348–432 The continvation of the forraine occurrents. &c. (Jan.–Sept. 1641).

64A.1 A continvation of the most remarkable passages (3 Dec. 1642).

66.1–2 A continvation of the true diurnall occvrrences (Feb.–Mar. 1642).

67.08–11* A continuation of the true diurnall occurrences (Feb.–Mar. 1642).

68.07–11B* A continuation of the true diurnall of all the passages in Parliament (Feb.–Mar. 1642).

69.2 A continuation of the true diurnall of passages in Parliament (24 Jan. 1642).

70.1 A continuation of the true diurnall of passages in Parliament (15 Aug. 1652).

71.09–10* A continuation of the true diurnall of proceedings in Parliament (Mar. 1642).

74.1 A continuation of true and speciall passages (29 Sept. 1642).

75.1–5 Continued heads of perfect passages in Parliament (Apr.–May 1649).

77.1 A coranto from beyond sea (9 June 1643).

78.1–2 The countrey foot-post/The countrey messenger (Oct. 1644).

81.01–12 The covrt mercurie (June–Oct. 1644).

86.1 The daily intelligencer of court, city, and countrey (30 Jan. 1643).

90.1–6 A declaration collected out of the journalls/Heads of a diarie (Nov. 1648–Jan. 1649).

94.1–2 A diarie, or an exact iournall, or the proceedings of the treaty (July 1647).

97.1–3 Diurnall occurrences in Parliament (Dec. 1641–Jan. 1642).

98.2* Diurnall occurrences in Parliament (10 Jan. 1642).

99.01–11* Diurnall occvrrances in Parliament (Jan.–Mar. 1642).

100.1–4 Diurnall occurrences in Parliament (May–June 1642).

101.1–2 The divrnal occvrrences, or, proceedings in Parliament/True diurnall (Jan. 1642).

102.1 The divrnal occvrrences, or proceedings in the Parliament (17 Jan. 1642).

103.1 The diurnal occvrrances: or, the heads of proceedings in Parliament (20 Dec. 1641).

104.1–6* Diurnal occvrrences; or, the heads of the proceedings/True diurnall (Jan.–Feb. 1642).

105.2–3* Diurnall occvrrences; or, the heads of the proceedings/A continuation of the true diurnal (Jan. 1642).

106.1–4 Diurnall occvrrances, touching the dayly proceedings in Parliament (Dec. 1641–Jan. 1642).

106A.1 Divrnall occvrrences, truly relating the most remarkable passages (5 Dec. 1642).

107.2* The divrnal occvrrances, touching the dailie proceedings in Parliament (Jan. 1642).

109.1–3 The diurnall: or, the heads of all the proceedings in Parliament (Dec. 1641).

110.1–2 A diurnall out of the North/A diurnall and particula of the last weekes (July 1642).

111.01–11 Diutinus Britanicus/Mercurius Diutinus (Nov. 1646–Feb. 1647).

111A.1 The divine penitential meditations . . . of his late sacred Majestie (18 June 1649).

124.01–22 England's moderate messenger/The moderate messenger (Apr.–Sept. 1649).

126.1–2 Englands remembrancer of Lon[d]ons integritie (Jan.–Feb. 1647).

142.1–2 An exact and true collection of the most remarkable proceedings (Jan.–Mar. 1646).

143.1–4 An exact and trve divrnall of the proceedings in Parliament (Aug.–Sept. 1642).

144.101–206 An exact diurnall/A diary, or an exact iovrnall (May 1644–Mar. 1646).

145.1–8 The exchange intelligencer (May–July 1645).

152.1 First decade of vseful observations raised out of modern experience (28 June 1649).

153.1 Five matters of note. As, first, a continuation of the weekely occurrences (23 May 1642).

155.1 The flying post conveying weekly packets to all forraigne nations (10 May 1644).

167.1–4 Generall nevves, from all parts of Christendome (May 1646).

172.1 A grand diurnall of the passages in Parliament (28 Nov. 1642).

173.1–2B Great Britaines paine-full messenger (Aug. 1649).

180.01–11 Heads of chiefe passages in Parliament/The kingdoms weekly account (Jan.–Mar. 1648).

181.101–208 The heads of severall proceedings/Divrnall occvrrences/Continuation of the divrnall (Nov. 1641–Feb. 1642).

182.1 Heads of severall proceedings in the present Parliament (29 Nov. 1641).

185.1 Hermes stratjcus; or, a scourge for Elencticus (17 Aug. 1648).

194.01–26 The impartiall intelligencer (Feb.–June 1649).

198.1 Informator rusticus: or, the countrey intelligencer (3 Nov. 1643).

204.1–2 The Irish monthly mercury/The Irish mercury (Dec. 1649–Feb. 1650).

205.1–3 Ianuaries accovnt/The monthly account of February/The generall account (Jan.–Mar. 1645).

206.1 Ieremiah revived: though in his prison (Apr. 1648).

J1113 A Iovrnall, Or a true and exact Relation (1644).

208.1 A jovrnall of Parliament (May 1648).

210.01–37 The kingdomes faithfull scout/The kingdomes faithfull and impartiall scout (Jan.–Oct. 1649).

213.1–3 The kingdomes scout. Perfectly communicating the proceedings in Parliament (Nov.–Dec. 1645).

214.001–332 The kingdomes vveekly intelligencer: sent abroad to prevent mis-information (Jan. 1643–Oct. 1649).

215.1–9B The kingdomes vveekly post: communicating the certain (Dec. 1647–Mar. 1648).

216.01–10 The kingdomes weekly post; faithfully communicating the affaires of the armies (Oct.–Dec. 1645).

217.1–9 The kingdomes weekly post, with his packet of letters (Nov. 1643–Jan. 1644).

219.1–2 Linx brittanicus (1648).

232.1–7 The London post, communicating the high counsells of both Parliaments (Dec. 1646–Feb. 1647).

233.101–204 The London post: faithfully communicating/The vveekely post-master (Aug. 1644–May 1645).

248.01–57 The man in the moon, discovering a world of knavery vnder the sunne (Apr. 1649–June 1650).

252.1 Martin nonsence, his collections which he saw with his brains (27 Nov. 1648).

258.101–373* Le Mercure anglois (June 1644–Dec. 1648).

259.1–2 Mercurio volpone (Oct. 1648).

260.01–14 Mercurius academicvs (Dec. 1645–Mar. 1646).

261.1 Mercurius academicus: communicating the intelligence and affairs of Oxford (Apr. 1648).

263.1 Mercvrivs Anglicvs. Communicating intelligence from all parts (3 Aug. 1648).

265.1–2 Mercurius Anglicus. Or, a post from the North (Feb. 1644).

267.1–3 Mercurius anti-Britanicus (Aug. 1645).

268.1 Mercvrivs anti-Melanchollicus. Or, newes from Westminster (Sept. 1647).

269.1–2 Mercurius anti-mercurius. Impartially communicating truth (Sept.–Oct. 1648).

270.01–19* Mercurius anti-Pragmaticvs (Oct. 1647–Feb. 1648).

271.1 Mercurius aquaticus (11 Aug. 1648).

272.1 Mercurius Aulico-mastix. Or, the vvhipping mercury (12 Apr. 1644).

273.01–15	Mercurius aulicus: againe communicating intelligence from all parts (Feb.–May 1648).
274.1–4	Mercvrivs avlicvs. Communicating intelligence from all parts (Aug. 1648).
275.000–319	Mercvrivs avlicvs, communicating the intelligence (Jan. 1643–Sept. 1645).
277.1–3	Mercurius aulicus. (For King Charls II.) (Aug.–Sept. 1649).
279.01–27	Mercurius bellicvs. Or, an alarum to all rebels (Nov. 1647–July 1648).
282.01–13	Mercurius Britanicus alive again/Mercurius Britanicus (May–Aug. 1648).
284.1	Mercurius Brittanicus. Communicating his most remarkable intelligence (7 Apr. 1648).
285.1–7	Mercurius Brittanicus. Communicating intelligence from all parts (May–June 1649).
286.001–130	Mercurius Britanicus: communicating the affaires of great Britaine (Aug. 1643–May 1646).
289.1–3	Mercurius Britanicus representing the affaires of great Britajne (June–July 1647).
292.1	Mercurius candidus (20 Nov. 1646).
293.1	Mercurius candidus (28 Jan. 1647).
294.1	Mercurius Carolinus (26 July 1649).
295.1–2	Mercurius Catholicus (Sept.–Dec. 1648).
296.1–3	Mercurius censorius. Or, newes from the Isle of Wight (June 1648).
298.001–183	Mercurius civicus, Londons intelligencer (May 1643–Dec. 1646).
301.1	Mercurius clericus, or, newes from Syon (24 Sept. 1647).
302.1	Mercurius clericus. Or, newes from the Assembly (25 Sept. 1647).
303.1–3*	Mercurius critticus, communicating intelligence (Apr.–May 1648).
309.1–4*	Mercurius dogmaticus (Jan.–Feb. 1648).
310.1	Mercurius domesticus, communicating intelligence concerning all affaires (5 June 1648).
311.01–69*	Mercurius elencticus, communicating intelligence from all parts (28 Feb. 1649).
312.01–59	Mercurius elencticus. Communicating the unparallell'd proceedings (Nov. 1647–Jan. 1649).
313.1	Mercurius elencticus communicating the unparallell'd proceedings (7 Feb. 1649).
314.01–56*	Mercurius elencticus. Communicating the unparalell'd proccedings (13 Feb. 1649).
315.1	Mercurius elencticus, communicating the unparalell'd proceedings of the rebells (11 Apr. 1649).
316.01–27	Mercurius elencticus. Communicating the unparralell'd proceedings of the rebbells (May–Nov. 1649).

317.1–2	Mercurius elencticus, (for King Charls II.) (May 1649).
320.01–11	Mercvrivs &c./Mercurius veridicus (Jan.–Apr. 1644).
321.1–2	Mercurius fidelicus. Truly and faithfully imparting to the kingdome intelligence (Aug. 1648).
326.2–3*	Mercurius Gallicus (May 1648).
329.1	Mercurius Hybernicus. Communicating intelligence chiefly from the kingdome of Ireland (6 Sept. 1649).
——	Mercvrivs Hibernicvs, Or, The Irish mercurie (14 Feb. 1645).
331.1–2	Mercurius honestus. Or, newes from Westminster (May 1648).
333.1	Mercurius Impartialis (Dec. 1648).
335.1–7*	Mercurius insanus, insanissimus (Mar.–May 1648).
339.1	Mercurius mastix: faithfully lashing all scouts, mercuriues, posts, spyes (27 Aug. 1652).
340.1–2	Mercurius medicus: or, a soveraigne salve (Oct. 1647).
342.1–3	Mercurius melancholicus. Communicating the generall affaires of the kingdome (Dec. 1648–Jan. 1649).
343.1–2	Mercurius melancholicus, for King Charles the Second (May–June 1649).
344.01–59B	Mercurius melancholicus: or, newes from Westminster (Sept. 1647–Nov. 1648).
345.1	Mercvrjvs melancholicvs. Or newes from Westminster (28 July 1648).
346.1–5	Mercurius militaris: comunicating from all parts/Mercurius militaris or the armies scout (Oct.–Nov. 1648).
347.1	Mercurius militaris communicating intelligence from the saints militant dissembled (28 Apr. 1648).
348.1–3	Mercurius militaris, or the people's scout (Apr.–May 1649).
349.1–3	Mercurius militaris. Or times only truth-teller/The metropolitan nuncio (May–June 1649).
350.1–4	Mercurius morbicus. Or, nevves from Westminster, and other parts (Sept. 1647).
353.1–2	Mercurius pacificus: impartially communicating unto the common-wealth of England (May 1649).
355.1–2	Mercurius philo-monarchicus: communicating intelligence from all parts (Apr.–May 1649).
360.1	Mercurius poeticus. Discovering the treasons of a thing call'd Parliament (13 May 1648)
361.001–615	Mercurius politicus (June 1650–Apr. 1660).
364.1	Mercurius populi. Or newes declaring plain truth to the people (Nov. 1647).
369.101–253	Mercurius pragmaticvs. Communicating intelligence from all parts (Sept. 1647–May 1649).
370.01–55	Mercurius pragmaticus, (for King Charles II.) (Apr. 1649–May 1650).
371.1–2	Mercurius pragmaticus, for King Charls II (Sept. 1649).

375.1–9 Mercurius psitacus. Or, the parotting mercurie (June–Aug. 1648).

377.1–3 Mercurius publicus, communicating emergent occurrences (May 1648).

382.1–5* Mercurius republicus. Communicating martiall actions (29 May 1649).

384.01–21 Mercvrivs rusticus, or the covntries complaint (May 1643–Mar. 1644).

385.1 Mercurius Scoticus. Imparting the proceedings of the northern armies (19 July 1648).

389.1 Mercurius urbanicus. Or, newes from London and Westminster, and other parts (9 May 1648).

390.1–2 Mercurius vapulans, survaying and recording the choysest actions and results (Nov. 1647).

391.1–3 Mercurivs veridicvs, communicating intelligence from all parts of Great Britaine (Apr.–May 1648).

394.101–210* Mercurius veridicus: or, true informations, of speciall and remarkable passages (Apr. 1645–May 1646).

401.1–2 The millitary actions of Europe, as also the councels made publique relating thereto (Oct.–Nov. 1646).

402.1–6 The military scribe (Feb.–Apr. 1644).

411.01–16 Mr. Peters report/A copie of the Kings commission/The Kings answer to the propositions/Heads of some notes of the citie scout/The city-scout (July–Nov. 1645).

—— Mr. Peters Last Report of the English Wars. [Bod.: Wood 501(26); Firth e.65(2)] (1645).

415.1–2 A moderate intelligence, impartially communicating martiall affairs (May 1649).

417.166–9* Moderate intelligencer: comprising the summe (Dec. 1652).

419.001–237 The moderate intelligencer: impartially communicating martiall affaires (Feb. 1645–Oct. 1649).

420.1 The moderate intelligencer: impartially communicating martiall affairs (5 June 1649).

421.1–2 The moderate mercury: faithfully communicating divers remarkable passages (June 1649).

424.1–4 The moderate messenger: impartially, communicating martiall affaires (Feb.–Mar. 1646).

431.1–7 The moderne intelligencer: faithfully communicating martiall affaires (Aug.–Sept. 1647).

433.01–25 A modest narrative of intelljgence: fitted for the republique (Apr.–Sept. 1649).

439.1 New Christian vses, upon the vveekly true passages, and proceedings (7 Oct. 1643).

442.1 Nevv nevvs, strange nevvs, true news (June 1648).

453.1 The northerne nuntio (Aug. 1643).

454.1001–2567* Nouvelles ordinaires de Londres/Nouvelles extraordinaires (July 1650–Jan. 1661).

464.3* Occvrrences from Ireland (Apr.–May 1642).

465.1001–5145 Occurrences of certain speciall and remarkable passages/ The perfect occurrences of Parliament/Perfect occurrences of some passages/Perfect occurrences of both Houses/Perfect occurrences of every dayes journall (Jan. 1644–Oct. 1649).

470.1 Oxford djurnall: communicating the intelligence (7 Jan. 1643).

479.1 A packet of letters from Sir Thomas Fairfax his quarter (30 Oct. 1645).

480.01–37 Packets of letters (Mar.–Nov. 1648).

480A.1–6 Papers from the Scots quarters/A continuation of papers from the Scots quarters/A continuation of a iournall of passages of the Parliament of Scotland (Oct.–Nov. 1646).

481.1–5 Papers of the resolution of the Parliament of Scotland/ Papers of surrendring the Kings majesty to English commissioners/Papers of the Kings Majesties answer/Papers concerning the debates of the Parliament of Scotland/Papers concerning the Scots commissioners (Jan.–Mar. 1647).

483.01–15 The Parliament-kite. Or the tell-tale bird, communicating intelligence (May–Aug. 1648).

484.1–4 The Parliament-porter: or the door-keeper of the House of Commons (Aug.–Sept. 1648).

485.01–84 The Parliament scout: communicating his intelligence to the kingdome (June 1643–Jan. 1645).

487.01–21 The Parliaments post: faithfully communicating to the kingdome the proceedings (May–Oct. 1645).

488.1 The Parliaments scouts discovery: or certain information from both armies (June 1643).

489.1–3 The Parliaments scrich-owle (June–July 1648).

490.1 The Parliaments vulture. Newes from all parts of the kingdome (22 June 1648).

492.1–7 A particular relation of the severall removes/The continuation of true intelligence/A particular relation of the most remarkable occurrences (May–Aug. 1644).

494.1 The passages in Parliament (10 Jan. 1642).

497.1–2* A perfect and more particular relation of the proceedings of the army in Ireland (Nov. 1649).

498.01–45 A perfect declaration of the proceedings in Parliament/ The true informer (Apr. 1645–Mar. 1646).

499.1 A perfect diary of passages of the Kings army (26 June 1648).

—— A perfect diurnall of all the proceedings of the English and Scotch armies in Ireland (18 July 1642).

502.1–2 A perfect diurnall of passages in Parliament (July 1649).

503.001–302 A perfect diurnall of some passages and proceedings of, and in relation to the armies (Dec. 1649–Sept. 1655).

504.001–324 A perfect diurnall of some passages in Parliament (July 1643–Nov. 1649).

507.01–12 A perfect diurnall of the passages in Parliament (Jan.–Mar. 1642).

508.1 A perfect divrnall of the passages in Parliament (7 Mar. 1642).

509.1–9C A perfect diurnall of the passages in Parliament (June–Aug. 1642).

510.6–9* A perfect diurnall of the passages in Parliament (July–Aug. 1642).

511.07–54* A perfect diurnall of the passages in Parliament (Aug. 1642–June 1643).

512.11–15* A perfect diurnall of the passages in Parliament (Aug.–Oct. 1642).

513.13–53B* A perfect diurnall of the passages in Parliament (Sept. 1642–June 1643).

514.1 A perfect diurnall of the passages in Parliament (27 Feb. 1643).

515.1–5* A paerfect/perfect diurnal of the proceedigns/proceedings in Parliament (Sept.–Oct. 1642).

517.1–2 A perfect diurnall or the proceedings in Parliament (July 1642).

518.1–3 A perfect narrative of the whole proceedings of the High Court of Iustice/A continvation of the narrative (Jan. 1649).

523.01–71 Perfect passages of each dayes proceedings in Parliament (Oct. 1644–Mar. 1646).

525.1 Perfect passages of state, and martiall affairs (4 Aug. 1646).

527.1–2 A perfect relation, or svmmarie of all the declarations/A perfect relation, or summary of 50 bookes (Sept.–Oct. 1642).

528.01–11 A perfect summary of chiefe passages in Parliament (July–Oct. 1647).

529.1 A perfect svmmarie of chiefe passages in Parliament (12 Feb. 1648).

530.01–27 A perfect summary of exact passages of Parliament/A perfect collection of exact passages of Parliament/A perfect summary impartially communicating/A perfect summary of an exact diurnall/A perfect summary of an exact dyarie (Jan.–Oct. 1649).

531.1 A perfect summarie of the most remarkable passages between the Kings Majesty (9 Oct. 1648).

532.1 A perfect tiurnall: or VVelch post. With her creat packet of letter (11 Feb. 1643).

533.01–82 The perfect weekly account containing/The perfect weekly account concerning (Mar. 1648–Oct. 1649).

540.1 The phoenix of Europe, or the forraigne intelligencer (16 Jan. 1646).

565.1–7 The proceedings of the army under the command of Sir Thomas Fairfax/An exact and perfect relation of the proceedings of the army/A continuation of the proceedings (July–Aug. 1645).

573.01–19 Publick adviser (May–Sept. 1657).

579.01–19 Quotidian occurrences in and about London/England's memorable accidents (Sept. 1642–Jan. 1643).

581.1–3 Remarkable occurrences from the high court of Parliament/The heads of all the proceedings in both Houses of Parliament/Remarkable passages in Parliament (May–June 1642).

582.1–8 Remarkable passages impartially relating/Remarkable passages published/Remarkable passages, of the occurrences (Nov.–Dec. 1643).

583.1 Remarkable passages, or, a perfect diurnall of the weekly proceedings (12 Sept. 1642).

587.1–7B The royall diurnall (for King Charls the II.) (Feb.–Apr. 1650).

588.1–5 The royall divrnall. Impartially imparting the affaires of England (July–Aug. 1648).

591.1 The Scotch mercury, communicating the affairs of Scotland (5 Oct. 1643).

592A.1–8 The Scots army advanced/A true relation of the late proceedings/A faithfull relation, of the late occurrences/The late proceedings of the Scottish army/Intelligence from the Scottish army/Extracts of letters dated at Edenburgh/Intelligence from the south borders of Scotland (Jan.–Apr. 1644).

594.001–162 The Scotish dove. Sent out, and returning/The Scotish dove sent out the last time (Oct. 1643–Dec. 1646).

595.1–3 The Scottish mercury. Relating the weekly intelligence/The Scotch intelligencer (Oct. 1643).

598.1 Severall new and good passages, or the weekly proceedings from divers places (27 Aug. 1642)

599.001–313 Severall proceedings in Parliament/Severall proceedings of state affaires/Perfect proceedings of state-affaires (Sept. 1649–Sept. 1655).

605.01–44 Some speciall and considerable passages/Speciall passages from divers parts/Some speciall passages/Speciall passages and certain informations from severall places (Aug. 1642–June 1643).

606.01–11B Some speciall passages from London/Westminster/Hull (May–Aug. 1642).

607.1	Speciall passages and certain informations (13 Sept. 1642).
609.01–22	The spie, communicating intelligence from Oxford (Jan.–June 1644).
612.1	The treaty traverst: or, newes from Newport in the Isle of VVight (26 Sept. 1648).
615.1	A true and perfect diurnall of all the chiefe passages in Lancashire (9 July 1642).
616.11*	A true and perfect diurnall of all the passages in Parliament (6 Sept. 1642).
618.1–2	A true and perfect journall of the [civill] vvarres in England (Apr. 1644).
T2577	True and remarkable passages (10 Sept. 1642).
620.3*	A trve divrnall occurrences, or proceedings in the Parliament this last weeke (31 Jan. 1642).
621.1–3	The true diurnal occvrrances: or, the heads of the proceedings (Jan.–Feb. 1642).
622.1	The true diurnall occvrrances or, the heads of the proceedings of both Hovses (21 Feb. 1642).
623.01A–11B	A trve diurnall of the last weeks passages in Parliament/A continuation of the true diurnall of passages in Parliament (Jan.–Mar. 1642).
624.3*	A trve diurnall of the last weekes passages in Parliament (31 Jan. 1642).
625.1–2	A true diurnall of the passages in Parliament (Mar. 1642).
626.10*	A true diurnall of the passages in Parliament (Mar. 1642).
627.3	A true diurnal or the passages in Parliament (Jan. 1642).
629.01–67	The true informer, continuing a collection of the most speciall and observable passages (Sept. 1643–Feb. 1645).
631.1	The true informer, or monthly mercury (8 Nov. 1648).
638.01–56	A trve relation of certaine speciall and remarkable passages/Certaine speciall and remarkable passages/A continvation of certaine speciall and remarkable pasages (Aug. 1642–Oct. 1643).
640.1–5	A true relation of the taking of Sherburne Castle/The second intelligence from Reading/The third intelligence from Reading/Mercurius bellicus. The fourth intelligence from Reading/Intelligence from the armie (Apr.–June 1643).
641.1–5	A Tuesdaies journall of perfect passages in Parliament (July–Aug. 1649).
668.1–6	Wandering Whore (?Nov. 1660–1663).
669.1–4	Wednesday's mercury. Or, speciall passages and certain informations/The speciall passages continved/Wednesdays mercury, or the speciall passages (July–Aug. 1643).
671.101–501	The weekly account/The perfect week[e]ly account (Sept. 1643–Jan. 1648).
673.1	A weekly accompt of certain special and remarkable passages (3 Aug. 1643).

676.1	A weekly accompt or perfect divrnall (10 July 1643).
686.1–2	Weekly intelligence from severall parts of this kingdome (Oct. 1642).
696.1–3	The weekly nevves, from severall parts beyond the seas (May 1644).
708.1–9	The Welch mercury, communicating remarkable intelligences and true newes/Mercurius Cambro-Brittanus, the Brittish mercury, or the VVelch diurnall (Oct. 1643–Jan. 1644).
709.1	The westerne informer. Containing the latest newes (Mar. 1646).
710.1–5*	VVestminster proiects, or the mysterie of Darby Hovse, discovered/Tricks of state; or, more Westminster projects/ Windsor projects, and Westminster practices (Mar.–June 1648).

STC PUBLICATIONS

3185. Traiano Boccalini. *The New-found Politicke.* [Trans. J. Florio, W. Vaughan, and T. Scott]. London, 1626.

3591. Richard Braithwait. *Whimzies: or, a New Cast of Characters.* London, 1631.

——Enrico Caterino Darila. *Historia delle guerre civili di Francia.* Venice, 1630.

7439. John Earle. *Micro-Cosmographie. Or, A Peece of the World Discovered; In Essayes and Characters.* London, 1628.

8921. *By the King. A Proclamation.* London, 1639.

12962. Richard Hawkins. *Observations of Sir R. Hawkins in his Voiage.* London, 1622.

13569. Raphael Holinshed. *The Third Volume of Chronicles.* London, 1587.

14753.5. Ben Jonson. *The Workes of Benjamin Jonson* [The second volume]. London, 1631.

16886. Thomas May. *Lucan's Pharsalia: or The Civil-Warres of Rome.* London, 1626.

16887. Thomas May. *Lucan's Pharsalia: or The Civil-Warres of Rome.* London, 1627.

17711. Thomas May. *A Continuation of Lucan's Historicall Poem till the Death of Julius Cæsar.* London, 1630.

18038. Richard Montagu. *A Gagg for the New Gospell? No: A New Gagg for an Old Goose.* London, 1624.

18030. Richard Montagu. *Apello Caesarem.* London, 1625.

18507.223. *The Continvation of our forreine Newes* 39, London, 19 Sept. 1631.

18507.238, 239. *The Continuation of our forraine avisoes* or *The Continuation of our forraine newes.* London, 24 and 30 Jan., 1642.

18507.277. *An abstract of some speciall forreigne occurrences* 1. London, 20 December 1638.

——*Mercurius Gallobelgicus: siue, rerum in gallia & Belgio potissimum: Hispania quoque, Italia, Anglia, Germania, Polonia, vicinisque locis ab anno 1588 vsque ad Martium . . . 1594 gestarum, Nuncius.* Cologne, 1594.
20469. William Prynne. *Newes from Ipswich.* 'Ipswich' [i.e. Edinburgh?], 1636.
20637. Sir Walter Raleigh. *The History of the World.* London, 1614.
22080. Thomas Scott, trans. *Newes from Pernassus.* 'Helicon' [i.e. Holland], 1622.
23740. John Taylor. *The Carriers Cosmographie.* 1637.
25325. Deggory Whear. *De ratione & methodo legendi historias dissertatio.* London, 1623.

WING PUBLICATIONS

A454. *The Actors Remonstrance.* London, 24 Jan. 1642.
A944. *All the memorable and wonder-strikinge Parliamentary Mercies effected & afforded unto this our English nation within this space of lesse then 2 years past A. 1641 & 1642.* London, 1642.
A2673. Naworth [George Wharton]. *A New Almanack.* Oxford, 1644.
A2674. George Wharton. *No Merline, nor Mercurie: but a New Almanac.* [?York], 1647.
A3062. *The Anatomy of the Westminster Ivncto . . . by Mercurius Elencticus.* London, 1648.
A3987. Elias Ashmole. *Theatrum Chemicum Britannicum.* London, 1652.
A4135. Richard Atkyns. *The Original and Growth of Printing: Collected out of History, and the Records of this Kingdome.* ?1660. London, 1664.
B804. Clement Barksdale. *Nympha Libethris: Or the Cotswold Muse.* London, 1651.
B1219. Richard Baxter. *A Christian Directory: Or, A Summ of Practical Theologie and Cases of Conscience.* London, 1673.
B2969. [John Berkenhead?] *Newes from Smith the Oxford Jaylor.* London, 1644[5].
B3032. *The Bishops Potion, Or, A Dialogue.* London, 1641.
B3728B. John Booker. *Mercurius Cœlicus; Or, A Caveat To all people of the Kingdome.* London, 1644.
B4850B. Alexander Brome, ed. *The Rump.* London, 1660.
B4851. Alexander Brome, ed. *Rump Songs.* London, 1662.
B5852. Gilbert Burnet. *Reflections on Mr. Varillas's History.* Amsterdam, 1686.
C460. *Canterburies Potion.* London, 1641.
C2026. *A Character of the New Oxford Libeller.* London, 1645.
C2021. John Cleveland. *The Character of Mercurius Politicus.* London, 1650.
C2467. *His Majesties Message to Parliament upon his Removall to the Citie of York.* London, 1642.
C2522. *The Kings Maiesties most gratious Speech to both Houses of Parliament. Whereunto is added the King and Queenes Royall loves returned to the worthy members of the City of London.* London, 1641.
C2772. *His Majestie's speciall Command to the Lord Major of London for the sending of precepts into the city to suppresse the tumultuous assemblies.* London, 1641.

C3808. [Attr. Francis Cheynell]. *Aulicus His Hue and Cry Sent forth after Britanicus.* London, 1645.
C3873. Joshua Childrey. *Indago Astrologica.* London, 1652.
C4426. Edward Hyde. *Mr. Edward Hyde's Speech at a Conference betweene both Houses, on Tuesday the 6th of July, 1641.* London, 1641.
C4657. John Cleveland. *A Character of a Diurnal-Maker.* London, 1654.
C4659. John Cleveland. *Character of a London Diurnall.* Oxford, 1644[5].
C4668. John Cleveland. *The Character of a Moderate Intelligencer.* London, 1647.
C5882. *The Connexion Being Choice Collections.* London, 1681.
C5998. Edward Cooke. *Memorabilia: Or, the most Remarkable Passages and Counsels Collected out of the several Declarations and Speeches That have been made by the King.* London, 1681.
C6206. *A Coppie of the Bill against the XIII Bishops, presented to the Lords, by the Commons.* London, 1641.
C6772. *Craftie Cromwell . . . Written by Mercurius Melancholicus.* London, 1648.
C7459. *The Cuckoos Nest at Westminster . . . By Mercurius Melancholicus.* London, 1648.
D1103, D1104. Edward Dering. *A Collection of speeches made by Sir Edward Dering in matter of religion.* London, 1642.
D1166. *A Description Of the Passage of Thomas late Earle of Strafford, over the River of Styx.* London, 1641.
D1216. *The Devill, and the Parliament; Or, The Parliament and the Devill. A Contestation between them for the precedencie.* London, 1648.
D1256. Sir Simonds D'Ewes. *Two Speeches Spoken.* London, 1642.
D1335. *A Dialogue between the Two Giants in Guildhall.* London, 1661.
D1495. *Ding Dong, or Sr. Pitifull Parliament, On his Death-Bed. . . . By Mercurius Melancholicus.* London, 1648.
D1637. *The Discovery of a Conspiracy at Edenburg in Scotland.* London, 1641.
D1845. *Don Pedro de Quixot, or in English the Right Reverend Hugh Peters.* London, 1660.
D2196. William Drummond. *The History of Scotland.* Preface by John Hall. London, 1655.
D2122. John Dryden. *Absalom and Achitophel.* London, 1681.
D2492. William Dugdale. *A Short View of the Late Troubles in England.* Oxford, 1681.
E228. Thomas Edwards. *Gangræna: or A Catalogue and Discovery of many of the Errours, Heresies, Blasphemies and pernicious Practices of the Sectaries of this time, vented and acted in England in these last four years.* London, 1646.
E234. Thomas Edwards. *The Second Part of Gangræna.* London, 1646.
[E971]. *An Act against unlicensed and scandalous books.* London, 1649. [Not separately published according to Wing 1994.]
E1286. *The Coppy of a Letter Sent by the Lords and Commons in Parliament to the Committees, now attending his Royall Majestie in Scotland. October 23. 1641. . . . Whereunto is annexed the Heads of severall proceedings in Parliament now Assembled, from October 20. to the 26.* London, 1641.
E1525. *The Diurnall Occurrences of every dayes proceeding in Parliament since the*

beginning thereof, being Tuesday the twentieth of Ianuary, which ended the tenth of March. Anno Dom. 1628. London, 1641.

E1526. *The Diurnall Occurrences, or Dayly Proceedings of both Houses, in this Great and Happy Parliament.* London, 1641.

E1802. *An Ordinance of the Lords and Commons . . . against unlicensed or scandalous pamphlets.* London, 1647.

E2070. *Ordinance . . . for the Utter Suppression and Abolishing of All Stage Plays and Interludes . . . 11 Feb. 1647.* London, 1648.

E2180. *The Petition of Parliament presented to the King with the Remonstrance.* London, 1641.

E2309. *Speeches and Passages Of this Great and Happy Parliament From the third of November, 1640, to this Instant June, 1641.* London, 1641.

F235. Thomas Lord Fairfax. *Short memorials of Thomas Lord Fairfax.* London, 1699.

F324. Lucius Cary, 2nd Viscount Falkland. *A Speech Made to the Hovse of Commons Concerning Episcopacy By the Lord Viscount Faulkeland.* London, 1642.

F582. *The Gentle Lash, Or the Vindication of Dr Featley.* London, 1644.

F594. Daniel Featley. *Sacra Nemesis.* Oxford, 1644.

F1231. Richard Flecknoe. *Miscellania.* London, 1653.

F2078. Thomas Frankland. *The Annals of King James and King Charles the First Both of Happy Memory.* London, 1681.

F2199. *A Fresh Whip For all scandalous Lyers. or, A true description of the two eminent Pamphleteers, or Squibtellers of this Kingdome.* London, 1647.

F2340. *A Fvll Answer to a Scandalous Pamphlet, Intituled, A Character of a London Diurnall.* London, 1645.

F2422. Thomas Fuller. *Ephemeris Parliamentaria.* London, 1654.

F2403 Thomas Fuller. *Andronicvs Or, The Vnfortunate Politician.* London, 1646.

F2410. Thomas Fuller. *Appeal of Iniured Innocence.* London, 1659.

F2416. Thomas Fuller. *The Church History of Britain; From the Birth of Jesus Christ until the year M.DC.XLVIII.* London, 1655.

F2423. Thomas Fuller. *A Fast Sermon Preached On Innocents day.* London, 1642.

F2443. Thomas Fuller. *The Holy State.* Cambridge, 1642.

F2451. Thomas Fuller. *Mixt Contemplations in Better Times.* London, 1660.

G1161. John Goodwin. *Cretensis.* London, 1646.

G1982A. L[ewis]. G[riffin]. *Essayes and Characters.* London, 1661.

H250. John Hall. *An Humble Motion to the Parliament of England Concerning the Advancement of Learning.* London, 1650.

H346. John Hall. *Grounds and Reasons of Monarchy.* Edinburgh, 1651.

——John Hall. *Peri hypsous Or Dionysius Longinus of the Height of Eloquence.* London, 1652. Wing L2999.

H1938. *Hierocles upon the golden verses of Pythagoras; Teaching a vertuous and worthy life.* Trans. John Hall. London, 1657.

H987. Samuel Hartlib. *A further Discoverie of the Office of Pvblick Addresse for Accommodations.* London, 1648.

H1289. *The Heads Of severall Petitions delivered by many of the Troopers against the Lord General And some other Officers of the Army. With the Answer which Mr. Pym Made to the severall Heads or Petitions, before the Committee on Tuesday, October 5. 1641.* London, 1641.

H1318. [James Heath]. *Brief Chronicle of all the Chief Actions so fatally Falling out in these three Kingdoms.* London, 1662.

H1319. 'H-I' [James Heath]. *A Brief Chronicle Of the Late Intestine War In The Three Kingdoms of England, Scotland & Ireland.* London, 1663.

——James Heath. *An Elegy On the Much lamented Death of Dr Sanderson.* London, 1662.

H1456. *A Copie of the Queens Letter from the Hague.* London, 1642.

H1689. Peter Heylin. *Cosmographie In Four Books.* London, 1652.

H1706, H1707. Peter Heylin. *Examen Historicum: Or A Discovery and Examination Of The Mistakes, Falsities, and Defects In some Modern Histories.* London, 1659.

H1938. *Hierocles Upon the Golden Verses of Pythagoras; Teaching a Vertuous and Worthy Life.* Trans. John Hall. London, 1657.

H2094B. *The Historians Guide: Or, Englands Remembrancer.* 1676. 2nd edn. London, 1679.

H2251. Thomas Hobbes. *The Life of Mr. Thomas Hobbes of Malmesbury. Written by himself in a Latine Poem. And now translated into English.* London, 1680.

H2430. *Sir Iohn Holland his Speech in Parliament, declaring the grievances of this Kingdome.* London, 1641.

H3068. James Howell. *Divers Historical Discourses.* London, 1661.

H3071. James Howell. *Epistolæ Ho Elianæ.* London, 1645.

H3093. James Howell. *Mercurius Hibernicus.* Bristol, 1644.

H3120. James Howell. *A Trance: or, Newes from Hell.* London, 1649.

I252. *Instrvctions Given Vnto the Commissioners of the Lords and Commons appointed to be imployed in the Parliament of Scotland, August. 18. 1641. Together With the proceedings in Parliament on Thursday, August 19.* London, 1641.

J1113. *A Iovrnall, Or a true and exact Relation.* London, 1644.

K324. *The Kentish Fayre. Or, The Parliament sold to their best worth.* London, 1648.

L492. *The last Newes from Ireland, being a relation of the proceedings of the rebellious Papists there.* London, 1641.

L498. *The Last News in London.* London, 1642.

L541. *A late and true Relation from Ireland.* London, 1641.

L559. *The Late Storie of Mr. William Lilly.* London, 1647[8].

L799. *A learned and witty Conference betwixt a Protestant and a Papist.* London, 1641.

L1299A. [Attr. Roger L'Estrange]. *A Rope For Pol. Or, A Hue and Cry after Marchemont Nedham. The late Scurrulous News-writer.* London, 1660.

L2081. John Lilburne. *An answer, to nine arguments: written by T. B. Written long since by J. Lilburne: now publ. by a well willer.* London, 1645.

L2324. *The Earl of Craford his Speech before the Parliament in Scotland upon his Examination concerning the late Conspiracie against the Marquise Hamilton, Earl of Argile, Lord Lowden and others.* London, 1641.

L2630. David Lloyd. *The Legend of Captaine Iones: Continued From his first part to his end.* London, 1648.

L2999. Dionysius Longinus. *Peri hypsous Or Dionysius Longinus on the Height of Eloquence.* Trans. John Hall. London, 1652.

L3460. Edmund Ludlow. *Memoirs of Edmund Ludlow Esq.* [London?], 1698.

M1395. Thomas May. *Breviary of the History of Parliament.* London, 1650.

M1400. Thomas May. *The Character of a Right Malignant.* London, 1645.
M1404. Thomas May. *A Discovrse Concerning the Svccesse of Former Parliaments.* London, 1642.
M1410. Thomas May. *The History of the Parliament of England Which began November the third, M.DC.XL.* London, 1647.
M1748. *Mercuries Message, or the Coppy of a Letter.* London, 1641.
M1752. *Mercurius Anti-Mercvrivs.* London 1648.
M1756. [Marchamont Nedham]. *Mercurius Britanicus, his apologie to all well-affected people.* London, 1645.
M1764. *Mercurius Diabolicus.* London, 1647.
——*Mercvrivs Hibernicvs, Or, The Irish mercurie.* London, 1645.
M1769. *Mercurius Propheticus, Or, A Collection of Some Old Predictions, O! May They Only Prove But Empty Fictions.* London, 1643.
M1882. Audley Mervin. *Irelands Complaint against Sir George Ratcliffe.* London, 1641.
M2281. *Mistris Parliament Brought to Bed of a Monstrous Childe of Reformation . . . By Mercurius Melancholicus,* London, 1648.
M2282. *Mistris Parliament Her Gossipping. . . . By Mercurius Melancholicus.* London, 1648.
M2283. *Mrs. Parliament Her Invitation of Mrs. London, To a Thanksgiving Dinner.* London, 1648.
M2284. *Mistris Parliament Presented in her Bed, after the sore travaile and hard labour which she endured last week, in the Birth of her Monstrous Off-spring, the Childe of Deformation. . . . By Mercurius Melancholicus.* London, 1648.
M2712. *More Newes from Ireland, or the bloody practices of the Papists.* London, 1641.
M2889. *Most fearefull Newes from the Bishoppricke of Durham.* London, 1641.
N106, N107. John Nalson. *An Impartial Collection of the Great Affairs of State, From the Beginning of the Scotch Rebellion In the Year MDCXXXIX. To the Murther of King Charles I.* 2 vols. London, 1682.
N381. Marchamont Nedham. *Certain Considerations Tendered in all humility, to an Honorable Member of the Councell of State.* London, 1649.
N392. Marchamont Nedham. *Interest will not Lie.* London, 1659.
N394. [Wrongly attributed to Marchamont Nedham]. *The Levellers levell'd, or, The Independents Conspiracie to root out Monarchie. An Interlude: Written by Mercurius Pragmaticus.* London,1647.
N404. Marchamont Nedham. *A Short History of the English Rebellion.* London, 1661.
N631. [Alexander Brome?] *A new Diurnall.* Oxford, 1643.
N670. *A New Mercury.* London, 1644.
N702. *A new Play Called Canterbury His Change of Diot.* London, 1641.
N1285. [Dudley, 4th Baron North]. *A Narrative of Some Passages in or Relating to the Long Parliament.* London, 1670.
O211. *Old Newes Newly Revived: Or, The discovery of all occurrences.* London, 1641.
O623. [Richard Overton?] *Articles of High Treason Exhibited against Cheap-Side Crosse.* London, 1642.
O620. [Richard Overton]. *The Araignement of Mr. Persecution.* London, 1645.

O851. *The Oxford Character Of the London Diurnall Examined and Answered.* London, 1645.
P336, P336A. *A Parallel Between the Late Troubles in Scotland, and the Present Trovbles in England, Written by a private Gentleman.* London, 1642.
P412. Henry Parker. *Observations upon some of his Majesties late Answers and Expresses.* London, 1642.
P425. [Henry Parker?] *To the High Court of Parliament: the humble remonstrance of the Company of Stationers.* London, 1643.
——*A perfect Diurnall of All the proceedings of the English and Scotch Armies in Ireland.* London, 18 July 1642.
——Hugh Peters. *M^r. Peters Last Report of the English Wars.* London, 1645.
P2224. Roger Pike. *A True Relation of the Proceedings of the Scots and English Forces in the North of Ireland.* London, 1642.
P2658C. William Pleydell. *The Speech of Mr Plydell.* London, 1641 [2].
P3293. *A Presse full of Pamphlets: Wherein, Are set Diversity of Prints, containing deformed and misfigured Letters: Composed into Books fraught with Libellous and Scandalous Sentences.* London, 1642.
P3926. William Prynne. *A Checke to Brittanicus.* London, 1644.
P4021A. William Prynne. *Nevves From Ipswich.* 'Ipswich' [?London], 1641.
P4039. William Prynne. *The Popish Royall Favourite.* London, 1643.
P4257A. John Pym. *The Copie of a Letter Written unto Sir Edward Deering, lately put out of the House, and committed unto the Tower, February 2. 1641.* London, 1642.
Q175. *Queres to be Considered.* London, 1647.
R164. Sir Walter Raleigh. *The History of the World.* 1614. Introduction by James Shirley. London, 1665.
R1821. Nathaniel Rogers. *A Letter, Discovering The Cause of Gods continuing wrath against the Nation, notwithstanding the present endeavours of Reformation.* London, 1644.
——*Sir Thomas Rowe His Speech At the Councell-Table touching Brasse-Money . . . Iuly, 1640.* London, 1641. Wing identifies this as part of *Speeches and Passages*, Wing E2309.
R2316A. John Rushworth. *Historical Collections.* First Part. London, 1659.
R2316. John Rushworth. *Historical Collections.* First Part. London, *c.*1675.
R2318. John Rushworth. *Historical Collections.* Second Part. 2 vols. London, 1680.
R2319. John Rushworth. *Historical Collections.* Third Part. 2 vols. London, 1691.
——John Rushworth. *Historical Collections.* Fourth Part. 2 vols. London, 1701.
R2333. John Rushworth. *The Tryal of Thomas Earl of Strafford . . . Faithfully Collected, and Impartially Published, Without Observation or Reflection.* London, 1680.
R2448. Bruno Ryves. *Mercurius Rusticus.* Oxford, 1646.
R2451. Brune Ryves. *Micro-Chronicon: Or, A briefe Chronology of the Time and Place of the Battels, Sieges, Conflicts, and other most remarkable Passages which have happened betwixt His Majestie and Parliament.* Oxford, 1647.
S646. William Sanderson. *A Compleat History of the Life and Raigne of King Charles From His Cradle to his Grave.* London, 1658.
S2294. *The Second part of Crafty Crvmwell. Or Oliver in his glory as king . . . Written by Mercurius Pragmaticus.* London, 1648.

S2318. *The Second Part of the Tragi-Comedy called New-Market Fayre, Or M[rs.] Parliaments New Figaryes . . . Written by the Man in the Moon.* London, 1649.
S3029. John Shawe. *Mistris Shawe's Tomb-Stone. Or, The Saints Remaines.* London, 1658.
S3160. Samuel Sheppard. *The Committee-Man Curried.* London, 1647.
S3168. Samuel Sheppard. *The Second Part of the Committee Man Curried.* London, 1647.
S3171. Samuel Sheppard. *The Weepers: Or, The bed of Snakes broken.* London, 1652.
S3597. *A Short History of the Anabaptists of High and Low Germany.* London, 1642.
S4264. *Newes from Smith.* London, 1644[5].
S4426. *The Souldiers' Language.* London, 1644.
S4552. *Some Passages that happened the 9th. of March between the Kings Majestie, and the committee.* London, 1642.
S4930. Sir Henry Spelman. *Reliquiæ Spelmannianæ.* Oxford, 1698.
S5070. Joshua Sprigge. *Anglia Rediviva; Englands Recovery: Being the History of the Motions, Actions, and Successes of the Army under the Immediate Conduct of His Excellency Sr Thomas Fairfax.* London, 1647.
T434aA. John Taylor. *A Brief Director.* London, ?1642.
T446. John Taylor. *Crop-Eare Curried, or, Tom Nash His Ghost.* London, 1644[5].
T481. John Taylor. *Mercvrivs Aqvaticvs; Or, the Water-Poets Answer to All that hath or shall be Writ by Mercurius Britanicus.* Oxford, 1643.
T486. John Taylor. *New Preachers, New.* London, 1641.
T498. John Taylor. *No Mercurius Aulicus, But some merry flashes of Intelligence . . . Also the breaking of Booker, the Asse-tronomicall London Figure-flinger.* Oxford, 1644.
T501. John Taylor. *Rebells Anathematized, And Anatomized.* Oxford, 1645.
T502. [Attr. John Taylor]. *A Recommendation to Mercurius Morbicus Together with a fair Character upon his worth.* London, 1647.
T514. John Taylor. *A Swarme of Sectaries and Schismatiqves.* London, 1641.
T627. Sir John Temple. *The Irish Rebellion.* London, 1646.
T1991. Heywood Townshend. *Historical Collections: or, An exact Account of the Proceedings of the Four last Parliaments of Q. Elizabeth Of Famous Memory.* London, 1680.
T2018. *A Tragi-Comedy, called New-Market-Fayre, Or a Parliament Out-Cry: of State-Commodities Set to Sale.* London, 1649.
T2577. *True and Remarkable Passages.* London, 10 Sept. 1642.
T2593. [Roger L'Estrange?]. *A True Catalogue.* London, 1659.
T2601. *The True Character of Mercurius Aulicus.* London, 1645.
V295. John Vicars. *The Burning-bush not Consumed.* London, 1641[2].
V307. John Vicars. *God in the Mount. Or, Englands Remembrancer.* London, 1641[2].
V309. John Vicars. *Gods Arke Overtopping the Worlds Waves.* London, 1646.
V313. John Vicars. *Jehovah-Jireh. God in the Mount. Or Englands Parliamentarie-Chronicle.* London, 1644.
V319. John Vicars. *Magnalia Dei Anglicana.* London, 1646.
V327. John Vicars. *A Sight of y[e] Transactions.* London, 1646.

V330. John Vicars. *A Summarie, or Short Survey of the Annalls.* London, 1646.
W324. Clement Walker. *The Compleat History of Independencie.* London, 1661.
W329. Clement Walker. *The History of Independency, With The Rise, Growth, and Practices of that powerfull and restlesse Faction.* London, 1648.
W1259. *Welcome, most welcome Newes. Mercurius Retrogradus.* London, 1647.
W1326. *The Welchmens Lamentation and Complaint.* London, 1643.
W1334. *The Welshmens Prave Resolution.* London, 1642.
W1338. *The Welch-mans publike Recantation.* London, 1642.
W1339. *The Welch-Mans Warning-Piece.* London, 1642.
W1343. *The Welsh Physitian.* London, 1647[8].
W1344. *The Welch Plunderer.* London, 1643.
W1544. George Wharton. *England's Iliads in a Nut-Shell.* Oxford, 1645.
W1550. George Wharton. *Mercurio-Cœlico Mastix. Or an Anti-Caveat.* Oxford, 1643[4].
W1986. Bulstrode Whitelocke. *Memorials of the English Affairs.* London, 1682.
W1992. Bulstrode Whitelocke. *The Speech of Bulstrode Whitelocke Esquire, To The Right Honourable the Lords, At a Conference of both Houses on Thursday the seventeenth of February last.* London, 1642.
W2030. Richard Whitlock. *Zootomia, Or, Observations on the Present Manners of the English.* London, 1654.
W3160. [Wrongly attributed to George Wither]. *The Great Assises Holden in Parnassus.* London, 1645.
W3171. George Wither. *Mercurius Rusticus: Or, A Countrey Messenger.* London, 1643.
W3204B. [Attr. George Wither]. *The Two Incomparable Generalissimo's of the world, with their Armies briefly described and embattailed, visibly opposing each other.* London, 1644.
W3641. [Attr. Sir Francis Wortley.] *Mercurius Britanicus His Welcome to Hell.* London, 1647.
W3681. *The Wren's Nest defil'd; or, Bishop Wren anatomiz'd, his life and actions dissected and laid open.* London, 1641.
W3685. Abraham Wright. *Five Sermons in Five Several Styles.* London, 1656.

POST-1700 PRIMARY SOMURCES

AUBREY, JOHN. *Brief Lives.* Ed. Andrew Clark. 2 vols. Oxford, 1898.
BACON, FRANCIS. *The Advancement of Learning and New Atlantis.* Ed. Arthur Johnston. Oxford, 1974.
BAILLIE, ROBERT. *The Letters and Journals of Robert Baillie . . . 1637–1662.* Ed. G. Laing. 3 vols. Edinburgh, 1841–2.
Barrington Family Letters 1628–1632. Ed. Arthur Searle. Camden Society[4], 28 (1983).
BAXTER, RICHARD. *A Holy Commonwealth.* 1659. Ed. William Lamont. Cambridge, 1994.
——*Autobiography of Richard Baxter.* Ed. J. M. Lloyd Thomas. London, 1925.
BIRCH, T., ed. *The Court and Times of Charles I.* 2 vols. London, 1848.

BUNYAN, JOHN. *The Miscellaneous Works of John Bunyan.* Vol. i. Ed. T. L. Underwood with the assistance of Roger Sharrock. Oxford, 1980.

BURNET, GILBERT. *The History of his Own Time.* 6 vols. Oxford, 1823.

Calendar of State Papers, Domestic Series, various.

Calendar of State Papers, Venetian, 1636–1639. London: HMSO, 1923.

CARLYLE, THOMAS, ed. *The Letters and Speeches Oliver Cromwell with Elucidations.* 1845. Ed. S. C. Lomas. 3 vols. New York, 1904.

CARTE, THOMAS, ed. *A Collection of Original Letters and Papers Concerning the Affairs of England From the Year 1641 to 1660.* 2 vols. London, 1739.

CAVENDISH, WILLIAM, 1st Earl of Newcastle. *Ideology and Politics on the Eve of Restoration: Newcastle's Advice to Charles II.* Ed. Thomas P. Slaughter. Philadelphia, 1984.

CLARENDON, EDWARD HYDE, Earl of. *The Life of Edward Earl of Clarendon.* 2 vols. Oxford, 1857.

——*History of the Rebellion and Civil Wars in England.* Ed. W. Dunn Macray. 6 vols. Oxford, 1888.

CLEVELAND, JOHN. *The Poems of John Cleveland.* Ed. B. Morris and E. Wittington. Oxford, 1967.

COATES, W. H., YOUNG, A. S., and SNOW, V. F., eds. *The Private Journals of the Long Parliament.* 3 vols. New Haven, 1982–92.

COPE, ESTHER S., and COATES, WILLSON H., eds. *Proceedings of the Short Parliament of 1640.* Camden Society[4], 19 (1977).

COWLEY, ABRAHAM. *The Civil War.* Ed. Allan Pritchard. Toronto, 1973.

CROMWELL, OLIVER. *The Writings and Speeches of Oliver Cromwell.* Ed. Wilbur Cortez Abbott. 4 vols. Cambridge, Mass., 1937–47.

DAVENANT, Sir WILLIAM. *Gondibert.* Ed. David. F. Gladish. Oxford, 1971.

D'EWES, Sir SIMONDS. *The Journal of Sir Simonds D'Ewes.* Ed. W. H. Coates. New Haven, 1942.

DONNE, JOHN. *The Satires, Epigrams and Verse Letters.* Ed. W. Milgate. Oxford, 1967.

DRYDEN, JOHN. *Life of Plutarch. The Works of John Dryden.* Vol. xvii. Ed. Samuel Holt Monk. Berkeley, 1971.

FFARINGTON, SUSAN MARIA, ed. *The Farington Papers.* Chetham Society, 39 (1856).

FIRTH, C. H., ed. *The Clarke Papers.* 4 vols. London, 1891–1901.

——and RAIT, R. S. *Acts and Ordinances of the Interregnum, 1642–1660.* 3 vols. London: HMSO, 1911.

FOX, GEORGE. *The Journal of George Fox.* Ed. Nigel Smith, forthcoming.

FOXE, JOHN. *The Acts and Monuments of John Foxe.* 4th edn. Ed. Revd Josiah Pratt. Introd. Revd John Stoughton. 8 vols. London, 1877.

FULLER, THOMAS. *The Church History of Britain.* 1655. Ed. J. S. Brewer. 6 vols. Oxford, 1845.

GARDINER, S. R. *Constitutional Documents of the Puritan Revolution 1625–1660.* Oxford, 1906.

The Great Assises Holden in Parnassus. 1645. Ed. Hugh Macdonald. Oxford, 1948. See Wing W3160.

GREG, W. W., ed., in collaboration with GILSON, J. P., JENKINSON, HILARY, MCKERROW, R. B., and POLLARD, A. W. *English Literary Autographs 1550–1650*. Part II. Oxford, 1928.

[HARINGTON, JOHN]. *The Diary of John Harington, MP., 1646–53*. Ed. Margaret F. Stieg. Somerset Record Society, 74 (1977).

HARLEY, BRILLIANA, Lady. *Letters of the Lady Brilliana Harley*. Ed. Thomas Taylor Lewis. Camden Society, 58 (1854).

Historical Manuscripts Commission: Fifth Report. Part I. London: HMSO, 1876.

Historical Manuscripts Commission: Seventh Report, Appendix. London: HMSO, 1879.

Historical Manuscripts Commission: Twelfth Report, Appendix, Part VII. The Manuscripts of S. H. Le Fleming, Esq., of Rydal Hall. London: HMSO, 1890.

Historical Manuscripts Commission: Fourteenth Report, Appendix, The Manuscripts of His Grace the Duke of Portland, Preserved at Welbeck Abbey. Vols. i–ii. London: HMSO, 1891–3.

Historical Manuscripts Commission: Report on the Manuscripts of the Duke of Buccleuch and Queensberry, K.G., K.T., Preserved at Montagu House, Whitehall. Vol. i. London: HMSO, 1899.

Historical Manuscripts Commission: Report on the Manuscripts of Lord Montagu of Beaulieu. London: HMSO, 1900.

Historical Manuscripts Commission: Report on the Manuscripts of the Earl of Verulam. London: HMSO, 1906.

HOBBES, THOMAS. *Leviathan*. 1651. Ed. Richard Tuck. Cambridge, 1991.

—— *Behemoth, or the Long Parliament*. Ed. Ferdinand Tönnies. Chicago, 1990.

HUTCHINSON, LUCY. *Memoirs of the Life of Colonel Hutchinson*. 1806. Ed. N. H. Keeble. London, 1995.

JONSON, BEN. *Ben Jonson*. Ed. C. H. Herford and Percy and Evelyn Simpson. 11 vols. Oxford, 1925–52.

JOSSELIN, RALPH. *The Diary of Ralph Josselin 1616–1683*. Ed. Alan Macfarlane. London, 1976.

LARKIN, JAMES F., ed. *Stuart Royal Proclamations*, vol. ii. *Royal Proclamations of King Charles I, 1625–1646*. Oxford, 1983.

—— and HUGHES, PAUL L., eds. *Stuart Royal Proclamations*, vol. i: *Royal Proclamations of King James I, 1603–1625*. Oxford, 1973.

LARKING, LAMBERT B., ed. *Proceedings Principally in the County of Kent in connection with the Parliaments Called in 1640*. Camden Society, 80 (1862).

LILLY, WILLIAM. *Mr. William Lilly's History of His Life and Times, From the Year 1602, to 1681*. London, 1715.

LUDLOW, EDMUND. *The Memoirs of Edmund Ludlow*. Ed. C. H. Firth. 2 vols. Oxford, 1894.

—— *A Voyce from the Watch Tower*. Ed. A. B. Worden. Camden Society[4], 21 (1978).

LUKE, Sir SAMUEL. *Journal of Sir Samuel Luke*. Ed. I. G. Philip. 3 vols. Oxfordshire Record Society, 29, 31, 33 (1950–3).

—— *The Letter Books of Sir Samuel Luke 1644–5*. Ed. H. G. Tibbutt. London: HMSO, 1963.

MACRAY, Rev W. DUNN, ed. *Calendar of the Clarendon State Papers.* Vols. 1–2. Oxford: Clarendon Press, 1869–72.

The Marprelate Tracts, 1588, 1589. Ed. William Pierce. London, 1911.

MARVELL, ANDREW. *Poems and Letters of Andrew Marvell.* Ed. H. M. Margoliouth, rev. Pierre Legois and E. E. Duncan Jones. 2 vols. Oxford, 1971.

—— *The Rehearsal Transpros'd.* Ed. D. I. B. Smith. Oxford, 1971.

MILTON, JOHN. *Complete Prose Works of John Milton.* 8 vols. General editor Don M. Wolfe. New Haven, 1953–82.

—— *The Complete Poetry of John Milton.* Ed. John T. Shawcross. New York, 1971.

MONTAIGNE, MICHEL DE. *The Complete Essays.* Trans. M. A. Screech. London, 1991.

NASHE, THOMAS. *Pierce Penilesse.* 1592. London, 1924.

The Nicholas Papers: Correspondence of Sir Edward Nicholas, Secretary of State. Ed. George F. Warner. Vol. i. Camden Society[2], 40 (1886).

NOTESTEIN, WALLACE, and RELPH, FRANCES HELEN, eds. *Commons Debates for 1629.* Minneapolis, 1921.

OLDENBURG, HENRY. *The Correspondence of Henry Oldenburg.* Ed. and trans. A. Rupert Hall and Marie Boas Hall. Vol. i: *1641–1662.* With the collaboration of Eberhard Reichmann. Madison, 1965.

OSBORNE, DOROTHY. *Letters of Dorothy Osborne to William Temple.* Ed. G. C. Moore Smith. Oxford, 1928.

The Oxinden and Peyton Letters 1642–1670. Ed. Dorothy Gardiner. London, 1937.

The Oxinden Letters 1607–1642. Ed. Dorothy Gardiner. London, 1933.

RAPIN DE THOYRAS, PAUL AUGUST. *Dissertation sur les Whigs & les Torys.* Trans. Mr Ozell. London, 1717.

—— *The History of England.* Trans. N. Tindal. 2nd edn. 2 vols. London, 1732–3.

ROLLINS, HYDER E. *Cavalier and Puritan: Ballads and Broadsides Illustrating the Period of the Great Rebellion, 1640–1660.* New York, 1923.

ROUS, JOHN. *Diary of John Rous.* Ed. Mary Anne Everett Green. Camden Society, 66 (1856).

RUGG, THOMAS. *The Diurnal of Thomas Rugg 1659–1661.* Ed. William L. Sachse. Camden Society[3], 91 (1961).

RUSHWORTH, JOHN. Letter to Sir Harbottle Grimston. Ed. S. R. Gardiner. *Notes and Queries*[6], 5 (1882), 325–6; also *HMC: Verulam*, 82–3.

SAINTSBURY, GEORGE, ed. *Minor Poets of the Caroline Period.* 3 vols. Oxford, 1905–21.

SALGADO, GAMINI, ed. *Cony-Catchers and Bawdy Baskets: An Anthology of Elizabethan Low Life.* Harmondsworth, 1972.

——ed. *The Elizabethan Underworld.* London, 1977.

SHAKESPEARE, WILLIAM. *A Midsummer Night's Dream.* London, 1967.

SIDNEY, Sir PHILIP. *Miscellaneous Prose of Sir Philip Sidney.* Ed. Katherine Duncan-Jones and Jan Van Dorsten. Oxford, 1973.

The Spectator. Ed. Donald F. Bond. 5 vols. Oxford, 1965.

SWIFT, JONATHAN, and SHERIDAN, THOMAS. *The Intelligencer.* Ed. James Woolley. Oxford, 1992.

Sydney Papers. Ed. R. W. Blencowe. London, 1825.

VERNEY, Sir RALPH. *Notes of Proceedings in the Long Parliament Temp. Charles I.* Ed. John Bruce. Camden Society, 31 (1845).
WALLINGTON, NEHEMIAH. *Historical Notices of Events Occurring Chiefly in the Reign of Charles I.* Ed. R. Webb. 2 vols. London, 1869.
WARWICK, Sir PHILIP. *Memoires of the reigne of King Charles I. With a Continuation to the Happy Restauration of King Charles II.* London, 1701.
WHARTON, NEHEMIAH. [Correspondence.] *Archæologia*, 35 (1853), 310–34.
WITHER, GEORGE. *Extracts from Juvenilia or Poems.* Ed. Alexander Dalrymple. 1785.
WOOD, ANTHONY. *Athenæ Oxonienses.* 3rd edn. Ed. Philip Bliss. 4 vols. London, 1813–20.
——*Fasti Oxonienses.* 3rd edn. Ed. Philip Bliss. London, 1815.

THESES

COTTON, A. N. B. 'London Newsbooks in the Civil War: Their Political Attitudes and Sources of Information'. D.Phil. thesis. Oxford, 1971.
FABER, BENNE KLAAS. 'The Poetics of Subversion and Conservatism: Popular Satire, c.1640–c.1649'. D.Phil. thesis. Oxford, 1992.
FREIST, DAGMAR. 'The World is Ruled and Governed by Opinion: The Formation of Opinions and the Communication Network in London 1637 to c.1645'. Ph.D. thesis. Cambridge, 1992.
HILL, MELRIN, 'The Poetry of John Hall (1627–1656)'. Ph.D. thesis. Columbia University, New York, 1963/4.
MANNING, B. S. 'Neutrals and Neutralism in the English Civil War 1642–1646'. D.Phil. thesis. Oxford, 1957.
MORGAN, VICTOR. 'Country, Court and Cambridge University, 1558–1640: A Study in the Evolution of a Political Culture'. Ph.D. thesis. 5 vols. Norwich, 1983.
ORCHARD, C. R. 'Literary Theory in the English Civil War 1642–1660'. M.Phil. thesis. Oxford, 1989.
PENDLETON, JOHN W. 'The Prose Works of John Hall of Durham'. B.Litt. thesis. Oxford, 1934.
SHAW, JOHN BURNHAM. 'The Life and Works of John Hall of Durham'. Ph.D. thesis. Johns Hopkins University, Baltimore, 1952.
STORMER, DAVID. 'The Faithful Scout, 1652–3: A Re-evaluation of a So-called Radical London Weekly'. MA thesis Victoria University of Wellington, 1987.

GENERAL BIBLIOGRAPHY

ACHINSTEIN, SHARON. *Milton and the Revolutionary Reader.* Princeton, 1994.
ADAMSON, J. S. A. 'Eminent Victorians: S. R. Gardiner and the Liberal as Hero'. *Historical Journal*, 33 (1990), 641–57.

ALLEN, DON CAMERON. *The Star-Crossed Renaissance.* Durham, NC, 1941.

ANDREWS, ALEXANDER. *The History of British Journalism, from the Foundation of the Newspaper Press in England, to the Repeal of the Stamp Act in 1855.* 1859. Grosse Point, Mich., 1968.

APPADURAI, ARJUN, ed. *The Social Life of Things: Commodities in Cultural Perspective.* Cambridge, 1986.

ARAM VEESER, H., ed. *The New Historicism.* London, 1989.

ARMITAGE, DAVID. 'The Cromwellian Protectorate and the Languages of Empire'. *Historical Journal,* 35 (1992), 531–55.

——with HIMY, ARMAND, and SKINNER, QUENTIN, eds. *Milton and Republicanism.* Cambridge, 1995.

ARMSTRONG, C. A. J. 'Some Examples of the Distribution and Speed of News in England at the Time of the Wars of the Roses'. *Studies in Medieval History: Presented Frederick Maurice Powicke.* Ed. R. W. Hunt, W. A. Pantin, and R. W. Southern. Oxford, 1948: 429–54.

ASHTON, ROBERT. *The English Civil War: Conservatism and Revolution 1603–1649.* 1978. 2nd edn. London, 1989.

——*Counter Revolution: The Second Civil War and its Origins, 1646–1648.* New Haven, 1994.

ATHERTON, IAN. 'Viscount Scudamore and the Collection of Newsletters in the Seventeenth Century'. Unpublished paper delivered at the History of the News seminar, Magdalen College, Oxford, 25 Nov. 1993.

AYLMER, G. E. *Rebellion or Revolution? England 1640–1660.* Oxford, 1986.

BAKER, HERSCHEL. *The Race of Time: Three Lectures on Renaissance Historiography.* Alexander Lectures, 1965. Toronto, 1967.

BAKHTIN, MIKHAIL. *Problems of Dostoevsky's Poetics.* 1963. Ed. and trans. Caryl Emerson. Manchester, 1984.

——*Rabelais and his World.* 1965. Trans. Hélène Iswolsky. Bloomington, Ind., 1984.

——*Speech Genres & Other Late Essays.* Trans. Vern W. McGee. Ed. Caryl Emerson and Michael Holquist. Austin, Tex., 1986.

BALIBAR, ÉTIENNE, and MACHEREY, PIERRE. 'On Literature as an Ideological Form'. *Untying the Text: A Post-Structuralist Reader.* Ed. Robert Young. London, 1981: 80–99.

BALLASTER, ROS. *Seductive Forms: Women's Amatory Fiction from 1684 to 1740.* Oxford, 1992.

BARWICK, GEORGE. 'Corantos'. *Library*[3], 4 (1913), 113–21.

BAUMANN, GERD, ed. *The Written Word: Literacy in Transition.* Oxford, 1986.

BELLANY, ALASTAIR. ' "Raylinge Rymes and Vaunting Verse": Libellous Politics in Early Stuart England, 1603–1628'. *Culture and Politics in Early Stuart England.* Ed. K. Sharpe and P. Lake. London, 1994: 284–310.

BENNET, H. S. *English Books and Readers,* 3 vols. 1965–70. Cambridge, 1989.

BENTLEY, GERALD EADES. *The Jacobean and Caroline Stage,* 7 vols. Oxford, 1941–68.

BERKOWITZ, DAVID SANDLER. *John Selden's Formative Years: Politics and Society in Early Seventeenth-Century England.* London, 1988.

BLACK, JEREMY. *The English Press in the Eighteenth Century.* London, 1987.

BLAGDEN, CYPRIAN. *The Stationers' Company: A History 1403–1959*. Stanford, Calif., 1960.
——'The Stationers' Company in the Civil War Period'. *Library*[5], 13 (1958), 1–17.
——'The Distribution of Almanacks in the Second Half of the Seventeenth Century'. *Studies in Bibliography*, 11 (1958), 107–16.
BLOCH, MARC. *The Historian's Craft*. Trans. Peter Putnam. 1954. Manchester, 1984.
BOND, RICHMOND P., ed. *Studies in the Early English Periodical*. Chapel Hill, NC, 1957.
——*Growth and Change in the Early English Press*. Lawrence, Kan., 1969.
BOSTON, RAY. *The Essential History of Fleet Street: Its History and Influence*. London, 1990.
BOURDIEU, PIERRE. *Outline of a Theory of Practice*. Trans. Richard Nice. New York, 1977.
——*Distinction: A Social Criticism of the Judgement of Taste*. Trans. Richard Nice. Cambridge, Mass., 1984.
BOURNE, H. R. FOX. *English Newspapers: Chapters in the History of Journalism*. London, 1887.
BOYCE, GEORGE, CURRAN, JAMES, and WINGATE, PAULINE, eds. *Newspaper History: From the Seventeenth Century to the Present Day*. London, 1978.
BRADFORD, ALAN T. 'Stuart Absolutism and the "Utility" of Tacitus'. *Huntington Library Quarterly*, 45 (1983), 127–55.
BRAILSFORD, H. N. *The Levellers and the English Revolution*. 1961. Ed. Christopher Hill. Nottingham, 1983.
BRAUDEL, FERNAND. *The Mediterranean and the Mediterranean World in the Age of Philip II*. 1949, 1966. Trans. Siân Reynolds. 2 vols. New York, 1972.
——*On History*. Trans. Sarah Matthews. Chicago, 1980.
BRENNER, ROBERT. *Merchants and Revolution: Commercial Change, Political Conflict, and London's Overseas Traders, 1550–1653*. Cambridge, 1993.
BRIGDEN, SUSAN. *London and the Reformation*. Oxford, 1989.
BROWNLEY, MARTINE WATSON. 'Sir Richard Baker's *Chronicle* and Later Seventeenth-Century English Historiography'. *Huntington Library Quarterly*, 52 (1989), 481–500.
BURKE, PETER. 'A Survey of the Popularity of Ancient Historians'. *History and Theory*, 5 (1966), 135–52.
——*Popular Culture in Early Modern Europe*. 1978. Aldershot, 1988.
——ed. *New Perspectives on Historical Writing*. Cambridge, 1991.
BUTLER, MARTIN. *Theatre and Crisis 1632–1642*. Cambridge, 1984.
Cambridge Bibliography of English Literature. Ed. F. W. Bateson. Vol. i: *600–1600*. Cambridge, 1940.
CAPP, BERNARD S. *The Fifth Monarchy Men: A Study in Seventeenth-Century English Millenarianism*. London, 1972.
——*Astrology and the Popular Press: English Almanacs 1500–1800*. London, 1979.
——*The World of John Taylor the Water-Poet, 1578–1653*. Oxford, 1994.
CAREY, JOHN. 'Sixteenth- and Seventeenth-Century Prose'. *English Poetry and Prose, 1550–1674*. Ed. Christopher Ricks. 1970. London, 1986: 329–411.

CARLSON, LELAND H. *Martin Marprelate Gentleman: Master Job Throkmorton Laid Open in his Colours.* San Marino, Calif., 1981.

CARLTON, CHARLES. *Going to the Wars: The Experience of the British Civil Wars, 1638–1651.* 1992. London, 1994.

CARUS-WILSON, ELEANOR M., ed. *Essays in Economic History.* Vol. ii. Economic History Society. London, 1962.

CHARTIER, ROGER. *The Cultural Uses of Print in Early Modern France.* Trans. Lydia G. Cochrane. Princeton, 1987.

——*Cultural History: Between Practices and Representations.* Trans. Lydia G. Cochrane. Cambridge, 1988.

——ed. *The Culture of Print: Power and the Uses of Print in Early Modern Europe.* Trans. Lydia G. Cochrane. Cambridge, 1989.

——ed. *Passions of the Renaissance.* Vol. iii of *A History of Private Life.* General eds. Philippe Ariès and George Duby. Cambridge, Mass., 1989.

——'Leisure and Sociability: Reading Aloud in Modern Europe'. Trans. Carol Mossman. *Urban Life in the Renaissance.* Ed. Susan Zimmerman and Ronald F. E. Weissman. Newark, NJ, 1989: 103–20.

——*The Cultural Origins of the French Revolution.* Trans. Lydia G. Cochrane. Durham, NC, 1991.

——*The Order of Books: Readers, Authors, and Libraries in Europe between the Fourteenth and Eighteenth Centuries.* Trans. Lydia G. Cochrane. Cambridge, 1994.

CHOUILLET, ANNE-MARIE, and FABRE, MADELEINE. 'Diffusion et réception des nouvelles et ouvrages britanniques par la presse spécialisée de langue française'. *La Diffusion et la lecture des journaux de langue française sous l'ancien régime.* Ed. Hans Bots. Amsterdam, 1988.

CLARK, J. C. D. *Revolution and Rebellion: State and Society in England in the Seventeenth and Eighteenth Centuries.* Cambridge, 1986.

CLARK, PETER. 'The Ownership of Books in England, 1560–1640: The Example of Some Kentish Townsfolk'. *Schooling and Society.* Ed. Lawrence Stone. Baltimore, 1976: 95–111.

CLARK, SANDRA. *The Elizabethan Pamphleteers: Popular Moralistic Pamphlets, 1580–1640.* London, 1983.

CLARK, STUART. 'Inversion, Misrule and the Meaning of Witchcraft'. *Past and Present,* 87 (1980), 98–127.

——'The *Annales* Historians'. *The Return of Grand Theory in the Human Sciences.* Ed. Quentin Skinner. 1985. Cambridge, 1990: 179–96.

CLUCAS, STEPHEN. 'Samuel Hartlib's Ephemerides, 1635–59, and the Pursuit of Scientific and Philosophical Manuscripts: The Religious Ethos of an Intelligencer'. *Seventeenth Century,* 6 (1991), 33–55.

CLYDE, WILLIAM M. 'Parliament and the Press'. *Library*[4], 13 (1932–3), 399–424; 14 (1933–4), 39–58.

——*The Struggle for the Freedom of the Press from Caxton to Cromwell.* London, 1934.

COGSWELL, THOMAS. 'The Politics of Propaganda: Charles I and the People in the 1620s'. *Journal of British Studies,* 29 (1990), 187–215.

COLLINS, D. C., ed. *Battle of Nieuport.* Shakespeare Association Facsimiles, 9. London, 1935.

CORNS, THOMAS. *Uncloistered Virtue: English Political Literature, 1640–1660*. Oxford, 1992.
COTTON, A. N. B. 'John Dillingham, Journalist of the Middle Group'. *English Historical Review*, 93 (1978), 817–34.
CRANFIELD, GEOFFREY A. *The Development of the Provincial Newspaper, 1700–1760*. Oxford, 1962.
—— *The Press & Society: From Caxton to Northcliffe*. London, 1978.
CRAWFORD, PATRICIA. ' "Charles Stuart, That Man of Blood" '. *Journal of British Studies*, 16 (1977), 41–61.
—— *Denzil Holles, 1598–1680: A Study of his Political Career*. Royal Historical Society, Studies in History, 16. London, 1979.
CRESSY, DAVID. *Literacy and the Social Order: Reading and Writing in Tudor and Stuart England*. Cambridge, 1980.
—— *Coming Over: Migration and Communication between England and New England in the Seventeenth Century*. Cambridge, 1987.
CROLL, MORRIS W. *Style, Rhetoric, and Rhythm: Essays by Morris W. Croll*. Ed. J. Max Patrick and Robert O. Evans, with John M. Wallace and R. J. Schoek. Princeton, 1966.
CROMARTIE, A. D. T. 'The Printing of Parliamentary Speeches November 1640–July 1642'. *Historical Journal*, 33 (1990), 23–44.
CURRY, PATRICK. *Prophecy and Power: Astrology in Early Modern England*. Cambridge, 1989.
CUST, RICHARD. 'News and Politics in Early Seventeenth-Century England'. *Past and Present*, 112 (1986), 60–90.
—— *The Forced Loan and English Politics, 1626–1628*. Oxford, 1987.
—— and HUGHES, ANN, eds. *Conflict in Early Stuart England: Studies in Religion and Politics 1603–1642*. London, 1989.
DAHL, FOLKE. 'Amsterdam: Cradle of English Newspapers'. *Library*[5], 4 (1949), 166–78.
—— *A Bibliography of English Corantos and Periodical Newsbooks 1620–1642*. London, 1952.
—— with PETIBON, FANNY, and BOULET, MARGUERITE. *Les Débuts de la presse française: Nouveaux Aperçus*. Acta Bibliothecae Gotoburgensis, 4. Göteborg, 1951.
DARNTON, ROBERT. 'Writing News and Telling Stories'. *Dædalus*, 104 (1975), 175–94.
—— *The Literary Underground of the Old Regime*. Cambridge, Mass., 1982.
—— *The Great Cat Massacre and Other Episodes in French Cultural History*. 1984. New York, 1985.
—— *The Kiss of Lamourette: Reflections in Cultural History*. New York, 1990.
—— 'History of Reading'. *New Perspectives on Historical Writing*. Ed. Peter Burke. Cambridge, 1991: 140–67.
DAVIS, NATALIE ZEMON. *Society and Culture in Early Modern France*. Stanford, Calif., 1975.
DE CERTEAU, MICHEL. *The Practice of Everyday Life*. Trans. Steven Rendall. Berkeley, 1988.
—— *The Writing of History*. Trans. Tom Conley. New York, 1988.

DIETHE, JURGEN. '*The Moderate*: Politics and Allegiances of a Revolutionary Newspaper'. *History of Political Thought*, 4 (1983), 247–94.

EAGLETON, TERRY. *The Function of Criticism: From the Spectator to Post-structuralism.* London, 1984.

EALES, JACQUELINE. *Puritans and Roundheads: The Harleys of Brampton Bryan and the Outbreak of the English Civil War.* Cambridge, 1990.

EARLE, PETER. *The Making of the English Middle Class: Business, Society and Family Life in London, 1660–1730.* London, 1989.

EDWARDS, PHILIP, BENTLEY, GERALD EADES, MCLUSKIE, KATHLEEN, and POTTER, LOIS. *The Revels History of Drama in English*, vol. iv: *The Revels History of Drama in English 1613–1660.* London, 1981.

EISENSTEIN, ELIZABETH L. *The Printing Press as an Agent of Change: Communications and Cultural Transformations in Early-Modern Europe.* 2 vols. Cambridge, 1979.

ELIAS, NORBERT. *The History of Manners.* Trans. Edmund Jephcott. New York, 1978.

EPSTEIN, EDWARD JAY. *Between Fact and Fiction: The Problem of Journalism.* New York, 1975.

EVERITT, ALAN. *The Local Community and the Great Rebellion.* London, 1969.

FEATHER, JOHN. *A History of British Publishing.* London, 1988.

——'The Country Trade in Books'. *Spreading the Word.* Ed. R. Myers and M. Harris. Winchester, 1990: 165–72.

FEBVRE, LUCIEN, and MARTIN, HENRI-JEAN. *The Coming of the Book: The Impact of Printing 1450–1800.* 1958. Trans. David Gerard. London, 1990.

FERDINAND, CHRISTINE. *Networking the News.* Oxford, 1996.

FEYEL, GILLES. *La 'Gazette' en province à travers ses réimpressions, 1631–1752.* Amsterdam, 1982.

FIELDING, JOHN. 'Opposition to the Personal Rule of Charles I: The Diary of Robert Woodford, 1637–1641'. *Historical Journal*, 31 (1988), 769–88.

FIRTH, C. H. 'The Development of the Study of Seventeenth-Century History'. *Transactions of the Royal Historical Society*[3], 7 (1913), 25–48.

FISH, STANLEY. *There's No Such Thing as Free Speech: And it's a Good Thing, Too.* New York, 1994.

FLETCHER, ANTHONY. *The Outbreak of the English Civil War.* 1981. London, 1985.

FORD, W. C. 'Benjamin Harris, Printer and Bookseller'. *Proceedings of the Massachusetts Historical Society*, 57 (1923), 34–68.

FORD, WYN. 'The Problem of Literacy in Early Modern England'. *History*, 78 (1993), 22–37.

FORTESCUE, G. K., ed. *Catalogue to the Thomason Tracts.* 2 vols. London, 1908.

FOSTER, ELIZABETH READ. 'Printing the Petition of Right'. *Huntington Library Quarterly*, 38 (1974), 81–3.

FOWLER, ROGER. *Language in the News: Discourse and Ideology in the Press.* London, 1991.

FOX, ADAM. 'Ballads, Libels and Popular Ridicule in Jacobean England'. *Past and Present*, 145 (1995), 47–83.

FOX, LEVI, ed. *English Historical Scholarship in the Sixteenth and Seventeenth Centuries.* London, 1956.

FRANK, JOSEPH. *The Levellers.* Cambridge, Mass., 1955.
——'An Early Newspaper Allusion to Shakespeare'. *Shakespeare Quarterly,* 7 (1956), 456.
——*The Beginnings of the English Newspaper, 1620–1660.* Cambridge, Mass., 1961.
——*Cromwell's Press Agent: A Critical Biography of Marchamont Nedham, 1620–1678.* Lanham, Md., 1980.
FRASER, PETER. *The Intelligence of the Secretaries of State and their Monopoly of Licensed News, 1600–1688.* Cambridge, 1956.
FREARSON, MICHAEL. 'The Distribution and Readership of London Corantos in the 1620s'. *Serials and their Readers, 1620–1914.* Ed. R. Myers and M. Harris. Winchester, 1993: 1–25.
FRIEDMAN, JEROME. *Miracles and the Pulp Press during the English Revolution: The Battle of the Frogs and Fairford's Flies.* London, 1993.
FUKUYAMA, FRANCIS. *The End of History and the Last Man.* London, 1992.
FURBANK, P. N., and OWENS, W. R. *The Canonization of Daniel Defoe.* New Haven, 1988.
FUSSNER, FRANK SMITH. *The Historical Revolution: English Historical Writing and Thought, 1580–1640.* London, 1962.
GALTUNG, JOHANN, and RUGE, MARI. 'Structuring and Selecting News'. *The Manufacture of News: Social Problems, Deviance, and the Mass Media.* Ed. Stanley Cohen and Jock Young. London, 1973: 62–72.
GARDINER, S. R. *History of England from the Accession of James I to the Outbreak of the Civil War 1603–1642.* 10 vols. London, 1883–4.
——*History of the Great Civil War.* 4 vols. London, 1986–7.
——*History of the Commonwealth and Protectorate.* 1903. 4 vols. Adlestrop, 1988–9.
GASKELL, PHILIP. *A New Introduction to Bibliography.* 1972. Oxford, 1985.
GEERTZ, CLIFFORD. *The Interpretation of Cultures.* New York, 1973.
GENTLES, IAN. *The New Model Army in England, Ireland and Scotland, 1645–1653.* Oxford, 1992.
GERRARD, CHRISTINE. *The Patriot Opposition to Walpole: Politics, Poetry, and National Myth, 1725–1742.* Oxford, 1994.
GINZBURG, CARLO. *The Cheese and the Worms: The Cosmos of a Sixteenth-Century Miller.* Trans. John and Anne Tedeschi. New York, 1982.
Gooch, G. P. *English Democratic Ideas in the Seventeenth Century.* 1898. 2nd edn. with supplementary notes and appendices by H. J. Laski. Cambridge, 1927.
GOODY, JACK. *The Domestication of the Savage Mind.* Cambridge, 1977.
——*The Logic of Writing and the Organization of Society.* Cambridge, 1986.
GOULD, MARK. *Revolution in the Development of Capitalism: The Coming of the English Revolution.* Berkeley, 1987.
GRAFTON, ANTHONY T. 'The Importance of Being Printed'. *Journal of Interdisciplinary History,* 11 (1980), 265–86.
GRAHAM, WALTER. *The Beginnings of English Literary Periodicals: A Study of Periodical Literature, 1665–1715.* Oxford, 1926.
GRANSDEN, ANTONIA. *Historical Writing in England,* vol. ii: *C. 1307 to the Early Sixteenth Century.* London, 1982.

GRANT, JAMES. *The Newspaper Press: Its Origin—Progress—and Present Position.* 2 vols. London, 1871.

GREENBERG, STEPHEN J. 'Dating Civil War Pamphlets, 1641–1644'. *Albion,* 20 (1988), 387–401.

——'The Thomason Collection'. [Debate with Michael Mendle.] *Albion,* 22 (1980), 85–98.

GREGG, W. W., GILSON, J. P., JENKINSON, HILARY, MCKERROW, R. B., and POLLARD, A. W., eds. *English Literary Autographs 1550–1650.* Part II. Oxford, 1928.

GUNN, J. A. W. *Politics and the Public Interest in the Seventeenth Century.* London, 1969.

HABERMAS, JÜRGEN. *The Structural Transformation of the Public Sphere: An Inquiry into a Category of Bourgeois Society.* Trans. Thomas Burger. Cambridge, Mass., 1989.

HALL, STUART, CRITCHER, CHAS, JEFFERSON, TONY, CLARKE, JOHN, and ROBERTS, BRIAN. *Policing the Crisis: Mugging, the State, and Law and Order.* London, 1978.

HALLER, WILLIAM. *Liberty and Reformation in the Puritan Revolution.* New York, 1955.

HAMPSON, GILLIAN. 'John Rushworth'. *History of Parliament: The House of Commons 1660–1690.* Ed. Basil Duke Henning. 3 vols. London, 1983: iii. 357–9.

HANDOVER, P. M. *Printing in London from 1476 to Modern Times.* London, 1960.

——*A History of the London Gazette, 1665–1965.* London: HMSO, 1965.

HANSON, LAURENCE. 'English Newsbooks, 1620–1642'. *Library*[4], 18 (1938), 355–84.

HARRIS, MICHAEL, and LEE, ALAN. *The Press in English Society from the Seventeenth to Nineteenth Centuries.* Cranbury, NJ, 1986.

HARRIS, TIM. *Politics under the Later Stuarts: Party Conflict in a Divided Society 1660–1715.* London, 1993.

HART, JIM ALLEE. *Views on the News: The Developing Editorial Syndrome, 1500–1800.* Foreword by Howard Rusk Long. Carbondale, Ill., 1970.

HARTH, ERICA. *Ideology and Culture in Seventeenth-Century France.* Ithaca, NY, 1983.

HARTMAN, JOAN E. 'Restyling the King: Clarendon Writes Charles I'. *Pamphlet Wars.* Ed. James Holstun. London, 1992: 45–59.

HEALY, THOMAS, and SAWDAY, JONATHAN, eds. *Literature and the English Civil War.* Cambridge, 1990.

HEINEMANN, MARGOT. *Puritanism and Theatre: Thomas Middleton and Opposition Drama under the Early Stuarts.* 1980. Cambridge, 1982.

HERD, HAROLD. *The March of Journalism: The Story of the British Press from 1622 to the Present Day.* London, 1952.

HEXTER, J. H. *The Reign of King Pym.* Cambridge, Mass., 1941.

——*Reappraisals in History.* London, 1961.

HIBBARD, CAROLINE. *Charles I and the Popish Plot.* Chapel Hill, NC, 1983.

HILL, CHRISTOPHER. *Society and Puritanism in Pre-revolutionary England.* London, 1964.

——*Intellectual Origins of the English Revolution.* Oxford, 1965.

——*Puritanism and Revolution.* 1958. London, 1968.
——*Religion and Politics in 17th Century England.* Brighton, 1986.
——'Political Discourse in Early Seventeenth-Century England'. *Politics and People in Revolutionary England.* Ed. C. Jones *et al.* Oxford, 1986: 41–64.
——*Change and Continuity in Seventeenth-Century England.* 1974. Rev. edn. New Haven, 1991.
——*The English Bible and the Seventeenth-Century Revolution.* London, 1993.
HINMAN, CHARLTON. *The Printing and Proof-Reading of the First Folio of Shakespeare.* 2 vols. Oxford, 1963.
HIRST, DEREK. 'The Defection of Sir Edward Dering, 1640–1641'. *Historical Journal,* 15 (1972), 193–208.
——*The Representative of the People? Voters and Voting in England under the Early Stuarts.* Cambridge, 1975.
——*Authority and Conflict: England, 1603–1658.* Cambridge, Mass., 1986.
HOLMES, CLIVE. 'The County Community in Stuart Historiography'. *Journal of British Studies,* 19 (1980), 54–73.
HOLSTUN, JAMES, ed. *Pamphlet Wars: Prose in the English Revolution.* London, 1992.
HOWELL, ROGER, Jr., and BREWSTER, DAVID E. 'Reconsidering the Levellers: The Evidence of *The Moderate*'. *Past and Present,* 46 (1970), 68–86.
HUGHES, ANN. *Government, Society and Civil War in Warwickshire 1620–1660.* Cambridge, 1987.
——*The Causes of the English Civil War.* Basingstoke, 1991.
HUNT, LYNN, ed. *The New Cultural History.* Berkeley, 1989.
HUPPERT, GEORGE. 'The Renaissance Background of Historicism', *History and Theory,* 5 (1966), 48–60.
HUTSON, LORNA. *The Usurer's Daughter: Male Friendship and Fictions of Women in Sixteenth-Century England.* London, 1994.
HUTTON, RONALD. *The Restoration: A Political and Religious History of England and Wales 1659–1667.* Oxford, 1985.
INGRAM, MARTIN. 'Ridings, Rough Music and Mocking Rhymes in Early Modern England'. *Popular Culture in Seventeenth-Century England.* Ed. Barry Reay. New York, 1985: 166–97.
JACKSON, H. J. 'Writing in Books and Other Marginal Activities'. *University of Toronto Quarterly,* 62 (1992/3), 217–31.
JARDINE, LISA, and GRAFTON, ANTHONY. '"Studied for Action": How Gabriel Harvey Read his Livy'. *Past and Present,* 129 (1990), 30–78.
JENKINS, GERAINT H. *The Foundations of Modern Wales.* Oxford, 1987.
JOHNSON, FRANCIS R. 'Notes on English Retail Book-Prices, 1550–1640'. *Library*[5], 5 (1950), 83–112.
JONES, COLIN, NEWITT, MALYN, and ROBERTS, STEPHEN, eds. *Politics and People in Revolutionary England: Essays in Honour of Ivan Roots.* Oxford, 1986.
JOYCE, HERBERT. *The History of the Post Office: From its Establishment down to 1836.* London, 1893.
KISHLANSKY, MARK A. *The Rise of the New Model Army.* Cambridge, 1979.
KNACHEL, PHILIP A. *England and the Fronde: The Impact of the English Civil War and Revolution on France.* Ithaca, NY, 1967.

KOPYTOFF, IGOR. 'The Cultural Biography of Things: Commoditization as Process'. *The Social Life of Things.* Ed. A. Appadurai. Cambridge, 1986: 64–91.

KROLL, RICHARD W. F. *The Material Word: Literate Culture in the Restoration and Early Eighteenth Century.* Baltimore, 1991.

LAMBERT, SHEILA. 'The Beginning of Printing for the House of Commons, 1640–42'. *Library*[6], 3 (1981), 43–61.

——'The Printers and the Government, 1604–1657'. *Aspects of Printing from 1600.* Ed. R. Myers and M. Harris. Oxford, 1987: 1–29.

——'Richard Montagu, Arminianism and Censorship'. *Past and Present,* 124 (1989), 36–68.

——'State Control of the Press in Theory and Practice: The Role of the Stationers' Company before 1640'. *Censorship and the Control of Print.* Ed. R. Myers and M. Harris. Winchester, 1992: 1–32.

LAMONT, WILLIAM M. *Godly Rule: Politics and Religion, 1603–1660.* London, 1969.

LEVI, GIOVANNI. 'On Microhistory'. *New Perspectives on Historical Writing.* Ed. Peter Burke. Cambridge, 1991: 93–113.

LÉVI-STRAUSS, Claude. *Structural Anthropology.* Trans. Claire Jackson and Brooke Grundfest Schoepf. Harmondsworth, 1977.

LEVY, F. J. *Tudor Historical Thought.* San Marino, Calif., 1967.

——'How Information Spread among the Gentry, 1550–1640'. *Journal of British Studies,* 21 (1982), 11–34.

LINDLEY, K. J. 'The Impact of the 1641 Rebellion upon England and Wales 1641–5'. *Irish Historical Studies,* 18 (1972), 143–76.

LOVE, HAROLD. *Scribal Publication in Seventeenth-Century England.* Oxford, 1993.

MACDONALD, HUGH. 'Another Aspect of Seventeenth-Century Prose'. *Review of English Studies,* 19 (1943), 33-43.

MCDOUGALL, WARREN. 'Scottish Books for America in the Mid 18th Century'. *Spreading the Word.* Ed. R. Myers and M. Harris. Winchester, 1990: 21–46.

MCENTEE, ANNE MARIE. ' "The [Un]Civill-Sisterhood of Oranges and Lemons": Female Petitioners and Demonstrators, 1642–53'. *Pamphlet Wars.* Ed. James Holstun. London, 1992: 92–111.

MACGILLIVRAY, ROYCE. *Restoration Historians and the English Civil War.* The Hague, 1974.

MCGINN, DONALD J. *John Penry and the Marprelate Controversy.* New Brunswick, NJ, 1966.

MCGREGOR, J. F., and REAY, B., eds. *Radical Religion in the English Revolution.* Oxford, 1984.

MCKENZIE, DONALD F. 'Printers of the Mind: Some Notes on Bibliographical Theories and Printing-House Practices'. *Studies in Bibliography,* 22 (1969), 1–75.

——' "The Staple of News" and the Late Plays'. *A Celebration of Ben Jonson.* Ed. W. Blissett, J. Patrick, and R. W. Van Fossen. Toronto, 1973: 83–128.

——'The London Book Trade in the Later Seventeenth Century'. Unpublished Sandars Lectures, 1976.

——*Bibliography and the Sociology of Texts.* The Panizzi Lectures, 1985. London, 1986.

——'Speech—Manuscript—Print'. *Library Chronicle*, 20 (1990), 87–109.
——'The Economies of Print, 1550–1750: Scales of Production and Conditions of Constraint'. *Productione e commercio della carta e del libro secc. XIII–XVIII.* Prato, 1992: 414–25.
McKEON, MICHAEL. *The Origins of the English Novel 1600–1740.* London, 1988.
MACLEAN, GERALD M. *Time's Witness: Historical Representation in English Poetry, 1603–1660.* Madison, 1990.
MADAN, FALCONER. *Oxford Books: A Bibliography*, 3 vols. Oxford, 1895–1931.
MALCOLM, JOYCE LEE. *Caesar's Due: Loyalty and King Charles 1642–1646.* Royal Historical Society, Studies in History, 38. London, 1983.
MALTZAHN, NICHOLAS VON. *Milton's* History of Britain: *Republican Historiography in the English Revolution.* Oxford, 1991.
MANNING, B. S. *1649: The Crisis of the English Revolution.* London, 1992.
MANWARING, G. E. 'Journalism in the Days of the Commonwealth'. *Edinburgh Review*, 244 (1926), 105–20.
MARCUS, LEAH S. *The Politics of Mirth: Jonson, Herrick, Milton, Marvell and Defence of Old Holiday Pastimes.* Chicago, 1986.
MARGOLIES, DAVID. *Novel and Society in Elizabethan England.* London, 1985.
MAROTTI, ARTHUR F. *Manuscript, Print, and the English Renaissance Lyric.* Ithaca, NY, 1995.
MARQUARDT, WILLIAM F. 'The First English Translators of Trajano Boccalini's *Ragguagli di Parnaso*: A Study of Literary Relationships'. *Huntington Library Quarterly*, 15 (1951), 1–19.
MARTIN, HEARI-JEAN. *Le Livre français sous l'ancien régime.* Paris, 1987.
——and CHARTIER, ROGER, eds. *Histoire de l'édition français*, vol. i: *Le Livre conquérant.* Paris, 1982.
MAUSS, MARCEL. *The Gift: The Form and Reason for Exchange in Archaic Societies.* Trans. W. D. Halls. Foreword by Mary Douglas. London, 1990.
MENDELSOHN, J. ANDREW. 'Alchemy and Politics in England 1649–1665'. *Past and Present*, 135 (1992), 30–78.
MENDLE, MICHAEL. 'The Thomason Collection'. [Debate with Stephen J. Greenberg.] *Albion*, 22 (1980), 85–98.
——'De Facto Freedom, De Facto Authority: Press and Parliament, 1640–1643'. *Historical Journal*, 38 (1995), 307–32.
MILLER, LUCASTA. 'The Shattered *Violl*: Print and Textuality in the 1640s'. *Literature and Censorship.* Ed. Nigel Smith. Essays and Studies[2], 46. Cambridge, 1993: 25–38.
MINER, EARL. 'Milton and the Histories'. *Politics of Discourse: The Literature and History of Seventeenth-Century England.* Ed. K. Sharpe and S. N. Zwicker. Berkeley, 1987: 181–203.
MORGAN, JOHN. *Godly Learning: Puritan Attitudes towards Reason, Learning, and Education, 1560–1640.* Cambridge, 1986.
MORISON, STANLEY. *Ichabod Dawks and his News-Letter: With an Account of the Dawks Family of Booksellers and Stationers 1635–1731.* Cambridge, 1931.
——*The English Newspaper.* Cambridge, 1932.
——*Origins of the Newspaper: Some Account of the Physical Development of Journals Printed in London between 1622 and the Present Day.* London, 1954.

——*Selected Essays on the History of Letter-Forms in Manuscript and Print.* Ed. David McKitterick. 2 vols. Cambridge, 1980.

MORRILL, J. S. *Cheshire 1630–1660: County Government and Society during the English Revolution.* Oxford, 1974.

——*The Revolt of the Provinces: Conservatives and Radicals in the English Civil Wars, 1630–1650.* 1976. London, 1980.

——*The Nature of the English Revolution.* London, 1993.

MOUSLEY, ANDREW. 'Self, State, and Seventeenth-Century News'. *Seventeenth Century,* 6 (1991), 149–68.

MUDDIMAN, J. G. *The King's Journalist 1659–1689: Studies in the Reign of Charles II.* London, 1923.

——'S. R. Gardiner's Historical Method'. *Notes and Queries*[13], 1 (1923), 23–5, 45–8, 69–70, 86–8, 107–8, 127–9, 149–50, 169–71, 185–8.

see also Williams, J. B.

MUGGLI, MARK Z. 'Ben Jonson and the Business of News'. *Studies in English Literature,* 32 (1992), 323–40.

MUNTER, ROBERT. *The History of the Irish Newspaper, 1685–1760.* Cambridge, 1967.

MYERS, ROBIN, and HARRIS, MICHAEL, eds. *Aspects of Printing from 1600.* Oxford, 1987.

——eds. *Spreading the Word: The Distribution Networks of Print 1550–1850.* Winchester, 1990.

——eds. *Censorship and the Control of Print: In England and France, 1600–1910.* Winchester, 1992.

——eds. *Serials and their Readers, 1620–1914.* Winchester, 1993.

NELSON, CAROLYN. 'American Readership of Early British Serials'. *Serials and their Readers.* Ed. R. Myers and M. Harris. Winchester, 1993: 27–44.

——and SECCOMBE, MATTHEW. *British Newspapers and Periodicals: A Short Title Catalogue.* New York, 1987.

————*Periodical Publications 1641–1700: A Survey with Illustrations.* Occasional Papers of the Bibliographical Society, 2. Oxford, 1986.

NEUBURG, VICTOR E. *Popular Literature: A History and Guide: From the Beginning of Printing to the Year 1897.* London, 1977.

New Cambridge Bibliography of English Literature. Ed. George Watson. Vol. i: *600–1600.* Cambridge, 1974.

NICHOLL, CHARLES. *A Cup of News: The Life of Thomas Nashe.* London, 1984.

NOBLE, MARK. *The Lives of the English Regicides and Other Commissioners of the Pretended High Court of Justice, Appointed to sit in Judgement upon their Sovereign, King Charles the First.* 2 vols. London, 1798.

NORBROOK, DAVID. *Poetry and Politics in the English Renaissance.* London, 1984.

——'Levelling Poetry: George Wither and the English Revolution, 1642–1649'. *English Literary Renaissance,* 21 (1991), 217–56.

——Selected and introd. David Norbrook, ed. H. R. Woudhuysen. *The Penguin Book of Renaissance Verse, 1509–1659.* London, 1992.

——'Lucan, Thomas May, and the Creation of a Republican Literary Culture'. *Culture and Politics in Early Stuart England.* Ed. K. Sharpe and P. Lake. London, 1994: 45–66.

——'*Areopagitica*, Censorship, and the Early Modern Public Sphere'. *The Administration of Aesthetics: Censorship, Political Criticism, and the Public Sphere.* Ed. Richard Burt. Cultural Politics, 7. Minneapolis, 1994: 3–33.

Nouvelle Biographie générale. Vol. xli. Paris, 1862.

NUGENT, LORD. *Some Memorials of John Hampden, his Party, and his Times.* 2nd edn. 2 vols. London, 1832.

ONG, WALTER J. *Orality & Literacy: The Technologizing of the Word.* London, 1982.

——'Writing is a Technology that Restructures Thought'. *The Written Word.* Ed. G. Baumann. Oxford, 1986: 23–50.

PATTERSON, ANNABEL. *Censorship and Interpretation.* Madison, 1984.

——*Reading between the Lines.* London, 1993.

PATTERSON, LYMAN RAY. *Copyright in Historical Perspective.* Nashville, 1968.

PEARL, VALERIE. *London and the Outbreak of the Puritan Revolution: City Government and National Politics, 1625–1643.* Oxford, 1961.

PIERCE, WILLIAM. *An Historical Introduction to the Marprelate Tracts: A Chapter in the Evolution of Religious and Civil Liberty in England.* London, 1908.

PLOMER, HENRY R. *A Dictionary of the Booksellers and Printers who Were at Work in England, Scotland and Ireland from 1641 to 1667.* Oxford, 1968.

——'Secret Printing during the Civil War'. *Library*[2], 5 (1904), 373–403.

——'An Analysis of the Civil War Newspaper "Mercurius Civicus"'. *Library*[2], 6 (1905), 184–207.

POCOCK, J. G. A., ed. *The Political Works of James Harrington.* Cambridge, 1977.

POLLARD, A. W., and REDGRAVE, G. R. *A Short-Title Catalogue of Books Printed in England, Scotland and Ireland: And of English Books Printed Abroad 1475–1640.* Rev. ed. 3 vols. London, 1976–91.

POOLEY, ROGER. *English Prose of the Seventeenth Century, 1590–1700.* London, 1992.

——'The Poet's Cromwell'. *Critical Survey,* 5 (1993), 223–34.

POPKIN, JEREMY D. *Revolutionary News: The Press in France, 1789–1799.* Durham, NC, 1990.

POPKIN, RICHARD H. *The History of Scepticism from Erasmus to Descartes.* Assen, 1960.

POTTER, LOIS. 'The Plays and the Playwrights, 1642–1660'. *The Revels History of Drama in English,* vol. iv: *1613–1660.* Ed. Philip Edwards *et al.* London, 1981: 263–93.

——*Secret Rites and Secret Writing: Royalist Literature, 1641–1660.* Cambridge, 1989.

POWELL, WILLIAM S. *John Pory 1572–1636: The Life and Letters of a Man of Many Parts.* Chapel Hill, NC, 1977.

PRICE, VINCENT. *Public Opinion.* Communication Concepts, 4. Newbury Park, Calif., 1992.

QUINT, DAVID. *Epic and Empire: Politics and Generic Form from Virgil to Milton.* Princeton, 1993.

RAYMOND, JOAD, ed. *Making the News: An Anthology of the Newsbooks of Revolutionary England, 1641–1660.* Moreton-in-Marsh, 1993.

——'Where is This Goodly Tower? Republican Theories of Education'. *Critical Survey*, 5 (1993), 289–97.
——'Some Corrections and Additions to *British Newspapers and Periodicals 1641–1700: A Short-Title Catalogue*'. *Notes and Queries*, 240 (1995), 451–3.
——'The Daily Muse; or, Seventeenth-Century Poets Read the News'. *Seventeenth Century*, 11 (1995), 1–30.
——'John Hall's "Method of History": A Book Lost and Found'. *ELR*, forthcoming.
REAY, BARRY, ed. *Popular Culture in Seventeenth-Century England.* London, 1985.
REEVE, L. J. *Charles I and the Road to Personal Rule.* Cambridge, 1989.
RHODES, NEIL. *Elizabethan Grotesque.* London, 1980.
RICHARDSON, Mrs HERBERT. *The Old English Newspaper.* London, 1929.
RICKS, CHRISTOPHER, ed. *English Poetry and Prose, 1540–1674*. Sphere History of English Literature, 2. London, 1986.
RICŒUR, PAUL. *Time and Narrative.* 3 vols. Trans. Kathleen McLaughlin and David Pellauer. Chicago, 1984–8.
ROBINSON, HOWARD. *The British Post Office: A History.* Princeton, 1948.
ROOTS, IVAN. 'English Politics 1625–1700'. *Into Another Mould: Change and Continuity in English Culture 1625–1700.* Ed. T. G. S. Cain and Ken Robinson. London, 1992: 18–52.
ROSTENBERG, LEONA. 'Nathaniel Butter and Nicholas Bourne, First "Masters of the Staple"'. *Library*[5], 12 (1957), 23–33.
——*Literary, Political, Scientific, Religious and Legal Publishing, Printing and Bookselling in England, 1551–1700: Twelve Studies.* 2 vols. New York, 1965.
RUOFF, J. E. 'Thomas Carew's Early Reputation'. *Notes and Queries*, 202 (1957), 61–2.
RUSSELL, CONRAD. *The Causes of the English Civil War.* Ford Lectures 1987–8. Oxford, 1990.
——*The Fall of the British Monarchies 1637–1642.* Oxford, 1991.
SALZMAN, PAUL. *English Prose Fiction 1558–1700: A Critical History.* Oxford, 1985.
SAMUEL, IRENE. 'Milton and the Ancients on the Writing of History'. *Milton Studies*, 2 (1970), 131–48.
SAWYER, JEFFREY K. *Printed Poison: Pamphlet Propaganda, Faction Politics, and the Public Sphere in Early Seventeenth-Century France.* Berkeley, 1990.
SCHAMA, SIMON. *Dead Certainties (Unwarranted Speculations).* London, 1991.
SCHILLER, DAN. *Objectivity and the News: The Public and the Rise of Commercial Journalism.* Philadelphia, 1981.
SCOTT, JONATHAN. *Algernon Sidney and the Restoration Crisis, 1677–1683.* Cambridge, 1991.
SEAVER, PAUL S. *Wallington's World: A Puritan Artisan in Seventeenth-Century London.* London, 1985.
SHAABER, MATTHIAS A. *Some Forerunners of the Newspaper in England 1476–1622.* Philadelphia, 1929.
——'The History of the First English Newspaper', *Studies in Philology*, 29 (1932), 551–87.

——'Some Forerunners of the Newspaper in America'. *Journalism Quarterly*, 11 (1934), 339–47.

SHAPIN, STEVEN. *A Social History of Truth: Civility and Science in Seventeenth-Century England.* Chicago, 1994.

——and SCHAFFER, SIMON. *Leviathan and the Air-Pump: Hobbes, Boyle, and the Experimental Life.* Princeton, 1985.

SHAPIRO, BARBARA J. *Probability and Certainty in Seventeenth-Century England.* Princeton, 1983.

SHARPE, J. A. '"Last Dying Speeches": Religion, Ideology and Public Executions in Seventeenth-Century England'. *Past and Present*, 107 (1985), 144–67.

SHARPE, KEVIN. *Sir Robert Cotton 1586–1631: History and Politics in Early Modern England.* Oxford, 1979.

——*Criticism and Compliment: The Politics of Literature in the England of Charles I.* Cambridge, 1987.

——*Politics and Ideas in Early Stuart England: Essay and Studies.* London, 1989.

——*The Personal Rule of Charles I.* New Haven, 1992.

——and LAKE, PETER, eds. *Culture and Politics in Early Stuart England.* London, 1994.

——and ZWICKER, STEVEN N., eds. *Politics of Discourse: The Literature and History of Seventeenth-Century England.* Berkeley, 1987.

SHARPE, REGINALD R. *London and the Kingdom.* 3 vols. London, 1894.

SIEBERT, F. S. *Freedom of the Press in England 1476–1776: The Rise and Decline of Government Controls.* Urbana, Ill., 1952.

SIMMONS, JUDITH. 'Publications of 1623'. *Library*[5], 21 (1966), 207–22.

SIRLUCK, E. 'Shakespeare and Jonson among the Pamphleteers of the First Civil War'. *Modern Philology*, 53 (1955–6), 88–99.

——'*To Your Tents, O Israel*: A Lost Pamphlet'. *Huntington Library Quarterly*, 19 (1955–6), 301–5.

SKERPAN, ELIZABETH. *The Rhetoric of Politics in the English Revolution 1642–1660.* Columbia, Mo., & London, 1992.

SMITH, ANTHONY. 'The Long Road to Objectivity and Back Again: The Kinds of Truth we Get in Journalism'. *Newspaper History: From the Seventeenth Century to the Present Day.* Ed. George Boyce *et al.* London, 1978: 153–71.

——*The Newspaper: An International History.* London, 1979.

SMITH, JEFFERY A. *Printers and Press Freedom: The Ideology of Early American Journalism.* New York, 1988.

SMITH, NIGEL. 'Richard Overton's Marpriest Tracts: Towards a History of Leveller Style'. *Prose Studies*, 9 (1986), 39–66.

——*Perfection Proclaimed: Language and English Radical Religion 1640–1660.* Oxford, 1989.

——'The Uses of Hebrew in the English Revolution'. *Language, Self and Society.* Ed. Peter Burke and Roy Porter. Oxford, 1991: 50–71.

——*Literature and Revolution in England, 1640–1660.* New Haven, 1994.

——'Popular Republicanism in the 1650s: John Streater's "Heroick Mechanicks"'. *Milton and Republicanism.* Ed. D. Armitage *et al.* Cambridge, 1995: 137–55.

SNOW, VERNON F. 'An Inventory of the Lord General's Library, 1646'. *Library*[3], 21 (1966), 115–23.

SOAMES, JANE. *The English Press: Newspapers and News.* Preface by Hilaire Belloc. 1936. London, 1938.

SOLOMON, HOWARD M. *Public Welfare, Science, and Propaganda in Seventeenth Century France.* Princeton, 1972.

SPALDING, RUTH. *Contemporaries of Bulstrode Whitelocke 1605–1675.* Oxford, 1990.

SPENCER, LOIS. 'The Professional and Literary Connections of George Thomason'. *Library*[5], 13 (1958), 102–18.

——'The Politics of George Thomason'. *Library*[5], 14 (1959), 11–27.

SPUFFORD, MARGARET. 'First Steps in Literacy: The Reading and Writing Experiences of the Humblest Seventeenth-Century Spiritual Autobiographers'. *Social History*, 4 (1979), 407–35.

——*Small Books and Pleasant Histories: Popular Fiction and its Readership in Seventeenth-Century England.* London, 1981.

STEARNS, RAYMOND PHINEAS. *The Strenuous Puritan: Hugh Peter, 1598–1660.* Urbana, Ill., 1954.

STEPHENS, MITCHELL. *A History of News: From the Drum to the Satellite.* New York, 1988.

STONE, J. M. W. *The Inland Posts, 1392–1672.* London, 1987.

STONE, LAWRENCE. *The Causes of the English Revolution 1539–1642.* 1972. London, 1986.

——ed. *Schooling and Society: Studies in the History of Education.* Baltimore, 1976.

SUTHERLAND, J. M. 'The Circulation of Newspapers and Literary Periodicals, 1700–30'. *Library*[4], 15 (1934–5), 110–24.

SUTHERLAND, JAMES. *The Restoration Newspaper and its Development.* Cambridge, 1986.

Tercentenary Handlist of English & Welsh Newspapers, Magazines & Reviews. London, 1920.

THIRSK, JOAN, ed. *The Agrarian History of England and Wales*, vol. iv: *1560–1640.* Cambridge, 1967.

——*Economic Policy and Projects: The Development of a Consumer Society in Early Modern England.* Oxford, 1978.

THOMAS, KEITH. *Religion and the Decline of Magic: Studies in Popular Beliefs in Sixteenth- and Seventeenth-Century England.* 1971. Harmondsworth, 1978.

——'The Meaning of Literacy in Early Modern England'. *The Written Word.* Ed. G. Baumann. Oxford, 1986: 97–131.

THOMAS, P. W. *Sir John Berkenhead 1617–1679: A Royalist Career in Politics and Polemics.* Oxford, 1969.

——*English Revolution*[3], *Newsbooks*[1]*: Oxford Royalist.* 4 vols. London, 1971.

THOMPSON, E. P. *Witness against the Beast: William Blake and the Moral Law.* Cambridge, 1993.

THOMPSON, HUNTER S. *Songs of the Doomed: More Notes on the Death of the American Dream.* New York, 1990.

THOMSON, OLIVER. *Mass Persuasion in History.* New York, 1977.

TREVOR-ROPER, H. R. *Religion, the Reformation and Social Change and Other Essays.* London, 1967.

——*From Counter-Reformation to Glorious Revolution.* London, 1992.
TUCHMAN, GAYE. *Making News: A Study in the Construction of Reality.* New York, 1978.
TUCK, RICHARD. *Philosophy and Government 1572–1651.* Cambridge, 1993.
TUCKER, NORMAN. *North Wales in the Civil War.* Wrexham, 1992.
TURNBULL, G. H. *Hartlib, Dury and Comenius: Gleanings from Hartlib's Papers.* London, 1947.
——'John Hall's Letters to Samuel Hartlib'. *Review of English Studies*[2], 4 (1953), 221–33.
TYACKE, NICHOLAS. *Anti-Calvinists: The Rise of English Arminianism, c.1590–1640.* 1987. Oxford, 1990.
UNDERDOWN, DAVID. *Pride's Purge.* 1971. London, 1985.
——'The Taming of the Scold'. *Order and Disorder in Early-Modern England.* Ed. Anthony Fletcher and John Stevenson. Cambridge, 1985: 116–36.
——*Revel, Riot and Rebellion: Popular Politics and Culture in England 1603–1660.* 1985. Oxford, 1987.
——'Popular Politics in Seventeenth-Century England'. Unpublished Ford Lectures, delivered in Oxford, 1992.
——'*The Man in the Moon*: Levelling, Gender and Popular Politics 1640–1660'. Ford Lecture, delivered in Oxford, Hilary Term 1992.
VAN STOCKUM, W. P., Jr., ed. *The First Newspapers of England Printed in Holland 1620–1621.* The Hague, 1914.
VARLEY, FREDERICK JOHN. *The Siege of Oxford.* London, 1931.
——*Mercurius Aulicus.* Oxford, 1948.
VEYNE, PAUL. *Writing History: Essay on Epistemology.* Trans. Mina Moore-Rinvolucri. Middletown, Conn., 1984.
VOLOSHINOV, V. N. *Marxism and the Philosophy of Language.* Trans. Ladislav Matejka and I. R. Titunik. Cambridge, Mass., 1986.
WALKER, R. B. 'The Newspaper Press in the Reign of William III'. *Historical Journal,* 17 (1974), 691–709.
WALLACE, JOHN M. *Destiny his Choice: The Loyalism of Andrew Marvell.* 1968. Cambridge, 1980.
WARBURTON, ELIOT. *Memoirs of Prince Rupert and the Cavaliers.* 3 vols. London, 1849.
WATT, TESSA. *Cheap Print and Popular Piety, 1550–1640.* Cambridge, 1991.
WATTS, THOMAS. *A Letter to Antonio Panizzi . . . on the Reputed Earliest Printed Newspaper: The English Mercurie 1588.* London, 1839.
WEBSTER, CHARLES, ed. *Samuel Hartlib and the Advancement of Learning.* Cambridge, 1970.
——'Macaria: Samuel Hartlib and the Great Reformation'. *Acta Comenia,* 26 (Prague, 1970), 147–64.
——*The Great Instauration: Science, Medicine and Reform 1626–1660.* London, 1975.
——'Benjamin Worsley: Engineering for Universal Reform from the Invisible College to the Navigation Act'. *Samuel Hartlib and Universal Reformation: Studies in Intellectual Communication.* Ed. Mark Greengrass, Michael Leslie, and Timothy Raylor. Cambridge, 1994: 213–46.

WEDGWOOD, C. V. *The King's Peace 1637–1641*. London, 1955.
——*The King's War, 1641–1647*. 1958. London, 1983.
——*Poetry and Politics under the Stuarts*. Cambridge, 1960.
WEED, KATHERINE KIRTLEY, and BOND, RICHMOND PUGH. *Studies of British Newspapers and Periodicals from their Beginning to 1800: A Bibliography*. Studies in Philology, Extra Series, 2. Chapel Hill, NC, 1946.
WERNHAM, R. B. 'The Public Record in the Sixteenth and Seventeenth Centuries'. *English Historical Scholarship in the Sixteenth and Seventeenth Centuries*. Ed. Levi Fox. London, 1956: 11–30.
WHITE, HAYDEN. *Metahistory: The Historical Imagination in Nineteenth-Century Europe*. Baltimore, 1973.
WHITELOCKE, BULSTRODE. *Diary of Bulstrode Whitelocke, 1605–1675*. Ed. Ruth Spalding. Oxford, 1990.
WILDING, MICHAEL. *Dragons Teeth: Literature in the English Revolution*. Oxford, 1987.
WILES, R. M. *Freshest Advices: Early Provincial Newspapers in England*. Columbus, Oh., 1965.
WILLAN, T. S. *The Inland Trade: Studies in English Internal Trade in the Sixteenth and Seventeenth Centuries*. Manchester, 1976.
WILLIAMS, FRANCIS. *Dangerous Estate: The Anatomy of Newspapers*. Foreword by Michael Foot. 1957; Cambridge, 1984.
WILLIAMS, J. B. *A History of English Journalism to the Foundation of the Gazette*. London, 1908.
—— 'Beginnings of English Journalism'. *The Cambridge History of English Literature*, vol. vii: *Cavalier and Puritan*. Ed. A. W. Ward and A. R. Waller. Cambridge, 1911: 389–415.
——'Benjamin Harris: The First American Journalist'. *Notes and Queries*, 163 (1932), 129–33, 147–50, 166–70, 223, 273–4.
see also Muddiman, J. G.
WILLIAMS, KEITH. *The English Newspaper: An Illustrated History to 1900*. London, 1977.
WILLIAMS, RAMOND. *Marxism and Literature*. Oxford, 1977.
——*Keywords*. London, 1976.
——*Culture*. Glasgow, 1981.
WILSON, F. P. 'Some English Mock-Prognostications'. *Library*[4], 19 (1938–9), 6–43.
WING, DONALD. *Short-Title Catalogue of Books Printed in England, Scotland, Ireland, Wales, and British America and of English Books Printed in Other Countries 1641–1700*. 3 vols. New York, 1972–94.
WISEMAN, SUSAN. '"Adam, the Father of All Flesh," Porno-Political Rhetoric and Political Theory in and after the English Civil War'. *Pamphlet Wars*. Ed. James Holstun. London, 1992: 134–57.
——'News, Pamphlets, Drama: Hybrid Forms and the News in the 1640s', forthcoming.
WOMERSLEY, DAVID. 'Sir Henry Savile's Translation of Tacitus and the Political Interpretation of Elizabethan Texts'. *Review of English Studies*[2], 42 (1991), 313–42.

WOODFIELD, DENNIS B. *Surreptitious Printing in England, 1550–1640*. New York, 1973.

WOOLF, DANIEL R. *The Idea of History in Early Stuart England: Erudition, Ideology, and 'The Light of Truth' from the Accession of James I to the Civil War.* Toronto, 1990.

——'Conscience, Constancy, and Ambition in the Career and Writings of James Howell'. *Public Duty and Private Conscience in Seventeenth-Century England: Essays Presented to G. E. Aylmer.* Ed. John Morrill, Paul Slack, and Daniel Woolf. Oxford, 1993: 243–78.

WOOTTON, DAVID. 'From Rebellion to Revolution: The Crisis of the Winter of 1642/3 and the Origins of Civil War Radicalism'. *English Historical Review*, 105 (1990), 654–69.

WORDEN, BLAIR. *The Rump Parliament 1648–1653*. Cambridge, 1974.

——'Literature and Political Censorship in Early Modern England'. *Too Mighty to be Free: Censorship and the Press in Britain and the Netherlands.* Ed. A. C. Duke and C. A. Tamse. Zutphen, 1987: 45–62.

——'Marchamont Nedham and the Beginnings of English Republicanism, 1649–1656'. *Republicanism, Liberty, and Commercial Society, 1649–1776*. Ed. David Wootton. Stanford, Calif., 1994: 45–81.

——' "Wit in a Roundhead": The Dilemma of Marchamont Nedham'. *Political Culture and Cultural Politics in Early-Modern England: Essays Presented to David Underdown.* Ed. Susan D. Amussen and Mark A. Kishlansky. Manchester, 1995: 301–37.

WRIGHT, LOUIS B. *Middle Class Culture in Elizabethan England.* Chapel Hill, NC, 1935.

WRIGHTSON, KEITH. *English Society 1580–1680*. London, 1982.

WÜRZBACH, NATASCHA. *The Rise of the English Street Ballad, 1550–1650*. Trans. Gayna Walls. Cambridge, 1990.

ZAGORIN, PEREZ. *The Court and the Country: The Beginning of the English Revolution.* London, 1969.

ZARET, DAVID. 'Religion, Science, and Printing in the Public Spheres of Seventeenth-Century England'. *Habermas and the Public Sphere.* Ed. C. Calhoun. Cambridge, Mass., 1992: 212–35.

——'Critical Theory and the Sociology of Culture'. *Current Perspectives in Social Theory*, 11 (1992), 1–28.

ZWICKER, STEVEN N. *Lines of Authority: Politics and English Literary Culture, 1649–1689*. Ithaca, NY, 1993.

General index

Index of newsbooks